The Odyssey of Shen Congwen

The Odyssey of
SHEN CONGWEN

Jeffrey C. Kinkley

Stanford University Press, Stanford, California

Stanford University Press
Stanford, California
© 1987 by the Board of Trustees of the
Leland Stanford Junior University

Printed in the United States of America

CIP data are at the end of the book

Published with the assistance of
the National Endowment for the Humanities

To My Parents
Harold Vernon Kinkley
Emily Jane Robinson Kinkley

Acknowledgments

I hope it is not presumptuous of me to thank so many Chinese scholars and writers for their help; they were speaking to posterity as well as to me, at a time when frank talk about Shen Congwen was hard to publish in Chinese.

I began reading Shen Congwen's works in a Harvard seminar on popular Chinese literature as witness to history, at the suggestion of Alexander Woodside, seconded by Ezra Vogel, Patrick Hanan, Yu Ying-shih, and Benjamin I. Schwartz. Professor Schwartz went on to direct my doctoral dissertation, which used Shen's literature and corroborating nonfiction materials to examine West Hunan and its special ethos. John K. Fairbank, Patrick Hanan, Roy M. Hofheinz, John C. Pelzel, David Deal, Donald A. Gibbs, Yun-chen Li Gibbs, Bonnie S. McDougall, Merle Goldman, Rulan Chao Pian, Ernst Wolff, William L. MacDonald, Hua-ling Nieh, Richard Cushman, Shao Lee Soo, Yang Chiu, Luk Kwok-sun, Perry Link, Richard Forde, Rev. Cormac Shanahan, C.P., Rev. Theophane Maguire, C.P., and Rev. Robert Carbonneau, C.P., also helped. Parts of some chapters in this book are revised from the dissertation, which still provides heavier documentation on ethnographic matters. That Shen to some degree wrote about the real lives of the Miao, as I argued there, now seems less controversial (see the interesting article by Mackerras).

In 1980 the Committee on Scholarly Communication with the People's Republic of China provided me with a rare opportunity to interview Shen Congwen, tour his home region for a week, and enjoy my first major scholarly interchange with Chinese writers and scholars (except for very useful talks in 1973–74 with the Hon. Chen Jiying and Sun Ling in Taiwan). The next winter, Mr. and

Mrs. Shen came to America. Thanks to Hans H. and Ch'ung-ho Chang Frankel (Mrs. Shen's sister), both of Yale University, I was able to talk to Shen Congwen several times more. Many of the interviews are on tape, so I have carefully documented information taken from them—still always giving preference to data from written sources, on first principles, and out of respect for the linguistic barrier that has befuddled even many Chinese who have interviewed Shen Congwen.

Howard Goldblatt kindly allowed me to use short excerpts from my article about Shen that he published in the second issue of *Modern Chinese Literature*. I also thank the China Committee of the American Council of Learned Societies and the Social Science Research Council for a Mellon Fellowship; the Mrs. Giles Whiting Foundation; and my colleagues at St. John's University—Rev. Thomas Hoar, C.M., Sr. Virginia Thérèse Johnson, M.M., Peter Nosco, Tu Nien-chung, and Yeh Chih-ying. Shen honored the university with a lecture, after which we retired to my little Flushing apartment and witnessed the spectacle of a famous author digging into my cheesecake—with chopsticks.

Besides Shen Congwen, I am indebted to his wife Zhang Zhaohe; his assistants Wang Xu and Wang Yarong; his relative Huang Yongyu; my Chinese colleagues Shao Huaqiang, Ling Yu, and Long Haiqing; Shen's friends and former students Ba Jin, Bian Zhilin, Cheng Yingliu (pseud. Liu Jin), Duanmu Hongliang, Feng Zhi, Jin Di, Li Huiying, Li Jianwu, Lin Pu (Ling Pu; Paul Lin), Ma Fenghua (Feng-hwa Mah), Qian Zhongshu, Shi Zhicun, Wu Xiaoling, Xiao Qian, Xu Jieyu (Kai-yu Hsu), Yang Yi, Yuan Kejia, Zhao Ruihong, Zhong Kailai (K. L. Chung), and Zhu Guangqian; Shen's nemeses Ding Ling, Huang Yuan, and Sun Xizhen; and some still straddling the fence, such as Zang Kejia. Feng Youlan kindly answered a few questions during a busy moment. Liang Shiqiu also contributed, by telephone.

I owe much to the Institute of Chinese Literature of the Chinese Academy of Social Sciences, which sponsored me while I was in China, the people and county committee of Fenghuang, Director Yu Guanghao, Chairman Long, the Shanjiang Commune Miao folk, the staff at Shen's old Wenchangge primary school, Tujia expert Yang Changxiong, and Fenghuang seminar speakers Li Daren, Long Zhian, Meng Muqiu, Tian Jingyang, Wu Rongzhen, and Wu Guangshi. Gao Peng of the Institute of Literature was an indispens-

Acknowledgments   ix

able right hand, and I especially thank Hu Qiaomu for facilitating Shen's return visit, a high point in Sino-American cultural exchange. Libraries at Harvard, Columbia, and other universities across the United States provided materials, as did the Peking Municipal, Peking University, Shanghai Public, Shanghai Teachers' College, Hunan, Zhejiang, Zhongshan, and Zhongshan University libraries, and the Academies of Social Science at Shanghai, Nanking, and Guangzhou. So did archivists of the Eastern Province of the Congregation of the Passion (formerly in Union City, New Jersey), the Evangelical and Reformed Historical Society (at the Lancaster Theological Seminary), and the Evangelical Church archives (now under the United Methodist Archives and History Center at Drew University). Chen Mengxiong provided many new leads, as did, above all, Shao Huaqiang, who nonetheless refused to let me name him co-compiler of the list of Shen's works. I thank Sheniana lovers Long Liangwei of Hong Kong, *Haineiwai* editor Yin Menglong, Rev. Paul Szeto, and Kang Chuchu, whom Rev. Szeto wedded to me in between my trips to China, in plenty of time for her to share my most trying moments. Leo Ou-fan Lee, Perry Link, Helen Tartar, Wes Peverieri, C. T. Hsia, Jonathan Spence, Thomas Gold, Peter Kahn, and others helped shape the book as it is today. Mr. Kahn not only pointed out defects in logic and style but proposed alternative wordings, some of which yielded, besides greater clarity, insights I hadn't discovered before myself.

J.C.K.

Contents

Introduction 1

ONE A Youth in West Hunan 8

TWO Adolescence: Shen Congwen and His Region Find Their Own Way 37

THREE The Romantic Young Man of Peking 67

FOUR The Origins of Shen Congwen's Literary Regionalism 111

FIVE Country Folk, Plain and Exotic 146

SIX Urban Man: Facing a Void Between Youth and Death 185

SEVEN Fighting for Autonomy 228

Conclusion 275

Notes 285 Selected Bibliography 369
A Chronological Listing of Shen Congwen's Works 387
Character List 439 Index 451

Eight pages of photographs follow p. 110

The Odyssey of Shen Congwen

When you ask for directions in West Hunan, folks
understand you better if you sing than if you speak.
  Shen Congwen (June 27, 1980)

  I worship vitality and love freedom. I extol the plucky
and the strong in heart. Any person who is vigorous
in his actions or spirit—who doesn't jockey for petty
advantage or care about material gain and public
prestige—if he can stiffen his backbone and go his
own way, straight as a ramrod, then I can accept him
as a friend, as a man. No matter that what he knows is
different from what I know, that his political ideology
is opposite to mine, or that his religious beliefs and
mine are in conflict. I love this kind of person. I
respect him. He might be a little wild, or a little crude,
but only people like him stand behind great
accomplishments and great literary works. He'll fail
sometimes, then try again. In fact he'll stumble often.
But he'll get up again immediately.
  Shen Congwen ("Preface to *Under the Eaves
  of Others*," 1934)

I have a rule. Once people are promoted to high office,
I no longer seek to have social intercourse with them.
  Shen Congwen (July 23, 1980)

Introduction

I THINK IT WAS in 1975 that I entered a New York Chinatown bookshop in search of works by Shen Congwen and was told by the manager: "Shen Congwen? Nobody reads *him* any more—he's an old man." Once I'd regained my composure, it consoled me to imagine what a bookseller might have said in Shen's own country: "Shen Congwen? Nobody reads *him* any more—he's a bourgeois." Or, "He writes about the *old* society." Or even, "He still believes in God." There'd be no books by Shen for sale in China (as in fact there were, in that Chinatown shop). Shen was more highly regarded in Taiwan, I knew (his works were proscribed, and therefore valuable), but a librarian there added this non sequitur to my collection: "Shen Congwen? He's a Communist—he didn't come to Taiwan." Good material for a story by Lu Xun, I said—to myself, since Lu Xun was forbidden, too. The funny thing was, when Sino-American relations improved and I was finally able to meet Shen Congwen, he seemed less an old man than a mischievous child, brimming over with irreverent comments about people in high places.*

In the West, Shen Congwen's most faithful readers are in the academy, and they generally agree that he is one of the half-dozen great authors of modern Chinese literature. Some have gone on to acclaim Lu Xun as "no. 1" and Shen Congwen as "no. 2," but even in that there is no escape from the political fairyland that impris-

---

* In the old Wade-Giles system, "Shen Congwen" was spelled "Shen Ts'ung-wen." I have used *pinyin* romanization throughout, except for Peking, Nanking, Canton, Kuomintang (KMT), Sun Yatsen, Chiang Kaishek, the Soong family, and Taoism. Dates given with titles of Shen's writings in the text are dates of composition, not publication.

ons Chinese literary reputations; few Sinologists will put their appraisals in writing, and an authority who eulogized Shen in those terms to my face in 1972 took it all back in the 1980's, when Shen and Chinese competitors were beginning to be discussed as possible Nobel Prize candidates.[1] Lu Xun's reputation itself now owes as much to received opinion as to critical reappraisals. Indeed, what place does any Chinese writer have in world literature? Sinologists are forced to ponder whether or not they are prone to judge Chinese writers by a double standard.

This is a book more of history than of literary criticism. It is the story of Shen Congwen's life, his times, his thought, and his art—considered whole, but, inevitably, with more space devoted to "facts" than evaluations, the more so since this is a pioneer biography and an all-but-authorized one to boot.[2] Shen's thought helps me to explicate his art, and vice versa, but I treat those topics also in order to illuminate the course of Chinese literature in this century. Indeed, Shen's life will be presented not just as the biography of a writer, but as a journey into large swaths of Chinese social history.

All the more reason, perhaps, for me to state my personal view of Shen's stature purely as a writer, not just for general readers, who cannot be referred to a consensus outside the field, but for the cognoscenti, who will want to know "where I stand." Shen Congwen's own taste ran from Daudet and France at the lower end on up to Shakespeare, Balzac, and Joyce. Surely he surpassed the former authors, though I cannot rank him with the latter group.* Those who share my taste for Shen will not be content to rank him with minor masters such as Maupassant and Gide. Shen was less consistent than Turgenev, and he was a master only of fiction, unlike his favorite Chekhov. But an author is to be judged by his best work. Shen's masterpieces rank with Chekhov's, I think, and I would place Lu Xun here, too—which is no insult to Lu Xun, who would be aghast to see all modern Chinese literary achievement (some of which he might not consider such an achievement) credited to him.

*Collectively, Shen Congwen and his fellow New Intellectuals contributed as much to the vocabulary of modern vernacular Chinese when they began using it as a language of literary expression as the Elizabethans contributed to English—though many innovations by the New Intellectuals were rejected by their successors as "bourgeois" or "un-Chinese." Shen Congwen's linguistic contributions may be his most obviously distinguishing mark of greatness, but that is a technical and subjective question which I leave to others. On China's literary languages, see Hanan, pp. 1–16.

A bigger difficulty for Shen's reputation than the fact that he wrote many flawed works is his chronic (though luckily not invariable) inattention to larger literary structures. Superstructural problems are hard to overlook, and therefore some critics praise Shen only as a "stylist"; indeed, as a mature author, he never even finished his major novels. *The Frontier City*, however, is reckoned by many to be nearly perfect in style and form, a classic of its kind that establishes Shen's greatness all by itself. We might, then, compare it with other solitary monuments. It is not a match for *The Dream of the Red Chamber*. What about *Madame Bovary*, *Tristram Shandy*, or *A la recherche du temps perdu*? Westerner that I am, I would be hard put to demonstrate that *The Frontier City* is as seminal as the first, as original as the second, or as substantial as the third. Yet I can imagine that critics in non-Western countries (in addition to China) might one day want to make the case for Shen; the reputations of Flaubert, Sterne, and Proust have had their ups and downs even in our part of the world.

In fact, Shen Congwen looms large in the history of Chinese literature not because he wrote an unusually monumental work, but, on the contrary, because his contributions to literature were so diverse and so pervasive. Diffuseness was Shen Congwen's weakness, but it also underlay much of his greatness. How his experiments, even in inferior works, contributed to Chinese literature when it so badly needed his innovative and undogmatic voice is part of the subject of this book. We ought, indeed, to reflect on how historicism affects artistic judgments. In China, from 1949 until the death of Mao, Lu Xun's works were idolized as the embodiment of what literature should be in an age of revolution against imperialism and feudalism, but they were deemed inappropriate for emulation in an era of socialism. In the West, we might delight in a newly discovered Mozart symphony, but pooh-pooh the same piece if it were found to have been written in the 1950's. Our own historicism works against the majority of modern Chinese authors, for they felt close to our nineteenth-century realists. On the other hand, because Shen Congwen was one of the very few Chinese authors to "break free"—as we say in the West—and experiment with avant-garde ideas and techniques, those with the biases of our era (myself included) can find rare merit in Shen's "creativity" even outside of his masterpieces. Shen Congwen actually discovered the idea of an avant-garde from his predecessors.

4   Introduction

But by the 1930's he felt, with some reason, that he was one of the last authors still interested in "liberation of thought" and new artistic frontiers.

It seems all the more paradoxical that Shen Congwen was so preoccupied with thoughts of home. He never went abroad (before 1980) or learned a foreign language. Indeed, his biography seems most closely intertwined with great events in Chinese social and literary history when his little native region, West Hunan, is the backdrop. Shen created a vision of the place so alluring that critics and readers still argue about how literally his regional works ought to be read. Only a novelist with a sure eye and a good ear could have created characters so indelibly marked by their homeland. Shen's works also interpret rural life in modern China as a whole, and even the existential plight of twentieth-century man. But in that, too, his regional vision takes command, supplying West Hunanese particulars as exemplifications of human universals. Shen's West Hunan fiction by itself presents a full and compelling statement about life. As has been said of Faulkner's works, "each novel, each long or short story, seems to reveal more than it states explicitly and to have a subject bigger than itself. All the separate works are like blocks of marble from the same quarry: they show the veins and faults of the mother rock."[3]

As an interpreter of his era, Shen Congwen also helps us to understand regionalism as a social force in Chinese history.[4] He first learned to identify with West Hunan while defending it as a warlord soldier; that part of his saga is a dark account of the militarization of China. Delightful in literature, often exasperating in real life (as Shen learned when he left home), regional particularism can lead to an escalating cycle of violence and finally to civil war. Yet regional sentiments have sometimes held Chinese society together at the local level when all else failed— prevented a descent into clan warfare and utter anarchy. Shen Congwen illustrates the uses and misuses of regional identification, while bringing his own favorite realm to life as a set of feelings. Indeed, his writings provide glimpses of the anarchy that could break out when even regional cement failed.

West Hunan in Shen Congwen's works is both more and less than an imaginary kingdom like Faulkner's Yoknapatawpha. On the positive side, one of the veins in the bedrock of Shen's oeuvre is intimate knowledge of local events. His region was small enough that Shen knew—if he was not related to—most of its major powerholders. Thus his regional works provide a brief history in the form of a roman-fleuve. They embody a fuller political apology for the cause of the Chinese Southwest than Faulkner's works do for the American South, and they lose nothing in interest or historical explanatory power for being subjective. Shen did not recycle stale regional self-images or local-color motifs impounded in the classical Chinese literature. West Hunan had its local equivalents of magnolias, mockingbirds, and cavalier myths (artemisia, dragon boats, shamans, and knights-errant), but it was Shen himself who first wove these together in creative works to present West Hunan as the modern descendant of an ancient kingdom and state of mind called Chu. Probably he created the first identity myth ever associated with West Hunan. One day he may even be recognized as the first author to create a local-color fiction in modern prose for any Chinese region.

It was not all imagination, for West Hunan in Republican times was an exceptional vessel for regional sentiment. Just as its exotic cultures uniquely fitted it for romantic mythmaking, the political birth of West Hunan as an independent region brought about conditions in which an abstract social and geographical idea of the region was waiting to be born. Indeed, Shen Congwen's regional works filled not just a West Hunanese but a more general Chinese need for regional literature and mythmaking.

Perhaps Shen Congwen the writer was *too* faithful to "reality" (though critics in his own country typically argue the opposite). Only Faulkner could draw a map of Yoknapatawpha. Its concreteness existed in his mind alone, where he was free to develop it as he pleased. Shen Congwen's literary West Hunan is bound to people and places that really existed. Sometimes he tried to make his despised fellow-regionals a cause célèbre, to capture his readers' imaginations with a few bold strokes, as Steinbeck did for the Okies. At other times Shen played James Fenimore Cooper to his region's Miao minority folk, making them out to be a dying race of noble savages. But if Shen Congwen is to be faulted for his vision of West Hunan, probably it will be not for his emotional engagement or subjectivity, but rather for not always letting his imagination go completely free.

And yet, Shen Congwen's works about the West Hunanese seem to me to have a broader symbolic meaning even in the realm of history. They may be read as parables about the whole Chinese people, who by the 1920's had grown dispirited because of their unenviable place in the world. Shen, like Lu Xun, was distressed to see his folk dwell on glories of that past before they were so tragically defeated by the better armed, more "materialistic" West. The Chinese nursed frustrated hopes for rebirth as a sovereign nation, yet (like partisans of America's Old South) still took refuge in fatuous "moral victories." It was right for his people to look inward for resources of the soul, Shen Congwen felt, but wrong to search for them only in the Old Civilization as conventionally defined. Though Shen's social and historical vision may strike today's readers as tragic, in its time it appeared particularly noteworthy because it offered grounds for hope—of national renewal for the Chinese as a people, or rather as a modern nation made up of many cultures and many peoples.

Optimism about China's future was not so rare during Shen's youth as when he became an adult. Forces of reform, rebirth, and renewal had arisen so suddenly at the turn of the twentieth century that it was fashionable in the West to speak of "Young China."[5] The phrase indicated in particular two forward-looking new elites that were beginning to form from among the scions of China's old literati class: modern military officers, and students. West Hunan was too isolated to have anything to do with "Young China" before the 1911 Revolution. Yet the intellectual currents that had energized China during those last years before she was cowed by imperialism and internal disunity did arrive in Shen Congwen's native region, about 20 years late. Social Darwinism, plans for home rule, Western education, and reform militarism invaded West Hunan all at once in the late 1910's, followed closely by the literary revolution and May Fourth movement of 1919. To many it seemed that China might be saved by fresh ideas; malleable young people would be in the vanguard, spreading the revival through new vernacular writings. All through the 1920's and 1930's, Shen Congwen, almost alone among his literary colleagues, continued to promulgate the original hopeful message of May Fourth. Even the Sino-Japanese War failed to divert him from his independent path.

Where did Shen Congwen's optimism, such as it was, come from? It might be traced to his religious faith. Or perhaps it was due to his educational upbringing. Shen Congwen appears to have been less a radical whose consciousness was formed by an era when it seemed shameful to be Chinese than one who still believed that the old in China (which was not to say the "Confucian" Old Civilization) could be redirected to serve new purposes, without fear of Westernization or social breakdown. The "Chineseness" of Shen's style and subject matter, and the easy and unquestioning way in which he assimilated ideas from abroad, are the mark of an artist who feared neither that China would succumb to imperialism, nor that she would lose her soul in the course of change. One could believe that in West Hunan; its regional culture was little threatened by the West, and its tribal society had never been fully subjugated by Confucianism itself.

Shen Congwen's regional fiction became the major vehicle for his own ideas about China's internal moral and cultural resources. He recreated the West Hunan he had known in childhood to recast it romantically and idealistically—as a young China, not an old China. Shen Congwen brought many Chinese readers to view their "traditional" heritage in a new light: to see themselves as potentially a young people, even as they yearned for salvation from a prison of accumulated customs, and to see the vitality of youthful creativity in the aspirations of their ancestors. Viewed from the right perspective, Shen's land of frontiersmen and tribespeople could evoke the quintessence of youth and vitality, of a cultural power beyond the brashness of the West and the obscurantism of the old Chinese scholar class. So, then, could all of China.

CHAPTER ONE

A Youth in West Hunan

NEARLY TEN YEARS after he had left his hometown for good, Shen Congwen reflected that "many people live there yet, but oftentimes I live in my impressions of its past."[1] Through those impressions, transformed by Shen's imagination in fiction, we know the riches in the background of this most provincial of China's modern writers better than we know the man himself. Shen Congwen constructed his tales from childhood memories, folktales told by his Miao (Hmong) nursemaid and country relatives, swagger-filled ransom notes he read while enlisted in the local warlord ranks, bits of legend connected with the places he visited while marching through the back country or drifting down its streams, snatches of street conversation and merchant patter he heard through the windows as he lay abed, and the imprecations exchanged by dueling soldiers and gangs of street urchins at high noon. From these he created the living image of a Chinese region.

West Hunan: Shen Congwen's World and Its Origins

Shen's native region made up the northwest quarter of Hunan province and was roughly coincident with the lands drained by the Yuan and Li rivers, excluding the Yuan headwaters up in Guizhou. Probably the region was not popularly known as West Hunan (Xiangxi) before the 1910's, when the Republic began appointing defense commissioners "of West Hunan." Of old, people simply spoke of Hunan west of the Snowy Peaks (Xuefengshan), or the place inhabited by the Barbarians of the Five Streams. Officially, the area was the Chen-Yuan-Yong-Jing military preparedness circuit in the Qing, and the Chen-Yuan circuit in the early Republic—

often popularly called Upper Hunan (Shang Hunan)—but the name West Hunan prevailed by the 1930's.[2]

Though still in search of a name, the region had been a single civil administrative territory (a circuit) since 1670; Hunan province itself was only six years older. The Snowy Peaks so obstructed east-west communication that the area west of them, during several dynasties prior to the Ming, was not yet politically yoked with the east (the Xiang basin, now Hunan), but was rather linked with the north (present Hubei). Few "aboriginal" peoples remained in eastern or central Hunan by Republican times, yet a million of them thrive in West Hunan today; they constitute half its uplands population. Even the several Chinese dialects of West Hunan are classed not with the Hunanese dialect of the east, but with the Southwestern Mandarin of Sichuan. The mountainous west is simply a different place from the Hunan that is called "China's rice bowl." Only 10 percent of West Hunan was cultivated in 1958, and less than half of that was in rice. Just a quarter or a sixth as densely populated as other parts of the province, West Hunan was, in a word, poor.[3]

Yet, a region is as much an imaginative construct as a geographical place, and the idea of West Hunan owed something to Shen Congwen himself; his romantic vision of the region as a cauldron of different ethnic groups is a good point of departure. To Shen, West Hunan was a cultural frontier where sophisticated Han people (the main Chinese stock, from the north and east) had since ancient times lived side by side with primitives like the Miao folk who still inhabited the hill country west of his hometown. The Miao had been subjugated a century before his birth, but many continued to resist acculturation.[4] So the frontier, as a meeting ground—a place where ways of life could mix, alloy, and struggle with each other—remained open, by Shen's formulation. West Hunan was to him a living evocation not just of China's great history, but of still greater primitive forces preceding it, underlying it—and waiting to drive it forward again.

The ethnic divide in West Hunan had for several centuries been a topographical one, between hill folk such as the Miao and more Sinified latecomers whose agriculture was tied to rivers and the low-lying fields they flooded. History and ethnography have not yet determined whether West Hunan's earliest tribal peoples, or even the Miao, were originally hill dwellers or were pushed to the uplands by newcomers. That the Miao still practiced a crude agriculture based on dry-farming crops such as corn and potatoes reinforced Chinese impressions that they were in a technologically pristine state. Yet these crops came to Asia only after the discovery of America; Miao technology had been far from static.[5] The Southwestern barbarians who first resisted the Han are known in the histories only as "Man" (barbarians from the South). Shen Congwen has a vision of the Han and the tribespeople that attributes to them not only comparably ancient ancestry, but common origins—if only they could see it. He invokes memories of the Chinese poet and minister Qu Yuan, and the great Han admiral Ma Yuan, who on going south two millennia ago found the barbarians to be a musical, artistic, hardy, and self-sufficient people making up a lyrical Southern cultural kingdom called Chu. Unfortunately the Southerners' and Northerners' consciousness of common humanity—not to mention common origins—became obscured by centuries of rivalry and armed conflict. This was inevitable, Shen's writings imply, once the two peoples chose different paths in their pursuit of life.

The Han chose the path of Confucianism and urbanization, of a cultural development that enabled them to dominate their fellow man. Yet their culture had, from Shen Congwen's frontier perspective, gradually declined and reached a point of crisis by the time of his youth (in the last decade of imperial China). The Han had become decadent, reliant on overdeveloped rites and the classics of their long-dead literary tradition. By contrast, the tribespeople retained vitality through their very primitiveness.

Shen Congwen describes a difference in the ethos of the Han and the Miao that is seconded by more objective observers:[6] the tribespeople do not read, seek to marry into a particular station, tell lies, or have the slightest idea of how to make a profit from a commercial transaction. Shen, however, endows these traits with moral import, seeing in them a directness undulled by inhibitions resulting from the literacy, acquisitiveness, and class distinctions of Han civilization. His Miao concern themselves only with working hard to subsist, appeasing the ubiquitous spirits and demons, and joining communally for emotional release through the simple pleasures of wine, song, group games, and spontaneous love-making. In his hands, the daily lives of the Miao appear rich in the creativity of untamed thinking and direct aesthetic apprehension of the world. At times their passion for life, best demonstrated at festival time, reaches a pitch of frenzied possession; it seems to represent a degree of success in uniting with the Infinite that the Han can only speak— or rather write—about.

It is before the Infinite that the cultural bankruptcy of the ritually overburdened Han stands most fully exposed, in Shen Congwen's vision. Man must confront the Infinite, whether among the primal elements at the Southwest frontier, or amid the sophisticated institutions of twentieth-century life. Though the Han identify themselves, and civilization itself, with their own economic prowess and empty rites, despising tribal folk as barbarians, the way of the Miao is no more than the elemental humanity of the simple life. Their culture and vitality once belonged to the Han, before the Han became insensitive and narrow of vision; the Miao way, in Shen's imagination, is that of the Chinese race when it was young.

Unfortunately, there is no reliable history of the Miao to use as a yardstick for evaluating Shen's poignant visions. Han and Miao historians of the past 500 years have typically concocted far more fanciful ethnic histories than he: myths that interlink the fate of their two "races" according to various forms of primordial enmity or sibling rivalry. The Miao have been traced back to the Han people's own mythic progenitor, the Yellow Emperor; to Chiyou, the Yellow Emperor's legendary aboriginal foe; to a wayward race from around Dongting Lake who were sent west by the Chinese Sage King Shun and chastised by Yu the Great; or to the dog Panhu, a totemistic ancestor more often acknowledged by the Yao tribes.[7]

Actually, though the word "Miao" appears in ancient Chinese classics, the Miao-speaking peoples of today are historically traceable only to the Song dynasty. Possibly they were "aboriginal" in West Hunan only to the extent of having migrated, from contiguous mountain homelands in the west, to the region's high western plateau (Upper West Hunan) just before the Han ascended to those parts during their Song era. Miao might have learned paddy agriculture, descended as far as the lower Yuan valley, and then been pushed by the Han back to where they came from. But there is no reason to assume that the Miao were the first tribal people to live in Lower, or even Upper, West Hunan. It is chiefly Ming-Qing Han historians who, fascinated by the resistant and resilient Miao, have reconstructed them into worthy foes (from a Chinese point of view) by conferring on them an ancient genealogy.

Probably Shen Congwen was wise to gloss over his hill folks' ancestry—and thus the unbridgeable cultural and racial gaps between them and the Han that some ethnically conscious people presumed must exist. His tribespeople, having ambiguous bloodlines, are the more powerful as modern cultural symbols of a lost happiness that might belong to any ethnic group, and harder to undermine through ethnographic fact or, more to the point, lack of facts. The Miao seem to the eye as exotic as they are independent. Their language is outside the Sino-Tibetan group. And yet, their tradition is in part a treasury of the culture of others. Much as Shen imagined, the Miao have preserved certain ancient Han customs that the Han long ago forgot. The Miao—and the Han—have also absorbed traits from colorful ancient Southwestern peoples in the Tai language group, those represented today by peoples spoken of in Mandarin as the Zhuang, Dai, and Zhongjia. So it is not contradictory to think of the Miao as culturally "ancient" but ethnically "young," and as ritually "conservative," however quick they have been to adapt to social and economic change.[8]

Behind the confusion about ethnic origins is the fact that hardly any of the Southwestern ethnic groups are culturally uniform or politically united amongst themselves; there lies part of their attractiveness to the modern mind. The Man who for millennia fought to keep the Han out of Lower West Hunan may have been Tai (who have been assimilated for centuries), and/or ancestors of the now nearly assimilated Tujia. Tujia live along some of the less inviting Yuan tributaries and the hills above them. Although they now speak Chinese more than their own tongue, they may be the source of much of the Southwestern cultural flavor West Hunan enjoys today. They were known as the Tu Man 50 years ago and have their own military history, having been sent east to fight the Japanese pirates under native heads during the Ming. Other peoples of demonstrably ancient residence in West Hunan include the Dong and mountain peoples like the Yao and Gelao (Kehlao), old foes of the Miao who have now almost disappeared. All these folk are offspring of ancient Chu, collective creators of the ethnically mixed exoticism that Chinese people associate with their Southwest.[9]

Better corroborated are the old histories' accounts of how Han people, in the last millennium, migrated up the valleys of the Yuan River and its tributaries, pushing those who stood in their way onto higher elevations. Finally, in the Ming and Qing dynasties, land-hungry Han climbed the mountain slopes to farm the rugged high plateaus that extend west beyond Hunan into the Miao redoubt of Guizhou province. The border mountains of Upper West Hunan, a fifty-mile-wide natural divide between the Yuan basin and the river systems of Guizhou farther west, became the final battleground between the master lettered race and the aborigines. The Han tried to end frontier conflict in 1615 by constructing an earthen wall (a lesser version of the Great Wall along the northern frontier), and forcibly moving all Miao west of it. The barrier lay within Miao territory—a few miles west of what would be Shen Congwen's birthplace—and the Miao destroyed it in 1628, when Ming power deteriorated. In the eighteenth century, the Han, under Manchu rule, struck back. To put it in the terms of a West Hunanese Miao legend that Shen adapted into a modern short story, the Han employed their most frightful weapons: soldiers and officials.[10]

The Qing planted frontier military outposts, from walled cities to watchtowers, deep in the Miao uplands. Among them was a town founded or refounded in 1700, to govern Miao of the Zhen Stream (Zhenqi) and the Gan Plain (Ganziping): "Zhen'gan." It became the focus of regionwide Han and Manchu power when the circuit taking in all of West Hunan was headquartered there in 1704. Though even in 1911 only 3,000–5,000 people lived inside Zhen'gan's walls, 7,000 regulation soldiers resided in the environs, to pacify not only the restive Miao uplands, but the "civilized" Yuan River lowlands, and neighboring provinces, too.[11]

Garrison cities symbolized imperial invasion in the most elemental cultural sense, for the tribespeople had not previously known urban concentrations. To the Han, cities at the frontier were, above all, fortresses protecting soldiers and farmer-soldiers. Moreover, as Shen Congwen is intent on pointing out, the merchants who followed on the heels of the soldiers and soon gained control of the local economy were not locals, but natives of faraway Jiangxi (those who monopolized trade in cloth), Guangdong (medicine), and Fujian (tobacco).[12]

The wall-building Han constructed smaller versions of their cities even in the countryside: *bao* (forts), *tun* (small forts), *diaobao* (blockhouses), and *yingxun* (guard stations). Anthropologists in the 1930's were startled to see how many still stood. *Bao* had a circular wall of earth or stone, with one gate at either end of a single through street. Larger *bao* had a cross street and three or four gates. It was in such a fortified village, called Huangluozhai, that Shen Congwen's father was nearly eaten by a tiger at the age of one or two. *Tun*, built in more sparsely settled areas, were only 100 or so feet wide and 100 to 300 feet long, big enough to accommodate a few dozen men, their animals, and stores of grain. *Tun* had walls of stone and brick four to five feet tall, with crenellations and musket holes. The smaller fortifications, placed at fixed intervals along hillcrests (*diaobao*) or along highways (*yingxun*), were no bigger than houses, but villages to house their garrisons grew up around them and remained anchored to the same spots in the twentieth century. By Shen's count, Zhen'gan oversaw about 1,000 blockhouses and over 300 guard stations. A century after bloody reprisals had ended the great Miao rebellion of 1795–1806, frontier militarism had become rather pastoral. The battlements dotting the upland ridges had crumbled into romantic ruins housing the descendants of the frontier soldiers and their families, many of whom remained on the military payroll after 1911. It was a landscape that let one "visualize the warning horns and drums, the torch alarm signals being communicated from one watchtower to the next."[13]

Besides providing a romantic physical backdrop for Shen Congwen's fiction, the walled settlements symbolically divided the populace into urban dwellers and those "in the country." The social chasm between city and country, universal in China, was originally an ethnic one in West Hunan. When many Miao assimilated, it became more a cultural one. Nonetheless, in twentieth-century West Hunan, "country folk" (*xiangxiaren*) was still a euphemism for "Miao."[14] "Country folk" to Shen Congwen, who considers himself one, means only the opposite of "folk from downstream," not necessarily Miao. But his country folk sound like Miao when he describes them: "'stupid,' awkward, incapacitated in society. Not in on city folks' etiquette, even the bare rules and regulations— hence unable to speak, and likely to get backed up into fights."[15] The Miao still suffered from intense discrimination unless they could pass for Han, but by Shen Congwen's time many had joined the army and moved into the cities (including Zhen'gan, where they were one-third of the urban residents).[16] In Shen's stories we see Miao tending fields just outside the city wall, running shops making bean curd, peddling buckwheat *baba* (coarse biscuits) in stands along the street, even acting as boatmen. Above all, intermarriage, cultural assimilation, and reverse assimilation (Han-to-Miao) had produced a hybrid Sino-Miao regional culture among the hardy agricultural folk outside the city wall. As a story of Shen's puts it, "you can almost say that there has been a mutual assimilation in customs and ethnic characteristics, like the alloying of tin and lead in the making of a pot."[17]

Meanwhile, up north and west of Zhen'gan, the unassimilated Miao continued in the way of their ancestors undisturbed. They still avoided the passes, post roads, and communications centers where Han had concentrated for defensive purposes, preferring security through isolation on the least accessible hillsides. Their villages, called *zhai* (stockades), had no regular streets like Chinese villages, but were a maze of alleys where strangers lost their way and could be ambushed. The Miao knew wet-field agriculture and even constructed waterwheels to irrigate mountain terraces, but many of them lived off the mountains with slash-and-burn technology. Perhaps they did this because it was their custom; perhaps because Han encroachment on their land forced them to regress. The Miao had paid a high price for their independence. Yet, they appeared no less cheerful for all that.[18]

Shen Congwen was not the first to create an image of West Hunan as a land forgotten by time, socially tranquil but full of "primitive" energy. West Hunan's scenic beauty, relatively unaffected by Chinese landscaping and literary commemoration, was by the twentieth century earning it the title of "China's Switzerland."[19] Foreign visitors in particular beat the drums for West Hunan as the most scenic area in all the Yangzi drainage system, perhaps because it was one of the few areas in China that remained closed to them until the twentieth century. The mountains of West Hunan are not high, but the waters have sculpted them into wondrous shapes and drenched them in green. Mountain caves, violent river rapids, and high cliffs plunging to stream beds complete a panorama most agreeable to the romantic temperament. Many of the scenic attractions are difficult of access even now. The Miao used to keep some of them secret from the Han.

West Hunan was also viewed, in the war-torn early years of the Republic, as a relatively undisturbed, independent "little kingdom." Some, mostly outsiders, even called it Shiwai Taoyuan, the Chinese Shangri-La.[20] Unaware that the retiring attitude of West Hunan's aborigines toward the outside world bespoke xenophobia as much as shyness, outsiders presumed that the folk who lived off the main highways must be as carefree as the lost villagers of the legendary Peach Blossom Spring, which was now said to be near the Yuan River town having that name (Taoyuan).

How could a land beset by conflicts between Miao and Han, hill and valley, and west and east, appear to anyone as a territory with a common regional identity? Multiethnicity and the fact that previous regional integration had come about through Han imperialism did retard the growth of regional self-consciousness. But as it happened, warlordism offered new opportunities for West Hunanese, including even the Miao, to rescue their region from imperial subjugation and win complete political autonomy.

Four conditions unique to West Hunan facilitated this remarkable transformation. First, the military nature of political rule in West Hunan persisted until the twentieth century, and the army was a local one—no modernized late-Qing New Army was ever introduced into the region. When sovereignty passed to the military throughout China, West Hunan's was already in place, with no competitors. Second, it was a strategic blessing that the longstanding administrative center at Zhen'gan was not in the economic core area of Lower West Hunan, but out of the way in the hills (there originally to watch over the hill folks' "counter-core").[21] Third, Zhen'gan's loss of subsidies from the national and provincial governments was more than made up for by a new economic resource: convoys of opium going down the Yuan. The Sino-Miao Zhen'ganese, long the object of eastern colonialism, turned the tables and acquired economic as well as imperial sway over the lowlanders. Fourth, the old Zhen'gan elite remained relatively cohesive. Thanks to their interrelatedness and links to old military institutions that the Qing neglected to modernize, they oversaw a smooth transition for their sons and protégés into the new local elite.

West Hunan's army had been created in the first three decades of the eighteenth century, when Chinese officials replaced native heads in the last unabsorbed Miao redoubts and created in this territory three new counties ("the three *ting*"), each directly ruled by the circuit and centered on a walled city: Zhen'gan, Qianzhou, and Yongsui. (When Yongsui subsequently proved indefensible, its garrison was moved to Chadong, which Shen Congwen immortalized as "The Frontier City.") Each city was protected by a contingent of Green Standard regular troops.

Following the Miao rebellion of 1795–1806, an army of 7,800 Green Standard regulars was assigned to remain in the three *ting* and two other upland counties. Half were stationed in Zhen'gan, under a brigade general answering to the commander-in-chief (*tidu*) of Hunan—who was not in Changsha but in Chenzhou, West Hunan, nearer the restiveness. The *tidu* in turn answered to the Huguang (Hubei-Hunan) governor-general in Wuchang to the north, not to the governor of Hunan. Militarily, then, West Hunan was again more closely linked with Hubei than with Hunan.

By 1849, on the eve of the Taiping Rebellion, all but five of the 53 battalions in the entire province of Hunan were commanded from cities west of the Snowy Peaks, 35 from Zhen'gan alone. Late-Qing military reform demobilized Green Standard armies all over China and replaced them with New Army troops, but the dynasty was overthrown before reform ever reached West Hunan. Therefore, when the link to the north was severed, the post of Zhen'gan brigade general evolved into that of defense commissioner of West Hunan, under the garrison system of the Chinese Republic; after West Hunan became independent under a warlord regime in 1917, the Zhen'gan defense commissioner took formal claim to the title of head of the military administration of West Hunan.[22]

These figures do not include a different sort of Green Standard army (a colony or *tuntian* army) that likewise dated back to the early nineteenth century. Although these troops did report to the governor of Hunan in Changsha, they escaped demobilization as did the regulars. They were particularly easy for the local elite to convert from imperial service to the local cause because their command was already centralized in Zhen'gan (under the circuit intendant), and because they were bound together with the very soil of West Hunan, in a great public agricultural settlement. The basis of it was over 100,000 *mou* of nationalized farms that were variously cultivated by soldiers or rented to civilians to subsidize the army.

Though its main force was a Han army of 8,000, the military colony had something of the appearance of a Han-Miao commonwealth in time of peace, for "good" Miao had been organized into a 5,000-man Miao *tuntian* army commanded by Miao officers. The

Miao had their own colony fields to plant, their own blockhouses to guard, and their own forts to live in. Virtually native heads, the Miao officers exercised judicial, taxation, and police power over all Miao in the five frontier counties, so as to serve as a buffer between the ethnic groups. Though they were not supposed to pass on their posts to their sons, they evidently became a continuous legitimate ruling group.

Most *tuntian* troops were assimilated with the regulars in a grand reorganization of 1912, but the colony itself—a public enterprise that parceled out land, paid soldiers and officials, and granted partial autonomy to the Miao—survived. Miao officers, still bearing old Qing dynasty titles that ought to have been abolished with the fall of the Manchus, remained in place under successive Han and Miao warlords until Nationalist armies took control of West Hunan in 1935.[23] In Shen's eyes, the colony had made his homeland the guardian of an antique social ethos that united Han with Miao, sword with plow, and city with country. Its demise, in 1936, did in fact mark the end of autonomous West Hunan and lead to 15 years of civil disorder—as well as Shen Congwen's last full-length novel, *Long River*.

Shen Congwen's Childhood

Shen Yuehuan (who in late adolescence styled himself "Congwen," the name we shall use from the outset) was born on December 28, 1902, to Shen Zongsi and a woman surnamed Huang who was known to her children only as "Mother." The fourth child of nine, Congwen was the second male, hence "Elder Brother No. 2" (Erge) to his younger siblings. He must have liked being called that; Liang Sicheng called him "Erge" when they became friends 20 years later, and Shen refers to his autobiographical persona as "Erge" in several of his early stories.[24]

The Shen family was proud of its past, though its historical roots were very shallow. The author tells us that there used to be a village of Shens, Han people, to the west of Zhen'gan. The villagers mined cinnabar for the government and may have been transported to the Miao frontier from the east as punishment. That is speculative, Shen Congwen admits, but the fact that he can trace his ancestry back only two generations, in a nation whose highborn like to claim genealogies going back the better part of a millennium, is indication enough of the humble origins of his family. Still, in as "young" a region as West Hunan, even the Shens passed for an "old family."[25] The family was suddenly established during the young manhood of Congwen's grandfather, Shen Hongfu. People called him Maogou, or "Hairy Dog" Shen. Imperiled by Taiping and other rebels during the 1850's and 1860's, the Qing allowed men like Hongfu who had proved themselves in battle to become generals of the Gan Army, with command over their own fellow-townsmen. That was a double concession, to nonliterary ability and to regionalism. In normal times military, like civil, leadership stemmed from success in the examination system, and postings assiduously guarded against possible ties between officers and their men. Says his grandson, with a touch of exaggeration, Shen Hongfu and three other heroic locals all rose from selling horse fodder to become Gan Army generals and commanders-in-chief of provinces around the age of 20.[26] After fighting Moslem, Miao, and Taiping rebels, Shen Hongfu was in fact named acting commander-in-chief of Guizhou province in 1863, when he was about 25. This came about when his commander Tian Xingshu, himself only 26, had to be cashiered for creating an international crisis for the Manchu court by persecuting Catholic missionaries. Of Shen Hongfu we can only confirm that, after his moment of glory at the provincial level, he fought on as a brigade commander for at least a year. A battle wound brought him home to a premature death.[27]

The "glory and property" Shen Hongfu won so dearly left his family in a position of local prominence. His widow adopted a son from his brother Shen Hongfang, Shen Zongsi, to become the heir, and Zongsi embarked on a course of literary and military study intended to make a general of him.[28] Though Shen Zongsi did become an officer, it was his misfortune to be assigned to the Dagu Forts, which fell to foreign troops during the 1900 Boxer crisis. His career in ruins, and having lost considerable family property, Zongsi returned home and fathered his second son.[29]

Congwen's family was still well-off during his childhood. The family land, seven miles outside of Fenghuang (as Zhen'gan was known after 1913), yielded an annual rent of about 300 piculs of grain, a third of which went to Shen Zongsi, who was able to give even his daughters some elementary classical education in private schools.[30] He had hopes of being elected to the provincial assembly after the 1911 Revolution, but when his bid failed he grew despondent and left for Peking, where he joined a cabal to assassinate President Yuan Shikai. After the plot was discovered by Yuan's spies, Zongsi escaped and hid out with friends in Rehe (Inner Mongolia). There he changed his name and started his officer's career over again at China's farthest frontiers: Manchuria, Mongolia, and Tibet. He never communicated with his family until after Yuan Shikai's death, when he wrote to mortgage the family land in repayment of a debt. He returned to West Hunan only when Congwen's elder brother, who worked as an artist in Manchuria, sought him out and brought him back. Shen Congwen saw his father just once more, in 1922, while going to Peking. Congwen himself got his father his last job, in a West Hunan military hospital. Shen Zongsi died about 1931. Hopes that the family would produce another general had already for some time been pinned on Congwen's younger brother, a Whampoa Military Academy graduate.[31]

Until the 1980's, Shen Congwen left this dark family matter unspoken, as he did another: his ethnicity. It is now clear that his ancestry is mostly non-Han, for his mother was a Tujia, and his paternal grandmother (the mother of Shen Zongsi) was a Miao. Tujia who could pass for Han were not despised as much as Miao, and Congwen's maternal grandfather, Huang Heqing, was even an educated man—the only one in Zhen'gan according to his grandson. (Presaging his grandson's love of place, Heqing compiled a gazetteer of Fenghuang *ting*). Shen's mother grew up better educated than his father, though she lived her early years in army camps with her military brother, Huang Jingming.* Still, when a Huang died, his name changed "back to Zhang," which evidently was the ancestors' name before one of them became a convict.[32] The real skeleton in the family closet, though, was Shen Congwen's paternal grandmother. When one of her sons became Shen Hongfu's heir, an elaborate cover-up had to be arranged. Once the Miao woman was safely removed to the countryside, she was pronounced dead and said to have been Han. There was a phony burial of an empty coffin in her name, which succeeded in fooling both the neighbors and later generations.[33]

Shen Congwen learned the full story of this from his mother on

*Huang Jingming was something of a progressive. He ran, out of the Shen home, Fenghuang's first postal drop and its first photography studio. Congwen's mother learned how to read from him, and even how to take pictures. Later Huang Jingming became the grandfather of the celebrated Fenghuang artist Huang Yongyu (Shen Congwen's first cousin once removed).

her deathbed in 1934, having only heard the first facts about it from his father at the age of 19—though he might have suspected something beforehand from his father's Miao connections in the countryside. Shen's autobiography (1932) drops a hint (and nothing more), by referring to a swarthy country cousin [Teng] Lenghan, who told him stories of the Miao people and could call up many Miao combatants. Congwen's mother's non-Han origins must have been apparent as well. Shen may even have thought her Miao, for he probably had a hand in the composition of a 1930 thumbnail biography that said his *maternal* grandmother and great-grandmother were Guizhou Miao. (Perhaps he, like many Han in West Hunan, was unclear about the distinction between Tujia and Miao, or perhaps the maternal side really was as complicated as the paternal.) Confused though he must have been, Shen even as a young writer felt a bond with the Miao. He expressed belligerent pride in their culture and sympathy for them as an oppressed people. Yet, he may also have felt ambivalence, perhaps embarrassment, about his "race." Only once, in a rare 1931 preface, did he directly acknowledge that he had Miao blood.[34]

Personal discomfiture may thus lie behind certain reticences in Shen Congwen's writings about family, although many of his first works are family reminiscences, or transformations of them. Later he took up imaginative family relationships, like that between the young heroine and her grandfather in his magnum opus, *The Frontier City*. As this last work exemplifies, the nuclear family, including its cross-generational misunderstandings, is very important in Shen's fiction. Yet he never composed an epic novel centered around a large, extended family, much less a major historical work within his regional oeuvre tracing the formation of his own or any other family from that crucial nineteenth-century era when foundations were being laid. He did not lack material. His father told him many stories about the exploits of Shen Hongfu and the "Long Hairs" (Taipings), and about what Zongsi himself had seen at the time of the Boxers. His household included at least a maternal grandmother and servants, and in the countryside nearby were three great uncle's sons, two aunts, and some maternal cousins. Nor is family saga unknown to Chinese literature: Shen's adulthood friend Ba Jin often trod a creative path between grand family history and fiction, and so did *The Dream of the Red Chamber*, one of Shen's favorite works of all time.[35]

Five characters recur in Shen's earliest family sketches: a mischievous Congwen persona; his little brother Dieyu, a companion; their long-suffering mother, full of maternal tenderness and sympathy; Congwen's elder brother Yunlu, whose duty it is to punish Congwen, as it was in real life; and Little Sister No. 9, the family pet, a sometime ally against elder brother and sometime vengeful brat. "Hearthside," a little story probably based on actual reminiscence, is illustrative. When Congwen and his little brother want an evening snack, they put Little Nine up to complaining that she is hungry. Mother loves her best and will be sure to have the young maid, Chunxiu, cook up a pot of bird's-nest or lotus-seed congee (rice gruel) for all to enjoy. But first Little Nine must be bribed. The emphasis on the warmth of interpersonal relations within the nuclear family, and the comedy of momentary bickering and personality clashes, seem to represent what Shen's own family meant to him—rather than the solemn permanency of the family as a corporate structure. Later, Congwen's elder brother, who has grown up and become an artist, appears in a more sympathetic role. The Congwen persona, a young man in his twenties, has nearly failed in his quest to become a published author in Peking, so elder brother invites him up to Manchuria to help him find a job. The tale seems realistic, until it takes a remarkable turn: big brother tries to initiate Congwen into sex by arranging an affair for him with the wife of a friend![36]

Finally, in works of the late 1920's, Shen puts Mother and Little Nine into his writings as they were at the time, sharing hard times with a young author. Most of the family land was sold by the time Shen Congwen took off for the army at 15; later the family went "bankrupt," so that Shen's mother and sister were actually reduced to coming to Peking to live off Congwen's meager manuscript fees. "A Woman's Diary," written in the voice of his sister-in-law, is another work rich in familial feeling, although seemingly farther afield from Shen's experience. It revolves around the same familiar characters: the diarist wonders how she can arrange a match for her brother-in-law, an author in Peking, evidently Shen himself.[37]

Prominent by their absence in all of this are Shen Congwen's father and the patriarchal family. Congwen really did feel closer to his mother than his father. He writes that she influenced him more. She taught him to read, told him many stories, explained the uses of medicinal plants, and even instilled in him "the decisiveness one must have to be a man." Shen Zongsi's failures under both the old and the new systems increased his wife's responsibility for the upbringing of his children. Probably they also made Shen Congwen desperate to succeed in an official career, to compensate. Family legend seems unfortunately to have exaggerated the measure of Shen Hongfu's success that his descendants would have to live up to: Congwen mistakenly believed that Hongfu had held the highest civil office in Guizhou.[38]

Whether or not Shen Zongsi was close enough to his children to communicate feelings of inadequacy of his own, Congwen always felt distanced from and inadequate before him. One of the author's strongest memories was of his father threatening to cut a finger off as punishment for playing hooky. This is less likely a reflection of Oedipal antagonism than one of filial guilt drummed into Congwen by his society. In the end, Congwen felt he "really wounded that soldier's heart." And then Shen Zongsi left him.[39]

Shen Congwen indeed liked to write of escape from the suffocating embrace of the family. Disobedience, and stratagems to avoid punishment after tasting forbidden fruits like gambling and hooky, are motifs found in many works besides "Hearthside." Likewise, the most interesting relatives in Shen's writings are not the members of his nuclear family, but semirespectable outliers: his illiterate "godfather," Fourth Uncle Teng, a friend of the family who sold herbal medicines, told fortunes, and taught the martial arts; a relative who beheaded people for a living; and Congwen's sister-in-law, an illiterate child bride (*tongyangxi*) who aspired to become a liberated woman, like Shen's child character Xiaoxiao.[40]

Religion in Shen's works, too, focuses more on communal celebration than on family-centered reverence and filial piety. Sometimes the appurtenances of periodic festivals, such as special holiday foods, appear in the warm context of family togetherness, as in the reminiscence "Holiday Fruit Congee." More often the author depicts outdoor festivals and bonds between ritual specialists and the community as a whole. This emphasis is regional as well as personal. Outdoor festivals were especially prevalent in the Southwest, owing to the tribal heritage, and the Han people of Shen's locale hired Miao shamans to conduct their rituals.[41]

Shen Congwen's works, though rich both in personal nostalgia and in regional myth, generally show little formal sense of history. His autobiography particularly stresses the influences from outside the high culture that helped form his temperament. The author emerges as a naughty little boy anxious to escape the control of straitlaced adult society. In this lies a strong anti-Confucian message from a New Intellectual reflecting on his life from the vantage point of his rebellious twenties. But as in the case of Hu Shi, a heavy dose of popular culture seems to have been a concomitant of being educated by women (besides his mother, Shen's first instructor was an uncle's wife who tutored his sisters). Congwen was unusually sensitive and curious about the world around him, and his eye for detail is part of his artistic genius. Young Shen was driven to poke into the secrets of town and country; he begged people to tell him stories, show him how to make something, tell him how things got to be the way they were. He found it thrilling to risk getting lost by venturing as far away from home as he could and finding his own way back, anonymously. When denied his freedom—as, for example, when he was forced to kneel in a corner by himself as punishment—his imagination would fill the void, spinning out entrancing visions of what he had seen earlier in the day. He did this during school, too, for memorizing texts was just too easy for him.[42]

Shen Congwen has not left us guessing about how he spent his childhood. His playmates included relatives and hefty country boys who were good companions for climbing trees, fighting, and picking bamboo shoots, berries, and medicinal herbs to heal the scrapes and wounds that resulted. In spring, the boys flew kites and went up into the mountains to pick flowers, having their way contested in gang wars of reasonably innocent dimensions. In summer, they caught crickets, went to puppet plays, or took off an afternoon to look for crabs and swim in the river. If you couldn't swim, you tied your trousers at the end and "inflated" them. But Congwen swam well and did so often, defying his family's worries about his safety. He learned to catch fish with his bare hands, and to model "guns" out of mud, like a little Miao boy. The object was to fashion the gun making the loudest "bang" when the sunbaked vessel was dashed on the ground.[43]

The gang also delighted in going to market, an opportunity that came twice a lunar week (every five days). The most intriguing market was a few miles to the west of Fenghuang. Miao chieftains arrived with their daughters on small boats and rafts, singing as they came, to exchange cattle, sheep, and tobacco—or perhaps wildcat and tiger skins—for salt and sugar. They dueled, gambled, and sold the prize fowl that would later appear in the city cockfighting arena. At special Miao festivals, Shen even saw bullfights and "bludgeoning the ox," ceremonies soon to be extinct. He knew just enough Miao language to get by—to purchase, more likely than not, a snack of dog meat. The narrator of "In a Private School" relates that a Miao headman might invite young Han folk of good breeding like himself onto a raft. There he offered the "young masters" his own pipe as well as sweet potatoes, sugarcane, and pears tended by his own daughter—for manual labor was honored, not despised, among the Miao. Miao women, few of whom bound their feet, briskly walked to market in ceremonial dress: embroidered tunics, oversized turbans, silver earrings the circumference of rice bowls, and silver-sequined skirts, "like military armor." The narrator remembers the vista as "seductive, savage, with an ethos of its own, ... simply a miracle within a dream!"[44]

Young boys on the loose in West Hunan also stole plums, peaches, and radishes, drank from the flooded fields, picked berries and wild cherries from the raised paths between, or gathered loquats by the road. When an angry peasant gave pursuit, young Congwen provoked him with a mountain song. The boys also emulated the combat of their elders. Duels were a common and socially accepted way of settling disputes in Fenghuang. They were fought in public, since honor was at stake, with children watching from the sidelines. Later Shen Congwen, for all his pacifism, pictured the dueling men as heroes straight out of *The Romance of the Three Kingdoms*—"generous and magnanimous, self-effacing and helpful to others, willing to exact vengeance for the sake of friendship, loving righteousness and given to offering alms, most of them extremely filial, too."[45]

If we can take the narrator of "My Primary School Education" at his word, boys in Fenghuang eleven years old and younger belonged to gangs organized according to street neighborhood. They regularly had rumbles to fight for turf, especially seating rights at the day-long puppet play on the tutelary deities' birthdays. Seats were allotted by street. Gangs tried to exclude children from outside the neighborhood at their own festival, and perhaps invade other neighborhoods on their holidays.

Shen himself often played the role of gang leader, or "military governor" (*dudu*). He was in charge of the minor expenses involved in providing each combatant with his weapon, a sharpened bamboo stake. (Fenghuang boys carried one concealed in their trousers at all times, for defense against "bad people and mean dogs.") Congwen also arranged practice drills. He positioned "warrior" friends and classmates astride stout country boys willing to serve as "horses." Opposing jousters locked in combat, oblivious to small flesh wounds. To test their strength, the boys arranged tugs-of-war or locked hands to encircle selected combatants, forcing them to fight with one hand tied behind their back, or maybe two-on-one; honor required that someone go home crying. They had of course watched soldiers drill with real weapons and shields, at the circuit yamen.

On the day of the play, the "military governor's" "regimental commanders" went door to door, declaiming mobilization orders as in the army: "Brothers! Before the gongs and drums open the event, you must go to the battleground with your weapons and uniforms, to defend the stage. . . . Those without weapons who do not go to the military governor to receive their proper allowance will be punished according to law." In an open space well away from the play itself, the combatants then paired off and dueled with their stakes, "putting their lives on the line like Miaozi* storming a *bao* fort!" This led to the formation of enmities, taunts out on the street between rival gang members, and duels like those among the frontier elders. To refuse a challenge was to lose face before friend and foe. According to "My Primary School Education," the group enforced bravery through regulations:

"He who sees the enemy but avoids him will be fined one copper.

"He who does not cry when wounded will be rewarded with one copper.

"He who is cornered when alone and attacked by two or more adversaries will be rewarded with two coppers.

"He who is thrice cursed but dares not engage in battle will be fined two coppers."[46]

Indeed, Shen seemed always to be testing his physical stamina. Measles had brought him near death at the age of five and worms kept him yellow and sickly, so that people called him "monkey" behind his back. Ever after, he remained concerned about appearing small and scrawny. Shen was not really so short, for a South-

---

*A diminutive epithet for "Miao," abusive or, as here, comical.

erner, but the army could only have increased his self-consciousness, for soldiers lined up by height, tallest first. Perhaps this explains his attraction to swimming and scrapping. In any case, Shen Congwen and company, however "martial," feared ghosts enough to restrict their play to daylight hours.[47]

Shen Congwen loved competition generally, unless his writings about cricket fights, quail fights (at the city god's temple), cockfights, and gambling were just psychic compensation for his later quietude as a scholar. He first bet on crickets, then graduated to gambling with dice. At first he put up money left over from his morning at the vegetable market. Later he began to bet all his shopping money. His maternal grandmother spoiled him by providing financial bailouts. But the truth came out, and Congwen's elder brother was assigned the task of whipping him and depriving him of food. Congwen's very association with the gamblers, and use of their gutter talk, embarrassed the whole family.[48]

Fortunately, the pack Shen ran with also enjoyed more laudable rural pastimes. They thought harvests interesting enough to go see them. Congwen learned how to identify crops and pests, catch grasshoppers and hedgehogs, and fish in flooded fields. He made little baskets from rice straw, like Uncle Teng's in *Long River*, and cylindrical whistles rolled from tung bark. His family hunted foxes, wild boars, deer, and wild pheasant, luring the latter with a whistle and a domesticated decoy. (Bird calls and tree identification would become a lifelong hobby.) Birds were brought down with homemade shot stuffed into a fowling piece.[49]

Later Shen Congwen liked to call himself a country person, but really he loved nothing more than the manufacturing processes he observed in town, from the extraction of tung oil to fireworks production. He made detours on his way to school to watch needle-grinding; the making of umbrellas, leather shoes, and dyes; the manufacture of bean curd and of soybean vermicelli; the making and peddling of sweets, such as lotus candies and sugar Buddhas; and the weaving of mats and ropes. Executions, butchering, barbering, bartering, and the construction of devotional objects and sedan chairs all fired his imagination. That he learned all the processes by heart will surprise no one who has seen his meticulous, sometimes even distracting descriptions of them in fictional works. Shen Congwen in particular shows young and old alike becoming rapt before two professions that were his favorites: milling grain and working iron and steel. Even when he was a young soldier, Shen spent his spare time watching smelting, forging, and smithing at small-scale furnaces. He would have us believe that he might just as easily have changed to that profession.[50] Two other passions of the author had yet really to develop. Shen claims that the world of water influenced him from childhood, but it was chiefly after going downstream with the army that he got to know boats and how to live on them. Later still, particularly after he could afford a phonograph in the 1940's, he discovered a love of music, including Western classical music. As a child he had gone to local West Hunanese operas (*Yangxi*) and the more extemporaneous Miao Nuo dramas. As with Lu Xun, though, fondness for local music and drama translated into disdain for the high-pitched droning of Peking (Northern) opera. Shen disliked the latter both for its musical qualities and its fashionable popularity among the Republican bourgeoisie. No doubt it is psychologically significant that Congwen's father dearly loved Peking opera and wanted his son to become a great opera singer.[51]

It is not surprising that West Hunan little influenced Shen Congwen's later classical predilections, for being in a military gentry family was different from belonging to the "scholar-gentry," and the whole region was deprived of high culture. There was assuredly no "West Hunan School" of learning, only Yan Ruyi's *Miao fangbei lan* (*Defense against the Miao*, 1843), a compilation of statecraft strategies and tactics that Shen Congwen read by the time he was 30 and even then found boring. In the early twentieth century, progressive local military officers were caught up in a national cult of emulating the great Ming-Qing soldier-scholars Wang Yangming and Zeng Guofan (a Hunanese); Shen Congwen's army buddies, and Mao Zedong, idolized Zeng Guofan even in 1920. What West Hunan did have was social stability: there were few bandits before 1916, or Young Turk cadets.[52]

Shen Congwen and His World in a Time of Transition

Reform came to West Hunan very late, even though military men were noted modernizers elsewhere in late-Qing China. One reason is that West Hunan, unlike other militarized Southwestern regions such as Yunnan, Sichuan, and Guangxi, had no military academy or modern military primary school. It had no New Army, and was not yet sending many native sons to military academies abroad.[53]

Primitive communications prolonged the region's archaism and made modern military tactics less useful than elsewhere in China. West Hunan lacked telegraphic communications until the 1920's, and it was only in 1972 that a railroad penetrated the region. The major towns of Upper West Hunan, including Fenghuang, are 50 rugged miles from a siding even today. West Hunan likewise remained inaccessible by automobile until the mid-1930's. Roads to Fenghuang and the other cities of Upper West Hunan awaited the advent of Communism, in the 1950's. All the while, nodes of administration were shifting away from the old garrison towns to commercial centers. In the 1930's, as in the 1950's, the building of roads only put Fenghuang more deeply in the shadow of more bustling commercial crossroads.[54]

For better or worse, hardly any foreign impact had been felt in Fenghuang. Finnish Lutherans set up outposts in the northwest corner of Hunan after 1902, and other sects visited Lower West Hunan before that, but after two nearly futile decades the first wave of missionaries was actually in retreat. Fenghuang, thanks to the anti-Christian tradition begun by Tian Xingshu, tolerated no permanent mission until the 1930's. Modern nationalism, on the other hand, took hold very slowly in these parts, precisely because foreign merchants and church people were so effectively kept out. At this internal frontier (as opposed to Yunnan, Guangxi, or Tibet), it was impossible to convey any sense that foreign imperialism was plunging China into crisis and international disgrace.[55]

The Revolution of 1911, far from precipitating West Hunan toward modern nationalism, was a throwback to frontier primitivism. In Fenghuang it was a very traditional kind of uprising, a secret society revolt. Miao were the cannon fodder, organized in the Gelaohui (Elder Brothers Society), with local gentry leadership. The targets were the yamens of the Manchus' circuit intendant and brigade commander. The intendant assumed command for the monarchists, after transferring downstream the troops of brigade commander Zhou Ruilong (who was suspected of being in league with his niece's husband, Tian Yingquan, a member of Sun Yatsen's Revolutionary Alliance and a "Dragon Head" in the Gelaohui; Tian was the eldest son of the Tian Xingshu who had commanded Congwen's grandfather). Shen Congwen says, accurately so far as we can tell, that his father, another Gelaohui leader, orchestrated the uprising of the Miao under Tang Lichen. Other plotters included Congwen's military uncles and his Miao cousin Teng Lenghan.[56] The plan was for the Miao to converge on the city from three directions and scale the wall in a surprise attack late at night. Swords, spears, and homemade guns were their weapons, although gentry like the Shens had hunting rifles. The revolt failed, with great loss of life, because the garrison army could not be won over, and partisans within the walls were prevented from offering assistance. When Congwen awoke the next morning, his brothers and sisters were already hiding in Miao caves. Some of his uncles were among the thousand revolutionaries killed. He searched for Lenghan's face among 410 bloody heads that dangled, as a public warning, from captured scaling ladders at the yamen, and he beheld a string of human ears. At the age of nine he suddenly understood what Chinese operas meant by the words "mountains of heads and rivers of blood."[57]

Yet the killing had just begun. The local officials were afraid to arrest the gentry, so they declared a state of "Miao rebellion" out in the *zhai*. Every day, about 100 Miao were rounded up and executed, all at once, by 20 swordsmen. Shen saw some prisoners escape because of the confusion; others, unable to understand Chinese, realized they were to die only when forced to kneel. It was getting cold, so the bodies were simply strewn along the riverbank without burial, 400 or 500 at any given time. Shen and his friends made a game of counting them from atop the city wall.

After a month of this genocide, the gentry conspirators jointly petitioned the governor that further killing be selective. The one or two hundred suspects being arrested daily were then made to submit to a trial by ordeal presided over by the god the Miao trusted most, the Heavenly King (Tian Wang). The accused were brought to his temple, on a hill overlooking the city, and made to cast divination sticks. Though they had one chance in four of being condemned, they accepted the death penalty in silence when their god handed it down. Shen Congwen was allowed outside to watch these ceremonies. Later he reflected that "When I began to understand 'human life,' this is what I knew."[58]

The revolutionary cause finally prevailed in Fenghuang during the third month of 1912, after Han patriots elsewhere had brought the dynasty down. Apart from the fact that army officers began to go around on horseback rather than in sedan chairs, the only effect in Fenghuang was to turn all the old institutions over to the local elite.[59] The region was if anything more isolated from the ebb and flow of national events than before. Tian Yingquan and his faction came to power, but for some reason not Shen Zongsi.

West Hunan had always been backward in education, and it remained so in the first decades of the twentieth century. Under the old examination system, besides the Hanlin scholar Xiong Xiling (who grew up in Yuanzhou), Fenghuang had produced only two metropolitan graduates (*jinshi*) and four "imperial students by special examination" (*bagongsheng*). Late-Qing China scrambled to build modern schools—Hunan had an average of ten lower primary schools per county by 1908—yet Fenghuang founded its first modern primary school only in 1914. Said a high school principal in the 1940's, "West Hunan may be a century behind central Hunan and its cities, but [Upper West Hunan] is two centuries behind the rest of West Hunan."[60]

Shen Congwen therefore grew up with education that both reformers and revolutionaries considered outmoded even before he embarked on it. It seems not to have absorbed much of his energy, however, or made a lasting impression on him. He learned to read at home, at the age of four *sui*, then went with his two elder sisters to study with the woman teacher. At six *sui*, having recovered from the measles, he was favored with a seat in a private family school (*sishu*). He did well, owing to his head start and good memory, but received his own "measure of all the mistreatments meted out to children in *sishu*," by which he no doubt means corporal punishment. The next year, he graduated to a *sishu* with older students.[61]

If "In a Private School" may be taken as autobiography—in view of the many details that reappeared in *Congwen's Autobiography*—Shen and 16 others were tutored by the husband of one of his mother's sisters at a yamen from which he managed some *tuntian* granaries. The school-day routine never varied, though it was interrupted by recesses for breakfast and lunch. In each session, after bowing to a Confucian tablet and the teacher, the pupils recited their lessons out loud, simultaneously but not in unison. Next they practiced their individual textual assignments in writing, reading, recitation, and punctuation of new materials, in that order. The texts included primers like *Jewels for Elementary Learning* and classics like the *Mencius, Analects, Book of Odes,* and *Book of History.* In the afternoon there was a period devoted to explaining what the memorized syllables of text really meant. The students recited two and one-half pages of their primer daily, learned 16 new characters, and filled in two pages of copybook. For relief, the narrator of "In a Private School" confides, he frequently asked for permission to go to the toilet. Actually he chased rabbits as they scampered under the granaries. After school, students were dismissed one by one, lest their pent-up energies lead to fistfights. The teacher so feared that his pupils would go off swimming during the lunch break that he painted a red character on their palms. The rascals therefore learned to swim with one hand out of the water.[62]

When Shen Congwen changed schools, the older group of boys he fell in with included a cousin named Zhang, who taught him to play hooky in earnest. At this time he gave up on school but became a good "storyteller" to cover his indiscretions: "My life that year formed the basis of my character and feelings for the rest of my days.... Having learned to use my eyes to take in everything in this world, to live amid all life, I found school unspeakably boring." Shen later reproached himself for letting down his family, and repaying his parents by becoming "a person who didn't respect himself at all." Thus when he was sent into the army as a foot soldier, he felt he was getting his just deserts.[63] Yet nearly all of China's New Intellectuals echoed Shen Congwen's dislike of the old system's rote learning, moral platitudes, unreasoning obedience to authority, and corporal punishment (in the case of hooky, flogging with a bamboo switch before the tablet of Confucius, sometimes followed by kneeling for as long as it took a stick of incense to burn out). The curriculum was useful only for passing a kind of civil service examination that had expired in 1904; the new doctrines of science, international political order, and Social Darwinism were nowhere to be found. "In a Private School" is unique for presenting the old education so engagingly. It intimately recollects the underside of traditional schooling, with the rascally humor loved by Chinese readers in Chapter Nine of *The Dream of the Red Chamber*, "Mudslinging Boys Brawl in the Classroom."

Shen Congwen did enter Fenghuang's new boys' elementary school in 1915, and its equally new higher primary school in 1916.

But the new subjects failed to capture his attention. Considering all the transfers into institutions just getting off the ground, where pedagogical methods were probably no better than under the old education, his boredom is not surprising. What Shen Congwen liked was the laxity of discipline in the new schools. There were so many opportunities for fighting during recess and on the new weekly day off that he no longer felt a need to play hooky. Two of the four teachers were his cousins.[64] More important, in this backwoods army outpost, was the fact that the military was finally being reformed and reinvigorated—at the end of the 1910's, just as modern political power was coming under military control throughout China. Shen Congwen began to dream of becoming a general, like his grandfather. He reflected, "Where I grew up, it was no disgrace to be a soldier. The glory of the locale had originally been won with the bravery of innumerable men of the past. Everyone wanted to be a soldier. It was a road open to a young man—the only road."[65]

Not reform or revolution, but the 1915–16 civil war against Yuan Shikai, fought just 50 miles south of Fenghuang in Mayang and Huangxian, prodded the local military into modernizing. Leading the fight against Yuan's monarchical pretensions was a fellow Hunanese, Cai E. Fenghuang hosted the Guizhou army, which was allied with Cai's Yunnan troops, and sent its own men to fend off the Northern soldiers and "protect the nation" with spears and pitchforks. The contrast with the reformed Northern troops and even the Guizhou "guests" made change seem imperative. Fenghuang founded separate officers' schools under the defense commissioner's and circuit (Tun Affairs Office) commands, a battalion for administering basic training, and an instruction corps for formally enrolled reserves (*jiaodaodui*). The spirit of patriotic, Japanese-style militarism finally came to West Hunan. Even shopkeepers conceded new prestige to the military as cadets proudly marched down the street in formation. Shen Congwen felt that "the atmosphere of [Fenghuang] was remade."[66]

Shen was only 13, too young for officers' training even by Southwestern standards, but not for after-school drill classes (*jishuban* or *buxizu*) conducted on the parade grounds outside the city wall by an instructor from the officers' training corps (under the circuit). At the urging of a classmate, Shen abandoned any civilian career goals he might have had and plunged resolutely into a military career. He began as a student or replacement soldier (*yubeibing* or *buchongbing*). Bimonthly examinations determined which trainees would formally join the army and receive pay. Congwen was beaten by other candidates in the three examinations he entered, but he still won a commendation and some family esteem. After he had been in training for eight months, his mother arranged with a local officer for Congwen to be taken on as a reservist at Chenzhou (now Yuanling).[67]

Prestige drew Shen Congwen to modern militarism, but role models like Fourth Uncle Teng made him love old-style soldiering more. When Congwen was about five, Teng had virtually become his guardian for a time; Shen's father handed the boy over so that Teng could rid him of intestinal roundworms. (It was Teng himself, as fortuneteller, who had announced that young Shen needed to eat "medicinal" chicken livers with him if he was to get well. Teng renamed the boy Maolin, which Shen would come to adopt as a pen name.) Later, though, Zongsi asked his son to shun this "vulgar illiterate" and his socially marginal trades.* Congwen, naturally, found Teng "rich in humanity and totally lovable," with a more "beautiful character" than anyone else in Fenghuang.[68]

Fenghuang's new craze for military training had provided Fourth Uncle with an irresistible new sideline: tutoring boys in the traditional martial arts. The techniques he taught blended mind with body and warrior with weapon, stressing individual mastery, the teacher-disciple relationship, and the importance of martial bearing. Uncle Teng did not teach annihilation through ballistics; he showed the boys how to handle themselves acrobatically and respect the different characteristics of the traditional weapons, which were no more interchangeable than people.† Shen learned about

---

*In his youth, Teng trained for the Qing exams—through such measures as sleeping curled up in a tub every night and eating eel's blood for breakfast—but some unnamed flaw in his social origins barred him from the military. That drove him into "gypsy" professions. Godfathering, to ward off evil spirits, was itself a subprofession in Fenghuang.

†Shen also learned about weapons from his relative the headsman, the model for Yang Jinbiao in "The New and the Old." Yang has a devil-headed "precious sword" that reveals portents of future executions. His firearm is a single-shot Guangdong-made musket, the Gan Army mainstay until modern (Hanyang) rifles finally arrived, after 1911. At a local gunpowder factory, Congwen observed the manufacture of *huoguan* (primitive grenades, or "stink-pots"), which were fuse-lit ceramic bottles stuffed with gunpowder and shrapnel.

the long spear, the eyebrow-high club, the flail, the iron-toothed rake, round shields woven of cane, decorated leather shields, bows and arrows, and javelins—in short, "every sort of elegant, eye-pleasing weapon."[69]

Once properly respectful of their weapons, Uncle Teng's wards learned combat as a traditional form of drama, consisting of set pieces. "Often one person held a shield and a lone sword, while the other took up the Guan Yu sickle-sword, or a lance, to rehearse the prescribed motions of 'the great sword scraping out the ears,' 'the lone lance breaking the shield,' or other interesting battle scenarios. While in combat, the two would shout 'chop,' 'kill,' 'fall,' or 'sit,' and when it came time for someone to turn a somersault, the other pulled back a step with agility, yielding his small bit of ground. When it was someone's turn to be defeated, the falling down of the defeated had its prescribed method, too, and it was performed with finesse and vitality."[70]

Since the old-style soldier had to know many skills, Uncle Teng taught boxing, swimming, gambling, fishing, and herbal medicine.

This teacher was a strange and interesting man. He could twist his body in midair effortlessly, with the turn of his head, while turning a somersault in any direction. He could climb a tree or reach the top of a boat's mast in an instant. He could stand on his head on a parapet or tower in the city wall, or in a crow's nest midway up the mast of a boat. There was no place he couldn't walk upside-down on his hands, for the longest time. He could dive or swim to the deepest bottoms in a splash.... He kept many kinds of estimable fighting cocks. He could plant flowers, graft fruit trees, and sculpt faces in clay [a passion of the local Miao, as well as of Shen Congwen and his schoolmates].[71]

Teng also had his old-style teaching methods. To encourage his disciples' self-esteem and valor, he had them wear embroidered costumes with different colors and designs, like soldiers practicing for the examinations in the old regime. He cultivated a personal relationship with his students and tried to transmit the ideal of the soldier's proper bearing through his own example. Wanting his students to feel dashing, not ashamed, and to love him as their teacher, he eschewed the physical punishments and standing at attention used in modern classes, saying they were ridiculous "foreign methods."[72]

Shen Congwen took little pleasure in the modern-style drill class, which tried to instill antithetical values: discipline, efficiency, and submergence of the individual soldier within the unit. Uniforms were gray and all alike. Training built stamina rather than rhythm and grace. Practical exercises were marching, hand-to-hand combat, and target practice. Shen disliked the time he had to spend in the classroom learning the "abstruse principles" of marksmanship and fortification, as well as all kinds of terms "not pleasing to the ear or relevant to everyday life."[73]

Still, even this new training was only semimodern. One of the practical skills taught, for instance, was walking across a "bridge in the sky," the high scaffolding that might have to be used to surmount a city wall. There was also much emphasis on acrobatics, including somersaults, headstands, and special stunts on the horizontal bar. The "new examinations" likewise tested old skills, and examinees were applauded for *tours de force*, much as in imperial times. One exam Shen took required tricks on the horizontal bar, vaulting over the wooden horse, crossing the "bridge in the sky," and doing headstands, as well as leading a file of men, marching, running, kneeling, and shouting out a report before the reviewing stand. One candidate placed first in an examination by excelling in the high jump and in pole vaulting. Another winner was as young as Shen and out of the competition until he took the judges' breath away with a single feat—alighting smoothly on the ground after turning several backward somersaults 20 feet up in the air on a "bridge in the sky."[74]

Modern soldiering, Shen gradually came to realize, was diverging from the profession of his ancestors. He bemoaned the fact that modern drill made soldiers into "wooden persons." One had even to accept orders to lie down in the mud, something quite out of bounds for the traditional warrior.[75] He should have suspected that he was not cut out for the job. Instead, Shen Congwen marched off to Chenzhou on September 2, 1917, expecting adventure and happy to be on his own.[76]

CHAPTER TWO

Adolescence: Shen Congwen and His Region Find Their Own Way

SHEN CONGWEN left for Chenzhou in 1917 with several hundred fellow-townsmen, led by a Gelaohui "Double-headed Dragon." On the march he fell in with 12 other young reservists, among whom were his older cousin Shen Wanlin and a tailor's son named Zhao Kaiming. All the boys developed a crush on a young shopkeeper's daughter at Luqi. Zhao Kaiming was most smitten; he vowed to return one day, when he was a dashing officer, and marry the pretty little girl. Sixteen years later, Shen recreated the two as Nuosong and Cuicui, the star-crossed lovers of *The Frontier City*. Zhao was in fact more fortunate than the other 11, every one of whom died in battle or in a hold-up before 1920.[1]

It was China's era of "high warlordism." Gan Army commanders, unimpeded by authorities in either Peking or Changsha (which was busy fending off the Northerners), raised their own troops and enforced their own laws—if they could. Subunits of the army not given ample spoils and autonomy would mutiny, forming bandit gangs with their old officers as "generals." They were "gentlemen bandits" to the foreigners whom they kidnapped for ransom, able to converse with their prey in German or Japanese. Shen's army friend Liu Yunting, an ex-highwayman, boasted of having killed 200 men but could sing opera and paint orchids. "A Tale of a Storyteller" and *Congwen's Autobiography* bring him to life, recounting his exploits as bodyguard and vassal of the general who captured him, spared him, and finally turned him into just another military casualty.[2]

Not all men under arms were so cultivated, by any means. One could become a bandit simply by buying or stealing one of the many rifles that Yuan Shikai's troops had left behind in 1916.[3] One illiterate chieftain, who settled in Yongshun with his five wives after taking it by force, began as a lowly mule-tender for another bandit and worked his way up the ranks through robbery and terror. Shen Congwen tells of a 17-year-old girl gang leader, and of a coal miner who became a bandit chief after false accusations forced him outside the law.[4] Bandit bosses commanded anywhere from 300 to 2,000 men, so army leaders found it prudent to co-opt them, usually by confirming their authority in the areas they preyed upon by assigning them to "garrison" the areas. The Miao had bandit chiefs, too. They became warlords among their own people and then were co-opted like the others. Conflicts over revenues nevertheless erupted into battles that leveled whole villages. When bandits captured a suspected spy, they dismembered him or skinned him alive. Still, they came into town to drink and gamble with old friends at the New Year, when there was a taboo on arrests. They might even be militia in their own county, robbers only next door.[5]

Because of the disorder, people of importance made friends with the local "general" (before bothering with any civil authorities) and procured a military escort before going on any trip. Merchants sent their goods down the Yuan in 50- to 300-boat convoys, paying as much as 5,000 yuan for a 130-mile escort by 300 soldiers. Missionaries, who frequently were murdered by men who scorned extraterritoriality, hired 30-man escorts for their trips overland. A several-hundred-mile trek cost one group of evangelizers only 153 yuan, but the soldiers fled as bandits approached. When travelers passed through bandit territories officially recognized by the military, however, they could get by with an escort of one soldier. He went ahead of the group to confer with bandit sentries, who would periodically send in a tally of the travelers they had let pass, "and receive in return a share of the money given in protection."[6] Chinese travelers required military-provided "passports" to go even short distances.

Shen Congwen's garrison duty in Chenzhou was part of what soon proved to be but an initial expansion of the Gan Army. Once they colonized the Yuan valley, the Fenghuang generals decided they must hire still more soldiers—which necessitated new revenues, and thus further expansion, in an endless cycle, until the army came up against rival warlord regimes that were expanding for the same reason. Yet, right up until 1935, the history of the region's leadership could be written using only six names. Three "old" families had got their start during the battles against the Taipings: the Tians and the Shens, who were in decline, and the Xiongs, who produced a premier of the Republic of China, a source of behind-the-scenes support at the capital. The other three names belonged to self-made men: Zhang Xueji, Shen Congwen's commander at Chenzhou; Chen Quzhen, who eliminated Zhang and became the "King of West Hunan" (which is another part of Shen's own story); and Chen's later rival, the legendary He Long, a bandit founder of the Red Army and, ultimately, of the People's Republic of China. Even these men once dwelt within a single West Hunanese leadership "family." The three old families united themselves by marriage, and the "self-made" men got their start by serving them. Perhaps the Gan military leadership was more insular, conservative, and tightly knit than in most Chinese regions, but only to a degree. One of Shen Congwen's gifts to posterity is that he actually recorded the web of obligations among his region's warlords—ties historians presume must have existed among warlords everywhere in China, but can seldom document. The Fenghuang elite's mutual entanglements seem byzantine, except that, as Shen Congwen once quipped, "it wasn't really so complicated, since it all boiled down to just the few of them!"[7]

The Tians clung to power through Tian Yingzhao (b. 1877), third son of Tian Xingshu and brother of the revolutionary Tian Yingquan. Educated at the Japan Army Officers' Academy, Tian Yingzhao supported the cause of Sun Yatsen in 1911 and again in 1913; he led the Gan Army north against Yuan Shikai while Hunan attacked Hubei during the Kuomintang (KMT) Second Revolution. After the Republic disintegrated and West Hunan became essentially independent, in 1917, Tian became defense commissioner, or head of the region's military administration. Yet he was too incompetent to retain power for long. An old-style scholar-general with many concubines, he enjoyed writing poetry with fellow officials in a park he built outside Fenghuang to commemorate his mother—one of his rather more martial father's spoils of war. About 1919, Tian Yingzhao was persuaded to hand over power to his younger and more talented chief of staff, Chen Quzhen. Tian retired to Sichuan, there to live off warlords like Liu Xiang, whom he had taught at a Sichuan officers' training school.[8]

Another scion of a nineteenth-century Zhen'gan army general of obscure origins was Xiong Xiling (b. 1870), Hunan's "boy genius" (a Hanlin scholar in Peking at the age of 24), who held the premiership in Yuan Shikai's "Celebrity Cabinet" of 1913–14. Titularly pacification commissioner of West Hunan in 1915, Xiong could not bring himself to join West Hunan's war to "protect the nation" from Yuan Shikai at the end of that year. He had, however, started his Yuanzhou friend Zhang Xueji on a Republican military career, and Zhang did take command of Fenghuang's regional defense against Yuan Shikai in 1916.[9] (According to Fenghuang legend, Zhang turned back the Northern soldiers with all available weapons, including the recoil of a bent-over tree.) Named circuit intendant at Fenghuang in 1917, Zhang was titular head of West Hunan's civil government, though his claim was really made good by the many troops he had raised (mostly ex-bandits). In 1918 he even proclaimed himself governor of Hunan, though he was in no position to fight his way into the capital at Changsha.[10]

The Shens were the odd men out in the Fenghuang power structure, thanks to Congwen's erratic father. Yet they remained part of the picture, if only because the Tians and the Xiongs still sought them out as relatives.* Shen Dieyu would nearly reestablish the military prestige of the Shens after all, in the 1930's; and, as we shall see, Shen Congwen was well on the way to doing that in the 1920's, until he decided to become a scholar instead.[11]

Congwen began his career auspiciously, as a bodyguard for Zhang

---

*Tian Xingshu, aware that part of his military glory had been won by Shen Congwen's grandfather, meant to marry his only daughter, Tian Yingbi, to Shen Zongsi. Shen Hongfu's widow objected because the girl had studied in Japan like her brothers and was "foreignized." (Yingbi admired Josephine Bonaparte—and sometimes dressed up like her.) The debt was repaid in the next generation; Shen Congwen's younger brother married a niece of warlord Tian Yingzhao. It was Xiong Xiling's younger brother no. 4, Xiong Xijing, who wedded Tian Yingbi. He was a Japan Army Officers' Academy graduate himself; Tian Yingbi once got him to pose for a portrait garbed as Napoleon. Xiling's younger brother no. 7 was matched with a younger sister of Shen Congwen's mother. Her brother, Huang Jingming, at one time managed Xiong Xiling's estate for him in Peking. Moreover, Nie Rende, a reformer friend of Xiling and *jinshi* of the same year, took another of Shen's maternal aunts to wife. He was Chen Quzhen's tutor and a teacher of Shen Congwen (see below). Surely he helped Congwen become Chen Quzhen's personal secretary. Congwen, in turn, got his younger brother and father jobs under Chen's regime. Another old bond between the Shens and Tians was secret-society membership in the Gelaohui. Shen Congwen, however, denies that he or Chen Quzhen were members.

Xueji. As squad leader of the reservists, he often figured among the 20 or 30 troops who escorted the commander whenever he left his yamen. The people Zhang wanted protection from, most likely, were his putative allies. Zhang Xueji commanded only the Second Army of the "United Army for Pacifying the Nation" (Jingguo Lianjun). The rival First Army, under Tian Yingzhao, was in Chenzhou, too, and so was a Guizhou brigade that did not return home until 1921, when Lu Tao, its commander, was named Guizhou's governor. The three forces were chiefly "united" against the 10,000 Beiyang soldiers of the "Christian General" Feng Yuxiang, who held Changde, near the mouth of the Yuan. Shen Congwen estimates that by 1918 there were nearly 50,000 troops in the whole region, not including the Guizhou guests or the bandits. Chenzhou was the major central place of the middle Yuan valley, but its urban population scarcely outnumbered the 20,000 soldiers of the three "friendly" forces occupying it. In that campaign, Shen Congwen remembers, "the troops on this side did not go downstream to attack [Feng Yuxiang], nor did the troops on the other side dare come upstream to launch an offensive; each side just clung to its base and waited for other opportunities," in typical warlord fashion. In the West Hunan camp, military police tried to insulate Zhang's troops from the other two contingents, but each army was itself of such mixed subregional composition that conflict was inevitable: soldiers wounded each other in fights when they lined up to get their rations, or trampled one another (and townspeople, including women and children) in the pandemonium that resulted every time Zhang Xueji allowed people to convert his worthless currency into hard cash.[12]

With the situation in Chenzhou becoming intolerable, the commanders agreed to divide the West Hunanese countryside into defense districts where their respective troops could be dispersed to live off the land and earn their keep by "pacifying the countryside." Zhang Xueji was quick to claim his native Yuanzhou (renamed Zhijiang in the 1940's), a prosperous river port that had the only bridge over the Yuan River in all West Hunan. Shen Congwen learned that he was to go with a unit assigned to pacify the banditry-prone rural districts east of Yuanzhou: Yushuwan (now Huaihua) and Huaihua (now Luyang). He happily converted his silver dollar transfer bonus into three pairs of straw sandals, a washcloth, and a little "yellow-eel-tail" dagger with a red-lacquered scabbard and satin flyer tied to its hilt. "What I most delighted in," he writes, "was having such a knife. With that in hand, it seemed nothing could get me down."[13]

At (old) Huaihua a literate soldier was needed to fill out forms, so Shen Congwen, at about the age of 16, was promoted to first-sergeant clerk. Probably by virtue of his rudimentary learning rather than his rank, he was able thenceforth to fraternize with the officers. But he also had to be present when prisoners were being tortured, to record their confessions.[14]

Shen Congwen and the Soldier's Life

The military career was traditionally despised in China and besmirched again by warlordism in the 1920's. This makes it easy to forget how much the Japanese example of progressive and nationalistic militarism had energized Young China just before and after the Revolution. Universal military education was a goal shared by monarchists and republicans.[15] The military calling had much appeal even in the 1930's, for militarists seemed still to be spearheading the national revival of Japan and Germany. Yet the original Japanese military discipline absorbed by China's first overseas students differed from 1920's militarism in a crucial way: it taught soldiers to preserve national unity by obeying civilian authorities without question.

Shen Congwen, no less than the Southwestern warlords, was slow to realize that his army was retarding, not leading, China's renewal. His ideals were those of the late Qing, or perhaps of his Gan Army forebears. He was young and intellectually innocent, unaware of options in the larger world, though not naïve about civil violence. His work was boring, yet he enjoyed physical proximity to the commander and soon was working with relatively well educated military officers who remembered the late-Qing dreams of disciplining China into revival. Indeed, Shen Congwen chose a military career a second time in 1920, during which he discovered reform militarism. He left the military in 1922, but only after a reevaluation of his own life. The alternative to a military career he sought then was not an updated way of forging a new national collectivism through modern party-armies. Rather it was an updated conception of the scholarly career—a career in pursuit of values that lay above the state, before which soldiers were but servants, as in old China, Young China, and the modern West. What Shen Congwen began to react against in his warlord career was not discipline—for the military life he knew was relaxed and relatively egalitarian, as "innocent" as he—but violence, and military participation in the affairs of state. He was preparing himself to reject both Nationalist and Communist solutions for China as well, and ultimately to become a pacifist.

We now draw on Shen Congwen's several detailed portraits of soldiering to learn the quality of that life and the different kinds of significance ascribed to it by Shen's young soldier personae. Exactly how the personae of the fictional works relate to Shen Congwen, who often took the pen name "Young Soldier," is moot, but each of his young soldiers is as innocent as the boy who took simple pleasure in his new eel-tail knife. Shen's works seem in fact to trace his own progress, from attraction to the military life to disillusionment. His earliest stories, of the mid-1920's, thus present raw and vivid scenes of frontier militarism, sometimes mixed with romantic evocations of, say, what it means to be a dashing officer enjoying the respect and perquisites of the uniform—one such perquisite being the amours of unattached local women, as described in "The Captain" (1927) and "Staff Officer" (1928). Shen paints a soldier's dream of rising through the ranks to ride a white horse like the Guizhou commander Lu Tao in "On Board the Boats" (1925), and creates a sense of the pleasures of simply being a foot soldier among comrades in "After Entering the Ranks" (1926). The poem "Mutineers" (1925), a partly heroic, partly comic scene of 42 deserters about to be executed, shows the men remembering the lovers they are leaving behind. "In a Separate Realm" (1926) and "Outlaws" (1927) make rural banditry exciting—though still with realistic, even documentary, narrative touches.

The elements of adventure, mystery, and the bizarre in Shen's early army stories provide a kind of formal plot interest quite uncharacteristic of his other early works. Probably Shen learned the art of oral storytelling while in Hunan, and felt moved to spin yarns ever after when the subject was soldiering. In "Night" [1] (1929?), a young soldier-narrator recounts eerie things that have happened to him, following a discursive preamble that tells part of his life story (most of which duplicates the author's) and relates peculiar incidents of cannibalism. One can almost picture the tale originating around a campfire, as a partly factual, partly fantastic offering traded with fellow NCOs and officers for their own ghost stories and sagas of great men of history. The romantic and nostalgic "Sentry" (1926), about a young soldier at the Fenghuang circuit yamen who fears ghosts, is like a bedtime tale. The better developed army stories, such as "Three Men and a Woman" (August 1930), one of Shen's first works to have a sustained, unified plot, still have hints of the traditional interest in "the strange," masquerading as a metaphysical evocation of the unknown.[16]

There is, however, a realistic stream in Shen Congwen's writing about army life, and the stories can be read as a serially produced *Bildungsroman*. Indeed, they culminate in "My Education" (summer 1929) and *Congwen's Autobiography* (1932). "Camp Messenger" (1926) and "The Day Before He Deserted" (April 1929) evoke the hopes and anxieties of a new-recruit persona, nostalgically lingering over the bugle calls, uniforms, roll calls, and antique weapons that Shen Congwen so loved. The "deserter" can hardly bear to leave camp sights and sounds that have become familiar to him. When we reach "My Education," however, the perspective is, if not disillusioned, at least skeptical, if only because of its awareness that *others* do not necessarily accept soldiers as liberators. "Staff Adviser" (1935), Shen's last close-up portrait of local militarism, gives his fullest account of corruption in the lives of officers, though it is still tempered with sympathetic caricature. To the end Shen was ambivalent about the military life. As late as 1933 he could still celebrate the glories of the Zhen'gan troops, even while apologizing for an incident of their looting. His interest in the reputation of his region prevailed over his disquiet over his profession.[17]

Shen Congwen's exposure of the dark side of militarism is thus less remarkable than his descriptions of its joys, its idealism, and what he thought of as its guilelessness. As his works indicate, Chinese soldiers seldom experienced the traumatic carnage that obsessed post–First World War European writers, only a slow sense of social decay and the occasional deaths of friends, a few at a time. Even so, Shen's army experience was intense enough to dominate his life, leaving him with a sense of identity, nostalgia, and loyalty. As a budding author, he took refuge in his army past as a substitute for the school ties society had denied him. He kept no diary while in West Hunan, but confirms today that his fictional one is based on fact. Wanting to instruct his younger readers about what he had seen—and perhaps, with a certain Fenghuangese pride, to deliver a reproof to better-read intellectuals who assumed such an easy air of superiority over military men—he had all the more reason to call his "diary" "My Education."[18]

The soldiers who came to "pacify" rural West Hunan dominated the scene, as one might expect of a detachment of some 500 men stationed in a market town of only 300 to 600 households. Such was the case in Huaihua, where Shen was billeted. Trade was conducted every fifth day, at the periodic market. Huaihua itself had but a dozen enterprises, including a traditional apothecary, a bean-curd factory, and a Southern goods store that sold lump and brown sugar, kelp, dried jellyfish skins, and stale lotus and walnut cookies. There was also an opium den in the town. Comments the diarist of "My Education": "There's only one street here, and if it isn't market day you can't even buy a *tangyuan* dumpling. The street is filthy. Stinking water has flowed out from the bean-curd factory to cover the whole street. Lots of dirty gray ducks stick their long, pink bills into the black and gray spume, sucking up edible matter."[19] Even market day was dominated not by the natural rhythms of rural commerce, but by the army's executions. They served as spectacle— and admonition. Commoners kept their distance from the enlisted men and addressed them respectfully as "assistant master" (*fuye*).

Troops were quartered in public buildings whenever possible. In the little towns of Yushuwan and Huaihua, the most capacious were a temple to the Queen of Heaven and a great clan ancestral hall big enough to have its own theater, where the officers set up their headquarters. It would have been symbolically more gratifying to take over the yamens of the old civil regime, particularly since the officers had to entertain gentry and militia captains and conduct trials in these places, but these towns were too small to have ever had administrative offices before.[20] The men slept atop planks covered with straw; every two men had a cotton-wadded coverlet. Rations were stale coarse rice and bean sprout soup, daily. At Chenzhou soldiers got four ounces of pork cooked into their soup on Sunday, and they could also afford the dumplings available on the street. In Huaihua there was sugar and evidently alcohol at the Southern goods store, but meat only every fifth day, at market. Since the diarist of "My Education" is a country fellow used to the primitive life, he describes the lodgings as "neither damp nor cold, and there is food and drink; naturally it's a very comfortable life once you're here, so everyone feels very satisfied...."[21]

Pay was not very good. Cooks had the lowest status in the ranks and earned only three dollars a month, half of which was deducted for rations. The savings of half a year, at most nine dollars, could easily be gambled away in a night. Young reserve soldiers earned almost a dollar a month more, and regular soldiers got twice as much as the cooks, or six dollars, but still not much more than $40 a year after deductions. (By contrast, even a local 12-year-old, notes the soldier-diarist, earned $4.60 monthly as an iron foundry apprentice and was headed for $8 monthly two years hence, when he'd be as old as the diarist.)[22] Wages of the higher ranks varied greatly. Under what Shen considered spartan conditions during his second enlistment, in Baojing, clerks like himself (*shuji*, at about the rank of sergeant) earned only $5 to $10 a month. Shen, still an adolescent, earned $6, less $2 for rations. Netting only $48 annually, he was hardly better off than when he was a foot soldier in Huaihua. The higher officers earned markedly more. Adjutants at Baojing took home $12 to $18 a month, and the staff adviser in Shen's story by that name $24 monthly. At these levels, too, irregular compensation extorted from prisoners or taken from camp enterprises could be as important as salary.[23]

Ordinary soldiers looked forward to the month's pay in advance that sweetened transfers, and the feasts that followed executions, when soldiers were allowed to get drunk. A survival of a barbarous Qing custom is observed in "My Education": the executioner makes the rounds of the butchers' tables at market, using his execution sword to cut off a few ounces of meat at each place as the camp's reward. Capturing a deserter also brought its reward—$300 divided among the whole camp in "My Education." The deserters Shen Congwen saw were mostly boys, though some of those were bandits before they entered the ranks. Typically their fate was to be shot or slowly bayoneted to death, as "My Education" shows. The chief loss in a desertion was not the man but his precious rifle; with that he could join a bandit gang and "live off the land" for himself. Conversely, the troops might pardon a deserter who left his weapon behind.[24]

Shen Congwen's comrades had so motley a group of weapons and so little ammunition that they seldom wasted real bullets on target practice. At Chenzhou they still used muskets of the old Guangdong Arsenal style, and local muzzle-loading types called "pig troughs." There were also Chinese-made breech-loading repeating rifles of various kinds, with nine- or five-round magazines, the latter mostly from the Hanyang Arsenal, with others coming from arsenals in Gongxian, Henan, and Manchuria. Then there were straight-pull (sliding bolt) rifles, Chinese- and German-made carbines, and "Japanese Springfield" (Arisaka) rifles. Missionaries often saw bandits sporting Colt revolvers. "One-shot," "five-bullet," or "nine-bullet" was about all a soldier had to know to call them when he filled out his arms depot receipt. "After Entering the Ranks" seems to suggest that a recruit either had to bring his own rifle or find an officer who would personally stand guarantor for him before he was issued one.[25]

Waiting, not fighting, was the usual lot of the warlord soldier. At Chenzhou, the daily routine began with reveille, roll call, a run around a track, and a set speech by the company commander, a Miao: "We soldiers are here to guard the nation and protect the people. There are many guest armies about that are here for the first time, so we must have regard for face in everything we do. When you go outside the camp, keep your uniform neat, buttons buttoned, belt tight, and leggings well bound. Those who make trouble will get their asses kicked."[26] The soldiers were issued their rifles after breakfast. They had little to do but clean them, and Shen Congwen used a lazy man's way by threading a clothesline through the bore. Afternoons were free. The diarist at Huaihua, supposedly on a mission of pacification, describes the routine there: "In the few days since we've lived in this ancestral temple, our activities have amounted to: (1) roll call (alternative: being made to kneel as punishment); (2) eating (mostly hot peppers for vegetables); (3) cleaning rifles, singing army songs; (4) going about having fun kicking up a little fuss (for instance, hitting someone's dog, or rolling over on their chicken). How long these days will last, not a one of us knows."[27] The soldiers of "After Entering the Ranks" practiced neither basic skills nor marksmanship, just boxing, led by an old master. Only the lowly cooks were incessantly busy, carrying and boiling water, preparing food, and cleaning up.[28]

In the afternoon, the soldiers washed their clothes in a nearby stream, a squad at a time, went into town, sat around trading ghost stories and singing army songs, or merely slept. Many of Shen's young soldier personae like to draw, as did the author himself.[29] Congwen the soldier evidently spent many hours outside camp. He and some apprentice friends his own age would meet at their ironworks and set out into the wilds, where they hunted for medicinal herbs and wildflowers. Sometimes the soldiers were ordered to gather firewood for the camp. Trapping weasels and wildcats by day and fishing by night were important pastimes, too.

To let off steam, the soldiers went to market, gambled at army-operated gaming tables there, and raised their own chickens and gamecocks—the former for eating and the latter for fighting and wagering. Soldiers in the naturalistic "My Education" secure the battalion commander's express permission to gamble at cards (of the traditional domino variety) in the camp itself, under the laxly observed conditions that there be no large stakes, cheating, or quarreling.[30] Towns as small as Huaihua had few regular prostitutes, but there were many camp followers. Officers were allowed to live with their wives. The opium pipe was a standard social amenity, but the addiction it led to is something Shen Congwen's fictional writings gloss over. In 1980 he recalled that 48 of the 60 to 70 men he served with in a secretariat in the 1920's were addicts. Opium was only 30 cents a *liang* (ounce), available to anyone who wanted it. And there was social pressure to smoke. Since the drug was taken until late into the night, some of the officers slept part of the day.[31]

Executions, too, were considered entertainment. Says the diarist, with a touch of irony but not necessarily a superior tone, "For excitement, other than decapitations there isn't anything that can stir up this very tough group of men."[32] Soldiers eagerly volunteered to guard the prisoners or even do the beheading, since it earned them prestige and pocket money. Shen may have delighted in shocking his bourgeois readers with these portraits of life in the raw, but he was not inventing. A missionary records that civilians, too, would afterward "tell their neighbors all about the execution and even pantomime the actions of the victim." Shen's characters throw the heads around like footballs and poke out the eyes; indeed, the diarist, in a moment of black humor, recounts that he injured his toe by kicking a head too hard. Even the officers did not try to disguise their fascination.[33]

For the most part, though, officers, in their bright brown uniforms, kept some distance from their gray-clad men. The higher ranks stayed within their yamen or temple headquarters, which at least relieved the soldiers of having to stand at attention as they passed. Soldiers often dealt with the adjutant, who divvied out to the camp proceeds from the fines levied on real and supposed bandits, and from the gaming tables his office managed at the market. His less popular role was to supervise and discipline the troops. The platoon leader, an NCO, was the main point of contact between officers and men. He might beat his men, but he formed special drinking relationships with some of them. One of Shen's narrators confides that the platoon leader tried to make friends with all his men, since to scold them too harshly would lead to his social isolation.[34]

Many among the officer class were well educated, and even Huaihua had some officers who had been magistrates once or twice, or had studied in Japan. Staff officers might even keep up the old literati distinction of wearing the long gown. Shen was able to observe the habits of the officers himself when he later served as a clerk. He cooked special meals of dog meat for them, and joined them in playing folk tunes on homemade flutes. Since the commander was illiterate, his subordinates played cards, told stories, drank, and smoked opium with him.[35]

Officers of this sort were not the kind of men to lead China into a new age. At Huaihua, only a staff secretary, an old clerk, and (after much prodding) young Shen Congwen cared to subscribe jointly to a newspaper. With a few deft, jocular strokes, the narrator of "The Day Before He Deserted" tells how officers at a camp a little larger than Huaihua's, who mostly quarreled and sang Peking opera among themselves, fit into the local community:

> Adjutants, judge advocates, staff advisers, envoy personnel, the paymaster, the quartermaster-sergeant, the battalion adjutant, the battalion commander, the detachment commander, the regiment commander ... if you wanted to learn the organization of the bandit pacification headquarters garrisoned here, you wouldn't need a personnel register, you could get it just by traveling the length of the street, going from shop to shop. They never had anything to do. A few dissipated their long days in heated gambling, but most passed the time at a shop counter, and not without a certain leisurely satisfaction. Their salaries didn't amount to much, but they didn't need any money. They only wanted to be happy. Three or four would go to the countryside in a group, on the pretext of surveying the land or taking a census. The captain of the militia or the like always

had sumptuous dishes ready to entertain them. The officers socialized with the local gentry; social occasions, whether for celebration or bereavement, gave a big boost to the number of banquets they could attend.[36]

The staff secretary at Huaihua, Wen by name, was partly responsible for turning Shen Congwen back toward the civil career of scholarship. Once more it was a character from old China who provided Shen with one of his social ideals: Secretary Wen donned a blue satin ceremonial riding jacket before making his rounds to pay respects, a comic anachronism in the eyes of fellow officers. Yet he taught young Shen to read not only newspapers but dictionaries for enjoyment, inculcating in him a classical respect for Chinese characters as artifacts and historical records in themselves.[37]

A more memorable (and probably more representative) character is the fictional head clerk of "The Day Before He Deserted." Good humored and easily able to fraternize with young soldiers on equal terms, he is not a bad sort. Evidently he had ideals during his youth. Like Secretary Wen, he acts as a kind of father figure and confidant to the youthful protagonist contemplating desertion. He lends him books, though his own taste seems to run not to the classics he touts, but to familiar vernacular and heroic novels. Yet his body is ravaged by opium. He has become a time-server, like the bureaucrats from the end of the old regime, though his generation does it for the military instead of the emperor.

This good-natured man was completely beclouded by opium; it had softened his heart and made him like a mother. Teaching him a joke was like telling a story to a child. This nonchalant disposition would forever limit him to the position he reached five years ago. Those who once worked with him had all become magistrates, but he was still a head clerk, copying out memos, making entries in the ledger, good-naturedly training the new copyists as they were appointed, having a cup of wine with the head messenger, taking his place at the card table with the commandant, chatting with a whole lot of soldiers—accumulating neither money nor virtue, only passing his days in peace. China has many types of people; he could represent one of them.[38]

Shen Congwen appears just as ambivalent when it comes to any general assessment of the military calling, or even its impact on the Chinese people. He documents his troops' taking of innocent lives even more fully and gruesomely than the more engagé leftist writers of his age. Yet he never draws the conclusion (as some, but surely not all would today) that local armies were the material cause of the breakdown of Chinese society in his era. In fact he emphasizes factors that tend to exculpate military—as opposed to civil—powerholders. He typically paints the foot soldier as more innocent than most other Chinese of his era.

The "pacification" armies seem parasitic at first glance. They came to the countryside to "seek their livelihood" (*jiushi*). Food and firewood were supplied to the troops directly by the captain of the local militia, or by the chamber of commerce in towns big enough to have one. In Huaihua, the troops' coverlets had been stripped right off the townspeople's beds. Even the militia captain "host" might have fines levied against him if he failed to play his part right. In Shen's fiction, he devotes himself single-mindedly to entertaining the troops (giving them money on their arrival, in "After Entering the Ranks"). In "My Education" he naturally is "all smiles," accosting "us soldiers as if we had just sworn blood brotherhood with him."[39]

But the local elite could manipulate the regulars when it came time to enforce the law. Sundry militia heads and landlords typically arrested and marched the accused to headquarters, where the adjutant had the unfortunates interrogated, tortured, and decapitated, at the direction of the judge advocate—once again in response to a petition from the captain of the militia. Ordinary criminal cases likewise led to military prosecution and execution, without any recourse to the quasi-civil institutions in the county city.[40] In "Day 13," Shen's diarist writes with deadpan irony: "Today seven more were sent over. Everyone seems very happy, for these bandits were arrested by the militia, which allows us to execute or fine them at will. The militia are very clear about the home background of these bandits, so there won't be any oversights or mistakes. Saves us a lot of trouble."[41]

In real life, the day after Shen Congwen's detachment arrived in Yushuwan, militia captains turned in 43 "artless country people," 27 of whom were summarily beheaded and five more of whom lost their heads on the next market day. The four or five executions every five days in "My Education" doubtless is no exaggeration.[42] It is Shen the autobiographer, not one of his fictional alter egos, who writes of Yushuwan: "The local people were extremely fierce and barbarous, so about 1914 a Chen-Yuan circuit intendant named Huang killed some 2,000 people there. In 1916 the Guizhou Army commander Wang Xiaoshan killed another 3,000, more or less; now it fell to our troops to do this sort of thing. When it was all over [after four months], *we'd* killed only 2,000!"[43] Shen as clerk recorded confessions to capital offenses of another 700 at Huaihua. His soldier personae in fiction express much doubt about the guilt of the people falling under the sword, and show a Mencian kind of sympathy even for those who may be guilty, since, as an honest merchant puts it, "at times there are more opportunities for those people to be rural bandits than for them to be good citizens."[44]

And "pacification" campaigns were diverted into far less straightforward activities than executions. Officers extorted money from the accused, after torturing them into making confessions. Sometimes the person would be asked to "reimburse" the troops with several clips of bullets or a rifle. A guarantor was found and he was set free. In practice, $1.50 "per clip" and $180 "per rifle" (near the real prices at the time) went directly to the adjutant and commissary officer. If the accused couldn't pay, or if local gentry had it in for him and paid the troops a bribe instead, his head came off.[45]

The victims were not allowed to spend their last days in peace, as Shen well knew. Confessions were extorted with the bamboo rod or ankle presses a day or two before the execution. Feet were beaten with a wooden club until the marrow was exposed, or broken with a blow from an iron bar. Burning incense sticks were stuck up the nostrils or applied to the chest. The executions were saved for market day partly as a demonstration that the troops were earning their keep. The diarist even speculates that some of the condemned were being "held over" to ensure executions enough for each fair.[46]

And though there were in truth plenty of bandits to be captured up in the hills—some of whom sniped at and killed a few men in Shen's detachment when it was on the march—the troops took no initiatives on behalf of law and order. For self-protection, they hired local informers to go to market and point out bandit gang members who had come to spy on the troops. (Hard-core gang members often could be identified by secret tattoos.) The Huaihua diary has a comic scene in which the soldiers are so bored that they actually ask leave to go up into the hills:

Roll call was particularly early this morning. I was commended for having a neat uniform. Made me very happy. Went with the others to the parade grounds and drilled for an hour. We all seem to need to have a little bit of responsibility to pass the time. Now I'm not necessarily this type, but

Adolescence 53

some of the other dumb guys can't keep in line unless you give them some work to do. And the weather's so good. We wanted to find something to do. Today we broke down and talked to the commander. We all asked to be sent out on patrol, to see if any bandits were making a disturbance in the neighborhood or not. This commander is a relative of mine. He's often eaten lumps of sugar off me in the name of our relationship. He answered,
  "Patrol duty is assigned, not requested."
  "Then we're requesting that you assign it to us."
  "Pack of idiots, what would you do if it were assigned? If there are any bandits around, the militia will tie them up and send them over. Could we catch any?"
  "What can we do?"
  "Go clean your rifles. Look how good the weather is! The inspection commissioner will be here soon. If he sees that your bayonets aren't shiny, won't that be a joke?"[47]

Shen does not depict his troops as undisciplined, but even the cooks were free to move around and presume on their uniform to short the merchants in commercial transactions—to get away with paying half-price, says the Huaihua diarist. Simple rules, like those later used in the Red Army, were repeated by the Huaihua NCO thrice daily: "(1) Do not flirt with other people's women outside camp; (2) do not take things from others [without paying]; (3) do not fight and cause trouble." A beating of 500 blows of the bamboo rod, enough to require medical treatment, was in store for violators. Yet the soldiers slapped literati in the face if they felt like it, while the officers invented pretexts for fining them. Reflects the diarist rather coldly: "Everyone says that garrison duty is an opportunity to make a fortune. Our time for it has now come. Since it has, there's nothing to do other than celebrate and have fun. But I also reflect that these people may hate us troops. Even if they do, though, they can't do anything about it. If they're not willing to pay their fines, we arrest them and kill them, and that's the end of that."[48]

Despite all this, Shen's stories, particularly the early ones, also show a happier side to the soldier's life. It was healthy, "as unbridled as a colt's." Even the diarist, who cynically notes the taking of human life, reflects on an occasion when "Our happiness was such that no one could prohibit it with regulations. We sang continuously as we entered the camp."[49] The inevitable fighting, and the picking on the poor cooks, is cast in a similar light. "They have nothing to do all day, so fighting really is unavoidable.... These men can fight and be on good terms tomorrow. Such is the temper of soldiers." The diarist is proud of the local character, which calls for a disgraceful epithet to be avenged with violence, and even of the unique "stupid society" of soldiery where "intelligence has no use": "Soldiers are particular about obedience. If they don't obey, they are beaten. This is the essential significance of our lives."[50] One could do worse than to accept fate, keeping one's sense of humor. The diarist records, with Shen's characteristic mix of irony and sympathy:

> Today the adjutant of the day punished someone by making him kneel in front of the temple with a bowl of water on his head. If he spilled the water then the time elapsed didn't count. Everyone felt this was very interesting. It created amusement. We all thanked the adjutant for having thought up such a good idea. Only in such matters can he show his intelligence. Other than this, he only eats and sleeps as we do.
> All of us are that artless and simple-minded.[51]

Shen Congwen the autobiographer took pity on his barracksmates for their ignorance and susceptibility; he found them "strong and simple" because they were raised in the countryside. Most were just adolescents, like himself, and too afraid to get into trouble. Those just down from the hills (many of them Miao) were even afraid to leave camp. Indeed, Shen himself had never seen a train, a steamship, an electric lamp, or a telephone. He learned about foreign army uniforms, torpedo boats, and balloons from Secretary Wen, trading in return lore such as how to extract a human gallbladder and kick it clear of the body with a blow from behind (so that it could be consumed, along with the deceased's vital essence).[52]

A soldier was not without his own honor: bravery brought face to his kin and his home village, even if he was being executed for crimes. One played out one's part in a drama. While awaiting the sword, it was best to speak a few fearless words, without showing emotion or cursing the officials, then kneel and stick out one's neck, lest one be thought a "softy shrinking-neck turtle." Adepts knew how to kneel so that their headless corpse would face up, benefiting reincarnation.[53] There was also much egalitarian camaraderie within the ranks. The soldiers healed each other's wounds, paid each other's gambling debts, and shared their wine and food. Officers saw to it that everyone in the camp, cooks included, got a share of the take from gaming tables, and punished those who didn't share money they happened to come into. "My Education" shows the whole camp getting a cut of the reward offered for the capture of a deserter, and subsequent burial of the executed deserter at the battalion commander's expense.[54]

Troop units were indeed familial in feeling. Fellow soldiers were one's "brothers," and officers and older soldiers were jokingly or respectfully called "Uncle." When traditional respect for age clashed with considerations of rank, as when an NCO oversaw some old privates, terms of address were problematic. For officers, the "family" even included servants—little orderlies or valets (*fubing*) to run errands. In fact, in any detachment of Chinese soldiers one might well find actual kinship relations, particularly among the officers. The traditional solidarity of common geographic origin was another strong social cement. Men of Gan thought themselves brave and heroic, fighting openly like knights instead of plotting secret assassinations "like the Northerners."[55]

Finally, the soldiers were bound together by a premodern kind of class solidarity from China's counterculture, a sort of bandit idealism. A postscript to "After Entering the Ranks" proclaims "the enemy" to be not militarists, but "all authority created by an unreasonable society." To the troops, the latter are the wealthy, whom they call "fat pigs" (as would the Communists in days to come). Says the narrator, "Unless you arrange a nice room for [the fat pigs] with bars on all four sides, it's really not so easy to get money from them!"[56] However self-servingly, the soldiers thought of themselves as righteous agents of social redistribution. Though Shen Congwen often satirized the military calling, even when he did he could not keep from recreating the youthful, anarchistic idealism he once found there.

Between Soldier and Scholar

In late adolescence, Shen Congwen kept up his haphazard book learning and began to think about alternatives to military service. He left the army and was nearly accepted as a member of the local gentry. Yet, ironically, it was during a second stint in the army that Shen was able to put his newly acquired traditional scholarly accomplishments—in calligraphy, history, and the classics—to work. His mastery of those subjects even flowered. Shen's Western learning, too, would progress a good deal while he was in uniform, thanks to his uncle, Nie Rende. But Shen soon realized that he had risen as far as he could. He forsook his uniform for good when it became clear to him that China's future, and careers for those who would be part of it, lay only in the big cities. Infatuated with modern ideas from the May Fourth movement and its literary revolution, he would then make his way to Peking.

Polemics would rage all about him in subsequent decades, but Shen Congwen would never become politically "revolutionary" like so many other young progressives who went to the city. He would study China's old literature, culture, and history harder than before, not to write scholarly books or create his own system of thought, but to absorb his predecessors' "ideals" so as to enrich his own creative writing. Shen's permanently youthful and eclectic quest for humane ideals wherever they were to be found, East or West, past or present, suggests that his intellectual temperament was largely fixed before he left Hunan. He absorbed the openminded, eclectic reformist spirit of his Young China officers and relatives: the Huangs, the Xiongs, his Uncle Nie. To them, the world was bigger than it had ever been before. Knowledge itself was expanding, without necessarily negating all the old learning or making the world Western. One of the main implications for Shen Congwen was simply that there were new things to be done in the world, photography and postal service being but minor examples. He would not even have to rebel against his family. After his first enlistment, he was its head.

Circumstance removed Shen from the military the first time by destroying his army. Zhang Xueji's Second Army had become unpopular in Yuanzhou and suffered internal divisions. Meanwhile, the First Army, having quietly passed from Tian Yingzhao to Chen Quzhen, was reformed and reinvigorated. Chen moved his troops down into the Yuan valley, putting pressure on Zhang. The latter chose to "aid Sichuan" rather than stand his ground; Shen Congwen remembers wrapping his feet in coir cloth for a hasty retreat across the snow. At the Yuan River, a fleet of tiny boats was waiting to rescue the troops and start them on the five-day trip downstream to Chenzhou. Shen Congwen was judged too young to proceed farther, on a dangerous mission into a "foreign" province. He was ordered to stay in Chenzhou, with "an old head adjutant, a crippled adjutant, a clerk who smoked opium, and 20 soldiers who were old or feeble," to man the army's rear liaison office.[57] This saved his life. A few months later, an army of *shenbing* (spirit soldiers), angry cultists of the Hunan-Hubei-Sichuan borderlands who believed themselves invulnerable to bullets, rose up and annihilated Zhang Xueji, his entire staff, and most of his troops near Laifeng, Hubei. Wiped out in a single morning in 1919 were Shen Congwen's battalion, regimental, and brigade commanders, an old judge advocate who had befriended him, and most of his army friends—some 8,000 in all on both sides, Shen says. One regiment escaped to mountainous Longshan to tell the tale.[58]

It seemed an omen. Gazing down wistfully at students playing at the Protestant mission high school in Chenzhou, Shen Congwen had already decided that he must seek a new life. What most Chinese outside Fenghuang thought of soldiers had been communicated to him by some young girls he encountered while strolling atop the city wall: they were afraid of him.

At that point I was completely embarrassed. I quickly turned my face against a parapet to make as if I were looking out an embrasure, so they could pass behind me. I felt a little apologetic on account of my uniform. I felt that I was a literatus, not deserving of the loathing of others. But how could I make those who didn't know me respect me? I thought of those two thick volumes of the *Ciyuan* [*Origins of Words*, a dictionary]. I thought of the *Shenbao* [a Shanghai newspaper] the three of us had subscribed to [at Huaihua]. I also thought of the *Qiushui xuan chidu* [*Letters from the Autumn Waters Studio*].[59]

A year later, at Changde, personal frustrations were to make Shen ambivalent about becoming a literatus, but by then he had acquired something of the appearance and manner of one that he had wanted so much in Chenzhou. Secretary Wen had begun the process of Shen's gentrification by correcting his young protégé's rough speech habits. Wen also taught him calligraphy, a literary skill he could practice without having to spend much money. It was the old judge advocate, Xiao Xuanqing, who first taught the boy to write classical poetry,* in return for stewed dog meat. Playing on the Confucian quotation after which Shen was originally named Yuehuan, Xiao further encouraged the lad by giving him

---

* When Xiao praised Shen's first poems for their "Tang [dynasty] taste," Shen misunderstood him as having said "sweet [*tang*] taste"!

the style Chongwen ("revering culture"). Shen himself changed this to Congwen ("dedicated to culture"), a name not only signifying his scholarly and literary resolve, but suggestive of civilian rather than military aspirations.[60] The judge advocate was killed in 1919, but later that year Shen went to Yuanzhou and acquired two new mentors. One, a younger brother (no. 7) of ex-premier Xiong Xiling, was Congwen's uncle by marriage and the most powerful man in town. The other, Huang Juchuan, was the son of a great-uncle on Congwen's mother's side; he was the Yuanzhou police commissioner, and he hired Shen as a police clerk.[61]

The job was not pleasant. Though Congwen had only to copy out forms indicating crimes and punishments and follow a patrolman through the prison at night to check off prisoners' names, he had once more to listen to the screams of men being tortured. Shackles and the cangue were still in use. But when the local tax on the slaughter of animals was earmarked as a police revenue, and the employee sent out to collect it proved dishonest, Shen was assigned to visit Yuanzhou's butchers in his place. The well-to-do shopkeepers, local gentry who drank with his uncles, were quick to entertain and otherwise ingratiate themselves with Shen Congwen. It was then Shen realized that, because of his rich and powerful relations, he was as good as a member of the gentry class himself.

Uncle Huang and Uncle Xiong gave him what they could of their gentry polish. Congwen copied out the poems they wrote in order to improve his calligraphy, and he left Yuanzhou able to cut seals and compose his own regulated verse. Though Uncle Huang died before long (which put an end to his "modern" police system), Shen stayed on as a petty functionary; when the gentry set up their own militia to keep order in the city, he found himself socializing with rich folk more than ever. He was ready for the final step— marriage to a wealthy gentry daughter. Uncle Xiong gave him a choice of four, including a daughter of his own. Shen Congwen was so close to success in gentry terms that his mother and little sister sold what remained of the family property in Fenghuang (for 3,000 yuan) and moved to Yuanzhou. The money was entrusted to Congwen to manage. In 1932 he reflected:

> Had I not been afflicted by fate, but been allowed to pass the months and years as I was then, I imagine that by now I'd be a petty member of the gentry there. My wife doubtless would be the daughter of a rich mer-

chant. I'd have been appointed magistrate twice, fathered four children or more, and learned to smoke opium, too. Circumstances suggested that my life would develop according to that formula. And this is not my own conjecture, but what my relative [Uncle Xiong] told me at the time.[62]

Shen threw it all away to pursue a love of his own, a beautiful maiden whom he wooed with love letters in classical poetry. Shen's relatives tried to warn him away from the girl, but nothing could distract the lad from his obsession, not even the siege of Yuanzhou by an 800-man bandit gang that was in progress at the time. Every day, when the brother of his beloved came to collect Shen's romantic epistles, Shen lent him money. When the debt amounted to about a third of the Shen family estate, the visits ended. The young woman, and the money, vanished.[63]

Shen Congwen lost face and started to flee to Peking, but his cousin Huang Yushu caught up to him in Changde and persuaded him to remain there. The two lived in a little hostel for five months, sharing "unemployment benefits" that Yushu's father, Huang Jingming, sent from up north, and learning how to live on credit, which would soon be essential to Shen in Peking. Meanwhile Yushu fell madly in love with an art teacher. He wooed her with love letters penned by Shen Congwen, about 30 in all, composed over the course of two months. This time Shen's epistolary skills culminated in a long-lasting marriage, although Congwen himself, fed up with his mooning cousin, left Changde before he knew the outcome.[64]

That literary courtship was a fitting prelude to Shen Congwen's later debut as romantic spokesman for the freedom of young love in defiance of gentry values. Shen Congwen was not yet ready to become a writer, least of all a modern vernacular writer, but he had become an avid and eclectic reader and was beginning to take as much pride in his literary sentiments as in his calligraphy. His first efforts in the manner of classical poetry showed their influence in his subsequent focus, as a fiction writer, on diction. Already preferring fresh poetic images to classical allusions, Shen inclined toward the difficult but original Li Shangyin, and other lyric poets who dared write of their subjective, even erotic, feelings. Later his Uncle Nie filled him with the Tongcheng School's literary ideas, which stressed the lyric style of old Tang and Song masters and the simple elegance of the ancient historian Sima Qian, whom Shen appreciated at this time and took as a model even as he began to write modern fiction.[65] Since the essence of the literary revolution was to substitute imaginative tropes for the set figures of speech through which traditional scholars demonstrated their classical learning, Shen was becoming predisposed toward the revolution even without knowing about it, or having yet come to love the twentieth-century vernacular.

Indeed, Shen had a taste for Ming-Qing vernacular fiction and much preferred it to the prose he had read in Classical Chinese. He confesses having read novels in the old vernacular as a child, including "classics" such as *The Dream of the Red Chamber*, *A Journey to the West*, *The Romance of the Three Kingdoms*, *The Water Margin*, and *Investiture of the Gods*; stories of the unusual such as *Strange Tales from a Chinese Studio* and *Wonders Old and New* (*Jingu qiguan*); popular historical novels such as *The Romance of Sui and Tang* and *The Chronicle of the Many States of the Eastern Zhou Period*; and knight-errant potboilers, from *Seven Knights-Errant and Five Gallants* (*Qi xia wu yi*) to *Five Young Gallants* (*Xiao wu yi*).[66]

Shen's taste ran to adventure and history—"the strange." The same curiosity led him into Western literature and Chinese history, in the library of a nearly defunct school that Xiong Xiling had founded in Yuanzhou. Shen Congwen devoured, with equal interest, the *Historical Records* of Sima Qian; the *History of the Han Dynasty* by Ban Gu; *The Thousand and One Nights*; and Lin Shu's Classical Chinese translations of Dickens. *Oliver Twist*, *A Christmas Carol*, *Nicholas Nickleby*, and *David Copperfield* became Shen Congwen's "bridge to a brand new world."[67] He liked the heroes, the sentiment, above all the twisting tales of success that came about through fate and self-help, in which young men in straitened circumstances "like himself" came out well in the end. The plot, social phenomena, and unspoken humanistic mores underlying it all were the more striking in the absence of the explicit moralizing he disliked in Chinese books. Being behind in his education, Shen Congwen only read the newer vernacular Chinese translations of Western fiction later; one consequence was that he learned to like Western literature before Chinese intellectuals divided into the camps of vernacular versus Classical and foreign versus native. Nor would Shen ever forsake the Dickensian (and Mencian) outlook that so suited his late-Qing mentors, but that became anathema to leftist writers in the 1930's—that humanity was one, and that it was good, whatever tribulations might come from society.

While Shen Congwen and Huang Yushu were struggling to

make ends meet in Changde, they made another fateful career choice. They learned that He Long, the famous "Robin Hood" militarist from the northwest corner of Hunan, had been co-opted by the Fenghuangese and appointed a regimental commander in the provincial army, with headquarters in Taoyuan, 30 miles up the Yuan from Changde.[68] Huang Yushu prevailed on a fellow-townsman and friend, who was a sworn brother of He Long, to write him and Shen a letter of introduction. Taking the Japanese-operated steam launch from Changde to Taoyuan, the cousins then went to see the commander. He Long agreed straight off to a $13-a-month job for Huang Yushu as counselor and a $9-a-month messenger position for the younger Shen. Since another of Shen's cousins, Cousin Nie, had a job at Taoyuan decoding telegrams, Congwen made several trips to the town and became familiar with the sights. In the end, neither Shen nor Huang took the job: Shen was still looking for a role model and preferred He Long's commander, General Zhang Ziqing (Shen noticed "special agility in his writing and rich experience behind his actions"); Huang Yushu became so infatuated with the art teacher that he would not leave Changde, even to work for He Long.[69] Zhang Ziqing did not, however, offer Shen a job. So, when Cousin Nie was transferred up to the Miao borderlands country at Baojing, where Chen Quzhen maintained military headquarters for the whole region, Congwen went along. They hitched a ride with Zeng Qinxuan, a fellow-townsman, soldier, and friend of the family who was headed up the You River with a boatload of uniforms. Zeng taught Shen a good deal of what he would later put into his stories about prostitutes, plus most of his obscene language. There was plenty of time. The hundred-mile trip upstream took them 40 days, owing to the many shipwrecks they encountered—including, finally, their own.[70]

Shen Congwen now sought out a military career for a second time, and again out of positive attraction. He was "moved" by the revival of martial spirit in West Hunan compared to what he had witnessed three years earlier. Arms and discipline were better, and so was the soldiers' "self-respect"; they worked inside the camp instead of wandering around town. Staff kept regular hours, and officers paid more attention to their public image. They "performed their duties to the limit without becoming dejected or falling into bad ways," even seemed "extremely aggressive and exuberant," though "eating coarse rice and passing crude and simple days." To Shen Congwen, it all seemed a result of "the personal example of the commander," Chen Quzhen. Most fellow regionals—and even foreign observers—agreed, though not all realized that Chen was trying to be not just a reformer but a latter-day Zeng Guofan or Wang Yangming.[71] Chen was born in Fenghuang in 1881, of humble origins. He was Han, but very popular among the Miao. Indeed, he had taken a local wife when stationed in Tibet, the new farther frontier where he, like the heroes of Shen's grandfather's generation, had his chance for glory "in fairy-tale situations of the sort found in novels." Yet he was also a Baoding Military Academy graduate. He combined the education of Tian Yingzhao and Zhang Xueji's generation, which he succeeded in 1919, with the limited ambitions and expectations of the relatively provincially-minded warlords then coming to power elsewhere in the Southwest.[72]

Upper West Hunan was Chen's base, never more impregnable than after he moved his capital out of Fenghuang, still keeping its military at his command. He won plaudits for disciplining and paring down his armies (and so taxes), while allowing small farmers to cash in on the profits of opium growing. Chen had two ways of dealing with the lesser warlords who rose to challenge him. Some he co-opted, such as Long Yunfei, a charismatic Miao from northwest of Fenghuang city whom Chen allowed to become "King of the Miao" after 1928. (Long retained his kingdom even after Chen lost his, in 1935.) Chen sent other troublemakers "traveling expenses" (bribes) and polite "congratulations for deciding to move to a better neighborhood" (a veiled threat). By the 1930's he had ushered in a new "golden age" when "doors could go unlocked and goods could be stored by the wayside" through his organization of extensive militia networks.[73]

It was largely the transit tax on Guizhou opium headed down the Yuan River to Wuhan that let Chen go easy on his own people, however. He held the transshipment points of Yuanzhou, Hongjiang, and Chenzhou when he could, but prudently let bandits and Guizhou militarists have the first two, and downriver Hunanese the last, when his strategic weakness so dictated. Changsha, powerless in the west and mollified by the gifts Chen sent, was usually happy to leave him to fend off the ambitious Guizhou generals and their troops, who were traditionally held to be especially brave and fierce. In 1924, Changsha did send an army across the Snowy Peaks to bring Chen under full control, but the attempt failed—as did subsequent expeditions by the Sichuan warlords, and indeed by Nationalist armies.[74]

In the early 1920's, while Shen was in Baojing, Chen Quzhen became a reformer. He founded modern high schools (staffed by young teachers from Changsha), three trade schools for demobilized soldiers, six factories, a modern forestry preserve, and a 6,000-man system of soldier-peasant brigades (probably yet another measure to keep ex-soldiers from becoming bandits). Regrettably, though in keeping with standard practice at the time, in 1925 Chen torched everything he built, from barracks to factories, to keep them out of the hands of the Sichuan warlords. But he rebuilt, and about 1932 he founded West Hunan's first modern bank. Two million yuan of his own money went to provide cooperative rural credit for agricultural reconstruction. Chen also initiated a geological survey to stimulate mining, built up local communications, and established an arsenal in Fenghuang, his capital in the 1930's.[75]

Chen was a political modernizer, too, though no democrat. Changsha in 1921 was promoting local self-government and federalism (literally, "self-rule under federated provinces") as quintessentially Hunanese solutions to end warlordism. Chen found the ideas useful. They had been the goals of his friend Xiong Xiling during the late 1890's, and now Xiong was reviving them in Changsha. Chen Quzhen enthusiastically began holding town meetings in preparation for subdividing the 13 counties under his control into "self-ruling" townships. But, Shen says, Chen was actually studying and taking inspiration from Shanxi warlord Yan Xishan's strategy, which was to use township government to bring local officials under tighter warlord control.[76] Just as "federalism" really justified Hunan's *independence* from Peking, so Chen's "self-rule" justified his independence from Changsha.

Many reformist warlords set up factories and schools, but Chen Quzhen (author of a book of poems) also supported the minimum goal of the May Fourth "literary revolution": use of modern vernacular Chinese in the media. In fact, he founded a newspaper and magazine to stir up enthusiasm for his reforms. In retrospect Shen Congwen spoke of after-ripples from the May Fourth movement reaching West Hunan at this time.[77] Chen, however, was up-to-date only in the educational and literary spheres; he was not purposely turning to new, Western solutions for changing culture or society. That aspect of May Fourth had yet to touch Shen Congwen, too. Though he admired Chen for trying new things, what really influenced him was "that rare spirit and character of [Chen's]," his "artless and simple" martial poise, his bravery, his disdain of luxury—in short, his traditional virtues. Chen reformed his men by personal example, and he dedicated much of the workday to study and self-improvement. That meant burying himself in his collection of old and new books, paintings, bronzes, and antiques, and listening to Shen's Uncle Nie, a heavy opium user, expound on Social Darwinism, Song metaphysics, even Buddhism. Chen also enjoyed friendships with Christian missionaries, and that put him at odds with city-educated young people, most of whom wanted to end all reminders of Western imperialism.[78]

The circumstances of Shen Congwen's second stint in the army were not at all such as to lead him straight down the path of progressivism to Peking. They only deepened the contradiction between his continuing naïve devotion to half-traditional, half-modern military heroes and the disillusioning insights into the realities of militarism that were building up in the back of his mind. It was direct contact with the new May Fourth consciousness, through its magazines and partisans, that broke his intellectual deadlock.

Shen had gone to Baojing hoping to serve in Chen's personal entourage, but he had great difficulty finding work. A cousin (yet another) was already clerking in Baojing, so Shen lived with him for half a year and helped with his work, just to pass the time. Eventually his fine calligraphy was noticed and he was put on the payroll too. Ironically, Shen was then able to get close to his earlier hero, Zhang Ziqing, as dispatch officer on an expedition into Sichuan. Finally the "King" himself happened to see Shen's calligraphy and recalled him to work as his own secretary. But Chen's use for Shen Congwen was not so much in assisting with his reforms as in cataloguing his collection of books and antiques, and copying out edifying classical phrases for later reference. Shen himself still felt his mission in life was to become a modern Wang Xizhi (that is, a great calligrapher).[79]

The dark side of militarism continued in evidence as Shen served Zhang Ziqing, a Guizhou man and Gelaohui member accepted by the Fenghuangese as one of their own.[80] Though Shen Congwen counted him a progressive, Zhang's exploits were ultimately disillusioning. Zhang, with He Long, led an expedition into Sichuan (ca. 1921-22), West Hunan's second. It was at the invitation of Sichuan warlord Tang Zimo, but had the ulterior motive of plundering the province to finance Chen Quzhen's reform program at home. Relations between Zhang's men and the allied Sichuanese were tense, so that Congwen hardly dared step outside his camp. He felt himself to be in a sense atoning for having cheated death when all his friends were sacrificed to Sichuan in Zhang Xueji's 1919 expedition. En route he observed the remains of an entire town massacred by "spirit soldiers," and he witnessed the execution of his friend Liu Yunting as punishment for getting into a fight with the Sichuanese. Shen didn't get to see Zhang Ziqing himself ambushed by his junior officer Tian Yiqing in 1924, machine-gunned to death as he stepped from his sedan chair in response to a phony dinner invitation.[81]

Where this was all leading dawned on Shen Congwen only gradually. He left before the famine of 1925-26, but he must have witnessed the tragic hunger of 1921-22 that left 40,000 dead around Yuanzhou. Aside from the foreign missionaries, local society seemed powerless to help. And Shen Congwen knew that social order itself was breaking down in West Hunan. Bandits swarmed in the no-man's-lands between garrison districts; one militarist after another conquered the Yuan valley with guns purchased from opium revenues—then was cut down, often by his own troops.[82]

Back from the expedition to Sichuan, Shen Congwen approached a turning point. His "personality seemed to have changed somewhat," his feelings "softened." Even his friends noticed his distracted "loneliness." Shen grew so envious of boyhood friends who had gone on to attend the new Baojing high school that he could not bear to visit them in their dormitories. He was not yet anti-military as such, but he was growing increasingly restless. His roommate, a young Changsha worker named Zhao Guiwu, the printer for Chen Quzhen's newspaper, had been propagandizing him. (Shen was the paper's proofreader; only he could decipher the "King's" hand, and it was largely Chen's pronouncements that saw print.) Zhao rubbed in the fact that Congwen couldn't even distinguish between Classical Chinese and the modern vernacular writing that Hu Shi had been promoting since 1917. Shen thought "the difference was that the one came to a stop with a *ye* or *yan*, the other with a *ya* or *a*. For the one, the briefer the better, while for the other, the more verbose the better." He had never seen a May Fourth periodical and could name no woman poet more recent than the disciples of Yuan Mei (1715–97).[83]

At the urging of his more progressive coworker, Shen Congwen began reading *Gaizao* ("La Reconstruo" was its Esperanto title), *Xin chao* (*New Tide* or "The Renaissance," a student magazine), and Creationist journals featuring Yu Dafu and Guo Moruo. At first he was offended by the freethinking re-examination of Chinese society and culture presented in these magazines, but soon the new books and their ideals "conquered" him. Shen felt a new surge of patriotism, too. He anonymously contributed ten days' wages to help sponsor a Shanghai program that aimed to create a new society through work-study corps among the masses.[84]

After narrowly escaping death from a 40-day attack of typhoid fever, and burying a close friend who died because of a dare, Shen came to a decision. He would take a dare himself rather than die at home. The challenge he would accept was to become a New Intellectual in Peking, a scholar "in opposition" to the "Confucian" establishment. Chen Quzhen had set up a program of scholarships for West Hunanese to go to Changsha or other provinces to study to become teachers, mechanics, or specialists in textile manufacture, sericulture, and other industries needed for local reconstruction. But this was too limiting for Shen Congwen; he wanted to break free completely, perhaps change the ideals of all society, not return to engage in piecemeal construction or, as Chen wanted him to do, manage his library for the rest of his life. Nonetheless, at Nie Rende's urging the "King of West Hunan" released his employee to go to Peking. Chen offered Shen tuition if he could enter a college, or his old job back if he failed. Even so the young soldier, much as he admired Chen Quzhen, sensed that the "King" did not want his subordinates so educated that they could think for themselves.[85] Indeed, given the change that had come over Shen Congwen, Chen may very well have felt relieved to see him go.

CHAPTER THREE

The Romantic Young Man of Peking

SHEN CONGWEN. Twenty *sui* old. Student, from Fenghuang, Hunan." So Shen identified himself at his first Peking lodging, in the early 1920's.[1] He would think like a student to the end of his days, but he never succeeded in enrolling. Perhaps that is why he was slow to recognize his success as a writer. Creative as he was in the 1920's, Shen claims that he began to write with critical consciousness only after 1929. Evidently he felt overwhelmed by the need to produce in volume just to live. He now refers to his early pieces as just "raw material," fast and unreflective reworkings of whatever he had just read, experienced, heard about, or imagined, churned out for 50 cents per thousand characters. Already in 1926 he was confessing that his "creative method" was simply "catching all the things of the past that have flickered before my eyes, like catching fireflies."[2]

The raw material of Shen Congwen's life still makes good reading. Even in technical terms these pieces have strengths that belie their author's modesty. The well-made lyrical fiction and essays most critics consider Shen's long suit do date from the 1930's, yet modern taste now esteems stylistic liberties of the sort Shen inclined toward before he "learned" about form. Happily, the author sought new frontiers again in the 1940's; even without knowing any foreign languages, Shen Congwen became aware that the Jamesian unities were out of style again—that the narrative voice itself was dissolving. He kept on experimenting, learning as he went, until society banned him.

Missteps on the Way to Joining the Chinese Renaissance

Shen Congwen went to Peking in 1922 with incompatible objectives and false hopes, partly because he believed what he had read in the newspapers about opportunities for study. His goal was to join the cultural renaissance that claimed to be remaking China's conceptions of truth, goodness, and beauty. A half-modern, half-traditional country literatus by background, Shen was quick to see literary revolution as a key element: overthrowing Classical Chinese would bring about the demise of its public, its sensibilities, and the very culture it represented, including traditional morality, politics, and family structure. These were the "ideals" that young Chinese out of power could agree upon, and though they were negative, young people thrilled at the prospect of finding new, positive goals on their own. Shen Congwen wanted to declare his personal independence, too—from his former life, with its military command structure, from his family and "the romantic schemes of women" (like the one in Yuanzhou)—from everything in the old gentry society that he had learned to look down on while in the army. Leaving West Hunan was itself an act of self-assertion. Shen says he was anxious not to take more money from Chen Quzhen or tie himself down with indebtedness to his Peking relatives, Huang Jingming and Xiong Xiling.[3]

Yet Shen Congwen had scholarly ambitions that required money. Writing and scholarship had always gone hand in hand; most progressive writers in the 1920's were professors who commanded respect through their learning. To Shen, it seemed obvious that he must join the academy. Even when Chinese universities locked him out, and he, almost of necessity, became a spokesman for creative writing as a fully independent profession, his ideals remained academic.[4] He measured literature by its seriousness, its ability to uplift and educate. After becoming a professor himself, in the 1930's, Shen Congwen still advocated the independence of literature from commercial and political control by appealing to the original spirit of May Fourth. By that he meant, with a touch of forgiveness and even nostalgia for the academic Peking of the 1920's, how well literature had developed in association with education.

Just getting into college may indeed have been Shen's main objective. Yu Dafu, in an "Open Letter to a Young Man in Literature" (November 1924), dissects Shen's original mix of youthful idealism and ambition with wicked satire. Shen had written a hardluck letter to Yu, a total stranger, asking for help. Yu Dafu was intrigued. He called on the 20-year-old in his hostel one morning, took him to lunch, and that very night composed an open letter sympathizing with Shen's plight but ridiculing his plans. (Shen is not identified by name; no one would have recognized it.) Yu Dafu writes: "What enticed you to Peking was [the thought of acquiring] the title of graduate of a national university. Graduation would at least solve your problem of livelihood. But the examinations are all over now, and you can't enter a single national university.... At such a time, and in such a state, you still go on about 'college education,' 'study,' or some such. I really admire your steadfast ambition. But all admiration aside, the simplicity and silly naïveté of your thinking are just as startling. You've now become a neuter, a semi-castrated literary man. You're not fit, for instance, to be a bandit or pull a rickshaw any more."[5]

Shen's good sense in coming to Peking had already been questioned by Huang Jingming, who had failed to find work in Peking for his own son—hence Huang Yushu's sojourn with his cousin Congwen in Changde. "I've come to seek ideals, and to study some," Shen said. "Oh, to study," Huang replied. "What ideals? And how will you study? You know there are 10,000 college students in Peking at this very moment, who after graduation will have nothing to do but go around looking worried and wondering what to do next. Professors get only a portion of their salaries, 36 yuan a month. Even that is wheedled [from the government] by bowing and scraping, or organizing and striking.... You'd have more of a future if you went back home and became a warlord!" "But how can I go back?" was Shen's rejoinder. "For six years I saw thousands of innocent commoners killed while I looked on. You can't learn anything from that, except for the impressions of cruelty and stupidity left behind by the executioners and the victims! There are plenty of smart people who can be the officials. The smarter they are, the stupider things get, while they act above it all, viewing all things as so many straw dogs [Laozi's phrase in reference to the inhumanity of Heaven and earth]." Or so Shen remembers the conversation.[6]

When Yu Dafu visited Shen Congwen in 1924, Shen must have

mentioned his relative Xiong Xiling, for Yu's letter facetiously advises his young friend to survive by stealing from people, beginning with his relative "H" (Xiong by the old spelling Hsiung), since H's wealth was itself gained by theft. (Yu Dafu may have been referring to the rumor abroad that Xiong had pilfered his great fortune from the Manchu summer palace in Rehe.) The "Open Letter" also discloses that Shen was in such desperate straits that he had in fact asked for outside help, although he got none: "Since the man who sent you traveling expenses [Chen Quzhen] is himself insecure back home and has no money to send you, you went to attach yourself to the mighty philanthropist H, your fellow-townsman and relative, but H wouldn't have you, so, down-and-out without a hope, you could only write a letter to me, a perfect stranger, and one you knew to be as poor as yourself."[7]

Ultimately Shen Congwen did succeed in going it alone, and over the next decade this encouraged his rebelliousness—though in the long run, it may have given him enough inner satisfaction to quiet the deeper personal outrage that made revolutionaries of many of his colleagues. In any case, a revolutionary had to take orders and be ready to die before making any other contribution to society. Shen Congwen had experienced that kind of subordination in the army; he was loath to submit to it again.

Shen Congwen could not attend college because he lacked money and formal education. He performed poorly in entrance tests at the private schools and could not even sit for examinations at the state-supported Peking University, since he lacked a primary school diploma. As if that were not bad enough, Shen had a mental block on learning foreign languages, which by itself was sufficient to bar him from many a scholarship. As he joked at the time, he couldn't even memorize the Roman alphabet. At one point two friends—the playwright Ding Xilin and Chen Yuan, a professor of English—personally tutored Shen in that language, hoping to send him to Cambridge, but their pupil still made no progress. Nor could he pass the entrance examination of the Yanjing University Chinese department (Shen's failing paper was marked by the philosophy professor Feng Youlan). When he did pass an examination, at the Franco-Chinese University (which might have sent him to France for study), Shen could not afford the tuition. These failures left an emotional scar on him. Later, when professors Gu Jiegang and Liu Tingfang tried to bring Shen Congwen onto the faculty at Yanjing, Shen's pride would not let him accept.[8] Yet the scholar status Shen lacked in the 1920's was intangible. His poverty was visible in his clothes; his low social position could be seen from his lack of metropolitan gentry manners; and his unprestigious geographical origins were evident in his accent. Only his non-Han ancestry was invisible, an embarrassment that must have troubled Shen under the surface.

Precisely how long Shen Congwen lived in Peking before he became a writer and how he spent his time are unclear. At first he must have been fully occupied preparing for college entrance examinations. Later he did odd jobs, such as working at the Jingzhou or Capital Printing Company. He had always intended to combine work with study. Evidently he applied for a job in a library, another kind of work he was familiar with from his Baojing days, but was turned away. One of Shen's published letters indicates that he endeavored to sit for examinations for local government clerical posts (this was in 1925), but found the positions already taken. A professor friend also helped him enroll in library science classes at a projected college summer session that never opened. Shen sold a few satirical articles about current local events to the Peking *Chenbao* (*Morning Post*), but not much before the *Post*'s literary supplement (*fukan*) began printing his literary works, at the end of 1924. Recent scholarship in China has yet to identify any examples of Shen's early reportage. He remembers that the *Post* only remunerated his work with book purchase certificates anyway, not with money.[9]

Shen Congwen was driven to consider becoming a policeman again, nearly entered a photography school, and, in his very darkest hours, almost reenlisted in the army. The Fengtian (Manchurian) and Zhili cliques were the local employers. Ragamuffins paraded in file behind a recruiting sergeant to help attract others, and Shen joined these sorry processions more than once. He even followed them to an inn for processing. Only when it came time to be fingerprinted and receive his food allowance did he steal away, resolving to hold on one day longer. Elder brother Shen Yunlu was already in the Fengtian Army, but as an artist; Congwen would have had to start over as a lowly foot soldier.[10]

Shen Congwen admits to having "wavered" in his quest to become a New Intellectual and author. Apparently he thought of returning to West Hunan to serve Chen Quzhen as late as 1926, only to be forced to stick it out in Peking when the KMT Northern Expedition prevented travel up the Yuan River. At that time Shen had already published several pieces in newspaper supplements. Later he dreamed of learning the Miao language and returning home professionally to record and study Miao songs and rituals, particularly the Nuo dramas. But then, as before, he lacked even travel fare to go home.[11]

The first known published work of Shen Congwen appeared in December 1924. He had spent much of that year writing and submitting pieces to a variety of publishers who simply destroyed them; his favorite anecdote involves Sun Fuyuan, the editor of the *Morning Post Literary Supplement* from 1920 to 1923, who gathered up a big pile of Shen's unpublished manuscripts at a meeting and demonstratively flung them into a wastebasket. Postage was not wasted on returning unused manuscripts, and Shen Congwen had no time to make copies, so he estimates that one-third or more of his early production was simply discarded.[12]

By 1925, however, the *Morning Post Literary Supplement* was publishing Shen Congwen's articles regularly, and paying him four to twelve yuan a month. His work was soon noticed by Lin Zaiping, a philosophy professor at Peking University. In May 1925, Lin praised Shen's writing in the *Morning Post Literary Supplement*, mistakenly assuming him to be a student. This was just the opportunity Congwen sought to open another line of correspondence focusing on his inability to contribute to society, as he had with Yu Dafu. Shen complained that he was flattered to be thought a student, but that evidently society didn't think him qualified for that status. Lin thereupon befriended the young man, inviting him to his house and offering him much compassion and advice. When Lin subsequently explained Shen's plight to the great elder statesman Liang Qichao, Liang recommended Shen to his friend Xiong Xiling, who just then needed a librarian at his Xiangshan Ciyouyuan (Fragrant Hills Orphanage). Thus did Shen Congwen come to work for his celebrated relative Xiong Xiling—through the offices of a new acquaintance (Lin) and a complete stranger (Liang, whom Shen would meet but once, in 1926).[13]

Shen came up into the Fragrant Hills, among the Western Hills outside Peking, in July 1925; he was put up in one small room of a temple gatehouse next door to Xiong Xiling's mansion Shuangqing (Double Clarity), where the Qianlong Emperor had once lived.

Xiong came out nightly to talk about current events, philosophy, and so forth. As they sat among the ancient pines, or on the stone steps that went up past Shen's lodging to the ruins of the Xiangshan Si (temple), Xiong probed Congwen's knowledge close onto midnight—gave him "examinations," as Shen later put it. Xiong also sent Congwen down to the Peking University Library, to study cataloguing and bibliography with Professor Yuan Tongli, who the next year was appointed head of China's new flagship modern library, the Peking Metropolitan Library. After September Shen lived right by the university, near the old Imperial Palace, but only for a few months. He was back in the Western Hills during the spring of 1926.[14]

Shen Congwen's days in the Western Hills were a time of personal enrichment for him. He wandered at will among the secluded shrines and pavilions of Xiangshan and put them into the date-and-place lines of his stories. Friends Hu Yepin and Ding Ling honeymooned nearby, sometimes skipping a meal to view a sunset. Transportation between Peking and the Western Hills was by mule in the 1920's, but since that took money, Shen would walk for the four hours when he wanted to browse at city newsstands. He was grateful for his rich relative's help, but he never felt socially accepted by Xiong's gentry set. And some unspoken barrier came between Shen and the Xiangshan staff that he couldn't quite understand. So when he had the opportunity to make a bare living in Peking working as a clerk for the *Xiandai pinglun* (*Modern Critic*) in mid-1926, Shen returned to his hostels. Library science had never claimed his full attention anyway. He had kept at his writing all the while, and together with Ding Ling and Hu Yepin had even begun to aspire to putting out a literary magazine. Indeed, it was precisely Shen's writing that cast a pall over his presence at Xiangshan. That he couldn't see this and thought he could get away with writing stories like "Cotton Shoes" and "Events to Be Filed Under 'A'" in the first place reveals the extent of his naïveté, or of his damn-the-torpedoes idealism. All Shen says today is that he left Xiong's establishment because he wanted his independence, and "because of some other reason."[15]

In "Cotton Shoes," the narrator fails to keep up social appearances because he cannot afford proper shoes. He plods around in an old cloth pair that earn him contempt from the Xiangshan librarian, quizzical stares from visitors, and an implicit reproof from his boss, the head of education at the orphanage. Even had the story been purely fictitious, the Xiangshan employees surely would have resented it for making them out to be snobbish gentry. But since it was based on fact, and since at the end the boss calls the narrator "Shen," Congwen's superiors must have seen "Cotton Shoes" as an impudent personal attack.

"Events to Be Filed Under 'A'" would have been even harder to ignore and forgive, expressing as it does contempt for a birthday celebration at Xiangshan. With 3,000 guests it must have been a major occasion, perhaps Xiong Xiling's fifty-fifth birthday. The anti-hero of the fiction is another socially despised alter ego of the author. The male gentry guests uniformly disgust him, but the perfumed, short-haired "modern young women" come close enough for him to imagine touching them, then embracing them, then.... The fictional narrator's lustful and aggressive attitudes toward his "social betters" are impertinent enough by the standards of the times, but it is tantalizing to speculate about the possibility that there really was "some other reason" for Shen's departure—perhaps an actual advance toward a well-to-do girl student that was rebuffed and got reported.[16]

Becoming a Writer While Staying Out of Writers' Groups

Instead of Xiangshan, Shen Congwen chose his old life of poverty. That he was very poor indeed at this time is not much in doubt, for he wrote several self-commiserating works about his hardships and made romantic heroes of friends who like him chose principle over comfort. He had already experienced straitened circumstances as a soldier, and unemployment at Changde and Baojing, but now he could not afford proper clothing or a stove to get through the Peking winter. (Later Ding Ling and Hu Yepin had a stove but no coal, so they burned old books when friends called.) Shen did his reading off the rack of a forgiving bookstall operator in eastern Peking, pretending to be making his selection. Sometimes he went a day or two without food. Colds and frequent nosebleeds weakened him right into his Shanghai days at the end of the 1920's. Shen held his pen in one hand and a rag to stop the blood in the other, while laboring to provide sustenance for his mother and sister. In Peking, he lacked even 20 cents to register at the hospital.[17] The respiratory ailment, however, was also part of the romantic syndrome in his autobiographical fiction.

When Shen Congwen first arrived in Peking, in 1922 by his reckoning, there was at least a *huiguan* (fellow-regional association) for him to stay at: West Hunan's Youxi Huiguan, which was separate from the main Hunanese *huiguan*. Shen stayed about six months, rent-free, for the proprietor was a distant relative. But thereafter, in 1924, much of 1925, and again in 1926–27, Shen lived in damp and dingy little rooms in the hostels ringing Peking's colleges, including the Qinghua, Yinzha, and Hanyuan Lodging Houses. The last, opened by a literature enthusiast next to the Peking University literature department, acquired a measure of immortality when three of Shen's protégés, He Qifang, Bian Zhilin, and Li Guangtian, named a book of their poems *Hanyuan ji*. But in one place, Shen's lodging was only a coal storage room that had a window poked into the wall. He was only a few months in any one location, sometimes being evicted for nonpayment of rent. He christened his rooms, collectively, The Cramped and Moldy Studio; Shen still lived the life of the student "class," however bitterly he resented his inability to afford education to match his aspirations.[18]

The greatest moral and physical support came from companions. Shen made a wide circle of friends and visited them in their dormitories, often at mealtime. Many were minor members of the Peking student subculture who are now long forgotten, not future writers, though most of his friends at the Peking, Yanjing, and Qinghua universities were in the Chinese departments. Ironically, Shen Congwen returned his friends' favors by writing their Chinese compositions, take-home examinations, and, to be sure, love letters.[19] One began by making friends through relatives and fellow-regionals, then moved outward. Huang Cunsheng, or Younger Brother Cun as the Shen persona calls him in "Cotton Shoes," was a student at the Peking Agricultural College and Congwen's second cousin. (Shen called him "brother" out of familiarity. The much-maligned shoes were Cunsheng's 1925 New Year's gift to Congwen, poignant symbols of a humanity transcending the indignity of poverty since Cunsheng purchased them with money he got from pawning his Western-style suit.) Although two years younger than Shen, Huang clued his cousin in on many aspects of city life and helped him move to the Peking University environs. He gave Shen meals when he needed them, and even a floor to sleep on for a week or two at a time.[20]

Entrée to the Agricultural College was most opportune. It yielded seven more fellow-provincial friends, and access to produce from the college farm plots. That included vegetables for the winter, since cabbages were carted into the city and buried underground near the dormitory. At Yanjing University, Shen got spiritual and physical sustenance from his close student friends Zhang Caizhen (from Hunan) and Dong Qiusi (a future translator of Tolstoy, from Hubei). Dong headed the student association; he introduced Shen to Situ Qiao, Liu Tingwei, Jiao Juyin, and many others. It was through shared literary interests that Shen made friends at Peking University, again mostly with Hunanese (such as Liu Mengwei, Li Jinming, and Wang Sanxin) and Sichuanese (whose dialect was like that of the West Hunanese—Chen Weimo, Zhao Qiwen, and Chen Xianghe). Congwen also had friends from Fenghuang itself: Man Shuyuan and Yin Yuangui. Man Shuyuan accompanied Shen on the trip to Peking and shared further hardships with him as they studied together in the *huiguan*. But Shuyuan had no way of living and had to return home, where he met an early death. Shen Congwen commemorated him in stories about their shared boyhood experiences. Shen's cousin Yin Yuangui likewise came to Peking with high hopes, only to see them dashed. However, he also brought Fenghuang folk songs with him, which Shen had published in Yuangui's name.[21]

But perhaps the most important friends Shen made were the editors of a literary supplement for the *Jingbao* (*Capital News*), Hu Yepin and Xiang Zhuo. Nearly as green as Shen himself, they cared enough to come calling at his tiny hostel room after accepting one of his literary submissions. Hu Yepin and his lover Ding Ling became more than good friends to Shen, though only in 1925, not as early as Shen's overwrought reminiscences of them imply. For the next five years they were his soulmates in plotting a joint conquest of the Chinese literary world. They could share his alienation because they, too, were aspiring but failed students. Following the period they spent together in the Fragrant Hills, the trio would slip in to Peking University to audit courses. They frequently lived in the same hostel, usually by way of Shen Congwen's introductions. This—and particularly the continued association and joint publication projects of the three in Shanghai in the late 1920's, plus the fact that constant moves made it necessary for them to bed down together from time to time—gave rise to rumors that they were a sexual *ménage à trois*. It may well be that Shen initially had a platonic infatuation with Ding Ling. He may even have written love poems to her.²² Being from the farthest downstream reaches of Lower West Hunan, Ding Ling was broadly speaking a fellow-regional, or so Shen tried to picture her; certainly she was one of the few liberated women from his parts. And she may have shown some teasing interest in Shen, if only to spur Hu Yepin's wild fits of jealous rage. Shen noted in 1931 that Ding Ling was the only person he had ever met who suggested he was good looking—and at the first meeting. Yet in Shen's reminiscences of his friends he depicts himself, quite credibly, in a passive role, as mediator during Hu's and Ding's marital spats. The three of them did share books, money, and plans for capitalizing a journal in such a way as to suggest that they may have pooled their meager income (from Shen's manuscript fees and Ding Ling's mother) for maximum effect. But they lived in separate rooms at the Hanyuan Lodging House, and in the late 1920's Shen's mother and sister Yuemeng (Little Sister No. 9) were living with Shen. That renders incredible the rumors about Shen's supposed affair with Ding Ling. Some who knew of Shen Congwen's arrangements indeed preferred to make up rumors about incest between him and pretty Jiujiu ("Little Nine").²³

Shen Congwen of course made some Communist friends. Dong Qiusi and Zhang Caizhen were among them. Later Shen met the Hunanese Li Da, a Party founder. When Hu Yepin was arrested in 1931, it was Li and Shi Cuntong who got Shen to inquire after Hu with Chen Lifu. One of Shen's three best friends during his Baojing days, too, was a Communist organizer at Wuhan in 1927. He wrote Shen in Peking, asking him to join the revolution (as did Dong Qiusi and others), but the letter was intercepted by the Peking police of Chu Yupu, a warlord of the Fengtian Clique. Shen was interrogated and his lodgings were searched four or five times, causing him to pack up and depart hastily for Shanghai. One of his reasons for shuddering to see Hu Yepin and Ding Ling take up Communist activities in the 1930's was his knowledge of the fate of other Red friends who had been organizing and trying to dodge arrest since before the Northern Expedition. Shen's accounts of Hu's and Ding's left-wing activities make them sound naïve—which they were—but if he further makes himself appear wiser than they, it is probably because he felt Hu Yepin was treating the Communist movement as if it had begun about the time he discovered it.²⁴

Within a few years in the late 1920's, Shen Congwen lost most of his leftist friends. Of many he simply received no more news—more often than not because they were dead. Six of his eight friends from the Agricultural College, for instance, became heads of agricultural associations in Hunan during the Northern Expedition in 1927. Whether Communist or just Left KMT, they were all executed during the 1927 KMT "Party purification." Shen's dozen Yanjing friends were revolutionary organizers at Wuhan in 1927, and then in the Canton Commune, which claimed the lives of most of them. In 1928–29 Shen would be able to talk over the events at Wuhan and Canton with Dong Qiusi and Zhang Caizhen, but only Dong would live to see Liberation. (And only he, in China's new official Communist establishment, would refrain from disowning Shen Congwen.) But what must have been even more difficult for Shen was learning, in letters from home, that nearly all the friends he had made before 1922 were lost to him, too. There were a lot of them, mostly fellow army officers and students from Chen Quzhen's highly militarized middle school. Among them were Shen's remaining two best friends at Baojing. They had become schoolteachers in Fenghuang, only to be executed for suspected Communist sympathies—though Fenghuang was far away from any Communist activity.[25]

Luckily, Shen Congwen found Peking itself to be a source of sustenance, another "book" of history. Certain streets were "a museum of the humanities for the two dynasties that made up the last 600 years"—and there was no admission fee. West of the *huiguan* where Shen first lodged were the famous antique shops of Liulichang. He dared not enter, but the outdoor displays exhibited ancient cracked porcelains and paintings such as he had never dreamed of in Baojing, enough to make him "go into a rapture, falling so in love with them that I forgot to go home." To the east was the great market of Qian Men Street, with its drink stands, instrumentalists who played to attract customers, and hawkers' calls, "a great chorus" to Shen's countrified ears. Peking had luxury shops that sold jewelry made from jade, pearls, ivory, and rhinoceros horn, and fans decorated with paintings that told a tale. Other stands cast a different light on society, with their used leather goods, satins no one wore any more, foreign-made serges, and out-of-date dresses. There were night markets, traveling temple fairs, and a row of firms that hired out bodyguards to private individuals. "Collectively it stood for the fall of the three-hundred-year-old

Qing," Shen felt. "In little more than ten years, everything produced in association with that dynasty had been scrapped, had lost its meaning." Real treasures, some from the imperial palaces, could be bought for next to nothing in those days. Shen Congwen did not become a collector until he had a steady job, in the 1930's, but the course of self-study in Chinese art history that he had begun in Chen Quzhen's library was already resuming.[26]

When Huang Cunsheng tried to rescue his cousin from these antiques and bring him up to date through immersion in a university environment, Shen found great freedom there, too. It was easy to audit classes at Cai Yuanpei's wide-open school, Peking University, where non-students outnumbered legitimate enrollees three to one. Shen, Ding, and Hu went to Japanese classes, for they dreamed of studying in Japan. They even attended lectures by the monarchist Gu Hongming. One could also purchase lecture notes and pass them around. Rules were so lax that Shen Congwen, pretending to be a student from another department, actually sat for some examinations, passed them, and was awarded the standard 35-cent prize intended for students. The Peking Metropolitan Library was his place for books—and for taking tea and keeping warm. Peking had so many poor students that people on the street didn't notice shabby clothes. Hostel owners were easily put off when the rent came due. These were "the good things about Peking" that Shen remembered as fondly as the excitement of the May Fourth movement and its student subculture. He saw Peking as the inheritor of a straightforward, noncommercial morality from China's past. It was the opposite of Shanghai, he said, when he had the opportunity to make the comparison.[27]

What ideas and philosophies kept Shen going in those days we can only guess. They must have been a chaotic mix of modern liberal ideals, perhaps with a whiff of the undoctrinaire but emotionally anarchistic individualism espoused by friends like Ding Ling. He "read everything he could digest," old and new, and never did give allegiance to a specific program, ideology, or philosophy. In 1980 he lowered his voice in speaking of Sun Yatsen, but Shen has never raised any "ism" except to ridicule it; certainly he never promoted Sun's Three Principles (literally, "Isms") of the People. To China's many pre-Communist governments, Shen was just another leftist malcontent like his colleagues.[28]

The foreign literary names recalled by Shen's fiction, through mention or characters whose eponyms are characters in Western literature, are a broad array of mostly Russian and French nineteenth-century fiction and drama masters, those most popular in China at the time: Chekhov, Turgenev, Tolstoy, Gogol, Gorky; Maupassant, Daudet, France, Flaubert, Gide; Ibsen, Wilde, and Hans Christian Andersen. The works of these authors offer social or plot interests, if not in all cases realism. Some are also notable for their wit. Shen says Chekhov was his favorite, for using sympathetic humor to temper his satire. When one of Shen's author characters caricatures people in the manner of Gogol, we appear to be seeing Shen's own method. In fact Shen Congwen was reading all the current student favorites—Tagore, Dewey, and Bertrand Russell. Shen conceived of the literary revolution as mostly linguistic, and so accorded nonfiction writers like Hu Shi, Chen Duxiu, Li Dazhao, and Qian Xuantong as much importance as he did creative writers. Shen was also aware of Western psychology. He referred to the subconscious in a story he wrote in the summer of 1925, and early in 1926 made an essay out of his own free association, highlighting his method as he went.[29]

But such clues merely hint at the catholicity of Shen Congwen's reading. He was, for instance, preoccupied with Western romanticism, though he mentions only Rousseau's *Confessions* by name. Shen's long poem "Dawn," in which a narrator describes true love to a prostitute, manages to allude not only to the courtesan Marguerite and her lover Armand (from *Camille*, by Dumas *fils*), but to Goethe's *Young Werther*. In Chinese literature, most of Shen's reading was in the May Fourth works of his contemporaries. Yet he also read Tang poetry and claims to have been influenced early on by Tang tales in the Classical language. Perhaps he was drawn to their relatively nondidactic, even "realistic" telling of fantastic events as if they were ordinary, as Průšek suggests; or perhaps he liked their accommodation of verse in the narrative.[30]

Indeed, Shen's favorite prose models were the Bible (Protestant, in vernacular Chinese translation) and Sima Qian's *Historical Record*, the two books he brought to Peking from Hunan. His style betrays indebtedness to the archaic vernacular of China's "classic" novels, and even to the Japanese-flavored vernacular Chinese that was used to translate Western novels in the early twentieth century. Shen Congwen's early works, in their unruly diversity, indicate that he was influenced by everything, but disciplined by nothing.[31]

Did Shen Congwen also like the Bible as a religious text? In 1957 he claimed, as was only politic at the time, that in his youth he read the Bible for its lyricism (and certainly his early works draw metaphors from books like The Song of Solomon). Zhou Zuoren's interest in the Bible was similarly literary, and though Shen continued to read the Bible daily in the 1980's (Huang Yongyu having supplied him with a copy after the Cultural Revolution), his literary explanation is credible. Still, in the 1920's Shen was depressed and looking for hope. Many characters in his works from that time carry a Bible; Christians must have approached him in Peking, if only at Xiangshan. Perhaps three pieces—but probably no more—have genuine Christian symbolism. Since Shen understood Christianity to be simply "universal love," an idea he would later embrace through a still more abstract pantheism, probably he was interested at least in that central tenet of the faith. However, he took no comfort from its institutional trappings or dogmas.[32]

Some aspects of Peking of course worked to Shen Congwen's disadvantage. Among the educated people and gentry at Peking's literary gatherings, Shen's shabby clothes and ignorance of manners were more noticeable. He especially despised the urban custom of tipping and made it the butt of his satire. No wonder: every month he had to tip the porter at the *Morning Post* 20 or 30 cents just to get past the door to receive his four to twelve yuan of manuscript fees. Above all, Shen Congwen hated the *guanxi*, or "connections" Peking society was based on, typically affiliations of native place, graduation from the same school, or some other quasi-familial tie. Though they had their own *huiguan*, West Hunanese could never hope to compete with people from wealthier districts of southeastern China at this game. Not having studied, Shen Congwen had no school ties at all. Yu Dafu agreed that without an introduction, Shen couldn't become a proofreader, library book boy, tutor, or nurse, not even a bellhop or errand boy. To paraphrase Shen's still rueful words 55 years later, "Even the beggars had their own organization. They wouldn't have let me in." His attempts to correspond with celebrities he'd never met ("try-my-luck letters," he called them) might seem to confirm how desperate the prison of *guanxi* had made him. But letters were his forte, and in this case there were historical precedents, even among his favorite Tang poets.[33]

Shen Congwen was distressed that lack of connections kept him from sitting for the Qinghua University exams, but the thought that *guanxi* were also determining what literary works got published was too much to bear. He felt, for instance, that influential Zhejiang writers such as Lu Xun (to cite an example that obsessed Shen) promoted only the careers of fellow Zhejiangese and personal friends. Regional and other forms of personal cliquishness, not political or ideological principle, formed the only real groups or "schools" (*pai*) in Chinese literature, Shen believed. All the rest was shadow play. He attributed his own initial difficulty in publishing to such factors—noting, pointedly, that his first story to be published by a major literary magazine (*Yusi*, or *Threads of Talk*, edited by Lu Xun and his brother Zhou Zuoren), saw print because Hu Yepin, through a connection, was able to deliver Shen's manuscript to Zhou Zuoren in person. Shen and Hu naturally dreamed of going it alone with their own magazine, where they could print whatever they wanted to "without prejudice." In the meantime, Hu Yepin's poetry found an outlet through Shen's connections, Xu Zhimo and the *Modern Critic* publishers.[34]

Shen was able to become a writer because things were not quite as bad as he pictured them; he gained the ear of open-minded New Intellectuals by the merits of his work. But from then on he tended to publish in their magazines, and to be seen, willy-nilly, as part of their "circle," so his perception was not wholly off the mark. That people who published together in China did so on the basis of factors other than shared ideology is a point now generally accepted everywhere but in China itself. So to explain how Shen Congwen succeeded as a professional writer, we again look to his friends.

The romantic poet Xu Zhimo, de facto editor of the *Morning Post Literary Supplement* in 1924 (he took the post officially in 1925), was instrumental in publishing Shen's first works. It was through him and his encouragement that Shen first earned a bare subsistence by his pen. Yu Dafu may have been Shen Congwen's first major literary "friend," but Shen's entry into literary circles was helped even more by Xu Zhimo's poetry-reading gatherings, which Shen attended around 1925–26, if not earlier. In Wen Yiduo's house he heard readings by Zhu Xiang, Liu Mengwei, Rao Mengkan, and probably many of the minor lyric poets who gave the *Morning Post* supplements their flavor. Chen Yuan and Ding Xilin were Shen's friends at the *Modern Critic*. Once in that "circle," Shen got to meet other American- or British-educated writers. Paradoxically, polemicists therefore associated Shen Congwen with an "Anglo-American Clique" and "their" subsequent non-revolutionary "Crescent School" (that is, those who published, as Shen did, in *Xinyue* [*Crescent Monthly*, est. 1928]). Yet he wrote no polemical antiradical articles of the sort Liang Shiqiu was known for, and in fact Shen seems to have remained relatively distant from Liang, though he was close to Liang's friend, Harvard-educated Wu Mi. Shen's career benefited from the relationship, despite the fact that Wu's literary ideals were too conservative for Shen or even the real Anglo-Americanophiles, lovers of romantic writing and bohemian life who sniggered at Wu's "classicism."[35]

By moving to Shanghai in 1928, Shen broadened his circle of friends to include the whole gamut of nonpartisan writers: Ba Jin (a good friend who roomed with Shen in 1933), Shi Zhicun, Hong Shen, Zhao Jingshen, and Yao Pengzi, to name just a few.[36] Shen was quite close to purveyors of American liberalism such as Hu Shi, and indeed to most of the people who published in the *Crescent Monthly*, including Ling Shuhua, Shao Xunmei, Ye Gongchao, and Pan Guangdan. However, it was not Hu Shi who first brought Shen Congwen into prominence, after meeting him at the Peking University Library, or in class, as some anecdotists have claimed. Hu Shi's great gift to Shen came later: in 1929, as president of the Woosung (Wusong) China Institute near Shanghai, Hu Shi gave Shen a position teaching creative writing and literature. That initial breaking of the rule that a professor must have a diploma was professionally decisive for Shen Congwen. It also lifted him back up into the middle class. Thereafter, literature professor Yang Zhensheng helped Shen get appointed at Qingdao University (Xu Zhimo helped, too), and then at Peking University itself.[37]

Often friends and associates led each other into new kinds of commitments; Wen Yiduo wanted to have such an impact on Shen Congwen, but in the end Shen was too resistant. The two men first mixed in circles that supposedly made "Crescentists" of them both. Later they became very close at Qingdao University; probably Wen had smoothed the way for Shen to partly fill the vacancy he left when he quit Wuhan University in 1930. In 1938, when Wen Yiduo accompanied a wartime trek into the Southwest, it was Shen's turn to invite Wen and his disciples to his home and urge them to train their folkloric interests on contemporary songs, including those of the local Miao. But Wen Yiduo then got involved in non-Communist left-wing political organizing of a sort quite beyond the experience of the "Anglo-Americans." He and Wu Han, a student of Shen's and a classmate of Shen's wife, tried to involve Shen in their political work. Only after much soul-searching did Shen Congwen reaffirm his fixed policy of staying out of all groups, even seemingly democratic ones.[38]

In late 1933, Shen Congwen himself became a major editor, head of the "Literature" Supplement of the Tianjin *Dagongbao* (*"L'Impartial"*). There he remembered his "Anglo-American" friends, such as Lin Huiyin, but remained open to articles from many quarters. Though he almost took a job editing Nanking's conservative *Wenyi yuekan* (*Literature Monthly*) in 1931, his avowed plan was to open it up to everyone and use it as an outlet for his polemics against the Shanghai-Nanking merchant-bureaucrat axis he felt was stifling independent writing. At the *Dagongbao*, Shen's contributors included dissidents Ai Wu, Ba Jin, Cao Juren, Jinyi, Lao She, Li Huiying, and Zhang Tianyi. Shen vowed to publish young unknowns as well. One of them was Lin Geng, the son of a friend (Lin Zaiping); another was a young Mongol named Xiao Qian, who succeeded Shen at the *Dagongbao* in 1936. By the nature of things, the authors Shen Congwen published became his friends if they were not before, just as the young people he introduced were considered his protégés. It may be that he gave his utmost attention to honing the writing skills of people like Xiao Qian and Liu Zuchun because their rural lyricism already seemed to echo his own. But Shen also favored young poets, since he felt poetry had the fewest outlets.[39]

Important as publication was to defining oneself as a writer, there was a psychological element to it, too, a commitment. This was particularly true for one who at first wanted to be a "professional" author, a serious writer outside the academy, perhaps outside the middle class. Shen names Liang Sicheng, whom he met through Xu Zhimo, as his "first critic," but attributes his initial resolve to continue writing despite all setbacks to the philosopher Lin Zaiping. Lin took issue with the self-centered pessimism of Shen's early work. Shen defended this as his right, and indeed continued to "complain" about the lot of little people like himself in his writings throughout the 1920's. But down deep he feared he was after all writing as much to keep himself alive as to further the literary revolution. Lin cut into Shen's self-pity. He sat the young man down and made him see that "finding the means to go on living is easy; what is difficult is knowing how to direct your Life once subsistence is no longer a problem." Shen says that Lin helped him to see creative writing not as just an occupation, but as a life mission through which he might define himself morally. Thereafter, on his way to pantheism, Shen felt drawn toward idealistic or metaphysical writers such as Xu Zhimo, Feng Zhi (another friend from the early 1920's), and young Chen Mengjia. He also formed friendships with men professionally learned in philosophy, such as Zhu Guangqian and Jin Yuelin, so long as they were not intellectually intimidating (like Qian Zhongshu).[40]

Several Peking academics besides the creative writers Ding Xilin and Xu Dishan introduced Shen Congwen to folklore, anthropology, and psychology, as the next chapter relates. But Shen says it was Lu Xun's writings (for instance, "Village Opera") that first showed him how rural themes could be treated in literature. Why Shen Congwen's talent was only grudgingly accepted by Lu Xun is an interesting tale. Political differences, Shen's closeness to Lu Xun's estranged brother Zhou Zuoren, and Shen's prideful disdain of a literary "authority" who showed favoritism, vanity, and loss of nerve might have been sufficient to produce a rift in any case. But it all began when Ding Ling took up Shen Congwen's practice of sending a letter to a literary lion from out of the blue. Lu Xun was her choice. Since she had never published before, under any name, and since her handwriting resembled Shen's, Lu Xun suspected that Shen had written the letter, to belittle him and test whether he could be taken in by the feminine writing and funny pseudonym "Ding Ling." (Others had thought even "Hu Yepin" to be one among Shen's dozens of pen names.) Lu Xun resented Shen's "presumption" and mentioned it in a letter to Qian Xuantong. Shen Congwen soon found out and felt hurt himself. It seems that the egos of both men were too fragile for either fully to "forgive" the other.[41]

The commitments and friendships that Shen shared with his more practiced colleagues do not, however, fully reveal the romantic, angry side of him that Lin Zaiping advised he suppress (as did Shen's other mentors later in the 1920's, to better effect). This was the Shen Congwen who befriended Hu Yepin and many other half-starving writers, some of whom died and some of whom dropped out of the literary revolution because they had nothing more to contribute than their rage. Shen and Hu saw themselves as mouthpieces for a new generation and a new China, one ready to defy the old people by going it alone. They viewed themselves as competitors of the writers who had more money and education, and later as adversaries of a capitalist Shanghai publishing establishment. The virtue they saw in writing was that it came from an individual mind. Being unaffected by *guanxi*, it was a perfect instrument of self-assertion. One could sing about freedom itself, or use one's own dreams and frustrations as "raw materials" to build a literature to replace the old. To write was to become a romantic. It was in this spirit that Shen first took up his pen.

Shen Congwen's First Modern-Style Works

Shen Congwen's earliest published works are a chaos of creativity, presented in nearly all the genres popular in his time. These tended to be short forms: two- or three-stanza lyric poems, one-act dramas, essays, and short stories. They were not, however, so short as to prevent Shen from borrowing literary conventions, characters, and linguistic styles with utter abandon. The result was quite unlike the disciplined realism espoused in theory by many of the other May Fourth writers, and evidently admired by Shen Congwen himself. Some might judge Shen to have chosen his elements of style naïvely and to have combined them haphazardly. He poured out his soul, writing in haste and insouciantly mixing points of view, genres, global literary traditions, and centuries—all in a single work. Is the literary result clumsy or experimental? Twentieth-century primitive or modernist? The method in his madness may remain a fine point of interpretation for critics for some time to come. Meanwhile, for the literary historian and biographer, Shen's early pieces leave an illuminating trail. And it is, indeed, an entertaining one.

Certainly Shen Congwen thought himself part of an avant-garde. He had gone to Peking as so many provincials in other countries had gone to their capitals, to join and learn from comrades-in-arms already dedicated to innovation and revolution. In 1920's China, after the failure of the political revolution and before the era of class revolution, innovation *was* the revolution, whether in ideals or in modes of expression. Like his colleagues, Shen saw modern literary works as weapons. Not only would new literature *épater les bourgeois*, its superior logic and beauty would prove decisive in the moderns' larger world of reality, which they saw granting survival to the fittest. All that was inferior in the old, cramped world of Chinese tradition would dissolve on contact with the new ideals and forms. Yet the atmosphere was libertarian, almost undiscriminating in its haste to assimilate foreign literature and social thought, literature from the underside of Chinese society, and even ancient philosophy that had been denied a place in the confined world of gentry orthodoxy. Reeling before such diversity, Shen Congwen learned to take pride in self-expression, and to identify innovation with utter freedom, perhaps with release from all "tyranny" of form.[42]

If the results of Shen's experimentation were primitive, he did create something new, even when borrowing old forms. The very genre of spoken drama that he took up in 1925–26 was new to China in the twentieth century. His poems are mostly nature poems, but they see the world afresh rather than through allusions, and typically take the shocking new form of unrhymed free verse. His essays often fall into intemperate rhetorical outbursts by the narrator, and his stories, after setting a scene and introducing characters, sometimes wander off into narratorial musing and even rhapsody, so dissipating the action that conventional expectations about plotting are completely frustrated. Nor do any of ancient China's erotic poets approximate Shen's explicitness about sexual craving.

Shen's style, too, is "new and Westernized," but with curious deviations. His language is modern vernacular, sometimes with dialect, Western concepts, and characters named Jack, Peter, and Tartarin. There is lengthy Western-style description in some works —analytical, rather than composed from set figures. More predominant, though, is chatty, subjective narration, not just vernacular but conversational in tone, accompanied by long passages of dialogue imitating real speech, with its sentence fragments and nuanced exclamatory particles. Shen's characters sometimes speak in paragraph-long run-on sentences, interrupting and correcting themselves midway, even changing the topic of their monologue. His narration, too, contains long periodic sentences, like Chinese translations from Western languages.

Shen Congwen used prepositions experimentally; throughout the 1920's, the unorthodox syntax of his long sentences was itself sufficient to keep his prose in a state of rebellion against all of China's literary traditions. He was au courant with various Western-inspired linguistic innovations today abandoned or partly abandoned, such as differentiating in writing between the homophonous pronouns "he," "she," and "it," and adopting a new word for "she" (*yi*). For adjectives, he favored onomatopoeia and colorful, resonant reduplicatives. Other modifiers of his are not only fresh but not in general use—disyllables that Shen evidently coined by creatively combining monosyllables (he liked to transpose the components of disyllables, too). To that extent his creativity is in the spirit of a lyrical writer in Classical Chinese. Indeed, his narrative prose is literary enough at points to omit or shorten syntactical words, in the manner of Liang Qichao, and to abridge abstract nouns for special effect (like shortening *shenghuo*, "life," into *sheng*). By establishing a contemporary conversational tone in his stories, Shen in the late 1920's was even able to incorporate some Classical words and archaic phrases from vernacular storytelling into the mix without overwhelming it. But he studiously avoided four-character set phrases, except to intensify ironic passages about old fogies through linguistic incongruity. The tropes and characters, like Zhen Guanxi, that he borrowed from China's "classic" vernacular novels evoke the feeling of popular storytelling.[43]

"Cotton Shoes" (1925) exemplifies Shen's discursive and eclectic composition in the short story form, although its self-deprecating vision is more deliciously ironic, and humorous, than most of his output.[44] Here Shen's diversions succeed in building suspense around a central mystery regarding the speaker's shoes. The structure is episodic, but the singularity and wit of each segment impels the reader through to the final resolution.

The speaker is the kind of modern, dramatized, first-person narrator familiar to us in the West, though his self-conscious rhetorical flourishes sound as though they are meant to be heard. Shen's regular readers and friends would recognize him as an alter ego of the author, the same person as the narrator of "Events to Be Filed Under 'A,'" who calls himself "Le Petit Chose" after Daudet and is far less able to poke fun at himself. This story, however, begins curiously: "As soon as I bring up the subject of these worn shoes I'm wearing now, I begin to feel sorry for myself. Sometimes I shed a few tears of self-pity as I rub the nearly bare leather soles, the unraveled threads, the many spots that have been sewn back together.

But whereas once I just pitied myself, now that these shoes have been unjustly insulted, I feel the injury done to them, too!"

The story relates how Younger Brother Cun bought the shoes and presented them to the narrator in his Cramped and Moldy Studio, where he lay in bed, rubbing his feet under the covers to keep them warm. Bantering dialogue, or rather monologue, dramatizes Cun's efforts to cheer up the narrator and make light of his being too poor to find a girlfriend.

"January, February, March ... I haven't parted with them yet," begins the next section. The narrator recalls that the shoes even accompanied him on a "shameful" trip to Jinzhou, Manchuria. What was so shameful about that is left to the imagination, modern style. (Perhaps he went to see his brother and investigate enlistment in the Fengtian Army.) The young man relates, first in paraphrase, then with sample dialogue, how he made up excuses to fend off those rude enough to ask why he didn't remove the warm shoes indoors. He told all comers that he needed protection from the dampness of his room. (One surmises that the narrator cannot afford socks.)

In the next segment, the narrator delves more deeply into his poverty, with self-effacing humor punctuated by pathetic accounts of how even the servant at his hostel disdained to keep on repairing the old shoes. The soles and uppers of one "part company." They are repaired. "Slip slop, slip slop, I can go to the telephone and the toilet again without fear of running into someone and having my big toe show itself shamelessly." The other shoe fails. We learn that the melancholic lad has moved out of the city now (to Xiangshan), for he laments that there is hardly any chance of picking up money. Time has been telescoped in modern narratorial fashion, and this leads to a rhetorical outburst, a tongue-in-cheek romantic lament: "In such a rural area, who would ever come drop his billfold on the ground for me to pick up? Woe is me! There aren't even any grounds for hope."

The narrator begins free-associating about his hopes at the outset of the next segment, interrupting himself as he begins to trail off. He also drops the names of famous pavilions at Xiangshan, as if appealing to the classical literary travel interest. Slip slop, slip slop, there is more comic onomatopoeia and self-deprecating humor, mixed with self-righteousness and fatalism, as the narrator approaches and describes the library. Dialogue is followed by a subtext delivered through interior monologue, without any markers to aid the reader unfamiliar with this new technique:

"I'd like to borrow some books."
"Fine, fine," said the mouth of the librarian, while his eyes drew a bead on my feet at first glance.
Ha ha, your eyesight is good, you've seen those things on my feet—it struck me as comic.

The young man recalls that he deliberately dragged his feet, just to create an annoyance. "Ta, ta, ta." The focal level shifts from the narrator to the librarian, but only through the old-fashioned rhetorical device of having the narrator address the reader: "You put yourself in his place. Except for procuring the books as quickly as possible, how else to get rid of me?"

In the next segment, the poor lad makes a witty play on the name of a building, and humorously compares the sound of its spring to an old country lady babbling late in the night, the better to satirize, through the same metaphor, the late-night philosophizing of gentlemen next door. Free association, functioning as a new kind of *entrelacement* (action used for linking purposes only), continues as the narrator reads poetry into our text. The poet is, remarkably, Bai Juyi of the Tang dynasty.[45]

> Among the wriggling water creatures are the useless frogs.
> Ugly and smelly, they go in and out of the mud.
> Come the torrential rains of summer,
> The frogs are in their element, no happier could they be!
> The earth swells their numbers and their kinds
> And heaven gives them voices to make a din....

An even bigger lapse from the story's modern ethos is the traditional narratorial comment that follows. It points out that Bai Juyi's poem (itself originally satirical) still has its uses. Shen then presents the balancing segment, the target of his satire. With prose he sets out the figures Bai would have stated in verse: "The summer rains must now be upon Peking, and so a lot of frogs! But everyone would be busy listening to the drums and flutes [Northern music], and the poets have already joined the croaking choruses, so who can write poetry for the creatures now?"

The next section dramatizes an abortive colloquy with literary sightseers. They move on after hearing the narrator's West Hunanese accent and seeing his disreputable shoes. The next segment, also depressing, describes a sunset, then some workers singing mountain songs but oblivious to the beauty of the moment, which makes the narrator feel close to them. Once more there is a traditional kind of poetic logic. A fresh and unrelated image is linked to the entire literary work when endowed with new meaning by another image in apposition.

Subsequently we experience the narrator's discomfiture and envy on coming across a pair of lovers in the dark. The incident sets him off on an imaginary conversation with them. He is so mortified that he refers to himself in the third person, not only in his interior monologue, but in the narration (possibly through a lapse in the concentration of the author in the latter instance): " 'What a lucky couple! Relax, no one else will disturb you. That one a moment ago was just careless, don't worry! There'll be no moon out tonight, only stars and fireflies.... Embrace more tightly, go all the way, let your bodies be moved, until you've spent all your heat.' He stole away."

Finally the young man invokes the climactic encounter with his boss. The boss "insults" the shoes by rapping them with his "dog-beating cane." A long, tongue-in-cheek display of outrage ends with the narrator exclaiming, "Ah. Ah. Pitiable shoes! Shoes whose fate is my own!" The piece could be called either an heir to traditional Chinese storytelling, with its episodic structure, or a precursor of modernistically fragmented stream-of-consciousness writing. It indulges in the most timeworn romantic clichés, even as it takes up free association. Yet the melancholia in pursuit of a serious social theme is a put-on, relieved by self-satire and, in the case of the librarian, even a bit of sympathy for the predicament of an "oppressor."

Sometimes Shen Congwen's works subtly play with narrator and focal levels in ways that deserve to be called experimental. An early diary of 1924 daringly introduces spoken phrases from several anonymous voices into its text, not marking them with quotation marks, or necessarily differentiating between spoken and silent thoughts. In time, one voice reveals himself as the diarist dramatized, for he mentions his own diary-writing. One gathers that the others are a servant in his hostel, and perhaps other guests. Only afterward does the diarist, as narrator, clearly indicate that the reader has not been overhearing a real conversation at all, but fantasy discourse played out in the diarist's imagination.[46] At the other extreme, Shen tried to recapture the magic of the old Chinese vernacular novel in some pieces through the use of an oral storyteller, like the one who addresses the reader directly while relating the bandit exploits of "In a Separate Realm" (1926). Says he, "I've yet to say a word about the mountain lair, and I'll bet everyone wants to know about it." However, the narrator does mix in modern self-consciousness with his timeless humor and suspense: "Now to characterize the bandit king's bedroom, it was simply a, simply a ... well, I don't know what to call it!" His main task is to introduce letters for the reader to peruse (ransom notes, some of them). Still, he describes the stationery so fastidiously, as if the letters were stage props, that some of the ethos of the old vernacular novel is captured once again. A story trying for the best of both narratorial worlds is "In a Private School" (1927). Its narrator gets chummy with the reader in a short prologue, yet a more modern first-person narrator tells the tale.[47]

Of equally mixed literary definition are Shen Congwen's one-act farces. They seem mostly copied from the contemporary plays of Ding Xilin. The plots of both writers revolve around misunderstandings and mistaken identities, with urban bourgeois society providing the setting, and modern courtship and marriage the mores to be satirized and turned upside-down. That did not stop Shen from giving one of his plays a prologue, in the traditional manner. It is metrical and partly rhymed, unlike most of Shen's early verse, but its content is modern, even shocking, and so therefore is its matter-of-fact attitude. The prologue actually sets the tone rather well for the play to follow: embarrassed amusement, tempered with covert sympathy.[48]

> Everything in this play comes from contemporary Peking;
> The father and mother are students in college.
> The young people fooled their folks and made love on the sly;
> Happily, but unhappily, they've now a baby.
> The mother has a plan to raise it in the house of a friend;
> She'll drop in for a look every day or two.

Shen Congwen might indeed have been confused about genres. His first book, *Duck*, groups the short works it anthologizes by genre, sometimes erroneously. "Huaihua Town," a piece of narratorial reminiscence and free association linked to a particular place in the author's past, is an essay, yet it appears under the fiction category. Similarly, placed among the essays is "The Little Grass and the Duckweed," a third-person narrative with dialogue between the two fantasy characters. Despite some narratorial asides at the outset, it is clearly fiction.

Although Shen Congwen reined in his frenzy of self-expression by 1930 (and wrote far less poetry and drama after the mid-1920's), let it not be assumed that he had been tightening up his prose all along. On the contrary, Shen's narratives in the late 1920's grew more digressive and wildly eclectic than ever. His sentences stayed long and his language became a complex melange of Classical, archaic vernacular, and modern vernacular vocabulary. The unconventionality and rebellious spirit of Shen's 1928 works, in form alone, approach those of the proto-novels of eighteenth-century writers such as Swift, Voltaire, Goethe, and Sterne. Shen Congwen must have seen them as fellow spirits. Probably the only line of a foreign language ever printed in a work of Shen's comes from Laurence Sterne (Shen used it as an epigraph).[49] The work is *Letters* (1928), one side of a lovers' correspondence, presented chronologically so as to form a novel, in the manner of *The Sorrows of Young Werther* (or *Pamela*, since the letters are a girl's). Each letter is its own prose poem, expressing in sequence moods of religiosity, love of art, and self-reproach. There are also such standard romantic poetic excesses as apostrophe, personification of the sun and spring as classical Western gods and goddesses (Mercury is named too, in English), use of foreign terms of endearment like "sweetheart," self-doubt about the act of writing itself (lifted onto a philosophical plane), and a high count of exclamation points.

More in the eighteenth-century pre-romantic spirit by content as well as form (though reminiscent, too, of China's late-Qing episodic satires, like *The Travels of Lao Can*) is another 1928 work of Shen's, *Alice's Adventures in China*. Having taken Alice from Lewis Carroll, Shen makes her rabbit companion into a comic but mildly sympathetic caricature of a gentry figure. Like his name, John Nuoxi ("Beloved of the Nuo Gods"), the rabbit and his manners are partly Chinese and partly British. Be that as it may, the companions in travel encounter a panoply of absurd Chinese types and learn of a Modest Proposal for feeding children of the Chinese poor to the imperialists and Chinese upper classes.[50] Satire of guidebooks, and Shen's mocking appeals to prospective patrons in other works he was writing at the time, may well reflect outright imitation of *Tristram Shandy*. More important, though, is the Shandean spirit in these culminating works of Shen's early period. *Alice in China* displays facetious wit, contempt for structure and plot line, unembarrassed outbursts, self-effacement, pleading with and mockery of the reader, burlesque of the manners of literary people and alleged testimonials from moralists that prove to be absurd parodies, juxtapositions of grotesque characters, references to people with satirically contrived and ridiculously long foreign names, topical philosophical digressions, and set pieces of sentimentality. The part of "the gentle soldier" is played by Shen himself, through his dramatized alter ego, Elder Brother No. 2. Missing for once is the Shandean narrator, which Shen was about to exploit to exhaustion in his *A Pre-posthumous Diary* and *Correspondence from a Born Talent*.

The wandering of Shen Congwen's mind and powerful observing eye may yet reflect a traditional sensibility, one simply exaggerated by the expansion of his imagination when he discovered a new literary language and international cornucopia of literary techniques. The importance of subjective, discursive belles-lettres forms in Shen's early writing suggests this. He began his publishing career with "A Letter Never Mailed," followed it with a satiric sketch and two diary-like prose-poem essays,[51] then continued with short lyric essays, sketches, narratives, and poems. His distinctive early period ended in 1929, after a flurry of diaries and collections of fictive letters that must have been partly responsible for his sobriquet, "prolific writer."

We have also seen how generic characteristics of the familiar essay could encroach on a narrative like "Cotton Shoes." The inventiveness of Shen's fiction would always lie in expression and observation, rather than in events or characters. And Shen found his first material by "dramatizing personal experiences," as Jaroslav Průšek styles Yu Dafu's method.[52] Yu and Shen's other friend, Zhou Zuoren, actually thought diaries and epistles superior to other genres, more authentic because they lacked narrative "artifice."[53]

No doubt Shen Congwen's early works partly imitated contemporary subjective writings by Yu Dafu, Zhou Zuoren, and the *Morning Post* lyric poets, who had their own Continental European and Japanese antecedents, as Průšek and Leo Ou-fan Lee have observed. Ding Ling's first efforts are yet another spin-off, possibly from Shen's own pieces.⁵⁴ But as an ex-gentry poetaster and romantic letter-writer, Shen Congwen was able not only to imitate, but to recapitulate the older, better educated writers' use of modern subjective writing to express traditional literary interests. What Shen shared with Zhou Zuoren will be discussed in the next chapter. First we take a closer look at the uninhibited and romantic "Yu Dafu side" of our author.

The Angry Young Man of Peking

An angry and upset young man emerges as the focus, and often narrator, of Shen Congwen's subjective writings. He is "modeled after [the author], in a tone of disgust and self-aversion; the hero, disillusioned by the social climate, confines himself to his own small room, delving into the rotten carnality of his own desire."⁵⁵ This description, so apt for a certain body of works by Shen Congwen, actually refers to the I-novel, a naturalistic genre dominant in literary Japan after 1906 and much admired by the 1920's Chinese avant-garde. The trend was "inward-looking, self-oriented, antisocial," but also avowedly progressive. It was avant-garde as much by its social pose, expressing the social and cultural rebellion of its authors, as by its literary qualities, which were often overshadowed by the taboos broken in subject matter.⁵⁶

Shen Congwen was not necessarily directly influenced by the Japanese, but by the time he took up his pen it was the rage for fashionable young men and women to compose diaries revealing their battles against feudal morals, nervous exhaustion, wet dreams that could not be told to friends in person, and real or imagined romantic conquests and rebuffs. Shen sketches such a love-and-anarchy diarist-litterateur in "Master Songzi" (1926). Songzi is treated comically, but Shen is careful to set him off as a "serious" author like Yu Dafu or himself, lest Songzi be confused with the subliterary writers whom Shen bemoans for their irresponsibility (and financial success) in adapting similar material to the pornographic interests of young people (Zhang Jingsheng, "Dr. Sex," is alluded to).⁵⁷

Shen Congwen maintains a serious literary stance and brings his own persona to life by dissecting him psychologically, often letting him express avant-garde abnormalities in his "own" rebellious and idiosyncratic voice. The afflictions of Shen's persona include unrelieved sexual desire, masturbation, insomnia, quasi-tubercular illness, spiritual lassitude, and paranoia—the basic Yu Dafu panoply, except for gambling, actual whoring, and alcoholism. Shen's young man lacks the means and the spirit to engage so actively in vice. Having desires that he can neither act upon nor forget, he cries himself to sleep at night, unable to keep the least bit of composure. This makes him fear he may lose control entirely, perhaps go insane and unleash his subconscious hostilities in antisocial behavior. That leads to still more self-reproach, until finally he dissolves in self-pity.

Because conventional norms of propriety and morality still hold him in their grip, the young man is continually overcome with guilt feelings: for coveting the girlfriends of others, for having sexual fantasies about young ladies he sees while out walking, and even for being unemployed, though his idleness is involuntary. He ultimately fears losing all self-respect, "falling into the dark, bottomless pit." Shen may have liked that apparent metaphor for Hell because it resonated with his Biblical reading, but as he and Ding Ling use it, it suggests the shattering of the self as a social being. It is above all a corporealized ego, nourished by outside psychosocial forces, that appears at risk. The persona's intellect remains intact. His ability to see through and dissect the inner rottenness of the outer world, as well as himself, is what keeps the narrative going. Though he reproaches himself for his weakness, he need not make the ultimate, Yu Dafu confession of self-deception, or appeal to his readers by invoking his own will to authenticity. That is not in question. Society has more to confess than he.[58]

The psychological wellsprings thus tapped are partly autobiographical, running deep and true to the extent that they transcend literary convention. Indeed, to young people who approached all subjective writing as if it were autobiography, Shen's penetration of the mask of ordinary social discourse was wholly a function of his willingness to present true revelations. But just how autobiographical are Shen Congwen's subjective pieces, except in the tautological sense that "all writing is autobiography," as Yu Dafu put it?[59]

Since Shen first developed his persona in works occupying a middle ground between his diaries and essays, the latter distinguished from the former by being filled with dreams and imagined conversations rather than remembrances of actual events, the question is less one of distinguishing fact from fiction than event from fancy, or Shen Congwen the many-sided person from his literary poses. Shen has muddied up these distinctions by studding all his subjective pieces, irrespective of genre, with hints that the writing is autobiographical. He drops references to Younger Brother Cun, his own family, and the "oppressors" at Xiangshan; his abodes and struggles to find work; his fallen social status, West Hunanese origins, and military background; and his habits, from trips to the library to get warm to hours spent gazing up at the clouds. In later works, one may encounter the young man persona as a writer very much in Shen's image, indeed as the author of stories identifiable to Shen Congwen aficionados as Shen's own.[60]

Certainly Shen put his real everyday life into his works. Consider "After Fasting" (1925), a narrative that pleads the case of a disconsolate, nearly starving autobiographical young man persona, and that midway through prints one of his letters, addressed to an older intellectual whose name is concealed. This letter takes up a third of the text and is a real one that Shen sent Lin Zaiping (not the first—though that letter, too, saw print in the *Morning Post Literary Supplement*). The "story" therefore originated as prologue and epilogue to an epistle. The narrative prologue gives its own clues about the young man's identity by listing his family members, and flashes back, via the persona's tortured memories, to frustrations and snubs soon to be related in the letter. It puts him under the microscope of a mercilessly clinical narrator who speaks in psychological terms, then lets the lad voice his own maledictions on the world through interior monologue. The letter, for its part, digresses into stylized lamentations, giving the young letter writer's visions of the succulent dishes he cannot afford, and his confession of disillusionment beyond tears. Yet the letter dims before the pyrotechnics of the epilogue, which lets the delirious lad conjure up friends who died before their time, goddesses, and imaginary reproofs from God and from his own better self, by whose lights he is a coward.[61] Thus autobiography, what was once document, has become literary, through elevation onto a higher plane—or a more elaborate rhetorical level.

Shen Congwen knew that many of his readers took his literary personae to be real. Certain of his gratuitous references to events from real life may be a sort of inside text put there for the special appreciation of a small circle of friends. One can imagine Lin Zaiping and Liang Sicheng perusing Shen's first works as "Red Inkstone" must have *The Dream of the Red Chamber*.[62] But most of Shen's readers were young and uninitiated. They were curious about actual social and moral transgressions by a real young author who voiced, and for all they knew acted out, their own forbidden fantasies. Shen's persistent dropping of autobiographical hints thus suggests that he was playing with his readers' curiosity. In *Past Dreams* he takes advantage of his aficionados' willing gullibility by creating realistic portraits of himself and his elder brother, only to have the characters resort to amazing schemes for sexual dalliance. Meanwhile Shen, Ding Ling, and Hu Yepin jokingly referred to one another by their comic pen names and published letters written to the others' personae. Hu Yepin seems even to have teased his companions—not to mention his readers—by writing and publishing fictitious letters from "Three People at Odds" that implied a love triangle among the young authors such as the gossip-mongers wrote about.[63] Shen's "After Entering the Ranks" plays with its author's persona in another way, by putting him into the story twice: first as the narrator, a young soldier, and then as "Elder Brother No. 2," a prisoner whose mother is like Shen Congwen's own and who becomes a fast friend of the first persona before coming to a tragic end. So, despite the official classification of, say, Shen's "Long Nights" as essay, one need not jump to the conclusion that it is factual when its Shen Congwen persona vents, with shocking frankness, envy of his own relatives and sexual hunger for their wives and girlfriends.[64]

Shen's "Master Songzi" is indeed a kind of warning (like "Lamp" [1929]) that an apparent *roman à clef* can be a total fabrication.[65] Songzi provokes the narrator, the oft-encountered Shen Congwen persona, into curiosity about Songzi's friend Mr. Zhou. The latter wants to rescue the beautiful young concubine of his cousin from a marriage of convenience; his own heroic true love is to be her deliverance. Unfortunately this concubine betrays Zhou's faithfulness by having liaisons with others, too. It develops that Songzi has written this all up into a story, in the form of Mr. Zhou's diary, evidently to provide his friend some spiritual recompense and to admonish society through these true deeds of dedication and betrayal. He finally hands it over to the narrator. There follows a long extract from the diary, so long, in fact, that one might question Shen Congwen's judgment in giving it so much space. (It may be filler, or a spoof of the love triangle formula.) When the narrator has finally become so caught up in this tragicomedy that he insists on meeting Mr. Zhou, Songzi admits having made up the whole story. In the final analysis, of course, this piece does less to close the door on subjective fiction as autobiography than to whet the reader's curiosity still further about the mystery of the creative process.

The persona of Shen Congwen's subjective writings could only be, in any event, one side of the author—Shen Congwen alone, thinking his thoughts, walking the streets, or withdrawing into his shell in the midst of social situations in which he feels estranged. Shen Congwen as a many-sided social being is scarcely visible. And although Shen's narrators like to dissect the world about them with their imagination, they do so with wit, making it clear they are as intent on entertaining as on holding up a mirror. Women's breasts are lambs wriggling around in the sheep's womb; the heat makes one feel one has been bottled for dry-steaming; sinewy muscles crawl like worms beneath the skin. Songzi wants to publish in a magazine called *Fragments of Speech* (cf. *Threads of Talk*). His conversation is analyzed by the narrator in reference to its dramatic effect: "filler" here, a "return to the main plot" there.[66]

In "Cotton Shoes," we observed, Shen Congwen uses a self-deprecating persona for humorous self-parody. Elsewhere intimations of irony are undone by the persona's conspicuous dedication to ponderous "ideals." This betrays yet another departure from autobiography. The young man is not just expressing himself, but trying to speak to, and for, young people. He voices their hopes for finding personal salvation in love between the sexes both spiritual and physical. He extols the beauty of the beloved with imagery reminiscent of the Bible, rendering her sacred. Love thus becomes a devotion important for its transcendence of the economic view of marriage. However many insults he must suffer, Shen's persona exemplifies a kind of dignity in his free self-determination. Shen Congwen even dropped his defenses and recast his persona as a recent college graduate in one story, as "Master Zhong." (Zhong learns that his education guarantees him neither work nor girlfriends.) More convincing, though, is Shen's sketch of a bored non-student who answers the telephone for college students in their dormitory. He envies them.[67]

The social definition of Shen Congwen's literary persona is what makes it distinctive. The young man's desolation is more the fault of society than of his own weakness, sensitivity, or genius. He does not quite reflect a general *Weltschmerz*, like a European Romantic, but takes the spirit of the times to be his personal enemy, like a Japanese I-novelist. Yet Shen's persona is not a personality in whom the author could take refuge, as Yu Dafu did in his, according to Leo Ou-fan Lee.[68] Shen's persona is not even bohemian (no more than the author himself). He has dropped out of society unwillingly, because of poverty and powerlessness. It is by fashioning his persona in reaction to such a strong and negative image of society that Shen Congwen sought to voice the discontents of China's young people as a whole. Their senses having been sharpened by oppression and powerlessness, he said, young people were uniquely equipped to "divine" the "brightness of the world of the future."[69] But the social consciousness of Shen's persona is also distinctively that of an uprooted country boy. Therein lies its special flavor, one the author would become conscious of himself in the 1930's.

In the eyes of Shen's persona, "society" is the streets of Peking and the pairings off of male and female that go on behind closed doors.[70] The world seems to consist only of people who are above him: well-to-do young men, their equally fortunate girlfriends, and the gentry. The urban poor are invisible, entirely subsumed within the persona himself. Society, in other words, is coterminous with "the oppressors." It has a monopoly on material comforts, the very basics of life, and on sexual partners, which it flaunts before the needy young man. Paunchy gentry even prevail over fashionable college students half their age. Says the narrator of one of Shen's "Long Nights" of a wealthy 43-year-old relative and his attractive 25-year-old wife, "although they're a little far apart in age, money is a counterweight when the sides are unbalanced, so it's no problem...."[71]

Pairing with the opposite sex might seem extravagantly romantic as a symbol of happiness, social success, and mental health too (one that naturally appealed to readers Shen's own age), but it takes on special weight because the young man lives in a Social Darwinist universe. Money and mates come only after grueling competition. Having "crawled out" of his "prison" school, Master Zhong learns that society is "a sea of people." He "tumbles into" its "competition for life." The diarist of "In a Lodging House," one of Shen's most autobiographical personae, likewise observes, "Victory goes to the strong, that's a phrase that needs no explanation. In this world, I need only beat you down, and then I can sit on top of you. I can control your fate. I can eat you. Love! Sympathy! Fairness! These words are just there to sound good. Who has ever really been rescued from abuse by words like 'sympathy' and 'love'? At most they help the abused ones to pity people still more pathetic."[72] Shen took this world view so much for granted that he could make jokes about it. Songzi's diary has Mr. Zhou fight the "sexual imperialism" of his cousin. A window "resists the authority" of the wind, in sympathy with the diarist of the lodging house, and another incarnation of the persona sees resistance even in tree leaves under the sun. He wishes he could summon up equal spirit in himself. Shen Congwen did think that competition, if conducted on fair terms, could foster the kind of human dignity and perseverance he admired.[73]

But his persona is in an unfair fight for survival. His manifest inferiority, evident in his hunger, cold, and lack of friends, turns his class consciousness into unshakable paranoia. He imagines well-bred young ladies, as well as gentry, giving him condescending stares. He actually follows a pair of damsels in one story, patronizing the shops they stop in and buying what they buy, as if to prove himself their equal. This provokes them into answering his interest with the sort of contemptuous grimaces that confirm him in his world view. One calls him a rogue, a reprobate. That acknowledgment of his existence is actually a victory of sorts, but the persona also realizes that his tortured soul has driven him to the brink of madness. So he returns to his little room, for his usual cry.[74]

The problem is that society judges people by their appearances. Put another way, people are irredeemably materialistic. Hence the wealthy's monopoly on sex. They "buy" their female companions with the glitter of their life-style. The persona, however, blames society and its false values for this bad state of things, not the women, who seem to him "prisoners" in gilded marital cages. No more would he blame prostitutes, who are victims of society, symbolic of the fallen state of woman in bourgeois society, like Marguerite. But if woman can be had by something other than money, the persona does not have that equalizer. He is too cowardly to approach women directly, and he is "old" (in his twenties and unengaged) or, in one story, "middle-aged" (that is, in his thirties).[75] The persona as moralist blames his pitiable condition on society, yet his Social Darwinism must reflect much of the blame back on him. He is suspended between anger and self-pity.

With these charges that society is materialistic and intent on reducing him to anonymity, we can begin to appreciate the persona's anomie as that of a displaced country boy in the city. The narrator of "Cotton Shoes" is ironically rueful about being isolated in a rural setting,[76] but many another persona is nostalgic about the countryside, or bewails the fact that his relatives are far away in Hunan. Besides hunger and cold, then, loneliness is the constant refrain in the young man's melancholia. It is a romantic spiritual loneliness, but with physical and social ramifications. The young man's little room, where he is thrown back on his own fantasies and neuroses, is his prison. He thinks in images of jails and cages, like Shen Congwen the author, who writes poems about prisoners and humiliates more than one of his autobiographical personae by actually seeing them locked up. It is the young man's obsession that society, having imprisoned him figuratively, will do so literally.[77] The real or imagined imprisonment, again, reflects a country boy's lack of organic relatedness in the city. The city will not let him take a job or make friends, particularly girlfriends, without a prior connection. The only social space it grants him is the street, which is just a torture, another reminder of his unrelatedness. He finds himself surrounded by goods and people in an abundance that makes him drool, but he must not touch any. Women, above all, appear on the streets in numbers and in states of dishabille (to his country eyes) that make his head swim. Even the "freedoms" of urban life thus drive the young man persona to distraction. He reads of liaisons in books, and may actually sit next to a stylish young lady on the bus, or stare at her bare neck, inches away from physical contact, if he takes a seat behind her in a theater. Yet, if he goes one step further, he will be rebuffed—threatened with jail.[78]

Many of the persona's psychosomatic illnesses are the result of unfamiliarity with the urban environment and homesickness. Hammering and pounding by craftsmen and construction workers may be no louder than the sounds of barnyard animals back home, and the noise of strangers that penetrates paper-thin urban walls may really be no more disruptive than family quarrels in the old homestead, but they drive Shen's persona to distraction, heightening his insomnia and weakening his emotional defenses.[79] Here we see how the deceptive glitter of the city has disoriented the hungry lad of "After Fasting." Things quite ordinary to the city person threaten his emotional equilibrium.

A yellow-suited policeman paced involuntarily, his expression changing in reaction to what he saw. What met his eyes hadn't changed an iota, and that was what prompted him to register surprise.... Jackets wafted in the breeze at a used-clothing store, seemingly as bored as the clerks. The man who ran a peep show stall kept on hoarsely calling out for customers, all the while humming a little tune to himself. Automobiles as usual dashed about at a deadly run, loaded with the living corpses of puppets, and still loudly making their shameless and arrogant sounds. Horses and men pulling carts and rickshaws sweated as always, sweated to move dead people. Multicolored advertisements just put up at the alleyway entrances now talked about "patriotism" or some such, so some hurrying passers-by still stopped to search those words for the benefits they promised. The fruit stands had added some round watermelons with rinds of blue-green jade, but they seemed no different from the ones that were there before; and the upside-down cups next to the jug of sour plum wine were arranged and sparkled just as before, too.... These things made his legs wobble and his stomach growl, they broke his heart with disappointment and loathing. Oh! Do these lifeless things yet lord it over people! In truth, living and lifeless things are both incapable of arrogance toward anyone; if only you set yourself to the task, you could approach them, possess them, assimilate them—but he could not admit of such transgressions, even if he spoke as if he knew all this.

Devilish crowds! Things from Hell! I want to leave you! Whereupon he returned to his damp and moldy little room, which was like a pigeon cage.[80]

This is extraordinary rage, only intensified by being repressed. It is the stronger because the persona thinks himself a typical social figure, without having established contact with fellow sufferers, or realized that he is fighting urban life itself. In "Events to Be Filed Under 'A,'" the persona finally acts out (mentally) the aggression against society he has so long suppressed. Hating the gentry up on Xiangshan just for existing, he clutches the pencil in his pocket, wishing it into a pistol so that he can shoot them one and all.[81] Here, in urban China, Shen Congwen had a negative mirror image of the life he would celebrate in his regional literature.

The Still Angrier Young Man in Shanghai

After Shen Congwen moved to Shanghai in 1928, his subjective writing culminated (or came to a dead end—perhaps none too soon) in longer works, *A Pre-posthumous Diary* (1928) and *Correspondence from a Born Talent* (1929). These books, told ramblingly and with little artifice by Shen the author in the first person, are little different from expository writing. The chronic discontents of poverty, tubercular illness, insomnia, and lack of satisfying contacts with the opposite sex and society generally are all present, but the content is strictly autobiographical. Mostly we see Shen's life as it meshed with those of the ailing family members he was supporting. Still, the narrator's voice, quarrelsome and repetitious, is not necessarily Shen Congwen's own voice. At most it expresses one of his moods; it may be an imaginative reconstruction (however unimaginative) of a mind disoriented by oppression. The persona has, however, begun to attribute his misfortune to his social role as a writer. This affords Shen opportunities for irony; his correspondent, for instance, mocks his publishers by writing drivel and confessing to it, reminding them (they are among his more-than-implied readers) that his assignment is to produce so many thousand characters rather than literature. He challenges his readers to accept the reality of his depressing life in place of their romantic fantasies about artists, to read about "life" instead of something more diverting.

Something else is new about Shen's Shanghai writing, besides an expression of disillusionment unprecedented even for Shen Congwen. These works do not stop at criticizing wealth and power, the nebulous "enemies" of the hungry young man. They move on to institutions. Shen's Shanghai persona drops snide comments about the care he must take in choosing his words, so as not to get himself censored by the government. He protests, in an injured tone, that people as critical of the status quo as he are likely to be branded Communist and liquidated. Directly addressing his publishers, he scathes them for exploitative pay scales and slavish pursuit of, even manufacture of, short-lived subliterary fads. (Though now a noted author, Shen Congwen earned only 100 yuan for every book he wrote—after selling away all his rights.)[82] Some works proceed to dwell on the evils of foreign imperialism.

Shen thus wrote a few realistic stories that seem at first glance, by subject and theme, right in the mainstream of late 1920's and early 1930's Chinese left-wing writing. He criticizes "masters" in several worker-employer relationships and, most bitingly, the exploitation of workers in the modern factory setting ("A Small Matter in a Big City," 1929). As one might expect from his later writing, Shen goes over and around the conventional Marxist class definition of exploitation, highlighting instead the noisome physical characteristics of a small steel factory: its cramped, dirty work space, its deafening noise and noxious air, its monotony and spiritual poisoning. The men are distracted to the point that they cannot sleep at night; their environment resembles the one inhabited by the young man persona in Shen's autobiographical stories. To better dramatize the workers' innocence and show how the factory stunts physical as well as mental growth, Shen chooses young apprentices as his focus. They are nearly dehumanized, getting into bloody fights after work. And yet Shen Congwen, though skeptical of conventional literary Marxist class consciousness, in one sense takes class antagonism more seriously than his colleagues: he probes its psychological origins, making it the centerpiece of his story. "A Small Matter" traces the growing anxiety about class conflict in the mind of the factory owner, who used to be a worker himself. Originally it was only a rumor of Communist conspiracy that planted a fear of rebellion in his mind. Yet a government spotter airplane circles overhead from time to time, a constant reminder of the civil war taking place. Feeling guilt for having tortured his men, the boss becomes increasingly paranoid. He starts trying to read the faces of his workers, wondering which may conceal the heart of a Communist. Surely there are at least two or three? He relaxes only when the government declares peace and he can head up a pro-government union in his factory—to "lead labor's resistance against capitalism." Closer to Fenghuang, "The Marble Carrying Boat" (1928?) has baseless rumors of a Communist threat gradually alienate relatives in a worker-manager relationship.[83]

This heightened political consciousness is not hard to account for. Shen had lost many friends to firing squads in 1927, and had himself been harassed by the Peking police, under suspicion of Communist sympathies. All Shanghai was radicalized by the May 30th movement of 1925, which Shen now belatedly began to mention in his fiction. Despite the executions, there were still enough leftist survivors among intellectuals to promote the banner of "proletarian literature" in Shanghai during the late 1920's. Like Shen, Hu Yepin, and Ding Ling, they found relative safety in the foreign concessions. Just by coming to Shanghai and taking up residence in the French Concession, Shen Congwen got his first glimpse of the full impact of imperialism in China.[84] He saw Chinese customs and faces replaced by foreign ones, and witnessed modern, "enlightened" changes in the uncaring wealthy classes that seemed to be no transformation at all. He began to fear that this might be China's future. Nothing suggested any role for him or his ideals in this particular kind of progress and enrichment.

The same factors enlarged the scope, and certainly the quantity, of Shen's satirical writings. Even at the beginning of his career he had penned a few satires without using the crutch of his young man persona. "The Family Precepts of Mr. San Bei" (1925), for example, savages a recently deceased small-town gentry notable. Judging by the Fenghuang setting and focus on stinginess and hypocrisy, San Bei could well be one of the author's ubiquitous distant relatives. But it is through its Olympian voice and relentlessly ironic use of Classical Chinese that the piece facetiously extols the rich man's "accumulated Virtue and its just Reward." Elegant funeral scrolls wax pious; testimonials from small peddlers he used to trade with are, on the contrary, unprintable. Mr. San Bei's relatives, though numerous and well-placed in the establishment, have their opinions, too. It seems their patriarch suffocated in his own anger because one of his sons wouldn't "return the money spent in raising him." Shen closes the piece with a mock-serious presentation of Mr. San Bei's admonitions for posterity, including "When in summer the nightsoil you collect is too thin to sell, mix in grasses and ashes; do remember to add in the price of these supplements when you make your sale."[85]

Shen Congwen's Peking works further include satires of bourgeois couples ("Lansheng and His Mrs.") and of stupidity and ennui among the bureaucrats ("Junzi" and "The Diary of Master Huang," the latter inspired by Shen's brother-in-law's experiences).[86] Using a device now better known from his cousin Huang Yongyu's 1962 "Animal Crackers," Shen even composed ingenious riddles to comment on current affairs. His reordering of unexceptionable "Words from the Old Testament" (1925), for instance, heaped ridicule on the conservative side in the famous 1925 Peking Women's Normal College controversy.[87] But these pieces are still minor compared to the book-length works of social criticism Shen wrote in Shanghai, such as *Alice's Adventures in China* (1928), *Diary of a Dumb Bureaucrat* (1929), and *The Life of an Actress*. The prefaces to the first book also contain what was for Shen strident criticism of the (KMT) government's white terror.[88]

Alice's Adventures in China is the most political, but also the most enigmatic of Shen's satires from this period. It has not one but several allegorical configurations of characters, all amusing but not consistent or developed fully enough to more than hint at a larger satiric purpose. A raucous meeting of Chinese literary savants is one high point in the novel; the participants discuss topical issues like "Love" entirely in verse, for they are birds. Some of the birds are comic Chinese regional types. A Yunnan fighting cock, like any militarist, wants to close the meeting down for subversion. A plump, middle-aged Nanking mother duck (from the capital) looks down her nose at him as a "Miaozi." There are swallows singing Suzhou dialect, Shaanxi hawks, a female swallow translator for the guest speaker, who twitters in Wu dialect, and a lonely grey stork (a Hunanese, whose plumage suggests the military calling; a sympathetic character, perhaps representing Shen's own background).

Shen is satirizing the Chinese literary forum, with special digs at China's self-important poets and at overrated multilingual experts like the guest speaker, a pugnacious and hyperactive Dr. Myna Bird. One may not enter into these weighty deliberations at all without rhyming one's words, so formal and dialect disputes rage over what are proper rhymes. Had Shen written the chapter just five years earlier, it might have been read as a send-up of his own friends, Xu Zhimo and Lin Huiyin, who hovered over Tagore. But there is also a stern Owl chairman, who wants to control the meeting; a rabble of half-breed proletarian birds who raise a ruckus to bring him down; Mandarin Ducks, representing pulp romancers, who embarrass everyone, particularly the snow-white Egret celibate faction, by necking in public; a Nietzschean Eagle; and a long-haired, homosexual, proudly tubercular pair, the Nightingale and the Lark, who only imitate European meadowlarks. The Grey Stork confides to Alice that "Birds of their species have never in China crooned / Their names, like their identities, are just assumed." "Can they, these poets of your country, Uncle Stork / Freely change their names, and make it work?" asks innocent Alice. "Over here there's many a thing thought odder / They only fear you [a foreigner] might think them a plodder."[89]

In more mordant chapters, the two guests from Britain are Shen's means of satirizing foreign imperialism, racism, and misguided affinities for the bankrupt tradition of China's past (like Bertrand Russell's). Alice has come to China to view kowtowing and superstition. Having seen quite a bit of it, she pronounces China "fun." The pair are also taken to see high-level Chinese gambling, that is, civil warfare, which foreigners are said to be particularly fond of watching and laying stakes on. A starving young man, yet another alter ego of the author, asks if he may rob the foreigners, so that they, or his own anti-Communist government, may execute him and so effect one facet of the Modest Proposal for relieving China of its poor.

On the other hand it is the Chinese who adulate foreigners or, like a native toad, find the sight of a Chinese duckling walking with a foreign girl "ugly." And the ridiculous "misperceptions" of China to which Alice and Nuoxi fall victim are but ironic exaggerations of real national ills the Chinese cannot see. Through this and devices like a dung beetle who argues with Alice that the Western practice of carrying nightsoil was taken from China, Shen Congwen paints a sorry picture of his nation. Yet, when Alice sees Chinese people pray to their gods, and children gamble, they seem to be having so much fun that one cannot be sure whether Shen is exposing vices or reliving childhood experiences he considers harmless and universally human. Despite its cutting anti-imperialist asides, *Alice* is far from nationalistic in total effect. It treats China and the West equally, with ironic but compassionate understanding of universal, and parallel, human foibles.

A quite different spirit and purpose fueled the most talked-about satiric form of the 1930's, the short, barbed essay (*zawen*). Lu Xun, a master of the form, used it to score ideological points by personally skewering his sparring partners. Shen Congwen eschewed *zawen* and indeed polemicized against short, satiric forms in principle, through his attacks on Lin Yutang's "humorous" essays. For his part, Shen continued writing diffuse, medium-length satires, such as "The Gentry Wife" and "A Lady of the City."[90] However, he did embed in his diaries some caustic repartee aimed, not coincidentally, at Lu Xun and Lu Xun's friend (at the time) Lin Yutang.

I had a dream about a birthday party for Lu Xun. Multitudes had come, distance being no object. They wore the uniform clothing appropriate for the celebration and kowtowed to him all day long. All wore knee pads.

Obeisances finished, they listened to the old man tell jokes and make a speech. They enjoyed that more than the birthday noodles. All said there'd been a literary renaissance, and sang the song of the literary renaissance. One Lin [Yutang] led the singing....
    I also dreamed of a flood. It drowned four members of the Creation Society. Three survivors from the society went about everywhere in a boat, shouting, "To Sichuan Road, for coffee à la mode, to Sichuan Road, for coffee à la mode!"[91]

These passages must parody Lu Xun's prose poems that begin "I dreamed...." In another work, Shen Congwen takes on the old master at his own game: "elevating" the level of discourse (Shen does it through psychological analysis instead of classical allusion, Lu Xun's forte) to gain apparent intellectual and moral superiority, while really striking below the belt.

It occurs to me that even if China today had one hundred Anatole Frances all able to speak satire, China would still be China....
    Now as to Lu Xun, I've been thinking,...
    When an official his age needs a woman, he can take a concubine, while a scholar can have an affair. But he seems unable to catch up to the one group, or get together with the other. It's really put him in a bad way. Nor can he do what Yu Dafu does, just yell out "I need one," and they come running. At this stage, no woman would be chasing after him, either. Some bored folks have read his articles and pronounced that "This chap is quite deep." But what use is that to him? Better that they were young and beautiful girls, those vulgarly called "Goddesses of Mercy," there stubbornly to love him, and follow after him bravely. That might do the old man some good. He's never spoken of his "need," but a girl like that could really be his salvation....[92]

Still, Shen ridiculed only "Lu Xun's Combat Actions,"[93] never Lu Xun the creative writer; he felt Lu Xun was wasting his talent.
    Probably Shen Congwen served his own talent best by abandoning both his topical lampoons and his tortured young man personae in the 1930's for what were literally greener "pastures." (Some publishers helped him make the choice, by sending him rejection notices.)[94] Satire became only a stylistic adjunct to lyrical and well-made fiction, except in such sketches of allegorical characters as "Big Ruan and Little Ruan" and "Portrait of Eight Steeds." Shen henceforth preferred realistic or symbolic approaches when he wanted to expose imperialism and congenital national weaknesses.[95] Humor, particularly "country humor" like that in *Long River*, he used for its own sake, and to impart the flavor of country life.

Shen Congwen did retain one thing in common with Lu Xun and the other, more engagé writers as he himself aged. All were struggling, through their literary works, to gain moral leadership over China's young people. As Shen saw it, therefore, the major challenge came not from other people's literature but from subliterature, the Mandarin Duck and Butterfly romances.[96]

Above, left: Shen Congwen as a young man in Peking, 1924.
Above, right: A typical West Hunan scene from Shen's youth: going down to the Yuan River for water, from *The Sign*, Feb. 1925.
Right: A West Hunanese bandit, mid-1920's, from *The Sign*, Mar. 1928.

Above, left: "Miao King" Long Yunfei (left) with Bishop Cuthbert O'Gara, from *The Sign*, Feb. 1939.
Above, right: Young West Hunanese soldiers in the 1920's, from *The Sign*, Mar. 1928.
Below: Houses on stilts by the Tuo River: a contemporary view of a scene virtually unchanged since Shen's youth.

Above, left: Shen and an older sister in 1934 (the child may be her son).
Above, right: Shen and his Little Sister No. 9 (Shen Yuemeng) by the sea in Qingdao, mid-1930's.
Right: Shen Congwen in 1947.
Below: Shen and his wife, Zhang Zhaohe, in 1934.

Top: A house in the village of Ala, west of Fenghuang.
Middle: A scenic valley in Xupu county, West Hunan, Aug. 1980.
Bottom: A *bao* (fortified town) west of Fenghuang.

Top: Miao people dressed up for market day, Shanjiang Commune (old Zongbingying), Fenghuang county.
Middle: Miao people at market, Shanjiang Commune.
Bottom: Boats on the Chen River at Mayang (old Gaocun), Aug. 1980.

Top: A Tujia village seen from a cornfield across the Tuo River.
Middle: Remnants of the Fenghuang city wall along the Tuo River, with a gate in the background.
Bottom: Houses along the river in Fenghuang.

Above, left: Shen Congwen in front of his old home in Fenghuang, 1982.
Above, right: Blacksmiths in Ala, just as Shen saw them in the late Qing.
Right: Shen with the author in Peking, 1980.
Below: Exhibition of Miao alternating singing: two men vie for a young beauty just as Tianbao and Nuosong vied for Cuicui in *The Frontier City*.

Top: Shen Congwen and his wife, Zhang Zhaohe, in 1980.
Bottom: A view of Shen's native Fenghuang, showing a bridge over the Tuo River.

CHAPTER FOUR

The Origins of Shen Congwen's Literary Regionalism

BESIDES FOCUSING ON the travails of modern urban living, Shen Congwen in his earliest works wrote of what he loved: he wrote of home. By the end of the 1920's, he had begun to create a vivid regional fiction. A few years more, and he was using West Hunanese landscapes and characters to frame universal questions of life and death, love and sexuality, permanence and change. Ultimately he conveyed a sense of his country folk as a moral community sitting in judgment on modern China. As he sought his own lyric voice, Shen extended the range of modern vernacular Chinese in its new role as a literary language.

At first Shen Congwen depicted and analyzed his roots in much the same spirit that had led him to become a Chinese I-fictionalist. Authenticity of self in his works was joined, then overshadowed, by authenticity of place. There was consolation in writing about the homeland and people he had left behind. Many a reader from rural South China must have taken similar comfort from his writings. But to most readers West Hunan was an exotic, semi-barbarian realm. And Shen was not necessarily loath to feed their curiosity. A literal-minded part of his audience had always read his works to get to "know" a young literary prodigy. Through Shen's local color sketches, they now had intimate access to the exotic background of "the Dumas of China."¹

In writing of his region, as of his persona, Shen Congwen still had reason to believe that his literary reach, if not his grasp, gave him common cause with the vanguard of the Chinese literary revolution and modern writers everywhere. He dealt in the Han and Miao "little traditions" of West Hunan: local dialect, folklore, religious customs, and the concerns of the mountain folk. He expressed a modern delight in "aboriginal" sexuality and artistic creativity. (Miao crafts won recognition as art in China as belatedly as African tribal art came to be appreciated in Europe. At market, Southwestern Han women actually ridiculed the breathtaking finery of Miao women's embroidery.)[2]

Peking's professors prepared Shen Congwen to look at his folk through social science, though his understanding of it was always that of an amateur. He had accepted Zhou Zuoren's (hence Havelock Ellis's) views on psychosexuality in the 1920's, and read Zhang Dongsun's book-length primer of psychoanalysis by 1930. Shen chatted about psychology with Yanjing University student Xia Yun; by the 1930's he knew Xia's teacher, Lu Zhiwei, who chaired the Yanjing psychology department and later became president of the university. Shen Congwen also saw Western psychological insights embodied in the fiction of Shi Zhicun and Zhou Zuoren's student Fei Ming (Feng Wenbing).[3]

As early as 1926, Shen Congwen was using the reasoning of Western mythographers and anthropologists to explain folklore motifs. Again, he must have taken his cue from his professor friends Zhou Zuoren and Gu Jiegang. They and Liu Bannong, whom Shen credits with beginning the use of folkloric materials in modern poetry, had initiated the modern Chinese interest in contemporary regional folklore. Influence from Western ethnography is also evident in Shen's acceptance of the idea that all art had its origins in the needs of ancient primitive man (the original outlet being primitive religion), and that art from contemporary tribal societies was therefore in the mainstream of world art. Shen went on in the 1930's to equate religion and art functionally, and even to name art as the successor to religion after the Death of God. Cai Yuanpei had argued this, though Shen says he was not influenced by Cai's ethnography or aesthetics. In truth there were many in the 1920's, above all Zhou Zuoren, who looked for the roots of human behavior in relatively "hard," physiological sciences of man, and who sought understanding of modern civilization by studying primitive and antique cultures as functional equivalents.[4]

Avant-garde and primitive are viewed benignly in the West (but not in China, even now) as complementary touchstones of modernism. Shen Congwen in the 1920's was not intellectually avant-garde by the international standards of his time, nor were his works. But if modernism is understood to be a total outlook on life, one that began in the West in the late nineteenth century, Shen Congwen may be said to have been inspired by the call of modernism.[5] Like many contemporaries in his own country and abroad, Shen yearned to stage a general revolt against the cultural complacency of upper-crust society. "Confucianism" was his explicit enemy. Like the Victorianism Xu Zhimo transcended in his "Anglo-American" world, Confucianism identified culture with morality, drawing clear lines between the civilized and the savage. In Southwest China, one of those lines divided "human" from Miao.[6] Yet Darwin had broken down the barrier between man and the animal kingdom itself, more rapidly in China than the West. It only remained for Freud, Nietzsche, Marx, and modern social science to probe the dark side of humanity, relativize culture, reveal vitality in "savagery," and derive spirituality itself from the primitive in man. The May Fourth generation was not just seeking cultural parity with the West, it was genuinely modernist, as intent as the Western avant-garde on promoting "pervasive cultural revolution" (Peter Gay) through "adversary culture" (Lionel Trilling). Shen, to be sure, loved modernism's "discovery and canonization of the primal, non-ethical energies" (Trilling).[7]

Shen Congwen's modernism is of course no more unequivocal than the larger tendency. Living in a technologically backward society, he never grew fearful of how science might affect human existence. Shen in his cosmopolitanism welcomed exotic techniques that were already "traditions." He absorbed them, when modernism might have called for him to transcend, purify, and ultimately "reject" them. He also loved nature above artificiality. And, though highly conscious of writing for the future, Shen did not seek for his art to annihilate history; he grappled with history as an inexorable force (as did American Southern modernists). If, however, the essence of modernism is to perceive and create in new languages—new words and new voices (Frederick Karl)—then we are very close to Shen Congwen's purpose in writing. In Hunan he first conceived of the literary revolution as a linguistic revolution. He broadened that by turning "linguistic" into "cultural." His split came with those who turned to revolutionary literature: art rooted in positivism. What makes the achievement of Shen's generation seem ephemeral is that their Communist successors are less modernist in spirit, not just doctrinally anti-modernist in the arts. The revolutionaries who came to power in 1949 lacked both modernism's "tragic sense of the pervasiveness of human evil" and its "preoccupation with exacting artistic craftsmanship" (D. J. Singal).⁸ Above all, the new generation craved what all modernists sought to escape: authority.

Regionalism, prizing the familiar and provincial, can clash with the modernist spirit. Yet Joyce, Woolf (*Mrs. Dalloway*), and Faulkner wrote with a sense of place, even topographically, as they dissolved consciousness itself (a task more ambitious than any Shen Congwen set himself at this time). The major obstruction to regional writing in Shen's society was nationalism, especially once unitary, revolutionary nationalism gained preeminence. Many politically conscious Chinese came to disdain modernism, too, after seeing its craftsmanship lead to the "self-sufficiency of the work" (Irving Howe) and so, allegedly, to art for art's sake and empty formalism.⁹ But converts to modernism in China's May Fourth generation saw themselves as latecomers to an international, "scientific" awareness, and so were afflicted with nationalistic anxiety of another kind: that world history had left their people behind culturally. Among those who were also self-conscious about being provincially backward, like Shen (and a generation of America's Southern writers, argues Singal), the call to modernism could even intensify one's sense of regional identity. Shen Congwen did not despair. The new thought from academic Peking gave his fellow-regionals an equivalence with other peoples they had never known before. By expanding the scope of culture to include the wit and lore of the folk, China's New Culture movement conferred the dignity of intelligence and creativity on China's tribespeople. They, the last, would be first, in folk song and art that touched the subterranean mind. Their culture was not only universally human; as Darwinism evidently indicated to Shen, they in their rudeness knew greater cultural vitality than the decadent Confucians he aspired to overthrow. So it was for Shen Congwen as author: his frontier roots were close to the wellsprings of that art which lay deepest in the human psyche. The New Culture movement would help him make a great leap, from provincial ignorance into the vanguard.¹⁰

Shen Congwen as Local Colorist

Shen Congwen's regional writing began humbly. He plumbed his memory for scenes and events from his life in West Hunan and wrote them up as short sketches and reminiscences. The earliest pieces are therefore nostalgic in tone, often simple remembrances of childhood innocence. They can be seen, at least, as preparation for the author's later sketches of child characters like Cuicui, Sansan, Lingling, and Xiaoxiao. But many of Shen's childhood pleasures were distinctly rural, and this led him into local color and dialect, which are all the more memorable for being unpolished.

Shen Congwen's family and friends, as he remembered them from childhood, figure among his first literary characters. "Roses and Little Sister No. 9" recalls a simple childhood pleasure Congwen shared with his brothers and little sister—planting roses around their own home and watching them bloom. Rather than indulge in direct narratorial sentimentalizing, Shen dramatizes his family. Elder Brother scratches peevish Little Nine, the family pet; Mother's tender love is shown by her skillful smoothing over of sibling rivalry. A third person narrates. Shen is here only as a minor dramatized child character, whose identity with the author is not highlighted. This piece, like many others, creates mood but not plot. There is, however, a twist at the very end: "The rose-hip candy that year was still made from a big basket of roses that Little Nine picked at Third Aunt's house."[11] With this hint that Mother loves the flowers planted by her own children too much to let them be picked, Shen lifts the significance of the hearthside roses onto a symbolic plane.

Shen used the dramatic genre itself to tell another episode, about how Little Nine made an alliance with him to smuggle a good fighting cricket into the household—despite family rules, Elder Brother's tattling, and the chirping of the uncooperative little warrior himself. Childish naughtiness is again played off against Mother's ironic and sympathetic understanding, but the emphasis is now on the farcical discomfiture of little Congwen as he tries to stifle the cricket and lie his way out of the predicament. Pre-modern dramatic devices—such as asides from the Congwen character, and his declamation of the panicky strategy-making going on in his head—add to the amusement.[12]

An entertaining storyteller-narrator relates "Holiday Fruit Congee."

From babies who've just learned how to call out for Papa, to big kids who can go outside to call for a rickshaw, to old children with a growth of white hair beneath their lip, who doesn't get a delicious taste of sweetness and oil in his mouth at the very mention of *laba zhou* (holiday fruit congee)?

You put millet, red lentils, red dates, chestnuts, sugar, and peanuts together in one big mess and cook them all up in a pot. When it bubbles and boils and sounds like it's hissing, just listening to it, or smelling the sweetness, is enough to get you swallowing in anticipation. What must it be to dip into it bowl after bowl, then send one big spoonful after another mouthward![13]

This is the stuff of local color, colloquially told, and still without much plot (this piece changes the subject to family dogs halfway through). Yet there is little West Hunanese dialect or reference to truly unique regional culture.

Shen Congwen had, in fact, begun to make use of these more exotic elements as early as the spring of 1925. Hot, peppery local cuisine, the colorful names of native poisonous snakes, and local fishing by sickle and torch appear in "Night Fishing" (Shen's first work by that name, written in March 1925). "Daigou" (April 1925) takes a Miao term of endearment for a child as its title, and includes a local mountain song, although not much dialect, in its sympathetic tale of a poverty-stricken little Miao boy forced to steal firewood by a father besotted with corn liquor. A panoramic view of the goods and people, Han and Miao, involved in local commerce makes up "At Market" (March 1925), and a pathetic but kindly neighborhood figure who used to call out the wee hours in old Zhen'gan (when sober) is remembered in "Ahan the Night Watch." Shen also moves his childhood family to this more colorful outdoor environment, to capture the scene "At the Butcher's Block" (April 1925). A sketch of a childhood friend, "Ruilong," turns to describing a vegetable market, a firewood market, childhood scrapping, tests of skill at splitting sugarcane, and so forth. The author's mother and siblings are back indoors in "Hearthside," a June 1926 work, but it is the calls of street vendors and thoughts of their savory delicacies that punctuate the domestic serenity at nightfall.

> [The candy peddler's] big wooden tray was partitioned into sections, each with its own kind of treat. Some had different flavors even though they were of the same color and shape. Others tasted the same but looked different. Mint candies, wrapped triangularly in red or green paper, were cool but sweet to the taste. Sliced ginger candy was slightly hot. There were all sorts of fruit candies, round or triangular, five or ten coppers for a big piece and one or two for a small one. Lotus root candies looked like the real thing, with a pock-marked pod and segmented root stalk. There were hollow hot pepper candies, red as a real chili. You could blow into

one and make a noise like a cow horn if you bit off the two ends, including the foot stalk. Eggplant candies were lots smaller than real eggplants, but they were just the same in shape and color. If you poured tea into one and then sucked it out, you'd have some sweet tea, too. Then there were treats molded into the shape of the gods. The smallest was the size of your thumb, but you'd need more than a catty of sugar to make the whip-wielding God of Wealth with his big belly. That Hubei candy peddler would put him right in the center, with the little gods and other candies arrayed around him in ranks.[14]

Soon Shen would blend his accounts of local products and their marketing, complete with prices, into the extended accounts of childhood freedom and games that we have already drawn on for biographical information: "My Primary School Education" (August 1926) and "In a Private School" (November 1927).

"Events Gone By" exemplifies how fully Shen had begun to use local color while still writing in his rambling nostalgic mode. The narrator, before dramatizing himself as a character we insiders can identify as the author in childhood ("Yuner"), recreates the scene. He does so evocatively if not invitingly, for it is Fenghuang during a pestilence. He remembers that he was about six *sui*; people still wore pigtails. Mother fears that her little boy will come down sick. He runs free and wild, with his little friend Ruilong, eating things at will from the stands of street vendors. So Yuner is carried, with his elder brother, in a basket on the back of his Uncle No. 4 to Tongren, deep in the Guizhou Miao country, where Yuner's sisters and father are already waiting. (Characteristically, the father figure hardly reveals his personality. He is in the shadow of the aunts and uncles. And they are not fictitious: Shen's Uncle No. 4 did live in Tongren.)[15]

Pointedly praising the flavor and climate of the countryside, the narrator is specific about the trees and animals to be seen—the species of bamboo, the ring-necked pheasants that come to the house to feed, the freshwater mussels whose shells are good for collecting. He bears witness to local beliefs: a tree on whose branches travelers place stones for relief from tiredness, and the house of a tutelary deity who helps wild boar hunters. Finally, we see two country scenes that Shen Congwen favored in all his subsequent regional fiction: a grist mill, and bamboo waterwheels used to lift water for irrigation.[16] As to dialect, suffice it to say that the author saw fit to append a little glossary of obscure terms.

Because these nostalgic works are set in the countryside, they are not only a reverse side to Shen's angry works about the city, they help explain his anomie, by cataloguing and romanticizing pleasures "unobtainable" in the city: the family ties, childhood confidences, camaraderie (even in the army)—in general, the sense of belonging and relatedness that the urbanized young man longs for. (The teller of "Holiday Fruit Congee" is more than homesick; he is hungry.) Even when Shen's young man persona is not dramatized as the reminiscer in these bucolic works, it is his distracted consciousness, his putting of dreams and memories on the same footing as more immediate visions, that creates the piece.

Shen Congwen as Lyricist

How Shen Congwen developed his literary technique to accommodate further these West Hunanese elements cannot be fully traced here, but he came at lyrical regionalism from many directions, poetry among them. Poetry does not quite have the place in Shen Congwen's early lyricism that it has in Faulkner's, but if one counts Shen's prose poems, and remembers that much of his discarded output must have been poetry, its importance looms large indeed. Like his contemporaries', Shen's poems are "revolutionary" simply in being vernacular. His subjects are those of the romantics and the Victorian love poets, from Byron to Browning: the beauty and inaccessibility of woman, the sensuousness of nature, the fleetingness of time, the transience of life and the seasons, the limits on the soul's freedom—and on one's worthiness as a lover. Occasionally Shen's heavy, reflective use of metaphors and similes turns erotic.[17]

> Your cleverness is like a deer,
> Your other virtues like a lamb;
> I would caress the lamb,
> But fear to startle the deer:
> Thus do I remain mute before you
> (In silence nearly despondent!).
> How could you know?
>
> "I Love You" (1926; first stanza of three)

> It was said a day would come,
> When your body would be my most familiar refuge,
> Its curves and cinches, its mounds and hillocks;
> I would know each tree, each blade of grass,

> And find my way, though it were dark.
> That day has come.
> "Ode" (1928[?]; first stanza of three)

Shen did not write autobiographical poetry. Nor do his poems invoke muses or mention the Greco-Roman pantheon, like his friend Hu Yepin's (or indeed like certain pieces of Shen's own fiction). Shen's lyric range is in fact not so European as it may appear at first glance. His vocabulary is mostly plain—visually and tactually suggestive, but not obscure. Sometimes there are echoes of Tagore's open philosophic musings and images, coming perhaps by way of Bing Xin's Tagore imitations. But there is none of Guo Moruo's Whitmanesque variation on Tagorean pantheism, no exaltation of the self or heroic transcendence of the natural world.[18]

> On the fisherman's hook,
> Hangs his bait, hangs his heart.
> "Embers" (1925), No. 11

> In Peking the June rains
> Are fierce, but not enough to rot down many walls or fences.
> "Embers," No. 9

> You said "I ask you, look at the grass beneath your feet,
> See how green it is already!
> Understand that,
> And you'll understand why I spend all day writing poetry."
> You say "Water cannot be silent on a fine day,
> It must ring;
> A bird cannot be silent on a fine day,
> It must sing;
> Why do you keep still,
> Would you have me be still?"
> "But that grass you speak of,
> It, too, is still."
> "Dialogue"

Much of Shen's imagery suggests The Song of Solomon, as in "Ode" (whose first stanza, already cited, could as well be addressed to God as to a lover).

> You are a branch of willow
> Swaying in the wind, swaying in the calm;

But once the tempest has its way with shaking you,
You will sway no further.
My thoughts are a wind unto eternity, your wind.

Not only did Shen Congwen favor imagery of lambs and other Western Old World animals ("I Love You," "The Little Lost Lamb"); his "Spring" (1927) is a pastoral in the full sense, a poem after the eclogue (singing-match) form. He must have thrilled to see a form so suggestive of the singing-match customs of his own Miao folk back home. His female singer at first uses a familiar Miao ploy to answer the male's extravagant use of natural metaphors and similes to praise her. She mocks him with her own metaphors, and exalts her status as daughter of the village chieftain. Yet true to the Greco-Roman tradition, Shen's singers are a shepherd and shepherdess. And this poem is lengthy, unlike Shen's usual lyrics, which are of only a few stanzas. The metaphors are a fascinating mix, uniform only in their rusticity: roses, lilies, and lambs from the West or its Biblical lands; and from the country people of Fenghuang, folk imagery of iron-soled shoes worn out in making a journey to keep a tryst, and a paraphrase, in modern vocabulary, of sections from two genuine Fenghuang mountain songs one uses to tease one's lover.[19]

Shen's poetry, like his prose, demonstrates versatility and willingness to experiment. He wrote satiric poems, too, as well as morbid ones developing his favorite themes of imprisonment and death —visions of personal undoing. And though free verse predominates in his poetry, he did try various rhyme patterns, even a few metrical poems whose lines are of uniform length and rhymed, like Wen Yiduo's. At points his poems gain economy from a word or two of plain Classical Chinese, as in "Spring Moon" (1925), which also presents images in sequence and leaves the connections unstated, as in traditional poetry.[20]

Into this international vocabulary of images and metaphors Shen Congwen began to introduce the language of his region, giving it equal poetic status. For example, he freely implanted the Miao word for "moon" in "Dusk" (1926), a poem that otherwise speaks in his cosmopolitan romantic voice. Another poem uses dialect to describe the Nuo exorcism, a rite over two millennia old that survived only in West Hunan and that Shen witnessed in childhood (it soon vanished, in the warlord years). Probably the rite continued as long as it did among the Hunan Miao because the Miao dedicated it to their own gods, Lord Nuo and the younger sister he took to wife. According to a myth common among circum-Pacific peoples (but locally unique to the Miao), the siblings were the only survivors of a primordial Flood. A heavenly sign condoned their incestuous union, in order that they might regenerate the human race. "Returning Thanks to the Gods" (1926), below, is the only published poem from the cycle Shen named "The Enlarged Songs of the South (*Chu ci*)," after the great regional lyric poems attributed to Qu Yuan. *Laogeng* is the polite Chinese term for a Miao in Fenghuang dialect. *Daipa* is a Sinitic rendering of the Miao-language word used to address a young unmarried woman. *Amei* is the equivalent Chinese word spoken by Fenghuang Han and Tujia folk, often found in their mountain songs.[21]

> Gongs and drums clamor as Miaozi *laogeng* thank the Nuo gods with sacrifices:
> *Daipa, amei*, in embroidered skirts and tunics, very young,
> Dance as if riding the winds, their breasts slightly swelling;
> After singing Miao songs, they smile, but only to themselves.
>
> *Suona* wail before the altar of Lord and Lady Nuo,
> A hundred celebrants lift their chopsticks as one, eating the pair of slaughtered pigs before the altar.
> A hoary priest, clothed in red robes and green hat, stabs the ox,
> While corn liquor is ladled to him and her, from crocks large and small.

After the 1920's, Shen Congwen published less modern poetry, though he never gave it up entirely. He attempted new kinds of metaphysical lyricism in modern verse even in the 1940's. Then, like others of his generation in the Communist years, he turned back to write poetry in centuries-old classical styles.[22]

We have seen that Shen in the 1920's made versatile use of the essay form, combining description of places and emotions, narrative, aesthetic reflection, reverie, and satire in a single work. His contemplative 1925 essays "Moon Over the Western Hills" and "Long Nights" Nos. 1, 2, and 5, with their poetic image-building and mood painting, deserve the name of romantic poems in prose.[23] Mostly eulogies on the beauty of nature and of woman, they incorporate nature metaphors, plaintive outcries about the injustice of life, verses from the Old Testament, and even Christian hymns. "Long Nights" No. 5 consciously or unconsciously quotes imagery from Tagore: "Lass! An instant of life is but the glimpse of a shooting star in the limitless void—but the flash of a spark in the pitch black of deepest night—yet I am already the prisoner of your soul!"[24] Exotic West Hunanese culture even comes together with Shen's distraught young urban man persona in one work, "Láo mei, zuohen!" (August 1926; the title is Romanized Miao, "Maiden, How Beautiful You Are!"). As a means of relief from his current anomie, the young man dreams of joining Miao young people in matchmaking festivities under the moon. To readers not familiar with the double-sided myth Shen was building around himself as author, the young man's means of escape must have seemed quite strange.[25]

Shen's interest in the ancient Greeks, the Bible, folkways, and the essay form so resemble Zhou Zuoren's that one must suspect his influence. Shen in fact acknowledges it, even though Zhou Zuoren is now far more a political pariah than Shen,[26] and he regards Zhou Zuoren as a founder of China's new poetry. No doubt he discovered prose poetry through Zhou's works, too, whose very titles (like "Rivulet" and "Essays from the Western Hills") Shen seems to have echoed. Zhou Zuoren even tried to implement the principles of Symbolism in his prose poems, so if Shen absorbed any of the Symbolists' way of understanding the world (and his poem "The Last Days of Winter" has a bit of synesthesia and certainly a "medley of metaphor" whose referent is ineffable), it was probably through such works rather than through theory.[27]

More prominent in Shen Congwen's essays are Zhou Zuoren's relatively concrete interests, or tastes: psychology, local color, street vendors' calls, and the small pleasures of life, from foods to games. (Zhou himself wrote an essay called "Speaking of Candy Selling," though a decade later than Shen.) But Shen had an aversion to classical allusions that was more than doctrinal. For all his eclecticism, he was too poorly educated to flavor his essays with erudition from either the tradition or international literature, as the older master did. He could only tell of regional scenes he had witnessed or imagined. The texture of Shen's prose most closely approximates Zhou Zuoren's when he is describing the minutiae of outfitting, sailing plans, and on-board customs of the different kinds of boats on the Yuan River.[28] Shen did, however, soon master the traditional essay technique of using something small, like a green vase (in an essay by that name), to symbolize larger issues of life. In that April 1926 piece, Shen's distraught young man persona contemplates a vase, thus broaching the theme of "emptiness." Where Zhou Zuoren would have been scholarly, Shen Congwen is expansive. From a flowerless vase, he proceeds to his tealess pot, his inkless inkpot, and finally to his own melancholia, unrelieved by female companionship. In another essay, Shen writes nostalgically of the sound of chickens. He realizes that he has missed them ever since moving to Peking, as if he were about to turn to the larger theme of city versus country. But with another deft twist, the essay becomes political allegory: Peking does have chickens, the narrator says, only they don't cry out. It was June of 1925, a time when Shen felt that more intellectuals should be speaking out for the protesters at the Peking Women's Normal College.[29]

Exactly how Shen Congwen made the leap to writing wholly fictive plots is unclear. He now modestly attributes it to practice and perseverance; becoming a teacher in 1929 made him financially more secure, which in turn allowed him to write more slowly, despite his new responsibilities. Shen's maturation must also have been rooted in greater self-confidence. At the time (1929), Shen attributed his rural lyricism in narrative writing to the influence of Fei Ming.[30]

From the Folk

Oral traditions of the West Hunanese folk were the other great stream leading into Shen Congwen's lyricism, and they contributed directly to its regional distinctiveness. Within the Chinese literary revolution, the issue of dialect transcended that of folkways as such, for the "revolution" lay in promoting a new vernacular language. The use of dialects was the revolution's anti-Classical extreme, for their diversity was potentially subversive of linguistic unity. It was symbolic of the conflict between regionalism and nationalism. Yet dialects were the only available building blocks for a new national language besides foreign languages and Classical Chinese. Peking dialect was the standard; how much the new vernacular language could absorb from other dialects without creating chaos remained to be seen. Shen Congwen implicitly made a case for Fenghuangese as a dialect with expressive nuances that could enrich the mix.

Exemplifying the spirit of the times was the *National Language Weekly*, a supplement of the *Jingbao* that especially welcomed dialect pieces and spelled out its title in newly invented phonetic characters. It was in that forum, during the summer of 1925, that Shen Congwen began to publish verse in pure dialect, his "Zhen'gan Songs" and "Summer in the Countryside (Rustic Dialect from Zhen'gan [Fenghuang])." Each verse appears to retell a folk anecdote or recreate rustic but witty repartee. We eavesdrop on the folk telling crude jokes, making provocative insults, and cursing at each other. The language is regional, sometimes scatological, and annotated by the author. Some verses can be identified as actual lyrics from Fenghuang folk songs. Others appear to contain folk song refrains; perhaps all are based on song, directly or in paraphrase. Shen's purpose seems to be to introduce West Hunan's dialect and wit to a national audience for its own sake, as regional tribute to the new national culture, and as a source from which to build the new national language. In a postscript he expresses fear lest "the life of our language atrophy from conventionality." "Skylarks, nightingales, angels, kissing, and embracing," have become nearly obligatory in China's vernacular poetry, he says.[31] His offerings:

> "Old shorty Yang No. 5,
> Stingy as all get out; you eat bean curd day after day;
> Why only bean curd?"
> "Bean curd is supposed to build you up."
>
> "Old Han, your peppers aren't so red;
> All the other peddlers' are red-a-ded-ded."
> "Yi-ai! My boy, you want the best of the brew,
> I'll throw in a few extra, that ought'a do!
> —'Old Han's peppers let you shit with the best of 'em.'"
>
> Who knows why they're in such a rush?
> Maybe cause they're under the heat,
> Maybe they got someone to meet:
> Miao folk comin', here's a brother, there's a brother,
> Sweat beads big as soybeans, here's another, there's another.
>
> Yeah! This ol' kid slips on into the water
> Catchin' fish, buildin' dams, splashin' water, laughin' out loud.
> Little doggy on the shore just watches, "prim and proud,"
> And wags his tail, as much as he's allowed.
>
> If a cute
> *Daipa* or *aya* [Miao: married woman] comes down the road

Maybe you, maybe I, will be a little devilish and "pull her hair."
We'll sing a mountain song to her, very low,
(Got to keep it low!):
> Big sis is coming, smi-smiling,
> Her pair of boobs, a stre-stretching,
> How I'd love to cop a feel,
> Oh my heart is leap-leaping.

See that *daipa* blush, all a-fluster,
See that *daipa* take off, in a bluster.

Here we can only convey Shen's folksy humor, not the dialect. In the 1930's, Shen would put teasing and naughty folk songs, including the one embedded in the verse just quoted, into his stories about frontier romance.

It was, however, the dialect interest—dialect for its own sake—that was already enlivening some of Shen's prose even in 1925. "Gamblers" is a vehicle for gamblers' slang. Other works, notably "The Sugar Peddler Sells Cane," draw on both the language and the wit of street hawkers.[32] Thematically, the last piece appears doubly indebted to Zhou Zuoren, for Shen calls it a "mime." But of course it was precisely in the realm of West Hunanese local color that Shen Congwen's memory and imagination were on their own.

The same might be observed of the farcical, one-act "folk dramas" Shen Congwen created. He wrote them up as *kyōgen*. Zhou Zuoren provided Shen with the genre, through translations from the Japanese.[33] The content Shen poured into the foreign literary vessel is native—mostly anecdotes from the West Hunanese folk. His plots, plus other dramatic conventions not so clearly Western or Japanese, may well have come from local Nuo dramas he observed, heard about, or saw mimicked. The suitability of the *kyogen* form for Shen's folkloric purposes itself may result from the underlying generic similarities—if not ancient genetic kinship—of the Japanese and ancient mainland folk dramas.

Shen's slapstick "Chinese *kyōgen*" pit stock characters against each other in battles of wits, with one player manipulating another's superstitious gullibility or misbegotten sense of face. The dialect is colorful and ribald, humorously plaintive or jocularly abusive, shot through with puns and allusions to local jokes and opera motifs. The players' asides impart a traditional, folk dramatic flavor and expose their rascality or foolishness, while inviting the audience to share in the victim's predicament. In "Duck," a roast-duck peddler fends off an overbearing army sergeant who wants to buy on credit. "New Year's" is about another soldier, who cannot control his gift for caricaturing senior officers, even to their face, and who ends up slapping himself a lot in atonement. "Inn of the Wilds" is the traveling salesman joke, told at the expense of Miao widows.[34]

Nuo rites, described in Shen's poem "Returning Thanks to the Gods," took place typically for three days and nights toward the end of the year (formerly in the spring as well). In his youth Shen saw Miao Nuos in the countryside, magnificent torch-lit ceremonies with hundreds in attendance. *The Shaman's Love* (1929) and a late, 1937, chapter of *Fengzi* detail the rites stage by stage, cataloguing the ritual masters' props (cow horns, magic swords, and "willow kerchiefs," just as in the anthropologists' accounts), the use of time, and the sociology of the affair, as in the relationship between the priest and the benefactor-host. Miao shaman-priests led the chanting, singing, and sacrifices to the gods, but the folk joined in singing unison choruses. The songs recited traditional lore, ranging from the Han story of Lady Meng Jiang to the Miao people's own tale of the Flood. To Shen Congwen, this very communal spectacle seemed like the *Chu ci*, with its presumed choruses. The dramas enacted on the occasion interested him even more. They were performed by masked players, but not professionals as among the Han. The folk themselves took the roles of stock characters, improvising humorous and satirical plays. Shen says the dramas were about, and sometimes made fun of, local customs. He also saw Nuo performances by Han puppeteers from the old Yuan River port of Pushi. Ordinarily they performed at *tudi* temples after the harvest, but at year's end they set aside their puppets to go house-to-house in Fenghuang, performing the Nuo without remuneration all night long, by torchlight. They dressed up as ordinary country folk. Again, amateurs could participate. At the end a Miao priest led unison singing. It reminded Shen Congwen of "the pageantry of the rustic dramas in *A Midsummer Night's Dream*. Carpenters, bricklayers, butchers, tailors—all take part in it."[35]

Shen wrote his folkloric farces in 1926, the year he spoke of wanting to "introduce to the outside world the comedies for requiting the gods of the Nuo." Today the author cannot remember if any of his plots were directly inspired by the Nuo plays he saw, or heard retold; but if any is, "The Xiao God" is a likely candidate.[36] The Xiaoshen, literally "Celestial gods" (or "little gods," according to another tradition), were the major gods of the Nuo sacrifice to some West Hunanese (though Shen Congwen was not aware of it, at least in 1980). The Xiao god imagined by the characters in Shen's play is less than a foot high, wearing a red cap and varicolored clothes. These gods were thought to love music and be mischievous. When displeased, they stole or ruined household objects until propitiated.[37] Shen's little drama also makes use of another common belief, that the Xiao gods could cause things to disappear into thin air and turn up elsewhere.[38]

Internal evidence in Shen's play indicates that it is to be performed at night, in front of the spirit tablet of a Xiao god, inside the house or courtyard of a well-to-do supplicant who has laid out sacrifices to the god. In a real Nuo play, the setting would be actual as well as symbolic, and the Xiao god would be in the audience, enjoying the spectacle (as *Fengzi* correctly points out). The sacrificial animals are themselves central props in Shen Congwen's drama; the play is a battle of wits to gain possession of them. Likewise the two characters are the typical honored guest and son of the host in religious sacrifices of the old Miao religion—a maternal uncle and his nephew. If a real uncle-nephew duo played themselves, making fun of each other's actual traits and social quarrels, the result might have been hilarious. That family relationship is much closer among the Miao than among the Han.

Fengzi gives a sample plot involving another relationship: a man and his potential son-in-law. The two gamble. If the latter loses, he must plant a mountain with tung trees, harvest them, and paint a ship with their oil, so the father-in-law can sail the ship to the "Taoyuan Cave" to ask for blessings from the Immortal there. Unfortunately the Immortal wants to marry his daughter, too, and *he* demands thousands of years' worth of tasks from the father. *Fengzi* says this play usually is performed by a young suitor and his actual father-in-law-to-be. In any event, Nuo plays heaped up as much satire and abuse as possible on the host of the ceremonies, say Fenghuang informants today.[39]

"The Xiao God" indeed seems to have inside jokes and references to the neighborhood, so that the players can involve other members of the audience in the satire, even as they ridicule each other. There is also much slapstick, including a chase at the end. The nephew is caught exiting with sacrificial meats he's stolen, but just beforehand he "unwittingly" insults his maternal uncle by singing, "Here go I, there go I, out the door I jog, run into a dog!" The play is hardly reverent toward the Xiao god, but this, too, is quite within the spirit of Southwestern Chinese tribal religion.

The skit opens with the nephew singing to himself:

"Ya, ya, ya, the time's not right and the luck's not right, the wife loves her outside man at night—" I, Pimply Zhu the Second, have no wife, though, so let it be. Goo loo goo loo [rumbling], my stomach is calling; it must be hungry. Stomach, oh stomach, about those silver [soldier's] rations of two taels, six cash, and three bits—in a single breath, like "a fast horse under the whip," I went up onto Great Bridge. Three hands of "casting tens" and one of "matching the six old gents" just wiped me out clean, and I have no hope of winning back my losses. Stomach, I may have wronged you, but you'll have to put up with it for the time being. That damned son-of-a-bitch Fifth Yang just isn't a man. He lets other people play on credit in a big way, it's only me, Zhu the Second, he looks down on. The day will come when luck strikes, "you can use a door plank to stop it, but even that won't do the trick." When that kind of luck comes, you dog-fucked Fifth Yang, you just wait and see![40]

The nephew hits on a plan. He'll visit his maternal uncle, pretend to have turned over a new leaf, and borrow money to win back his losses. Unlike his brash nephew, the uncle is now seen reciting a pious prayer to the Xiao god. The nephew then envisions another, more farcical deception:

With hastened footsteps, as if mounting the clouds and riding the mists, I've arrived at the entrance of Wang Family Lane. A gold character for "happiness" is pasted on the front gate. Mustn't this be Maternal Uncle's house? Let me go in for a look. Hai, the gate is closed. Let me have a look through the crack in the door. Hai, he's kneeling. Let me listen to what he's saying. He's h ... m, h ... m, intoning prayers to Xiaoshen! If Xiaoshen may be entreated, wait till tomorrow and I, too, will buy three cash worth of incense and two of spirit money, and go to do a kowtow. Goo loo, goo loo, my stomach is rumbling again. Aren't the chicken and the pig spread out in the middle of the room awfully good-smelling sacrificial beasts? "There was a beautiful woman, her face like the hibiscus,"* you can look but you can't touch, isn't this frustrating? Let me think (dramatic action of bowing the head), first this, then that ..., and then this ..., and then that ..., I've got a plan. Why don't I take this opportunity to sneak into the house, climb the stairs, and take the place of Xiaoshen for a while? I'll manifest a bit of the August Power to trick Uncle out of a little wine and food. If discovered, I'll

---

*An amalgam of lines from the *Book of Odes*; odes 94 and 83.

say I was in a trance, not in control of my faculties, and had been forced to go upstairs in Uncle's house under the influence of the god. Dai, dai, don't turn around, don't turn around! Made it.⁴¹

There is more irreverence. The nephew throws down brickbats at his uncle to scare him away from the tender meats. The uncle, made to look foolish for taking this to be a sign of the Xiao god's displeasure, does the god no courtesy by assuming him to be drunk today! But his nephew is a very bad shot. His missiles only serve to knock over the spirit tablet and the wine pot. Running out of objects to throw, he tosses down his hat and a shoe. Uncle thinks Xiaoshen has been up to his old tricks, stealing things from passers-by and giving them to others. Having unwittingly denuded his nephew, no doubt to the amusement of the audience, he hurries off to the home of Village Head Liang, who has just smoked several fine hams. Can he not use the "magic vestments" from the god to displace a few of those hams into his own house? He promises to repay Xiaoshen with sacrifices—if the garb proves efficacious. The nephew then descends to rescue the "lonely" meats on the altar, and sample them, to the accompaniment of outrageous lip smacking. But his uncle returns prematurely, having been ridiculed by some villagers, whose names he calls out (perhaps members of the audience). He feels some sprite must have tricked him. Finally there is the discovery, the nephew's unconvincing explanation that he, half bare, deserves pity because the Xiao god has stolen his clothing, and ultimately a grand chase.

It seems a pity that Shen Congwen wrote no more such plays after the mid-1920's. They are hilarious on their own terms, and probably his closest approach to the West Hunanese folk mind. Shen continued putting "rural humor" into his stories, but typically only one joke at a time.

Shen's more academic, if still amateur, folkloric interest is visible in his 1926 rewriting of a Jataka in *kyōgen* form⁴² (a precursor of his Jataka adaptations in *Under Moonlight*, 1933–34), his introduction of a Miao folktale about "how we got the flute" into a melancholic essay, and his publication of 41 mountain songs from home, discussed below.⁴³ The author never studied his region's folklore professionally, nor does he seem to have continued trying to collect it. It may be, however, that West Hunanese folklore themes have had a more diffuse, often unacknowledged impact on Shen Congwen's storytelling. The plot of "Ajin," for instance, about a country fellow who wants to marry a widow but gambles away the bride-price, sounds as if it might be from the folk. I told the story to two Chinese-speaking Miao, a young man and an older fellow, at the general store in Ala (Yala), the Miao town west of Fenghuang that Shen chose as the setting for his tale. Both knew the story (as well as the scenarios of "The Xiao God" and "Duck"), though they had never heard of the all-but-proscribed author Shen Congwen.[44]

When in the 1930's Shen Congwen, having become a famous writer, published *The Frontier City, Discursive Notes on a Trip Through Hunan, West Hunan,* and *Long River,* all with characters speaking in authentic local dialect, it seemed to some readers that he was developing a new style, having just discovered the dialect and local color of his own region. Actually the reverse is true. Never again would Shen Congwen so fill his pieces with dialect and folklore as he did at the start of his career. Increasing psychological distance from West Hunan as time passed may be one reason. Another seems to be that national readers simply were not interested in dialect from outside their own region. They found Shen's dialect in particular to be uncouth and hard to understand. Lu Xun, for one, took some interest in Shen's bucolic writings, but not necessarily in his West Hunanese dialect. In a letter to a friend, he poked fun at "Nunu [Kiddy] A-wen," using Shen's own patois.[45] It was in the course of finding his audience that Shen Congwen shifted to more visual and imaginative aspects of his regional inheritance, to create a regional fiction that would appeal to the national reader.

Narrative Development and Didacticism

In the late 1920's, Shen Congwen's fiction became more complex. He concentrated more on plotting, and as early as the fall of 1927 gave a new intellectual dimension to some of his regional works by using them to critique Chinese society. How distinctively regional to make his settings and characters, however, was nearly as problematic as the political question of local autonomy in an age striving for national unity. Were regions building blocks or stumbling blocks in the construction of a New China? Ultimately, Shen's depiction of regional landscapes was pulled in two directions: having encountered anti-Southern prejudice in Peking, he was all the more intent on describing his homeland as a special place, with a unique and tragic destiny befitting its aboriginal apartness; yet dedicating his writing to a single region, like writing in dialect, might constrict the significance of his moral message and narrow his readership. In many stories, therefore, he rendered his region's exotic culture diffusely, allowing it to blend into and symbolize the vastness of China's hinterland, the better to dramatize the apartness of all rural China. The distance between rural China and the cities stood as a reproof to the inhuman forces accompanying modernization. Still, it was in the apartness of his own rural folk, above all the Miao, that Shen conceived an anti-traditionalist critique of China's *old* urban civilization and its Confucian moral basis.

Shen Congwen's most explicit statements elevating country life at the expense of city mores actually occur in some of the earliest specimens of his more developed storytelling art, like "Snow" (October 1927) and "Aboard and on Shore" (December 1927). He used Southern landscapes to taunt his many Northern readers even earlier. But it was in the 1930's that Shen would build a fuller critique of urban China, buttressed by Social Darwinism, a transcendental view of morality, and finally a Freudian approach that found conventional social mores to be excessively inhibiting.

In "Snow," "Aboard and on Shore," and "The Marble Carrying Boat" (1928), Shen Congwen began to create extended local-color mood pieces. Dialect has been left behind in these stories, and exotic customs seldom intrude. The sights, sounds, and evocative placenames of the Yuan River, vividly remembered and subjectively but poetically drawn into mutual associations, convey a sense of place that is nonurban, though tied to the waters. There is the telling of lore, providing a sense of authenticity, as in discussion of the origin of the name of a Yuan River port where an alter ego named Shen and his friend Man Shuyuan laid over one night on their trip to Peking, in "Aboard and on Shore." But it is boatmen's lore, not that of the mountain folk. The story goes on to discuss the town's local products with the conscientiousness of a gazetteer. In a setting of natural symbols like wild cormorants winging on the horizon, and familiar, haunting images of beauty like melancholy rowers' chants and work signals heard under moonlight, the calls of snack sellers plying the waterfront in sampans, the stillness of the piers, and the smell of fish frying on board, it settles into treating the traditional theme of homesickness. The boys recall the household pets, even the fishing poles, they have left behind. Such a piece could appeal to a wide audience.[46]

Shen dramatizes the moral superiority of country people in "Aboard and on Shore" through the person of a street vendor, an old lady who sells pears. Her wares are hardly superior, but there is virtue even in this, that of familiarity. "Shen" and Shuyuan return to the docks, eating as they go, when the narrator reflects, "We were acting like boatmen. Only a boatman would have eaten those pears! They were terribly sour, but that was just how we liked them. If we hadn't known there was mandarin fish for supper, we could have eaten ten more apiece."[47] The old woman, likewise, reminds the narrator of a country aunt he has left behind on his journey downstream. Her motherliness leaves Shuyuan weeping at the end of the story. The didactic point, however, is her honesty toward strangers. This is the observation of the "Shen" narrator as author, after his urbanization—for how could he have known about urban life before he left West Hunan? Making ironic use of the city literati's sanctimonious mode of discourse—Classical Chinese—the narrator ponders the old lady's refusal to make as much from her financial transactions as the market will bear:

These honest words, from the mouth of a country woman like her, made me unaccountably disturbed. Why must the countryside and the city be unlike in all things? Why didn't this woman want to get a little more money [out of the deal]? And those people in the city, the ones they call philanthropists—what about the way they treat themselves, and others . . . ? Some beneficent people of the city market rice abroad in secret, to make a little profit, and sell clothes intended for relief of the poor to profit their private estate. And these people are respected. The radiance of virtue shines on their faces; "blessings and longevity" are their reward. Why did this sincerity, this thing city people won't stoop to bother with, take root only in the heart of an old country woman? This thing called conscience is a constituent of poverty. Those in the city "whom we style moralists" all dread that they should ever truly get caught up in it. Should they suffer a small loss, they must with great bombast proclaim to the whole world that they are doing good: as I see it, if this woman wasn't awfully stupid, then these city people must be awfully clever and practiced.[48]

This figure of maternal integrity is recast as Shuyuan's mother when the Congwen narrator persona goes to visit Shuyuan in his own country home in "Snow." The incompatibility of urban and rural styles of life reappears, but in this context the narrator (a Fenghuangese) is a "city boy." Shuyuan makes fun of him as such, when the narrator wants to wash before breakfast, for instance. The narrator had feared boredom in the countryside, but country pleasures such as trapping, fishing, and eating roasted chestnuts in snow-blanketed woods not only conquer but liberate his spirit.

If Shen the country boy reacts defensively against the Chinese city, Shen the regionalist feels estranged from the North, China's arbiter of politics, language, and education. He derides the oppressive Beiyang armies, while calling his own West Hunanese troops "lovable."[49] Prefatory to his reminiscences of West Hunan's "Huaihua Town" (April 1926), he defiantly proclaims that he will not bother to locate the subject of his piece on the map. "This place is beyond the imagination of you Northerners. And precisely because it is so far beyond the realm of thought of so many Northerners (and not only Northerners), I'm just saying it's very far away."[50] More colorfully, in June 1925, he turns a reminiscence of the Duanyang holiday (associated with his home region, Qu Yuan's place of exile, Chu) against the North. Peking's summer rains (already encountered in "Cotton Shoes") remind the narrator of the summer rains of home. Down South, summer rains feed the major streams upon which the dragon boats race at the festival, he observes, but Peking's noisome precipitation creates no stream sufficient for the festivities. This was but the beginning of a career-long celebration of the gentle Southern rains and rivers of West Hunan, in contrast to the arid North, the land of dust and the cold north wind, "this very, very lifeless desert called Peking."[51]

Shen Congwen's Social Darwinist love of vigor further sharpened his apology for his own region. West Hunan's "regional character" (*minzuxing* or *minxing*) was often said to be fierceness, barbarism, a proneness to banditry, dueling, ethnic uprisings, and violence against the social order generally. This regional reputation originated among disparaging outsiders; but at a time when Chinese were accusing themselves of weakness, the ferocity of West Hunan and its armed bands could be appreciated as primitive "strength," a folk vitality not yet worn down by the prissy classical tradition. So it appeared even in the late 1940's to Li Zhenyi. Violent recalcitrance, along with cultural distinctiveness from the mixed Tujia, Miao, and Han influences, are what Shen Congwen, too, cited as the major elements of his people's character when he was asked for a definition in 1980. Regional refractoriness, he points out, is the result of regional oppression by outsider governmental and military forces, who used violence themselves because they misunderstood local culture. Hence the violent barbarism ultimately reflects West Hunan's virtuous position as a victim of other regions. In more modern, Communist terms, the refusal of the locals to accept their fate passively—their willingness to take up arms to fight "feudal oppression" (as Shen himself put it in 1980)—is virtuous on first principles.[52]

It still may come as a surprise that as early as in his "Letter" (of January 1926), Shen Congwen began to write about West Hunan's violence, and recast it romantically, as a manifestation of folk mores. "Letter" describes a barbarous perversion of the Duanyang Festival that Shen witnessed as a child at Shiyangshao, a village near Fenghuang. In most other localities, pent-up competitiveness and hostility among social groups found healthy release on that day, through dragon boat races. But in Shiyangshao, the festival was the time for avenging blood debts. Feuding villagers would get into their respective dragon boats and hurl rocks and oar fragments at each other, causing one or two fatalities annually, and renewing the zeal for vengeance in the next year's race. Shen calls it a bad custom, but makes it look interesting. He asks his addressee if it has any basis in legend, and indeed confesses that "even now it seems to me that such naïve, nearly mindless melees are no worse than the fraud and intimidation that is accomplished in Society through polite manners and other tricks."[53]

Shen went on to pen romantic accounts of West Hunanese banditry, glorifying the "naïveté" of the open, honorable fighting in his region. Even his relatively idyllic *Fengzi* (1932) features dueling (chapter 9). And Tianbao, a hero of *The Frontier City*, is good at defending himself. Shen's acceptance of this much of the martial ethic may explain why he felt, even in the 1940's, that the hope of his region lay with its brave and idealistic young military officers.

It is not expressly in their violence, though, that Shen Congwen pictures country people as leading lives that are "vital." He sees vitality, too, in their unreflecting willingness to go to extremes at the crucial, appropriate moment—for country folk avoid excessive behavior in their daily lives. Like certain dissenters in the Chinese literary tradition, Shen values the "childlike mind" of the country person over urban sophistication, and thus naïveté and guileless sincerity, even unto foolishness and "stupidity" (*tianzhen, laoshi, dai, chi*). For Shen, however, the apparent impassiveness of this state of mind masks a deeper spiritual engagement. Indeed, China's own romances, and *The Dream of the Red Chamber*, had already teased new, positive connotations out of *dai* and *chi*. As applied to newly legitimized romantic feelings, being "agape" before the world shaded from irrationality into infatuation, purblindness, even being crazy—wonderfully, helplessly so. For Shen, too, being "stupid" is a virtue, and at root it signifies intensity in living, not blandness. He sees a continuum, fully positive, from purblindness, rapture, and transfixion before the ideal, to true lunacy (*fengkuang*), his characterization of man's naked contemplation of the beautiful or God without the mediation of "sane," worldly taste. This is the virtue of the eponymic hero of "The Simpleton." Entranced by the spiritual beauty of two females, he naïvely follows them. The girls summon the police, mistaking him for a lunatic. Yet, in a sense, he is. Shen Congwen finds the same sort of obliviousness to the material world, bespeaking elemental vigor, in the zest of his country people as they worship and play. Once again, country observances of the Duanyang Festival are his example. The country folk row with a fanatical absorption in the moment. They are vulnerable to those whose purposes are more complicated, but their lives are uniquely full of passion, one that approaches madness.[54]

Shen Congwen so loved activity and motion that he was drawn time and again to describe the excitement of commerce. Old shopkeepers, their innocently nubile daughters, and even wharfmasters like Shunshun of *The Frontier City*, a Gelaohui "Dragon Head," are among his most memorable characters. (Small wonder; Shunshun is probably modeled after Shen's favorite Uncle No. 4, the one in "Events Gone By." He was head of the stevedores in Tongren.)[55] The hero and intended victim in *Long River*, too, is a prosperous owner of tangerine groves who transports his own crop to market, a worthy survivor of Social Darwinist competition. Now commerce may not be inherently urban, but its world ought to be rather foreign to a true country person, though Shen's favorable vignettes of substantial commerce are all attached to the cleansing waters of the Yuan. In effect his concept of the "country folk" broadens into a state of mind, to include West Hunan's farm laborers, mill owners, boatmen, artisans, and military officers (except those sent by Changsha)—one vast rural *region* standing in opposition to a parasitic urban world downstream, the latter evidently including Changsha, but not Changde. We can only be grateful for his making honorary country folk out of blacksmiths and boat owners, for it is by adding detailed portraits of West Hunanese urban landscapes and waterfront life to his sketches of the frontier that Shen has created a full regional literature. And in China, as in America, cities have been important in the development even of the frontier, serving as symbols of the expanding race's conquest of natural, and human, obstacles.

Along the river, Shen smooths over social contradictions with still more doses of Social Darwinism, plus a little regional pride that once again partakes of West Hunan's martial rather than literary heritage. He focuses on boatmen, who bravely face the rapids. He classifies them and even their boats according to their sloth or vigor, finding most merit in the Miao people's Dong River boats, which have to be light and agile (small and adaptable as the Miao themselves) in order to get through the rapids. He deplores the wide scows (Chenqi boats) downstream that transport dirty bulk goods. Their state of disrepair and lack of individuality, like a "fallen household," has rubbed off onto their boatmen, whom he finds lazy, dirty, and unpunctual, "lethargic in spirit." Similarly, passenger boatmen downstream serve the wealthy who seek sex and opium. For that reason, and even more because calm downstream waters offer few dangers to be overcome, "the temperament of the boatmen is very lackadaisical," he says. The crucial social problem for Shen to rationalize, though, is the monopoly over much Yuan River trade by boat owners (who captain their own vessels) from Mayang, a prosperous group most all of whom are named Teng. He resolves this, too, with reference to the "matchless vitality" of the Mayang people, adding that "all success requires struggle." He finds the Mayangese courageous, strong, and unyielding in countenance, but of cheerful disposition, loyal to fellow-townsmen, and able to "eat, drink, act, and fight." They are "good singers, swimmers, brawlers, and cussers. In water, they're like a fish; on land, with a woman, like a little boar." As men who have built the waterfront with their own hands (or fists, according to Changde legend), they are water-borne counterparts of Shen's Fenghuang military class on land: "If you can't find anyone at hand with the fervent, classical earnestness of the people of Chu, characterized by magnanimity, love of righteousness, and knight-errantry in the service of avenging the weak, you can discover it in the men from these two places [Fenghuang and Mayang]."[56]

From finding value in duels and trancelike religious behavior, it was but one step more for Shen to proclaim full independence from conventional, urban morality. He liked to provoke his urban readers, as in his autobiography, by challenging them to understand the bizarre, seemingly barbarous acts that he represented as part of everyday country life. Could his readers transcend their own moral sensibilities and see life from the point of view of the country folk? Yet in calling for a shucking off of urban pretensions, Shen does not necessarily imply that country folk have a mystical or transcendental understanding of life and death—other than the Wordsworthian acceptance of the natural world (as Hsia and MacDonald put it) available to us all. The transcendent vision that Shen Congwen probably did espouse regarded beauty, and the incompatibility of conventional, often hypocritical, "moral" approaches to life with a higher, aesthetic view. He saw the world idealistically, as being both noumenal ("the Abstract," he called it) and phenomenal. He also had a Kantian notion that noumenal Beauty, the sublime, might exist in what was on the surface ugly and violent. It was from this aesthetic viewpoint—amoral in conventional terms— that he sought to defend not any separate rural "morality" but his own right, aesthetically, to delineate the reality of rural regional life—including aspects of it that were indeed very dark in the view of conventional "urban" morality.[57]

Singing Matches and Other Regional Mating Customs

Shen Congwen also elevated West Hunan through his liberal views on sex. Nearly all May Fourth intellectuals decried traditional arranged marriages, but Shen went well beyond the consensus. He valued sex for its own sake and let his literary characters, particularly young folk not yet ready to tie themselves down and young women prematurely widowed, enjoy the act outside of marriage without paying any price for it. The West Hunanese mountain folk back home pursued these pleasures freely, as sexually inhibited Shen Congwen, who had grown up in a military gentry family far above such behavior, was only too aware. Ultimately he was able to depict the poor mountain folk's mores in ways that contribute a unique social interest and even regional authenticity to his works (though they are more of a romantic than of a realistic stripe). Shen's stories of frontier romance did not spring from his imagination full-blown, however; he learned to integrate the romantic interest with his regional fiction over the course of a decade.

Shen of course advocated sexual freedom not because he was from West Hunan, or because of personal sexual experience he acquired in Peking (probably he had none), but because of what he had absorbed of Western theories of abnormal psychology. He may well have counseled friends to have love affairs to cure their cases of nerves, but, except for the rumors about him and Ding Ling, all suggestions that Shen might have practiced what he preached refer to the period after he got married and gained more self-confidence.[58] Shen's own timidity must indeed be given credit for keeping his imagination working overtime, inside the young man persona and out. His fervid writing about Ding Ling and her tumultuous marriage, for instance, reads like the sublimation of an inchoate desire that he surely could not have bared any more directly than in writing. (As a professor he even wooed his future wife through letters.) Thus it was Shen Congwen's imagination, as well as his intuitive grasp of psychology and such understanding of the folk as he did achieve, that allowed him to create such lifelike portraits of humble people making love, enjoying the unself-consciousness about sex he was so at pains to achieve himself.

Eroticism as a literary effect must have nourished his imagination well before he was much influenced by Freud. Shen's moralistic detractors were quick to point out that he often conveyed sensuality for its own sake. The roots of this lay not just in his modern poetry (like "Ode"), but in the classical love poetry he wrote in Hunan, though we have no extant samples to analyze. Substantial eroticism entered Shen's fiction only with *Long Summer* (summer 1927) and *Past Dreams* (1928). "Inn of the Wilds" appeared earlier, in 1925, and is a fascinating glimpse of a West Hunanese Miao woman sparring with her lover, in dialect. But the plot is more humorous than erotic. Since Shen Congwen disdained much contemporary fiction as cheap erotic subliterature (including the works of Zhang Ziping and Zhang Yiping), he probably refrained from developing his sensuous descriptive talents as long as he could, until the financial pressure of supporting his family in Shanghai "drove" him to it.[59]

Shen's early erotic fiction is not subliterature. However, some works are more successful than others. If *Past Dreams*, about an unconsummated extramarital affair, is to be rationalized as "seriously" literary where Zhang Ziping's triangular love stories are not, it must be so on the basis of style, satire of manners, and depth of psychological dissection of the usual young man persona. *Long Summer*'s eroticism already lies elsewhere, in the poetry of its metaphors, conveyed in lovers' talk that resonates with the climate and natural scene about them. It is this lyric, sometimes innocently explicit eroticism that Shen Congwen would develop to describe love affairs among the mountain folk, beginning with a cycle of 1928 stories about his young montagnard lovers, Ahei and Wuming.[60] (The characters of *Long Summer* and *Past Dreams* are intellectual urbanites.) Shen as psychologist probed the folk's passions, as he did those of his urban characters, but this time he found no tortured inhibitions, only straightforward desires and affects expressible through simple nature metaphors. Simple on the surface, that is, like classical erotic poetry—but on further analysis, charged with the subliminal mystery and primal vigor of symbolic thinking in the subconscious mind, all the more active for its being at work among "primitive" people.

Romance at the frontier is well documented anthropologically, for it is most open among the "tribal" Miao. Academia Sinica fieldworkers visited the West Hunan Miao in 1933 and published a detailed report many years later, long after Shen wrote his Miao stories. The Miao were already much Sinicized and the anthropologists' stay was brief; some local informants today say the Academia Sinica book mixes up Tujia rites with Miao ones. But Miao in Guizhou, whence the West Hunan Miao migrated, were the subject of detailed, if not professional, ethnographic reports too, and these indicate a rich variety of non-Sinitic customs of the sort Shen Congwen's imagination worked with. Nineteenth-century West Hunan gazetteers likewise describe customs that are now extinct locally but verifiable in the Guizhou homeland.[61]

Chinese had long been amazed to see that the Miao, Yao, Gelao, and other Southwestern peoples, such as the Tai, let young people of both sexes work and play together, not only in childhood but after puberty. Premarital friendships with the opposite sex were allowed and sometimes even encouraged by the parents. Little hedged about by convention, teenagers flirted in public and enjoyed sexual relations in private. Most young people got married by their late teens, but they selected their own mate, perhaps after considerable experimentation with different partners. (West Hunan Miao were, however, succumbing to the Chinese view of marriage as a property settlement to be handled by the parents, working through go-betweens. While customs were in transition, elopements and litigation were frequent.) In fact marriage was not quite so permanent among the Miao as among the Chinese. There were extramarital affairs and many divorces, followed by remarriages. Among one group of Miao in Sichuan, men had secret extramarital relations with paternal aunts and maternal cousins. Just as shocking to Chinese was the sexual freedom enjoyed by widows. A Miao widow might seek a new partner—even begin experimenting—when her husband had scarcely breathed his last. Upper-class Chinese would have had her remain true to her deceased first husband forever.[62]

But it was the special Miao singing customs and pairing institutions that set Chinese imaginations on fire. (The Sinologist Marcel Granet detected signs of similar customs among the ancient Han in the love songs of the *Book of Odes*—more evidence for Shen Congwen's vision of Miao life as that of the Han when they were "young.") Even the Communist revolution did not deter Han interest in *yao malang* encounters, a form of behavior so foreign to the Han that they have no native Chinese word for it. Below is Ma Shaoqiao's 1956 description. Ma declines to point out that the activity on the hillsides leads to sexual intercourse, but he is not coy. He extols Miao freedom in order to attack "feudal" Chinese mores, much as Shen Congwen did decades earlier.

> In Guizhou, the love songs sung by boys and girls when they feel affection for each other are called *"malang* songs." Each village furnishes its young men and women a meadow in which they may freely mix, called the *"malang* hillside." When young men and women freely mix, it is called *"yao malang."* Each year, during the agricultural slack season, young men form groups to go from village to village to *"yao malang."* When they arrive in a village, they play their reed organs (*lusheng*) out on the *"malang* hillside." The teenage girls of the village put on their best and go out to meet them. The two sides begin to sing; their songs speak of love. Meeting by meeting, year by year, their feelings and thoughts come into accord. Then they may speak of marriage. In principle, their parents may not interfere.[63]

As Ma says, there were no such hillsides in West Hunan (during this century, anyway): "However, when young men and women meet at market, at assemblies, while gathering bracken and wild onions in the spring or cutting grass and chopping wood in winter, or while tending or hunting animals, they can use songs both beautiful and rich in sentiment to express their affection to each other. Gradually they come closer, establish their affection, and arrange *rendez-vous*. After the two sides come to an understanding, they exchange gifts and ask a go-between to obtain their parents' permission. [If it is denied, they elope.]"[64] This lyric passage is nearly worthy of Shen himself. A custom of some *malang* hillsides that we do see reflected in at least one Shen Congwen story is informal chaperoning. Chaperoning was done, at a distance, despite the young people's sexual freedom, partly to verify "who was going with whom." As in Shen's stories, the young people's teasing, chasing, and delight in sex itself, which might be initiated by the girl if she were so disposed, did not keep young folk from exchanging vows of faithfulness and physical tokens such as a ring, handkerchief, or embroidered ball (from the girl).[65]

In nineteenth-century West Hunan, there seem to have been many institutions for young people to meet each other, including perhaps even youth houses (*malang*) where young unmarrieds might go to meet, sing, and make love without parental interference. Generally young people met each other at fixed times and sites, for example, during religious festivals like those at the New Year and for "bludgeoning the ox." It was not easy for hard-working and widely dispersed mountain folk to come together otherwise. An observer of Indochina Miao went so far as to speak of "marriage fairs." Shen Congwen's stories show the more typical pairing off of boys and girls individually, using alternating songs to measure each other's personalities and present teasing challenges, dares, or rebuffs to the potential sexual partner. Shen also took up the Miao association of romance with festival time, and with the moon and moon festivals. The passage from his "Long Zhu" below is accurate, as far as it goes. Above all it captures the importance of singing ability in mate selection.

> The boys and girls of the Langjia tribe came together through singing. At the time of the Greater New Year's Festival, Duanyang, the Mid-Autumn Festival of the eighth month, and the great sacrifices of Dancing for the New Year and Stabbing the Ox, boys and girls would form into groups to sing and dance. Each of the girls would be decked out in a tunic and skirt of tribal brocade, with flowers in her hair and powder on her face, to offer herself to a boy. Ordinarily, when the weather was good, whether it was early or late in the day, in a deep mountain valley or by a riverbank,

boys and girls would be drawn together by their singing. Then, under sunlight or moonlight, they could come to know each other and do those things that can only be done by the most intimate of lovers. Under such customs, a boy who could not sing was in disgrace, and a girl who could not sing could not get a good husband. Plucking out one's heart and tendering it to one's lover depended not on money, appearance, family status, or anything of pretense, only on genuine and passionate songs. What was sung was vigorous and happy, or sad, angry, irritated, and tearful. In any event, it was still a song. A passionate bird is not a silent bird. A person without the strength and courage to express his love has no hopes to speak of, in any endeavor whatsoever. Such a person is no good![66]

Hence songs are the other element of frontier lovemaking that Shen later used to lend regional flavor and eroticism to his fictional romances. It was through Chinese-language mountain songs (whose music and verse forms differ from those of Miao language songs, but whose occasion and spirit are influenced by the Miao and Tujia traditions) that he first explored and praised frontier sexuality, deprecating urban repression. That was in 1926, well before Shen thought of putting his songs into his fiction. At first he simply explained, for his Peking audience, the dialect and erotic metaphors of songs he had collected, and their social function: picking up someone of the opposite sex, teasing a lover, or suggesting a tryst, as in Miao "songs sung along the road" and "songs of seduction" of the sort well known in Guizhou and Guangxi. All these songs carry on their repartee through double entendres, typically botanical metaphors. (It is the metaphors that are reminiscent of the *Book of Odes*.) Here are a couple of examples from the Guizhou and Guangxi Miao, respectively. The singer usually refers to both parties in the singing match obliquely, in the third person.[67]

> For a long time I have been coming here.
> The cool water produces cool melons.
> If one opens the melon he may drink cool water.
> If you will not be my sweetheart, I shall not come again.

> Elder brother [this singer, "I"] is a spring atop a tall mountain,
> Younger sister [you, my opposite] is a field at the foot of the mountain.
> The spring water flows down the mountain,
> If younger sister doesn't keep it, it'll be a waste.

In one of Shen's West Hunan songs, the sexual symbolism of water is even more suggestive, for it comes from a (female) orifice:

> There's a well by the roadside that has very cool water,
> People come to drink from it, but no one comes to keep it in repair:
> This little lad is of a mind to come fix it up,
> He is afraid the well water won't keep on flowing!

The following was a favorite of Shen's. He put it into several of his stories:

> Clouds soar in the sky;—cloud on top of cloud,
> Graves are dug underground;—grave on top of grave,
> Dainty younger sister [you] washes bowls;—bowl on top of bowl,
> Dainty younger sister is on the bed;—lover on top of lover.
>
> Clouds soar in the sky, and from them, flowers,
> Peapods are sown among a forest of corn stalks,
> The peapods wrap themselves around the stalks, smothering them,
> Sister wraps herself around the lad [me], smothering him.

One can use the following to entice a *daipa* one sees washing clothes on the riverbank, Shen says.

> [I'm] singing a mountain song to get a rise out of the maiden,
> To see if she'll raise her head or not:
> If a horse doesn't raise his head, he's eating tender hay,
> If a girl doesn't raise her head, she's not amorous!

In the following song, a girl mocks a boy's timidity, and evidently his male organ (sparrow). In the next, she seems to find its length sufficient.

> Little bitty sparrow, just left the nest,
> Winging to a field, he alit for a rest,
> Sparrow's so 'fraidy, looks quite distressed,
> The grain is ripe, but sparrow won't test.
>
> Planting turnips in the big fields and on the big slopes,
> The turnip has grown yards and yards tall.
> If only my lover elder brother is willing,
> How can he fear journeying ten days for a meeting!

Suppose the lovers differ in complexion, or age:

> Dainty younger sister has grown whiter than white,
> Your lover, the lad, is blacker than black:
> When black ink is written on white paper,
> Don't you think they go together well?

Dainty younger sister is 18, the lad is 17,
Yap, yap, she scolds me for not being up-to-age!
In the mountains, tree leaves are not all the same size,
And how can the ten fingers all be of equal length?

Shen Congwen provides examples of how first lines of songs are used to link a series, or build alternating verses, as in the following, the first to be sung by the female lover, and the second by the male:

The peppers are green in the field apart,
Hot peppers, peppery stomach, peppery heart!
You've a wife in your bed, but your mind's elsewhere,
On your dew-drop [illicit] lover [me], that little tart!

The peppers are yellow in the field 'cross the rut,
Hot peppers, peppery stomach, peppery gut!
You've a husband in your bed, but your mind's elsewhere,
On your dew-drop lover, that awful lout!

Above all, the songs provide good ribald humor.

When you go to pick flowers, pick enough to adore,
When lighting up your pipe, you smoke three or four;
Three or four girls, too, when making love,
If this 'un's too weak, maybe that 'un has more.

Shen Congwen brought his advocacy of vigor, sexuality, and the virtues of the simple country life all together in "After Rain," a charming 1928 story whose very title has erotic overtones. It tells of the pleasant seduction of a girl who gathers bracken out on the mountain slopes. The reader is put in the position of a voyeur as Shen relates the vulgar but arch counterpoint of the lovers' talk, the boy's impertinent flirtations and the girl's coy responses, the teasing and feigned petulance of an eternal drama on its way to a natural climax under the open sky. (The boy and girl are seemingly, but not explicitly, Miao.) There appears to be Freudian symbolism in the young woman's pigtail, a "snake" that might "bite" her lover, Fourth Dog. But Fourth Dog's conquest symbolizes a larger battle, between the high culture of the literate people and the more vital, popular culture of the mountain folk. From a written poem, necessarily in Chinese, the girl has learned a decadent idea from the high culture, that women are like flowers. Reminded that she, too, must one day wither, she becomes spiritually enervated. She ceases to enjoy the pleasures of the moment, the joy of being under clear skies, the strength of her own and Fourth Dog's body. Illiterate Fourth Dog, too "dumb" to understand, remains incorruptible in his primitive vitality. He overcomes his lover's inhibitions with the more straightforward oral traditions of Zhen'gan (a song like those just cited) and the gift of his own body. Once her instinctual desires take command, the girl forgets the Chinese poem and is made strong again through union with the savagery of Fourth Dog. Symbolism invoking the skies and, incongruously, the vast sea make the union a cosmic marriage. A later version wisely excises Shen's unnecessary explanation: "To be deeply in love, but still feel it is not enough—this is the fault of literacy. Fourth Dog was fortunate to be illiterate. Otherwise, this couple would not have known how to find the happiness due them under this kind of weather." [68]

CHAPTER FIVE

Country Folk, Plain and Exotic

OF SHEN CONGWEN'S many works, those set in West Hunan have attracted by far the most critical attention. Not surprisingly, it is in these pieces that Shen Congwen grapples most profoundly with the meaning of his personal past and his people's history. Yet we encounter abstract human and cosmological concerns here, too, and perhaps the best integration of Shen's search for meaning with the formal demands of his art. C. T. Hsia has sympathetically traced the gradual artistic maturation of this fiction.[1] Few other critics have grasped the variety of effects Shen Congwen drew out of seemingly similar regional landscapes and characters. He spoke in different voices, for different ends, and to different audiences, too.

In China, critics typically treat Shen's literature as if it were nonfiction, to negate the workings of his imagination in the realm of Chinese social life. Read as prescriptive sociologies like the Marxist and Nationalist morality tales that politically conscious critics feel were "needed" (in their time), Shen's West Hunan works long ago lost the right in China even to co-exist, as modest regional historical monographs, beside the panoramic epics written for the revolution. Had simple regional realism been tolerated by the revolutionaries, Shen Congwen might actually have acquitted himself fairly well. Su Xuelin's complaint, for instance, that he could not well convey the essence of Chinese militarism, since he never was rigorously trained or fought a pitched battle, surely could have been refuted by those who knew the desultory nature of 1920's warlordism.[2]

But such simplistic approaches to works of literature are unfair from the first. To say nothing of the complex overall effect of Shen's fiction as art, its explicitly intellectual dimensions address aesthetic and moral questions as often as social theory and ideology. Even when he is delineating social relations among seemingly realistic characters, as between city people and country folk, one cannot assume Shen to have his eye only on the sociology of twentieth-century China, or to be pursuing truths that add up to historical science. Surely he does convey heartfelt images of China's contemporary predicament. But his social classes are not the same as Lenin's and Mao's. It never occurred to him, as it did to Engels, to represent the social typicality of characters by how frequently they appear in the text. Determining how much weight to give the social attributes of Shen's characters is, to be sure, complicated. He has a moral purpose in writing, even as he warns against the high morality of civilization. He seeks to render lower-class people as ordinary, hence *understandably* human to his urban readers, yet also as humanly individual, as well as different—aesthetically colorful and culturally apart from city people. And the West Hunanese social types he wants to introduce to his readers are diverse, their identities subject to confusion. Above all, Shen Congwen does not limit himself to realistic literary modes when portraying other patterns of life. His stories about the Miao have drawn special fire for being unrealistic. Yet in their very farfetchedness these fanciful plots are most imitative of folklore. One could joke that the folk should be told to create more realistic, up-to-date, less frivolous lore, except that during the Cultural Revolution they were asked to do just that.

A few critics, mostly in the West, have read Shen Congwen's works symbolically, finding Taoism in them, or even Existentialism. Those two ways of seeing life are rich enough of themselves to provide fruitful approaches to reading Shen's works, but these sorts of interpretation can also be carried too far. Shen valued dynamism over passiveness. He loved the *Zhuangzi*, an imaginative, some would say pantheistic, work of literature, but he deplored Taoism as a tradition, just as he did other traditions. The strangeness and distraction of his country folk on the other hand suggest the mystery of the ghost stories he heard while in the army more than a metaphysical sense of the Absurd. Shen was a pantheist who was thoroughly disillusioned with academic philosophy, though he might have found it interesting to look for Absurdity in social relations. More rewarding is Hua-ling Nieh's analysis of the natural and psychological symbolism pervading Shen's art.[3]

In truth Shen Congwen's vast oeuvre does contain moments, in fiction as well as nonfiction, in which he acts merely as gazetteerist, chronicler, or apologist for his own folk. He can scarcely bring himself to write about evil. At times he lapses into sentimentality, catalogues social customs for their own sake, even repeats himself, though the situation is usually rescued by his precise, vivid, and original language. Nearly always, though, Shen Congwen creates a literary world of his own, no more a plain recounting of what he has seen and heard than it is a mere reflection of his own wishful thinking. When he simplifies social reality, sometimes it is to press a point about rural Chinese mores, sometimes to let "us see our modern and complex problems mirrored in a simpler and more primitive world."[4] The latter is what Cleanth Brooks defines as pastoral. Brooks would remind us that it is more appropriate to seek "truth of coherence" in Shen's fictional works than the "truth of reference" we expect of his nonfiction.[5] Yet in the final analysis Shen Congwen's works, even the idyllic ones, are rendered coherent by the author's knowledge of, and ability to reinvent, his "references": West Hunanese and panhuman "realities," both plain and extraordinary.

One cannot call Shen a writer in the realist tradition. He loved "ideals" and the realm of myth. It was with fanciful stories of Miao singing masters, star-crossed lovers, and fighting brothers that he most explicitly delineated the regional myth summarized in Chapter One, of the great contradiction between tribal vigor and Confucian decadence. Yet he generally espoused the doctrine of realism in theory, as did most of his colleagues. Probably for that very reason he seldom attempted "realistic" stories about the Miao. Shen did not "know" their social life, only their stories, so he kept the Miao for his fairy tales. By "Miao" we mean unassimilated Miao, not the more numerous mountain-folk characters whose culture simply has a Miao or Southwestern ethnic flavor. Zhu Guangqian was one of many Chinese readers who loved *The Frontier City*, among other works, partly for its national minority ethos,[6] although no character in the novel (not even the Wang daughter, who lives up in the hills) is explicitly called non-Han. (Chadong, the "Frontier City," is in real life a Han island town within a sea of Miao.) In Shen's realistic or relatively realistic works, the characters are indeed quite likely to be of unclear ethnicity—typical Sino-Miao mulatto folk who would rather be considered Chinese. The great divide in Shen Congwen's works set in the Chinese countryside thus lies not between stories of Miao life and Han life, but between literary modes, between legends and mimetic works. This distinction, as it happens, is sharpened not by ethnic culture as such, but by ethnic and cultural identity: his heroes in the one realm are untamed, not yet "detribalized" folk (whether Miao or Tujia); in the other, they are Sino-Tujia-Miao plain folk, of Han culture with an ethnic tinge, but, more importantly, at the mercy of a larger world dominated by cities and Confucianism. It was the latter kind of folk that Shen really knew, the former about whom he felt free to dream.

The Untamed Tribespeople: Shen Congwen's Legends and Romances

Centuries before Shen Congwen took up his pen, there was a Chinese gentry tradition of writing about the tribespeople. It noted, with some fascination, variant dress styles, lore, and social customs among all the montagnards, as well as colorful distinctions among different groups of Miao themselves. Many reports indeed proceeded to quasi-clinical, seemingly detached curiosity about the Miao's sexual customs. This brought certain Confucian authors to cover some of the same anthropological ground as Shen Congwen. But on closer examination, the gentry appear to have based their writings on centuries-old accounts copied and recopied without updating, including many unverified stories—literate people's own legends about the primitives. Chinese classifications of the Miao according to dress, into "Red," "White," "Blue," and so forth, have not squared with social reality for more than a century, if they ever did. Descriptions of social customs turn out to emphasize the degree of the tribespeople's assimilation to Han Confucian norms. The literati, in good Lévi-Strauss binary fashion, literally divided the Miao into the "raw" and the "cooked" (the culturally "underdone" and the well-done). The gentry's detached curiosity about Miao mating habits, too, bespeaks less a tolerant moratorium on moralizing than a zoological fascination comparable to the Victorians' patronizing curiosity about the South Sea islanders.[7]

Established Han curiosity about the Miao did help Shen Congwen create an atmosphere of myth and legend in his frontier romances, yet his attitude is fundamentally different. He mythologizes the tribespeople by setting them apart from ordinary society, then accepts the validity of their way of life, trying for once to render them "human": in a traditional sense, as living by ramified social norms comprehending familiar concepts such as loyalty and piety; and in a more modern sense, as having their own complex mental lives, and their own dignity as unique individuals with aspirations, ideals, and devotions. Having little firsthand information about the interior lives of the "tribal" Miao, Shen Congwen was thrown back on the resources of his own imagination, what he knew of the tribespeople's own legends, and such elements of their dreams and thought processes as he thought he could derive from those legends. Yet, even now we have no more sophisticated literary or anthropological probings of the Miao mind by which to measure the extent of his achievement in cross-cultural representation.

Special controversy has centered on the songs Shen has his Miao and other tribal heroes sing. The music and lyrics of real Miao songs, some traditional, others extemporized to fit the occasion, differ from those of the Chinese-language Zhen'gan songs.[8] Shen could have known the former only in paraphrase, except insofar as their spirit and occasion, and way of constructing erotic double entendres through botanical metaphors, have influenced the Chinese songs. In fact the invented "Miao songs" in Shen's works are deliberately exotic—non-Chinese—expressed in free verse, or sometimes just in paraphrase, to distance us from the lyrics, reminding us that the "song" is a translation from a foreign tongue. But the metaphors in the songs are extravagant. Are real folk songs as florid, and their double entendres as obvious, as in Shen Congwen's verses?

> A dragon should be hidden in the clouds,
> And you should be hidden in my heart.[9]
>
> With their wings birds fly into the sky,
> Without wings I fly into your heart.
> I shall not ask where Paradise is,
> For I am sitting at its gate.[10]

The metaphors, indeed the verses as a whole, are close enough to Shen's free-verse romantic poems to have been wholly invented. The meteor imagery could be from Tagore, the metaphors of riches and animals from the commercial Islamic world of the *Thousand*

and One Nights ("Nuo You's bag was full of glittering pearls and rare stones [i.e., possible mates], and just because their number was too large, he was somewhat at a loss to choose among them and was slightly embarrassed"). Still other images could derive from The Song of Solomon ("her body appeared to have been carved from mingled white jade, milk cream, delicious fruits, and sweet flowers").[11] Other elements, like the *diaobao* fortifications and quotations of sayings of the "country folk," are authentically regional if not ethnic.[12] Heavenly metaphors are not unknown to the Miao, however, as we see from this genuine Miao song from Thailand:

Now I have to leave your village, and whenever I remember your embraces, my soul will be happy. Now I must leave, but I shall think only of returning. My soul wanders in the clouds (meaning: you have bewitched me) and not on earth. And when I return and hold your hand, I shall not be able to stop the flow of words until the end of my life (meaning: he will take her as his wife for life). What are you going to give me then to fill my soul and to stop the flow of my words? (a clear allusion to the sexual act, the only moment when the lovers are silent). Whatever you give me I shall give back to you all my life long.[13]

Behind Shen Congwen's sometimes puerile erotic lyrics and unsubtle metaphors ("At this moment their lips found another use, and they remained silent for a short while"; "His songs had become the cradle for the girl to sleep in")[14] lies the spirit, probably more than the substance, of the Miao formal mode of discourse through metaphor. It is a mode of communication often delivered through song, as when arriving, parting, wooing, or attending ceremonies. It requires two-level translation and has been little studied, partly because the Han of West Hunan have so little interest in learning any more than "marketplace Miao," and probably too because the Miao are less than anxious to expose their intimate thoughts to outsiders. Miao teachers in Fenghuang provided the following example in 1980. When encountering a stranger, one does not ask his or her honorable name, like the Han, but tells a symbolic story. "I'm a swallow who has flown into the master's home." The reply: "No, you're a bee, bringing good luck," etc.[15] Shen seems to have duplicated such discourse when his city stranger meets a "country girl" (ethnicity unspecified, but living in the pure Miao pale of West Hunan) in *Fengzi*: "You're like an immortal in moonlight, or a spirit under sunlight—since you're not a shooting star, this stranger from afar would like to know where you've come from and where you're going, and might you not stop a while? ... Before I'd only heard of intoxicating mushrooms, but today I've heard intoxicating songs." The girl: "Good mushrooms sprout only when the air is damp. Who knows whether it will rain or clear up?"[16]

The three-line question-song of Shen's Miao singer Long Zhu (reproduced by the narrator in paraphrase), followed by a one-line response, does exist in the West Hunanese (Chinese) folk tradition.[17]

What Long Zhu's song conveyed was:
> All good wine goes to the best singer to drink,
> And all good meat [flesh?] goes to the best singer to eat, too,
> But you, lovely and beautiful girl, to whom will you go?

The woman answered with a song whose drift was: Good women can only be matched with good men.[18]

Fengzi no doubt means to instruct us ethnographically when it enumerates three kinds of songs among its "country folk": "four- or five-line songs with seven syllables to the line, of the sort children sing on impulse while tending the cows, cutting firewood, or preparing fodder for the pigs; alternating lovers' songs, with double entendres or citations of ancient words or deeds, sung by adult men and women when they want to express their love; and songs whose words are few but sustained, sung to eulogize the gods or convey bereavement. The first calls for quick-wittedness; the second, passion; the third, a good voice."[19] Worrying too much about the "realism" of these stories, however, can obfuscate their more unshakable literary basis in imagination.

"Under Moonlight" is lifted onto the plane of fable and legend from the outset. It unfolds among "the remnants of a people long neglected by mankind and forgotten by history."[20] Their ethnicity is not specified, but they fear the Han, "who would kill them as aborigines" (the hero has a West Hunanese name, Nuoyou, "Protected by the Nuo Gods").[21] Ethnic apartness and geographic isolation, however, are merely the material causes of these people's more unique significance, which is that they had lived in a physical and spiritual world beyond ordinary Chinese history: "They had been living in this corner of the world for many, many years, speaking a language of their own, following their own customs and dreaming their own dreams."[22]

Shen's character Long Zhu is explicitly Miao, a master of song with a reputation for musicality and lyric inventiveness known throughout the border Miao pale, one publicly established in individual singing matches and village-against-village competitions. Such people exist even today, and truly are culture heroes among the Miao. (The Deng Xiaoping regime has ferreted out the remaining few, grandly lifting them out of the obscurity in which they took refuge when ethnic culture was attacked during the Cultural Revolution.)[23] But Shen's piece is literature, of Frye's "high mimetic" mode, if not fully mythic.[24] Long Zhu is above the rest of us, the son of a chieftain, so beautiful, so intelligent (inventive at song), and in all so perfect that women fear to approach him. The narrator compares him with gods, and characters in other stories by Shen sing Long Zhu's praises.[25] His perfection would be a tragic flaw, but for the saccharine ending. And Long Zhu's predicament is accentuated, while comically relieved, by a Shakespearean foil, the prince's loyal dwarf slave. Possessing singing powers that are great but not so impressive as to frighten women away, the slave shares his master's loneliness in that he is kept apart from womankind by his deformity. Yet he is a good vocal go-between, just the person to woo a perfect princess in Long Zhu's stead. His voice expresses the purity nature has denied his body.

Shen's prose is pure, but not heroic or archaic. "Long Zhu" is cast as a fairy tale suitable for, among others, young people in high school. Without being didactic, it offers them uplift through healthful "ideals" to free their imaginations. A fanciful but elegant, memorably atmospheric inspirational piece, "Long Zhu" may have a more deeply idealistic didactic end than that. Considered in his mortality, as a person with emotions and frustrations, Long Zhu evidences Deity within man, and so foreshadows Shen's later pantheistic works, which explore the divinity in all people and things.

These stories, set in the countryside, are not simply "pastoral." "Under Moonlight" actually mystifies nature. It creates a slightly eerie mood as it paints the moonlight spreading across the landscape from behind the *diaobao* (appropriately rendered by Jin Di and Robert Payne as "castles").[26] This is soon ramified with legends about humans of old chasing the sun and seeking the moon. Man is above nature itself; he tries not to accommodate himself to it, but to "conquer" it, and with his own prowess rather than devices.

Shen's plots likewise unfold as legend. "Under Moonlight" actually is West Hunanese folklore retold. The story was passed down through Congwen's grandfather's line, at Huangluozhai. Informants at Fenghuang today say that the village may originally have been Tujia, which, if true, might explain the tribal, but not explicitly Miao, ethos.[27] A legend-within-the-legend is told near the beginning of the story, as cosmological and historical background for musings about the moon by Nuoyou, the hero. It foreshadows the central moral insight under which Nuoyou's tragedy will unfold: man perpetuates evil customs, but going against the way of the gods takes its toll. "And this was the story he had been told," says the narrator: In ancient times, a man who had attained all mortal happiness tried to catch the sun and the moon, with the result that the whole human race was punished for its hubris. The moon god and the devil hit upon a punishment; "the reason for hating the sun but not the moon, according to the natives' explanation, is that humanity has slowly become less divine, and more evil."[28] Lack of materials precludes authentication of this legend, but the motifs of hunting the sun and the moon, and falling from grace with the gods, are ubiquitous in Southwestern minority folklore, and found among the Han, too.[29]

Then commences the main story, of the star-crossed lovers Nuoyou and his girl. As the amorous associations of the moon come into play, the lovers flatter each other with florid sung metaphors and similes. There is a reference to the *lusheng* reed pipe, nearly unique in Shen's stories. The instrument is now found mostly among Guizhou minorities.[30]

"Under Moonlight" then relates the "ancient custom" of the tribespeople, which engenders the lovers' dilemma: one may not marry the person with whom one has lost one's virginity. Paraphrasing Zhou Zuoren's theory regarding *jus primae noctis* (the right of the first night), which links the *jus* to fear of virgins, Shen as amateur anthropologist intervenes in the text, as narrator, to speculate that the local taboo on marrying the first lover is a further transformation of "fear of virgins." He cannot resist adding his own psychoanalytic speculation: the noxious duty of deflowering virgins, once undertaken among this people by altruistic (unafraid) headmen and sexually repressed shaman-priests, ultimately was transferred to stranger-males at large, so long as they did not proceed to marry their sexual partner. That would incur the death penalty for both of them.[31] Again, specific local folkloric confirmation of Shen's legend is not available, but historical reports abound of ritual defloration rituals among Southeast Asian peoples, from Tibet to the

Philippines. Some groups of Miao probably did grant sexual freedom to brides, until they bore their first child, and at least one group of West Hunan Miao, like some Miao elsewhere, is said to have disinherited the first-born (who was assumed to be illegitimate). Above all, the folklore of several Southwestern ethnic groups exemplifies the concept Eberhard puts under his Yao rubric as "contagion": "every virgin carries in herself a certain poison which she passes on to the first man possessing her. This man must die, and therefore no man marries a virgin."[32] Shen's legend, however, proceeds not to the motif of death from virginal sexual intercourse, but to an even more prevalent Southwestern folkloric motif, love suicide.[33] Nuoyou and his girl are so in love that they cannot wait for strangers to deflower them before joining their bodies with vows of permanent faithfulness; nor would they suffer their lover to have intercourse with another in the first place. Therefore they make love, choosing the natural way of the gods, in disregard of the consequences under the evil and distorted customs of men. More legends-within-the-legend examine the possibilities of escape, only to reject them one and all. "The tribesmen possessed an ancient song in which human desire, a desire which contained all the significance of life and which each man who wanted to live must possess, was interpreted in terms of death, indicating that the greed for life could only be satisfied in death."[34] To escape the world of men and more easily find each other in the afterlife, the lovers blissfully commit double suicide. Fenghuang informants in 1980 still noted that Huangluozhai was well-known for its double suicides and stories about them.[35]

Though "Long Zhu," too, reads like a legend, it is not folklore. "It's just romantic," Shen says now, with a chuckle.[36] Given the mythic power of the hero (Shen named his first son after him), the tale is virtually "invented folklore" of the author's own. Unfortunately, Shen simply cannot remember the origin of "Meijin, Baozi, and the White Kid." It is even more consciously folkloric in the telling, a masterpiece of quasi-folklore, if not the real thing. Like "Under Moonlight," it exalts faithfulness in love through a tale of double suicide. Again the hero and heroine are nearly perfect. Meijin is the girl, a Miao beauty of the White-faced tribe (quite likely a tribal name that Shen invented). Her lover is Baozi, or "Wildcat," a lad from Fenghuang Battalion, a *tuntian* village west of Zhen'gan. The tragedy is brought on by the inability of the young people to consummate their first union in love-making, a mutual deflowering that Meijin and Baozi take to be, in effect, the beginning of an eternal union in marriage. Their failure to keep the first tryst is the result of Baozi's obsessive quest for a perfect gift for his "bride." He wants to give his lover a white, unspotted kid, in exchange for her virginal blood; evidently the kid is to be sacrificed. Meijin and Baozi's tryst is of special import, and Baozi's belated arrival particularly subject to misunderstanding, because the lovers have never met before face-to-face. They have fallen in love while gazing at each other from afar, across opposite hillsides, listening to each other's extemporized alternating songs. Baozi conquered Meijin by the end of their singing match. She submitted with the erotic verse, "Red leaves pass over the hills, helpless before the winds of autumn / I will be made a woman only by you...."[37] Come the night of the tryst, Baozi is fated to discover his perfect gift so late that Meijin mistakenly judges herself to have been forsaken. For the sake of the love that might have been, she plunges a knife into her breast, sacrificing herself, instead of the kid. When Baozi arrives, she is just conscious enough to smile on the spectacle of her true love making ready to join her in the next life, like Romeo, or Nuoyou.

In addition to extolling true love, the tale is a parable about manly decisiveness. An old fortuneteller who knows Baozi gives him early warning, and then repeated, increasingly urgent and suspense-building late warnings, that Baozi must not be too fastidious in finding something to exchange for Meijin's virginity. It is his masculinity that she really wants. Chalk it up to fate, as the old man does, or to subconscious fear on Baozi's part of losing his own virginity—Baozi's neglect of his lover's womanly needs is the real cause of his failure to achieve manhood.

The tale is the more intriguing in having a single narrator, but two successive focal levels. The narrator begins the story as folklorist. He addresses us directly, with some lyrical and windy rhetorical flourishes appropriate to an involved, professional storyteller, but later concentrates fairly objectively on storytelling as an act, instead of dramatizing himself. "One who is truly familiar with stories among the Miao could tell you 50 stories about Miao girls who were ugly, though they conquered men of legendary manly beauty with their sweet singing. He could tell you 50 more about handsome men driven to distraction by the songs of Miao women of the White-faced tribe [Meijin's]. But if he left one out, no doubt it would be for having forgotten to tell you the tale of Meijin and Baozi."[38] Our storyteller indicates that some comparative compilation has already been undertaken. He rather deliberately sorts out alternative versions of the legend, and, after noting that the White-faced tribe has a taboo on eating goat meat, owing to the lovers' tragedy, injects a skeptical note about the tribe's subsequent custom of exchanging kids as betrothal gifts, saying that even the sex of the first kid is unknown. He concludes, "Let me write it out as I know it. My version comes from the bandit Wu Rou. Wu Rou is descended from the man who acquired Baozi's kid after the event, and that man was also Baozi's martial arts instructor. Naturally his story is more reliable in most of the details. What follows is his story."[39]

That the outline of the tale is thus pretold, in a relatively modern voice (both modern in outlook and temporally near), softens the fact that the supplied threefold reason-for-being of the myth in functional social-science terms is uncannily convenient—cause for suspicion about the tale's authenticity. This tale not only rationalizes social mores with its romantic exemplars; it explains the origin of strange customs, such as the taboo on goat meat and the use of goats as betrothal presents, and the significance of a pair of deities, namely Meijin and Baozi, now worshipped at the cave where they belatedly kept their tryst. The focal level hereafter, in effect the voice, changes to that of a folksier traditional-style storyteller. Partly the effect is achieved through language—phrases like *qie shuo* ("let us now talk about"). Partly it is conveyed by periodic traditional narratorial intervention, in the form of a didactic refrain alleging the decline of the good old customs of the past. "Like good women, they must gradually wither." The narrator attests that Baozi and Meijin's souls would not have wanted their cave, so ideal for the enjoyment of young people, to have been given over to religious purposes, even for the commemoration of their own love. "As I said, the good customs are dying out, and so are the passions of the race. The women are slowly becoming like Chinese women [revised edition: Han women], consigning their love to empty things like cattle and sheep, gold and silver. The passion of love has already declined. Beautiful songs, like beautiful bodies, have become useless things, overcome by material objects."[40]

How well the stories succeed as fiction is a separate question from their folkloric authenticity, which is nebulous enough. A revised version of "Meijin" wisely deletes a passage that quite incongruously speaks in Shen Congwen's own literati voice, to note that the clever, rumor-mongering Shanghai litterateurs of the twentieth century could hardly imagine the beauty of one such as Meijin.[41] There remains a facetious reference, more in the voice of the storyteller, to how attractive Han men still find Miao women, though compared to Meijin they are now only "the dregs of the dregs."[42]

Shen's style nevertheless remains at all times elegant. His symbolism, too, is carried to a fine point: when Baozi finds his perfect gift, in the wee morning hours, it is by accident. And his white kid is wounded, as is Meijin by this time, spiritually if not yet physically. For all the excesses, one can scarcely doubt that Shen Congwen has caught a little of the pathos inherent in the extinction of Southwestern Chinese tribal culture. In another tale, "Seven Barbarians and the Last Rite of Spring," which is authentic folklore, we see Miao experts and singing masters retreat to the wilderness to drink, revel, hunt, practice martial arts, and set up cave hideaways for lovers. They curse the coming of officials from the lowlands people, the "race that enjoys botheration." The Miao predict the prompt and utter destruction of their race: degeneracy among males and indolence among females, "as among the Han." Miao folk will now learn how to swindle, plunder, beg, and sell their children into prostitution and slavery, like the folk who know cities.[43] Shen Congwen's regional myth of frontier superiority could not be more explicit.

The Plain Country Folk: Their Place in Society and the Landscape

In moral terms, the rural characters of Shen Congwen's other, nonmythic regional stories are like his tribespeople, a pastoral redemptive community of West Hunanese standing in opposition to urban materialism from the north and east. They are not so easy to identify socially, though, as rich or poor, or even Han or Miao. To lie ambiguously athwart economic and ethnic continua is part of their lot. Many indeed seem to be of mixed origins. Nevertheless, the detribalized folk are not just a moral but a social community. Paradoxically, they stand even more passively before the corruption and complications of city society than the tribespeople, for they are, and consider themselves to be, plain folk, or as Shen would have it, "country folk." Tribal people are pitted against the cities, alone but independent. "Country folk," on the other hand, even the more prosperous among them, lead an existence that they themselves recognize to be a less complicated, indeed a "lesser" variant of a culture whose apex is in the cities.[44] They know that they stand apart from cities in values and sensibilities; many, perhaps most, of the country folk in Shen's works think themselves morally and physically superior to city people. Even so, they must take their place within an urban scheme of things. They are *humble* folk, something to which the tribespeople would never admit. The more fortunate country folk may spend most of their lives oblivious to the fact that they are ultimately at the mercy of cities and literate people. But in many of Shen's stories, powerful city people intrude upon the scene to take their property, do business with them, perhaps lure them into the city world itself with offers of marriage or employment. To retain their way of life, country folk must struggle against forces more gradual and insidious than ethnic warfare and taxation. Their social existence is not the totality of their lives, any more than social questions are the totality of Shen's concern as a writer, but the nuances of their social identity, like the more political one inherent in their regional identity, conditions the way in which they face, or ponder, universal human problems.

Mary C. Wright has demonstrated that traditional Confucian thought recognized the importance of agriculture as the basis of the state and took the humble peasant to be "a rational and perfectible human being." Chinese gentry created Taoist images idealizing the contentments of country life and, unlike conservatives in the West, showed little fear of mass education.[45] But for reasons not yet fully studied—perhaps owing to modern urbanization, if not Westernization itself—China's early-twentieth-century city people disdained country folk as stupid and ineducable.

Shen Congwen inverted this prejudice, turning the social liabilities of country folk into moral virtues—modern ones—of individual dignity and self-determination. His most famous definition of the country person occurs in his 1936 "Preface to My Exercises," wherein he defiantly proclaims himself to be one: "A country fellow is by nature an inveterate country bumpkin. What he likes or dislikes, and what brings him sorrow, or happiness, is distinctly up to him, quite at odds with the tastes of a city person! He's conservative, and stubborn; he loves the soil; he's no pushover, but trickiness is beyond him. He takes everything to heart, almost too much to heart, which in some instances may make him out to be a 'simpleton.'"[46] Mao Zedong was similarly given to restating peasant liabilities as virtues, but instead of seeing country people as leading dignified and stable lives on their own terms, he praised them for quite the opposite characteristic: a revolutionary *malleability* predicated on precisely the view Shen Congwen wanted to contradict, that country folk were culturally "poor and blank." Shen agreed that his country folk were not necessarily "intelligent" in the city folk's practical terms, but he insisted that they led rich imaginative lives all their own. A major weakness in his portraits of rural characters may well be that between his careful treatment of rural community and custom on the one hand, and his extraordinary delineation of rural interior lives on the other, he lets the exterior personality traits of his characters fall into stereotypes: strong, outspoken martial "brothers" (like Tianbao of *The Frontier City*), and beautiful, intelligent, and imaginative Miao bards (like Nuosong of the same novel); dreamy adolescent girls and earthy old men; and so forth. In other words, Shen's rural folk are too like their opposite numbers in the mythic pieces. Few critics, though, would fault the sensitivity of his psychological portraits, even of relationships between generationally stereotyped characters.[47]

What particularly caught readers' attention was Shen's extension of "country virtues" to boatmen, prostitutes, soldiers, and others apt to be considered drifters. If the old gentry were more sympathetic than modern urbanites toward people who were rooted in the soil, they were quite intolerant of people lacking a fixed abode and known origins. Modern city dwellers, meanwhile, were acquiring new, Western viewpoints with which to despise those who sold their bodies or lived apart from bourgeois society. Shen Congwen had more liberal views on sex, and a Social Darwinist respect for people who lived beyond the comforts of society and risked their very lives. Intimating that his (and "their") very unbourgeois morality was of the folk, he linked boatmen and prostitutes to their rural forebears. Popular writers had blazed this trail before, but the seriousness with which Shen made his point was still startling in his time.

In addition to occasional stereotyping, Shen Congwen at times overstresses his "country" characters' innocence, to the point that they become dull. He felt such an identity with the rural lower classes that some of the views and sensibilities he attributes to them appear to be his own. But to that extent the "country folks' world" illuminates Shen's own values.

Leftist critics have charged Shen Congwen with being less sensitive to questions of social class than the other writers of his era. Yet Shen as storyteller also appears less class-conscious than his characters; the illusion that we are viewing a society without class (or more accurately, social status) distinctions begins to unravel. Indeed, Shen often *tells* us who are "plain folk," and who have city wealth and manners.

Though most of Shen's characters who work the land are poor by urban standards, they are not, like his river and army-camp-follower folk, in straits that directly evoke pity. (The Miao father in *Alice's Adventures in China*, who must sell his daughter into slavery, and the starving beggars helped by "Ahan the Night Watch," who himself squats in the Zhen'gan *tudi* [tutelary] temple, are exceptions.) Though they may be seen eating a poor man's diet of sweet potatoes, or gathering bracken (a fern, mostly consumed in time of famine), the very poorest do not dwell on their poverty, not even Guisheng, the irregular laborer. Indeed, Shen Congwen includes relatively uncapitalized, self-made proprietors of country crossroads shops among his country folk, if they share the origins, regional identity, and values of his peasants (as in "Guisheng"). Of course Shen would have had difficulty depicting human dignity among the starving, of whom he must have seen many in West Hunan in the 1920's. Yet, his most memorable country-folk characters are, as the Marxists have pointed out, usually not the poorer ones, but those who are rather comfortably supplied with the simple necessities of food and clothing. The eponymic heroine of "Sansan," for instance, is sought after for a bride because her dowry will be her deceased father's mill. The mill would enrich any local groom well beyond the level of his peers. What emerges is not, however, an apology for landlords and capitalists, but a picture of a society in which low class status is a function more of powerlessness than of poverty. Not that humble rural people seek to rise above their station, for that would be to enter an unknown world plain folk consider both "above them" and somehow morally questionable.[48]

For all their prosperity, Sansan and her widowed mother, who live close by a *bao* in the Miao borderlands, are conscious of living in a class society in which the major social divide is still far above their heads. They are not Miao, but still plain folk, among the ruled rather than the rulers. Independent amid nature, they are dependent among men—doubly so, as women. They *dream* about the manners of the rural powerholding class. It lives apart, in fortifications (Long Yunfei would be a historical example). Like other country folk, people of Sansan's mother's station address the rural ruling class, who own most of the local property, with honorific phraseology. The narrative voice of "Guisheng" has its title hero (a laborer but also a free spirit, in no way dragged down by economic servitude) "entreatingly report" (*bing gao*) to Fifth Master that Master's tung nuts are ripe. He fears to dirty Master's floor by treading on it. Shen typically depicts these "lords" (to adopt Jin Di and Robert Payne's terminology, which is not far off the mark) as decadent, though reasonably generous to their laborers, with whom they have long-standing relationships and for whom they may provide housing. Their gifts, however, are often cast-off items— old clothing, for Guisheng. The masters vulgarly treat lower-class women as their sexual playthings, as "pigtail merchandise"; and, because they can afford concubines, they in effect take wives from poor folk. Above all, the rural ruling class provides the country folk no leadership in fending off bourgeois modernization. On the contrary, the rural masters are allied with the city people, that other, still less fathomable class above Sansan's people, exemplified in her story by a sick young rich man, evidently an opium addict. Wanting to recuperate, he moves in with the local rural "lord." He seeks, at first, the good country air, and then, inevitably, beautiful young Sansan for his wife. The deteriorating young man would, however, take her off into his own decadent, unhealthy world. Sansan senses the threat he represents.[49]

"Health": this is really a modern author's moral category. What chiefly binds Sansan and her mother to the commoners instead of the rural upper class is psychosocial "health and dignity" that come from not only living on the land, but laboring on it. The riches of the soil (and the waters, in "Sansan," which produce fish) result from the folk's own labor and loving upkeep. This is not to say that prosperity is a Calvinist or Social Darwinist proof of moral virtue in Shen's vision. The decadent ruling class have the riches, whereas the surpluses from nature that the country folk reap remain just that: grains and fruits, or eggs and fishes in Sansan's case, symbols of her sexual maturation. They are not cashed in for silver, fine clothes, or opium. Sansan does not even hanker after the finer things of life, but fears them. Country folk value things more than money. Shen represents the simplicity of their habits through such symbols as the countryman's pipe (versus the city man's cigarette), and Sansan's pumpkin seeds (versus the city folk's melon seeds). As he would have it, the country folk's attachments, other than to each other, are to their animals: Cuicui (*The Frontier City*) to her dog, Huiming ("Huiming") and Old Mrs. Wang ("A Country Town") to their respective chickens, the protagonist of "Ox" to his draft animal.[50]

Sansan's environment is not very rough or exotic, nor has she done much living yet. For Shen's representative "lovable country auntie," of the kind Shen admits he likes to "so often praise," let us therefore consider "Maodi's ma," a character in "Mountain Spirit." Culturally, she is fairly far toward the Miao end of the Sino-Miao spectrum, judging by her cooking, dress, mountain habitat, and the author's claim that she has "all the virtues that the gods in heaven have given the country women who inhabit that part of China's southland adjoining the Miao districts."[51] Probably she is a mulatto, or a woman of Miao blood who is culturally Han and has had her genealogy redone. (Shen's emphasis on her hygienic standards may be a considered refutation of the Han prejudice against Miao as being dirty.) Like Sansan, and many of Shen's widows (the object of Ajin's love, or the innkeeper woman of "The Inn"),[52] Maodi's ma is of the petty propertied "class" among the peasants. Still, she is "country folk," leading a hard life and enjoying its rewards as nature allows—spiritual and psychosocial, not material ones.

These women know how to make sour dishes from *jiaotou* [a tuber, like a turnip], fermented bean curd, and rice wine, and how to knead *baba* biscuits. Besides this, they can make a great many other dishes that are both sanitary and tasty. There is an inborn habit of cleanliness about them that is most appealing. They're not too tall, and very thin. The face retains a healthy red color from being burned by the clean air and unsparing sunlight. At 45 years of age, the hair is as a rule partly greyed. Now the clothing: according to the customs of the small landowners' wives of the countryside in the western parts of Hunan, one always wears a colored checkered turban, regardless of the season. Clothes are made from cotton in winter, and from the mountain grass-cloth nettle or from ramie in the summer. The color is blue in winter and white in summer. The clothes are coarse but sturdy. Usually the sleeves are rolled up above the elbows. The wrists, strong enough to turn a mill, being thus exposed to the elements, turn the same color as the face. Yes, this old marm had been born with a pair of hands for working, and besides those hands, she had a pair of big feet for running up and down the mountains, which were very much to be esteemed, too!

The rewards:

Although she was nearing middle age, she had none of the maladies of middle-aged women of the city, neither illness nor ache. Whenever she felt a little indisposed, she would sip some ginger broth with ground pepper and sugar. After drinking it down hot and sleeping a while, she would be completely well. Her waist was hard and firm, from carrying water from the well daily. She spoke in somewhat of a rush, but this wasn't inappropriate to the dignity of a head of a household.... Health, stamina, frugality at home and generosity toward outsiders: you could see them all in her. She was good at conversation, too.[53]

Nature is of course important to the country way of life, but it bears a different face to Shen Congwen the artist, and yet a third to the author as moralist. To begin with, his folk do not live shut in behind walls, or crowded among one another. This is a blessing that boatmen, even prostitutes (spiritually purified by the waters of the Yuan River by which their kind live, following the paths of the merchants), share with the peasants. Housing is a curious blank spot in Shen's otherwise visually rich and ethnographically detailed accounts of rural life. He shows neither the squalor of thatched-roof hovels nor visions of peasant abodes rising up organically from the earth, the provider of building material. Riverside dwellings, which do rise up from the water, on stilts, are his only structures of note. Perhaps Shen found peasant houses unexemplary; perhaps he deliberately neglected the indoor life. Among his fondest memories from his days of soldiering were those of sleeping under the stars while on the march, or on board a boat.[54]

The great outdoors, all the greater at the frontier, "socializes" the country folk, sometimes in lieu of society. Cuicui ("Blue-jade green"), the pubescent heroine of *The Frontier City*, is introduced as having nearly Rousseauean virtues, though Shen's prose locates her amid nature using the appositional logic of a Classical Chinese poem. "Her skin was very dark, from growing up under the wind and the sun; so were her eyes clear as crystal, from the verdant mountains and turquoise waters they beheld. Reared and educated by nature, she was innocent and vivacious, in every way like a little creature of the forest. Gentle as a mountain deer, she had never known cruelty, nor felt anxiety, or anger. Should a stranger on the ferry take an interest in her, she would stare back at him with those brilliant eyes, as if to turn tail at any moment and flee deep into the mountains. But once she knew he meant her no harm, she would calmly resume her play by the shore."[55]

Yet even *The Frontier City* does not develop the idea of an ideal "state of nature." It is more the isolation of youth than of nature that has kept Cuicui from knowing distress and melancholy. As she matures, the more complicated emotions begin to unfold. She becomes wary of her sexual feelings, and sensible of death. The borderlands people are no strangers to human misunderstandings and tragic feuding, which intrude even on this deliberately idyllic work. Living amid the elements promises not happiness or a Taoist "emptying of the mind," only freedom from the urban nervous pathologies of Shen Congwen's young man personae—insomnia, paranoia, and morbid unfulfillable sexual preoccupation.

Enjoying mental health and dignity as their birthright, Shen Congwen's country folk do not commune with nature, or need it to heal them; their souls are not distraught in the romantic manner of the city person. Nature does give life, and rest, as well as that play of the senses that city folk lack, with the result that their psychic development leads in "unhealthy" directions. Above all nature creates a positive, vigorous resiliency in the people who adapt to it. Cuicui is typical of Shen Congwen's heroines: dark, like Yaoyao (of *Long River*), Sansan, and, in real life, Zhang Zhaohe, Shen's bride. Their beauty runs counter to the Chinese ideal. So does that of the ethnically tinged men Shen presents as his model West Hunanese soldier males. They are short-limbed, spry, monkey-like fellows who resemble Congwen's cousin Lenghan (and He Long, in his memory), men well suited for mountain warfare.[56]

Adaptation draws on an inborn vitality inherent in life, which develops through struggle with exterior, often natural, forces. Harmony with nature is not easy. It requires discipline, as human relations require "love." Shen often speaks of country folk challenging the elements, like boatmen going against the Yuan River rapids. Even the rivertown folk of *The Frontier City* have many opportunities for heroics, as during floods, when they risk all to save the lives and property of others. Premonitions of death fill the country people's dreams, as ruination in the rapids fills the songs of the boatmen. It is during a flood that Cuicui's grandfather, her guardian, quietly passes away. The folk view of nature is not itself Darwinist, like Shen's, but it is still practical. Nature has rules unto itself and is not of this world, but it is practical, too. It consists of the spirits of "winds and waters." They can be propitiated, but not understood.

It is thus Shen Congwen the author, not his characters, who concentrates nature into one abstract and powerful force. But he does not further rarify the natural world, like a Western arcadian, into a virginal existence subject to rape by mankind, not even when he critiques the advance of industrialism in the countryside. Of course permanent scarring of the land by strip mines, railroads, and rows of telephone poles lay decades in the future. Nor was West Hunan a natural wilderness. Man had been deforesting and burning off even the mountain "wilds" for centuries, always abandoning them to return to scrub. However, Shen's regional pride, nostalgia, and desire to make his art uplifting did lead him to fructify nature. He tells of natural disasters but seldom depicts them. Wanting to reveal the variety of nature, particularly the local species of West Hunan, he lapses into listing them, and so, perhaps unintentionally, portrays nature as bountiful. "Many fruits and melons grew wild in the mountains, and it was not unusual to find chestnuts and hazelnuts up there. In the third month, [Guisheng] picked big strawberries for [his friend, the shopkeeper's daughter]. He sent her ground-growing loquats in the sixth month, and in the fall there was the famous local specialty, the August melon. It looked like a dried sea slug, bleached white as jade, or snow."[57] Nature is friendly in this story. Even tiny shrimp are anthropomorphized. The epitome of Shen Congwen's humanistic nostalgia is his regret for the passing, not of wilderness, but of old towns, like the river port of Pushi. Shen lends regional interest to his works by citing authentic place names, but he also seems to be trying to give these places extended life.[58]

Shen's works of the 1930's tend further to blur the distinctions between man and nature, creating plotless, still landscapes of vivid sensory impressions—minutiae that conjure up an atmosphere of rural comfort and familiarity. He increasingly writes in a folksy tone, stopping to repeat peasant aphorisms and local jokes connected with the names of things. On the other hand, having acquired traditional literary and artistic sensibilities, and a pantheistic view of life, he humanizes nature itself, as aesthetic experience (though always maintaining in theory that art can never capture the beauty of nature). *Man*, sometimes, is rendered magically, or divinely, through the mystery of his interior life. If Shen Congwen the moralist loves the mountain folk best, as artist he prefers picturesque landscapes by the waters, where nature—meaning both man and the land, with animals playing an important role, too—forms an ordered, cultivated pattern. In the description below, the eye beholds beauties that are really the comforts of a traveler. Our voyager is of classical, educated sensibilities. What he sees, however, are commonplaces of life, related in simple language, including a folk expression.

The White River is the famous You Shui of history. After reaching Yuanling, where it joins the River Yuan, its water grows turbid, being "spring water far from its mountain source." But if you trace the stream backward, you can see to the very bottom of its pools 30, 50, or however many feet deep, so clear is the water. In sunlight, even the tiny white pebbles and marble cornelian gems on the river bottom can be seen distinctly. The fish dart back and forth, as if floating in air. Tall mountains abound on either bank as you go, covered with delicate, thin bamboos from which paper can be made. They are of a deep verdure all year round, compelling the traveler to fix his gaze on them. The dwellings near the stream are set amid peach and apricot trees, so that in spring, wherever you see peach blossoms, you know there are people, and wherever there are people, a place to stop and have a drink. In summer, the dazzling embroidered purple tunics and trousers of the womenfolk hung up to dry in the sunlight can serve as ensigns marking the whereabouts of man. In the autumn and winter, the eye finds pleasure in the cottages, whether perched on the cliffs or down at the water level. They have yellow mud walls and pitch-black roof tiles; their placement is in a proper order for all time, and so completely in harmony with the surroundings that it fills the heart with delight. A traveler with any feeling at all for poetry or painting can curl up in the bottom of his little boat for the whole of the 30 days' voyage upstream, without ever becoming bored, for there are miracles to be discovered at every turn. Captivating and endearing, the boldness and craftsmanship of nature are with you at every stage, every moment of the journey.[59]

 Shen's country folk do not idealize nature, however. With the exception of attachments between the sexes, which Shen says can drive even prostitutes to suicide, and moments of transcendental frenzy, as during the Dragon Boat Festival, they see the world with practical, "anti-romantic" eyes. When Huiming and other soldier characters (like those of "Dark Night") think of death, it is of the bodies being reduced to elements by maggots. "Ox" features a peasant comically named "Uncle Big Ox," like his draft animal, worrying over the beast like a person, after he in a moment of anger beats it too hard, dealing a permanent wound to a rear hoof. Yet he fights off sentimentality, so that the ox will not be so "spoiled" as to feel the world owes it a living. And in "Knowledge," a city boy steeped in Nietzsche is "enlightened" when peasants teach him the unimportance of death, since it is beyond human control, even that of a "superman," evidently.[60]

The author does, however, let his country folk join him in humanizing, if not romanticizing, nature. They mark the passing of calendrical time not just by the passing of the seasons and the crops, but by annual folk festivals: human commemorations, or reinterpretations, of the import of the seasons. Thus to adolescent heroines like Cuicui, Sansan, and Xiaoxiao, autumn is the season not just of harvest, but of marriages. Cuicui's emotional maturation is related year by year, against the clock of Dragon Boat Festivals. The festival evokes associations of Chu regionalism, the striving of men against the elements and each other (in the boat races), and the riverine, watery symbolism that Shen bends toward the purposes of delineating Cuicui's erotic awakening instead of the historical associations of Qu Yuan. (He has already set the scene by associating the annual festivals with Southwestern lovemaking festivities for young people.) Despite the regional exoticism of both the natural and human worlds he depicts, simply by humanizing nature Shen has rendered his work comfortably "Chinese" rather than Western.

The World of the Plain Country Folk

What Shen Congwen's country folk have that is uniquely theirs (and to which young girls like Cuicui and Sansan are privy, despite, or rather especially because of, their youth) is a simpler understanding of things. From a sophisticated urban viewpoint, their grasp of the world is partial, their understanding of newborn social forces especially incomplete. When country folk misinterpret city folk's drift, they can get backed up into rural "stubbornness." Yet the folk's "simpler" view of the world recasts everyday phenomena in different, sometimes creative, forms—into new, poetic associations of images to which urban people might remain blind. This is what makes Shen Congwen's regional universe "pastoral." At the same time, Shen argues two social points on behalf of his country folk: they are very vulnerable in the modern world, yet they have sensitivities and sensibilities of their own that are overlooked by the world of commercial value. From here, Shen goes beyond pastoralism to structural irony. The strange incapacities and unorthodox insights of his innocent country folk in the modern world cast a bittersweet perspective on modern change—and on human nature, too.

Sansan, for instance, cannot comprehend the function of a nurse who waits on the convalescing city stranger who comes into her world. She reasons that the young lady must be a concubine, something just as mysterious to one her age. The man's incapacitation itself remains vague to her (and to us) because his decadent life-style is so foreign to her; but this, too, creates a new perspective on what is usual and what is strange. Sansan's idea of what a city must be is particularly interesting. She imagines a larger version of the strongholds of the local ruling class, foremost a giant, sturdy *wall*, enclosing many fine houses, with their idle lords and servants, carts and horses, foreigners, and great yamens full of judges.[61]

Being uneducated, Sansan's people must draw much of their happiness from the routine of their daily lives.[62] Shen Congwen takes every opportunity to depict it as rich in lore and techniques—colorful, even musical. Operas are not often performed in rural areas (the city, to Sansan, is "where operas are performed day and night"), but that makes them all the more memorable to the folk, who sing the tunes and lyrics as they do army and wedding songs. When resting from work, they play homemade flutes and practice handicrafts such as weaving animals out of reeds. Shen's adolescent heroines, between dreams, build miniature dams and pick flowers. His country folk who are spiritually alone, like Huiming the soldier and Guisheng the bare-stick (unmarried) hired laborer, are likely to be portrayed as unskilled and indeed rather "poor and blank." But when Shen depicts the plain folk in their communities, especially in family situations, their world comes alive.

"Fishing" recreates a scene of a whole community in the Sino-Tujia-Miao borderlands, a *zhai*, going down to the river on a summer's night: men, women, and children, bearing knives, baskets, and crackling torches. At the signal of drums from the mountainside temple of Tian Wang (the Heavenly King; a god now held in special reverence by the Miao, possibly of Tujia origins), the folk, from not one but two feuding clans in their separate *zhai* on opposite sides of the river, cooperate in spreading square netting across the river. Shen turns to the story of twin brothers from the lesser clan, whose members, "because of the competition for survival," are relatively hardy, "like tigers and wildcats." Awaiting a signal shot a mile upstream, they prepare to overturn a boatload of lime, knotgrass (polygonum), and wood resins. These make a poison to stun the fish and send them floating on the surface toward the nets. The boys are good swimmers and fighters, familiar as only country folk can be with the sounds of the wild animals in the mountains. They can tell time by the stars and from the burning of incense. This equips them to play their role in the drama at the time required.[63]

Although he insists that the hard labor of country life is what makes country people strong, Shen Congwen seldom chooses rural toil and sweat as a literary subject (the way he does, for instance, the back-breaking work of boatmen and trackers). Toil presents the animal brutishness of peasants instead of their internal capabilities. And, like hunger, the subject is incompatible with Shen's desire to provide hope. By the 1930's, he in fact had his ideological back up against proletarian writers who extolled the "sanctity of labor."[64] Probably he found the concept hypocritical, coming as it did from foreign-educated intellectuals, and a kind of empty idealization itself, even a rationalization of drudgery as the common people's "lot." Moreover, the slogan, meant to celebrate industrial labor, offered no solutions for the signal diminution, in the eyes of modern people, of the dignity of farm labor.

Hence the rural labor that enters Shen's works relies on quick hands more than strong arms (a Southerner's asset): we see handicrafts; women washing laundry by the riverside; men neatly piling wood and hanging tobacco out to cure, or twisting twine into rope; young people gathering bracken out on the hillsides; farmhands fashioning straw sandals; and prostitutes embroidering shoes with phoenixes on them. This labor evokes a small-town atmosphere simply because the work is comfortingly routinized, but we also see these tasks performed out-of-doors. All but the shoe and rope manufacture are explicitly riverside, mountainside, or forest work. Human labor is virtually incorporated into nature, in the telltale fires of spring that appear in Shen's landscapes, indicating the burning off of mountain brush. Such picturesque scenes freeze the country folk and their routines in time, as if in a painting. But there is a deliberately sociological element to it as well. Particularly in Shen's mature works of the 1930's, country labor enters the already humanized landscapes in bird's-eye-view panoramas of small-town and village scenes that serve as preamble to the action later to unfold. As he moves from street to street, from one class of people to another, Shen generalizes about the activities by which each group makes its living, sometimes even quantifying their income. The vignettes are fascinating for readers pursuing sociological interests, although close to becoming set pieces not much related to the story.

Though country folk take pleasure and pride in their daily routines, Shen Congwen observes in "Sansan," "they also take pleasure in their dreams (*huanxiang*)."[65] His adolescent heroines—like Cuicui, who searches for shapes in the clouds—live within their dreams and fantasies. These contain inchoate mixings of their hopes and fears, like Cuicui's previsions of being bitten by a fish (losing her sexual innocence), and of her grandfather's death. The dreams in turn present Shen's vision of the country folk's own interior world, one closer to the basics of elemental vitality, and having (in the 1930's works, like *The Frontier City*) subliminal Freudian meaning. Not fully conscious of their own feelings, and unable to put outsiders' social behavior into recognizable categories, country folk analyze these things into their elements, imposing new kinds of meaning on them. Sansan remembers her deceased father, the miller, as a man always covered in white dust, the ashen-complected stranger as one with a camellia-colored face, his nurse as the one in the white cap—the color white bearing, evidently, her own premonitions of death, which bear comparison to Cuicui's.

The bucolic metaphors of peasant language are themselves a point of interest and authenticity in the folksier dialogue of Shen Congwen's later 1930's stories, though that dialogue seems at times self-consciously rustic (unlike that in the 1920's dialect pieces). These passages are thus something of a forerunner of peasant speech in Mao-era socialist-realist novels. Shen does at least give an impression of country folk thinking and speaking in their own metaphors, like the Miao. In *The Frontier City*, courtship by singing contest is "the rook's move," arranged marriage "the knight's move."[66] Country folk will often make their point with a rhyming aphorism, like Uncle Duck Feathers in "Guisheng": "Fry up chives or fry up beef; the one or t'other, by your lief. It's not painted ladies what get money off our Fifth Master [unlike you folks' Fourth Master], it's those painted mah-jongg tiles!"[67] Later, a shopkeeper parries Guisheng's disbelief that anyone would marry a mere laborer, and quietly warns him not to be too tardy in going about wooing his daughter:

"Who would [ordinarily] believe that the Heavenly Dog could eat the moon [the folk explanation for an eclipse]? You might not believe it, but when the time comes, and the Heavenly Dog really does eat the moon, you won't find a doubter anywhere. I'm telling you, up in the mountains, when a bamboo sparrow wants a mate, he has to sing his own song. You keep an eye out![68]

Guisheng finally gets the message, just a little too late. He conceptualizes it a little more crudely: "*baba* biscuits have to be shaped while the rice is still hot. You can't put it off till too late."[69] Later he inadvertently speaks an insightful truth; a double-meaning in his words is discovered by another character who "misunderstands" him, a favorite device of Shen's. Guisheng has just discovered that Fifth Master has taken the shopkeeper's daughter, Guisheng's favorite, as a concubine during Guisheng's absence. Guisheng was just readying his gifts to propose to her. "Guisheng's foot slipped a little as he trod on a melon rind. He cursed himself under his breath, 'The devil with me. [I] didn't recognize a good thing when it was right here.' Uncle Duck Feathers, thinking Guisheng was cursing Proprietor Du's daughter, said, 'Actually good *things* [the master's bride price] is what they do recognize, rather than good *people*."[70]

Shen has of course created comic rural characters, like Uncle Big Ox, Huiming, and "Uncle" [West Hunanese dialect: "Manman"] in *Long River*. Country folk's "simpler" view of things leads to rustic malapropisms and unintended synecdoches ("big boxes that take you where you want to go"—automobiles),[71] but then, they enjoy a good joke themselves. And just as Sansan is an unconscious poet, the folk of *Long River* are unwitting prophets of the fate of great policies of state. They "misunderstand" the New Life movement, making it much too concrete, until it looms up as a great engine for robbing them of all their life dreams. Not so much intuition as experience with city folk's politics, and ability to see through the refined slogans to the essentials, leads them to this prescient insight.[72]

The country folk's unique handicrafts, too, are partly to be valued because they enrich their makers' dreams. They are more proof that the humble people are neither blind to the beauty around them nor unable to create their own. Yet handicrafts do serve life. They are not ends of life in themselves, as for anti-industrialists like William Morris. Nor does Shen give a Ruskin-style rationale for handicrafts (however much he may have been the Englishman's fellow-spirit in appreciating the shapes of clouds); for Shen Congwen, the little Fenghuang boy who was enthralled by every manufacturing technique and device in West Hunan, iron foundries most of all, could never have found ugliness in machine production as such. Shen the idealist sees Beauty everywhere. This was to undermine his naturalistic attempts to portray urban slums, his negative mirror image of country life. In "Mud" and "Rot," he focuses on slime, garbage, and human excrement. Yet, unable to forsake his poetic descriptive style, he gives even these things an eerie beauty, like the copper-toned scum on Wen Yiduo's "Stagnant Water." Likewise, from showing a dehumanized, scabby little boy picking out his dinner from a refuse pile, his humanism drives him to show the little boy finding his own amusements. In *Long River*, Shen does criticize the replacement of rural industry by city manufacture, but he faults the machines for their *economic* impact on the countryside, for good measure adding to them the stigma of being instruments of "bureaucratic capitalism" (but not, characteristically for Shen though not his colleagues, symbols of a foreign, imperialistic threat to China).[73]

Shen's country people are too conservative for many of their dreams to be about acquiring learning, above all for women. The older characters in "Xiaoxiao," and the heroine of "Sansan" too, scoff at "girl students" and literate women like the nurse in the latter story. But Xiaoxiao herself begins to entertain visions of becoming just such a student, to escape her sorry predicament. Huiming, the quintessential "idiot" countryman, has ideals, too. He serves as a mere cook-boy in the army and is the butt of others' jokes, appearing the more foolish because he has an incongruously good physiognomy and stature, sufficient for a general. Yet he has patriotic visions of fighting imperialism and opening virgin frontier territories. That these dreams were implanted in his mind by a Hunanese patriot-warlord, Cai E, years ago, merely testifies to the stubborn and selfless tenacity of his idealism. (In the 1920's, Feng Yuxiang and Yan Xishan promoted similar colonization schemes for the Northwest.) Huiming also has an innate respect for living things, like his chicks.[74]

Ultimately Shen Congwen is less concerned about the disappearance of the country people's way of life, even their handicrafts and harmony with the land, than about the decline of the uncalculating morality and spontaneous interpersonal relationships he associates with their simpler life, "that element of honesty, big-hearted genuineness, simple sincerity, and plain uprightness"—"the primitive personality," as he says in reference to assimilated Miao boatmen—which "because they live in the mountains, they retain ... a little more than city people."[75] Shen's country people do not lie, or even dissemble. They like good-natured joshing, but do not play tricks, especially on strangers—so far removed are they from urban practice. This is clear from their customs about exchanging the fruits of nature. They will not seek the main chance; still less would they seek a *small* advantage, particularly in selling that which is not scarce, thanks to the bounty of nature. *Long River* symbolizes this in the locals' refusal to take money for tangerines during the season when they rot from oversupply. Nor do country folk like to take charity. When Guisheng receives gifts from his landlord, he insists on returning gifts of his own. The folk hardly know how to deal with people of commercial bent, like the officers from Changsha. These outsiders know ways of exploiting even the country people's bumper harvests, to the point of actual injury to the growers.[76]

This idealizes the country folk, though there is a kernel of truth here. Observers of the Miao, in particular, have commented on their openness, even gullibility, and un-Confucian willingness to ruin their families to provide hospitality for non-relatives.[77] However, Shen Congwen does explore poor-peasant materialism in "Ox" and "Guisheng." His peasants can count. They worry over how the market conditions will affect their income. They also like to dream about being rich, though they partake little of the acquisitive mentality of the bourgeoisie. One non-bourgeois attitude is even held in common with the rural upper class: if one makes a fortune, it is the result of the workings of fate (unlike subsistence, which comes to him who works). Big money is easy come, easy go, and it may have nothing to do with one's social station. The lower-class people of "Guisheng" gather in the masters' kitchen to marvel, and cluck, at the masters' profligacy at gambling and purchase of the service of big-city prostitutes. They can scarcely imagine such waste. But since the loss of money is in their final analysis just as fated as life and death, they do not in the end blame the upper class. When, in one comic episode, a master brings on his mother's death by driving her to distraction with his gambling losses, he parts with another vast part of his fortune, consigning it all to ashes so that his mother's ghost may have spirit money to spend and spirit servants to wait on her in the next life. This is all the more proof that the whole scenario was fated, and that the master has played his proper role, by the plain folk's lights. It is *hoarding* that they find repugnant and inexplicable: "A spotted-leg dog's not a white-faced cat. Each has its own temper. When a fortune comes to yuh, yuh spend it, jingly jangly jing, how can yuh not? Your fortune's in your fate. If your fate tells the money to come, even a door plank won't block it. If your fate tells that money to go, you can't keep it tied up, not with a rope, not even with a chain!"[78]

Of course the humble people's materialism otherwise is rather different from the upper class's. Much of their realistic calculating, like that by Uncle Big Ox, who "hard-heartedly" begins thinking of butchering his faithful plow animal, is brought on by fear of losing their slender margin of subsistence. If Uncle Big Ox dreams of striking it rich, it is but a wonderful abstraction, not a calculation serving acquisitiveness. It boggles his mind just to try imagining the biggest numbers he can think of.

"Hit it a hundred times? Sure, my ox would still work for me even if I hit it a hundred blows."
"Even a thousand? Yeah, it could stand it, I bet you still couldn't hurt that ox of yours."
"A thousand blows? Why, sure ... "
"Even two thousand blows, and more than that!"
"Two thousand blows, sure ... "
At this point the two men laughed. They could think up enormous numbers in this idle exchange, and almost picture themselves talking about "pieces of silver," or "bushels of wheat."[79]

Constancy is another virtue of the country folk: they are loyal and dependable. Shen symbolizes the routine, constant nature of their lives by giving them occupations like ferrying and driving mill wheels. It is the familiarity of life they enjoy, the comforts of the known challenge, the intensity of the moment, of life itself. Dependability shades into obsession: stubbornness and single-mindedness, like Ajin's pursuit of his widow, undone by another obsession, gambling. More typically, the country folk avoid gambling big stakes, lest they follow in the path of Fifth Master in "Guisheng"—not that they have much to gamble in the first place.

The folk do become fully absorbed in their festivals, as in all other aspects of life they pursue. This inimitable state of rapture brings them close to God, but religious devotion as such does not dictate their lives (except perhaps in *Fengzi*, whose setting is the Miao pale). City folk see country people as "children," but not as having child-like "faith" like the European peasant of literature. Instead, country folk are distinguished by a more inchoate religious sense, that all life is drama—acted out before the gods, perhaps, but anyway performed for its visual effect in a higher dimension. Thus when depicting formal folk "religion," Shen makes it seem routine, a keeping of faith with custom as much as with the gods, an occasion, too, for families and communities to act as one.

The family had no particular religious faith, but come the birthday of the Goddess of Mercy, the God of Wealth, the Bodhisattva of Healing, or any other god or Buddha known from legend, they followed the local custom, offering incense and avoiding meat, and contributing to those in charge of the association for the observance. They quite piously observed all the holidays and taboos connected with village society and respectfully played their part. They went out traveling in the first month of the New Year, but only after consulting the almanac to find an auspicious day on which to set out. During the Time of the Excited Insects, they would eat sweet cakes. At the Time of Eating Food Cold and the Qingming Festival right afterward, they would go up to their ancestors' graves, gathering there for a picnic of boiled Hunan preserved pork. On the Dragon Boat Festival they wrapped glutinous rice dumplings and hung seasonal artemisia on the door. At noon on the Double Fifth, they put the five kinds of creepy-crawlers and eight treasures into a jar to fight to the death, producing a medicine to go with the Six-One fever-reducer, as gifts to be given during the midsummer heat. When the whole family had drunk [the traditional] wine with realgar in it [to provide a year's protection from poisonous snakes and insects], they changed into new clothes for the occasion and went up to Lüjiaping to see the dragon boat race and cheer the crew from their own village. When it was time to eat the Seasonal Food of the Sixth Month, they ate carp, eggplant, corn, and rice fresh from the fields. At harvest time, they brewed a crock of glutinous rice wine for their long-term laborers, to give them cool, liquid refreshment to ladle out when they were resting from their work. On the festival of the ides of the seventh month, the Ghost Festival, they would burn spirit money for ancestors and the deceased, for relatives of every degree of closeness. Womenfolk would be busy with the preparations for some time, everybody having fun wrapping the packets of riches for the ghosts, folding tinfoil into mock ingots of gold and silver and so forth. They waited till dusk before carrying them to the riverside to be sent up in flames. They made lotus flower lanterns, too, and set them afloat in the river, to light the lost souls' way to the Western Paradise. When it came time to honor the moon in the eighth month, someone was sent to town to buy moon cakes and get the other festival things. The whole family would gather around to enjoy the full moon. On the Mountain-Climbing Festival of the ninth month, there'd be a picnic of duck braised in purple-sprout ginger. Up there in the clear, crisp autumn air, it was a world all its own. At the Time of Winter Hibernation, they sprinkled lime in an arc around the doorsill, to kill the hundred insects. On the Eighth-day Year-end Festival, they made holiday fruit congee, and festival beans.... By keeping all the customs and doing everything by the almanac, without being sloppy about it, the whole family felt the happiness of release and the mood of solemnity that went with the occasion.[80]

The recounting is itself solemn, less interesting (artistically, if not sociologically) than the sort of list the author was wont to give in the 1920's. Shen wrote more spontaneously and more as a regionalist in his early pieces, endowing his festivities with all the expectations of youth:

What child doesn't look forward to New Year's? Some people say that a lot of China's happy festival times are just for children. True enough! I still think there're a lot of festivals that little children can't appreciate yet, but New Year's is one that any tot will admit is exciting! At Duanwu, you can drink realgar wine and watch the dragon boats; at Mid-Autumn you can eat moon cakes; at Qingming you can go up into the mountains and play; at weddings, you can see lots and lots of dowry things, all draped in red and green, and the embouchures of the *suona* players when they swell up like little balloons, and you can eat Four Happiness Balls; at the Nuo rites you can see Old Master Guangxing put on his red religious robes and turn somersaults, and you can steal firecrackers to set off yourself—but when you come down to it, New Year's is the most exciting, and lasts the longest.[81]

Like tribal folk, country folk take their entertainment, too, in the form of communal celebrations, as detailed in "Village Opera," the final chapter of *Long River*. Here one finds not so much a hint of a *Volksgeist*, not even one emerging from folk handicrafts and collective dreams (the operas come to town through outsiders, itinerant troupes), as a sense of communal mores and self-protection. The folk's community spirit is an adjunct to their willingness to care for one another as individuals. They chip in to repair flood damage, rebuild the pagoda behind Cuicui's home, and so forth.

Shen Congwen's caution in regard to religion reflects his interest not in reviving religion, but in finding new forms of it, or substitutes, for modern man. "Guisheng," in fact, is an ironic extended parable about the evils of superstition. The laborer fatally delays proposing to the proprietor's daughter he so loves only because her horoscope says that she will bring misfortune to her husband. Superstition, moreover, is a foolish evil held in common with the rural upper class, one that precipitates Guisheng's loss from above as well as below. Regardless of her sign, the proprietor's daughter is a virgin—her first blood is just what Fifth Master needs, he believes, to "wash away" his bad luck at gambling. So he takes Guisheng's love away from him. Yet, by this same folk "science," Guisheng was already in the clear, for his birth animal is the tiger, a cat twice over, more than a match for the rat that is the young girl's horoscope animal. He must not even be present at Fifth Master's marriage, lest he jinx it by terrifying the "rat." As a final irony, Uncle Duck Feathers suggests that Guisheng's tardiness, too, must have been declared by fate. Such a view might have reconciled Guisheng to accepting his misfortune. Instead, he leaves the wedding in anger. At the end of the story, the celebrants witness fires that have broken out at the country store, and at Guisheng's shack. We do not know if there are any survivors, but we do see the jinxed young woman blamed for the calamity instead of Guisheng.

However, this superstitious gullibility is less prominent among Shen's country folk than thoroughgoing skepticism—about men, especially city folk, and even the gods. The superstitious propitiations in the list from *Long River* themselves suggest a cautious, conscientious piety, based on respect for fate, precedent, and authority—but always authority as a distant, stabilizing, ultimately unapproachable force, not an immanent and earth-moving power. As the *Autobiography* puts it, "The local authorities are of several types: highest are the gods, then the officials, and then the village heads and the workers of magic who serve the gods. Everyone keeps himself in check and believes in the gods, and likewise respects the laws and loves the officials."[82] The country folk listen to their social and celestial "betters," treating them with an openness that seems to betray naïveté, while inwardly remaining skeptical in temperament. Perhaps it is because of this, and the fact that gods are even more distant and unpredictable than officials, that country folk feel at liberty to play jokes on spirits.

Country people are wary enough of mortals to want to inquire into their background, and this, too, is reflected in Shen's later works. We have seen how the author's passion for social detail (possibly reinforced by the example of the classic vernacular novels he was teaching about in class) could lead him into gazetteer-like list-making, as of local products, festivals, funeral customs, and even the genres of songs the Yuan River prostitutes have learned (a map of the social origins of their customers). In stories of the 1930's, Shen would recite his characters' life histories as he introduced them into his text. Thus he added a time dimension to his social landscapes—typical scenarios of gentry sons and daughters moving out of the community, choosing their own mates, becoming revolutionaries, and finally returning home to a formidable generation gap, if not execution by uncomprehending local authorities. For all the pedagogical overtones, these life histories communicate concern for people's origins in a folkish sort of way. How and when did Proprietor Wang come to these parts? How did he come by his money? Did he begin as one of us, or did he inherit his wealth in the city? And how has urban living changed Young Mistress Zhang's hairstyle and the way she treats Venerable Lady Zhang? Shen once wrote that country people, unlike city folk, do not pry into other people's personal affairs, but this may well have been the inverse of his personal complaint against Shanghai rumor-mongers. In *Fengzi*'s Sino-Miao realm somewhere west of Fenghuang, Shen has a local character tell a city stranger that locals by custom let travelers from afar ask quite intimate questions of them. Country folk's lives are open books.[83]

Shen seldom has his free-spirited country people create their own forms of family oppression. "Xiaoxiao" is one of the few stories featuring patriarchal control. Most of Shen's country folk live in a nuclear family. Relations in it are based on love and mutual caring, seldom authority; the family is often disrupted by death, so each member is precious. Yet, fathers encourage their sons to go out into the wilds and face the rapids, to make men of themselves. They grant their young folk independence, leaving their survival up to fate. Rarely do they arrange marriages. In *The Frontier City*, courtship by singing match is the favored custom, employment of go-betweens the coward's way out.

The sociability of Shen's country folk as such may appear to be debatable. Guisheng and Huiming, as well as Cuicui and Sansan, have undeveloped social skills. Shen enjoys probing generational misunderstandings and communications gaps, even impasses, as between Cuicui and her granddad. *The Frontier City* as a whole explores the isolation of human souls. But in Shen's fuller social landscapes, country folk enjoy gathering to exchange gossip at designated spots, like Maple Tree Hollow along the highway and the periodic markets so vividly described in *Long River*, or the country store and Fifth Master's kitchen in "Guisheng." They enjoy tall tales and jokes. Like Maodi's ma, most are good at conversation.

In his very exploration of the metaphysical isolation of human souls, Shen Congwen points up the ways in which his country folk, especially in a family setting, are able to communicate their moods and feelings without much recourse to speech. Their intuition, psychological sensitivity to gestures and offhand remarks, and imaginative ability to enter each other's minds, are sufficient. Shen holds that silence "nourishes" the country folk's dreams. In the last chapter we examined the "foolish" silence and "idiot's" smile as spiritual states of rapture, and Hua-ling Nieh has gone so far as to see these as signs that the country people experience Existentialist quandaries.[84] Huiming and Guisheng are close to being simpletons; they are so recognized by their friends. Cuicui and Sansan, of course, are immature, just on the brink of their young womanhood.

Shen Congwen indeed finds silence (which he happened also to be praising in his literary commentary, meaning refusal to join in literary polemics) to be a state of blessedness, representative of innocence. He puts it rather explicitly in "Ox." Uncle Big Ox is able sincerely to make amends to the one he has injured only because he does not speak: too often speech is used for lies and excuses. He communicates his concern by pushing the plow a little harder from behind. That the one whom he has hurt is a dumb animal incapable of understanding speech is beside the point, for in Shen's parable the ox is fully anthropomorphized.[85]

Finally, the dumbness of the rustic before the city person can be understood partly as a social response, indicative of a social and cultural gap and even a relative power relationship. It is the humble folk's way of avoiding further discomfiting communication with their betters, who because of their different life cannot understand a country person's feelings. Only a loquacious city person would ask a country fellow to verbalize an inexpressible feeling. To a beancurd peddler, why did he exhume his dead lover? To Sansan and her mother, why have they not come to visit the great lord in his "castle"? Unable to avail themselves of urban circumlocutions and insincerity, they can only "keep silent, and, like all country folk faced with such a question, return a smile."[86] Among themselves the country folk are not so impassive. Indeed, they marvel at the reserve of "modern" young ladies, who "do not curse or cry when they've been wronged."[87] When the country folk go to market, too, "transacting business requires a lot of shouting and cursing, and swearing oaths before the gods. After the sale is made, the parties go to a food stand nearby to drink up and celebrate the deal, so it's exciting as well as very noisy."[88]

In the previous chapter we spoke of sex as another symbol of folk vigor. Sex is rendered mysterious and wonderful in Shen's tales about adolescent country girls, down-to-earth and essential to vitality in tales about rougher folk like the title hero of "Baizi," a boatman. Society does not segregate the sexes in Shen's fiction. Poor farmhands have the opportunity, in "Xiaoxiao" and "After Rain," to seduce young farm girls. In "Baizi," "The Husband," and *The Frontier City*, Shen Congwen is intent on pointing out that even the sale of sex (an economic necessity to those in the trade) does not inhibit "country folk" from forming long-term attachments to lovers. Prostitutes enjoy both the thrill of sex and the true love of fully human relationships with their steady boyfriends, even as they earn their living from the merchants. The title character in "The Husband," too, is subject to jealousy, but not prudery.[89]

"The Lovers" and "Xiaoxiao" present folk who have much more conservative, Confucian attitudes censuring sex outside of marriage. Yet, in the latter story, which points up the unnaturalness of the custom of child brides, punishment comes only with pregnancy, and when the outcome is successful procreation of a male child, any sin can be forgiven. Of course the sex of the child is determined by fate; the story underscores the perilousness of Xiaoxiao's powerless situation, which drives her to escape through becoming a student. Elsewhere, however, in the erotic Ahei/Wuming cycle of stories about frontier mountain folk, adults seem actually to condone extra-marital sexual experimentation, especially among adolescents and widows.

Shen's female adolescent "innocents" are highly sexed, too, with swelling bosoms and so forth. In works like *The Frontier City*, they are allowed some initiative in mating, though this is unusual in ordinary Han society (less so among the Miao). The erotic stories about Ahei indeed highlight the fact that she is older and more experienced than Wuming, her male lover. Yet in "Gathering Bracken," little Wuming is the one insistent on coupling. This adds still more innocence to the act of love. Shen Congwen the urban author, meanwhile, paints sexual intercourse as a natural response to the weather, one in resonance with the warm sun that reappears after a rain, along with new bracken sprouts the rain has created. The young woman takes sexual intercourse more seriously than Wuming, perhaps "too seriously." She is outwardly ambivalent about making love to a "baby" like Wuming. But she finds him immature partly because, after all his tiresome persuading, he seems reluctant to be silent and take what is his![90]

The menfolk, especially the boatmen, are given to crude, sexually explicit language. This was one aspect of Yuan valley life Shen had brushed up against several times. The lower-class people's curses, like their comic nicknames, show their creativity, he tells us. The colorful dialogue seems to prove his point. Too, the cursing, like the plain folk's capacity for fighting, drinking, and lovemaking, lends a heroic (if sometimes a burlesque, mock-heroic) aspect to their lives, as does their bravery in time of crisis. Unlike city folk, they are willing to take a chance, to brave the elements on a dare, or to leave their fortunes entirely up to fate, like Ajin.

What, then, of forbearance? Impassive acceptance by country people of their harsh fate has been counted another form of heroism in Chinese tradition. In the twentieth century, however, this "virtue" came to look like a defect in the Darwinian struggle for national survival, one bespeaking cowardice. Shen Congwen's country characters, as is only realistic, often speak of their lives as subject to abstract "fate," or even Buddhist "retribution" for sins in previous lives (in the round-table discussion about the follies of the rich folk in "Guisheng"). Shen does seem to count belief in fate as a force helping poor folk to survive, though his nonfiction *West Hunan* criticizes a defensive and conservative resignation, an attitude of "self-abandonment," among his fellow locals.[91] In "Huiming," fiction, Shen Congwen redefines the issue, characteristically letting his protagonist appear heroic in two ways. Huiming suffers insults from nearly all his comrades in silence, yet he transcends their complacency by holding to those martial ideals of Cai E's that no one else can any longer understand.

Shen Congwen does not entirely obscure the dark side of the country person. Guisheng, "unable to control (*zhipei*) himself," as the author tells us in an interview,[92] evidently commits arson, and possibly murder and suicide. "The Lovers" shows an evil side to communal rural morality: unforgiving ostracism of outsiders who do not observe the conservative local code. "Ox" projects perhaps the most complex image of the "country person." As his name suggests, Uncle Big Ox lives rather like a brute himself. He is poor, dwelling in a mountain *zhai* and mixing sweet potatoes with his rice—staring ruination in the face when his ox begins to ail. In this story, though, he, the country person, is the "oppressor," for he has injured his own dependent "laborer." He recognizes his guilt in stages, after first fearing to show the "weakness" of conscience before his beast. Is the ox not trying to play him for a fool? But the country *person* wisely keeps his peace, and puts his whole property at risk to save the one he now calls his "friend." He seems to be fighting to redeem more than just an investment. Yet the story ends with the yamen requisitioning all oxen, and Uncle Big Ox wishing he'd killed the beast when he had the chance. In this story, it is not simply the country person's mentality that is laid bare with special realism, but the country person's social position, above all the psychology of the master-servant relationship. Here the *ox* is the plain folk, the plowman a symbol of the class of masters, perhaps even the Kuomintang government, in this piece written in 1929, a high point of class consciousness in Shen's work.[93]

When all is said and done, Shen Congwen cannot be called a "realistic" writer in the same sense as a successful doctrinal realist like Zhang Tianyi, who created convincing portraits of country people as a rather crude and physically dirty breed. Shen acknowledges that *The Frontier City* creates a "pattern of life" that is "beautiful, healthy, natural, and not contrary to human nature," that is, one selectively remembered, though not created from fantasy.[94] He sometimes writes sentimentally and with regional bias, always searching for hope from among a hypothetical "innocent" social group within China. Yet he also writes out of informed social concern for the plight of China's hinterlands. If he idealized the lower classes at all because of guilt feelings about his own elevated status, one looks in vain for evidence of it in autobiographical vignettes that show the author among his social inferiors. Even when little Congwen and his siblings in their childish ignorance take advantage of their social position as "young masters" to poke fun at the nightwatch caller, Ahan, in Shen's story about him (1926), no injury is done, and no retrospective sadness or regret is evoked.[95] Some have missed the realistic dimension of Shen Congwen's writing, since he insisted that China's humble folk survived because they were more than just material, social beings. To ignore the social dimension, however, is to miss much of the moral significance of his work. And, without Shen Congwen's gazetteerist interests in his region, many Chinese would know far less about how West Hunanese country people look, talk, act—and feel.

CHAPTER SIX

Urban Man: Facing a Void Between Youth and Death

To all appearances, the 1930's were years of personal triumph for Shen Congwen. At the height of his creative powers during his Qingdao-Peking period, 1931–34, he began to write the well-made, stylistically dazzling works that are today most highly regarded by critics, anthologists, and the author himself. Yet new kinds of frustrations came to replace the ones Shen had surmounted. He was, for instance, very ill at ease as a professor. His lectures were rambling and largely extemporaneous, delivered with little dramatic emphasis and in a voice not much louder than a whisper. Perhaps it was on purpose that he failed to complete his thoughts, to force his students to deduce the point for themselves in the Confucian dialogue manner. At least his zest for delving into concrete problems, reactively, served him well when he sat down to criticize student writing exercises. But Shen was so shy on his first day of teaching at Wusong that he mumbled a few sentences and dismissed class without even beginning his lecture. Teaching evidently heightened his sense of intellectual inadequacy.[1]

Shen Congwen also became alienated from his main profession, writing. He felt estranged not only from editors and publishers, but from many Chinese authors, and readers, too, though his works remained quite popular. By the war years, he was fundamentally at odds with the spirit of the times—meditating, in rhapsodic essays, about drawing nearer to his God. And he wrote less, above all less fiction. Nevertheless, Shen Congwen's discontents gave his work a fresh dimension. He was able now to analyze urban alienation sympathetically, from within—with more complex language, and more complicated views of man, consciousness, and the universe.

The estrangement between Shen Congwen and the Marxist litterateurs who were fast assuming the right to speak for all Chinese writers was mutual. (The same was true of the minority on the government side, whom Shen dismissed as fascists.) The left charged Shen Congwen with cowardice, bourgeois leanings toward obscurity and art for art's sake, and retreating from social "reality" into his own private world.[2] That was a misunderstanding, possibly deliberate. Shen Congwen's social criticism, like the frequency of his publication more generally, slackened during the later 1930's in part precisely because politics had come to govern literature. He got a foretaste of the double bind that would inhibit writers of his generation in decades to come: criticism of what one wrote, and didn't write. Still, the thirties and forties were not the fifties and sixties. Shen remained an activist, as teacher, critic, and encourager of young writers. Far from retreating, he was diversifying, both intellectually and as a writer. Recent literary excavations indicate that he was more vocal than most imagined. His goal was positive and well defined, though hopeless of achievement: restoring the spirit of the New Culture movement as the force behind literary creation, in place of marketing and politics.

Shen Congwen idealized the New Culture era of the 1920's as a time when all writers were unified. This was nostalgic. Yet Shen shared his more radical colleagues' sense that the minimum goals of the 1920's "literary revolution" had already been won—that it was time to move on to a new "stage." Let literature continue to speak in its new key and move society forward, but let it now push toward more profound and permanent human goals, he argued, through works conveying a deeper understanding of man and his final purpose on earth. This was a large, ordinarily quite controversial bit of ground that Shen and his antagonists had in common. But the majority, armed with historical science predicated on the inevitability of Communist or Nationalist revolution, thought they had already seen the future. The mission of literature was to reflect and hasten the inevitable; imagination had a subordinate role. They made Shen Congwen out to be not a dreamer but an old fogy, like Liang Qichao and his Young China generation—a reformer, left behind by an age of revolution.

Shen did remain a reformer, but he turned to his own social scientists for updated notions about man and his ultimate ends. The wide assortment of theorists he read are not all remembered today. Besides Freud, they tended to be Americans (many associated with Dewey) or Europeans of the Enlightenment tradition, not Russians. Typically they were abstract thinkers who spanned the fields of psychology, literature, religion, epistemology and symbolism, social anthropology, political theory and anthropology, and so forth. Pushed to show off his intellectual sources, Shen would come up with names like James Harvey Robinson (an American historian favored by Gu Jiegang, interested in psychology and the primitive mind), James Rowland Angell and Joseph Collins (early popularizers of psychology, American), John Gould Fletcher (an American Imagist poet and critic), Eric Voegelin (a theorist of political history, in Dewey's circle), the Goncourt brothers, Flaubert, Dickens, Carlyle, Goethe, and Nietzsche—all read in translation. As Shen Congwen slowly gained confidence in his ability to work with ideas, he put them into his fiction. His were not materialist ideas, but explorations of the more mysterious recesses of being—the subconscious, and behind that, the divine. This led him to Freud, and, in a different direction, toward religion.[3]

What really changed was Shen Congwen's image, in the light of his times. Shen had closed out his, and the century's, twenties in Shanghai, as the "Young Soldier," the "Dumas of China." In those days he composed caustic satires and scenes of the lower depths—pacification, prostitution, and penury—while joining the budding leftists Hu Yepin and Ding Ling as co-editor in direct challenges to the literary establishment. After writing "My Education" and *Congwen's Autobiography*, Shen was modern China's most famous literary autodidact, a good candidate for the title "China's Gorky" had there not been so many writers farther left, struggling for the revolutionary high ground. The very titles of some of Shen's, and Ding Ling's, works appear to echo the Russian's.[4] But whereas Hu Yepin and Ding Ling recapitulated Gorky's progression toward rosy socialist heroic writing, Shen Congwen in the 1930's kept developing the gently ironic realism and skill at minute emotional depiction that he and Gorky had so admired in Chekhov. Shen did agree with much of the Marxist criticism of society, though not its Critique. He wrote only negatively of the Kuomintang government, and after 1945 warned America not to intervene in the Chinese Civil War. Though he wore the long gown of the traditional scholar, he also wore his hair long, like a student rebel. Even so, China's leftists thought they detected in Professor Shen a hardening of the arteries and deafness to the cry of the proletariat. Shen did dread their revolutionary agenda. He thought them too violent and purblind in their idealism, when not altogether too skilled at manipulating the idealism of others. He doubted the power of politics to work a real revolution; he doubted, and feared, the power of politics over literature.

All this subtly affected Shen's writing. Far from being deaf to the new literary tendencies, he was all too conscious of being outside the leftist and rightist mainstreams they defined, the more defensive because his critics, revolutionaries included, still outranked him socially and educationally. At times they seem to have nearly convinced Shen himself that the times had passed him by. When he apologized for being "behind in the ranks" (summoning up a phrase from Lu Xun), Shen must have been speaking ironically, yet if we dig down to yet a third level, there is more than a hint that Shen Congwen really feared he had become middle-aged. He said as much in 1936, when he was 33, a stripling by Chinese standards.[5]

Probably events aged him as much as anything. Shen was 28 in 1931, when Hu Yepin was executed; 30 when Ding Ling was kidnapped and presumed executed; 31 when he became a major shaper of other people's careers as editor of the Tianjin *Dagongbao* "Literature" Supplement; 34 when the war with Japan broke out; and still just 39 when America entered the war. But this was no ordinary era. Shen Congwen's sense of time had sped up, as it had for all of his generation. They were no longer China's youngest rebels. The dream of one new generation leading another in strictly cultural rebellion was itself a holdover from the May Fourth period. Had Shen been able to visit Japan, as he and Ding Ling once planned, he might have seen how far China was from being able to emulate Japan's generationwide youth protest, for want of a comparable national education system to bind young people together with shared experience. Even in modernizing Japan, student cohorts stratified themselves according to age.[6] But then, it was part of the May Fourth fantasy to think of literature not only as an adjunct to education, but as its vanguard—even a substitute for it.

Intimations that he and his works were passé struck Shen Congwen with special force because he feared "middle age" on a more personal level—as in his relations with women. Sexual love was Shen Congwen's favorite literary epiphany, yet he married very late himself (so he felt, at 30) and after a long, nearly unsuccessful courtship, the embarrassing frustrations of which he confesses in such stories as "Restless" (1931) and "Xianxian" (1932). Once the marriage was concluded, on the other hand (September 9, 1933), it must have relieved Shen of part of the demon within him, even encouraged the smugness with which he advised colleagues to get married or have an affair to cure what ailed them. Yet the woman who had put him off (though she never twitted him as Ding Ling had) was one of his students, eight years younger than he. If "Housewife" is as autobiographical as it appears, Shen's marriage to Zhang Zhaohe must have done little to make him feel youthful. The story's author-narrator is beset by unresolved desires and frustrations, some of them stemming from the "immaturity" of his wife. She still manages to deliver telling complaints about his absorption in writing and connoisseurship. Evidently Shen felt guilty about his comfortable and sedentary, middle-class and "middle-aged" life-style. He was particularly sensitive about his attachment to his art collections, of quite "material" antique porcelain, silk, paper, and lacquerware.[7]

Shen Congwen also lost his parents in the 1930's, and many friends. Xu Zhimo died in an airplane crash in 1931. Hu Yepin and Ding Ling had gone their separate ideological way the year before. Shen feared for their lives, and perhaps his own, from the moment they took up Communist organization work. Seeing them silenced before their time must have left him feeling survivor's guilt, particularly since he took a safer path. Imagine his further disillusionment when, having just finished two volumes about Ding Ling's selfless idealism, leading up to her presumed martyrdom, he saw her living under house arrest, in the arms of the lover who had betrayed her to the KMT.

For all this, Shen Congwen's diminished productivity suggests not burnout so much as absorption in the responsibilities of a senior man of letters. A true editor, he meticulously revised younger colleagues' manuscript submissions and kept reworking his own—in several different literary venues.[8] As a professor teaching writing and Chinese literature, he prepared for class and broadened his own stylistic range and subject matter by continuing his self-education in ancient literature. Even his interest in art objects was a resumption of a long-standing serious interest in Chinese history and its artifacts. In the mid-1930's, Shen began to write about art education in China, partly to broaden the definition of "art" so that schools might heighten public awareness of beauty in handicrafts, architecture, and the entire realm of the visual—wherein lay the great, *Chinese* art legacy, he felt. The late 1940's saw him discussing calligraphy, art history, and museum preservation. He was getting ready, it turned out, for his post-1949 career.[9] Artifacts also sent him back to China's classic histories and their lessons about narrative.

Shen wrote less *fiction* partly owing to his new involvement, or reinvolvement, with other, more essayistic genres. Literary criticism, commentary, and letters, even a few poems, began competing with fiction for his time as early as 1930–31, while he was still composing short stories at breakneck speed. When he became a major editor, Shen had to take stands on literary issues and write occasional pieces. That part of his 1930's nonfiction is minor. But *Remembering Hu Yepin* (1931), *Congwen's Autobiography* (1932), and *Remembering Ding Ling* (2 vols., 1933) match the narrative art of *Long River*, Shen's foreshortened novel. *Discursive Notes on a Trip Through Hunan* (1933–34) helped pioneer China's new reportage literature, though the title (with its ironic hint that the subject matter may be nonserious) also resonates with the classical Chinese travelogue tradition.

It was in Shen's own eyes that fiction remained the measure of his accomplishment, for at the end of 1936 he confessed (with some exaggeration, however construed) to having fallen silent for two years. He must have meant "silent" like Lu Xun, whose turn to *zawen* he found disappointing. Shen avowed, however, that he was not retiring from creative writing, merely gearing up for new initiatives.[10] And so he was, if we judge him not by the quantity of his 1940's writing (with or without adjustments for KMT censorship), nor perhaps even by its quality, but by the new technical vistas he began to explore, until he had to stop.

The artistic dividends from Shen's "mid-life" malaise are several. His fiction began to treat growth, aging, and death. His plots explored, and many of his characters pondered aloud, the meaning of life and love; the nature of God and man; the relative importance of words and actions; the relationship of art to life and the human spirit; and the origins of social commitment, decadence, and suicide. Often it is middle-aged professors, Westernized city professionals, and other elements of the noncommercial bourgeoisie who ask these questions. Shen's range of characters was broadening, in step with his own new circles of friends now that he, too, was an urban intellectual. Previously he had rarely put the bourgeoisie into his stories for any other purpose than satire. Now his new citified characters had the leisure to ponder the meaning of life in the most abstract, erudite terms. Were those not uniquely "bourgeois" problems, political critics asked? Or were such abstract concerns panhuman, bourgeois only insofar as Shen's realistic characters conceptualized them in their own inimitably sophisticated vocabulary? On this ideological point turned many an evaluation of Shen's mature stories. Yet Shen Congwen was trying to use literature to unsettle, instruct, or, as he liked to think, "cure" the middle-class people in his intended readership. Nor did he give up his habit of lightly caricaturing bourgeois habits of living and thinking. Wu Mi worried that he personally was being satirized in one story. Shen's most revealing stories *à clef*, though, are the works in which he dissects himself, and his family.[11]

Ultimately the left was irked less by the change in Shen's writing than by its constancy. Young people remained his most important intended audience—very young people in books like *Under Moonlight*. He sought to reestablish literature as an idealistic medium to inspire youth, not a "realistic" one to indoctrinate them. Shen did want to aid the war cause, but without compromising his art. How he solved the dilemma appears now to have prefigured his response to the Communist revolution in 1950. He chose a different career for his patriotic work. In 1937, it was secondary education: he edited textbooks, though much of his work was not printed by the KMT government, on the grounds that it was insufficiently political. Party propaganda departments were likewise unmollified. Yet even when he could not publish his own work, Shen Congwen engaged in literature vicariously, by overseeing a circle of young writers who gathered around him at Kunming. That was the worst offense: independent leadership.[12]

Shen Congwen Cultivates His Own "Tendencies"

The literary criticism Shen Congwen wrote in the 1930's is weak in theories but rich in nuances and suggestive contemporary and historical comparisons. Shen wrote about works and authors individually, by generation, according to the sentiments and aspirations they voiced, and their contributions to a linear, or multilinear, stream of progress in developing literary technique and a new vernacular language. Remarkably, he tended to ignore the political and clique affiliations of authors. When discussing the building of a new language, he even blurred the distinctions between poets, fiction writers, and essayists. These critical essays, later collected in the inappropriately named *Froth* (1934), originally were Shen's university lectures at Wusong (1929) and Wuhan (1930).* The exceptional case in which Shen Congwen abandoned the equanimity of the classroom for polemics was a quarrel he picked all by himself. It was grounded in his regionalism.

The political signals Shen sent were deliberately mixed; his views on current events are intriguing partly because of his public reticence about them. One could almost be fooled into thinking that Shen tried not to be interested, the more so after Liberation, but one automobile tour with him through Peking is enough to dispel that illusion. Associations of geography and incongruities of history come tumbling out in a running satirical commentary on the human landscape of foible and folly. See how they like to put up incompetent calligraphy by officials, he chuckles, pointing to inscriptions by Mao Dun and Guo Moruo. Over there was a stand of ancient trees, until warlord Fu Zuoyi cut it down, he sighs. Yonder is an elegant imperial mansion occupied by a People's Liberation Army (PLA) general whose daughter committed suicide in the Cultural Revolution. The naughty little boy of Zhen'gan remains unreconstructed even in the 1980's.

Shen Congwen in the 1930's first of all remained true to his cultural iconoclasm. "Don't weaken yourself with memory," he wrote to one correspondent, "all memories are hurtful. And stay away from old books. We're no longer obligated to take up the intellectual burden of men gone by from times gone by. If, while we're still young ourselves, we read too many of those books written in a Taoist or Buddhist spirit leading out of the world and into the grave, by old men tortured with our overlong national history, it's a surer path than memory itself to premature senility."[13]

Give up your faith in old systems and devote yourself to new ones, he repeated. Dissecting intellectual friends' malaise, using the figures of youth and age that so concerned him, Shen archly noted their absorption in old poetry. The Chinese tradition, he claimed, bespoke physical and philosophical "malnutrition." Authors must

---

*Later Shen Congwen taught at Qingdao University; Peking University, 1937; Southwestern Union University in Kunming, 1938–45; and Peking again, after 1946.

therefore use literature to discover flaws in the national character itself: laziness, pusillanimity, and reluctance to think.[14] Still, what stood out about Shen Congwen in the 1930's was his lack of overt engagement, for his theme of cultural revolution was no longer new. It had even been co-opted by his new cultural villains, bureaucrats and businessmen.

Shen Congwen's higher criticism was mostly aesthetic. His most persistent message was a call to excellence, in diction, structure, and other aspects of "form." One must rely, he emphasized, not on the first efforts of one's "genius" or "inspiration," but on the hard work of practicing and polishing; this was "bravery in writing" coupled with "caution in publishing." The dichotomy was easily understood in traditional terms, as Li Bai's presumed method (insight) versus Du Fu's (deliberation). Shen was coming down heavily on the antiromantic side. Not that he was compromising his cultural iconoclasm, as he was soon to show in his own works. What he meant by "practicing" was experimenting with new literary forms, not imitating old ones. Caution in publishing was a natural concomitant of innovation. Publication might well entail difficulty, as he was to discover when presenting his own modest *Ulysses* ("Gazing at a Rainbow").[15]

Indeed, Shen criticized romantic excesses from a realist standpoint as often as from a formalist one. A revealing essay of Shen's about the creative process fully embraces his colleagues' realist reductionism. Content is by no means less important than form, he affirms, going on to suggest that writers consciously acquire literary content by collecting "material." Adopt the style of a favorite literary model, then write about what is around you, he tells a correspondent in Southeast Asia: "Get to know your Southeast Asian social organizations in detail, the rites of joy and mourning, people's concepts and beliefs, everything about the upper crust and the low life. Once you understand all that fully and deeply, use that special atmosphere as your background. Add an appropriate imaginative element, and you'll be able to write a moving story as a matter of course."[16] Shen's fiction, tending more and more toward intellectualism and pantheism, was not primarily aesthetic in conception, either. He emphasized form mostly out of conviction that failure of craft was undermining nearly all Chinese literature in his time.

That opinion, widely embraced now, was controversial then. Had not Shen Congwen himself, the angry young man of the 1920's, declared war on the niceties of form? It was particularly ironic for him to be warning young writers not to simply pour out their complaints against society.[17] This was the major literary fault he had had to overcome himself. That he made an about-face allowed him to continue developing as a writer, and indeed to give advice on form to many who badly needed it. But his advocacy of literary form was staid, whereas his practice had been untrammeled. And in essays, as in fiction, argument was his weak suit—too weak, at least, to convert the public to ideas so unpopular.

Having stressed craft in art, and innovation in life and morals as well as in art, Shen Congwen went on to insist that authors do their own thinking, take responsibility for it, and otherwise maintain their integrity. His was a message of moderation, of deliberate disengagement from any group or writers' association, left, right, or even center, that might divert authors from their own creative visions. Typical was his reaction to the leftist polemic urging adoption of a "mass language" (*dazhongyu*). Many literary works in the modern vernacular *were* stiff, unnatural, and Europeanized, Shen agreed, but he blamed it on bad writing. That the May Fourth vernacular was best spoken by the bourgeoisie did not diminish that language as a medium for the fiction of a country boy like him. Nor did he see any threat in translations of the works of the international bourgeoisie. Indeed, Shen's solution was more and better translations. He wanted to elevate the masses to international standards of excellence, though he admitted that "half" of them were "about as bad off as refugees, with no work or food." Time would weed out the bad works. Why did those favoring a purer vernacular not write model fiction as an example, instead of carping manifestos?[18]

The major polemic that Shen did take as his own was against China's "Shanghai School" of literature (Hai Pai; "Shanghai Types," as Yang Xianyi and Gladys Yang so well translate it).[19] It may seem fitting that China's great regionalist and self-styled "country person" led the assault on China's Paris-cum-Moscow—or, as he saw it, Chinese Gotham. Yet, mentorship over an opposing Peking, or Academic School, was the mantle thereby thrust on Shen Congwen— the Hunanese who shunned groups and never went to high school.

From literary Shanghai's point of view, the polemic began early in 1934, after Shen Congwen intimated that the city was in the clutches of a Shanghai School: "what you get when you cross the artiness of celebrity scholars with the auctioneering of merchants."[20] Shanghai's taking offense was what initiated the polemic then, for Shen had been deriding its bad writing for years. Many who passed for authors there were amateurs and idlers "fooling around" (*boxiang*) with literature, he had been saying since 1931, using a word unique to Shanghai dialect that Lu Xun, too, had picked up in 1933. Writers in Shanghai countered with definitions of Shen and "his" Peking Types. Soon the polemic ran its course and gave way to new issues —from Shanghai's point of view.[21]

Not so for Shen Congwen. He took seriously his idea of a baleful Shanghai influence on modern literature; otherwise he might have jettisoned the regional epithet, which was offensive to so many of China's writers, in order to save his critique. "Shanghai" let Shen conceptualize and vent regional pride and prejudice; smoldering resentments against publishers; perturbation at the demeaned status of writers since May Fourth; reservations about cultural change; and complaints against writers themselves, as a group. His polemic has overtones of contempt not only for the leftist litterateurs, but also for capitalism and imperialism. The attack on Shanghai writing may even indicate a rift within the ranks of Chinese modernism. We usually have to infer just whom Shen was inveighing against, for he seldom accused individuals, even obliquely, except for Jiang Guangci, Lin Yutang, and the Creationists, especially Zhang Ziping.[22] (Probably he regarded these people more highly than those he wouldn't name.) Shen's polemic was abstract, not just a cover for settling scores with competitors. He even tried to bolster his concept of a Shanghai School with a theory of literary history. That, of course, made the term seem all the more invidious to writers in Shanghai. When so many of them came to power, in 1949, Shen's words came back to haunt him.[23]

The crusade as Shen tried to shape it began in the summer of 1929, when he first identified a "New Hai Pai" ("Xin Hai Pai"; shortened to "Hai Pai" in his writings after 1930).[24] Few writers were listening, or perhaps few disagreed, for criticism of the world of the concessions, home to the "School," was hardly novel. Shen was living in Shanghai himself. He wanted all the more to define himself in opposition to Shanghai: not as a Peking writer, but as a hinterlander, from Shanghai's real antithesis.

Shen's implication that the "Hai Pai" had a predecessor shows him in his new role as historian of Chinese literature,[25] a subject he had begun to teach in college. But he was not really so detached.

His first polemics came right after Shanghai inflicted a major psychological defeat on him. In 1928–29, Hu Yepin, Ding Ling, and he had been busy co-editing the literary journals *Honghei* (*Red and Black*) and *Renjian yuekan* (*The World of Man*). Proudly proclaiming independence from any particular tendency, they had printed only creative works, including Shen's own painfully authentic diaristic complaints against society. The magazines went under in just a year. Shen went into debt; his friends, into politics.[26]

Unable to imagine that in a few years he and Ding Ling would have more influential journals to edit, Shen Congwen blamed their defeat on unfair competition: capitalists' marketing muscle and officials' behind-the-scenes influence. Like the Marxists, he said the two were in collusion; but he also blamed the left, who as "officials out of power" had their own publishers in their pocket.[27] Attacking the competition as Shanghai Types regionalized Shen's old war on the literary establishment. Now he blamed the authors themselves, not just their backstage support.

It was also in Shanghai that Shen's own works received criticism, and some rejection slips, even as a Shanghai publisher was out promoting Shen as a "genius," as if he, too, were a Shanghai-Type literary prodigy of the Bund.[28] Everything seemed to revolve around influence and money, little of which ever went to the writer. Shen knew that he was indeed writing too fast—with too little craft—and he resented the Shanghai publishers for making him do it. Jobs up north soon rescued Shen from the "evil" city, but he felt guilty about the struggling "professional" writers Hu Yepin and Ding Ling he left behind. Shanghai's queer extraterritoriality (*seeming* extraterritoriality, he worried, prophetically) had mesmerized them into a false optimism and sense of security, even as it drew them toward disaster from the merchant-police-underworld combine that most people thought ran the place.[29] Their ultimate fate in the International Settlement confirmed his suspicions that Shanghai literary activity was just another racket in the city's world of shadows.

What Shen wanted was a return to 1920's Peking, when writers enjoyed high status and stood united as a bloc, leading society. Shanghai Types were litterateurs who gathered rumors about real authors, then wrote them up as "literary news"; who plagiarized Chinese works, or translated foreign ones, for presentation as their own creations; who organized and promoted themselves, when not gossiping and drinking tea at over-publicized literary gatherings;

who in general undermined the dignity of authorship through distracting sideline activities. Such people hung out with movie starlets and gangsters, maybe even got ahead through them.[30]

Defining a "school" by its activities instead of its literary style is the action of a moralist rather than a critic, but Shen's point was that in Shanghai people became "writers" through KMT subsidy or left-wing promotion, without yet having produced any works. No real author belonged to the Shanghai School, not Mao Dun, Ye Shaojun, Lu Xun, or Su Wen, Shen had to reassure them in 1934. He warned that journal space devoted to their true literature might come to be squeezed out by columns reporting on personalities and events. Indeed, he later observed in 1936, journal publication of serious, nonpartisan fiction was dying out.[31]

The ultimate "literary" sideline activity was dabbling in topical essays. Too lightweight to be literarily or politically courageous, such essays were as fully a diversion from the cultural task at hand as movie-star gossip, in Shen Congwen's view; they inevitably propped up the status quo. His 1929 reproofs of *zagan* polemicists, minor critics, and people who engaged in personal attacks became in the 1930's a full crusade against "humorous" essays. That meant Lin Yutang. Perhaps Shen was trying to nudge his friend Shi Zhicun away from the genre, too.[32]

Shen Congwen especially deplored Shanghai authors who pandered to "base interests" or frequently changed style to stay current. He savaged the Liangyou Press's journals for their photos of college beauties and movie stars kissing; writers who switched from triangular romance to radical chic (Zhang Ziping); and, after Feng Da's presumed betrayal of Ding Ling, "sentimental leftists, brave as lions, who recant the moment the wind shifts and turn in their friends for profit—these too are the Hai Pai." Styles, genres, ideologies—nothing was sacred. Publishers now promoted satire, now children's literature; now foolish–son-in-law stories, now "classics illustrated" comics; now Nietzschean heroism, now Baudelairean decadence—as "taste" dictated. Shen wanted literature to be a profession. Having lambasted amateurish trifling, he actually had to take care only to defend serious writers from playboys, not old pros from new blood.[33]

Shanghai was not a new target. Images of urban meretriciousness already clung to the "Shanghai School" of Chinese opera. It was said to be "well-known for mechanical devices of theatrical production, and stretching a play to an incredible number of acts, full of bustle and movement, ... through which the applause of the audience was stimulated by rather disreputable methods, and in which the form of the traditional opera disappeared completely." Shanghai acting was thus a perversion of a "Peking School" that "emphasized singing and acting technique, in which they preserved the traditional excellences of grace and precision."[34]

By analogy, the 1930's Shanghai School in literature perverted Peking's May Fourth tradition, just for reader applause.[35] Shen did not shun titular leadership over the School of Peking, his second spiritual home. To him the city symbolized the independence, individualism, and links between literature and education of May Fourth. Revival of New Culture movement support for literature was just his remedy for Shanghai's outsize influence.[36] At peace with academia, having scaled its heights from outside, Shen had finally got inside the literary-cultural movement he was too young and poorly educated to join at its height.

Shen Congwen's masterstroke, then, was to recall Shanghai's pre–May Fourth past, the better to strip the city of its pretensions of being up-to-date and progressive. He had from the beginning portrayed the Shanghai School as successor to the Mandarin Duck and Butterfly pulp romancers of the 1910's. The latter published in *Saturday* magazine, whose admitted purpose was to help readers pass the time on the Chinese day of rest. Shen made the connection by naming his 1930's Shanghai nemesis the New Saturday School. By further calling it the New Hai Pai, he implied that the "school" could even be traced to an Old Hai Pai that went back to 1890's compradorial Shanghai or before, a literary world of bohemian, *fin de siècle* "geniuses of the Bund" who, as Lu Xun put it, dreamed of celebrity scholardom and parties with famous demimondaines. Shen also liked to foster historical associations by using Shanghai's old-fashioned name, "Haishang," when deriding "Haishang Taste" and so forth. Further, the "Hai" (sea) at the start reminded one that Shanghai was only littoral, not heartland.[37]

By early 1931, Shen had ready a whole literary history in outline. The May Fourth movement had taken hold only in Peking, Sichuan, and Hunan (thanks to the favorable Hunanese character, or *minzuxing*), he said. In Shanghai, the Saturday Types were never displaced. Their Classical language gave way to Peking's vernacular, but their Shanghai Taste continued, culminating in a New Hai

Pai.[38] Later that year he claimed for the original Peking May Fourth literature (Jing Yang, or Peking Style, not yet a Peking School, and never a mere Peking Taste) the good tradition of "humane literature" (i.e., what Zhou Zuoren had advocated). The Hai Pai replaced it with a romantic literature, under the stimulus of the Creation Society's hyperbole and bohemian life-style. Like Lu Xun and Liu Bannong, Shen went on to deride empty proletarian poetry (Guo Moruo), as well as the KMT's Nationalist literature.[39] Shen was no longer just moralizing against trifling activities and lifestyles; he was attacking literary styles, for the 1890's and 1910's authors were not "writers without writings," and neither was Guo Moruo, though most Nationalist writers were.

Now rumors, news of literary soirees, minor criticism, and literary fads were spread by a growing Shanghai popular press, its lesser tabloids and broadsides called "the mosquito press." (Nearly all of it was quite literally ephemeral; it is a good guess, though, that the Shen-Ding-Hu relationship and the private lives of Shen's "Anglo-American" friends were among the topics of gossip.) There are many hints that Shen's polemic was partly a reaction against lowbrow, commercial culture—the world of pulp romances, flamboyant covers, full-page advertisements, chitchat, movie stars, scandals, confabs, literary celebrity, book-review payola, and American popular music (which Shen, like his leftist and rightist colleagues, found culturally unhealthy). He worried that serious writing could not co-exist with this, or, worse, that competition between publishers might alter the direction of serious writing itself.[40]

The Shanghai-Type writing Shen deprecated was also foreignized, not of "us outside the concessions." In 1930, he criticized an alleged flood of second-rate commercial translations and trendy new ideologies (some evidently "proletarian"), blaming them on Japanese periodicals and literary criticism.[41] He had joined the May Fourth army to fight against tradition, never anticipating war on this second front, against a newer, slicker enemy whose foreign-derived innovations and quick adaptability to changing taste threatened to make *him* seem "behind in the ranks."

Was Shen Congwen fighting the left, then? He derided *zagan*, and later criticized Lu Xun by name. (He did not of course imply that Lu Xun was a Shanghai Type, only that he was being dragged down by the meeting-hoppers and criticasters.)[42] Shen liked to imply that "proletarian literature" was a slogan promoted by the capitalists, to boost new book sales. So he probably did not mean to exclude the polemical Shanghai left from his Shanghai Types. They wore their ideology on their sleeve, accepted questionable converts, and stayed close by the concessions long after their mass base moved inland. But the "naïve" left (e.g., Hu Yepin) was still Shen's sentimental favorite over the "venal" right. When the right renewed its killing of leftist writers, his criticism gave more than equal time to attacking the right, if only as apology for not joining the left (as the left may have suspected, and not forgiven). In 1932, for instance, Shen deplored how lowbrow saturation was making it difficult for "leftist works of merit," like Mao Dun's and Ding Ling's, to find an outlet.[43]

Contrary to received opinion in China, the left did not wholly disagree with Shen Congwen about Shanghai writers. Shen's most prejudiced insinuations, that Shanghai was reactionary and compradorial, were probably just what kept Lu Xun from counterattacking too vigorously; he may well have recognized many of Shen's innuendoes as his own.[44] In 1934 it was not the left, but the self-styled nonpartisan ("third force") litterateur Dai Kechong (pseuds. Su Wen, Du Heng) who took offense at Shen's allegations. During the Second World War, the leftist Tang Tao actually revived Shen's anti–Hai Pai rhetoric to attack Shanghai collaborationist writers.[45]

Why did Su Wen think Shen might have been criticizing him? Su co-edited the Shanghai literary journal *Xiandai* (*"Les Contemporains,"* literally *"Modern"*). As the title implies, the magazine's contributors—notably Shi Zhicun, Mu Shiying, and Liu Naou—meant to be part of the international modernist movement, with special acknowledgments to the French. Leo Ou-fan Lee and Harry Kaplan, in their separate research, see the Contemporains' fiction as relatively experimental: carefully contrived, but plotless, with influences from Symbolism and stream-of-consciousness writing. What might have concerned Shen was that they also dabbled in Decadence, gloried in "urban" sophistication, and dropped knowing Western cultural (even linguistic) asides. As Kaplan notes, some of Mu Shiying's stories, with their ballroom encounters, unfathomable illnesses, and wilting flowers, do look like Mandarin Duck and Butterfly romances in new aesthetic clothes.[46] One of Shen Congwen's most mean-spirited literary reviews is of Mu Shiying's fiction (1935). Shen found things to praise, but he also wrote that Mu's

"Haishang romances" were best suited to "pictorial, fashion, women's, movie, and games magazines"; they looked good amid illustrations. Perhaps Shen, the Peking modernist, was criticizing Shanghai modernism. His own technique in the mid-1930's, considered apart from the Freudian and other modernist intellectual influences, was "well-made," not so experimental. Shen began imitating Joyce only during the war, when Shanghai modernism was already dead. Without much regard for preaching what he practiced, Shen in 1935 even faulted the style of Mu Shiying (and Shen's Peking modernist friend Fei Ming) for "abnormality" (*xiepi*). But there is no evidence that Shen really meant his polemics for the Contemporains, Frenchified though they were. If Su Wen felt the Hai Pai shoe fit him, perhaps it is because he printed art gossip from Paris and literary news—but so did all magazine editors, North and South.[47]

What Su Wen could not help was his address. Much as one may appreciate Shen's lamentations over the might-have-beens of the 1930's, or marvel at the flashes of insight in his criticisms, one must suspect that regional bias is the underlying basis of his polemic. In 1929 he wrote:

In the Miao country, swine are black. Jiangsu and Zhejiang have black swine, too. People from Jiangsu and Zhejiang make good officials. Also good revolutionaries. When Hunanese make revolution, they're killed. When people from Jiangsu and Zhejiang make revolution, they become commissioners. It's not strange when you really think about it. Zhejiang and Jiangsu people are a little smarter.... Hunanese are fools. Those who won't admit it, like X X X (can you guess who this is?), are even bigger fools. In the future Communist dictatorship, just wait and see, there'll still be Zhejiang and Jiangsu people at the top.[48]

Shen Congwen here betrays an old Hunanese fear of political, economic, and cultural domination by Jiangnan. In many parts of China, the success and aftermath of the Northern Expedition created images of Ningbo bankers, Shanghai gangsters and imperialists, and Zhejiang militarists conspiring to form a Shanghai-Nanking axis. In culture there was Lu Xun, whom Shen disliked personally as a "typical Shaoxing man." Lin Yutang was a Southeasterner who created a personality cult of Lu Xun. Of course Xu Zhimo, Zhou Zuoren, and Cai Yuanpei were Zhejiang men, too, but regional prejudice does not feed on logic. If further proof of Shen Congwen's Hunanese outlook were needed, he provided it in his 1945 sketch of Hunan's contribution to modern Chinese literature. Shen celebrates nearly every writer Hunan ever produced; he begins with the 1895–98 Young China reformers at Changsha, but soon proceeds to praise Xiang Kairan—a writer of knight-errantry novels and model "genius of the Bund."⁴⁹

Run-ins with the Government

Shen Congwen's feelings against Chiang Kaishek ran deep, as his talk of swine suggests. Shen disapproved of Mao Zedong and his tactics, but Mao was an idealist, a "country person," and Hunanese. In any contest with the no. 1 blood-letting Zhejiangese, Shen would have to side with his fellow-provincial. To the surprise of many, that was his choice in 1949: Mao instead of Chiang, and China instead of Hu Shi and the "Anglo-American" world.

In the background lay not just a regionalist but a personal grudge against the man who ran the Nanking regime. In his late-1930's and 1940's dissent, Shen Congwen focused on the vision of the future held by Chiang's most fanatical, protofascist partisans (many of them army officers trained in 1930's Germany), the Blue Shirts. Their ideology was a cult of the Leader, which Shen Congwen objected to in principle. In 1934 he even had a premonition that China's craving for a savior dictator had yet to be satisfied: "The benighted majority are hoping for a miracle. Let there come a leader, a hero, and they will hand over the fate of the whole nation to such a person. Out of ignorance, and on the evidence of all the things accomplished by such leaders in places far away [Germany, Italy, Russia], they await the coming of this man. They believe that some day he will arrive."⁵⁰ But in 1934, one could not attack the cult of the Leader without implicitly attacking Chiang Kaishek. Contrary, then, to opinions held about him on the left, Shen often wrote about the government in the 1930's, and always to rebuke it. Even his fictional oeuvre contains a small but hard-hitting, not very discreet body of dissent. Shen never asked for literature to eschew political themes, only for authors not to neglect "that which makes a literary work a good literary work."⁵¹

What put things on a personal level for Shen Congwen was the continued persecution of his friends. Though the purges of the late 1920's had left him indignant, his anger might have gradually dissipated as the left took up armed struggle of its own in the 1930's. Shen began a new life up north in 1930. He started publishing nonleftist literary criticism, some of it in Nanking journals. But then came more tragedies. The most awful symbols of Chiang Kaishek's personalistic style of ruling China were his secret operatives. Some came from the underworld, and it seemed only the Generalissimo and his cronies could rein them in. When those particular weapons were used to silence Hu Yepin and Ding Ling, Shen Congwen's reaction was predictable.

He was not too surprised when Hu Yepin was made to disappear, on January 17, 1931. One evening a year before, Hu had dashed into Shen's apartment. He was being tailed—had to change into Congwen's clothes and slip out a back door Congwen didn't even know existed! After Hu was kidnapped, Shen came south. He and Ding Ling worked frantically to learn of Hu's location and secure his release. In Nanking, Shen Congwen made inquiries through Cai Yuanpei, president of the Academia Sinica. He also solicited bail money. Friends Xu Zhimo and Wang Jizhen (in America) contributed. Shen himself donated the copyrights of *The Marble Carrying Boat* and *The Inn*. Before long, he found himself face-to-face with both the extreme left (Hu's and Ding's friends, who were afraid to come forward themselves) and, after further trips to Nanking, the far-right KMT: party leader Shao Lizi, and secret police czar Chen Lifu. Unfortunately, Chen's agents were not the ones responsible. Hu Yepin was martyred on February 7—buried alive, by one account. How the money was spent is not certain, but one could not ride the train to Nanking, or call on the police, for free.[52]

After 1929 Shen had drifted fairly far away from Hu and Ding, but now he was deeply involved in Ding Ling's personal life again. He lost his job in Wuhan after spending the beginning of the semester looking for Hu Yepin, so he stayed in Shanghai, letting Ding Ling and her baby son lodge with him. Afterward he fled with them to Hunan, so the infant could be left with Ding's mother. Then Ding Ling lived with Shen Congwen's relatives in Shanghai for a time. As a monument to the idealism of his martyred friend, and to provide money for his widow, Shen composed *Remembering Hu Yepin*. It was really a fond reminiscence of their three-way friendship, with special attention to the stormy love of Hu and Ding, and the creative beginnings of both of them. Shen made them appear lovably naïve—temperamental and all too human. But Ding Ling pre-approved the manuscript. At the end, Shen Congwen promised to continue the story in a future biography of Ding Ling.[53]

From there, Ding Ling continued with leftist literary work. She joined the Communist Party in the spring of 1932, while Shen remained in Qingdao, teaching and writing nonleftist fiction. Their paths thus diverged once more, only to cross again, still more spectacularly, when KMT Blue Shirts kidnapped Ding Ling herself, in the International Settlement where the Chinese government had no jurisdiction, on May 14, 1933. Ironically, Shen's other big personal involvement all the while was his pursuit of Zhang Zhaohe. It seemed nearly to crisscross with his Ding Ling escapades, in life as in his fiction. The courtship had got off to a rocky start in 1929, and Shen was wooing Zhang, still without much success, when the 1931 crisis reinvolved him with Ding Ling's affairs. The final irony is that Zhang Zhaohe married Shen Congwen on September 9, 1933, not four months after Ding disappeared. Shen's preoccupation with saving his older female friend that summer must have delayed his marriage—if Ding's presumed demise did not somehow expedite it.

Shen Congwen refuses to discuss how he responded to Ding Ling's 1933 predicament.[54] He was up north on May 14; letters from Shanghai informed him of the kidnapping. He wrote two articles accusing the government (which was feigning ignorance of the matter) and pleading for protests. The first was written on May 25 and published on June 4. It was of this tenor:

> These past few years, the government has had a uniform policy for dealing with the Communist Party. Whatever the explanation given, whether to the Party [KMT], the nation, or the people, it has adopted extreme measures of extermination. By now hardly any degree of cruelty would be beyond belief. A friend of mine in Jiangxi, for instance, saw with his own eyes how an army unit "settled" a group of more than 200 deserters in a giant vat of lime. "This is war!" he said....
>
> This terribly stupid policy has already taken its toll in dead! But if all authors who want to improve themselves, who are dissatisfied with the status quo, and who dare hope for the future end up as missing persons, those left will be a pack of mediocrities. When the nation has to brace itself to survive, they'll still be putting on their little acts, pretending to be sophisticated, commenting on the city lights here, dashing off a few *ci* [old-style poems] or making up a rumor there, drawing on their feel for the vulgar. Pretending to be worthy scholars, but taking literature to be a plaything, they'll run their periodicals for the government and, according to the length and nimbleness of their fingers, snatch a few royalties from the accountants who keep the Party's so-called literary policy. When they

run out of things to do, they can while away their days at conferences, advancing enlightened theories about Greece and Rome. Thus will the tastes and mentality of two or three Shanghai rentiers and idlers set the tastes and mentality of our country's youth. With the government intervening positively, to kill off all writers with promise, and negatively, to cultivate these bums and loafers using the national treasure, need more be said about the nation's future?[55]

By May 29 newspapers were already reporting that Ding Ling had been betrayed by one Feng Da and captured by government secret agents. Public Security Bureau inspector Ma Shaowu, a notorious ex-gangster and Blue Shirt, was suspected as the chief operative; he came to public attention more than ever when he was murdered by his own thugs in front of a brothel on the night of June 14. It was also rumored that Chen Lifu had come to Shanghai to try to turn Ding Ling and get her to work for the government.[56] All this was mortifying for Shen Congwen. He knew that Ding Ling and the putative leftist Feng Da had been lovers before the arrest. Shen had chanced to bring the two together, when the journalist Agnes Smedley asked Shen for an introduction to Ding Ling; Feng was Smedley's interpreter, and Ding was still lying low, living with Shen's Little Sister No. 9. Shen Congwen had disliked the Feng-Ding liaison to begin with, probably because he liked Hu Yepin so much better and cherished the memory. Smedley also disapproved. She fired Feng because of his relationship with Ding Ling.[57]

Literary evidence in the story "Three Women" (June 1933), the most explicit elements of which were deleted in reprint editions, suggests that Shen shuttled between Shanghai and Nanking in May and June as he had two years before, for Hu Yepin. The story takes place in Qingdao; the characters hope that Shen's autobiographical persona, "Xuanruo" (a pen name of Shen's) can post bail for a masculine, leftist woman called "Mengke" (like one of Ding Ling's personae). Finally Xuanruo wires from Nanking that Mengke is dead. By the end of June it was generally, though falsely, rumored that Ding Ling had been executed, in connection with the death of Ma Shaowu.[58]

Meanwhile Shen was dashing off, if he had not already written, *Remembering Ding Ling*, whose postscript has a date-and-place line reading "June 1933, Qingdao." He may well have thought Ding Ling dead by the time he finished that first volume, though he began the book to stir up public indignation and so forestall her execution.[59] Perhaps Shen also raised bail money with it. Installments did not see print until July 24, 1933, however, and they were censored, though the book was written with the circumlocutions and tentativeness about causality of a good Japanese psychological novel. Shen then completed volume two, the first installment of which appeared on October 9, on December 13.[60] We do not know how he spent the money from the book (if it was not already pledged in advance), but it would have been out of character for him to give it to anyone but Ding Ling, her family, or maybe those who had Ding in their clutches.[61] Counteracting the vicious rumors about what Ding Ling had supposedly done in her "final days" was reason enough for completing volume two.[62] Shen once more made his heroine look fallible and even weak at times, but he was careful to depict her as "not Feng Da's type" (i.e., not one to knowingly become enamored of a turncoat and KMT informer). Yet Shen ended his story before coming to Ding's abduction and presumed execution, and his implicit criticism of Feng Da in the final chapters is peculiarly measured. After Ding Ling was reunited with the Communist movement, she repudiated the book and took offense at its author. Her animus would bring Shen much pain in the late 1940's, and for 35 years after that.[63]

Ding Ling in late 1933 was in fact sharing rooms in Nanking with her lover Feng Da, evidently under a loose sort of house arrest. Not only was this rumored about, though we cannot say how early, but Shen Congwen visited her while she was in this situation, probably as early as December 1933, while he was en route to Hunan. Ding Ling was living in reasonable comfort, with her personal effects. It is possible that the government allowed the visit in order to get Shen Congwen to stop writing about her or to induce him to say that she was happy in her new circumstances; thereafter he wrote nothing more about Ding Ling's mishaps, but neither did he write about the Nanking visit, to confirm that she was alive, until she resurfaced in Yan'an at the end of 1936.[64] Most intriguing of all the possibilities opened up by this chronological reconstruction is that Shen Congwen may have written the final chapters of his second volume, including the sections about Feng Da, with the hope that Ding Ling herself might read them.[65] Moreover, if Shen Congwen knew where Ding Ling was being held, others may have found out also, including the Communists. They, however, were led by a faction not necessarily well disposed toward Ding Ling. Whatever conclusions Shen Congwen may have come to about Ding Ling at this time, he must have turned more cynical than ever about the doings of people in politics.

As the government in 1934–35 moved further to the right, toward the Leader cult and military solutions for domestic problems, Shen Congwen stepped up his dissent. Like the politicians, he decried "international capitalism" and foreign "airplanes, artillery, products, and preachers,"[66] but still he criticized the inner degradation of the Chinese people more than he did external threats, just as he had worried more about cultural than political imperialism in the 1920's. Long-term historical problems such as opium, superstition, and resistance to change concerned him most. What worried Shen Congwen politically was polarization and violence. The banning of books, which he protested at considerable length, warning that the Nationalists might go down in history next to the tyrant Qin Shi Huangdi, symbolized his own alienation from the government, and his profession's, for the government "stupidly" imagined that mere literature was turning the young into Communists. Yet Shen, too, worried that left-wing ideology was becoming "general" among college and high-school students—the result of the government telling them to get out of politics, he thought. His growing distance from those youngest of the "troops"—another "falling behind in the ranks"—caused him the most anguish. He had always been at war with "the officials." Now the very fact that he occasionally tried to reason with them, besides berate them, was offensive to the left. That was what Shen feared.[67]

Besides political control of literature, the subject Shen Congwen was most vitriolic in denouncing was the re-Confucianization of education. Generals—above all the warlord He Jian, governor of Shen's fellow-provincials (and object of his special contempt, as we relate in the next chapter)—were leading the movement to restore classics to the heart of the curriculum at all levels. Shen minced no words in pointing up the hypocrisy of this. Reading the ancient books was not just a waste of young people's time that left them unprepared to cope with China's unpleasant future, he said, it actually harmed them, stripped them of their vitality and ingenuity. "To put into effect study of the classics in this day and age is tantamount to national suicide." "It shows we're really in the Middle Ages, that history is running backwards," he added.[68]

From this he proceeded to criticize Chiang Kaishek's attempt to restore ancient thought, morals, and concepts of loyalty and hierarchy as the basis of a disciplined corporate harmony between Leader and masses. This was the New Life movement. Its mixture of old Confucian and YMCA-Christian disciplines, violent practice, and crypto-totalitarian aims so offended Shen that he kept pursuing this nemesis in the 1940's, when the movement had largely died out. To treat it seriously, as the symbol of Kuomintang China, instead of merely ridiculing it, as most intellectuals did, was Shen's way of crossing swords with several adversaries: the Blue Shirts, who had persecuted his friends and were leading the New Life movement in rural Hunan and Jiangxi (using it to give their counterrevolutionary violence a touch of punitive fascist zeal, he felt); the YMCA, which Shen had long scorned for producing foreignized young men with slick hair and ingratiating smiles; the governor of Hunan, He Jian; and finally Chiang Kaishek himself. Most telling was Shen's fictional attack on the movement, "The New and the Old." His weapon is subtle symbolism, or "pointing at the mulberry to revile the ash." [69]

On the surface, the story is vintage Shen Congwen pastoralism. The setting is old Zhen'gan, with lushly described surroundings and a proud young country-lad protagonist, a Gan Army *tuntian* warrior named Yang Jinbiao. Shen builds on the strength of his own culturally exotic background (having had an executioner relative), picking and choosing from among actual ethnographic details to create a slightly surrealistic atmosphere.

Young Yang Jinbiao's late-Qing world is a moral one. Life itself is a play acted out before the gods. When there is an execution, the Gan community ritually atones for it before the forces higher than law by having Yang, the executioner, run with his bloodied sword into the temple of the city god. There Yang must confess murder to the god and his earthly counterpart, the magistrate, and undergo a ritual beating for god and man to see. Shen Congwen reverently dramatizes, and explains, the ancient (real) custom as a socially therapeutic act. Then he turns to the present era, for ironic contrast.

In the Republic, criminals are casually shot to death "by the dozen." There being no ritual, not even any technique, to execution, nor amelioration of the bloodletting through social compact or religious act, the state now takes lives without any moral basis. This is dramatized when the local authorities face an unprecedented challenge: alleged Communism, in the form of two young and evidently innocent schoolteachers. They must be liquidated by "new," exceptional means. So Yang Jinbiao, now grown old, is recalled to behead them with his ancient weapon. Beheading seems especially terrible and minatory in the modern age because the process is no longer understood. But neither is the ritual atonement act, which Yang tries to reenact, as in the old days, only to be misunderstood and even considered insane. Shen leaves no doubt about which society, the new or the old, is barbarous. Cowardly modern soldiers go into the temple with guns to flush out the man who is armed only with his magic sword and old-style conscience. The story is so powerful a commentary on the moral dilemma of modernization and social change that it can be read without any reference to politics. The more brilliant is its moral condemnation of the New Life movement: a movement promoting Christo-Confucian morality the better to spill young blood, and reviving old customs as "new life." Many would agree that China's old regime failed precisely because it tried to solve new problems by reviving ideas whose moral basis had passed into history.[70]

Shen Congwen's Idea Fiction

Although Shen Congwen was pessimistic about China's future, many of his 1930's creative works are, in their own way, quite as "positive" as the heroic revolutionary fiction of which he was so leery. Shen asked authors to put "religious emotion" into their works—to create literary "amulets" for "mesmerizing" Chinese readers, imbuing them with the faith to go forth and change the world. He was still enamored of the doctrine of literary realism; as late as 1941 he defined fiction as "very appropriately recording human events in words." However, human events, he said, consisted equally of social phenomena and dream phenomena. And the realities that interested him (much more than any theory) now included "higher" realities, or "the Abstract." In the spirit of Plato—an author he recommended to revolutionaries—Shen yearned to reintegrate, even transcend, the fleeting, war-torn phenomenal world by realizing a more permanent, noumenal one of Beauty. He admitted that he himself wrote from emotions "just like religious ones." He sought, in other words, to create light in a time of darkness.[71]

This ethical and philosophical idealism evoked a nearly forgotten aspect of the original May Fourth spirit. Radicals of 1919, too, intended literature to create new intellectual forms directly, without the mediation of treacherous social forces. Indeed, intellectualism better characterizes Shen's later works than worldly optimism. Although his essays write of God, his fiction wistfully contemplates the ironies of existence. In the 1940's, Shen was reading in Buddhism, classical literature, and, no doubt, Western philosophy, for one of the textbooks he prepared was about logic. Yet Shen as cultural innovator so liked to experiment that one must ask: Were the ideas in his literature just experiments, too—elements of craft—or do they truly represent his own search for meaning? If on the other hand he understood works instrumentally, functionally, even anthropologically, as *means* to the Abstract, does this mean that his *craft* was merely phenomenal?

At bottom, Shen cared little for the philosophic process that might definitively answer such questions. What attracted him was philosophic uplift, the "ideas" themselves, whether revealed by God or science. He "loved" his Abstractions, meaning by that both literary works and the ideas in them, just as he was genuinely curious about the social behavior he probed in his other writings. He had no French Symbolist notion of art restructuring life or constructing "a new edifice into which the artist can escape from life."[72] Though his 1940's fiction-essays in the "Nightmare" cycle seem to evoke mystical union with color metaphors, their art, too, is within life. It may be that Shen Congwen's alienation from his society, its writers, and even its readers ultimately encouraged him to ignore public opinion and take refuge in the role of modern avant-garde writer. Still, Shen always explained himself by invoking common sense—resistance to being stampeded into going with the times—not genius, prophecy, or indeed God.

Professional consciousness and involvement with literary history did certainly make Shen's intellectualized purpose in writing more urgent. He began to wonder if China's new writing would speak to future generations as *literature*. As he aged, his own mortality began to haunt him. Did his life have historical significance? This led back to the Abstract. Major artists had a special path to immortality, he observed, for their works outlasted the deeds of most other people, notably politicians. There was, moreover, something exhilarating about the creative process. To Shen, this confirmed that life had a spiritual dimension that was not readily apparent.

Shen Congwen therefore took the 1930's as a time for establishing the meaning of his own life and work, irrespective of the war. He had become better read in all kinds of literature, developed many literary styles, and updated his understanding of man, consciousness, and the universe. But he had yet to achieve a synthesis that would lift his previous "exercises" onto the plane of true literature, he thought. This self-assessment was at once humble and hopeful about his ability to progress. One may of course question Shen's use of problem fiction, and tidier plots, to achieve his ends. Critics had long asked for this "thought" that he was now putting into his works (though they really meant ideology), but had that not betrayed incompetence on their part in penetrating modern "Western" indeterminacy in plot and meaning?[73]

Shen Congwen's 1930's stories certainly are not as modernist in technique as subsequent stories were to become. Yet a psychological microstructure of minutely observed human relations, heightened by subtle images evoking subconscious responses, often underlies his well-made superstructures. And plots so often based, like Lu Xun's, on reminiscence turn out on closer analysis to have a nearly Proustian self-consciousness about time. Ultimately the intellectual ethos takes over, giving Shen's writing a modern, if not really an avant-garde, feel. Of the ideas he voices directly, not all were original or fresh, even in the 1930's. But the characters' very act of questioning—their sense of uncertainty about reality itself—conveys a modern anomie locating them squarely in our own world. Life is random, and so is joy; Shen's positiveness is a rarified delight in the boundlessness of possibility. Sometimes we observe the author using literature to seek meaning in his own life. At the center of all progress is something inner, not exterior: the creative mind, Shen says (like James Harvey Robinson) in his essays, and "demonstrates" in fiction, through his characters.

Many of these elements appear together in the story "Portrait of Eight Steeds" (Qingdao, 1933?).[74] It scrutinizes, even plays a psychological experiment upon, "Mr. Dashi," a Qingdao University summer-school professor. He loves his fiancée, Yuanyuan, but is tempted by another woman. When, at the end, he stays by the sea to have an affair with the latter, his decision is made to seem not just an ethical choice, but a philosophical commitment and a dose of emotional therapy. Dashi, moreover, is a professional writer resembling Shen Congwen. He sorts himself out by writing, as in letters to Yuanyuan we get to read—three the first day. As with

Shen, Dashi likes to think of writers as doctors who minister to illnesses of the psyche.[75] Not that "Portrait of Eight Steeds" is entirely self-justification. Dashi's very name is ironic, for it can be construed as "Accomplished Scholar" (preceded by the surname Zhou, "All-around"). The story thus probes modern situation ethics; presents a psychological view of the nature of man; explores an intellectual, even "psychiatric" view of the role of the writer; and satirizes China's modern intellectual class—all at once.

Dashi stakes out his position in life through one-on-one colloquies with the seven male faculty members who lodge with him by the sea. All but one are sexually repressed—odd if not neurotic, Dashi writes Yuanyuan, exulting. He also tags them sociologically, as middle-aged "transitional" men caught out by the sexual revolution (their sons and daughters are better adjusted, he imagines). Dashi pretends that his meticulous reports are a keeping of faith with his lover, not just romantically, but as her literary window on the human condition. In fact the letters could be his vicarious way of winning arguments that he may or may not have won in person.

The point that the other professors think too much and act too little is well made by Shen as satirist. Dashi understands physics professor A from exterior symptoms: fat wife, erotica by the bed, headache medicine. Biologist B he knows by the obsessions hidden in his words. "Shanghai girls don't seem to be bothered by cold" means "their state of dishabille makes me nervous"; "It's beautiful by the sea" decodes as "The girls in their bathing suits are alluring." Professor C, a moral philosopher who thinks sex dirty, rationalizes with the thought that he is old, and gently advances the ideal of Platonic love—not directly, but through a story about how sex ruined "a friend." He keeps a nude picture of Venus in his room. In asking Dashi if he knows a particular student, he unintentionally reveals his desire for her. And so on, to historian D, who has pledged himself to a philosophy of self-control but will not commit himself to a woman while she is still beautiful; divorced literary historian E, who dislikes having to submit to a woman's needs; a "quite mad" historian H; and economist G, the only healthy one, evidently because he has a girlfriend. In this puzzle the missing piece is *ji*—"F," or "self": Dashi.

Mr. Dashi becomes infatuated with G's beautiful woman friend. We suspect this after reading a letter of Yuanyuan's. She has sensed an unusual reticence about Professor G. Meanwhile Dashi applies medical metaphors to himself, seemingly unaware of how they seem now to echo his colleagues' rationalizations. He will never again become "lovesick," he says, for he is "immunized." His responsibility to Woman (his fiancée) is precisely what denies him the right to love again, and so forth. When Dashi reverses himself and prepares to have a fling with G's lover, conventional moralistic readers conclude that Dashi himself has indeed become "sick." But Shen's Freudian logic is of course quite the reverse. Faced with the alternative of banishing his emotions, Mr. Dashi has healed himself by taking the plunge.

Mr. Dashi's victory is one of instinct over intellect, a replay of illiterate Fourth Dog's triumph over his lover's refined doubts in "After Rain." But Dashi is not a country boy. His psychiatric understanding of his friends' modern malaise is rare and penetrating. Indeed we appreciate his insights because Shen, through narrative selectivity, leads us to the same conclusions after letting us enjoy inductive reasoning for ourselves. Dashi's wit lies in his ability to screen out the "noise," leaving just the fat wife, bedside erotica, and headache balm. Likewise, when Dashi and B bare their souls, we hear only B's side of the conversation. Having to infer what he is talking about, it is but one step more for us to infer what he is *really* talking about. Dashi is the skilled analyst who can elicit such responses. The device of partial dialogue must have puzzled some readers, but Shen uses it in a simpler context at the outset, when Dashi is welcomed by a garrulous houseboy, who truly gives one no chance to get a word in edgewise.

In fact the intellectualizations of the professors that Dashi seeks to refute are not so easily brushed off as the poem in "After Rain." Dashi's solution to the problem of life must take all their contemporary theories into account and transcend them. Hence the importance of his remaining true to his human insight. Freudianism becomes a philosophy of life and morals.

Symbolism, too, lifts Mr. Dashi's personal, seemingly selfish choice onto a cosmological plane, affirming that his behavior is moral despite evidence that he does have human weaknesses. The vast, beautiful, therapeutic sea is ever-present, as backdrop. Recurring references to it are subliminally premonitory, linking the sea not just with death but with suicide, the mid-life alternative to life and health that Shen's stories often raise. The houseboy reads a book called *Casting [Oneself?] into the Sea*. He jokes with Dashi about the danger of falling in. Soon Dashi imagines he sees a woman walking into the sea. He jests about falling into the sea in a letter to Yuanyuan. Finally, to make a point in a dispute with a colleague about one's freedom to harm oneself, Dashi selects "throwing oneself into the sea" as his hypothetical example. He has also been reading Lao She's *Divorce*, a hint of trouble in his relationship with Yuanyuan. (When published or republished in 1935, this story must have led some readers to question the health of Shen Congwen's own two-year-old marriage.)

Once the other woman comes on the scene, there is a reversal. Merger with the sea is still the image evoked, but now it portends not demise but salvation. She takes the initiative, with an anonymous letter: "The semester will soon be over. Can you really leave the sea?" Later she etches in the sand an invitation to a tryst, asking Dashi to practice what he preaches (in his novels, which she knows well): "Some cannot love the sea, for they do not understand it. Others understand the sea, but *dare* not love it." Merger with the new and unknown thus becomes a moral reconciling of action with principle, and sexual intercourse a cosmic union. In fact the sea is part of Shen Congwen's recurring private (though hardly esoteric) symbolic world, its vastness representing, he said in 1980, "emancipation of thought, and of the feelings."[76] Other, more enigmatic symbols, such as colors, awaken Dashi's sense of wonder and expectation, setting him to free associating. These are, perhaps, a Symbolist technique in prose. At one point a color and an odor send him into a Proustian reverie about a failure in love, indicating how much in flux this fiancé really is.

Many readers read such stories à *clef*, including "Professors A, B, C, and D." Shen confesses that he lost their friendship—exaggerating, no doubt, since two of the eight steeds seem to be Wen Yiduo and Liang Shiqiu (with their academic fields altered). Easier to identify are the characters of "Three Women." This story features philosophical discourse, as does "Eight Steeds," but among the three most important young women in Shen's life: his Little Sister No. 9 ("Yiqing"), studying French at a missionary high school, pretty and delicate but slightly pettish; Shen's fiancée, Zhang Zhaohe ("Heifeng," Black Phoenix), dark, beautiful, dreamy, and musical, but cautious; and Ding Ling ("Pujing"), the oldest, stout, mannish, unsentimental, and always in charge—but dressed in white, the color of death. There are indeed two alter egos of Ding Ling in this piece, just as there are two of Congwen in "After Entering the Ranks." As Pujing, Ding Ling speaks "her" mind at the Qingdao seaside, in dialogue with the other two women. Yet the occasion for this soul-searching is Ding Ling's own sacrifice to her revolutionary artistic cause: the arrest down south of an undramatized "Mengke," who is masculine and leftist, like Pujing. "Xuanruo," Heifeng's undramatized fiancé, is away trying to rescue Mengke, while Pujing keeps up a brave front, as if to demonstrate that Ding Ling's indomitable spirit will live on, no matter what.[77]

There the factuality ends, of course. Ding Ling was indeed imprisoned down south, far from Qingdao, and she met Zhang Zhaohe only once (as the story says of Heifeng and Mengke), though Ding was well acquainted with Little Nine. Shen has brought the three women together through imagination, to contrast their psychologies, to explore their views (e.g., their attitude toward the writing profession and its risks and choices—his profession, as well as Ding Ling's), and possibly to ponder their influence upon him. "Three Women" provides Shen's remaining women friends with their own memorial to Ding Ling, reconciling them to her memory in death, though in Zhaohe's case a meeting of minds may not have occurred in life. The story also seems to be Shen's way of encouraging his little sister's budding literary interests.

Again, symbolism furthers argument. Pujing, the collectivist, *leads* her friends onward, toward the emancipating sea, that they may in more than one sense "lose themselves" in it. Then the young women debate the meaning of art. Pujing of course feels that art helps one dissolve the self. Heifeng worries that art may be a sacrilege to beauty. Yiqing argues for art as a means of elevation. All accept Shen's own views of ever-present beauty in nature, and the difficulty of really capturing it in words. Ultimately the piece focuses on Heifeng: her doubts about her usefulness, in view of Mengke's example, and her worries about whether or not her beauty distracts people from taking her seriously. Mengke's character, too, is examined, or rather praised, in her absence. Her alter ego Pujing presents a tough, revolutionary view of her, while the other women conjure up fond memories of Mengke's sincerity and softer virtues. The ethos is one of mutual love, respect, and good humor. What renders "Three Women" unlike Shen's other idea stories, perhaps, is its reticence about love between the sexes.

A pervasively Freudian way of seeing the world, as in "Eight

Steeds," appears quite frequently, probably under the influence of Zhu Guangqian as well as Lu Zhiwei, in the stories Shen wrote after moving to Qingdao in 1931. As he now admits, Freudianism flavors even the regional *Frontier City*—his "representative" work, and in the eyes of the unsuspecting a quite innocent one. The novel explores the psychological development of its pubescent heroine, Cuicui, against the background of the aging and gradual decline of her grandfather, the village ferryman. Thoughts of death, and the need to arrange for Cuicui's well-being, begin to preoccupy him. Meanwhile she, too, has subliminal premonitions of impending loss: of Granddad, and of her innocence. Shen fills Cuicui's world with images of being "bitten by a fish," erotic love songs, bridal processions, and phalli, from flutes to racing dragon boats. There is sexual symbolism in her daydreams: "She had no idea how large Dongting Lake might be, nor had she ever seen one of those large boats [of which she dreamed]. What was even stranger, she herself didn't know why she had come to think of these things." She begins to realize, and fear, her blossoming sexuality. "[S]he thought of many things. Of stories of tigers eating people, of the four-line mountain songs used by people to curse each other, of the square pit in a papermaking factory, of the molten iron being let out of the smelting furnace of an iron works. She seemed to want to go over everything she had heard and seen." Indeed, she goes through a stage of hostility toward her own grandfather, before finally accepting her new role as the one responsible not only for herself but for him. Finally, love songs she hears while sleeping lift her subconscious mind up to pick erotically red saxifrage. Through symbolism already adumbrated in *Fengzi*, these wildflowers represent love and its hidden dangers. Cuicui "absentmindedly" gathers some, in combination with whip-shaped bamboo shoots. When a flood carries away the landing and marks the death of Granddad, Cuicui is torn loose from her mooring, ready to face an indefinite future of love and ever-present death.[78]

More programmatic than *The Frontier City* in celebrating the benefits of love are Shen's classic stories "Spring" and "Dr. Ruomo," published the previous year, in 1932. ("Spring," however, shows few signs of Freud.) These stories in turn follow "Chill" (1930) and "No. 4" (1930?), which argue a point both romantic and psychological: that the way to love is to be decisive and take a woman physically, not waste time with sweet words.[79] "Chill" sketches a listless woman high school teacher, with her dreams—of being taken by force—and frustrations. While strolling in a park, she notices and admires a virile military officer, but must instead suffer the attentions of an excessively inhibited colleague, a physics teacher. He flees when she tacitly challenges him to be a man. The woman sits down next to the soldier. When he begins to flirt, she teases him and withholds her name. But she will meet him again.

"No. 4" is more complex. It purports to be scenario no. 4 in the author-narrator's notebook, the tale of a garrulous friend from whose experience the author has often taken his literary plots. The talkative one likes to avoid mention of his own experience with women, but goes on and on about what makes them tick. His philosophy is one of "decisiveness rather than words," unlikely as that seems, coming from him. Finally he tells his story. He fell in love and had an affair with the wife of a minister friend. Two days before they were to elope, she was injured in a bus accident. She confessed all, in a "crazy dream." The preacher nursed her and pretended not to understand. He gave her the chance to leave; thus did he gain the psychological upper hand over the lovers. Confesses the author's proud friend, it was his first defeat in the game of love. He was changed by it; could never love again. Some time later, the author-narrator prepares to send him a newspaper clipping. The minister has been killed by soldiers. The writer destroys it, however, on learning that his friend is engaged to be married to someone else. By *telling* his story, it seems, the inhibited "garrulous" one had cured himself.

"Spring" is a more lighthearted, even frothy, yet elegantly crafted work featuring entertaining dialogue in a psychological standoff between a male medical student and his elegant ladyfriend. The story could be called a city-folks' "Long Zhu." Confident of his powers of flattery, the boy begins ebulliently. He pretends to envy his love's caged bird, a "songbird" like himself. The girl is too hemmed in by bourgeois conventions herself to communicate her passion directly, but clearly she is impatient, ready for the relationship to move ahead. It amuses her to make fun of her suitor, parrying his flattery of her as his "princess." He becomes ever more flustered. When finally he is completely tongue-tied, the girl rescues him. She knew all along that he had come to propose marriage. Her father has agreed. Thus encouraged, the medical student finds the nerve to kiss her. The story ends with him in command, and nature ready to take its course.

"Dr. Ruomo" is more militantly Freudian, and more philosophical and autobiographical in its implications—halfway to "Portrait of Eight Steeds." Like the latter, "Dr. Ruomo" tells of talks by the Qingdao seashore between an autobiographical narrator and a staid, repressed professional, a medical doctor. The narrator plays him philosophically and psychiatrically like an instrument. Ruomo has a psychological crutch: his pipe. The narrator thinks it makes him seem too old, too serious and unnatural. When Ruomo argues, though, out comes the pipe—the more reason for the narrator to engage him in debate, and so loosen him up. The subjects are politics and sex. Interestingly, Shen Congwen's alter ego, who does represent the author's own views, is a left-wing idealist foil to Dr. Ruomo as cynical rightist. Ruomo wants a clear "direction" and strong leader for the state. He cannot tolerate decadent trends like dancing, nor Christians, nor adherents of the "new faith" (Communism?) born of the Death of God. He asks for government by experts and wonders why the narrator is unwilling to give the Leader (Chiang Kaishek) time to solve the nation's problems. What experts? And is 20 years not a long time for a republic? Thus counters the narrator, who disagrees on every point.

Their other argument is over women. Serious Dr. Ruomo dislikes these "gods to poets and wastrels," fearing the power they might exert over him. His anality and political conservatism thus are traced to a blockage of libido. Just as he confounded Ruomo's politics with its own contradictions, the narrator manages to get him interested in a nubile minister's daughter. The doctor in the end surrenders his pipe, his arguments, and his celibacy.

This all appears in yet another dimension. Shen Congwen's plot elaborately frames the talks with Dr. Ruomo as a reminiscence by the narrator about deceased friends and their orphans—like the late Dr. Ruomo and his only child, the sole issue from his "conversion." The narrator's past encounter with Ruomo has special autobiographical poignancy because Shen, who at the time of writing was still frustrated in his attempt to marry, has the narrator reflect on his own "country-boy" ineptness with women. Fiction appears to mimic reality in the matter of the minister's daughter, too. The minister is the narrator's friend. Aware that the narrator (Shen's alter ego) has recently been hurt in an affair of the heart, the minister has sent his daughter as a possible match for him. As in an actual event from Shen Congwen's life, the girl mistakes Ruomo for the narrator, increasing the latter's pain.[80] Moreover, the story ends with the narrator confessing that he has recorded everything about Ruomo's romance in his diary. He was, quite possibly, sublimating his own desires by writing. "Dr. Ruomo," with "No. 4," appears to present yet another psychiatric justification for authorship. It is an author's therapy for himself.

For all their similarities in subject matter and world view, "Dr. Ruomo" and "Portrait of Eight Steeds" are not quite the same. Surely it is no coincidence that "Dr. Ruomo," written in July 1931 while Shen was still unsuccessfully courting Zhang Zhaohe, explores the anxiety of being single, whereas "Portrait," written just before his marriage, and given its first major publication (possibly revised) two years afterward, raises the frustration of being tied down. Because Shen kept feeding his immediate life interests into his stories, 1933 marks a general watershed.

A recurring theme after 1933 is the necessity of *jingya* ("wonderment," "surprise") for romantic love and attraction to beauty. Habituation dulls these feelings. Such is the case with psychology professor Liu and his unhappily married friends, middle-aged like himself, in "Suicide" (1935). Liu's friends have spoken of suicide as an alternative to divorce. Liu's own marriage appears rather shaky, from clues in the interaction with his wife that Shen dramatizes, and unusual narrative coincidences. His baby, for instance, is just learning to talk, but seems presciently to allude to the departure of marital fidelity (and also longevity) by mimicking Liu's mention of having seen a white crane fly: "Flies! Flies! Papa flies." The wife is beautiful, but that beauty now bores Liu, in a way he never could have imagined. When he takes an interest in a teenage girl orphaned by a double suicide, Mrs. Liu, too, like the wife in Lu Xun's "Soap," fears for the marriage. Before going to bed, they each suggest, with ambiguous seriousness, that they have been thinking about suicide. This is the story that Wu Mi feared might be about him. Readers in the know must have wondered if it reflected Shen Congwen's own anomie.[81]

So autobiographically factual in all exterior details is the story "Housewife" (1937) that one is tempted to read it as Shen Congwen's confession of having himself lost the heady infatuation, the *jingya*, that initially attracted him to Zhang Zhaohe (now his wife of three years). Shen explores the psychology of the marriage by entering the minds of both parties. The wife's case is presented first. She rehearses her own life and the place of the marriage within it, her husband's foibles, the clash of temperaments, the sorrows and joys. Then the husband persona, after somewhat patronizingly interpreting his wife's experience as psychological "growth," proceeds in a tender spirit of reconciliation with self-criticism and apology. He, Shen's alter ego, has a revealing nightmare about one of his precious antiques being smashed; he awakens and counts his treasures. They number almost 300 items, enough to be "a sandbag weighing down his soul, scissors shearing off his imagination." He, however, would deflect further consideration of tensions in the marriage onto a more abstract plane.

He wondered, When a breeze from one person's heart blows into another's life, is it by chance, or of necessity? Who is being reasonable—the one so often controlled by her surroundings and youth, or the one who seems to be forever illimitable? Is it the human ideal for the emotions to be reined in, or for them to roam unbounded? ...

Looking up at the blue sky, his feelings swam out without hugging the shore. It was as if he could freely proceed anywhere—into the past, the future, into the void. He was himself an Abstraction.[82]

Is the subject philosophy or romance? Though Shen in the 1930's liked to raise Aristotelian ideas about man's need for self-control, if not external control, he invoked such concepts metaphorically, to describe his wonderfully rapt "enslavements"—to a woman, Beauty, or ideals. He never meant seriously to consider any creed of the limited life. Hence the "other interests" he wants freedom to pursue might well include other women.[83]

This typifies the role of philosophy in Shen Congwen's works. Searching questions are asked, or suggested, without follow-through. For instance, Shen does not, like Proust, proceed from the role of mystery and enigma in love to the idea that love itself may be focused on an idealized image in the imagination instead of a real person—much as he is fascinated with unattainability. Instead he conveys his own sense of wonder at the power of memory to keep the loved one in her original state.

Temperamentally assimilative and impressionable rather than systematic or analytical, Shen likewise borrows the vocabulary of dualism to show that the cosmos is reflected in a dewdrop, that the noumenal is one with the phenomenal. The "beauty" that feeds on wonder is for him *both* the physical beauty of his wife and noumenal Beauty, or the sublime. He seeks the magic of the commonplace, of the hidden life. Says the husband in "Housewife":

"Beauty is an indefinite and limitless term. Any event or thing that can stir a person's emotions, leading to wonderment and a feeling of comfort, is beauty." About 1940, Shen explained it, in words reminiscent of Cai Yuanpei, as "perhaps a person, an object, or an assembled arrangement of abstract symbols" that commands reverence from the viewer. "This beauty perhaps has been produced by the creating hands of God. A slab of bronze, a piece of rock, a bundle of threads, an arrangement of sounds—though they are small as matter, [in them] may be seen the vastness and completeness of the world. Perhaps it is 'Creation' (*Zaowu*), most directly, most simply, 'Man.' A shooting star is gone in the lightning-flash of a moment; in this it manifests a beautiful sacredness, and man is the same. A smile, a frown—nothing is incapable of manifesting this sacredness." [84]

Idea fiction constitutes only a minority even of Shen's mid-1930's works, but "ideas" subtly flavor much of his writing. His social satire, for instance, has more historical perspective than before. Not that Shen discarded analyses of static social landscapes. "Sons of the Rich" is one, a Chinese *Volpone* about the people preying on a degenerate landlord's son, who ends up as an agricultural "expert" with "experimental plots" to tend. This leads to a new round of wasteful folly, from the purchase of expensive grass-cutting machinery to a junket to study Soviet collective farms. "An Ordinary Story," about snobbery, frivolity, cliquishness, and romantic mores at a missionary school (like Little Nine's?) similarly resembles Shen's 1920's satires, with an ironic twist at the end about the meaning of it all. But Shen also began more imaginatively creating comparative life histories that spanned decades, as in "Big Ruan and Little Ruan." Sons of the gentry, this uncle and nephew pass through an elite high school at about the same time, yet diverge in practice, helpless before the social forces of their time. One, literarily inclined, ends up as a Shanghai-Type writer, penning little essays and consorting with prostitutes. He marries the daughter of a Nanking official and is in every sense corrupt and self-serving, unfaithful even to the memory of his nephew—who became a Communist organizer and rashly sacrificed his life. It is a panoramic, not very sympathetic, vision of China's old ruling class and the historical split in it. [85]

Continuing with autobiographical fiction, Shen Congwen now explored the meaning, or rather the ironies, in events. This includes mistaken identities, as in "Tiger Cub" (1931) and "The Visitor" (1933), and generational misunderstandings, as in "Lamp" (originally 1929), which he revised in such a way as to tease readers who took all his writings to be autobiography. Shen Congwen's own persona in "Lamp" is visited by a young woman who resembles Ding Ling. Her presence raises false hopes in the mind of a quasi-factual old soldier servant that the girl and the Shen persona might get married. At the end, the reminiscing narrator, the Shen persona, has to explain all this away as a fantasy—to a Zhang Zhaohe persona![86]

Shen Congwen also exercised his technical and linguistic talents in ineffable mood pieces like "Living" (1933) and "Quiet" (1932), the latter C. T. Hsia's favorite. The poignant "Rurui" (1933) uses scents, colors, and wilting flowers to capture a sensitive young couple: a woman just past her prime, and the one she loves, a strong young man. He is younger than she, not ready for romance, until he lies poisoned in a hospital—flowers by his bed. There he belatedly confesses love to the fading beauty. Rurui chooses to leave him. The deft psychological portrait of a strong, unattainable woman and an indecisive man is particularly intriguing because Shen may have poured into it his feelings on learning of Ding Ling's "death."[87]

These pieces draw on, if not Shen's "ideas," his universe of ethereal imagery. A 1946 work proceeds to link color symbolism to Buddhist allegory. But the religious element in most of Shen Congwen's work is still more elusive than the philosophic, until 1940, when he speaks explicitly of pantheism (he did again in 1980). Shen had been rewriting Buddhist tales in 1933–34; Anthony J. Prince's definitive study even finds a Buddhist model for one of Shen's pieces of philosophical fiction, "Knowledge" (1934). Yet Shen seems only to have borrowed Buddhist plots, symbols, and perhaps the pantheistic idea of Indira's web, not any sort of asceticism that might have reined in his love of sentient existence. In the early 1940's he wrote, in essays, and in poems he published under an obscure pen name, not of one but of two life forces. One was "living" (*shenghuo*), man's existence as an animal, seeking food and sex. The other was a higher force, "Life" (*shengming*)—that which seeks "the Abstract." No more than Mencius or Freud would Shen force man into abnormality by denying physical living. Yet he depicts the more exalted Life as willingness to forsake mere living. In its oblivion to material gain and focus on higher ideals, Life is like a form of madness. It alone partakes of divinity. Using Tagorean metaphors, Shen describes Life as a pantheistic spirit: a flame, radiating into the lives of others.[88]

Life is present in all people; it is in fact omnipresent, realizes the pantheist. But few transcend living to know Life—very few city people. Their senses are dulled by the environment without, while their spirit within "crawls" along at the level of seeking petty advantage for mere existence. Lacking Life within, they cannot link up with the Life without. Primitive man, however, seeks the divine in his frenzied rites. As pantheist, he finds Life everywhere in nature. Yet he does have fellow spirits in the modern age. Among them are great authors and artists, who in their own "madness" seek the Abstract ideals of truth and beauty, or the disinterested ideals of helping the downtrodden in society (through realistic writings). Creativity is thus a divine expression of the Life force. And it is not in the final analysis counter-evolutionary. One creates to overcome death, to achieve immortality through works. Creativity fills a psychic need. Its origin lies, biologically, in "sexual instinct."[89]

These views helped Shen Congwen transcend his time by integrating his faith with science. They hallowed the tribal folk from which he sprang, and the scholar he had become. They also justified his unengaged writings, as altruistic and permanent in a way that anti-Japanese literature was not. Shen argued that transcendent literature reduced the isolation of the self: by reaching upward, to the Ultimate, and outward, to break down the barriers between one's own Life and that of others. "By making contact with another kind of human life through a literary work, a reader has a revelation. He can gain a deeper understanding of human life, or of Life itself."[90] Finally, by defining Deity not only as good, but as aesthetic, Shen provided a rationale for craft and imagination in literature, without making them ends in themselves (rather their Beauty was). His Abstract, he said, *was* the Beautiful. This was the one check on his freedom he could accept. He would be limited by no code or person (except for her beauty). "In my life I have discovered 'the Beautiful,' that whose form and shape represent the highest virtue, and which causes men to delight in being controlled by it, in being governed by it." It was abstract indeed: better captured in mathematics than writing; better still, he said (like Kant), in music. Shen was not consistent, however. Elsewhere, he still argued for literature as the best art form for prodding mankind forward, or literally "upward" (*xiang shang*).[91]

Besides the references to Jesus's "universal love" in his earliest works, we have noted Shen's depiction of man as divine in "Long Zhu" (1929). In many subsequent works he approaches and describes all things with a conscious sense of "wonder," if not religion as such. In *Fengzi* (1932), the characters' self-consciousness about the role of metaphors in seeing the world could itself be a metaphor for art as a method of meditation. But more directly, the *Autobiography* already presages Shen Congwen's pantheistic language of the war years, and so marks a watershed in 1932: "Each kind of life nourished this soul of mine, causing it to sense a spark of light and flame from everything it touched." And, "I got an elementary knowledge of how this people, over a vast stretch of time, created all kinds of art, through an individual life, using a patch of color, a bundle of threads, a piece of bronze, a heap of clay—or a group of words." *The Frontier City*, too, Shen explains, was written to explain "love"—surely not just Cuicui's blooming sexuality, nor yet the love of grandfather and granddaughter, but a larger pantheistic love that subsumes all the others.[92]

Pantheism in Shen's works is, however, subtle—difficult to trace, or disentangle from his general, expansive celebration of "Life." Shen Congwen was familiar with Henri Bergson's theory of *élan vital* and "creative evolution" early on, from Lin Zaiping —perhaps even earlier, from reading with his Uncle Nie in West Hunan. A 1932 work further hints that Shen sought emotional refuge in Buddhist writings when he went to Qingdao, in 1931. The 1932 upsurge of metaphysical and ethereal, often typically Tagorean, images in Shen's work—including love, freedom, beauty, stars, shooting stars, human beings coming together "by chance," and so forth—may on the other hand partly reflect the profound impact of Xu Zhimo's death upon him. Xu Zhimo had been Shen's most helpful professional friend and a source literally of inspiration. He was himself a man of faith, an advocate of "creative idealism" who dealt in these images. Shen Congwen wrote hardly any commemorative pieces about his friend. Instead, Shen later wrote, he tried to assimilate the "afterglow" of Xu Zhimo's life into his own works.[93] It is precisely in Xu Zhimo's poems, though, that one may suspect the cosmological metaphors of being artifice.[94] When Shen used cosmic symbols, he did so more solemnly, though not more profoundly. The main evidence, before 1940, is his *Fengzi*.

Fengzi is Shen Congwen's *A la recherche du temps perdu*, at least in spirit.[95] A complex work in psychological and symbolic texture to begin with (and unfinished), *Fengzi* is not simply a first-person allegorical venture into the meaning of the author's past; the integration of memories occurs through yet a second veil of allegory. There is, to begin with, the story of a young West Hunanese made disconsolate by a failure in love. Using indirect third-person narrative, Shen weaves in and out of his mind while the lad spiritually convalesces by absorbing the brilliance of nature at the Qingdao seashore. Further exploration of the young man's background paradoxically turns away from him, to the reminiscences of a second "hermit," a gentry fellow whom the young man meets by the sea: not a West Hunanese, but a middle-aged city aristocrat whose manhood has been shaped by a long sojourn in fabled West Hunan during his youth. The friendship between the young hermit and the older one is one of life's magic coincidences ("by chances"). And it was preceded by another, one evening at dusk, when the sun covered the sea in brilliant gold. The young man had chanced to overhear a middle-aged man discussing the meaning of life with a 20-year-old young woman. Several months later, he learns that he had been eavesdropping on a conversation between his new gentry acquaintance and the beautiful Fengzi—a vision of Zhang Zhaohe, the woman Shen still hoped to marry. It remains to be added that, far away and long ago, the gentryman was initiated into the mysteries of West Hunan (when he was about 30, the present age of the forlorn native West Hunanese protagonist) by a Miao chieftain in his fifties. The young gentryman had been sent into the Miao pale after the revolution by the provincial bureau of mines. His guide, the lord of all he surveyed, became his mentor. The present Qingdao friendship between young man and elder, wayfarer and aristocrat, is thus not only a mutual reawakening of memory, but a psychological recapitulation of the life story that the Qingdao gentryman is about to relate. It is a paternal relationship, one Shen Congwen sorely missed in his own life, but seems to have created from imagination.[96]

Fengzi deals with many things: the dying spirit of the Chinese countryside, the local character of West Hunan and its people, the imperatives of romance, the inadequacies of art, the nature of God, and the wisdom that comes with age. The last two issues are first dramatized in the overheard conversations between the middle-aged gentryman and Fengzi (chapter 2). The man wants her to appreciate God's handiwork in the ever-present natural beauty. She acknowledges the beauty, but because it is so "natural," can it also be sublimely startling—a source of "wonderment"? An interesting point, but the man sighs that she is too young to understand. Perhaps this is Shen Congwen, "middle-aged" already, as usual pressing his Zhang Zhaohe to "catch up" so that they may have a meeting of minds.

Many of Shen Congwen's subsequently recurring cosmic symbols appear in *Fengzi*, with their referents. Grains of sand on the beach represent faraway lives meeting "by chance," and stars, individual lives. Meteors are symbols of life's fleeting brilliance. Rainbows, likewise, show transient and uncapturable beauty. Finally, as if to win the argument with Fengzi, wildflowers appear as miracles of nature evoking "wonderment." In chapter 7, the gentryman as a young man explores the Miao chieftain's "theology": "God is nature" (which is not meant to contradict the other proposition, that God is the creator of nature). Will science replace theology, the young man asks? In the city, perhaps, says the chieftain, where the Chinese have already lost their faith in the gods and in themselves. But not in the countryside, where the politicians' rule does not extend, and the gods are still acknowledged to be in control. For "God, according to the XX-ese [West Hunanese], besides controlling nature, is only an abstraction: uprightness, sincerity, and love. Science is truth, which is a legacy culled from Deity. But however advanced science becomes, it cannot take away uprightness and love, so our God here will last forever. He [They] cannot be extinguished." The chieftain makes a "rash" prediction. The atheists returned from abroad, who think they can refashion China's faith by simply remaking her social organization, are bound to fail. What will be the outcome? Thirty years of anarchy, perhaps. And the countryside? It will not be destroyed from within, but from without: economically, in the turmoil of the revolution.[97]

There is, finally, a more contentious question to face. Was Shen Congwen in his idea fiction developing as a writer, or just "unfolding" (to borrow Frye's term)?[98] As his subject matter grew more abstract, so did his language—"flowery," some called it.[99] Something was gained from his new intellectuality, but was the comic and realistic bite of his earliest works lost? When Shen scaled new technical heights in the 1940's, it was through yet another turn inward, toward psychological autobiography. Did this mean that he lacked "the confidence and toughness to build imaginary worlds,"[100] even regional ones, like Faulkner's? Perhaps. And yet, however fascinating the exotic realities he had "recorded," much of Shen Congwen's greatness had always rested with his powers as mythmaker. As one of the few modern Chinese writers touched by post-Freudian consciousness, he was able to continue engaging his readers with universal dreams of life, love, and death, communicated through shared images at the subconscious level. Yet, though young people in particular did continue to interact with literature at the level of myth, as when they read Ba Jin's popular works, Shen Congwen's social myths were no longer the ones that inflamed them. Youth wanted to dream of entering the world of political action and revolution, or simply to enjoy the new opportunities that capitalism had already built for the lucky ones among them in China's coastal cities. In this changed context, it probably made little difference to most of his readers that Shen, no longer content to plumb the symbols and myths of his subconscious, felt compelled to deal with explicit "ideas." Unfortunately ideas—nonmaterialist ones—struck the Communists as a challenge in their own realm: that of world view.

CHAPTER SEVEN

Fighting for Autonomy

SHEN CONGWEN's idea fiction was headed toward ever more remote realms of eroticism and technical experimentation, as we shall relate. Yet no sooner did he reach the frontiers, in the early 1940's, than he fled them, under unanimous censure from China's literary left, right, and center. His regional writing was more sustained and less controversial. It lasted through 1947—longer than autonomous West Hunan. In the regional works one did not have to put up with the "obscurity" and "abnormality" with which Western modernism had, Shen's friends and readers felt, infected his stories about urban people. The home-grown opacities, such as dialect, were already long since muted. Ultimately, though, Shen made his own artistic choices. Faulkner's fiction is proof enough that regionalism is compatible with literary modernism at its most difficult. Shen Congwen put avant-garde technique into his regional writing once or twice, but he had hardly made a start of it when the Communist revolution silenced him entirely.

Shen's late 1930's and 1940's regional works diverged from the "abstraction" of his urban fiction in yet another way. Though their realism was still pervaded with lyricism and comedy, the regional works were becoming "engaged." They were politically more vulnerable in their specifics, though perhaps less so in principle, since engagement was, some now said, required of literature.

It was not the literary climate, though, but Shen's return trips home, in 1933–34 and early 1938, that turned his regional fiction toward harsher "realities." He got caught up on, and in 1938 caught up in, local history. It was a tragic history, much less reconcilable now with his regional myths. In 1935, West Hunan lost all power of self-determination. Its new military overlords did not love the region or easily tolerate the Miao. The region was heading toward continuous social violence and anarchy, which would end only in the 1950's. Telling that story, or at least the first part of it, was the final goal Shen Congwen set himself as a regional writer. More than ever, he took West Hunan to be its own political entity. He was nearly writing a sectional literature for his region. Yet the more Shen explored the rights and wrongs in the relationship between his region and central power, the more he was delving into a fundamental problem of the Chinese state, rather than West Hunan's special case, based on its regional peculiarities. Shen Congwen was not necessarily aware of that, however. If he was, he did not let the generalizing power of political theory turn him into a propagandist. Shen discovered his generalizations while writing. He did not write to embody the sociologies of others, not even the apostles of democracy from whom he took his own political ideas.

West Hunan Before and After the Fall

The visit home in 1933–34 that so affected Shen Congwen's writing was his first return to the uplands region of West Hunan in ten years. Previously, much of his regional fiction had been nostalgic, recreating Shen's carefree days of childhood as often as his more troubling experiences as a soldier, and seldom hinting that social disintegration lay ahead.

The Frontier City appropriately marks the end of that period. It is literally on the "borderline," the last work Shen composed during his ten-year absence from home. (It was in fact not yet complete when Shen left Peking for home in late 1933.) Shen lingered over each word, writing under the date and locust trees in the yard close by his honeymoon lodgings. To Shen Congwen in 1933, West Hunan was a set of memories: a girl he once fancied, a fellow soldier in love, border ferries traversing crystal-clear streams, soft rains, riverside prostitutes cursing their steady boyfriends, country folk bravely battling floods, haunting bugle calls, mountain songs, and melodies from an old man's flute. This West Hunan was not really Shen's home, but the region he had glimpsed from the perspective of a soldier, living one day at a time in a kind of never-never land. Nor is the novel set in the 1920's, when Shen actually passed through Chadong with his unit. It unfolds during the much more pacific first years of the Republic.[1]

Perhaps the bittersweet ending to *The Frontier City* reflects the disquieting things Shen saw on his 1934 trip home. *Fengzi*, written a year and a half earlier, is more idyllic. In both works, however, distance from West Hunan seems to have brought detachment, along with idealization. It is in those pre-1934 works—not in *Long River* (1939–42)—that the technical barriers between Shen's lyrically realistic regional writing and his Westernized idea fiction were starting to dissolve.

Introspection suits *Fengzi*, for this work is about Shen Congwen's real native place. It was for *Fengzi* that he composed the panoramic description of old Zhen'gan now famous as the opening to his autobiography. The novel proceeds all the way back to Shen's roots, in the border Miao pale west of Fenghuang. Along its forest and mountain paths, the city stranger (the gentryman in his youth) meets a "country girl" and dreams of a dalliance, even of giving up his old life to settle down with a local beauty. One major backdrop is a *baozhai*, or fortified Miao village, in which dwells the sage chieftain who initiates the young city man into the lore and ways of the natives. It is just after the 1911 Revolution, but the Miao lord is still addressed by the old Qing title of "Zongye" ("Honorable Sergeant"; from *qianzong*, the second-highest Miao *tuntian* officer, of whom Fenghuang had 20 by statute). He has inherited the position from his father, who had it from his father, and so on for seven generations; on the site of his castle once stood a native head's (*tusi*'s) palace. The city guest is educated and gentrified, though, so His Honor addresses the lad, with no irony intended, as "Teacher." [2]

A government cinnabar mine is another focal point. This is a hallowed site for the Shens, for according to family tradition it was in such a place that they were transplanted into local history—took root and became nativized. The mines, like the *luguan* music and Miao discourse through song, which Shen abstracts into a pervasively metaphoric mode of apprehending reality and human relations, flavor *Fengzi* with Chu mysticism—with the ancient ethos of China's Southlands, a place where God is not yet dead. Mercury, believed to have magic powers 2,000 years ago, especially links the region to the past and to the gods. Miners plumb that treasure with methods hallowed by millennia, their very drudgery revealing the strength in immutability. Yet mercury's properties are prized by modern science, too. How long can the past and present coexist?, Shen asks.[3]

Fengzi is a regional apologia—but not for banditry, poverty, or civil war. Rather it accounts for more barbaric (that is to say, romantic) regional images and legends, like blood feuds and the *gu* poison cult.[4] The natives, and the city convert, want outsiders to understand the region and put aside their fearful wariness. As to realities—all these scenes are reminiscences conjured up at the Qingdao seaside. The characters are aware, and fearful, that *their* West Hunan may already have been destroyed. Shen expresses not so much a historical as a cultural nostalgia, his yearning for an antidote to the unprecedented twentieth-century wasteland. It is not, indeed, so far removed from his modernism.

How different is the West Hunan Shen Congwen depicted after going home. It was three years before he undertook another major work of regional fiction. That was *Xiaozhai* ("Little Stockade," the name of a village), begun in the summer of 1937.[5] When Japan attacked, he abandoned the work to join his university (then Peking University) in retreat to the Southwest. *Xiaozhai* was to have been a long novel: when Shen gave it up, after five chapters, he had not even introduced the village that evidently was to have been his focus. The central locale of the completed part is an unnamed city and its environs, almost certainly Wangcun, a You River port just a hundred miles downriver from Chadong. This town, however, is an opposite mirror image of the picturesque and sturdy "Frontier City"; not idyll, but anti-utopia, beginning with cave-dwelling country people outside town whose existence is subhuman. Other major actors include a corrupt military detachment sent by Changsha (that is, an occupation force of "foreigners"); a diseased prostitute from the countryside whom the boatmen consider worn-out at the age of eighteen; her madam; and a grotesque—a boy with dropsy who works at the customs office, also now under Changsha control. The boy is just learning how to presume on his tiny measure of official status to cheat the peasants at market. The scene is thus set for further demoralization of the locals, as they become more "realistic" in order to defend themselves against the new, leeching opportunism that has intruded on West Hunan from the more developed world. Perhaps (if we may be permitted to extrapolate from Shen's other writings, and local history) the locals will learn to strike back at the Changsha troops and bad officials. We might envision them leaving their wretched caves to take to the hills and found a bandit lair, perhaps called Xiaozhai. The prostitute, after being coveted by the customs inspector, would end up as the mistress of the stockade. Shen never wrote this, but he did write the following, in 1937.

Living on the street by the wharf are customs officials and some Jiangxi moneylenders. Most of the rest are small businessmen. They vend food and drink so that people can eat, and opium to numb their souls and ruin their bodies. Those who sell their lower parts relieve the boatmen's weariness and spread the gonorrhea and syphilis prevalent among the thoroughly moderns. When people splurge on a meal of meat, it's from a piglet dead of smallpox or the stinking internal organs of a cow. Most of the opium is labeled as being from Yunnan or Sichuan, but really it's just local stuff, mixed with distillates of pumpkin and pigskin. As to the flesh trade, even women over the age of forty have the opportunity to join in this competition for survival.[6]

For an understanding of what it was that brought Shen Congwen from the relatively happy mental state of *The Frontier City* to the disillusionment of *Xiaozhai*, one must turn to his *Discursive Notes on a Trip Through Hunan* (1934), a nonfiction account of what he saw in January 1934, revised from letters he wrote to his wife en route.[7] The *Discursive Notes* actually conceal Shen's most important reunions—with his brothers, at their new home in Chenzhou (Yuanling); with his dying mother, in Fenghuang; and with his old superior, Chen Quzhen, still "King of West Hunan," in Fenghuang. There is no mention of Shen's emotional visit to a pavilion commemorating several of his friends, evidently killed by bandits, or the difficulties he encountered in Fenghuang after being suspected of Communist sympathies (so much so that he avoided contact with relatives and cut his visit to three days). Instead, Shen dramatizes himself, juxtaposing mental images from past and present, and moves between conversations with representative common people and what he *imagines* they must be doing and thinking out of earshot. The *Discursive Notes* are a very literary bridge between Shen Congwen's pastoralism and his subsequent naturalism, an internal journey into the people and places of his whole life experience rather than a documentary about what dispirited him. His 60 letters yielded but a dozen chapters. Only one chapter is set in Fenghuang, and it was omitted from the book.[8]

The *Discursive Notes* are thus less fascinating for the social phenomena they reveal than for how Shen Congwen refracts them—

sometimes through his past, sometimes through prophetic apprehensions about the future. Many of the images signify lack of change: a Miao customs inspector; a young boatman who expresses grudging love for a prostitute; a lovely young prostitute who dreams of Shen, the city stranger, delivering her from bondage; boatmen who brave the rapids, one of them 76 years old; and the *memory* of dragon boat races that Shen once saw at a particular village, since the reality is now inaccessible. The region has not kept up with Shen. Yet, to find strangeness in these scenes is to discover alienation from a part of himself. He reflects sadly on the consequences of aging, just a step away from his ultimate fear: that he, Shen Congwen, is now a "city person." "Trackers passed over the stone shoals, their backs bent. These poor creatures seemed to be outside of history. They were now as they had been a hundred years ago, and would be a hundred years from now.... It made me feel a bit anxious—everything in this place was unchanged, whereas I perhaps had changed a little too much." [9]

Immutability can be attractive. Reflecting on the Yuan River fauna and the dragon boat races, Shen imagines that time has stood still in West Hunan since Qu Yuan visited some 2,000 years ago. But as Social Darwinist, he reasons that his fellow-regionals, having made peace with nature, must now founder in the "struggle for existence." At their doorstep is another species of humanity: those who struggle *against* nature, making history instead of existing outside it. As they have conquered the elements, so will they conquer the West Hunanese.[10]

The real subject, then, is Shen Congwen's sense of what is to come. He arrives in each isolated Yuan River port with a sense of its impending doom. How much historical consciousness do the locals have of their coming "fate"? Shen's idea of what that fate may be slowly takes form between the lines. He is imagining what the fifth anti-Communist "extermination campaign" might do if it came to his region. Revolution and counterrevolution were invisible once he got to West Hunan, but that was precisely the danger. Nanking and Changsha were just then mobilizing 600,000 troops against the Central Soviet in neighboring Jiangxi province. The state of emergency nearly prevented Shen from arriving, and must have fed the suspicions that he was a fellow traveler. Surely central KMT armies would soon be coming to attack He Long, in northern West Hunan. Already a motor road was being extended into the region, giving Changsha's governor He Jian ("butcher of men," Shen calls him) his first access to Chen Quzhen's warlord kingdom, as well as to He Long's soviet. In 1936, plans were even announced for a railroad (to be completed in three years, but delayed for 40 once Japan struck). Already Shen's old commander was weak from local warfare, and from conflicts with He Long and with Guizhou. The "golden age" he had brought to West Hunan was about to end, Shen Congwen warned the "King of West Hunan."[11]

Shen in fact warns not just against stasis, but against harmful change, for "civil war, the Poison [opium], flood, and famine" have led his folk down "the road of moral degeneracy and extinction."[12] This narrative thread, too, intensifies from one Yuan River stop to the next. Zeng Qinxuan, once Shen's "living dictionary" of obscenities, has become a Changde hotel manager and lost his childlike directness (*tongxin*). Taoyuan has built its old literary associations and new accessibility (from the new automobile road) into a giant flesh trade; Shen ironically juxtaposes the classical and carnal visits of literati tourists. Pushi and Luqi have declined commercially. They now call to mind only robbery and mayhem. One of the local notables is a wounded veteran from the anti-Communist wars who has retired to a profitable and illegal life of opium-running. Then there is Shen's childhood army buddy, after whom he created Nuosong. "Cuicui" has just died; opium has so ravaged "Nuosong" that Shen cannot bear to identify himself to his old friend. He also learns that his younger brother's valet, whom Congwen once tried to make into an educated man, is a ruffian, murderer, and ex-bandit; so is a man who now rows Shen's boat. The coup de grace is a reencounter with a Baojing friend who once served Mao Zedong and tried to convert Shen to Communism. He has given up and become a tax collector and opium addict; his new habit will help him shed his leftist image, the man explains.

And Fenghuang? Shen hastens to the site of his godfather Teng's herbal medicine shop. How he loved to visit the neighboring firecracker store, salt vendor, butcher, tailor, and barber. Uncle Teng and his wife are dead. One of their sons has become a rich landlord outside Chenzhou, thanks to a lucrative job as head official for "opium suppression." (The city he exploits is Wangcun. Probably Shen got his "materials" for *Xiaozhai* while passing through Chenzhou on his way back.) Shen chats with another survivor, about friends killed for alleged Communist sympathies. The *Discursive Notes* close with the subsequent exchange:

I asked him why all the shops on the bridge had changed into residences. He told me that ten opium dens stood there now; three sold morphine. Five other establishments sold opium paraphernalia. Going over to the city wall after exiting the shop, I chanced upon an opium convoy. Two companies of soldiers, armed with the latest semiautomatic rifles—made locally—served as escort. It was a long, long caravan of men and horses, bearing over 320 loads of the black merchandise, all of it from Guizhou.

I had wanted to photograph this long bridge and keep it for a souvenir. But I looked up at that pier section, where "pitcher chestnuts" [opium poppies] were raised 27 years ago [by Uncle Teng, when opium was just a medicinal curiosity]. Then I thought of the ten opium dens and five paraphernalia shops. My courage and interest in the project evaporated.[13]

The Civil Unrest in West Hunan, 1934–46

Truly massive and punitive counterrevolution never spread to West Hunan. When Mao Zedong's forces passed through Hunan in October 1934, Chiang Kaishek's central armies pursued them out of the province, leaving Hunan to He Jian's devices. Even so, history unfolded much as Shen Congwen predicted, except on a smaller scale and along a more desultory—and less heroic—path.

The beginning of the end for Chen Quzhen came in October 1934, when He Long reoccupied his old base around Sangzhi and Dayong in far northwestern Hunan. Reinforced with troops from the Jiangxi Soviet under Xiao Ke, the Communists marched south to capture Chenzhou. Defending, on Chen Quzhen's side, was Shen Congwen's cousin Dai Jitao (not the similarly named KMT ideologist). Chenzhou held firm on December 7, after frantic fighting right up to the city walls. He Long therefore thrust toward the heart of the province. He took Taoyuan, imperiling Changde.[14] Shaken, He Jian ordered two divisions of his own provincial armies, under Liu Jianxu and Liu's subordinate, Tao Guang, from southern Hunan to Chenzhou. They arrived on December 22. Chen Quzhen kept out of their way, up in Guzhang.[15] He Long and Xiao Ke retreated that spring, to the Hubei-Sichuan-Guizhou border. They would fight more battles, but would finally leave. He Jian's men, by contrast, had come to stay. Road-building crews pushed deep into West Hunan, and with them still more anti-Communist troops—some 50,000 by March 1935.[16]

When his troops were in place, He Jian ordered Chen Quzhen to take up headquarters in the Communist nest, so that the red and white West Hunanese could annihilate each other. Instead, Chen retreated up to the Miao country. He Jian announced a time limit, then four extensions. Two months went by while the "King of West Hunan" weighed his options. He could make a suicidal charge directly into He Long's base and end up like Zhang Xueji in 1919; wage war against the easterners, as most locals expected him to do; or retire and disband his troops.[17] Shen Congwen celebrates his old commander's decision, which was to step down, in *Long River*. Says a downriver intellectual to a West Hunanese:

> Five years ago, when that Old Marshal from these parts [Chen Quzhen] ran your area, he wanted his cut, but he was one of you, and there was a limit to it. When he was satisfied, he went on about his job. But he couldn't be allowed to get the credit for it. The provincial government feared he'd win favor from the people. Once he got powerful, they wouldn't be able to control him. The Chairman [He Jian] feared his own position would be unstable. Therefore he sent two divisions up [to West Hunan], to force [Chen] to hand over his military authority, retire from public life, and forgo further involvement. If he wasn't willing to retire, they'd fight him. If they'd actually gone to war then, there's no telling whose kingdom it might have ended up as. The young army officers from around here all said they were ready for a fight; they happily awaited the outcome. But your Old Marshal felt constrained by the central government [Nanking], if not the Chairman; not by any man, but by the law—the law of the nation, and military law. He felt he ought not to make trouble for the Generalissimo [Chiang Kaishek]. A fair settlement could always be made. So he retired. All alone, he was driven in an automobile to the provincial capital, to be a commissioner and never again to interfere in military matters. Some of his troops were reorganized and the others transferred. Soon it was all over. Not long afterward the Peace Preservation Corps [Changsha troops] arrived.[18]

What does not ring true here is Shen's claim that Chen Quzhen was loyal to Chiang Kaishek. Probably Chen's position was close to Shen Congwen's, disdainful of the Nationalist regime. Chen was less concerned with abstractions than with practical benefits for his region; he would not spill his own people's blood in a hopeless cause. Like some other warlords, he responded to the decline of the Nationalists in 1949 by covertly aiding the Communist side and appealing to his former lieutenants to submit.[19] Thus did he cast ideology to the winds, to get his region off on the right foot with yet another regime—and perhaps have the last laugh on the KMT.

Upon the breakup of its old warlord kingdom in 1935, West Hunan descended into anarchy. It all climaxed, but by no means ended, in a 1937 "Miao rebellion." He Jian was then forced out of his warlord-governorship, for having failed to restore order to a province that stood astride the Japanese invasion route. Chiang Kaishek was only too happy to replace He with a more loyal general, Zhang Zhizhong, but the situation was desperate. The "King of West Hunan" had to be recalled to restore the peace. Things quieted down in the early 1940's, but by the end of the war, banditry serious enough to cut off whole counties had resumed. Order was restored only by drastic political and military pacification measures under the Communists in the 1950's; they sealed off West Hunan as a "special zone."

The causes of this anarchy are moot, but Shen Congwen intended to write up his version as a final chapter to his regional saga. Like his fellow-regionals, he blamed the disorders on He Jian's new regime, with its draconian military suppression, ruthless taxation, and economic exploitation by carpetbaggers. The Changsha officials felt no sympathy for the West Hunanese, Shen said, and were always being transferred anyway. The central Hunanese, on the other hand, attributed the unrest to West Hunan's regional character: rebellious, xenophobic, and prone to banditry in the best of times. Both sides agreed, however, that mutual antipathy and the loss of locally legitimate leadership lay at the heart of the problem. The region was, in other words, in rebellion against national (or really provincial) integration. And the 1937 rising was fairly successful. The rebel chief, Long Yunfei, remained undisputed "King of the Miao" through 1950—long enough to lead regional resistance against the Communists.[20]

In 1935, two demographic problems aggravated the tensions. Thousands of West Hunanese who had long made their living toting guns for Chen Quzhen were suddenly demobilized and left without any ready way of making a living. Feeling no loyalty to the new military government, many turned to banditry. Meanwhile, thousands of central Hunanese regular troops and armed constabulary forces (Peace Preservation Divisions and Corps), more than the region had ever supported before, were shipped in from Changsha. They, too, had to support themselves on West Hunan's meager surpluses. Conflict was inevitable.

Military rule it was, as even KMT sources admit. On May

23, 1935, Chen Quzhen's former kingdom was carved up into administrative inspectorate districts, a new level of civil-military administration between province and county peculiar to designated "Bandit (i.e., Communist) Extermination Provinces" like Hunan. At the head of these inspectorate districts was the frankly military West Hunan Pacification Office (Xiangxi Suijingchu), established on July 22 and seated in Yuanling, as Chenzhou was now called. Provincial regulars were stationed in all West Hunanese counties to disarm the locals and set up a *baojia* system of mutual surveillance. Much of the pacification work was concentrated in Fenghuang, where there were no Communists.[21]

Chen Quzhen's old "34th Division" of the National Army was reorganized and mostly disarmed by the central Hunanese in the spring of 1935. More than half the soldiers were sent home. The others, including Shen Congwen's younger brother Shen Dieyu, a Whampoa graduate, were sent east to Chiang Kaishek's home province of Zhejiang—indeed to Chiang's home county of Fenghua, and nearby Ningbo.[22] Some of the dispersed West Hunanese troops, however, regrouped around Mayang, hoping to force He Jian to reinstate their old "King." Less organized banditry had already broken out in 1934, when Chen Quzhen moved his troops north to defend against He Long. The new regime gave Chen a titular post up in the Miao country, as head of the hoary Tun Affairs Office, but his Miao Defense (Miao) and Tun Affairs (Han) armies were very small. His task was the delicate one of raising Miao taxes.[23]

Hence Chen, ironically, had to deal with the first overt resistance to the new regime. In Yongsui on June 24, 1936, Miao people disarmed his soldiers while they were collecting taxes. Chen resigned and there was some fighting, but General Tao Guang soon had provincial troops on hand to disperse the Miao rebels. Two county governments came under martial law.[24]

Shen Congwen, and informants in Fenghuang today, confirm that the Miao were really rising up not against their old lord, Chen Quzhen, but against his new masters from Changsha.[25] Locals were forced to accept depreciating provincial paper money and to pay taxes allegedly in arrears, as well as "taxes in advance." Above all, the old *tuntian* armies were replaced in April 1936 with new Peace Preservation forces. The whole system of Miao governance was to be abolished; displaced Miao leaders naturally led the rebellion.[26] Though the provincial regime forgave the "back taxes," it sent still more regulars into Yongsui and organized new militias.[27] But Yongsui was only the beginning: Miao and Han bandit gangs arose and did battle in four other counties by the end of 1936. In Guzhang, bandits defeated militia from two counties and two battalions of provincial regulars. Four or five thousand Miao and Han rose in Mayang, proclaiming themselves "spirit soldiers" able to swallow swords and spit fire. When they nearly took Gaocun (Fenghuang's link to the outside world), Chen Quzhen's successor resigned in his turn.[28] Meanwhile, up in the Han-Tujia realm in the You River valley, Chen Quzhen's old officers were setting themselves up as bandit-king "generals." Endemic banditry made river traffic unsafe as far east as Wangcun; the city itself was looted in broad daylight. Soon one ex-soldier bandit chief was killed and two or three others were co-opted and transferred downriver, but 3,000 renegade troops remained at large at the start of 1937, pillaging and kidnapping for ransom.[29] Nor did the Yuan and Chen river valleys quickly recover from the early 1936 destruction caused by He Long. The Communists, too, had deserters, and the Nationalist Air Force for its part bombed He Long's villages.[30] Yet the big trouble was still to come.

With the help of KMT Miao representatives like Shi Honggui, Changsha drew up its plans for a permanent advance into the West: the Reconstruction Program of July 3, 1936, which called on the Miao people to learn Chinese, intermarry with the Han, and give up their traditional sacrifices, "undesirable marriage customs," and "improper amusements." The Miao were to be educated, but also pacified and culturally assimilated. That military control was an important part of the program was evident from provisions for building blockhouses, as in the anti-Communist campaigns. Shen Congwen's worst fears seemed about to be fulfilled after all.[31]

The larger rebellion commenced one month after Changsha announced, on July 16, 1937, its new system of Miao taxation and governance. The *tuntian* system was to be abolished and the provincial financial commissioner would carry out a detailed cadastral survey. Much newly reclaimed land that had been tax-free would now be taxed. Most important, the Miao would have to purchase any *tuntian* land they farmed.[32]

A Miao army representing 48 *zhai* rose up on August 9. Leading them was "Miao King" Long Yunfei, and secondly a Miao called Wu Hengliang. Long's army captured the county city of Qiancheng and held it for three weeks. Mayang was besieged (accounts vary on whether it fell) and Fenghuang was attacked but not taken, as 20,000 Miao from the surrounding counties rose up to do battle with the Peace Preservation troops. At stake was more than taxes. Many saw it as a war of regional revenge against the "downriver people" sent by Changsha. In the highland cities, some locals threatened a massacre of all extraregionals. Their slogan was "kill the sand-heads" (Changsha being literally the city of "Long Sands").[33]

With the revolt still raging in November, the Generalissimo replaced He Jian with Zhang Zhizhong. The new governor co-opted the main rebel forces in December 1937, just as Chen Quzhen had done a decade earlier. Long Yunfei and troops became a brigade in the provincial forces, and Wu Hengliang's forces a regiment. Tax-collection quotas were drastically reduced. In 1938, Zhang brought back the "King of West Hunan" as titular regional leader, too, but only to direct a new Yuanling Field Office, not to lead troops. Chen Quzhen was to reorganize West Hunan's county administrations and disarm the various extralegal military forces (many led by his old lieutenants) in order to disband them—or, better, reenlist them to fight the Japanese, who had taken Nanking and were pressing up the Yangzi, soon to threaten Changsha itself.[34]

West Hunan, particularly the Mayang and You river valleys, remained very unsettled in 1938. Lüjiaping, which was to be the setting for *Long River*, was the headquarters of a thousand-man bandit gang under a self-styled "general." (Yaoyao, the pretty heroine and chief victim of the novel, may be modeled after a noted young beauty who was kidnapped from Yuanling by a 400-man bandit gang late in 1937.) People were beginning to write of West Hunan as a place where "the bandits are the people, and the people are the bandits"—just because his people refused to submit to the Changsha/Nanking tyranny, Shen said. After he dined in Changsha with a friend in late 1937, someone called Shen Congwen a "West Hunan bandit." He vowed to counteract the negative press and wild rumors about West Hunan, and if possible create sympathy and understanding for the region among the refugees and cadres pouring in from the east. The result was *West Hunan*, a literary gazetteer that Shen finished in the spring of 1938, after moving to Kunming.[35]

In early 1938 Shen Congwen even played a small political role in his region's history. He gave talks on the national war crisis at his brother's house in Yuanling, the Yunlu Estate, in which he urged his fellow regionals to "unify"—that is, broaden their perspective and support the war effort, lest all West Hunan be disgraced for helping the Japanese. Even before he came to West Hunan, Shen wrote an especially moving letter from Changsha. Addressed to any and all West Hunanese army officers contemplating setting themselves up as bandit kings, it cajoles, dares, shames, and pleads: "Do Not Scorn This Once-in-a-Lifetime Opportunity to Repay Your Country."[36]

About this time, Shen Congwen was appointed to the Hunan provincial assembly. He refused that honor, but more importantly, he brought Long Yunfei and Chen Quzhen together for four hours of "unification talks" over dinner at the Yunlu Estate. Congwen had known Long Yunfei since the 1920's, when he led only 300 men; Shen Yunlu had been advising Chen Quzhen ever since Hunan provincial organs started moving west to Yuanling. The Shen brothers hoped to persuade Long to lead West Hunan's "heroes" down from their mountaintops and onward to the front. Ultimately Long Yunfei did marshal his men against the Japanese, and even Communist sources admit that he won victories at Changsha, Shimen, and Lixian.[37]

Precisely what else Shen's hero Long Yunfei stood for is an interesting puzzle. An informant at Long's old homestead says Long's ancestry includes Miao *tuntian* officers, but that his father was just a bean-curd miller, though also a member of the Gelaohui. (Long Yunfei was not necessarily a member.) Shen Congwen traces Long Yunfei's beginnings as a bandit-warlord to membership in a band led by Tian Sannu, who was a "Double-headed Dragon." Tian was assassinated by men sent by Tang Lichen, who at one time followed the lead of Shen Zongsi. That did not keep Shen Congwen from immortalizing Tian as a model Zhen'gan brave: small, tough, and chivalrous, "the last of the knights-errant." Long Yunfei inherited Tian's style of going out of his way to "right wrongs" and "protect the weak," Shen asserts. Communist historiography gives it all a negative twist, claiming that Long made his fortune gambling and beat people up when he didn't win. By all accounts, wherever there was gambling or hand-to-hand combat, Tian Sannu, Long Yunfei, and their ilk were sure to be in on the action.[38]

After the "King of West Hunan" spared Long and gave him a commission in the Gan Army (plus control of the Tun Affairs

Office), Long returned the favor by helping Chen Quzhen, and the region's few foreigners, hide out from the KMT Northern Expedition in 1927. Unstoppable in his own Miao realm, Long ultimately proved to have a more secure political base than Chen. Though quick to add that Long was an opportunist, revisionist Communist historians credit Long with setting out deliberately to topple He Jian after 1935. They say that in 1937 he even raised the apparently precocious slogan of *kang Ri dao He* ("resist Japan; overthrow He Jian"). Long and fellow rebel Wu Hengliang felt that the KMT generals were racially prejudiced against the Miao and were giving them an unfair burden in the war, say these historians, seconded by Miao elders. But Long and his son continued their historic separatist mission and opposed the CCP in 1949. That last resistance was of course decisive in subsequent Communist thinking. Long Yunfei became the great counterrevolutionary pariah of modern Miao history, complete with an antimemorial at a tree where he allegedly skinned alive an honest man of hired-laborer class background. The locals may not be aware that Long was a sworn brother of He Long. Yet, post–Cultural Revolution revisionism has already gone far down the path of remembering the "progressive" days of Long Yunfei. Could old political scores be set aside, probably the regional view of Long Yunfei would be the one Shen Congwen holds yet today: a symbol of the dignity of West Hunanese regional and ethnic resistance; parochial, but "having his reasons."[39]

Sending Long Yunfei to the front did not bring civil order. He, after all, was one of the few who could command bandits to lay down their arms. Chen Quzhen had to retire again. The Nationalist government now diverted whole divisions of its armies from the war against Japan, and even winning generals such as Li Yannian, to bring about a definitive solution to the West Hunan problem. Heading the operation, from a new Hubei-Hunan-Sichuan-Guizhou Border Region Pacification Office established in Zhijiang (old Yuanzhou) in February 1939, was General Gu Zhenglun—old KMT revolutionary, Guizhou army commander, member of the KMT Central Executive Committee, and "father of the Chinese military police." Large forces of his MPs joined the crack troops up in the hills. The initial reckoning with the bandits was successful enough for Gu to be rewarded with the governorship of Gansu. But the northern realm became unsettled again in 1940, and more generals had to be brought in to set up northern and southern pacification districts in Yongsui and Zhijiang. Particularly disturbed was Yushuwan (new Huaihua), where Shen Congwen had first learned about pacification two decades before. Prefiguring the early 1950's were "reindoctrination camps" into which rebels were herded, preparatory to conscription as soldiers. One location was the temple of the Heavenly King in Yongsui. It came into public view in 1944 when its hundred-odd inmates, accused of plotting escape, were executed en masse.[40]

The cities of West Hunan were burdened with refugees, outbreaks of cholera, and bombing by the Japanese air force, but it was in the countryside that public order began to unravel again, in 1942-43. Even the American press corps in Chongqing caught wind of "what seemed to be the first large peasant rebellion against the Kuomintang." All that was known for sure was that the Hunan-Guizhou motor road had been cut for a month, and that fleeing missionaries thought the rebels antiforeign, "believing all foreigners to be pro-Kuomintang."[41] At the time Fenghuang was torn by a Miao rebellion against press-gangs and the new government salt monopoly. Again proclaiming themselves "spirit soldiers" invulnerable to modern arms fire, those Miao may well have hated foreigners. They had only a thousand men, but tens of thousands arose north of the Miao pale, both "spirit soldiers" and professional bandits. KMT pacifiers called in troops from the front again in 1945, and thousands died. Civil order remained elusive in 1946, and no wonder: as many as 20,000 KMT soldiers were simply loosed on the countryside, to make their own way home, if they still had one.[42]

So much for West Hunan as "China's Switzerland." Yet to Shen Congwen, "Shiwai Taoyuan" also meant the Gan Army. He identified with that army and thought it the only repository of idealism among his region's young people. West Hunan had its students. They had sought Shen out as he passed through Changsha and Changde in 1934. He found them trifling and degenerate, interested only in rumors and literary lions. The region's young military officers were of different mettle—sufficiently aware of their own degeneration to be able to save themselves if offered adequate leadership, as he put it.[43] So for Shen Congwen, there could be no greater blow to West Hunan than the destruction of its young officer corps. That took but a week.

The place was Jiashan, near Jiaxing, on the line of reinforced concrete bunkers built to protect Zhejiang and the upper Yangzi in case Shanghai fell. Named "the Hindenburg Line," these fortifications were Chiang Kaishek's Maginot: massive, costly, immovable, and protecting the territory he cared about most—the more spectacularly useless therefore in the end, and not just from bad strategy, but from the fact (it was said) that those who kept the keys to the concrete doors were nowhere to be found when the Japanese advanced. The bungle was seldom written about, but the story of "the keys" became legend on the national grapevine. Shen wrote his version after the war, in "Material for a Fairy Tale."[44]

As Shen Congwen tells it (following the account of Shen Dieyu, who commanded a regiment), while Chinese armies were retreating from Shanghai in November 1937, the remnant Gan Army was rushed up to the front from Hangzhou on a midnight freight train. The troops were now called the 128th or Ningguo Division, having previously been transferred from Fenghua to Ningguo, Anhui. Liu Jianxu commanded, but two West Hunanese actually led the troops: Gu Jiaqi (Gu Xiuzhi), and Shen's cousin Dai Jitao. Both had been seconds in command to the deposed "King of West Hunan." Awaiting the bewildered Sino-Miao boys at the Jiashan station was the magistrate—no one else, military or civil. He did have "the keys," which he gave to Shen's brother before speeding away in a waiting truck, but nothing else, not even blueprints for the concealed bunker doors. A suicide regiment discovered the doors by trial and error while the enemy commenced seven days of aerial bombing. The Gan folk's "Miao fanaticism" then made up for the stupidity and cowardice of their predecessors. Shen Congwen says that one battalion, reduced by bombing and artillery fire to 16 men, emerged from cover to fight hand-to-hand. He gives these casualty figures: all four regimental commanders wounded; of their four deputies, three dead, one wounded; all twelve battalion commanders wounded, seven of them dead; two-thirds of the captains and sergeants killed, the rest wounded. As for the men, there were 120 survivors among the 1,500 Shen Dieyu once commanded. The order to retreat came much too late. What was left of the army was dissolved by General Xue Yue, who charged it with "laggardness in prosecuting the war." Dai Jitao was removed from command.[45]

Shen Congwen felt that "his" troops were being used as cannon fodder in the defense of Chiang Kaishek's home, whereas Chiang's own troops were being spared. He was also appalled to see his wounded brother and other heroes of Jiashan called back to Changde time after time to fill vacancies in the ranks of the new "Honor Divisions" and to fight again and again without respite— at Nanchang, Yichang, the west bank of Dongting, the south bank, the battles of Changsha, and so on. Concerned not to give Chiang Kaishek an excuse to disband their units and extinguish the Gan Army for good, the officers kept filling up the spaces. Shen Congwen felt Chiang was purposely, maybe even genocidally, annihilating his own Sino-Miao folk. No doubt Fenghuang turned into a city of widows and orphans, as he claims. This was something Shen had to write about.[46]

Shen Congwen's 1940's Regional Writing

Long River (1939-42) is Shen Congwen's finest achievement in pastoral comedy, justly praised by C. T. Hsia above Shen's other long works as "the most richly inclusive of the many facets of his talent."[47] As pastoral, it presents Shen's most vivid, observant, and extended scenes of country life: fields ablaze with the color of tangerines; a rural fair, with its many wares and goings-on behind closed tent doors; the village of Lüjiaping and its hamlet, Turnip Creek, lovingly sketched in topographical detail. The opening chapters, "The People and the Land" and "Autumn," are nearly monographic about their respective subjects. They present in full typical life histories, or "fates," along with local customs, the background of debts and obligations among the major characters, their nicknames, and their reputations. The change of seasons, the dawning and setting of the sun, the atmosphere of expectation as a boat convoy approaches, even the blush on an adolescent girl's face—all this Shen renders in a mature narrative voice.

As comedy, the novel shuttles from manners to burlesque, the latter providing comic relief from the ominous initiatives launched by city people. At the center are Shen's stolid country folk—pretty and innocent adolescent girls, old men rich in life experience, and wharfside people and ex-soldiers who have become pillars of the community in middle age. In just enough dialect to move a West Hunanese without alienating the general reader, they tease each other, speculate about carryings-on in the city, and worry about the tax collectors. Shen almost parodies his own pastoralism when he refers to a country woman "eating so many oranges that her eyes sparkled."[48] There is, one commentator notes, movement between land and water as well as town and country. The waters bring risk and opportunity, and the land, stability.[49]

Yet *Long River* is also Shen Congwen's most historically conscious novel, his requiem for a region and its old way of life. It has four threads of social and historical criticism. One is the theme of social decay brought by the new masters from Changsha. The novel is fixed exactly in time and place: it is the fall of 1936, one year after the transition from local to provincial rule. By now the dockside scene is decadent and full of parasites. Shen attributes it to change—to the introduction of outsiders, and the evils of garrisoning localities with soldiers who have no roots there. One of the most obviously censored passages occurs at this point.[50] Accordingly, the chief villain is an outsider Peace Preservation officer. His first imposition seems harmless enough: he wants some tangerines. Already Shen has made these fruits into symbols of country generosity. But tangerines, and the folk, can be squeezed. The Changsha man wants a whole boatload. He begins to dally with pretty little Yaoyao, the tangerine grower's daughter. The subtlety of this oppression might be thought a calculated, literary restraint (if not the result of censorship), but Chinese readers are more apt to call Shen's rendering of conversations between the new warlord and his victims an achievement in social realism. That is precisely how the more intelligent officials talked, Shen says: How better to deliver a threat, without prejudice to one's pseudo-literati mien, than by using a young girl as the messenger?[51]

Another thread is the coming of "New Life." *Long River*'s country bumpkins "misconstrue" New Life as something powerful and animate that chases Communists, and maybe even He Jian's provincials. They fear that New Life may destroy their dreams. It promises burning and killing, just like the Communist revolution they also fear.[52] New Life thus signifies violent rural counterrevolution, as in Jiangxi. This is far more serious than the urban manifestations of the movement that Shen also ridicules, like boy scouts who rap country folk on the knuckles for walking on the wrong side of the street or going around bare-chested—comic relief indeed.[53] At one point, Shen "obliquely" (enough to get it past the censors, evidently) casts aspersions on the movement's leader, Chiang Kaishek. The Generalissimo appears in the person of an anonymous commandant astride a white horse who proclaims, "Comrades, I am the 'New Life.' "⁵⁴

The name of the ill-fated movement was of course too convenient for Shen to pass over as a more abstract symbol of the evils of modernity. He attributes decadence to commerce and prosperity, and lets his characters worry about how the coming of a mechanized oil press will affect the local economy.⁵⁵ Yet this broader social theme is relatively undeveloped. Even more neglected is a fourth thread, which Shen's preface claims was to be his major theme: change and corruption of the country folk themselves. He felt, after his return visits to West Hunan, that the old morality was vanishing. Even women somehow changed, he believed, once clothing and oil could be store-bought. Released from their traditional work patterns, people seemed to him to have lost the old work ethic.⁵⁶

Shen blames many of the reticences in *Long River* on the censors. They did certainly disrupt the structural logic of the novel. Some chapters hardly advance the plot. The final one, in particular, is a relatively bright, very much out-of-place segment that Shen evidently moved to the end (closest to the "future") to protect himself from charges that he was pessimistic about his nation. Rewriting covered over smaller excisions, rendering individual chapters more successful than the book as a whole, but he never began the two final volumes of his trilogy. Even the one he completed was banned for most of the war. Shen Congwen was able to depict West Hunan and its "good old customs"—the subject of volume one—but not the changes that were, he thought, steadily undermining his folk physically and morally.⁵⁷

Had Shen been able to write *Long River* unimpeded, he might have let local history supply the plot his novel now lacks. In 1980, he said he meant for the later volumes to describe Chiang Kaishek's brutal occupation of West Hunan and deliberate destruction of Sino-Miao and other warlord (*zapai*) troops in the maw of the Japanese armies, that is, Chiang's regionalist crimes against Shen's folk.⁵⁸ Volume one already sets the scene for a confrontation between locals and outsider officials. It hints that government forces may suppress a Miao uprising.⁵⁹ The novel seems about to turn into an apology for West Hunan's late 1930's rebellions and banditry. Fenghuang's sacrifices at Jiashan and subsequent battles might have furnished the climax, for mention of them is ubiquitous in Shen's other 1940's writing. He wanted so much to write the full story of the effects of the war on his West Hunanese country folk that he conceived a plan to go live and write in America for two or three years. It would free him from censorship and, he hoped, also let him tell the American allies something they needed to know about what they were doing to China.[60]

A completed *Long River* might thus have been interesting not only as a sectionalist novel, but as engaged, anti-Japanese (if also anti-KMT) war literature of the sort Shen Congwen otherwise refused in principle to write. Interesting, but not necessarily great literature—though it is a paradox to say so, since the nearly inchoate political intimations of the novel as it stands are a refreshing change from the explicit propagandizing that marred most wartime Chinese writing. Still, Shen might have done better simply to write a local history. He wanted to do just that, after the war, with a Whampoa graduate friend. The focus was to be "how thousands of stout lads from that little mountain town [Fenghuang] continually sacrificed themselves to protect the nation." This plan was not fulfilled, either. Shen's collaborator, Fenghuang's KMT general Tian Junjian, was ordered off to an early engagement in the Civil War and killed before he could retire.[61]

At least three fictional pieces do, however, contain sentiments and content that fit Shen's stated plan for *Long River*. *Yunlu Chronicles* (published in 1947, some years after Shen wrote it) is the weakest as narrative, and not coincidentally the longest—another incomplete novel ravaged by censorship.[62] Built around real events in the life of Congwen's elder brother, it explores history and character in its author's well-tested biographical voice, beginning with a clash, nearly a fight, between Congwen's "busybody" brother and two overpoliticized and arrogant high school students who claim status as KMT cadres. Simply because they cannot quite grasp the local dialect, the young outsiders despise Yunlu, and the people of Yuanling generally. That motif recurs in Shen's late writing. Right in the midst of the war, Shen's "A Country Town" (1940; written under the anonymity of a new pen name) criticized wartime mobilizers and propagandists. The story tiptoes around the theme of older officers' corrupt "war requisitioning" by letting young cadres' vacuity and insensitivity occupy center-stage. (This, too, is part of Shen's great historical roman-fleuve; one of his young relatives from a propaganda team was the source.)[63] The unwieldy *Yunlu Chronicles*, however, goes off on tangents (in the original 1947 version), so that Shen's zest to document nearly smothers his imagination. One chapter provides a whole outline history of the failure of Chinese democracy, from 1890's constitutionalism to 1940's authoritarianism, by having it flash through Yunlu's mind.[64]

"Stirrings" (1943) is Shen's most exquisite piece of wartime fiction. It shows a Gan Army colonel who has survived the battle of Jiashan quietly letting his wounds heal during a two-month furlough in Yuanling. His country orders him up to the front to fight the Japanese again. The soldier unobtrusively gathers up his men and leaves the next day, before the Party Branch (KMT) can organize its propaganda rallies. The young activists are discomfited; perhaps they are abashed. Only the future will tell.

This is a vision of Shen Dieyu, convalescing at the Yunlu Estate. However, the subject is not identified: "Stirrings" is an abstract contemplation of a whole army's sacrifice, not a personal tribute. And, unlike genre "National Defense Literature," "Stirrings" lacks action. It is a still mood painting similar to "Quiet," beginning and ending with mists that come up from the river nightly, wrapping the town in a blanket of illusory protection—up to, but no higher than, the rooftops. Such stillness contrasts with the war's bleeding away downriver of the town's good men when the fog lifts, and with the noisy agents of purpose from the Party Branch. "Stirrings" does not just contemplate change, however. It fixes on the new generation, posing alternative visions of their future. Will they in their book-fed ignorance continue to romanticize warfare and heroism, and so actually abandon any chance to take hold of their future? Or will the example of the wounded colonel shock them into a new wisdom? The Dieyu persona, like Shen Yunlu in *Yunlu Chronicles*, is at first scorned by the young intellectuals. Eyeing his leisure with suspicion, they disdain him both as a lowly soldier and as a "worthless" "petty bourgeois." The shame they feel on learning that he is a wounded war hero causes them to do an about-face. They adopt him as a model—a hero—but then he throws cold water on their romanticism. He becomes therefore a fallen idol, until his answer to his country's call a second time silences the young folk for good. Thus does Shen argue two causes that would later turn him into an obtrusively didactic author: opposition to hero worship, and pacifism. (He may also have been subtly reproving left-wing students for running off to fight "romantically" for the Communists, instead of facing the enemy head-on, in the major engagements.)

The doctor asked the army officer to tell how he felt about these young people. "Our young friends are all quite lovable," he said, "full of vigor, and high aspirations. And guts. They're the cream of the local youth, the raw material for our future nation-building. They tell me they want to give up their studies to go into the army. I try to persuade them to go get military academy training first, but they won't have it. *They* want to fight guerrilla war. As we'd say in school, that's romanticism. It's suitable for a poet, not a good junior officer. But that's how they think at that age. They all think I understand them, and sympathize with them. Begging their pardon, I do sympathize with them, but I really don't understand them. Their view of war won't easily mesh with ours. It's too lyrical, too out of accord with reality."

"But they all worship you!" said the doctor.

The officer only smiled. He indicated complete agreement, but he held back part of what he was thinking: "This worship is meaningless. At the very least, it's of no use to them. The problems we face today can't be solved just with worship! The situation calls for deeds!"[65]

However severe the censorship, one suspects—and Shen confesses—that his own emotional conflicts would not *let* him depict the corruption of his own people without compensating comedy and hope.[66] This is another cause of the structural weaknesses and intellectual puzzlements in *Long River*. The more gratifying is it then to see a more complex web of historical and social causation in *After Snow*, Shen's last major regional work (1946–47).

The four extant chapters of the novel set the stage for a protracted blood feud between Man and Tian clans in the mining country west of Fenghuang. This work, too, is historical, even partly autobiographical. It begins brightly, with Shen's trip home to Fenghuang from Chenzhou about 1919, to attend the wedding of his friend Man Shuyuan's elder brother. Congwen begins to fall in love with a pretty orphaned country girl who serves the lady of the household (the mother in Shen's early story "Snow"). But the bridegroom, head of the militia, gets drawn into a bloody and pointless feud when another militiaman and the opium he is escorting are taken for ransom by local rowdies, the Tian brothers. Both Mans and Tians are landed gentry, but that class is splitting, Shen tells us. It happens that a friend of the Tian gang elopes with the orphan girl. Soon the magistrate is called in. A peaceful solution has eluded the locals' grasp; revenge is inevitable. The extant chapters do not get to it, but in real life Militia Captain Man was hacked to death by his enemies as he lay ill in bed.[67]

After Snow is unusual among Shen's regional works for its realism. It explores corruption within village society, that change in morals that *Long River* never got to. Shen still traces the *beginnings* of evil to influences from outside the region. But in *After Snow*, no outsider has penetrated the Miao pale in person, either to force the locals to give up their old morality for self-defense, or even to set a bad example. Locals do the opium-toting. The clownish magistrate exploits the villagers in the name of pacifying the countryside, but he, too, is a local. Corruption thus enters by way of an abstract social condition rather than extraregional oppressors, and that condition is national social and economic decay. This decline has led, Shen says as narrator, to reliance on soldiers for peace and opium for revenues. Technological change, meanwhile, has only created new opportunities for exploiting people, as by force of arms.

The armed bands who swear blood brotherhood in this novel are not knights-errant, as in *West Hunan*. Shen calls them a new, rootless class of people, aware of new ways of getting rich without working. Some began poor; others, "local despots," were already rich. Even good landed folk like the Mans have become "more adept at safeguarding their wealth. They sent their sons and nephews to military schools, and raised money to buy guns to protect their estates—actually to safeguard their special rights as well."[68] But they "work for a living," unlike the parasites. Shen's is a vision of quasi-class conflict, with two sides forming on the basis of Darwinist rather than economic or historical criteria. He even speaks of social "contradictions" (*maodun*), though his view of rural violence is meant to be an alternative to the Communists'. Class divisions themselves do not predestine the people toward conflict, he argues; violence is a social force itself. Formerly, class-based and non-class-based (clan and personal) conflicts could be settled by forbearance and a little money (or the murder of a woman who broke the moral code—like the orphan girl's mother, in this thoroughly unidyllic story). People declined to fight on principle, and because they felt regional solidarity as "kinsmen" (*jiabianren*). Now there is polarization, of whatever social origin. Violence has become a disease affecting all people, leading to "the slow decomposition of society."⁶⁹ That is the phenomenon Shen Congwen intends to explore. We know because he tells us his moral before dramatizing it. That, perhaps, is the chief weakness in these late regional works. Shen has grown so anxious about the course of history that he feels he must directly instruct.

Shen Congwen and the Place of Unengaged Writing in Reconstructing China

The onset of the Sino-Japanese War (1937–45) at first seemed to heal Shen Congwen's rifts with both the government and the Communist Party (CCP). He was on the government payroll as a university professor and now also as a textbook editor, even as he came into closer contact with leftist writers and the CCP itself. Friends like He Qifang, for instance, resided at the Communist capital in Yan'an. Shen received letters asking him to go there to do his writing. And the CCP was not necessarily offended that he did not accept. In December 1937, Shen Congwen and the playwright Cao Yu called on the Communist elder Xu Teli, CCP liaison officer in Changsha (since the KMT and CCP were now formally allied against Japan). Xu invited them and eight others, including Mao Dun, Lao She, and Xiao Qian, to Yan'an, but added that there was much anti-Japanese United Front work for them to do in the white areas if they preferred. Hunanese like his student Mao Zedong, Xu could see the use of Shen's going home, since the rebellion there was disrupting what might one day be a frontline battlefield.⁷⁰ Shen Congwen had already put aside his old policy of eschewing political writing, by agreeing to compose ten articles on behalf of the United Front for a Changsha newspaper supplement run by his radical friend Wang Luyan. Wang, however, was harassed by the Blue Shirts. His enterprise was shut down by the government within months, after Shen had published only four pieces.⁷¹

Soon Shen, too, was on the outs with Chongqing. Government critics sniped at him. Three of his books were banned, including his major wartime works *Long River* and *Gazing at Clouds in Yunnan* (the third was *Sequel to Remembering Ding Ling*). Censors also held up publication of Shen's collected works, in thirty-odd volumes, for at least four years. Nine stories about rural China, though printed before, were labeled "irrelevant to the war." Shen became disillusioned with the wartime conduct of the government as early as 1938, while living with his brothers in Yuanling. Shen Yunlu was involved with a national art school that had moved inland to that town. Congwen only alludes to the unpleasantness that developed—a political demonstration against the school, spying by government agents, and so forth. (The unfinished *Yunlu Chronicles* seems to be working up to it.)[72]

Yet Shen's deepening rift with the KMT won him no credit later on with the CCP, particularly its writers. What would stick in their minds was his prewar skepticism about left-wing United Front agitation. Shen saw it as just another round of politicking, with one Marxist faction attacking another, to see which could excel in "sideline activities." Borrowing a phrase from Hu Shi, Shen even warned that an epidemic of patriotic "about-the-same-itis" (*chabuduo*) was making writing as formulaic as the old eight-legged essay. Leftists in particular felt impugned. They came to regard Shen Congwen as simply unpatriotic when he refused to join even the broadest of anti-Japanese United Front writers' organizations, which otherwise managed to enroll nearly all major KMT, CCP, third-party, and neutral writers. Shen feared that such groups would be used to control writers. That the left and right had joined forces was hardly of any comfort on that score.[73]

Luckily Shen Congwen spent most of the war in Kunming, a city controlled by the warlord Long Yun, a third political force neither Nationalist nor Communist. Later Shen was accused of helping edit *Zhanguoce* (*Intrigues of the Warring States*), a Kunming journal that after 1949 was pegged as fascist. He strongly denies being an editor, and there is no evidence that he was. The journal was really in Long Yun's pocket, Shen Congwen believed—precisely why he refused to get involved with it. Similar suspicions caused him to shun the non-Communist left-wing "democratic parties," the "neutral" groups that later called for Chiang Kaishek to cease making civil war and form a coalition government with the Communists. Shen basically agreed with their democratic slogans and peace platform, and he was not concerned that third-party adherents might be fellow travelers. Rather he feared that they fronted for other political forces: in Kunming, Long Yun. But then Shen distrusted political parties as such. That probably was apparent in his newspaper article "What We Need Is a *Fourth* Party," though we shall never know for sure. The title appeared above a big empty space; 100 percent of the text was excised. Thus did Long Yun hold Shen Congwen strictly accountable to his professed moratorium on politics.[74]

Scores left over from Shen Congwen's polemics against conformism would be settled after 1949. What aroused antipathy toward him during the war itself was his own nonregional writing. Not only did that body of work fail to cheer on the troops against Japan, some of it just did not "make sense"—intellectually, artistically, or in subject matter ("if it had any"). These were Shen Congwen's further experiments, influenced by Freud and Joyce. Shen's will to be modern had finally brought him to the frontiers of literary technique itself. He had to fight for toleration of "difficult" literature, a battle still waged by China's allegedly "obscure" modernist poets in the 1980's. Then, as now, it was usually poets who manned the front lines; Shen felt called on to defend Bian Zhilin and He Qifang as early as the summer of 1937. Soon, though, he was hard put to justify his own fiction. "Gazing at a Rainbow" and "Plucking a Star" (1940?) were seldom, if ever, reprinted, and no Chinese text of them has survived.[75]

Fortunately—and fittingly—we have "Gazing at a Rainbow" in an English translation by Shen's younger poet friend, Jin Di. The microstructure of the text was so unfamiliar to Chinese readers that Shen gave his readers a crutch at the outset ("the words meant") as he split his dialogue into separate conscious and subconscious levels of discourse. The speakers are an autobiographical author persona and a beautiful young woman.

> "In hot weather you are much less troubled." But the words meant: "In hot weather you never wear stockings and your feet are still nicer."
> The hem curled up again. "Oh much less troubled in hot weather." ("Everyone says my feet are nice-looking, but really they are not nice-looking at all.") "And then fashions are always changing." [pp. 179–80]

Here the unspoken stream of discourse appears, from its simple subliminal sexuality, to be a fully unconscious response to the presence of the other person. But soon the unspoken dialogue becomes more purposive and intellectual, as if already risen to the surface of consciousness—but not speech. Shen now drops the quotation marks around the interior dialogue.

> "My dear, every nation is squandering millions and millions of dollars on things which are entirely unimportant, so what does it matter whether

there is a change in stockings?" (Why do you mind the expense, since it adorns you? An artist in a stocking factory contributes no less to human welfare than an engineer.) "This is all too deep for me. I just like kicking the sand barefoot when I reach the seashore." (I am not afraid of being gazed at or being kissed, but not everywhere.) [p. 180]

The couple exchange thoughts and desires through glances, words, and a fictional piece about the hunting of a doe written by the author persona. As the woman reads it, the writer's surroundings—the galloping horses on his lover's curtains, her green gown (the color of life), the snow outside held off by the warmth of her room, the fragrance of plum blossoms, the flames in her fireplace—all come alive to him.

Might not the dialogue itself be fantasy? While his lover ponders the story of the doe, the author quietly "reads" "the colored horses on the curtains," which seem to vanish "into the limitless expanse of green reeds."

He seemed to feel a need for continuing imaginary conversations.
—Too beautiful. As a rule a beautiful woman rarely realises how much vexation her beauty causes to others, and how much happiness.
—Really? You are joking! What do you mean by gazing so steadily at my feet? You are artless in appearance, but you are a romantic at heart. I know you once kissed my whole body, but what you said was: "The horses are drawn with gusto and seem to be running away in all directions." What ran away was your heart! You are travelling the same road again. [p. 182]

Perhaps the entire dramatized encounter is imagined, for the passages that frame it are meditative, like Shen's 1930's idea fiction. The prologue has the narrator (first-person, not third-person, as in the main, dramatized body of the story) walking home at New Year's. He smells plum blossoms amid the snow. That is the link; the following story is a reverie recalled by that sense impression. He steps through an archway into "nothingness" and begins to read "a strange book," on whose first page are the words "We are spirits of flame!" The image of flame transports the narrator back to the fireplace in his lover's home, but more figuratively, it also communicates to him a pantheistic vision of Life as energy: beauty that burns itself out, while manifesting a short-lived and unfathomable radiance. Moreover, his lover first comes into view through a mirror.

The I-narrator of the frame appears to be Shen Congwen in Kunming, 1940. The "remembered" tryst, however, might be an evocation of any one of several of Shen's past extramarital encounters with female beauty—or perhaps an imagining of a tryst that never took place—transplanted into his 1940 living room. The woman might be a vision of Gao Qingzi, a former student he was often seen with during his Kunming days (but never in his home); of a radiant "by chance" (*ouran*) who flashed before his eyes as a "white rainbow" when their paths crossed at the Xiong Xiling residence in Peking, about 1935; or even of a lovely young woman in green who tempted Shen at the Qingdao seashore shortly before he was to marry in 1933.[76]

"Gazing at a Rainbow" and its companion piece rocked Kunming. Even Shen's friends advised him to take another direction. Not only were the stories "obscure"; what *could* be fathomed in them seemed pornographic. One young author charged him with imitating D. H. Lawrence.[77] Shen's eroticism was actually tantalizingly suggestive rather than explicit. But because he often spoke up on behalf of sexual liberation, and was imagined by the academic community to be pursuing the lovely Miss Gao and perhaps others, most readers misread the story as a simple autobiographical confession.

The only direct account of Shen Congwen's extramarital yearnings available to us is his own "Water and Clouds: How I Create Stories, and How They Create Me," an apologia he wrote in 1942. Yet, as might be guessed from the subtitle, this piece is a psychological autobiography that makes imaginings concrete and dissolves events into abstract ideas, so that the line between fact and fantasy becomes more problematic than before. The three "by chances" mentioned above, for instance, appear at first to be different women, but Shen's prose is so obscure that he could be referring to a single woman (or idea of a woman) who reappeared at different periods in his life, establishing a different kind of relationship each time: "When one of the 'by chances' chose 'security' for the past, I discovered the beauty of restraint. When another 'by chance' 'threw caution to the winds' for the sake of the present, I discovered the beauty of commitment. And in the 'prudence' desired for the future by [or 'at'] the third 'by chance,' I discovered the beauty of the bravery and wisdom that inhere in modesty."[78]

"Water and Clouds" may be called experimental because of the three voices that do the narrating. One dramatizes the author's interactions with the "by chances"; their concrete existence is vaguer than the education they provide, and some actually may be lost opportunities. Another voice is the author's, split into two opposite personalities who narrate in alternation, in order to argue with each other: an optimistic Shen, eager to love and confident of his ability to shape life to suit him, and a fatalistic Shen, who scoffs at his other half for believing in free will. Finally, there is the author as an integrated and maturing consciousness, periodically taking stock of emotional and artistic lessons until self-doubt splits him into two again, or a chance encounter leads to a new crisis or a new epiphany. The narrative does not unfold chronologically, but is told in episodes that mark time according to two unsynchronized kinds of mileposts. The beguiling chance encounters are one kind of marker. They bring about a ten-year suppression of the Shen Congwen who believes in self-determination (ca. 1933-42), in favor of a self who is resigned to learning from women, like Jia Baoyu dreaming of the Twelve Beauties of Jinling. Shen's major writings are the other mileposts. Some works began as sublimations of libido. He wrote "Portrait of Eight Steeds," for instance, as a way of "resisting" the Qingdao beauty who tempted him to break off his engagement to Zhang Zhaohe; Shen let Mr. Dashi act out a fantasy he could not allow himself. The other side of him, however, intervened to warn that, by writing in order to sublimate his desires, he was surrendering "control." Hence he wrote *The Frontier City*, evoking sadness during a time of happiness (his honeymoon), virtually as a test of will.

Regrettably, after writing the controversial Kunming stories Shen seems after all to have followed the critics instead of his own will. He ceased writing fiction in the mold of "Gazing at a Rainbow," though he continued experimenting with structure, symbolism, and fragmented consciousness, and still pursued private religious and philosophical concerns. Mostly he contemplated the disillusionments and decline of faith wrought by war, and their diminution of the human spirit. The result was meditative autobiographical essays that he called "Nightmares." Conceptually they are of a piece with Shen's 1930's idea fiction, though they differ in being self-consciously unconventional in form. There is no unitary plot, only alternation between chronicle and interior monologue, between sensation and meaning.[79] Shen's experimentation continued in its own channel, quite separate from such regional works as *Long River*. The two creative streams came together for a brief moment in "After Snow" (1946), but that story is less impressive than "Qiaoxiu and Dongsheng" and "Truth Is Stranger Than Fiction," pieces written in his more practiced, lyric-cum-realistic voice.

Shen Congwen's writings about God in *The Candle Extinguished*, and even about the war, set him still further apart from his colleagues. He had always found prowar, anti-Japanese literature difficult to stomach, on both moral and literary grounds. Literature ought to elevate people above war, he reasoned. As the Japanese threat receded, Shen reflected anew on his lifetime of encounters with organized killing. He wrote newspaper essays criticizing the way in which wartime confusion was creating spiritual and material opportunism among his fellow-countrymen. By the end of the war, he was actively voicing antiwar sentiments. When peace gave way to civil war, he redoubled his efforts. Shen Congwen had become a pacifist.[80]

This was a change. Shen's stories of the early 1930's—e.g., "Dark Night"; "Morning: A Soldier on a Mound of Earth"; and "The One Who Crossed Over the Mountains"—had celebrated Chinese military heroism. A piece he wrote following the loss of Manchuria might have been written by a Marxist. In it, local authorities lock up all anti-Japanese patriots as "anti-government." Their comrades stage a strike that collapses when wealthy merchants withdraw support.[81]

In the 1946–49 Civil War, though, it was his pacifism that put Shen on the left. He pleaded his case in the literary supplements he edited, for the Tianjin and Shanghai *Dagongbao*, the Tianjin *Yishibao* (*Social Welfare*, a Catholic newspaper), and the Peking *Pingming ribao* (*The Dawn*). China was headed for the abyss, Shen wrote. Its values were now wholly corrupted by selfishness, degeneracy, and thirst for "organized group suicide" (civil war). For one thing, a new class of sybarites ("who 20 years ago would have been called compradors") had fanned out and taken office throughout China. They had been created by the United States, which still wanted to build China into "a democratic country, its biggest customer on the other side of the Pacific, its satellite." Americans listened to these people they had brought into being and to no one else; George Marshall himself simply encouraged the KMT in its unregeneracy. Becoming dimly aware of its error, the United

States then belatedly tried to organize China's liberal intellectuals into a third force for democracy. But they, too, were divorced from the real China, the hungry and humiliated millions. Even educated young people were beginning to hate America, as the prolonger of China's Civil War and rebuilder of Japan. Here Shen spoke not just for his students, whom he "polled" through writing assignments, but for himself. His views were in accord with non-Communist leftist intellectual ideology. Yet, by his own analysis, to join China's Westernized intellectuals was to be cut off from China. He had learned that lesson while taking a Western road in literature. He did not mind being ahead of the masses intellectually, but he saw no reason to be divided from them politically, too. He shunned the "democratic parties" to the end.[82]

In the main, Shen Congwen preferred not to analyze society in political terms. He felt himself spiritually a "nineteenth-century man" trying to hold back the debilitating disease of the twentieth century. China's 1940's bloodlust and materialism were but the outer signs of a modern decline in character, he felt, a failure of world civilization. Shanghai culture was an early Chinese manifestation of it. Now the baseness of modern vapidity was being imitated directly, from American movies. Young people walked, talked, dressed, and acted like their favorite stars; they gave up reading and "ideals"; and they were content to adapt to society so long as they could earn enough money to stay fashionable. Not wholly unlike T. S. Eliot, Shen Congwen clung to tradition for modernist reasons.[83]

Thus it is in the name of an ancient that Shen voiced one of his last, and most affecting, meditations on the human condition: "Socrates Discusses What Peking Needs" (1948). With polite nods to fellow unheeded sages Jesus, Laozi, and Buddha—and sly bows to latter-day "fellow Western" fix-it-alls like John Leighton Stuart, George Marshall, and Albert Wedemeyer—"Socrates" lays out a Reorganization Plan for Peking's civic and educational institutions. A philosopher should be made mayor, and an architect vice-mayor, to beautify and rebuild the city. Socrates' candidate for the latter post is wholly unknown to the Chinese government, though internationally famous for his work on the United Nations building in New York: Shen's friend Liang Sicheng.* The city

---

*Ironically, after 1949 Liang was put in charge of Peking's civic architecture, and given a seat on the Municipal Council.

might still be ruled by the police, but Peking should be cultivated as the "garden" that history had meant it to be. So policemen's wages must be raised to the level of gardeners'. Let the chief be a former stage director or musical conductor instead of a Party flunky, and let the station houses be covered with flowers. Police might check private residences (as they had some of Shen's students'), but only to give advice on sanitation and vegetable patches. At scheduled hours, police radios might receive Beethoven and pipe it out to the citizenry.

The seeming levity of Shen Congwen's vision of "flower power" masks not just inverted criticism of the old regime, but a lament over the Battle of Peking that seemed to be on the horizon. Most people feared that the great city and its half-millennium of cultural history would be obliterated in a last-ditch stand.* The essay therefore begins with Shen's shock on seeing the physical decay of Peking when he returned in 1946. Wartime civic and moral diseases, too, had "spread" to his favorite city. And now the government, which ought to be setting a moral example, was extorting fresh levies from the city's most destitute citizens, to build defense works that could only prolong the destruction.[84]

Mostly, though, "Socrates" keeps to Shen Congwen's own ken, art and education. He would build a new kind of Academy for the Applied Arts:

> In charge of the school would be a noted philosopher-poet. Ordinarily he would not get involved in running the school. Instead, not only would his glorious integrity reflect credit on the school, his avant-garde views on poetry and the arts, and enthusiastic discourse on the progress of Oriental Art, would have an international impact. The old manner of settling curricular matters would be changed. The practice of doing it through squabbling would be long forgotten. Chinese and foreign approaches would both be represented; you don't, after all, hear of Chinese and Foreign Language departments in regular universities waging war with each other and creating an embarrassing scene. Hands would be trained purely through apprenticeship. Eyes and intellect would be trained purely through tutorial. The combination of the two would be strengthened, and liberal arts subjects for the intellect, like literature, philosophy, history, and folklore, would be taught as conscientiously as in regular universities. (Most professorial chairs would be funded jointly by public and private arts organi-

---

*As it happened, Peking was surrendered to the Communists without much destruction—except for that done in advance by KMT general Fu Zuoyi's building of fortifications. Shen Congwen had not forgiven him even in 1980.

zations, and handicrafts industries.) For the feelings, students in all departments would undergo higher training in music. Students who don't react to the great classical works and like only jibbering pop songs, who write uncalligraphic calligraphy, call themselves by foreign names, flatter teachers and deans too much, or secretly take government money for reporting on people, would be considered spiritually unfit—sick in the head—to be cured by a specialist or, if incurable, expelled. Those who lack aesthetic sensibilities and only talk drivel, imitate and plagiarize, and write theoretical articles that don't make sense, be they student or teacher, would be uniformly judged unsuited for the art world. The counseling office would ask them to change profession and enroll in propaganda classes at a cadre school, or in the advertising department of some newspaper. [There would be resources for faculty development and student exhibitions. The president would in time step down and become director of publications for a New Art movement.][85]

Using aesthetic education to cure moral ills, Cai Yuanpei's Chinese variation on Kantian idealism, evidently overshadows Platonic idealism in this utopia of Shen's. However, the idea of beautifying Peking with great public lawns is very Western, and Shen ends on a note that seems genuinely Socratic. Hu Shi and Mei Yiqi (presidents of Peking and Qinghua universities) are to clarify "differences and similarities between capitalism and socialism" by convening an uncensored public debate on that issue. Yet, whereas a good Athenian would seek actively to participate in such a debate, Shen Congwen probably would not, himself: he would fill the polis with civic responsibility, only to purge it of politics. To Cai Yuanpei's slogan, "aesthetic education as a substitute for religion," Shen explicitly adds a rider: "and also as a substitute for politics"—for war, above all. ("Socrates" wants to commission public sculptures that illustrate twentieth-century cultural innovators triumphing over war.) Democracy did not concern Shen Congwen as much as it did Hu Shi. Shen's ideals, on the eve of the revolution, were beauty, love, virtue, freedom, and peace.

The Last Chapter: Two Tales of Resistance, One Active, One Passive

Throughout history, the West Hunan Miao had resisted every new regime that meant to tighten political control over them. The People's Republic was but the latest. Upper West Hunan therefore took its "Liberation" about as badly as any region in China, save the still larger minority areas, such as Tibet. Many who did not revolt sympathized with the rebels. Communism aside, they resented the new "descent on the South" (*nanxia*) by Northern soldiers.

But first came one last revolt against the Nationalists. Those who led the uprising opposed Communist rule, and would soon prove it. Why, then, did they attack the KMT in March 1949, as Communist armies prepared to cross the Yangzi? Perhaps because their scores against the KMT were historical and concrete, whereas those against the CCP were still hypothetical. Furthermore, bemoans a pro-KMT source, the last KMT general all but invited the locals to strike out at him in self-defense.

This final KMT pacifier was General Li Moan, a Changsha appointee. Li had his own troops in Changde and an array of uncertain allies in particular upriver towns, but in the chaotic 1940's Changsha no longer controlled the countryside—not even the Peace Preservation Corps. Many of the latter were led by local bandit generals, or holdovers from Chen Quzhen's old regime; Li headed a pyramid of power whose foundations were beyond his grasp. Even so, he had county assembly heads in Upper West Hunan seized, prosecuted, and in some cases executed. Meanwhile, a wave of unexplained assassinations felled, among others, Gu Jiaqi, a hero of Jiashan. When Gu's old boss, the former "King of West Hunan," barely escaped from an ambush en route to talks with the KMT, the atmosphere became tense. Li was not necessarily behind that plot, but finally he completely overstepped himself, by trying to replace several local heads of peacekeeping forces with his own men.[86]

The result was a mutiny that wrested Yuanling from the KMT and shook Nationalist confidence throughout the Southwest—the March 2d Incident. The chief rebel was Peace Preservation Corps commander Wang Yuanhua, who raised his standard when he learned that he was to be replaced. Militia heads in the northwest joined him, as did "Miao King" Long Yunfei, despite his position as one of Li Moan's five division commanders. Cao Zhenya of Yongshun, also on Li's list to be eliminated, proclaimed a West Hunan People's Anti-Oppression Committee up in the hills. Wang and Cao marched on Changde itself, but had to settle for Yuanling, much of which Cao burned to the ground on March 2d. Shen Congwen's cousin Dai Jitao, formerly Wang's commander, was sent to negotiate with the rebels; he regained control of Yuanling by promoting both rebels to deputy brigade commander. Li Moan then pinned the blame on Dai, until Governor Cheng Qian intervened to save him.

By now, though, the Miao were up in arms. Their "King" had taken Mayang. Wu Hengliang, the other rebel chief of 1937, led 2,000 Miao in the capture of Yongsui. Luo Wenjie, another of Li Moan's division commanders, took Guzhang. Baojing fell to a militia head. Most unnerving, a combined bandit force of 2,000 seized the government's arsenal, at Chenqi. With its 8,000 rifles, they ravaged Xupu, Huaihua, Qianyang, and Hongjiang, looting, burning, and raping. In April the serious power brokers organized themselves, in the Miao hills between Fenghuang and Qiancheng, into a Hunan-Hubei-Sichuan-Guizhou Self-Defense Military Administration Committee. Old Chen Quzhen, the one man around whom they could unite, was titular "King" again. His "commanders" included his former subordinates Long Yunfei and Zhou Xieqing; Luo Wenjie, of the old warlord regimes farther north; and the rebels of March 2d, Wang and Cao.

The rebels "won": in May, when KMT General Song Xilian arrived to organize a new military government for the four-province border area, he appointed the rebel chiefs as division and brigade commanders. But their units could hardly be united to fight the PLA, and Chen Quzhen and Dai Jitao temporized when asked to join last-ditch KMT war councils with Bai Chongxi. They did not have long to wait: Liu Bocheng's and Lin Biao's Communist soldiers swept into West Hunan's cities in October 1949.[87]

Very like the KMT in 1935, the CCP set about governing West Hunan from a West Hunan Field Office in Yuanling, headquarters of a special subprovincial West Hunan Military District. Household registration was expedited, "bandit registration stations" were set up in the hills, and a breathtaking 18,000 firearms were taken from citizens in 14 West Hunan counties during the first three months of 1950. Some 60,000 PLA troops mopped up in the hills, but the region would remain too unsettled for land reform to begin before 1951.[88]

Chen Quzhen, aware of the larger political situation and no stranger to defeat, came over to the Communist side before the official "Liberation." By the end of 1949, he and Dai Jitao were in Yuanling, helping to mediate the new PLA-imposed peace. The

"King" was rewarded with a symbolic post in the new provincial government. This restored some of his long-lost official prestige, but he was unable to deliver the biggest prize: Long Yunfei and the son who stood to inherit his aura among the Miao, Long Enpu. It is said that Chen Quzhen tried repeatedly to arrange a meeting with the "Miao King," but to no avail. On the third try, Long killed the messenger. Wu Hengliang, however, sided with the CCP.[89]

Even without Chen's faction, the "resistance to Communism" was almost identical with the March resistance to the KMT. Its leaders included Long Yunfei and his son; Zhou Xieqing; Luo Wenjie; and Wang Yuanhua, Cao Zhenya, and the other local bosses from the You River counties. A would-be eulogizer betrays the bandit origins of many of the lesser "heroes" by speaking of their return to permanent bases up on Bamian Mountain. A 4,000-man anti-Communist force did retake the county city of Guzhang and sever the Hunan-Sichuan road in the spring of 1950. But by then the You River bosses and most of the remaining Gan Army officers had surrendered. Still unpacified were the Miao pale and the permanent bandit realm in the Hunan-Hubei hills, spirit-soldier country. In April, Long Yunfei announced the creation of a Sichuan-Hunan-Guizhou Border Region People's Anti-Communist Self-Defense Army. He resisted for his own reasons, Shen Congwen says, not to help the Nationalists. The Miao recovered their Fenghuang pale, cut communications between counties, and kept the PLA cooped up in the cities.

The Communists were on the spot; their troops had to leave for Korea. They responded by setting up militias under the officers Chen Quzhen brought over and establishing tight controls on foodstuffs and travel. They also terrorized rebel family members, sympathizers, and designated counterrevolutionaries. The Miao rebellion was finally crushed in November 1950, after a 17-day battle. Long Yunfei committed suicide and his family was put to death.[90]

And yet—Long Enpu, his son, escaped and swore vengeance. We have only one, KMT, account. It claims that Enpu met secretly with a repentant Chen Quzhen in Changsha, then hid out in the boat people's underworld. Back in the hills, Long prepared for a last stand. His hideouts were taken only with the help of Soviet arms and military advisers, in the bloody summer of 1951. When Long was executed in Yuanling, West Hunan was finally pacified. Or mostly pacified. Up in Dayong, a Han bandit chief from the pre-Liberation era and his wife were exterminated only in 1964. The cost of resistance was high. Shen Congwen estimates that 30,000 of his people, mostly Miao, died during the Liberation. Thousands more were eliminated up in the Hunan-Hubei border country.[91]

Shen Congwen's fate at this time is similarly obscure. The only account of this darkest period of his life, when he attempted suicide, was published years after the fact in Taiwan, by his former student Ma Fenghua. For 30 years, except for the appearance of his name on the spines of a few art history books, Shen Congwen virtually disappeared from public view. No one could even dispute a 1968 report from Taiwan that he had died.[92] Yet it was in his own country that Shen Congwen's memory vanished most completely.

At the start of 1948, a full year before Peking changed color, Shen Congwen had already written his last piece of fiction. Hence it is not exactly clear what killed the author in him. He was thoroughly depressed by China's continued descent into civil violence and social and moral breakdown. Even that part of the old society he thought good seemed powerless to save itself. He was also afraid of what the Communists would do once in power, particularly to intellectuals like him. He did not, however, modify his opinions ahead of time to suit them. At a literary forum convened just two months before the January 1949 surrender of Peking, at which Zhu Guangqian spoke of European literature as having entered a period of decadence and Feng Zhi allowed as how Symbolism had had an unhealthy influence, Shen Congwen hammered away against the idea that politics had the right to direct literature. He spoke of traffic signals, as if about to concede that individual behavior must accept certain basic restraints. Instead he caught his colleagues up short: Can't stoplights be manipulated? And, "Perhaps there are those who think that travel goes better without stoplights...?"[93]

Shen's friends did not, however, think him clinically depressed at this time. Though he was retiring from fiction writing, he was more absorbed than ever in his reading, his interests in art history and architecture, and calligraphy. Shen's grass script had become nearly as prized as his fiction. To help relieve the great Hunan famine of 1946, he had donated 100 scrolls of it, to be sold for 10,000 yuan each. He remained close to his friends (Zhu Guangqian, Jin Yuelin, and Fei Ming, among others), to the young writers he published (such as Wang Zengqi, Jin Di, and Yuan Kejia), and to the college students to whom he taught composition. The young were radicalizing rapidly (many were underground Communists), and Shen's closeness to them may have increased his self-doubt about his "worth" at this time when, as he all too readily acknowledged, old values were crumbling. A whole generation was on trial, and Shen could not help feeling himself on the wrong side of the line—damned, as part of the old.[94]

At the November 1948 forum, though, Shen went beyond the issue of politics controlling literature to address the idea of literature reforming politics—of authors leading *society*. Yet by 1948 he surely realized that his kind of literature was not having even the remotest effect on the swift flow of events. Judged in the light of his own exaggerated hopes, his life as a writer was now "irrelevant"—useless to his highest goal, reform. Perhaps it was that realization that moved Shen out of literature and into art—in 1948, before he lost confidence in himself.

When Communist troops began the siege of Peking in December 1948, Shen's mental state must have reached the point of "three parts relief and seven parts fearful apprehension." Surely apprehension was in the ascendancy after the spring of 1948. Guo Moruo, citing "Plucking a Star," labeled Shen a reactionary pornographer (a "peach-pink" writer) and propagator of a fourth-party stance above the revolution. Xia Yan's words wounded deeper still: he said Shen had defended fascism and besmirched the memory of his martyred friend Wen Yiduo by undermining Wen's third-party movement. Friends and KMT intermediaries pleaded with Shen to follow the government south. But his estimate of the KMT's longevity, never sanguine, could hardly have been on the rise, nor his estimate of how much use that regime would have for him. "As I see it, it's no use to escape," Shen wrote a young student during the siege of Peking. Summoning up his positive, idealistic, literary voice, he went on to speak of rebuilding China.[95]

Shen later pointed out, with a sense of having been betrayed, that he had never had a good word for the KMT, had no close surviving landlord relatives, but did know some Communists. Even so, as Peking came under siege, a war of psychological terror opened up against him. In private, Shen received hate mail and at least one death threat. In public, at Peking University, wall posters said he was "peach-pink," "uncommitted" to the New China, and had "prostituted" himself as an author. Close to a nervous breakdown, he left the campus for a rest in the suburbs, at Jin Yuelin's place.[96]

When the PLA moved in, a commissar (an old friend of Mrs. Shen, Ma Fenghua says) came by to have "heart-to-heart talks" with Shen Congwen and to convince Zhang Zhaohe to get Marxist training, so she could get in on the ground floor of China's reconstruction. The friend also wanted them to hand their children over to a boarding school, where they might get a good revolutionary upbringing. Zhang Zhaohe did leave home for North China University, though the children stayed behind with their father. Like many of her classmates, Zhang was excited about the prospect of leaving the household and holding down a career to serve the New China. Ultimately she became an editor for *People's Literature*. But the immediate effect of her enthusiasm for the revolution, Ma Fenghua says, was the development of marital discord that opened a second front of psychological struggle against Shen Congwen. Even his children promised their teachers to argue with their father until he saw the light. Distraught, Shen could only take refuge in his Western classical music. He tried to write again, late at night, but destroyed everything the next morning. The one piece he showed Ma was a long poem, an elegy about his old life. He may have been trying to put the sentiments of his "Nightmare" series into verse.[97]

At this point—sometime in the early months of 1949, while Zhang Zhaohe was away at study classes—Shen Congwen's colleagues learned that he had tried to kill himself by drinking kerosene and slitting his wrists and throat. Unconscious in the hospital for days, he awoke thinking that he was in prison. His classes were canceled at Peking University. At some point he resigned from that institution (perhaps as late as 1951), as he had, earlier, from his other post at Furen University. It was in 1950 that Shen Congwen was assigned to the National Historical Museum and given a small work space just outside the Wu Gate of the palace. For several years, he was asked only to label artifacts and take the general public on museum tours. (One such visitor, in 1953, was a Korean War veteran named Wang Xu; he stayed on as Shen's permanent assistant.) Shen took pleasure in the rare privilege of being able to handle the kinds of antiques he had so loved as a collector. But there were political pressures to face as well, so in the fall of 1950, he bit the bullet and enrolled himself in political classes at the Revolutionary University.[98]

This was the turning point. Shen's grades were low, but just passing relieved the pressure on him. Far from being brainwashed, Shen Congwen emerged with the same impishly ironic perspective on China's great social upheaval with which he delighted his friends in the 1980's. He had found his strategy: self-effacement and avoidance of ladders of social mobility—"retreat to the second line," as he likes to say now, playing on the euphemism used by Mao Zedong for *his* late 1950's semi-retirement. By keeping out of sight, Shen could maintain his own inner life intact—even his old policy of staying out of organizations. Cleaning latrines was no punishment for Shen Congwen. He could think his thoughts again, just as when he knelt in the corner as a little boy. He had entered his classes full of self-doubt, but it turned out not to be the Marxist intellectuals he so despised and feared who were running the show, only semiliterate peasants. Professor Shen realized that his taskmasters did not *understand* what they were saying; yet they were perfectly happy to do all the talking for him—even insisted on it. He smiled when the dormitory cooks ridiculed his intellectuality. Paradoxically, Shen Congwen was free at last from his feelings of inadequacy.

Shen's confession, however, must have gone through many rewrites before it was deemed acceptable. It appeared only in November 1951. It is long, but not especially cringing. In fact it seems loaded with filler, such as a pointlessly long recitation of various historical incidents he didn't fully understand. And, as in certain other confessions of the day, Shen relates his "mistaken old ideas" with such a flourish that one has to wonder if he is not being ironic, seizing the occasion to justify himself, or putting himself on record for posterity. He reiterates how thoroughly he opposed Chiang Kaishek with this and that, though higher insight would of course have told him that objectively he was really helping Chiang Kaishek. "I've come to understand a lot of things. I've particularly come to understand the profound meaning for the nation of the statements, 'politics is above all else,' 'everything is subordinate to politics,' and 'literary art must follow politics and serve the interests of the broad masses.'" Had he not indeed. "In the last 20 years I wrote a lot of articles and made a lot of mistakes." Even this concedes very little. The word "mistake" came easily, as in Shen's stock answer today, delivered with a chuckle, to anyone who asks him why he no longer writes: "Demands have changed. It's easy to make a mistake!"

Shen's confession about his background is lyric, hardly a confession at all. He describes his native place, the injustices done to the Miao, and how the Hunanese despise all Fenghuang people as "Zhen'gan Miaozi." He gets by with a classification of himself as from a *bankrupt* landlord-military family, and tells how horrible were the circumstances in which he was brought up. If he had not gone against "reality," he would have ended up a warlord bully who smoked opium. But he did oppose reality. So this is really testimony about his strength of character, except that this did lead him to "mistake" all politics as being only "control." Shen provides yet more filler—a thumbnail history of the entire New Culture movement. Its words about the new villain Hu Shi are unexceptionable: "One group thought that conditions were not ripe for social revolution. They found more hope in the road of capitalist democracy. They advocated academic freedom to save the nation and did their utmost to promote the overthrow of Confucius and Sons, though they stayed away from encouraging the head-on struggle of class revolution. Hu Shi and Wu Zhihui exemplify this group."

Never having been abroad, Shen did not have to confess to being a tool of imperialism, only to being a model old-style intellectual and pseudoliberal separated from the masses, "a mixture of [Turgenev's 'superfluous' hero] Rudin and Don Quixote." He bumbled into retarding the revolution; had unclear thought; misled young people (with his idealism); and was influenced by Freud and Joyce. By habit of association with intellectuals who fawned on the KMT ruling elite, he "came very close to" aiding the Four Families (which is not to say that he actually did). In the end, the confession depicts Shen's recent Marxist "study" as but the final stage in a whole lifetime devoted to "experimentation" and writing "exercises." His life has been one long learning process, he humbly submits; that is to say, he has not just now been "reborn." [99]

In literature, Shen Congwen's name was anathema in any case. Except for Zhu Guangqian, Yang Zhensheng, Fei Ming, Li Jianwu, Ba Jin, and a few others, his old colleagues would have nothing more to do with him. So it was with most of the young writers whose careers Shen had helped launch. Even Ding Ling wrote an article that, in Jonathan Spence's carefully chosen words, "denigrate[d] Shen Congwen in what seems to have been a gratuitous way." In 1953, the Kaiming Press in Shanghai wrote to announce the burning of the inventory and printing plates for all Shen's works, since they were "passé." (Meanwhile, Taiwan proscribed all his works, too.) Shen's name virtually disappeared from mainland literary history books, except for one or two that stopped to criticize him in passing. That was still mostly true in the 1980's.[100]

Shen Congwen replied by burying himself in his new career. By the mid-1950's, he was actively publishing articles on the materials of and artistic and folk custom motifs embedded in Chinese material history; on architecture, the city of Peking, and historical preservation; and on how literary evidence and archaeology could be used to corroborate each other, a methodological approach he took as his new cause. He compiled whole books, on lacquerware (1954?), textile designs (1957), Tang and Song dynasty mirrors (1958), Ming dynasty brocades (1959), and folk art (1960). He was an editor of the journal *Zhuangshi* (*Decoration*) during its entire run, from July 1958 to May 1960, and became a member of the Chinese Writers' Association and even the People's Political Consultative Conference, which occasioned a trip home to Fenghuang in 1957. In 1957 he also published two topical essays in *People's Literature*. One, "Supporting Actors," may contain covert satire. Ostensibly it is a recherché piece about reform of Peking opera. Shen argues against excessive emphasis on the star. Opera would be more interesting if bit players had interesting parts, too. But when he gets to talking about the stars making spectacles of themselves, and the bit actors doing somersaults in sympathy, he just might have his eye on something else. He starts the piece with the self-effacing observation that he, for one, is just a "supporting actor."[101]

Otherwise, it was in the mid- and late 1950's that Shen Congwen and the new regime came to their greatest mutual accommodation. Shen's praises of Chairman Mao and the CCP are mostly to be found in his articles from these years. However, his encomiums are brief and perfunctory, not enthusiastic, like Ba Jin's early 1950's writings. When friends Ding Xilin and Zhang Xiruo invited him to apply for membership in the Communist Party, Shen was not interested. Yet he evidently felt a genuine surge of patriotism, because China had "stood up"—rid itself of civil war, imperialism, starvation, and opium. For its part People's China, in the spirit of the Hundred Flowers, reissued a volume of Shen Congwen's old short stories. He responded by "updating" them, making his criticism of the old order more explicit. Most stories were touched only in a few spots, though Hua-ling Nieh thinks the damage fairly serious. Shen had the good judgment to undo this tampering in all 1980's reissues.[102]

Would he ever undertake new creative writing, though? Between formal sessions of a big literary meeting Shen attended, Mao Zedong and Zhou Enlai summoned 12 writers they wanted to meet and encourage. They asked Shen to resume writing. He tried, in 1961. With 18 younger writers, he ascended the Maoist shrine of Jinggangshan (Mt. Jinggang), intending to stay for three years and write a novel about a Communist martyr in his wife's family. Three months later he destroyed what he had written and came down the mountain. He could not bring himself to write the sort of thing he was expected to.[103]

The trip did, however, inspire some ancient verse in Classical Chinese. And Shen kept it up. In 1980, he showed me a drawerful —reams of old-style poems. Some refer obliquely to the injustices and humiliations he suffered. Some even contain social and political satire. That was not so surprising in 1980, but many of the poems were written in the early 1970's, at cadre school, when Shen Congwen was supposed to be "reforming" himself. Even his 1960's poems are deliciously suspect. The ostensible subject of the one below is the Tang dynasty "people's poet" Bai Juyi. As Bai ascends Mt. Lu (Lushan), he recalls the ancient poet Tao Qian, who must have enjoyed the very same scenery. Tao was thought to have lived nearby, at Lili. Both poets liked wine and the lute; Shen nails down his historical allusions through annotations, so that the poems will be understood as the moldy relics that they appear to be. Yet he could not get his prefaces cleared, though it was early 1962, almost open season on Mao Zedong himself.

> The poet, enjoying his solitude, joyfully makes the climb, upon his cane,
> Shirking not the arduousness of the trek, he marvels that his vision is still so clear.
> Mountain springs ring clear, like clacking jade, as tender peaches greet the early spring.
> Looked back on with fond nostalgia, it has a beauty all its own.

A pure lute sounds a tune; he pours another cup of thick wine.
He cherishes the memory of the Lushan meeting, but it is hard to meet up with the man of Lili;
Often he experiences a common loneliness, his career having encountered equal hardship.
The two worthies did not live at the same time, but both will be remembered for a thousand autumns.
[Their] great poetry being close to the people, the people deeply cherish their memory![104]

Is Bai Juyi, or Mao Zedong, "the poet" after Tao Qian? Mao had recalled and, by some readings, even put himself above Tao in his own poem, "Ascending Mt. Lu" (July 1959). It was at the Lushan Meeting (Eighth Plenum) convened just afterward that Mao renewed his foolish Great Leap Forward and purged Peng Dehuai, the major critic of the people's communes. Those acts, however, were Mao's final exercise of will before the other Communist leaders began to treat him like a "departed ancestor."

Shen's student Wu Han had already ridiculed Mao's senile pigheadedness in a play. Shen seems to have scoffed at the Leader's poetry, too. There exists an unpublished alternative last line for Shen's poem. It shifts abruptly from Classical Chinese to post-Liberation slogan-vernacular: "[Your] great poetry being close to the people, the people fervently love you!" (*re ai ni!*)[105]

As China's writers, including Ding Ling, were humiliated one by one in purges, Shen Congwen's low profile came to look like the greatest wisdom—above all during the Cultural Revolution. He did not of course escape persecution. (Fortunately for him, he did not seek protection from Jiang Qing—Mme. Mao—whom he once taught writing at Qingdao University.) In 1966 he was assigned to clean the toilets again, for a year. In the course of eight raids on his house, he had to relinquish most of his books. (He had given his antiques to museums years ago.) People who worked with Shen in the museum, mostly artists who made illustrations for him, attacked him from year to year when called upon to do so. (More constant was Wang Yarong, who has painted for Shen since 1974.) And, when he had nearly completed his master multivolume book on the history of Chinese costume in 1969, Shen Congwen was sent down to a May Seventh Cadre School for "reform." Unlike his wife, he did not have to do much hard labor (Kai-yu Hsu says he was sent to something of a resort); but Shen was separated from his family, poorly fed, without medicine for his high blood pressure, and not allowed to take along his work materials. Since his survival strategy had always been to bury himself in work, he reconstructed much of his recently confiscated writing from memory. It was a time for writing poems, too. Shen even began a long Huang family history. Had he been kept in the countryside for a few more years (and survived), Shen Congwen might have produced one more great prose narrative, *The Dream of the Red Chamber* for the Huang clan, as his relatives jokingly called it.[106]

Back in Peking after three years, Shen was given a one-room house not much more than twice the size of his double bed—and he half filled that with books. The house became a legend on the Peking grapevine. Zhang Zhaohe, released the next year (1972), preferred to live in a house of her own; Shen walked half a mile to take the meals she prepared for him. Mrs. Shen, whatever marital difficulties may have occurred before, affectionately looked after her aged but stubbornly lovable mate with the conscientiousness of a nurse and the dogged protectiveness of a bodyguard. Having survived, Shen Congwen seemed deliriously happy. The treasures of China's ancient palaces were wholly at his disposal, to learn from as he could. In 1973, he struck Kai-yu Hsu as "Like a religious devotee who has just seen God's grace" when he talked about his artifacts. He felt protected, and "given unusual opportunities to work," perhaps because his book on costume had been given priority by Zhou Enlai. Even so, the book—or the first volume of it—saw print only in 1981. Still in the 1980's, by underlining phrases like "*works still waiting to be wrapped up*" in letters to his friends, Shen revealed his frustration that politics was continuing to delay his publications. The problem was never-ending.[107]

In 1979–80, though, partly because of the prestige his old works enjoyed in foreign countries, there was a revival in China of interest in Shen Congwen's fiction. A few scholars began to do research on him; most of his literary works were republished, for the first time since 1949, in a twelve-volume edition; and a film was made of *The Frontier City*. (Shen, characteristically, twice returned his royalties from a prior film version of his novel, by a famous Shanghai director, because it was unfaithful and overpoliticized. Presumably his fastidiousness was decisive in getting the inferior film killed.)[108]

Still, Shen's rehabilitation was only partial. Print runs of his works were small. His name loomed larger in the Panda Books series, intended for foreign consumption, than in native cultural circles. Indeed, when the campaign against "spiritual pollution" descended in 1983, old criticisms of Shen were aired again. The "excessive" new interest in his works was widely faulted, a provincial press reneged on its decision to print a book about him, and even in Hong Kong the reprinting of Shen's works ran into serious roadblocks for a time. The Hunanese, however, and not just the West Hunanese, were a good deal more constant. Shen Congwen became a hero in Fenghuang, a symbol of West Hunan and the Miao. Several local writers, and Gu Hua, who hails from another mountain district of Hunan, were said to be writing in Shen's tradition. Shen Congwen's less class-conscious regional writing was acknowledged *as* a tradition: not "peasant[-class] literature," but "native-soil" or "rural" literature (*xiangtu wenxue*). Until Shen Congwen is reabsorbed into China's literary histories and textbooks, though, the best guess is that in future decades no high school students, few college students in the sciences, and not all students in Chinese departments will even recognize his name—as is the case now.[109]

Yet Shen Congwen is a major figure in the People's Republic because of his other career. By serving a materialist regime explicitly in the realm of material culture, he has even managed, to a remarkable degree, to pursue his own goals. He can afford now to support the revolution—as the embodiment of China's history, the custodian of her future, and the sometime promoter and popularizer of his own cause, which is aesthetic resistance to the tide of mediocrity that he sees in all the media. Shen felt no compunction about representing his country on a study-lecture tour of America (1980–81), once it was resolved that he could go alone, with his wife, and decide for himself precisely how, and how far, he would act as official spokesperson. He has refused, however, to enter more abstract realms on behalf of the New China. In view of his unchanged idealistic values, this is an act of passive resistance. It goes beyond noncompliance with Marxist literary policy. While serving the revolution in his own way, Shen Congwen resists its claim to embody a new truth. There he remains in the mid-1980's: still tirelessly continuing his historical studies and revising his old works, though half paralyzed by a stroke; still stubbornly refusing to write to order.[110]

Conclusion

WERE LIFE POETRY, it might seem fitting that Shen Congwen, China's "Miao" author, went down to defeat alone. The heights he defended were not an ivory tower, as some critics still allege, but a "primitive" realm of individualism, eroticism, and religion. Politically, too, Shen's is more a world of "primitive anarchism" than of modern democracy. Access to those taboo literary frontiers requires some effort on the part of the reader. But the equipment most needed for the climb is imagination, not learning.

Shen Congwen's artistic journey was a long one. To the end he kept his resolve to be always on the move: to stay abreast, as well as he could in Chinese, of avant-garde trends in world literature, and also to see what he could learn from ancient Chinese literature. Starting out as a warlord soldier unable to punctuate, in the 1920's Shen developed and abandoned one new linguistic style after another. He ended up being called a stylist—a pastoral, "very Chinese" writer. Yet in 1940 he reemerged on the other side, with Western style and Western fragmentation of consciousness.

Shen Congwen's concentration on his craft led some to mistake him for an aestheticist. He did consider craft to be the sine qua non of literature, having its own innovations and development. He also had a passion for the visual arts and espoused holistic aesthetic theories. Yet Shen Congwen was interested not just in the arts, but in many intellectual concerns, such as the nature of man, consciousness, and the cosmos. Had his temperament been different, or had he enjoyed a better formal education and known foreign languages, he might have turned away from literature in the 1940's and written philosophy. As it was, he wrote a book on logic and infused his late creative works with religious sentiments. Beauty was Shen

Congwen's God, but his God was also Life. He advocated art not for phenomenal "art's sake," but for God's sake, a God who dwelt in human Life.

Shen Congwen was not politically stationary, either. Just when he seemed to be emerging as a full-fledged radical writer in the late 1920's, he took a turn toward the least engaged writing of his career, in the early 1930's. Yet in the late 1940's, though he chose to remain ideologically in a state of maximum tension with the Communists, his political views were unmistakably leftist again. Shen Congwen defies classification because he stayed out of groups. He was every faction's enemy, but no faction's archenemy.

While this bespeaks remarkable independence of will, keeping abreast also meant keeping sensitive to the currents of thought around him. Shen cared what his colleagues thought. When they told him it was not a good thing to become the D. H. Lawrence of China, he set aside his "rainbows," at least temporarily. He remained watchful of the political and social situation, too. There, in particular, his own skepticism, feelings of inferiority, and openness to all sides fed self-doubt—though not to such an extent as to drive him into the fold of any group; his old defense was to think of himself as really closer to China's masses than the Nationalists, the Communists, or, above all, those most like himself, the third-force intellectuals. But self-doubt must have played some part in his decision to stop writing, and then to attempt suicide. It did not, however, terminate his thinking—not even about the revolution that in 1949 took him so by surprise. In the end, Shen emerged as a commentator on the manners of People's China quite as sensitive and witty as his more embittered colleagues, though his commentary remains private (or, rather, it will remain private until his poems can be fully interpreted).

One could say on the other hand that Shen Congwen changed little in all these years, or even that he returned to the intellectual roots of his Young China upbringing. He was raised on reform militarism, like his mentors. Also like them, he graduated to a newer instrument of reform—not constitutional government, in his era, but "literary revolution." Shen Congwen believed in the power of literary idealism. When his colleagues lost faith in it, he saw his world as one afflicted with the Death of God. It was as if the materialists, the Western-educated people who were not really interested in the inner life, had combined with political organizers and commercial interests to steal the literary movement away from him. Revolution and sociology began as updated forms of idealism, he reasoned, but ended up replacing, even opposing, literature. Shen continued to espouse reform, science, and individual freedom, and he rediscovered holistic cosmology. The 1940's actually found him reinvestigating much of the ground covered by his Uncle Nie: Darwinian vitalism, local self-government, cosmology, and Buddhism. Shen Congwen started and ended with faith in humanity—a faith that he could reconcile with biological science, Christian love and pacifism, and the cosmic holism of the Indian faiths—a belief system to keep society heading dynamically forward in a world of struggle and energy, but also to unify it and lift it up toward higher things.

In time, Shen Congwen began to think of his own literary movement as the product of Liang Qichao's generation, not just Hu Shi's and Chen Duxiu's.[1] It was the older generation who began to reform China's ideals, and Liang himself who designated fiction as those ideals' handmaiden, and who even started the shift to the vernacular. Shen's own style, in his late writings, was beginning to meet Liang halfway. He avoided set phrases as always, but was no longer so opposed to borrowing from Classical syntax.

Many of Shen Congwen's political perspectives remained constant, too. Pacifist or not, he always liked soldiers and distrusted Western-educated intellectuals. Immune to romanticism about the masses seizing power, he took it for granted that Chinese government throughout his lifetime would turn on the wise or foolish doings of emperors and would-be emperors: Yuan Shikai, Chiang Kaishek, and Mao Zedong. Blocs and pressure groups—"politics"—bored him. The acts of emperors and their armies did not. Shen's deepening sense of historical irony allowed him to penetrate the inconstancies and charades of twentieth-century politics, though better, perhaps, in allegorical than in realistic writing.

For the sake of his "ideals," Shen Congwen sacrificed his writing career. The choice, in the final analysis, was his. He was seemingly driven to keep on working, but, quite the opposite of his old friend Ding Ling, he did not feel "compelled to write under all circumstances."[2] Though slow to admit that literature was not the great tool for remolding ideals he had hoped it was, he seems to have quietly bowed to that reality in his own life. He began subordinating literature to a broader quest for Beauty as early as the 1930's.

Literature was but one route to Beauty, he said, and inferior to mathematics and music at that—to mention two of the few arts he was not yet pursuing himself, as a creator. It is not clear precisely what factors moved him in that direction, though—traditional outlooks on the unity of the arts; his holistic aesthetic cosmology; disillusionment with the literary climate; his new historical and antique-collecting avocations; or his Huang family artist's genes. It was, in the end, the revolution that locked him into his "more traditional" lifework.

The irony did not escape Shen Congwen that, just as he left the field, literature at last acquired the social role and ideological authority of his dreams. In a 1962 letter to relatives, he marveled at the expansion of the reading public and the hold that fiction had acquired over youth. Young people now went directly to fiction for their role models, he said. A novel could actually create a social disturbance.[3] Perhaps that was why he had felt tempted to resume his writing the year before. But, he realized, the victory had not gone to China's authors, to express their own will (*yan zhi*). Literature once more had to "promulgate the Way" (*zai Dao*).[4]

Under those post-1949 conditions, Shen Congwen surely could not have further developed his art. He had been hard put, even in the 1940's, to combine his cosmopolitan, experimental technique with native, rural subject matter. Under Mao's literary line, that gulf, partly one between East and West, grew until it became unbridgeable. Literary modernism, "obscurity," stream-of-consciousness—all techniques not deemed realistic—have no sure footing in Chinese socialist poetics even in the 1980's. Religious motifs, too, are today still ideologically suspect. And so, of course, is eroticism. The status of Freud in the meantime is clear from the heralding, in 1985, of a book that "introduces Freud to Chinese readers for the first time."[5]

Regionalism, on the other hand, became a major current in post-1949 literature, thanks to Mao's emphasis on peasants and patriotism. (The regional realism in Shen Congwen's works greatly furthered his partial rehabilitation in 1979.) Shen, however, valued regional writing for evoking not just a feeling of organic relatedness, but a sense of particularity and autonomy. Mao's "regional socialist realism" tolerated only the former. Dialect was in, but subjective definitions of regions were out. Sectional identity was simply subversive. Shen Congwen was out of phase: dialect was among the first elements of regional writing that he had learned to jettison. The literature of New China did not much interest *him*, either. He did not, and does not, read it.[6]

Literary greatness, however, rests on more than an ability to see the truth. It requires a spark of creativity whose nature still eludes us. Did Shen Congwen still have his, at the end of the 1940's? Precisely because he so often set his own goals, there will always be a nagging doubt that inner blocks, not just the bad environment, hindered his further development. To be sure, censorship inhibited Shen Congwen from enriching his regional writing with the political and social themes of his choice. And public disapproval promised to deprive him of critical and popular success if he pursued his interest in the Western avant-garde. Yet no one literally forced him to stop mining those literary veins. He might have continued writing "for the drawer"—as he did in the 1970's, when even his art books had no hope of publication—had he still had faith in himself, and in posterity. Probably that is what he lost for a time, in 1949. In any case, Shen Congwen in 1947 was down to formulas when asked for advice on how to write a regional novel about Mongolia. Heed the background, he said; play the action off against the four seasons, the rising and setting of the sun; put in some border love songs to heighten the lyricism; use psychology, including abnormal psychology, to dig into the people; and observe the customs of trade, to indicate the feelings in social relationships. This is a caricature of his own accomplishment, saved only by a more inventive further suggestion to use the musical technique of polyphony, so that motifs in "contradiction" may harmonize within a larger theme.[7] Perhaps Shen's own choices in the 1940's, to explicate history through realism in some works, and to express his religious faith in other writings, would have smothered his imagination in any society. Or was Shen's writing in this decade, too, as much a response to his environment as to his feelings within? The inner and outer factors are not so easily divisible.

Shen Congwen has in any case made a lasting contribution to Chinese literature and to world literature. As teacher and mentor, he also influenced many of China's most important fiction writers and poets, as well as two generations of West Hunan local colorists, in the 1940's and 1980's. He introduced literary techniques that seem avant-garde in China even in the 1980's, and provided an intense personal example of how literature could be an independent professional activity. Perhaps his most lasting contribution of all was his remolding of modern Chinese as a literary language.

Apart from masterpieces such as *The Frontier City* and *Long River*, Shen Congwen will be remembered more for his tales, portraits, mood paintings, and essays than for his grand constructions, but the whole is greater than the sum of the parts. Already in the 1940's he noted that the trend was toward greater length in fiction. Hindsight confirms that observation; poetry grew long, too, and it was not always for the better. Shen Congwen deliberately espoused the short story. The genre was another of his unpopular "causes."[8]

To view all modern Chinese *history* from a West Hunanese perspective is to look at China from the margins, and to see it through Shen Congwen's eyes, doubly so. Still, a reading of Shen's regional saga as witness to history can take us by surprise, even when it reminds us of what we thought we knew. The level of violence and social "decomposition" in his time is an example. Shen Congwen outlived nearly all his friends and relatives—and has done so "all his life." It is also startling to reflect on the importance of Communism in West Hunanese history. Outside He Long's realm, West Hunan, particularly Upper West Hunan, was all but untouched by the Communist peasant movement.[9] The region had no proletariat, nor is there any record of boat people or secret society lodges turning "red" before Liberation. West Hunan became Communist only as a result of Northern military occupation—a point that rankles still. Yet the idea of Communism weighed heavily on the minds and souls of Fenghuang's ruling class. Several of Shen Congwen's more educated soldier and upper-class friends joined the cause at one time or another, and many others became enthusiastic Left-KMT revolutionaries before the 1927 "purification." Those in the upper classes who did not enlist were unnerved by the idea of revolution, obsessed with the thought that it might spread to their territory. The social atmosphere became uneasy on that account. West Hunan's experience reflects even on the revolution from which it, like much of South China, was seemingly so far removed.

The locals' anti-Communist leanings seem on the other hand to have been quite irrelevant to how they felt about the Nationalists. West Hunan fought the KMT right up until the Communist conquest. Regional parochialism made the Nationalists seem like outlanders, and the KMT's links to America made it seem un-Chinese even to the cosmopolitan Shen Congwen himself. The Kuomintang, for its part, acted as if bent on alienating the affections of Shen, his officer friends at home, and most others in the middle.

Part of Shen Congwen's pastoral appeal is that he depicts a smaller, more manageable world. Nostalgia aside, his China was in fact a smaller and less populous country than the one we know today. His regional "kingdom," unlike the Autonomous West Hunan Prefecture that today runs factories, mines, and even a university, could be managed by a few families. Similarly, the literary profession he describes, before writers had national congresses and county branches, was far cozier than what the literary histories would lead us to expect. For all its factions and polemics, the writers' profession of his day emerges looking like a small and fragile fraternity. The lot of writers was unenviable; many had to abandon their profession. When they did, they were missed, even by their "opponents." Shen Congwen was no exception. So it seemed to me in 1980, when I was summoned to the hospital bedside of an old leftist polemicist who insisted on having his chance, before he went to see Marx, to set the record straight about Shen Congwen's ideological "errors." The old man glowed as he recalled the 1930's. In those days, everybody knew who was attacking whom. Shen Congwen the writer was, in a word, missed.[10]

What, then, of West Hunan? It remains "backward," of course. Even as roadbuilding, power projects, and a new railroad were transforming the region in 1980, blacksmiths worked their bellows much as Shen Congwen remembered them from the Qing.[11] The new economic policies will surely hasten the pace of change, but they may also cause West Hunan to be economically outstripped by littoral China as never before. Whatever the future may hold, the sights and sounds, and fears and hopes, of West Hunan's old society are preserved in literature. Few other Chinese regions are so blessed.

Reference Matter

Notes

For full forms of works cited in the Notes, see the Selected Bibliography, pp. 369–85. Where Shen's works are cited, dates in parentheses directly after the titles are dates of composition. The following abbreviations are used in all the Reference Matter.

CF	*Chenbao fukan* ([Peking] *Morning Post Literary Supplement*)
Ch. cal.	Chinese calendar date
DF	*Dongfang zazhi* ("*Eastern Miscellany*")
DGB	*Dagongbao* ("*L'Impartial*")
GW	*Guowen zhoubao* (*Kuo-wen Weekly*)
int. 1980.vi.20	Interview with Shen Congwen on June 20, 1980
letter 1984.viii.13	Letter from Shen Congwen, signed August 13, 1984, and penned by Zhang Zhaohe from dictation
W. cal.	Western calendar date
WJ	*Shen Congwen wenji* (*The Works of Shen Congwen*), Shao Huaqiang and Ling Yu, eds., 12 vols.
XFC	*Xin feiyou cundi* (*New Letters Never Mailed*), part of *Yunnan kan yun ji* (*Gazing at Clouds in Yunnan*)
XP	*Xiandai pinglun* (*Contemporary Review*)
XS	*Xiaoshuo yuebao* (*Short Story Monthly*)
ZZ	Shen Congwen, *Congwen zizhuan* (*Congwen's Autobiography*), rev. 1980 ed. (Beijing: Renmin wenxue chubanshe, 1981)

Introduction

1. My own mention of Lu Xun and Shen Congwen as authors of comparable merit is one of the few statements in my doctoral dissertation that had to be deleted or altered before the book could be considered publishable in China.

2. Shen Congwen has exercised judgment while speaking as I have while writing, but he has never sought to tell me what to write. I have, however, enjoyed many of the advantages of an authorized biographer, for after 1980 Shen became selective about whom he saw. I interviewed him in Peking 12 times during the summer of 1980. Most visits were three or four hours long. We took day trips together to the Great Wall, Xiangshan, and the Temple of Heaven. At the Frankel home in New Haven, Conn., I interviewed Shen six times more, often alone, during the winter of 1980–81. On a return trip to Peking in the summer of 1981, I visited the Shens a couple of times more.

Shen, at 77 and 78 years of age, remembered the names of old army and literary associates, and the Fenghuang curiosities and Peking antiques he gaped at in the marketplace, as if he had seen them all yesterday. He had forgotten many other things from 50 or more years ago, including some of his works of the 1920's. That was compounded by reluctance to be associated with his "immature" writing. Shen has for some time considered many of his early works too minor to take seriously. In his *Ji Hu Yepin*, *WJ* 9: 60, for instance, he appears to have confused his early work "Di'er ge Feifei" with another, "'Feifei' de beiai." (The work he really describes is a sort of sequel to the former, "Yong 'A' zi jixialai de shi.") I consider Shen's memory of dates unreliable; certain aspects of his family knowledge also appear surprisingly shaky, suggesting something more complicated than forgetfulness. These idiosyncratic and isolable lapses do not compromise his reliability as an autobiographer and biographer (of Ding Ling and Hu Yepin). His memory of the 1930's and 1940's was still solid in 1981, and his recall of the past 20 years appeared scarcely inferior to the average person's. Currently, in 1986, Shen is continuing his researches into Chinese history despite a serious stroke in 1983 that left him paralyzed on one side of his body. Since the stroke, he has corresponded with me by dictating letters to Zhang Zhaohe, his wife.

3. Cowley, ed., p. xv.

4. On Chinese regionalism economically defined, see Skinner, ed., especially Skinner's own chapters. For explicit studies of regionalism during the era that concerns us, see Lary and Schoppa. On regional warlordism, see Gillin, Kapp, Hall, McCormack, and Sutton. Solinger treats surviving political regionalism under the People's Republic. There are hardly any modern studies of regionalism in traditional Chinese literature, except for Schafer's delightful books about regional phenomena in Tang literature. Time-honored classifications of poets into Northern and Southern, etc., are no longer taken seriously. Interesting adjuncts are Nivison's revelations about regional schools in traditional Chinese thought. There are no books about regionalism in modern Chinese literature, but this reflects the true lack of that phenomenon, except for post-Liberation "regional socialist realism" like Hao Ran's. For articles on the subject, see

Goldblatt, and Kinkley, "Shen Congwen and the Uses of Regionalism." (Shen agrees that the literature of his time was impoverished in regionalism and local color; int. 1980.vii.20.) Hsia, a pioneer in the study of regionalism, has so far given us "*The Korchin Banner Plains.*" Xiao Qian believes that besides the Northeastern writers, the 1940's saw the rise of Inner Mongolian, Yunnanese, and Cantonese groups of writers (letter, 1983.v.31).

5. The foreign-language press in China commonly spoke of Young China during the first three decades of the twentieth century, but the term is not fashionable now. Unlike Mazzini's Young Italy of the 1830's or the Young Turks of the early twentieth century, Young China was not a group of people who took the name for themselves. The term was nebulous, evoking a general sense of hope that China was becoming nationalistic and progressive. Yet another precedent was the concept of Meiji Youth popular among journalists in turn-of-the-century Japan (Powell, *Writers and Society in Modern Japan,* pp. 6–8). Some used "Young China" to refer specifically to constitutionalists who espoused the ideals of 1898 (the "Young China Party"), but the term also took in progressive youth, Western-oriented Christians, etc. "Young China" brought to mind nationwide cultural rebirth rather than clandestine activities by exiles, which gave it more in common with, say, Young Italy than with the Young Turks, but China was another "sick man of Asia," and Young China, like the Young Turks, was thought to be particularly strong among young military officers (who made up a large proportion of China's foreign-educated during the late Qing). China's democratic revolutionaries in exile were, however, included under the term. The hope embodied in it focused on them after 1911. J. O. P. Bland optimistically began to refer to the Chinese nation as "Young China." Later, Bertrand Russell and Lancelot Forester saw the young people who participated in the May Fourth movement of 1919 as a manifestation of Young China. I do not refer to the Young China Society of the May Fourth movement, which was but one intellectual group among many.

Mary Wright revived the idea that China was undergoing national rebirth in the 1900–1911 period, but not the term "Young China," in her introduction to *China in Revolution.* Subsequent research has emphasized the 1915–49 national disintegration instead (Sheridan, *China in Disintegration*). Still, Philip Kuhn, Albert Feuerwerker, and Frederic Wakeman, Jr., have found long-term modernizing trends. See the books by Rozman, ed., and Zhang Pengyuan.

Chapter One

1. ZZ, p. 3. This edition, revised in May 1980, a month before I arrived to interview Shen, adds information about Shen's family and corrects a

few numbers and dates. It deletes only one phrase, "raping women," at a point clearly indicated on p. 96.

2. Kinkley, "Vision," pp. 3–4; see Wiens for maps, following p. 393. Upper Hunan: *Jiekai shizong de mimi*, p. 114. Recent administrative geography is well laid out in the *Hunan Province Gazetteer*, vol. 2. Note that the West Hunan Autonomous Prefecture (Autonomous Zhou) founded by the People's Republic in 1952 is only half the size of pre-1949 West Hunan. The prefecture roughly corresponds to the area that I refer to, in keeping with pre-1949 usage, as "Upper West Hunan" (Shang Xiangxi).

3. For details see Kinkley, "Vision," pp. 1, 2, 5, and Sun Ching-chih, ed., pp. 353–55, 357.

4. Kinkley, "Vision," esp. pp. 237–370, summarizes ethnographic information on the Miao and other groups of West Hunan that might be of interest to Shen's readers. For a compilation and preliminary sifting of data on all the ethnic groups, see LeBar et al. The only full anthropological study of the Miao in Shen's area, based on 1933 fieldwork, is that by Ling Chunsheng and Rui Yifu. The ethnic identity of the Miao is uncertain; Eberhard, in *The Local Cultures of South and East China*, takes Miao culture to be a late or derivative culture, not a seminal early one of South China. Even the genetic classification of the Miao language is in dispute; Chinese nationalism has influenced some studies.

I use the terms "tribe" and "tribal" in the loose, Southeast Asian sense, to signify non-literate peoples, not tribally organized ones. I also feel uneasy using the Chinese term "Miao," since it is thought to be derogatory in origin. In America, "Miao" has generally been supplanted by "Hmong," as the Southeast Asian Méo call themselves. However, the West Hunan Miao are the one major group of "Miao" who call themselves not "Hmong" but "Kexiong" or "Guoxiong." Han folk (including those I spoke to in West Hunan in 1980) deny that the term "Miao" has any derogatory ring. I can only take them at their word when they say that "Miao" has become a neutral term.

5. Ho, pp. 143–52, 187–90. Miao throughout Southeast Asia learned opium cultivation, too, and regrettably became renowned for it (as U.S. allies in Laos).

6. Kinkley, "Vision," pp. 281–83, citing a variety of missionaries, Chinese cadres, and journalists who wrote about the Miao of West Hunan and Guizhou. See also de Beauclair and Bernatzik (on Thailand Miao).

7. Kinkley, "Vision," pp. 460–61; Ling and Rui, pp. 1–14; Wiens, pp. 81–83.

8. The now "distinctively Miao" Nuo rite is a long-abandoned Han ritual. See Kinkley, "Vision," pp. 297–306. The *gu* poison cult, which is a Miao cult in West Hunan, similarly originated in ancient times among other ethnic groups. Kinkley, "Vision," pp. 473–74, nn.113–22. The West

Hunan Miao themselves divide their religion into native beliefs and those learned from the "guest people" (Han); Ling and Rui, pp. 128–30.

9. Kinkley, "Vision," pp. 264–66, 460–63. Originally the Miao of West Hunan were not culturally or linguistically uniform. Gazetteers indicate the reason: different subcultures of Miao migrated to West Hunan from different areas of Guizhou. Since the Qing migrations, which continued at least into the nineteenth century, there has evidently been some mutual assimilation among the West Hunan Miao, more cultural than political. Ling and Rui, pp. 12–25. Perhaps assimilation to Chinese culture is the strongest unifying force the Miao have ever known.

The identity of the Tujia, or "Tu" folk, is moot. The Tuhua they speak (a term usually referring to Tai elsewhere in China) is said to be in the Tibeto-Burman group (like the Yi or Luoluo language). The Tujia were not even identified as an ethnic group until about 1957, when the West Hunan Miao Nationality Autonomous Prefecture was renamed the West Hunan Tujia and Miao Nationalities Autonomous Prefecture. Yet the histories indicate that "Tu" people, whoever their descendants (if any) may be now, made much of the history of West Hunan and shaped its regional religion. That is how Shen Congwen sees the role of the Tujia; int. 1980.xii.13. On the other ethnic groups, see the works of LeBar et al., de Beauclair, and Eberhard. None of these works mentions Tujia; only Sheng Xiangzi's articles possibly refer to them, under the term "Tu Miao."

10. Kinkley, "Vision," p. 6. Ling and Rui, pp. 30–32, 113–15. Short story: "Qi ge yeren yu zuihou yi ge yingchunjie," *WJ* 8: 316–26. Confirmed as Miao legend: int. 1980.vi.27.

11. Kinkley, "Vision," pp. 6–8. Ma Shaoqiao, pp. 38–44. Figures from *ZZ*, pp. 1, 3. The urban population of Zhen'gan (called Fenghuang after 1913) grew only to 5,000–6,000 in the 1920's. In 1980 the population was 14,000; courtesy Fenghuang Revolutionary Committee Director Yu Guanghao, 1980.viii.14, who convened a week of seminars on Shen Congwen and local ethnic culture (hereafter referred to as "Fenghuang seminars"). Other participants were Li Daren (retired schoolteacher), Long Zhian (Miao), Meng Muqiu (Jishou University professor), Tian Jingyang (brother of Shen Congwen's younger brother's wife), Wu Guangshi (Miao), and Wu Rongzhen (Miao). In 1947, Shen wrote that Fenghuang's urban population just before the war (1937) was under 20,000; "Yi ge chuanqi de benshi," *WJ* 10: 155. He may not have overestimated it, since the war greatly depopulated Fenghuang. Parts of the city wall, including two impressive gates, still stand; hence Fenghuang has a unique antique appearance and is a favorite subject of painters Zheng Shufang and Huang Yongyu. Huang paints Fenghuang on-camera in the television series "The Heart of the Dragon."

12. *ZZ*, pp. 2–3.

13. Settlements: Ling and Rui, pp. 33–35. Huangluozhai (home of several of Shen's father's cousins): ZZ, p. 18. Tigers are now extinct in Fenghuang, although wildcats are not. Shen's figures (revised downward since the 1932 edition): ZZ, p. 1. Quotation: ZZ, p. 2.

14. Rev. Cormac Shanahan, C. P., "From My Mission Gate [Gaocun]," *The Sign* 12, no. 9 (Apr. 1933): 547. Rev. Ward Hartman reported from Yongsui that Miao called *themselves* "country people," to avoid being classed as Miao, as the Chinese would call them regardless of their state of assimilation. Cited in Casselman, "From Six to Sixty to Six," p. 92.

15. Int. 1980.vi.20. ZZ, p. 24, also seems to use "country people" for "Miao."

16. "Wo de xiaoxue jiaoyu," *WJ* 2: 22. Rev. William Westhoven, C. P., "Missionary Notes," *The Sign* 8, no. 4 (Nov. 1928): 253, estimated that the Miao made up half of Fenghuang city. According to Shen, the Miao and Han lived interspersed in Fenghuang. A missionary, however, reported that Chinese and (mostly assimilated) Miao in Yongsui (Huayuan) "mainly live[d] apart, as it were, in ghetto districts." Beck, p. C.2.4.

Despite the relative quiet of the Hunan-Guizhou Miao pale in the nineteenth century, there were lesser uprisings, mostly to protest taxes and injustices, in 1847–48, 1855–56, 1866, and 1880 (the last was in Fenghuang *ting*). *Hunan sheng zhi*, vol. 1: 15–16, 61, 64–65, 94–95, 112.

17. "Wo de xiaoxue jiaoyu," *WJ* 2: 22. Shen gives evidence for Eberhard's thesis that China's regional cultures (little traditions) vary because they have inherited characteristics from regional ethnic groups; see his *China's Minorities*. On reverse assimilation, see Ling and Rui, p. 93, and Sheng Xiangzi, "Hunan Miao Yao wenti kaoshu," p. 14. Sheng notes that the Chadong area, the setting for Shen's *The Frontier City*, has such people. Garrison soldiers were particularly likely to intermarry and partially assimilate with the "aborigines." The Lao Han Ren of neighboring Guizhou are the classic example. See Mickey, p. 6, and de Beauclair, p. 177.

18. Ling and Rui, pp. 35 (*zhai*), 54–92 (economics), 202–39, 362–415 (amusements, songs). Missionaries, and de Beauclair, p. 115, who claimed support from other observers, were fascinated by the cheerfulness of the Miao in the face of hardship. Kinkley, "Vision," pp. 282–83.

19. Hu Guisheng, pp. 2, 10.

20. Li Zhenyi, pp. 8, 63; Shi Honggui, p. 11; Hu Guisheng, p. 23.

21. The frontier situation reveals both the genius and the limitations of Skinner's seminal core/periphery dichotomy.

22. Kinkley, "Vision," pp. 7–12; Wade, pp. 383–84; Sheng Xiangzi, "Zuijin Hunan de Miaomin kaihua yundong," p. 56.

23. Kinkley, "Vision," pp. 12–17; Ling and Rui, pp. 108–26. The *tuntian* troops were the last surviving remnant of the Green Standard Army in China; ZZ, p. 3. Residence doors in Fenghuang bore unusual colored

plaques indicating each family's *tuntian* status, even in Republican times; *ZZ*, p. 25; int. 1981.i.16.

24. It was not uncommon for Chinese in traditional families not to know what we think of as "the name" (i.e., the legal name) of their mother. This reflects not a disrespect for mothers, but a preference for family appellations ("Mother," "Elder Brother No. 2") instead of legal names, and a view of women as domestic creatures of no importance under the law. A child never heard his father, or any relative, call his mother "by name." As can be seen in Shen's story "Shangui" (discussed below in Chapter 5), according to local custom Shen Zongsi might have called his wife "XX's ma," XX being his favorite nickname for his favorite son. Letter 1985.iii.9 finally proffered Huang Suying as the name of Shen's mother. I suspect it came from Huang Yongyu's family register.

For the last 20–30 years (but not earlier; see Kinkley, "Vision," pp. 401–2, n. 10), Shen has said he was born on the 29th of the 11th month, 1902. Then when Ling Yu interviewed him, Shen added that it was "Chinese calendar 29th of the 11th month" (W. cal. 1902.xii.28). Just so; the Ch. cal. Guangxu 28.xii.19 birthdate (W. cal. 1903.i.17) Mrs. Frankel told me matches—after transposing a one and a two (11 mo. 29 day for 12 mo. 19 day).

Shen's autobiography tells time by stating how old Shen was without clearly giving his birthdate; years are vaguer than months, as one might expect from a "country person." The time Shen says elapsed while he was in the service simply does not add up. And surely he was not just "a little over 14 *sui*" (12 or 13 years old) when he went to Chenzhou, as *ZZ*, p. 47, says, even if he did go in 1917 instead of 1918. Perhaps he thought he was born in 1903 or 1904 in 1932, when he wrote his autobiography, but has learned better since. Shen supports everything in the article by Huang Cunsheng (Congwen's second cousin) *except* Huang's claim that Shen's pen name Jiachen, which could refer to 1904, indicates his birth year. Shen cannot explain why he chose that name. He says he thought in terms of Chinese *sui* when he wrote *ZZ*; int. 1980.vi.27.

Father's name, place in the family: int. 1980.vi.21; *ZZ*, pp. 4–5; Huang Cunsheng. Congwen was third among the five Shen children who survived to adulthood. Liang: int. 1980.vii.14.

25. Int. 1980.vi.20. "Old family": *ZZ*, p. 72.

26. *ZZ*, p. 4, amends "before the age of 20" in the 1932 edition to "around 20." It says Shen's grandfather had been appointed garrison commander in Zhaotong, Yunnan, at the age of 21. During int. 1981.i.16, Shen mentioned "Maogou" and claimed that Shen Hongfu, Tian Xingshu, Liu Shiqi, and Zhang Wende all provided fodder, then were promoted, after fighting their way into the Taiping capital of Nanking, where they all got rich through plunder. *ZZ*, p. 36, obliquely repeats this point,

which I cannot confirm. The Gan Army was titularly part of Zeng Guofan's Hunan Army, though really separate. The Taiping era evidently spurred the creation of a local military elite and forged ties between it and men under arms, but the Taiping-era Gan Army was more a precursor than a progenitor of the warlords' Gan Army.

27. *Qing shi*, 421: 4810 (1), 4809 (6); 21: 298 (1); 425: 4839 (1–2), corroborates Shen Hongfu's 1863 Guizhou post and his further battles. See Cohen, pp. 113–20, for the spectacular career of Tian. At 23 Tian became commander-in-chief and imperial commissioner of military affairs of Guizhou.

28. *ZZ*, p. 4. Shen Zongsi changed households at the age of four *sui*. He was Hongfang's second son; the first was mentally ill. Hongfu's widow was surnamed Zhou. Int. 1980.vi.21; 1980.vii.2. Congwen's Little Sister No. 9 (Jiumei), Shen Yuemeng, went insane, too, in middle age.

29. *ZZ*, p. 5. At Dagu, Shen Zongsi was deputy commander to Luo Rongguang, a West Hunanese from neighboring Qianzhou *ting* who had served in the Hunan and Ever Victorious armies. Luo Ergang, p. 61. Shen Congwen does not say why his father had so much of the family property with him at Dagu.

30. *ZZ*, p. 27 (new info. in 1980 ed.); daughters: *ZZ*, pp. 6, 35.

31. *ZZ*, pp. 24–25; int. 1980.vi.20. About 1922 Shen Zongsi was hired as a medic, then as an administrator, at a Chenzhou hospital under Congwen's former commander, Zhang Ziqing; int. 1981.i.16. The 1932 edition of *Congwen's Autobiography* seems to say that Shen Zongsi died in 1931, although the phrasing is ambiguous (and it is doubly so in the amended 1980 *ZZ*, pp. 7–8). *Ji Hu Yepin*, *WJ* 9: 91, confirms that Congwen learned, secondhand, that his father died in 1931 while saving someone. But *ZZ*, and int. 1980.xi.15, have Zongsi dying quietly in the countryside. In an interview, Shen counted out "1933 or 1934" as the date of his father's death, but that was off the cuff. I tentatively opt for the date given in writing.

32. Tujia: int. 1980.vi.20, 1980.vi.21. Huang Heqing won a lower civil-service degree (*gongshen*) and was in charge of the Zhen'gan Confucian temple, where he ran an academy of sorts. He compiled the 16-chapter 1892 *Fenghuang ting xu zhi*. It was a sequel to the 20-chapter 1824 *Fenghuang ting zhi* compiled by Sun Junquan and revised in 1875 by Huang Yingpei (no known relation). Int. 1980.vii.2. Mother and Jingming: int. 1980.vi.21, 1980.vii.2, 1980.xi.14; *ZZ*, p. 5. Huang name change: int. 1980.vi.21, 1980.xi.15. See also "Yi ge chuanqi de benshi," *WJ* 10: 153.

33. Int. 1980.vi.20, 1980.vi.21, 1980.vii.2. Much of this has been added to the revised *ZZ*, p. 4. Note that, contrary to our usage, Shen Congwen calls Ms. Zhou (Hongfu's widow)—not his Miao blood grandmother—his "real grandmother." (He means "legal" grandmother.) The Shens got rid of the Miao woman, whose name no one bothered to record, by marrying her off to someone else.

34. Here we get into some contradictions. *ZZ*, p. 4, says Shen's father told him about the empty "grandmother's grave" in 1922. Zongsi must indeed have divulged that he (and Zongsi's adoptive father, too) were born of Miao women, for Shen gives that information in his 1931 preface to "Long Zhu," *WJ* 2: 362 (omitted in most reprints prior to *WJ*). Yet, "Wo de Erge" (1930; first extant publication 1934, in Shen's *Momo ji*, pp. 100–103) says instead that Congwen had some Miao *maternal* relatives. Since that piece appeared under the name of Shen Yuemeng, Shen Congwen was able to answer my repeated questions (int. 1980.vi.20, 1980.vi.21) with "she must have got it mixed up." But the piece could hardly have been printed without Congwen's help, and Zhang Zhaohe (Mrs. Shen) says, credibly, that he wrote the article himself, in his sister's voice (int. 1980.xi.7). Anyway, Shen told me his mother straightened him out on the details of his ancestry just before she died (1934), though he already knew most of it (int. 1980.vi.20, 1980.xi.15). Wang Yarong says Shen told her the same thing. Shen's cousin: *ZZ*, p. 18; identified as Teng Lenghan (locally pronounced Nyium-han): int. 1980.vi.21.

35. Father's stories: *ZZ*, p. 7. The paternal aunts were born to a mother different from Shen Zongsi's. Int. 1980.vii.2. *Dream*: "Xiaoshuo zuozhe he duzhe," *Zhu xu* (1941 ed.), pp. 85, 93.

36. The generally used names of Zongsi's three male children were Yuepu (Yunlu), Yuehuan (Congwen), and Yuequan (Dieyu); letter 1985.vi.14. For other names of Congwen's brothers, see Huang Cunsheng. "Lubian," *WJ* 2: 67–73. The novel set in Manchuria is *Jiu meng* (1928; published as a book in 1930).

37. "Yi ge furen de riji," *WJ* 1: 186–200; *ZZ*, p. 25.

38. *ZZ*, pp. 4, 5. Congwen says that once when Shen Zongsi was challenged to a fight by a warlord, Zongsi's stepmother intervened and protected him; int. 1981.i.16. On the Guizhou post, see note 27; Shen Hongfu held provincial-level office, but it was neither civil nor permanent.

39. *ZZ*, p. 7. A poignant episode showing a Congwen persona being scolded by his father is "Zai sishu," *WJ* 1: 181–83. I asked Shen if he really played truant as often as his works imply, or if he just found it fun to write about. He said he did, and that he truly liked to gamble, with three, four, or six dice; int. 1981.i.16.

40. For the martial arts teacher and the executioner, see the discussion of Fourth Uncle Teng and Yang Jinbiao, respectively, below. Child bride of Shen's elder brother: int. 1981.i.24. See "Xiaoxiao," *WJ* 6: 220–35.

41. "Laba zhou," *WJ* 1: 23–27. Shamans: *ZZ*, p. 2.

42. Hu Shi and Yu Dafu were educated mostly by their mothers. Grieder, pp. 8–12, and Doležalová, p. 135. *ZZ*, pp. 6, 9, 10, 15.

43. "Zai sishu," *WJ* 1: 175; *ZZ*, pp. 26–27, 30, 32. "Wo de xiaoxue jiaoyu," *WJ* 2: 28. Mud guns: "Fusheng," *WJ* 8: 10; see also Ling and Rui, p. 235. For missionary accounts of little West Hunanese boys at play,

The Sign 3, no. 3 (Oct. 1923): 128; 8, no. 6 (Jan. 1929): 381; 8, no. 8 (Mar. 1929): 501–2.

44. *ZZ*, p. 32. Bullfights and *zhui niu*: int. 1980.vii.23. Knowledge of Miao: int. 1980.vi.27. "Zai sishu," *WJ* 1: 176–77.

45. *ZZ*, pp. 15, 33; duels, pp. 16–17. The new edition singles out soldiers and Gelaohui members for praise.

46. "Wo de xiaoxue jiaoyu," *WJ* 2: 20–30, quotations pp. 24, 23, 25. Sharp stakes, and country boys as horses: *ZZ*, pp. 16, 28.

47. *ZZ*, p. 6, says Shen got worms and later, at six *sui*, measles; "Teng Huishengtang jinxi," *WJ* 9: 320, says he got worms at six *sui*. Ghosts: *ZZ*, p. 35. Shen in int. 1981.i.16 said he and his friends found the gods simply "amusing." However, when playing hooky they stored their book bags in the temple of the tutelary deities (*tudi*), since no urchin would dare steal them from that sacred place; *ZZ*, p. 10.

48. "Zai sishu," *WJ* 1: 180–85; *ZZ*, pp. 13–14, 34–35, on crickets and dice. See also "Huashi jia xiong," *WJ* 8: 23. Shen at age 79 happily recalled that short-legged cocks were the best fighters. They were trained to walk away fast, then suddenly turn back and snap at their surprised foe. Int. 1981.i.16.

49. *ZZ*, pp. 27–28. Shen seems to care as much for trees as for people. And as we toured Xiangshan, 1980.vii.17, he suddenly broke into bird calls.

50. *ZZ*, pp. 9, 10–13, 15–16, 26, 31–33; smelter, pp. 61–62.

51. "Wo de xiezuo yu shui de guanxi," *ZZ*, pp. 141–43. Love of music: int. 1981.i.16. Shen himself forgot, until reminded by a friend for whom he played a tune around 1925, that he learned to play the Chinese lute or *pipa* after coming to Peking. Later he gave it up. "Yi Xianghe," *WJ* 10: 246. Shen's 1940's works refer to Western classical composers like Bach, Brahms, Mozart, Schubert, etc. See also "Dinghe [Zhang Zhaohe's younger brother] shi ge yinyuemi," Shanghai *DGB*, 20 Aug. 1946. The Zhangs were a musical family, too, the sisters having an interest in *Kunqu* opera. Unsympathetic to Northern music is "Wo de lin," *WJ* 1: 156–62. Father's hopes (new to 1980 ed.): *ZZ*, p. 7. This, like a favorable reference to the Gelaohui, does not appear in the official English translation, Gladys Yang, trans., *Recollections of West Hunan*, pp. 18, 31.

52. Shen on Yan: *ZZ*, p. 1. Wang-Zeng cult: *ZZ*, pp. 103, 106; Sutton, pp. 18–19, 83–86. Zeng's maxims were issued to 1924 Whampoa cadets by Chiang Kaishek. On Mao's admiration of Zeng in 1919, see Schram, p. 45.

53. Shen says a few West Hunanese graduated from the Japan Army Officers' Academy (Nihon Rikugun Shikan Gakkō), including Cai E's chief of staff, Zhu Xiangqi; others graduated from the Baoding Military Academy and the Yunnan Military Course. "Yi ge chuanqi de benshi,"

WJ 10: 154–55; *ZZ*, p. 36. For the kind of late-Qing military modernization West Hunan did not get, see Ch'en, *Yuan Shih-k'ai*, pp. 29–43; Powell; Sutton, pp. 27–73; Lary, pp. 37–40; and Kapp, pp. 26–27.

54. Kinkley, "Vision," p. 251. I rode the fine railroad (described in *New China's First Quarter-Century*, pp. 108–18), which was built during the evidently overstated "Ten Year Catastrophe." Road-building in Upper West Hunan since Liberation has transformed the landscape. It still takes three hours to drive the 80 km. from Fenghuang to the railraod at Huaihua (old Yushuwan), but the road is paved. There are even unpaved roads out past Ala to a reservoir at the Guizhou border. Before the 1950's, West Hunan knew only foot-hardened trails and old flagstone imperial post roads, which had deteriorated since the end of the Qing. At some points they had staircases; see photo in *The Sign* 5, no. 2 (Sept. 1925): 49.

55. Spanish Augustinians who arrived in West Hunan in 1879 spent much of their time hiding from angry mobs. They established a mission as far up the Yuan River as Luqi, but in 1922 retreated to Changde and other towns near Dongting Lake (*The Sign* 10, no. 8 [Mar. 1931]: 504), after handing over their only real church, at Chenzhou (est. before 1902; Beck, p. B.5.1), to their successors, the American Passionists. *The Sign* 1, no. 8 (Aug. 1922): 40.

The Protestant story begins with Mr. Adam Dorward, who entered Hunan in 1880 and was driven out in 1883. A Mr. Gimmel of the China Inland Mission worked in Chenzhou in 1898, but his successors, Messrs. Bruce and Lowis, were stoned to death by a Chenzhou mob in 1902. (A. H. Butzbach, "Sketch of the Evangelical Association Mission in China," *The Evangelical-Messenger*, 27 Feb. 1922, p. 7.) The indemnity built a hospital in Chenzhou for the Reformed Church (later Evangelical and Reformed Church, now United Church of Christ, an American denomination but then still partly German-speaking). At first the hospital was run by Presbyterians; Reformed missionaries arrived in Chenzhou only in 1903 or 1904 (Casselman, pp. 1–20). Meanwhile, the Finnish Missionary Society was down to 25 workers in four counties by 1913; most withdrew by the end of the 1920's (see Carlsberg). American missionaries of German background in the Evangelical Church (eventually absorbed by the United Methodist Church) arrived in Chenzhou in 1905; in 1913 some resided in Tongren, Guizhou, but Chenzhou was their only other permanent mission.

It was in the 1920's that the Passionists (with a few Sisters of Charity and Sisters of St. Joseph), the Reformed Church, and the Evangelical Church established permanent churches widely in the Yuan valley. After 1919, the Evangelical Church was at work in Chenqi, Pushi, Luqi, Xupu, and finally Jiangkou and Gaocun (Butzbach, p. 7; Beck, p. B.5.1). Reformed Church missionaries built beachheads in Upper West Hunan at

Baojing in 1916 and, after 1920, in Yongsui. Rev. Hartman began work among the Miao; see Snyder, pp. 23–79. By 1923 Passionists had set up shop in Yuanzhou, Yongshun, and Baojing, though the local military had to suppress resulting anti-imperialist demonstrations in Baojing. Fenghuang was visited by a Passionist in 1928, but no land for a mission could be bought until 1933. (Yet a grandson of Tian Xingshu was converted to Catholicism; *The Sign* 8, no. 8 [Mar. 1929]: 509.) The Evangelical Church also tried to work in Fenghuang but succeeded in building a mission only in 1934. Catholics, however, became firmly established in Upper West Hunan as good friends of the Miao militarist Long Yunfei. Long sold the Catholics their land in Fenghuang (*The Sign* 12, no. 6 [Jan. 1933]: 356) and relief rice during a famine. But Bishop Cuthbert O'Gara, C.P., must have come to rue the day he had himself photographed with his arm around Long (*The Sign* 18, no. 7 [Feb. 1939]: 419), for Long became the Communists' no. 1 enemy. See Chapter 7 below.

Missionary writings suggest that West Hunan was penetrated by just a few foreign salesmen (e.g., from the British-American Tobacco Co., *The Sign* 3, no. 2 [Sept. 1923]: 83). American Standard Oil lamps made it into West Hunan, we know from *Bian cheng*. About the only anti-imperialists in West Hunan were the Changsha students at Baojing. Compare this to the late-Qing anti-imperialism in Yunnan; Sutton, pp. 27–51.

56. Huang Muru, pp. 129–35, largely corroborates Shen's account in *ZZ*, pp. 19–25. Huang speaks of a person named Tang leading the Miao and cites Shen Zongsi as a major plotter. Shen told me his father commanded Tang Lichen in int. 1980.vi.27 and 1980.xi.14. Miao under Gelaohui: interview in Shanjiang Commune, Fenghuang, 1980.viii.17. Confirmed Miao were Gelaohui, Shen Zongsi a member: int. 1980.xi.14. Tian Yingquan a "Dragon Head": Fenghuang seminars, 1980.viii.16, attended by Yingquan's son, Tian Jingyang. Other main forces of the revolution were merchants from the coastal provinces and Jiangxi, where Han nationalism was relatively well developed, and local merchants such as Zhang Shenglin, the neighbor mentioned in *ZZ*—the name appears in Huang Muru and was confirmed by Li Daren in a letter of 1986.i.15.

57. *ZZ*, p. 22.

58. Ibid., pp. 22–24. The 1980 revision amends "two chances in three" (of being saved) to the mathematically correct "three in four." *WJ* 9: 126. The gutted shell of the Tian Wang temple still stood in 1980.

59. Ibid., p. 25. Sedan chairs: int. 1981.i.16.

60. Old scholars: *ZZ*, p. 36. Modern schools: *The Cambridge History of China*, vol. 11: 560; for Hunan, see Zhang Pengyuan, p. 173. *ZZ*, p. 25. Quotation: Li Zhenyi, p. 39.

61. *ZZ*, pp. 6–7.

62. "Zai sishu"; "Fusheng"; *ZZ*, pp. 8–9. Informants at the Fenghuang

seminars, 1980.viii.16, said Shen's *sishu* teacher was the noted Fenghuang poet Tian Xingliu, but letter 1985.iii.9 denies that. Hometown tales about Shen have now grown into legends (mostly favorable). Shen did respect Tian Xingliu's accomplishment; see *Xiangxi, WJ* 9: 412.

63. *ZZ*, pp. 7-8, 36, 45. Actually, *ZZ* itself undermines Shen's suggestion, on pp. 7-8, that he was a family pet who fell from grace because of his own naughtiness. In keeping with custom, Shen family finances favored Congwen's elder brother, who enjoyed the luxury of schooling in Changsha after he graduated from Fenghuang's art school ("Huashi jia xiong," *WJ* 8: 22-25). Also quite naturally, Congwen's younger brother succeeded him as family pet. Dieyu was stronger—better material for a soldier; *ZZ*, p. 7.

64. *ZZ*, pp. 25-27, 35. The higher primary school has become the Wenchangge School of today.

65. *ZZ*, p. 36.

66. *Ibid.*, pp. 35-36. Wen Gongzhi, vol. 2: 70-71. *Jiaodaodui*: int. 1981.i.16. The Tun Affairs Office (the old circuit yamen) was right by the Shen residence; Huang Cunsheng, p. 15.

67. *ZZ*, pp. 36-41, 45-46. About 100 boys trained with Shen under the circuit command officer. A slightly less prestigious class was drilled by an officer under the brigade's (defense commissioner's) officer training school. There was also a third group under Uncle Teng, described below. The three rival classes of trainees were in competition with each other at the examinations. Note that Shen Congwen—and his father, uncles, brothers, and indeed nearly all his male relatives—were soldiers from childhood. Most "professional" Japan- and Baoding-educated warlords were not.

68. *ZZ*, pp. 42-46; "Teng Huishengtang jinxi," *WJ* 9: 320-27; int. 1981.i.16. Later Shen was close to Teng's son-in-law, Zhou Binchen, onetime deputy battalion commander under warlord Tian Yingzhao; letter 1985.vi.14.

69. *ZZ*, p. 42. "Teng Huishengtang jinxi," *WJ* 9: 322. Headsman: int. 1981.i.16. "Xin yu jiu," *WJ* 6: 253, 254. Old weapons, Hanyang rifles, and grenades: int. 1981.i.16; Ball, pp. 41-42.

70. *ZZ*, pp. 42-43. Yang Jinbiao's martial arts practice is similarly filled with a sense of battle as a visual drama for spectators, a spectacle governed by etiquette; "Xin yu jiu," *WJ* 6: 251.

71. *ZZ*, p. 43. Miao sculpting: Ling and Rui, p. 235; Shen's passion for sculpting: *ZZ*, p. 27.

72. *ZZ*, p. 44.

73. *Ibid.*, pp. 37-39; quotation, p. 44.

74. *Ibid.*, pp. 37-40.

75. *Ibid.*, pp. 42, 44.

76. *Ibid.*, p. 46. I converted the Chinese date to its Western equivalent; the year 1917 is new to the 1980 *ZZ*, p. 25, but matches "Mo cuoguo zhe qianzainanfeng de baoguo jihui," *WJ* 12: 361 (which gives the season as fall, not summer). A more wistful rendering of Shen's situation on the eve of his departure is "Zuwu," *WJ* 2: 317–40.

Chapter Two

1. "Laoban," *WJ* 9: 295–98. Earlier editions omit the name of the cousin and call the girl and boy who fell in love "Cuicui" and "Nuoyou." (Nuoyou is the hero of "Under Moonlight"; I assume that Shen meant Nuosong). For Zhao's actual bittersweet fate, see Chapter 7 below.

2. On "high warlordism," see Sutton, Part 5. Major studies are Sheridan, *Chinese Warlord*; Ch'en, "Defining Chinese Warlords"; and Ch'i. As Xiong Kewu came through West Hunan in 1925, his soldiers were "deserting by the hundreds, and infesting the neighboring country as bandits." *The Sign* 5, no. 5 (Dec. 1925): 23. "Gentlemen bandits": *The Sign* 3, no. 2 (Sept. 1923): 83; 4, no. 9 (Apr. 1925): 390. Note the story of former-officer bandits who robbed missionaries clean but returned eyeglasses to a nun in need, in *The Sign* 4, no. 7 (Feb. 1925): 305, and 4, no. 8 (Mar. 1925): 349. Reformed Church missionaries being held captive for ransom in 1926 reported that some "well-dressed and most gracious-mannered young men dropped in to chat with us. They apologized: 'Don't blame us too much. If the world weren't in such a sorry state, we wouldn't be doing this sort of business. We do it because we can't do anything else and make a living.'" Casselman, p. 233. An Evangelical Church missionary similarly got an apology from a bandit chief who held him for five weeks; Dr. E. W. Schmalzried, letter, *The Evangelical-Messenger*, 23 Feb. 1924, p. 2. Liu Yunting: "Shuo gushi ren de gushi," *WJ* 2: 419–28; *ZZ*, pp. 91–102.

3. *Xiangxi*, in *WJ* 9: 388; Li Zhenyi, p. 13.

4. Agatho Purthill, C.P., "Yungshunfu: Illiteracy and Insanity," *The Sign* 6, no. 7 (Feb. 1927): 439. Girl: *ZZ*, pp. 97–99. Miner: "Wu ge junguan yu yi ge meikuang gongren," *WJ* 9: 287–93.

5. Few Miao rose to high office through the Gan Army ranks, except for Ma Pizhai, a Japan Army Officers' Academy graduate; int. 1980.vi.20. *ZZ*, p. 74, mentions bandit outrages, as do many numbers of *The Sign*, e.g. 3, no. 1 (Aug. 1923): 42 (village destroyed; some villagers carried off while all Yuanzhou besieged); 3, no. 9 (Apr. 1924): 393 (bandits destroy what they can't carry away); 18, no. 6 (Jan. 1939): 355 (bandit fires destroy one-third of Gaocun, though they make Mayang valley uniquely free of cholera, since war refugees fear to approach); 5, no. 7 (Feb. 1926): 299 (bandits dismember boy, feed him to pigs before his grandfather can collect the pieces); 6, no. 2 (Sept. 1926): 122 (dismemberments); 8, no. 10 (May 1929): 629–30 (nearly half of Luqi takes flight; skinnings alive; slow

death by multiple stab wounds during crucifixion); 10, no. 3 (Oct. 1930): 190; 4, no. 4 (Nov. 1924): 171 (splints under fingernails, hanging by thumbs). Bandits blackmail cities, asking from 3,000 to 300,000 yuan: *The Sign* 6, no. 4 (Nov. 1926): 246, 248. Taboo: *The Sign* 3, no. 3 (Oct. 1923): 127.

Militia at home, bandits abroad (in the rural slack season): *The Sign* 10, no. 10 (May 1931): 631, referring to Gaocun (now Mayang), river port to Fenghuang; also *The Sign* 3, no. 3 (Dec. 1923): 215. In a Baojing incident, villagers called in militia to ward off bandits; when the militia started robbing them, the villagers recalled the bandits to drive out the militia and replace them—*The Sign* 18, no. 2 (Sept. 1938): 97. In int. 1980.vii.24, Shen criticized Xu Changlin's screenplay for *Bian cheng* for showing indiscriminate robbing by local bandits. Bandits don't rob their own people, he said, "they go to a different county" (*gai yi ge xian*).

On co-optation: an American priest kidnapped by bandits reencountered them one year later when they had become "good soldiers"; they met the priest and escorted him through town "with all honors," after he first paid respects to the officer (ex-bandit) in charge, who "almost cried as he deplored the outrage committed against me last year!" *The Sign* 7, no. 6 (Jan. 1928): 374.

6. It was actually the custom to pay respects to the local military leader before seeing the district magistrate; Rev. Quentin Olwell, C.P., "Founding a Mission," in *Eyes East*, p. 59. On the 5,000-yuan escort: *The Sign* 8, no. 10 (May 1929): 632. Bandits might attack convoys even if they did have an escort of 300 soldiers, for the boats would be strung out over a long distance. On 153 yuan for 30 troops, in Sept. 1926: Casselman, p. 231. Quotation (on tallies, Mayang to Yuanzhou): *The Sign* 5, no. 6 (Jan. 1926): 260.

7. Int. 1980.vi.27.

8. Tian Yingzhao, born the year Tian Xingshu died of his battle wounds, inherited his father's eighth-rank title of *Yunjiwei*. According to Shen, "Yi ge chuanqi de benshi," *WJ* 10: 154, Yingzhao graduated from the Japanese academy one class behind Cai E, became a regimental commander in the New Army, and joined the revolutionary attack on Nanking in 1911 (while Yingquan was plotting the putsch in Fenghuang). Congwen's elder brother was a young officer in Yingzhao's expedition to the Hubei border; ironically, he was quartered in Linli, at the home of a cousin of Ding Ling; *Ji Ding Ling* (1934 ed.), pp. 2–8. Shen says Tian might have profited from his relationship with Cai E to rise to high office, but Cai disliked Tian's bureaucratic airs and incompetence. Tian loved new-fangled, arty, foreign things. He opened a coal mine, porcelain factory, foreign imports shop, and even an art school, presumably the one where Shen Yunlu and Huang Yongyu studied. Most of these enterprises

failed. Tian Yingzhao's nickname was "Three-Beard Tian," Shen says, after the handlebar mustache and goatee he wore after his return from Japan. ("Yi ge chuanqi de benshi.") Career details: Li Zhenyi, p. 62; Gaimushō Jōhōbu, *Gendai Shina jimmeikan* (1928), pp. 758–59. Retirement: int. 1980.xi.14. Yang Changxiong, convener of a seminar on the Tujia held at the Mujiangping Commune of Fenghuang county, 1980.viii.18, told me that villagers of Bailin claim Tian Xingshu was born there, a Tujia. The Tujia blood was denied at the Fenghuang seminars by Tian Jingyang, Yingquan's son (imprisoned 20 years by the Communists because of his landlord background, I learned only in int. 1980.xi.14).

9. "Zhijiangxian de Xiong gongguan," *WJ* 10: 168. Boorman, ed., vol. 2: 108–10. Sheng Xiangzi, *Xiangxi Miaoqu*, p. 26, suggests Xiong Xiling's father was Miao, as does Payne, p. 8. Shen thinks Xiong may have been Tujia; int. 1980.vi.21. Zhang Xueji and his Yuanzhou friend, the Japan-educated Chenzhou customs inspector Zhang Boliang (who turned his revenues over to the cause), went so far as to plead jointly with Xiong to help lead the 1915–16 fight against Yuan's monarchical plans, but to no avail. Li Zhenyi, pp. 57–58, 60–61. Xiong's aid to Zhang: int. 1980.vi.21. Xiong Xiling is said later to have helped Chen Quzhen, too, perhaps with money. For Shen's subsequent encounter with Xiong when he was a Peking philanthropist, see Chapter 3.

10. Zhang Xueji studied at a Hunan training camp for noncommissioned officers, then graduated from an accelerated normal school course in Japan. It was probably there that he joined Sun Yatsen's Revolutionary Alliance. Under the old regime, he was an "imperial scholar by special examination" (*bagong*) and military governor of Yantai. After Zhang rose to military power in Fenghuang in 1917, he set up a *mufu* (field cabinet) with Revolutionary Alliance elder and future Hunan governor Tan Yankai. This led in turn to a military appointment from the Canton government of Sun Yatsen (who was in reality powerless to appoint anyone). Sun also "authorized" the 1919 Sichuan campaign that led to Zhang's undoing (see below). Gaimushō Jōhōbu, *Gendai Shina jimmeikan*, 1916 ed.: 116; 1928 ed.: 152. Li Zhenyi, pp. 60–62. *ZZ*, pp. 51–52. Zhang as "Governor" of Hunan: *DF* 15, no. 11 (Nov. 1918): 210.

11. Int. 1980.vi.21; Fenghuang seminars. Shen wrote all the relationships out on paper for me, int. 1980.xi.14. The wife of Shen Dieyu was a daughter of Tian Yingquan, i.e., a sister of Tian Jingyang. Shen saw the portraits of Xiong Xijing and Tian Yingbi as Napoleon and Josephine in Yuanzhou; "Zhijiangxian de Xiong gongguan," *WJ* 10: 166. Huang Jingming and Xiong: int. 1981.xi.15. Nie Rende (Nie Jiantang): letter 1985.iii.9. Nie was the first elected head of the Fenghuang county municipal council after the 1911 Revolution. Younger brother: *ZZ*, p. 105. Shen's translator, the late Robert Payne (who once taught at Southwestern Union

University), was Shen's relative, too. Payne married a daughter of Xiong Xiling; int. 1980.vi.21. Shen Congwen not in Gelaohui: int. 1980.xi.14. Chen Quzhen not in Gelaohui: int. 1980.xii.13.

12. *ZZ*, pp. 51–52; p. 52 of this 1980 edition still claims that there were 100,000 troops occupying West Hunan at the time, far too high a figure. In Kinkley, "Vision," p. 61, I suggested halving the number; Shen, in int. 1980.xi.15, agreed, adding that there were "less than 50,000." In any event, there were clearly tens of thousands. Calculating from 1928 Hunan provincial government statistics cited in Fu Juejin, pp. 10–12 (Kinkley, "Vision," p. 409, n.29), over one percent of the population in this rather unproductive territory was in the army. Feng Yuxiang arrived in Changde in June 1918; Sheridan, *Chinese Warlord*, pp. 74–96.

13. *ZZ*, p. 52; quotation, p. 53.

14. *Ibid.*, pp. 62–63.

15. Duiker, pp. 44–47; Kinkley, "Vision," pp. 192–93.

16. "Lianzhang," *WJ* 1: 144–55; "Canjun," *WJ* 2: 384–91; "Chuanshang," *WJ* 1: 28–33; "Ruwuhou," *WJ* 2: 2–19; "Panbing"; "Louluo," *WJ* 2: 308–16; "Zai bie yi ge guodu li," *WJ* 8: 146–72. "Ye" [1] (not to be confused with a work of identical title in *WJ* 3), *Shen Congwen jia ji*; "Shaobing," *WJ* 8: 116–29. "San ge nanren he yi ge nüren," *WJ* 6: 25–49.

17. "Chuanshibing," *WJ* 2: 80–87; "Tao de qian yi tian," *WJ* 8: 366–83; "Wo de jiaoyu," *WJ* 3: 114–42; "Guwenguan," *WJ* 6: 209–18. *Ji Ding Ling* (1934 ed. cited throughout), pp. 2–6.

18. It strikes me that Shen was haunted by his army experience somewhat in the way that British writers, from Coleridge and Lamb to Orwell and the Waughs, were obsessed with the all-boy experience of the public school—a phenomenon christened "The Theory of Permanent Adolescence" in Connolly, p. 253. Kinkley, "Vision," pp. 66–70, corroborates social and geographical details in Shen's more realistic army stories with nonfiction sources and indicates more fully how they may be read for historical data. In int. 1980.vi.20, Shen said that "Wo de jiaoyu" was based very closely on life, although he kept no diary while a soldier. *ZZ*, p. 56, refers to "Wo de jiaoyu" as a "record" of what Shen experienced.

19. "Ruwuhou," *WJ* 2: 4. *ZZ*, p. 56, revises Shen's earlier estimate of Huaihua having 600 households downward to 300. When I visited in 1980, the place hadn't grown much. Most buying and selling was done by peasants peddling their wares in the street. Yushuwan (now Huaihua), once about the same size, has grown much faster, for it became a county seat in 1942. It has recently become a major railroad and administrative center. Quotation: "Wo de jiaoyu," *WJ* 3: 115.

20. *ZZ*, pp. 53, 56. "Ruwuhou," *WJ* 2: 4. For a description of how the temples were divided into offices, see *ZZ*, p. 95, or Kinkley, "Vision," p. 72.

21. Bedding: "Wo de jiaoyu," *WJ* 3: 114. In "Ruwuhou," *WJ* 2: 5, each man has his own quilt—enough to keep warm, says the narrator. At Chenzhou the men slept under straw mats, on planks raised off the ground by bricks. The rooms were squalid. *ZZ*, p. 49. Food: *ZZ*, pp. 50–51; "Wo de jiaoyu," *WJ* 3: 116–18, quotation p. 114. The narrator of "Ruwuhou," *WJ* 2: 5, also remarks that he is well fed.

22. Cooks: "Wo de jiaoyu," *WJ* 3: 127. "Tao de qian yi tian," *WJ* 8: 369, quotes a figure of $4.80 for cooks. However, "Ruwuhou," *WJ* 2: 4, agrees with the $3 figure; reservists get $3.74. Regulars, foundry worker: "Wo de jiaoyu," *WJ* 3: 135, 129.

23. *ZZ*, p. 85; when promoted to dispatch officer, Shen earned $9 a month and was exempted from deductions for food; p. 91. "Guwenguan," *WJ* 6: 214. Extortion: *ZZ*, p. 59.

24. Extra pay and feasts: *ZZ*, pp. 92, 58–59; "Wo de jiaoyu," *WJ* 3: 129–30. Deserters: "Wo de jiaoyu," p. 135. Bayoneted: int. 1980.vii.24. Excused if rifle left: *The Sign* 10, no. 4 (Nov. 1930): 248.

25. *ZZ*, p. 51. Int. 1981.i.16. *The Sign* 4, no. 7 (Feb. 1925): 301. "Ruwuhou," *WJ* 2: 14–15. Militia and Miao continued to use swords, spears, muskets, and halberds through the 1920's. Shen became familiar with the kinds of rifles through filling out armaments forms; *ZZ*, p. 56. Machine guns and artillery were slow to enter West Hunan. Even in 1923 Chenzhou had only three machine guns; *The Sign* 3, no. 7 (Feb. 1924): 306. Shen said his unit had no machine guns yet, in int. 1980.vii.20 and 1981.i.16.

26. *ZZ*, p. 50. See also Kinkley, "Vision," pp. 75–78.

27. "Wo de jiaoyu," *WJ* 3: 119.

28. "Ruwuhou," *WJ* 2: 4–5. A cook accompanied each squad (ten men and a squad leader, commanded by an NCO [*paizhang*]), and did all menial chores. He might be middle-aged. Besides being the butt of jokes and torments, he was envied by the soldiers for his access to food. Kinkley, "Vision," pp. 86–87.

29. "Shuo gushi ren de gushi," *WJ* 2: 420, has its young soldier protagonist draw pictures in his spare time; the whole episode later became a chapter of Shen's autobiography, "Yi ge da wang," *ZZ*, pp. 91–102. See also "Wo de jiaoyu," *WJ* 3: 119; "Ruwuhou," *WJ* 2: 5; *ZZ*, p. 66. At times Shen yearned to become a painter; "Chi yan," *WJ* 7: 356–62 (story affirmed to be strictly autobiographical in int. 1980.vi.20). Wang Chichen (Jizhen) kept a few sketches Shen made early on while he was a writer, now in the possession of the Hans Frankels. Huang Yongyu, "Taiyang xia de fengjing," in *ZZ*, p. 163, says that Shen still paints, though he quickly hides his work when finished; we evidently see Shen adding calligraphy to one of his own paintings in the television series "The Heart of the Dragon." It was an artistic family: artists included Huang Yongyu, Yongyu's father and mother, and Shen's elder brother Yunlu, not to mention Huang Jingming, the photographer.

30. "Wo de jiaoyu," *WJ* 3: 118, 127; "Tao de qian yi tian," *WJ* 8: 380–82.

31. *The Sign* 11, no. 10 (May 1932): 635. Maguire, p. 117. (Priests were offered the opium pipe, too.) Int. 1980.vii.17; 1980.xi.14; 1980.xi.15.

32. "Wo de jiaoyu," *WJ* 3: 121.

33. *Ibid.*, pp. 121, 123 (toe), 128–29, 130. Pantomime: *The Sign* 9, no. 1 (Aug. 1929): 57. Officers: *ZZ*, p. 58.

34. Officers distant: int. 1981.i.16. "Wo de jiaoyu," *WJ* 3: 120: "The commander's office is in the rear hall; soldiers don't go there except on business." Prestige of the brown uniform: "Tangxiong," *WJ* 8: 76–78. Spoils: *ZZ*, p. 59. "Wo de jiaoyu," *WJ* 3. 113. NCO: "Wo de jiaoyu," pp. 114–15, 131. "Ruwuhou," *WJ* 2: 5.

35. *ZZ*, p. 59; officer education confirmed in *The Sign* 6, no. 3 (Oct. 1926): 186. Long gowns: *ZZ*, p. 48; "Wo de jiaoyu," *WJ* 3: 129.

36. "Tao de qian yi tian," *WJ* 8: 377. See also "Ruwuhou," *WJ* 2: 5, and *ZZ*, p. 59.

37. *ZZ*, pp. 64–66.

38. "Tao de qian yi tian," *WJ* 8: 372.

39. *ZZ*, p. 67. "Ruwuhou," *WJ* 2: 3, 6–7, 8–9. "Wo de jiaoyu," *WJ* 3: 119, 125. Coverlets: "Wo de jiaoyu," *WJ* 3: 114. Quotation: "Wo de jiaoyu," p. 125.

40. *ZZ*, pp. 54–55. "Wo de jiaoyu," *WJ* 3: 120–21, 125, 128.

41. "Wo de jiaoyu," *WJ* 3: 128.

42. *ZZ*, pp. 53–54.

43. *Ibid.* The last figure was corrected in the 1980 edition.

44. *Ibid.*, p. 56. "Wo de jiaoyu," *WJ* 3: 128.

45. *ZZ*, p. 54. See also "Wo de jiaoyu," *WJ* 3: 125. *ZZ*, p. 99, gives rough figures that work out to $143 as the actual cost of a rifle (in 1921).

46. *ZZ*, pp. 54, 62–63. "Wo de jiaoyu," *WJ* 3: 131.

47. *ZZ*, pp. 53, 54. Quotation: "Wo de jiaoyu," *WJ* 3: 132–33.

48. Overbearing soldiers: "Wo de jiaoyu," *WJ* 3: 118, 126–27, 140–41. Rules, punishment: pp. 114–115, 125. Quotation: p. 125.

49. The narrator of "Ruwuhou" (*WJ* 2: 5) says, "in my whole life I never felt healthier or happier." Quotations: "Ruwuhou," p. 6; "Wo de jiaoyu," *WJ* 3: 133.

50. "Wo de jiaoyu," *WJ* 3: 115, 122, 127, 130, 138–39. Pride in avenging small insults is part of the spirit of the secret societies.

51. *Ibid.*, p. 131.

52. In 1931 an American priest at Yuanzhou still found the soldiers to be "mostly boys, 16, 17, 18 years of age." *The Sign* 10, no. 11 (June 1931): 700. The same was noted of Guizhou soldiers in West Hunan in 1923; *The Sign* 3, no. 10 (May 1924): 435. Shen's reserve contingent at Chenzhou was aged 12 to 21; *ZZ*, pp. 49–50. A postscript (in the voice of the author) to "Ruwuhou," *WJ* 2: 17, says the writer led a squad of 10 men at the age

of 16 (as Shen seems to have done at Chenzhou). I have turned Chinese *sui* into approximate English years by subtracting one year.

53. *ZZ*, pp. 50, 64, 65. See "Wo de jiaoyu," *WJ* 3: 124–25, 130. A condemned man might wear straw sandals to his execution, to escape pursuing devils in the next life; *The Sign* 11, no. 4 (Nov. 1931): 251.

54. "Wo de jiaoyu," *WJ* 3: 131. Gambling proceeds: *ZZ*, p. 59. Sharing: "Wo de jiaoyu," *WJ* 3: 115; 137, 138–39.

55. "Ruwuhou," *WJ* 2: 3, 5. There are actual blood relations in this story. A member of the narrator's squad, son of the battalion commander and nephew of the judge advocate, is soon promoted to captain. Shen denies that *he* served among relatives while a soldier, despite what one might speculate after reading "Tangxiong"; int. 1981.i.16. *Fubing*: *ZZ*, pp. 59, 64; "Tao de qian yi tian," *WJ* 8: 371, 375; "Tangxiong," *WJ* 8: 79. Open fighting, no assassinations: *ZZ*, p. 17; maintained in int. 1980.xi.14.

56. "Ruwuhou," *WJ* 2: 17; "fat pigs": p. 6. The diarist of "Wo de jiaoyu," *WJ* 3: 125, wants to make something of himself: to "become a knight-errant."

57. *ZZ*, p. 67.

58. *Ibid.*, p. 70. Li Zhenyi, p. 61. Shen offered the 8,000-man figure in int. 1980.vi.21. Another account is "Laoban," *WJ* 9: 298. It says 3,000 West Hunanese troops were killed in one morning, and 7,000 locals thereafter, in retaliation. The date of the debacle was 1918 or 1919. Li Zhenyi says Zhang went north in 1918; *DF* 15, no. 11 (Nov. 1918): 210, has Zhang in Hubei at the end of Sept. 1918. Even if Zhang was killed as late as 1919, this throws doubt on *ZZ*, p. 56, which says that Shen was in Huaihua 16 months. "Zhijiangxian de Xiong gongguan," *WJ* 10: 172, says Shen was at Xiong's Yuanzhou mansion (see below) in 1919, but I doubt that, too; 1920 is more like it. These dating problems cannot presently be resolved.

59. *ZZ*, p. 69. The last work is by Xu Simei, of the late Qing.

60. *ZZ*, pp. 78–79, 64–67. Int. 1981.i.24. Name: int. 1980.vi.27; 1981.i.16. *Tang wei*: int. 1981.i.16; also Ma Fenghua, "Chongwu," p. 39. The judge advocate of "Guwenguan" is a sketch of Xiao, Shen says.

The "*huan*" in Shen's name Yuehuan suggested to the judge advocate a passage from Confucius' *Analects*, VIII: 19. The Master said, of the Sage King Yao, "*huanhu qi you wenzhang*," or "dazzling [were] the insignia of his culture!" That is, he "revered culture," *chongwen*. *Congwen* means nearly the same thing, but could also suggest an inversion of the stock phrase, *qiwen congwu* ("put aside his pen to take up arms," the patriotic scholar's response to a national crisis). Shen was doing the opposite: putting aside his weapon to take up a literary career, that is, *congwen*. Shen's pen name "Huanhu" must have come from the *Analects* quote, too.

61. *ZZ*, pp. 70–71. Kinkley, "Vision," pp. 107–10. Shen's experience at this time must be reflected in his grim story about a jail, "Jieri," *WJ* 5:

348–57. Huang Juchuan: letter 1984.viii.13. Shen called Juchuan his *Jiu* No. 3 (though he was not a *qin jiu*; evidently only the Oldest or *Da Jiu*, Huang Jingming, was in that category). Juchuan was the son of a brother of Huang Heqing, Shen's maternal grandfather. He had been magistrate of Yuanzhou.

62. *ZZ*, pp. 72–73. The 1980 revision says the family property was 3,000 yuan, not 1,000. So Shen only lost a third of it through foolish loans.

63. *ZZ*, pp. 73–75. The girl who jilted Shen was Ma Zehui; int. 1980.xi.14. Zhang Zhaohe says there was also something between Congwen and the Tian Xingshu granddaughter who later married his younger brother; int. 1980.vi.20.

64. *ZZ*, pp. 76–77. "Yi ge chuanqi de benshi," *WJ* 10: 144–47. Huang Yushu and his sweetheart became the parents of Huang Yongyu.

65. *ZZ*, pp. 91–92. Shen also mentions a work by the Ming erotic poet Wang Yanhong. Nie: int. 1980.xi.15; 1980.xii.13. "*Shen Congwen xiaoshuo xuan ji* tiji," in *ZZ*, p. 135.

66. Int. 1981.i.16. "*Shen Congwen xiaoshuo xuan ji* tiji," in *ZZ*, p. 137. Shen liked to reread *A Journey to the West* in his spare time while a soldier; *ZZ*, p. 66.

67. *ZZ*, p. 72. "Zhijiangxian de Xiong gongguan," *WJ* 10: 170–73, quotation p. 173. Shen indicates that Xiong's Yuanzhou school was named after the renowned reformers' school in Changsha; that would be the Shiwu Xuetang, or Academy of Current Affairs. Yet Shen calls the Yuanzhou school the *Wushi* Academy. I can't say where the mistake lies. Note that though Communist commentaries (e.g., Feng Naichao's) have criticized "Xiong gongguan," Shen's essay in fact satirizes his gentry subject. See Kinkley, "Vision," pp. 108–9.

68. He Long (1896–1969; killed in the Cultural Revolution) was the semiliterate son of a Qing army officer (or peasant, or tailor, as Communist sources prefer to say; Gu Zhibiao, 1b: 618). He rose to be the head of secret society brothers in the tri-province area around his family homestead at Sangzhi, Hunan. The area is north of the Miao pale, home to many Tujia, and it has been traditionally hard for central power to control. After 1927, He declared himself a member of the Red Army and turned his bandit kingdom into a soviet. Boorman, ed., 2: 69–72; Klein and Clark, eds., 1: 297–303; *Chinese Communists Who's Who*, 1: 246–48. Shen Congwen says that He Long got his start grooming horses for the bandit chief Wang Zhengya, who was defense commissioner of northwestern Hunan by 1916, and killed in 1920; *DF* 17, no. 21 (10 Nov. 1920): 136. He Long left Wang before that, Shen says; "Xiangziyan," *WJ* 9: 286; int. 1980.vi.21. Shen worked this tale into *Chang he*, *WJ* 7: 136.

By most accounts, the He family rose to power under He Long's father, who (like Shen's father) was not just an officer but a Gelaohui leader, a status to which his son succeeded. In int. 1980.xi.14, I asked Shen if He Long was a Gelaohui and Shen said, "No, he was a brother, not necessarily a Gelaohui." Smedley, *The Great Road*, p. 184, says He Long was a Double-headed Dragon in the Gelaohui (its highest title). Fenghuang informants, 1980.viii.17, also said He Long was a Gelaohui. The distinction may be a fine one, as I understand it from Shen, in that the Gelaohui had contracted, splintered, or modified itself by He Long's time. Anyway, He's "spirit soldiers," who with their amulets and red armbands (red was their religious color and later their political color) knelt in prayer before joining battle, frightened the superstitious Sino-Miao Gan Army "white" soldiers. See He Long, 1b: 611–12; Liao Hansheng, 1b: 653–56; He Xunchen, 1b: 650–51; and *The Sign* 10, no. 3 (Oct. 1930): 190.

Shen, like other observers, found He Long a man of great charisma, short (*wuduan shencai* or "short all five ways," i.e., short of stature and short in the limbs), and dark but handsome; int. 1980.vi.21. Shen was proud enough of his fellow-regional to say, in a 1928 story ("Shuo gushi ren de gushi," *WJ* 2: 419) that he saw He daily, gambling at mah-jongg in West Hunan's East Sichuan headquarters, and never observed that "the great man had fangs hanging out of his mouth or horns growing out of his forehead").

69. *ZZ*, pp. 79–80. I can only speculate that Shen in previous editions of his autobiography *denied* that He Long offered him a job because he feared KMT reprisals, particularly against Shen Dieyu. Congwen did give the full details as he tells them now in "Yi ge chuanqi de benshi," *WJ* 10: 146, and in int. 1980.xi.15. The introduction to He Long came from a Japan-educated Gan Army officer, Xiang Yingsheng (whose name is misprinted in "Yi ge chuanqi de benshi"). Cousin Nie was a son of Nie Rende.

70. *ZZ*, pp. 81–84; int. 1980.vii.14. The hero of a chapter of *Xiang xing san ji*, *WJ* 9: 226–33, Zeng still fills Shen's thoughts today.

71. *ZZ*, pp. 80, 85, 103 (Wang-Zeng). Rev. Raphael Vance, C.P., "Paotsing Progress," *The Sign* 5, no. 5 (Dec. 1925): 212, says that Chen made Baojing "synonymous with peace and prosperity."

72. Li Zhenyi, pp. 62–65 ("novels," p. 62). Hu Naian, pp. 100–105. Gaimushō Jōhōbu, *Gendai Chūka Minkoku Manshūkoku jimmeikan*, p. 259. I have borrowed the dichotomy of first- and second-generation warlords from Kapp, pp. 11–13, 25–27. See also Lary, pp. 9–10, 34–42.

73. "Traveling expenses": Hu Naian, p. 104. "Golden age": Li Zhenyi, pp. 62–63. Militias: *The Sign* 8, no. 10 (May 1929): 632; 11, no. 12 (July 1932): 762; 7, no. 4 (Nov. 1927): 248; 8, no. 6 (Jan. 1929): 379. Sheng Xiangzi, "Zuijin," p. 56, says Chen (in the quieter early 1930's?) hired only 9,000 troops, with monthly military expenses of only 20,000 yuan.

74. Guizhou reputation: *The Sign* 3, no. 9 (Apr. 1924): 389; 3, no. 10 (May 1924): 435. Attack by Zhao Hengti, 1924: *The Sign* 3, no. 9 (Apr. 1924): 387; 10, no. 7 (Feb. 1931): 439–40.

In 1925, a rapacious Sichuan band invaded, under onetime revolutionary Xiong Kewu, Tang Zimo, and the Hunan warlord Zhou Zhaowu. He Long came with them, but ceased attacking when he reached Chen Quzhen's domain. He even occupied his former liege lord's capital, to save it from the Sichuanese. *The Sign* 4, no. 12 (July 1925): 520; 5, no. 5 (Dec. 1925): 211–12.

Chen hid out in Miao country again during the 1926–27 Northern Expedition, when KMT armies and radical students created a short-lived ruckus in Lower West Hunan as far upriver as Yuanzhou. Shi Honggui, p. 11; *The Sign* 6, no. 5 (Dec. 1926): 309. The major threat after that was He Long's soviet. In July 1929, He routed Chen Quzhen's regimental commander, Xiang Ziyun. See He Long, pp. 612–13; Liao Hansheng, 1b: 653–56; *The Sign* 9, no. 4 (Nov. 1929): 245–48. Finally, Guizhou mounted a major attack in 1933; "Sanwen xuanyi xu," *WJ* 11: 84.

75. *ZZ*, pp. 106–7, 110; Kinkley, "Vision," pp. 123–26. While Shen was at Baojing, the principal of the middle school was Li Yunhang; letter 1985.iii.9. *The Sign* 4, no. 12 (July 1925): 521, calls Baojing the most up-to-date city in West Hunan (setting it above Yuanzhou and Chenzhou) and compares its schools favorably with Changsha's. Scorched earth: *The Sign* 5, no. 5 (Dec. 1925): 211–12. Later reforms: Li Zhenyi, p. 64; *The Sign* 12, no. 6 (Jan. 1933): 356. "The Bank of West Hunan for the Farming Community" (main branch in Fenghuang): *The Sign* 15, no. 5 (Dec. 1935): 289.

76. *ZZ*, p. 106. At Xiong's urging, Hunan in 1922 promulgated a Western-style provincial constitution, in hopes that other provinces would follow suit and federate. Yan Xishan: int. 1980.xii.13.

77. Int. 1980.vi.21. *ZZ*, p. 107. "*Shen Congwen xiaoshuo xuan ji* tiji," in *ZZ*, p. 135. "Yi ge aixi bizi de pengyou," *WJ* 9: 310–19.

78. Chen's character: *ZZ*, pp. 103–4, 105. Nie, opium: int. 1980.xi.15. Chen saved missionaries from radicals many times: *The Sign* 4, no. 12 (July 1925): 521; 5, no. 2 (Sept. 1925): 52; 6, no. 10 (May 1927): 629; 7, no. 1 (Aug. 1927): 2 (letter from Chen Quzhen, "Tzen Twen Tzen"); 8, no. 6 (Jan. 1929): 376–79 (Catholics enter Fenghuang with Chen personally standing behind them). In 1924, Chen asked Reformed Church missionaries to set up a hospital with him in Baojing, but they were reluctant to enter into a joint enterprise in principle, disliked Chen's raising of revenues from opium taxes, and feared Chen's rule might not last long. *Minutes of the Annual Mission Meeting of the Reformed Church of the U.S.*, p. 31.

79. *ZZ*, pp. 85–86, 103. Wang Xizhi: *ZZ*, p. 87.

80. Int. 1980.vi.21; 1980.xi.15. American missionaries gave Zhang some instruction in Catholicism; they didn't view him as such a progressive; *The Sign* 4, no. 3 (Oct. 1924): 128.

81. *ZZ*, pp. 91–102. On the Zhang assassination: *The Sign* 4, no. 3

(Oct. 1924): 127–28; 5, no. 7 (Feb. 1926): 304. Beck, pp. B.7.2–4. Revs. Karl H. Beck and George Snyder were accidentally shot while trying to mediate in the civil war following the assassination; *The Outlook of Missions* 16, no. 8 (Aug. 1924): 355. Shen Zongsi, who was working in Zhang's hospital at the time, also tried to prevent the civil war; int. 1980.vi.27; 1980.xii.13. A year later, Tian was executed by exactly the same ruse, a phony dinner invitation; *The Sign* 5, no. 7 (Feb. 1926): 304; and Maguire, p. 58, who confirms Shen's version in *ZZ*, p. 102. Tian Yiqing was a lesser warlord, not descended from Tian Xingshu.

82. Famines: *Hunan sheng zhi*, 1: 462–64, 479–80. *Eyes East*, p. 65. *The Sign* 1, no. 7 (July 1922): 36–39; 1, no. 12 (Dec. 1922): 219; 3, no. 7 (Feb. 1924): 302–3; 5, no. 2 (Sept. 1925): 84; 5, no. 10 (May 1926): 434–35; 6, no. 2 (Sept. 1926): 115–16. *The Outlook of Missions* 13, no. 12 (Dec. 1921): 555–56; 14, no. 10 (Oct. 1922): 461; 18, no. 3 (Mar. 1926): 99. Casselman, pp. 223–26. Bandits especially arose along the Yuan between Taoyuan and Chenzhou, and at Hongjiang and Qianyang, opium transshipment points beyond the control of Changsha, Baojing, Guiyang, or Nanning. Guizhou militarists who rose to power on the basis of the latter revenues were Lu Tao, Wang Dianlun, Wang Xiaoshan, Zhou Xicheng (later governor of Guizhou), and Wang Jialie. West Hunanese who took the area were Cai Juyou, Zhou Zefan, and Chen Hanzhang. (Int. 1980.vi.21; *Xiangxi*, in *WJ* 9: 386.) The last two were assassinated in Hongjiang, Chen on 25 March 1930 by the troops of his Yuanzhou subordinate, Li Baochen. Guizhou troops exited, leaving Chen's loyal Qianyang commander to besiege Li at Yuanzhou. There was civil war up and down the valley. *The Sign* 10, no. 1 (Aug. 1930): 55–59; 10, no. 2 (Sept. 1930): 125–26. In 1933, a rebel bombed Yuanzhou from an airplane; *The Sign* 13, no. 5 (Dec. 1933): 288–89.

83. *ZZ*, pp. 104–6, 108–11. Zhao's name: letter 1985.iii.9.

84. *ZZ*, pp. 109–10. On such work-study corps, see Chow, p. 191.

85. *ZZ*, pp. 37–38, 110–12. Shen was reluctant to criticize anything Chen did in relation to himself, but he repeatedly spoke of Chen's unwillingness to be surrounded by people as smart as he was. Chen wanted Shen to manage his library: int. 1980.xi.15. In int. 1980.xii.13, Shen said Nie "pleaded with Chen Quzhen, 'send these young people out, and give them 20 yuan a month. Let them keep on learning, don't keep them here with you.' But what the King of West Hunan feared most was these intellectuals.... It was on [Nie's] account that I was allowed to go off [for further study]." Also int. 1980.vi.21, 1980.xi.14.

Chapter Three

1. *ZZ*, p. 113. Dates in Shen's life are open to question. Shen insists that he arrived in Peking in 1922, though 1923 is just as plausible, if not more

so. For instance, *ZZ*, p. 109, has Shen reading the *Chuangzao zhoubao* (*Creation Weekly*, founded in 1923) before he left West Hunan. However, he might have mistaken the *Creation Weekly* for the *Creation Monthly*, so this is not conclusive. Arguing for 1923 is Long Haiqing, "Bu shou suiyue jiban de ren," p. 43. Shen disputed Long's conclusion in int. 1980.vi.27. Yet in "Ershi niandai de Zhongguo xin wenxue," *WJ* 10: 32, Shen said he arrived in Peking in the *summer* of 1922; if it was in a season as early as that, it seems all the more likely that the year was 1923. Then again, I think it was more likely winter; cf. "Xue," *WJ* 1: 126, which puts Shen in the *huiguan* during cold weather.

One can even make a case for a summer 1924 arrival, from "Gongyu zhong," *CF*, 30 Jan. 1925; the autobiographical diarist says, in a 16 Nov. [1924] entry, that he arrived in Peking five months earlier. But he also says he is 20 years old on 25 Dec. [1924], which contradicts Shen's actual age (*CF*, 31 Jan. 1925, p. 4). This might all be explained if Shen originally thought he was born in 1904 and in the 1930's learned he was wrong.

2. Volume of output: Hsia, *A History*, pp. 194, 196–97. "That's all just raw material, not literature" (*Na dou shi yuan ziliao, bushi zuopin*), Shen said when I asked him about "Yi ge furen de riji" (*WJ* 1: 186–200); int. 1980.vii.24. He feels that way about most of his early works, saying they were written just to earn money (he kept many of them out of *WJ*, too); int. 1980.vi.20; 1980.vi.21. He says 1929 is the watershed year for maturation of his works; int. 1980.vi.21; 1980.vii.24; 1980.xi.15. Fireflies: "Di'er ge Feifei yin" (1926), *WJ* 11: 3.

3. Newspapers: "Cong xianshi xuexi," *WJ* 10: 301. Desire for independence: int. 1980.vi.21; 1980.vii.20. In "Ershi niandai de Zhongguo xin wenxue," *WJ* 10: 327, Shen speaks of his broad desire to get away from authority. Disillusionment with women: int. 1981.i.16; *Ji Ding Ling*, p. 38. Desire for financial independence from Chen and Xiong: int. 1980.vi.20; 1980.xi.15.

4. On "professional writers," those who did nothing but write, see "*Shen Congwen xiaoshuo xuan ji* tiji," *ZZ*, p. 136; "Dao shijie shang zixu," *CF*, 27 Oct. 1927. Shen considers himself, Hu Yepin, and Ding Ling to have been modern China's first "serious" professional writers; Hsu, *Our China Trip*, p. 114. Also int. 1980.vi.20. Sima Changfeng, *Zhongguo xin wenxue shi*, vol. 1: 160, agrees that Shen was probably the first.

5. Yu Dafu, "Gei yi wei wenxue qingnian de gongkai zhuang," vol. 1: 3–4. Letter mentioned in "Cong xianshi xuexi," *WJ* 10: 302, and in int. 1980.vi.20. Identified in Kinkley, "Vision," pp. 146–48. Later Shen and his friends gave Yu Dafu a meal of West Hunanese specialties at the Peking Agricultural College; "Yi Xianghe," *WJ* 10: 242.

6. "Cong xianshi xuexi," *WJ* 10: 300. Speaker identified in int. 1980.xi.15. Yu Dafu, p. 8, also indicates that Shen was outspoken about

his ideals at this time, so perhaps Shen has not exaggerated the conversation.

7. Yu Dafu, p. 9. Rehe rumors: Boorman, ed., 2: 108. People from Fenghuang were proud of their "Xiong Fenghuang" (Xiong Xiling of Fenghuang, a pun on "Papa Phoenix"), but they also blamed Xiong for his passivity toward Yuan Shikai and for not doing more to uplift his native region; Li Zhenyi, p. 58. Shen criticized Xiong in that vein; int. 1980.xi.7. Huang Yushu, similarly, called Xiong a "capon"; "Yi ge chuanqi de benshi," WJ 10: 149. Shen even satirized Peking "philanthropic circles"; see Kinkley, "Vision," pp. 210, 452, n. 237. Once, though, Shen eulogized Xiong, in "Xindang zhong yi ge Hunan xiangxiaren" (1948). Quotation: Yu Dafu, p. 3.

8. Peking University: interview with Wang Yarong, Peking, 1980.vi.21. Inability to master the Roman alphabet: int. 1980.vi.20. After 1949, Shen tried again to learn English to further his research in art history, but again he made no headway; interview with Wang Yarong, 1980.vii.16. Ding and Chen: int. 1980.vi.20; 1980.vii.20. Feng: int. 1980.vii.23; Feng Youlan himself graciously acknowledged the incident during a brief interview in New York City, 1982.ix.10. See also "Ershi niandai Zhongguo xin wenxue," WJ 10: 329. The Franco-Chinese University was near Shen's residence at Xiangshan; int. 1980.vi.20; 1980.vii.17; 1980.xi.15. Gu Jiegang: int. 1980.vii.23.

9. "Half-work, half-study" was Shen's plan; "Cong xianshi xuexi," WJ 10: 300. Jingzhou company: int. 1980.xi.14. Failure to get a job as a library runner: "Zhi Weigang xiansheng" (a letter to Lin Zaiping), WJ 10: 261. Information on the examinations and summer session comes from a letter dated 23 July [1925] that according to int. 1980.vii.24 is another real letter Shen sent to Lin Zaiping. It appears in "Jueshi yihou." On the *Morning Post*: Ji Hu Yepin, WJ 9: 54; Wang Zhefu, p. 318; int. 1980.xi.15. Shao Huaqiang showed Shen some articles from the "Peking Section" he contributed to, to jog his memory, but Shen could not recognize any as his. The column was instituted only on 1 Dec. 1924, though Shen might have contributed to some predecessor. In "Ershi niandai de Zhongguo xin wenxue," WJ 10: 329, Shen added a new wrinkle, saying that he first published in *Morning Post* columns *like* (my emphasis) "Xiao gongyuan" (Little Public Garden), after the paper's editorship passed to Liu Mianji and Qu Shiying. Yet Shen must have published something in the "Peking Section" before the literary supplement published his "Yi feng wei ceng fuyou de xin" (see below, note 12), for Shao Huaqiang found a notice in the "Peking Section" asking Shen to pick up his remuneration (book gift certificates). Interview with Shao Huaqiang in Peking, 1981.vii.9.

10. Policeman: ZZ, p. 112; "Congwen xiaoshuo xizuo xuanji daixu," in ZZ, p. 123. Photography: *Ji Hu Yepin*, WJ 9: 54; int. 1980.vi.20. Chapter

1 has mentioned that Huang Jingming preceded Shen in the field of photography. Huang also had set up a police force in Changde; int. 1980.vi.21; letter 1984.viii.13. I asked if Huang Jingming had anything to do with Shen's explorations of the photography or police careers at this time in his life. No, said letter 1985.vi.14. Army: "Cong xianshi xuexi," *WJ* 10: 302; *Ji Hu Yepin*, *WJ* 9: 58; "Shen Congwen zai Jishou Daxue de jianghua," *Jishou Daxue xuebao* 12 (Mar. 1985): 3. In "Zhi Weigang xiansheng," *WJ* 10: 261, Shen indicates that he might have entered the Northern armies but for the lack of a guarantor.

11. Shen wavers: int. 1980.xi.15. Return: "Di'er ge Feifei yin," *WJ* 11: 2. Shen also seems to have considered returning home in 1924 and 1925, but then, too, Chen Quzhen's cause seemed to be lost, owing to civil war. Yu Dafu (written 13 Nov. 1924), p. 7; "Zhi Weigang xiansheng" (8 May 1925), *WJ* 10: 261. Miao: "Ganren yaoqu," *CF*, 25 Dec. 1926, p. 60.

12. First work known to me: "Yi feng wei ceng fuyou de xin," *CF*, 22 Dec. 1924, in *WJ* 10: 2–5. "Ershi niandai de Zhongguo xin wenxue," *WJ* 10: 329, mentions the incident of Shen's manuscripts being thrown in the wastebasket, but gives the date as "about 1925" and does not name Sun Fuyuan. Shen named Sun at the Columbia lecture on which "Ershi niandai" is based, 1980.xi.7, and spoke of the incident once or twice in Peking in 1980. One cannot take Sun's action as evidence that Shen was sending out articles in 1923, for the incident may have taken place while Sun was editor of the literary supplement of the *Jingbao* in 1925. One-third discarded: *Ji Hu Yepin*, *WJ* 9: 65.

13. Income: *Ji Hu Yepin*, *WJ* 9: 58–59. Shen's first letter to Lin Zaiping is the one published as "Zhi Weigang xiansheng"; from it one gathers that Lin's prior letter was published in the 4 May 1925 issue of the *CF*. How Shen got his job: int. 1980.vii.2, written down by Zhang Zhaohe and Wang Yarong. Also int. 1980.vii.17. Huang family informants provide the intriguing fact that Huang Jingming was general manager at the Xiangshan Ciyouyuan just when Shen went to Peking. I do not know how deeply Huang was involved in orphanage affairs when Shen went to work there in 1925, or if Huang was still at Xiangshan. Letter 1984.viii.13. Shen's one meeting with Liang Qichao (at Xu Zhimo's wedding): int. 1980.vii.17. It is interesting that one thumbnail biography of Shen mentions, out of the blue, that Shen was highly regarded by Liang Qichao: Acton and Ch'en, p. 172.

14. *Ji Hu Yepin*, *WJ* 9: 59, says Shen lived at Xiangshan from April through August (1925). This chronology is contradicted by the fact that the Shen-Lin contact did not come about until May (see previous note), and by the date-and-place lines of Shen's works, which indicate that he lived in Peking until June, *then* at Xiangshan, where he remained through September. The date-and-place line of "Dao fenmu qu," *CF*, 23 July 1925,

p. 120, is "July 1925, while going to Peking." Date-and-place lines also contradict the written statement acquired at int. 1980.vii.2, which says that Shen went to study library science in Peking *before* going to Xiangshan. Probably Shen was at Xiangshan from July through September, then was sent to the Peking University Library for further study in the fall of 1925. His literary output slackened in the fall, and the few works he did write, such as "Ruilong" (*CF*, 26 Nov. 1925, in *WJ* 8: 57–66) and "Meigui yu Jiumei" (*CF*, 19 Nov. 1925), have date-and-place lines indicating composition in the "The Cramped and Moldy Little Studio, Peking," not the Western Hills. When Shen was back in the hills, in early 1926 (as numerous date-and-place lines attest), he might have taken up his Xiangshan library job again (he says that his literary audacity caught up with him somewhat after the fact), or he might have already been let go and simply gone to live with Hu Yepin and Ding Ling.

Living arrangements: int. 1980.vi.21; 1980.vii.17 at Xiangshan, where Shen took me on a tour. The Xiangshan Ciyouyuan had become the Xiangshan Restaurant. The library was on the second floor. Shuangqing is now close by a hotel built by I. M. Pei. "Examinations": int. 1980.vii.2 and 1980.vii.17. Peking University Library study: int. 1980.vi.27; 1980.vii.2; 1980.vii.23; interview with Hon. Ch'en Chi-ying (Chen Jiying), Taibei, 1974.v.28. Shen says he made friends with writer Yan Wenjing while there; int. 1980.vii.23.

15. *Ji Hu Yepin*, *WJ* 9: 59–62, 65, 68–69. In int. 1980.vii.17, Shen said he also visited Liang Sicheng and his bride Lin Huiyin in the Western Hills, at Northeastern University, but I am not sure if it was in the 1920's or the 1930's. Editing plans: *Ji Ding Ling*, pp. 57–60. Int. 1980.vi.21; 1980.vii.17. *Ji Hu Yepin* says Shen got his comeuppance for writing "Cotton Shoes" and "Feifei's Sadness," but Shen's description of the content of the second piece fits "Events to Be Filed Under 'A.'" "Mian xie," *WJ* 8: 26–33 ("5 September, from the Western Building of the Jingyi Garden in the Western Hills [at Xiangshan]"). "Yong 'A' zi jixialai de shi," *CF*, 5 Sept. 1925, pp. 4–6 ("Morning of 14 August, from Shibawan at Xiangshan"). A Feifei story that might have got Shen into trouble is "Di'er ge Feifei," *WJ* 8: 12–16, since its date-and-place line says "The Xiangshan Ciyouyuan." Shen's explanation, quoted: int. 1980.vii.2, written statement.

16. This may appear a peculiar speculation in view of Shen's apparent lack of self-confidence around women, but later Shen persisted in courting his future wife, Zhang Zhaohe (his student at the Woosung China Institute), through letters long after she made it clear that his attentions were not wanted. (Shen denies that she complained about him to the president, Hu Shi, much less demanded his resignation, as anecdotists like to say. Shen says Hu Shi argued on his behalf; int. 1980.vi.20. Also 1980.xii.2

talk with Rev. Paul Szeto about his interview with Shen Congwen and Zhang Zhaohe in New Haven, 1980.xi.25. However, Mrs. Ch'ung-ho Chang Frankel, Zhaohe's sister, in a 1975.i.21 New Haven interview, said that Zhaohe did complain to Hu Shi that Shen was bothering her.)

17. Shen's life of poverty: *Ji Hu Yepin, WJ* 9: 55, 71–72; "Cong xianshi xuexi," *WJ* 10: 301–2; *Ji Ding Ling*, pp. 124, 37 (burning books). Peking nosebleeds: "Ganren yaoqu," p. 60. Shen's later nosebleeds are commemorated in his complaining *Yi ge tiancai de tongxin*, pp. 4–5, and *Bu si riji*, pp. 2–3. Also int. 1980.vii.24; *Alisi Zhongguo youji, WJ* 1: 346; "Shengming de mo tiji," *WJ* 11: 7. *Bu si riji* said to be true, and nosebleeds attributed to poverty: int. 1981.i.16.

18. Youxi: "Ershi niandai de Zhongguo xin wenxue," *WJ* 10: 324; int. 1980.xi.14. Hostels: *Ji Hu Yepin, WJ* 9: 53, 69, 71, 73. The date-and-place line of "Gongyu zhong," *CF*, 30 Jan. 1925, p. 3, and 31 Jan. 1925, pp. 3–4, says "Christmas, at the Qinghua Gongyu." Shen moved there through Qinghua connections Xu Zhimo and Liang Sicheng; int. 1980.vii.14. Shen sketches his friend the Hanyuan Gongyu proprietor in *Ji Hu Yepin, WJ* 9: 64–65, and in *Ji Ding Ling*, pp. 111–18. The proprietor's son was Parker Huang (Huang Bofei), who today teaches at Yale University; see his "Que shi you yuan," and Shen's new note in *Ji Hu Yepin, WJ* 9: 73. Hanhuayuan was the name of the neighborhood, and later of a street. Coal room: "Yi Xianghe," *WJ* 10: 241. It should be added that hostels, however dingy, usually came equipped with a concierge, servants, and a house telephone.

19. "Ershi niandai de Zhongguo xin wenxue," *WJ* 10: 326; int. 1980.vi.27.

20. "Mian xie": int. 1980.vi.21. "Ershi niandai de Zhongguo xin wenxue," *WJ* 10: 326; int. 1980.vi.27. Letter 1984.viii.13 relates that Huang Cunsheng was born the son of Huang Juchuan, Congwen's *Jiu* No. 3 (as Shen loosely called him), the Yuanzhou policeman. Cunsheng was then adopted by Huang Xinyu, whom Congwen loosely called his *Jiu* No. 5. I presume that happened after Juchuan died, ca. 1919, as *ZZ* relates. Juchuan and Xinyu were sons of a great-uncle (or great-uncles) of Congwen, that is, nephews of Shen's grandfather Huang Heqing.

21. "Yi Xianghe," *WJ* 10: 241–48. Dong and Zhang: int. 1980.vi.2; 1980.vii.14; "Ershi niandai de Zhongguo xin wenxue," *WJ* 10: 326. Man Shuyuan: int. 1980.vi.21; *Ji Hu Yepin, WJ* 9: 59; commemorated in stories "Chuanshang anshang" and "Xue," *WJ* 1: 126–43. Shen wrote about Shuyuan's brother in "Qiaoxiu he Dongsheng," *WJ* 7: 363–81. Yuangui: int. 1980.vi.20; letter 1985.vi.14. See [Yin] Yuangui. I presume Yuangui was the cousin in the Gan armies who collected some of the extra folk songs for Shen's own "Ganren yaoqu." Yuangui became an artilleryman in the Fengtian warlord army.

22. Hu and Xiang (whom Shen particularly liked since they were former naval students, and he was an ex-soldier): *Ji Hu Yepin, WJ* 9: 52–53. 1925: Kinkley, "Vision," p. 150. In March 1926, Shen wrote a love poem called "Cheng Xiao Sha," which I think might be translated as "Humbly Offered to Sophie." In the winter of 1927–28, Ding Ling would create a Sophie who would be her most intimate "autobiographical" persona. But all this is speculative. In literature, what comes to mind is Rousseau's Sophie, his surrogate for womankind in *Émile*. The second stanza of Shen's poem:

> You are the source of all life.
> Brightness follows by your side:
> Men go mute before you,
> Reverent, as if before God—
> The one who stands behind you, bearing his cross,
> Shall silently let that cross grow moldy and decay.

23. Shen celebrates Ding as a West Hunanese: *Ji Ding Ling*, pp. 7, 18. *Ji Hu Yepin, WJ* 9: 56; "good looking," p. 55. It actually appears that Ding Ling was too busy pursuing other loves, when she was not with Hu Yepin, to have time for Shen; see *Ji Ding Ling*, p. 129. For a typical source of rumors about a Shen-Ding romance, see *Zuojia nishi*, pp. 18–23. Another who makes incorrect inferences about names in *Ji Ding Ling* censored out with x's is Zhou Fennuo. According to int. 1980.xi.15, seconded by Ding Ling in a New York interview, 1981.xi.6, Shen's Yang X X is Yang Daicheng, not Yang Kaihui.

One editor printed an excerpted, out-of-context letter from a group of fictitious ones (I think; int. 1980.vi.20; 1981.i.16) that originally were published under the name of Hu Yepin. Probably Hu wanted to play a joke on Shen and Ding, and capitalize on the public's desire to believe that they had a love triangle going. The original work is Hu Yepin, "San ge bu tongyi de renwu." The "letters" are signed with names similar to the three's pen names, but the girl has a name suggestive of one of Shen's pen names (Qi*lin*, as in Shen Mao*lin*). The anonymous excerpter, in *Wenxuejia de qingshu*, pp. 203–7, has taken a letter meant by Hu to look like a letter from the girl to "Shen," named Bo or Xuanbo (cf. Shen's pen name Xuanruo), and by printing it out of context, as simply a letter from Lin to Bo (ambiguous without the "Xuan"), made it look like a letter from Shen *to* Ding.

Separate rooms: Huang Bofei, p. 27. Huang was only an adolescent, but he was aware of people's comings and goings; he remembers that Hu and Ding slept with each other, but that Shen was not part of the picture. Interview with Rev. Paul Szeto, 1980.xii.2, about his and Huang Bofei's 1980.xi.25 meeting with the Shens. Fabrications about incest: Sun Ling, a writer who was a friend of Ba Jin and Shen (so he said), still insisted that

Congwen and Yuemeng were lovers when I interviewed him in Taibei, 1974.vi.14. He said this in front of his wife, adding, "of course you can't write this."

24. Dong and Zhang: int. 1980.vi.27; 1980.vii.14. Li Da: int. 1980.vii.5; 1980.xi.15. Hu Yepin arrest: int. 1981.vii.17; 1981.vii.18. Letter and harassment: "Yi ge aixi bizi de pengyou," *WJ* 9: 315–16. This essay, p. 316, also mentions Gu Qianli as a Communist friend from the early days. Other letters: *Ji Ding Ling*, pp. 122–23. Chu Yupu: int. 1980.vi.27. Of course Shen may have emphasized his friends' naïveté to get the last word in, for they chided *him* for being a bookworm. And he may have subconsciously invited their derision, if he did secretly love Ding Ling—by playing the role of "martyr," the romantic odd man out.

25. "Yi Xianghe," *WJ* 10: 242–43. Zhang Caizhen was killed at about the same time as Hu Yepin; *Ji Ding Ling xuji*, p. 112. It was Dong and Zhang who introduced Shen to Agnes Smedley. Friends killed at home: "Yi ge aixi bizi de pengyou," *WJ* 9: 312–19. Other friends became bandits. Shen claimed retrospectively (*ibid.*, p. 314) that it all had struck him as "quite unsurprising and yet quite interesting. Time was remaking everything, letting the strong climb to the top and the weak perish. At that time I was in even more turmoil than those little fellow-townsmen, so none of their activities shocked or surprised me."

26. Quotations from "Ershi niandai de Zhongguo xin wenxue," *WJ* 10: 324–26. See also *Ji Hu Yepin*, *WJ* 9: 58.

27. Shen said auditors outnumbered enrollees 3 to 1, and added that lecture notes cost 30 cents (more than he could afford, but one could share), in his Columbia University speech, 1980.xi.7. Auditing, Japanese: int. 1980.vi.20; 1980.vii.23. The trio got their own tutor in Japanese; *Ji Ding Ling*, pp. 136–38; on their "empty fantasy of going to Japan," see pp. 127, 137. Gu Hongming: "Ershi niandai de Zhongguo xin wenxue," *WJ* 10: 328. Feng Zhi, in a 1980.vii.2 Peking interview, remembered that he audited Zhou Zuoren's lectures and that Shen Congwen was there, too. He agreed that there were so many auditors that real students were nearly crowded out. Shen got scholarships though not a student: "Shen Congwen zai Jishou Daxue de jianghua," p. 2. Library: int. 1980.vi.27. "Chuanshang anshang," *WJ* 1: 126; "*Shen Congwen xiaoshuo xuan ji* tiji," *ZZ*, p. 135. See also "Yaoye," no. 1, in *Yazi*, *WJ* 9: 19. The diarist of "Gongyu zhong" has to save his money to pay the library's entrance fee. Advantages of Peking: int. 1980.vii.17; *Ji Hu Yepin*, *WJ* 9: 73; *Ji Ding Ling*, pp. 37, 127.

28. "Everything he could digest": int. 1981.i.16. Sun: int. 1980.vi.20; 1980.vii.17. (Also "Qiong yu yu," *WJ* 12: 385–90.) Ridicule of "isms": *Alisi Zhongguo you ji* (1928), *WJ* 1: 382.

29. Shen named Chekhov as a special influence on him, citing humor:

int. 1980.vi.21; 1980.vi.27; 1980.vii.24. Gogol: "Songzi jun," *WJ* 2: 54. Shen says that he learned from Turgenev's *A Sportsman's Sketches* how to combine descriptions of scenery with storytelling. Interview with Ling Yu, 1980.vii.18. See also Ling Yu, "Shen Congwen tan ziji de chuangzuo." Tagore, Dewey, Russell: int. 1980.xi.14; 1981.i.16. Hu Shi et al.: "Baihuawen wenti," *Zhu xu* (1941 ed. cited throughout), pp. 79–80. Subconscious: "Yong 'A' zi jixialai de shi," p. 4. Free association: "Huaihuazhen," *WJ* 1: 42.

30. The *Confessions*: "Lun Guo Moruo," p. 9. "Shu," *XP*, 2d anniversary edition (July 1927), pp. 245–46. Lee points out the importance of *Camille* to all young Chinese readers, and calls *The Sorrows of Young Werther* "the bible of modern Chinese youth," p. 188. Tang *chuanqi*: int. 1981.i.24. Through genius, luck, or his scholarly fixation on traditional Chinese narrative, Jaroslav Průšek made the unlikely connection between *chuanqi* and Shen's fiction in his *Dictionary*, vol. 1: 152. Shen mentioned *chuanqi* out of the blue, without any prompting on my part.

31. Bible and *Shi ji*: interview with Rev. Paul Szeto, 1980.xii.2, after his 1980.xi.25 interview with Shen. "*Shen Congwen xiaoshuo xuan ji* tiji," in *ZZ*, p. 135, highlights the same two books, but says that Shen got his Bible from friends at Yanjing. For an example of the influence of classic vernacular novels, see *Jiu meng*. Influence of translations acknowledged: int. 1981.i.16.

32. Literary only: "*Shen Congwen xiaoshuo xuan ji* tiji," *ZZ*, p. 135. Daily reading: interviews with Shen's friends, Peking, 1980.vi.27; 1980.vii.12. Mrs. Shen steered us away from this topic during the interviews. Christian symbolism: "Meng'en de haizi," analyzed in Kinkley, "Vision," pp. 184–85. "Cheng Xiao Sha" (see note 22 above). Also "Yaoye," no. 5. Christian universal love is mentioned in "Gongyu zhong," *CF*, 31 Jan. 1925, p. 4. Shen confirmed his stand on religion when Rev. Paul Szeto interviewed him, 1980.xi.25. Shen satirized institutional Christianity in "Jianshe," *WJ* 4: 46–87; "Guwenguan," *WJ* 6: 212–13; and *Chang he*, *WJ* 7: 98–99. Talking about institutional Christianity now, Shen often mentions imperialist excesses; this comes from his own perception, for he subscribes to no theory of imperialism; int. 1980.vii.20; 1981.i.16. Probably for social, not religious reasons, Shen's 1930's essays express singular dislike of the YMCA. He evidently agreed with Bertrand Russell (*The Problem of China*, p. 81), who decried "something which exists equally in imperialism, Bolshevism, and the Y.M.C.A.... the habit of regarding mankind as raw material."

33. Satire of tipping: *Alisi Zhongguo youji*, vol. 1, ch. 3, in *WJ* 1: 227–36. Porter's 20 cents: *Ji Hu Yepin*, *WJ* 9: 58–59. Yu Dafu, p. 5. *Guanxi*: int. 1980.vii.20; 1981.i.16. Beggars: int. 1980.vi.21. On the common Tang dynasty practice of seeking a patron by letter, see Mair. The diary "Gongyu zhong," *CF*, 31 Jan. 1925, p. 3, refers to a "try-my-luck letter" written

to yet another person, named Chen (Chen Yuan?). A nonfiction preface of Shen's confesses that he wrote letters to nearly everyone he knew—over 30 in all—to find work. Over half were to relatives, who proved unresponsive. Among the others, four took pity on Shen. "Dao shijie shang zixu," *CF*, 27 Oct. 1927, p. 43. "Yi feng wei ceng fuyou de xin" contains a try-my-luck letter; I don't know that it was in fact "never mailed."

34. Qinghua exams: "Ershi niandai de Zhongguo xin wenxue," *WJ* 10: 327. Lu Xun: int. 1981.i.16. Real basis of "schools": int. 1980.vi.20; 1980.xi.15. Just *guanxi*, especially from Jiangnan: int. 1980.xi.14; 1981.i.16; 1981.i.24. The story published by Zhou Zuoren was "Fusheng" (1925). On its publication, see *Ji Hu Yepin*, *WJ* 9: 66–67; Shen helps Hu, p. 69.

35. Xu: int. 1980.vii.20; 1980.xi.14; 1980.xi.15; "Congwen xiaoshuo xizuo xuanji dai xu," *ZZ*, p. 123 (mentions Xu with Yu, Lin, Chen, Hu, Ding Xilin); Liang Shiqiu, p. 2. Poetry-reading sessions: "Tan langsong shi," *WJ* 11: 248–49; int. 1980.vii.20. Shen says he went to the poetry sessions before he was writing himself. He felt the poets were very far above him. Liang: int. 1980.vi.21; 1981.i.24. Ba Jin confirms that Shen was in no sense affiliated with some "Crescent School," and that he was distant from Liang Shiqiu. Ba Jin says he advised Shen against the appearance of closeness to the Anglo-Americans, when in 1929 Shen went to live with them at the China Institute (out in Wusong, some distance from Shanghai). Interview with Ba Jin in Shanghai, 1981.vii.9. Shen may have felt intimidated by Liang's learning and pugnaciousness. Wu Mi: in int. 1980.vii.23, Shen said that Wu Mi was the literature editor for the Tianjin *DGB*, ca. 1932–33. Shen suggested that the friendship helped Shen become the *DGB* "Wenyi" editor, seemingly beginning 1 Jan. 1934. Shao Huaqiang's letter of 1985.xi.11 instead emphasizes the role of Yang Zhensheng. Shao says that Yang was the editor before he turned the supplement over to Shen on 23 Sept. 1933. Anyway, Shen and Wu Mi were close friends.

36. Sun Ling, in a 1974.vi.14 Taibei interview, reaffirmed the closeness between Shen and Ba Jin. Letter 1985.vi.14 says that Ba Jin was a guest at the Shens' when Congwen moved to Peking after marrying in September 1933. When Shen's elder sister and her husband came to live, Ba Jin moved out and roomed nearby with Jinyi (Zhang Fangxu), Cao Yu, Bian Zhilin, and others. (Shen's protégés He Qifang and Li Guangtian, and friend Zheng Xidi, were frequent visitors.) This is related in Shen's "Dao Jinyi," *WJ* 10: 218. Mrs. Ch'ung-ho Chang Frankel, in a 1975.i.21 New Haven interview, said that Ba Jin lived in Shen's study about half a year before his marriage (that would have been in Qingdao), and that Shen also lived with Yang Zhensheng in Qingdao. Yang gave Shen a wedding ring, but Shen was so hard up he pawned it. The ticket was discovered by Shen's laundryman, Yang's servant. Yang bawled Shen out for not asking for a

loan outright. Shen met Hong and Zhao at the Woosung China Institute. He also taught at Jinan University, about 1929–30. Yao Pengzi: int. 1981.i.16; *Ji Hu Yepin, WJ* 9: 83, omits the passage concerning Shen's friendship with Yao Pengzi in the original 1932 ed. of *Ji Hu Yepin*, p. 68. With Bian Zhilin, Ba Jin, Li Jianwu, Jinyi and Zheng Zhenduo, Shen co-edited *Shuixing* (Beiping, Wenhua shuju), first issue 10 Oct. 1934. Shen often let poor students crash at his house, Mrs. Frankel says.

From *Ji Hu Yepin, WJ* 9: 73, one could get the impression that Shen moved to Shanghai in 1927, but his date-and-place lines indicate that he continued to live in Peking until 1928. Perhaps he made a short trip and returned to Peking in 1927, or perhaps this is just another instance of his poor memory for dates. See *Ji Ding Ling xuji*, pp. 171–73.

37. Shen and Ding Ling stopped to see Ling Shuhua after Hu Yepin's execution; *Ji Ding Ling xuji*, p. 135. Cheng Yingliu (pseud. Liu Jin), a creative writer who was a protégé of Shen's in the early 1930's and is now a history professor at Shanghai Normal University, in a 1980.vii.31 Shanghai interview remembered that Shen in the fall of 1930 lived at Ling Shuhua's house in Wuhan. Ling Shuhua became the wife of Shen's old friend Chen Yuan. Pan: int. 1981.i.16. For false anecdotes about Shen in the library, and about Shen and Hu, see Hu Zili, p. 333; Yang Jialuo, vol. 2: 10–12; Tandangdang zhaizhu, p. 223. Shen published several books before Hu Shi sought him out; int. 1980.vi.20; 1980.xi.15. Yang Zhensheng: int. 1980.vi.21. Xu Zhimo: Liang Shiqiu, p. 2.

38. In Hsu, *The Chinese Literary Scene*, p. 134, Shen remembers having been with Wen Yiduo at Wuhan University. This couldn't be true if he means that the two worked there at the same time, for when Shen worked in Wuhan it was the fall of 1930; Wen had already left his job (as dean of the college of arts and chairman of the Chinese department) in the spring. See Hsu, *Wen I-to*. All this probably does indicate that a closeness had developed between the two before Shen took his post. Wen and some of his students visited Shen Congwen at Shen Yunlu's home in Yuanling in March 1938. Int. 1981.ii; Wen Yiduo, *Wen Yiduo quanji*, vol. 1, chronology, p. 63. On the folk songs collected, see Wen Yiduo, "Xi'nan caifeng luxu," in Zhong Jingwen, ed., pp. 209–13. Wen, and Zhang Zhaohe's China Institute classmate Wu Han, visited Shen outside Kunming during the war to ask him to join the Democratic League: int. 1980.vi.21; 1980.vii.23; 1981.i.16. According to Mrs. Frankel, New Haven interview 1975.i.25, Wu Han had had a crush on her sister Zhang Zhaohe at the China Institute. Zhaohe spurned Wu Han (as she did Shen, at the time). Hence an unconfirmed story that after Wu Han became an assistant mayor of Peking in 1949, he made trouble for Shen Congwen out of jealousy. Shen, however, still regarded Wu Han as his good friend after Liberation. He claims to be the one who persuaded Wu Han to come to Peking

and says that Wu didn't visit him after 1949 because he "didn't dare." Int. 1980.vii.23. Wu Han was Shen's student: int. 1980.vi.21.

39. *Wenyi yuekan*: *Ji Ding Ling xuji*, pp. 136–37; the journal can be identified from the less censored version of *Ji Ding Ling xuji* in *GW* 48 (4 Dec. 1933), and from Shen's heavy use of the *Wenyi yuekan* for his literary criticism. Unknowns: Shen's editor's note, "Qishi" (1936), says that he had been devoting the Wednesday editions of his literary supplement to unknown writers, including factory workers and shop clerks who wrote in their spare time. Cheng Yingliu remembers that Shen carefully polished Xiao Qian's *Under the Eaves of Others* before publication. Shen did that for many young writers. According to Shao Huaqiang, Shen and Xiao Qian were joint editors of the "Wenyi" supplement after late 1935; Xiao was sole editor in name, beginning 1 Apr. 1936, but Shen told Shao that he, Shen, continued to solicit manuscripts and so forth until the war. (It should be noted that Shen and Xiao are now estranged.) Xiao went on to edit the Hong Kong *DGB* supplement when the war broke out, from August 1938 until September 1939, when Yang Gang took it over. Shen helped install another protégé, Chen Jiying (interview, 1974.v.28), as editor of the literary column of the Chongqing edition of the *DGB* during the war. Poets: int. 1980.vi.20; interview with Zhao Ruihong and Yang Yi, Nanking, 1980.viii.4.

40. "First critic": int. 1980.vii.14. Lin: int. 1980.vii.2; 1980.vii.17. Chen Mengjia: int. 1980.vi.27. Shen says he became a friend of Feng Zhi as early as 1923: int. 1980.vi.21. Zhu Guangqian published Shen's works in his *Wenxue zazhi* (1937, 1947). He again stuck his neck out and defended Shen in his "Cong Shen Congwen xiansheng de renge kan ta de wenyi fengge." Int. 1980.vii.17. Zhu Guangqian, interview in Peking, 1980.vii.16, said that he did not talk philosophy with Shen, though they lived together in a dormitory with Yang Zhensheng, about 1934, and edited the *Dagongbao* supplement together. He says Shen talked philosophy with He Lin, a friend in the Peking University philosophy department, and with the school's vice president, Tang Yongtong, who studied Buddhism. Jin Yuelin: int. 1980.xii.13; 1981.i.16; 1981.i.24. Both Shen and Qian Zhongshu taught at Southwestern Union University during the Sino-Japanese War and knew each other, but they were not close; int. 1980.vii.4; 1980.xi.15; 1981.i.24. In a Peking interview, 1980.vi.23, Qian stated, persuasively, that Shen had an inferiority complex. In his essay "Mao," Qian satirized Shen. See Gunn, pp. 245, 294, citing a work by C. T. Hsia.

41. Ding Xilin: int. 1980.vi.21. Lu Xun and rural themes: "*Shen Congwen xiaoshuo xuan ji* tiji," *ZZ*, p. 137; repeated in int. 1980.vi.27. Ding Ling's letter: Long Haiqing, "Shen Congwen and Lu Xun." *Ji Hu Yepin, WJ* 9: 68–69, notes the confusion between Shen and Hu and vaguely alludes to the Ding Ling incident. Int. 1980.vi.20; 1980.vi.27; 1980.xii.8 (at

Harvard); 1981.i.24. Lu Xun's letters are dated 12 July and 20 July 1925; see *Lu Xun shuxin ji*, vol. 1: 71–72; also Jing Shan, pp. 298–300. Lu Xun did finally cite Shen Congwen as one of China's best writers, in Snow, ed., *Living China*, pp. 347–48. But Lu Xun offended Shen by not selecting his works for the *Great Compendium of the New Chinese Literature*. See Sima Changfeng, "Lu Xun bu xuan Shen Congwen," pp. 181–82.

Shen was even more ambivalent about Lu Xun. He admitted he didn't like Lu Xun much, in int. 1981.i.24. But Lu Xun heads most of Shen's lists of contributors to modern Chinese creative writing, as in "Xin de wenxue yundong yu xin de wenxueguan," *Zhu xu* (1941 ed.), p. 61, and "Baihuawen wenti," *Zhu xu*, p. 79. Shen also praised the older writer in "Xue Lu Xun" (1947), *WJ* 11: 232–34. But he also put Lu Xun in his place by making his contributions to literature seem mostly historical in "Lun Zhongguo chuangzuo xiaoshuo," pp. 4–5. And *Ji Ding Ling*, p. 167, seems to be deploring Lu Xun's misuse of his talent without naming him. Shen speaks of one who fights with a knight-errant spirit, seemingly at the front lines carrying a torch to enlighten humanity, who nevertheless seems unable to write himself, and so is unable to point the way for China's monumental works of the future. For Shen's outright ridicule of Lu Xun, see the end of this chapter.

42. Shen still used a warfare metaphor in reference to writing in int. 1980.xi.14. See also "Shen Congwen xiaoshuo xuan ji tiji," in *ZZ*, p. 136. The theory of literature as expression was quite common in China during the early twentieth century; see McDougall. On provincial contributions to the early Soviet avant-garde, see Williams, esp. pp. ix, 3–22.

43. Xu Zhimo exclaimed that Shen's sentences were Europeanized, and Shen admitted it; he'd "read all the European translations" and didn't "pay any attention to grammar." See Gao Zhi.

44. "Mian xie," *WJ* 8: 26–33 (written 5 Sept. 1925). I describe formal features of narrative using vocabulary from Hanan, pp. 16–22, and Booth. They of course are not responsible for any misapplications of their terms.

45. The poem is "Hama," from *Changqing ji (Poems from the Changqing Reign Period)*. Reprinted in *Bai Juyi ji*, vol. 1: 24–25.

46. "Gongyu zhong," *CF*, 31 Jan. 1925, p. 3.

47. "Zai bie yi ge guodu li," *WJ* 8: 146–72, quotations, p. 154. "Zai sishu," *WJ* 1: 163.

48. "Muqin" [1], *CF*, 10 Mar. 1926, p. 22. Other farcical Ding Xilin-style well-made plays are "Mangren"; a completely different play also called "Muqin" ("Muqin" [2]); and "Zhiwu" (March 1926). For a Ding Xilin play, see "Oppression."

49. *Xin* (1928, published in 1933), p. 443.

50. *Alisi Zhongguo youji*, vol. 1, *WJ* 1: 264–71.

51. "Yi feng wei ceng fuyou de xin." Sketch: "Wo hen ta de shi...." Diaries: "Gongyu zhong"; "Yao ye," nos. 1–5. "Pingfan gushi" [1] may belong here too, but I have not seen it and do not know its date of composition.
52. Průšek, *Three Sketches*, pp. 48–58, phrase cited from p. 52.
53. Pollard, p. 53, and Doležalová, p. 107. See also Průšek, "Subjectivism and Individualism"; Lee; and Wolff.
54. Shen's possible influence on Ding Ling was of much interest in China. I asked Shen if he had influenced Ding Ling early in her career and he chuckled "no comment"; int. 1981.i.24. Su Xuelin wrote that Ding was influenced by Shen in Schyns, p. xxiii. Author Xie Bingying, a friend of Shen's now in Taiwan, said in a 1960's Taiwan newspaper article clipped by Mrs. Ch'ung-ho Chang Frankel that Shen edited Ding Ling's early works. Su Xuelin's "Shen Congwen lun" (1934), p. 134, also says that "Ding Ling's style is evidently influenced by Shen Congwen's." Su does not say this in order to diminish Ding Ling's accomplishment, for she adds (strangely, for 1934) that Ding Ling's position in the Chinese literary world had surpassed Shen's.

Conversely, perhaps Shen's long hack diaries of 1928–29 (see *Dong de kongjian*, *WJ* 3: 143–268) were an attempt on his part to repeat the success of Ding Ling's diaries such as "The Diary of Miss Sophie," published in February 1928. "Sophie" was longer than most of Shen's diaries up until then and, as Feuerwerker points out, Ding Ling was relatively reflective about the existential plight of the author as author.
55. Maruyama, p. 508.
56. Powell, *Writers and Society in Modern Japan*, pp. 26–30. See Cheng for a discussion of Japanese influence on Yu Dafu.
57. "Songzi jun," *WJ* 2: 40–59.
58. The pathologies are to be found throughout Shen's subjective works of this type; see Kinkley, "Vision," p. 448, n. 202. Shen put most of the pathologies into a single work, "Gongyu zhong." It mentions the "bottomless pit"; *CF*, 30 Jan. 1925, p. 3, entry for 16 Nov. 1924.
59. Lee, p. 110.
60. The persona referred to here is the hero of "Laoshi ren," *WJ* 1: 92–125. A literary work said to have been written by the fictional persona, described on p. 111, appears to be Shen's own "Yi ge wanhui," *WJ* 8: 130–43.
61. "Jueshi yihou." Int. 1980.vii.24, on the authenticity of the letter.
62. *The Dream of the Red Chamber* originally circulated as a manuscript annotated by one "Red Inkstone." He (or she) is not now identifiable, but scholars assume that the person who commented so personally on Cao Xueqin's text, as if it were a sort of history of real events, must have been a relative or close friend of the author's. See Hawkes.

63. An example of what seems to be an inside joke for Huang Cunsheng's benefit, for instance, is a reference by one of Shen's dramatic characters to a popular poet "often compared with Browning," one "Cunsheng"; in "Mangren," *Yazi* (1926 ed.), p. 16. Poems written to Shen: Hu Yepin, "Gei Maolin." Jun (pseud. of an unknown author—Shen himself, for all we know), "Gei Xuanruo." Hu Yepin's joke: Hu Yepin, "San ge bu tongyi de renwu." See note 23 above.

64. "Yaoye," no. 4.
65. "Songzi jun." "Deng," *WJ* 4: 23–45.
66. Lambs: "Zhong jun," *CF*, 7 Apr. 1926, p. 15. Heat: "Songzi jun," *WJ* 2: 40. Muscles: "Feifei de beiai," *XP* 3, no. 61: 170. "Fragments," etc.: "Songzi jun," *WJ* 2: 52–53.
67. "Zhong jun." "Yu," *WJ* 1: 2–4.
68. Lee, p. 123.
69. "Dao shijie shang zixu," *CF*, 27 Oct. 1927, p. 43.
70. The following characterizations of Shen's persona are found in most of the works mentioned in this section.
71. "Yaoye," no. 4, p. 4.
72. "Zhong jun," p. 14. "Gongyu zhong," *CF*, 31 Jan. 1925, p. 3, entry for 2 Dec. 1924.
73. "Songzi jun," *WJ* 2: 55. "Gongyu zhong," *ibid.* "Lü de huaping," *WJ* 9: 49. Glorification of competition: "Yi tian shi zhe yang guo de," reprinted as "Yi tian," *WJ* 9: 31–33.
74. "Qie han." "Laoshi ren" similarly has a wretched autobiographical persona who follows young ladies.
75. Women prisoners: "Yaoye," no. 3. "Old" in his twenties: "Gongyu zhong," *CF*, 31 Jan. 1925, p. 4, entry for Christmas 1924. "Middle-aged" in his thirties: "Qie han," *CF*, 27 June 1927, p. 46.
76. "Mian xie," *WJ* 8: 28. The point is made more clearly in the original version, in *CF*, 21 Sept. 1925, p. 4.
77. "Laoshi ren"; "Ruwuhou"; "Qiuren"; "Yaoye," no. 9.
78. Bus: "Yaoye," no. 5. Mixed seating: "Yong 'A' zi jixialai de shi."
79. E.g., "Lü de huaping," *WJ* 9: 50. Complaint about noise is a constant refrain in *Bu si riji, Yi ge tiancai de tongxin*, and "Wo de lin," *WJ* 1: 156–62.
80. "Jueshi yihou," *CF*, 4 Aug. 1925, p. 8.
81. "Yong 'A' zi jixialai de shi," *CF*, 5 Sept. 1925, p. 5.
82. All unreasonable authority as the "enemy": "Ruwuhou," *WJ* 1: 17. "San Bei xiansheng jiaxun," *WJ* 8: 4. 100 yuan: "Zai Jishou Daxue de jianghua," p. 3; int. 1980.vi.20.
83. "Da cheng zhong de xiao shiqing," *WJ* 8: 235–40. "Shizi chuan," *WJ* 3: 2–15.

84. Shen volunteered that he never really saw the full impact of imperialism until he came to Shanghai, in int. 1981.i.16.

85. "San Bei xiansheng jiaxun," *WJ* 8: 2–5, quotation p. 4.

86. "Lansheng tong Lansheng taitai," *WJ* 2: 31–39. "Junzi," *WJ* 8: 85–98. "Huang jun riji," *WJ* 2: 185–249. The latter was identified in letter 1985.iii.9 as a partly fictionalized account of the experiences of Tian Zhenyi, husband of Shen's elder sister. I also asked: "Is there really a Junzi, or a person after whom he's partly modeled?" Answer: "China has a lot of people like Junzi."

87. Below I translate Verse Four of "Jiuyue jiju," *CF*, 12 Sept. 1925, p. 72, which Shen composed by rearranging verses 48 and 16; 37 and 38; 48; and 49, from Psalm 18 (I cite the Authorized King James Version; the match is close, but not perfect). The "enemies" are female, for Shen wrote the word "them" with a woman radical; hence my identification of the Women's Normal College as Shen's subject (about which see Mills, pp. 201–3). Verse Four is to be spoken by the College President. Her authority did indeed have to be rescued by a lord on high: Minister of Education Zhang Shizhao.

> "He delivereth me from mine enemies, he drew me out of many waters.
> "I have pursued mine enemies, I have wounded them that were not able to rise.
> "Thou liftest me up above those that rise up against me:
> "Therefore will I give thanks unto thee, ... among the heathen [in Chinese, 'foreigners']."

Other verses take aim at Zhang's alleged corruption, and at the uselessness of the professors. Shen's conclusion asks that the ire of all oppressed people "rain" upon "The Enemies of the Students." The controversy is now remembered for having led Lu Xun, who backed the student radicals, to attack Chen Yuan's allegedly "Anglo-Saxon," "gentlemanly" (conservative) response to the events. If Shen's satire fully reflects his position, he must not have shared his friend Chen's moderate attitude.

The Huang Yongyu riddles (which became famous after the death of Mao) are "Dongwu pian." For others by Shen, see "Dao fenmu de lu" (1925).

88. *Dai guan riji. Yi ge nü juyuan de shenghuo*, *WJ* 3: 299–426.

89. *Alisi Zhongguo youji*, vol. 1, *WJ* 1: 303. The Nanking Duck might represent the government. She is overfed, cries oily tears, and doesn't always understand the jokes other birds make about her. But she, and particularly her niece, the Ugly Duckling (befriended by Alice), are at least partly sympathetic characters. The satire is neither pointed nor consistent.

It is all too possible that the lack of a central thread in *Alice* resulted from Shen writing the book a chapter at a time, each chapter just ahead of a deadline. Note that the allegedly conservative Crescent Publishing House published both the serial and the book edition of *Alice*, one of Shen's most leftist works.

90. For Shen's attacks on "humorous" essays, see Chapter 6. "Shenshi de taitai," *WJ* 4: 88–118. "Dushi yi furen," *WJ* 4: 214–38.

91. *Yi ge tiancai de tongxin*, pp. 84–85. The Creation Society had been dissolved by the government when Shen wrote.

92. *Bu si riji*, pp. 14–15.

93. "Lu Xun de zhandou," *Momo ji*, pp. 30–39.

94. "Houji," *Shizi chuan*, *WJ* 3: 89–90.

95. Shen did return to satire much later, as in his masterful send-up of Chinese politics (and sex), "Xing yu zhengzhi" (1947).

96. Int. 1980.vi.20.

Chapter Four

1. "Before the age of thirty Shen Ts'ung-wen was called the Dumas [*père*] of China, for he had already produced more than forty books." Snow, ed., *Living China*, p. 181. Besides being a "fiction factory," Shen loved adventure and was the son of a mulatto army officer. (The mother of Alexandre's father, General Dumas, was a West Indian slave.)

2. Graham ("The Customs of the Ch'uan Miao," p. 26) found on a return trip to a Miao village in Sichuan that Miao women were rapidly abandoning their native embroidery, which was finer than that of neighboring Han folk, because it was time-consuming and also because Han people ridiculed it.

3. See Chapter 5 on Shen Congwen's retelling of the West Hunan legend "Yuexia xiaojing" using Zhou Zuoren's psychological theory of *jus primae noctis*. For Zhou's debt to Ellis, and concern about abnormal psychology's origins in sexual repression, see Pollard, pp. 125–26, 130.

Shao Huaqiang asked Shen what psychology books he had read and jogged his memory by showing some to him (Shao letter of 1982.vii.1). Shen first discussed Freud with Xu Zhimo. (Shao points out that such theory was broadly introduced piecemeal in the 1920's, in the "Xue deng" supplement of the Shanghai *Shishi xinbao*, the *Chenbao fukan*, and other periodicals.) Shen recalled that his first major exposure to Freud was Zhang Dongsun, *Jingshen fenxixue ABC* (1929), which he read while teaching at the Woosung China Institute. That would be 1929–30. For the information about Lu and Xia, I am grateful for interviews with Shen and Shao Huaqiang in Peking, 1981.vii.17. According to int. 1980.vii.20, Shen was good friends with Feng Wenbing. Feng inveighed against Confucianism and advised Shen to write from the heart. For more on Shen Congwen and Freud, see Chapter 6 below.

4. Liu: "Tan langsong shi" (1938), *WJ* 11: 250. Zhou, Gu, Liu: Schneider, pp. 135–36; Wolff, p. 20. Shen and Gu: int. 1980.vii.23. On the importance of Western ethnography, mythology, and biology to Zhou Zuoren's thought, see Pollard, p. 129; Wolff, pp. 39–42; Kinkley, "Vision," pp. 172–73. Shen's view of aesthetics: Kinkley, "Vision," pp. 176–81. Cai Yuanpei's theory was heavily grounded in his ethnographic study. See Kinkley, "Vision," and *Cai Yuanpei minzuxue lunzhu*. In int. 1980.vi.21 and 1980.vii.20, Shen denied influence from Cai, though during int. 1980.xi.14 he said Cai's liberal spirit influenced him. At the very least, Cai's aesthetic theory was on Shen's mind in the early 1940's. See "Mei yu ai," *WJ* 11: 379.

5. This broader definition of modernism, from intellectual rather than literary history, is consonant with the views of Karl, Singal, and Howe. On the role of the primitive in modernism, see Howe, pp. 32–33, and Woodcock. "Modernism" was singled out for vilification in China even during the relatively liberal post-Mao era, in the 1983–84 campaign against "spiritual pollution."

6. The Miao writer Tang Yi, p. 230, movingly tells how Han "racism" brought him to the brink of doubting that he was fully human.

7. Singal, pp. 4–5, citing Trilling, p. 19, and Gay, pp. 21–26.

8. Karl, pp. xi, 101. Singal, p. 84.

9. On topographical aspects of British literature, see Daiches and Flower. Howe, pp. 27–29. On modernism versus Marxism, see Lunn.

10. See my "Shen Congwen and the Uses of Regionalism," pp. 162–65.

11. "Meigui yu Jiumei," *WJ* 1: 13.

12. "Xishuai," *Yazi* (1926 ed.), pp. 79–93.

13. "Laba zhou," *WJ* 1: 23.

14. "Ye yu," *WJ* 1: 14–18. "Daigou," *WJ* 1: 19–22. "Shiji," *WJ* 10: 10–15 (this volume puts the piece in the "essay" category). "Gengfu Ahan," *WJ* 8: 99–106. "Tuzhuobian," *WJ* 2: 60–66. "Ruilong," *WJ* 8: 57–66. (Ruilong was a little neighbor boy; int. 1980.vii.24. Another friend Shen wrote a reminiscence of is Lu Tao; see *ZZ*, p. 111. The story is "Ji Lu Tao," *WJ* 2: 74–79, with a new, 1981 postscript by Shen.) "Lubian," *WJ* 2: 67–73, quotation p. 71.

15. "Wangshi," *WJ* 1: 5–9. Uncle No. 4: letter 1985.iii.9.

16. Mills and waterwheels figure in "Shuiche," *WJ* 9: 23–26; in "Sansan"; in *Bian cheng*, ch. 10; in the Ahei cycle, notably in "Youfang," *WJ* 5: 194–204; and in *Chang he*. A talking waterwheel seems to represent the Buddhist wheel of life in *Alisi Zhongguo youji*, vol. 2, *WJ* 1: 429–43. Note

that Shen often echoes themes from Daudet, and that Daudet wrote *Letters from My Mill*. In one story from that collection, "The Secret of Maître Cornille," an old mill stands for an old style of life in opposition to urban mechanization, as in Shen's *Chang he*, *WJ* 7: 88–89.

17. "Wo xihuan ni," *Yazi* (1926 ed.), p. 285. "Song."
18. "Yujin"; "Duihua."
19. "Shilu de xiao gaoyang." The third passage for the male, "Chun," p. 52, uses imagery of "iron-soled shoes" and *baba*, evidently derived from the Zhen'gan folk songs nos. 17 and 31 recorded in Shen's folk song collection "Ganren yaoqu."
20. "Chun yue," *Yazi*, p. 282.
21. "Bomu," *Yazi*, p. 283. "Huan yuan." Shen says that Nuo rites disappeared in his home area after 1911; int. 1980.vi.27. Drama specialist Wu Xiaoling says that the Nuo lasted for a long time in Shanxi, too. "*Amei*" in Tujia love songs: Tian Maozhong. Another modern poem of Shen's with local color subject matter is "Xiang" (1928).
22. A metaphysical poem Shen wrote under a new pen name ("Yongyu," confirmed in int. 1980.vi.20) is "Kan hong" (1941). He also continued to publish a few poems under his own name, such as "Huai Kunming" (1946). Shen published most of his modern poetry of the 1930's under the pen name "Shangguan Bi." For his post-Liberation poetry in Classical Chinese, see *WJ* 10: 342–68.
23. "Xishan de yue," *WJ* 10: 22–26. "Yaoye," nos. 1–2, *WJ* 9: 18–22. "Yaoye," no. 5. Shen puzzled over the concept of prose poems in "Xiang jian de xia," p. 6.
24. "Yaoye," no. 5, p. 4. Christian hymns are in "Yuexia," *WJ* 9: 2–5.
25. "Láo mei, zuohen!" *WJ* 10: 27–33.
26. Int. 1980.vi.21; 1980.vi.27; 1980.vii.23. Zhou Zuoren is stigmatized in China for allegedly having collaborated with Japan during the war.
27. Wolff, p. 29. "Medley of metaphor" is Edmund Wilson's term. It may be more than coincidence that even Shen's late work *Yunnan kan yun ji* (1943) echoes a title of Zhou Zuoren's, *Kan yun ji* (1932).
28. Zhou on candy selling: Wolff, p. 29. Shen describes the kinds of boats on the Yuan River most fully in *Xiangxi*; Kinkley, "Vision," pp. 225–37.
29. "Lü de huaping," *WJ* 9: 48–50. A similar green vase has a nearly Proustian function of stirring the memory in "Huaihuazhen." "Qiebuzhe biji—jisheng," *WJ* 10: 20–21.
30. "Fufu," *XS* 20, no. 11 (10 Nov. 1929): 1734. Shen told Ling Yu that Fei Ming influenced him heavily. Interview with Ling Yu in Peking, 1980.vii.18. Also int. 1980.vii.20.
31. "Xiang jian de xia," p. 6. The first two poems translated are from

"Zhen'gan de ge" (1925), pp. 5–6. The last three are from "Xiang jian de xia," pp. 5–6.

32. "Dutu" (play; "mime"), *Yazi* (1926), pp. 34–42. "Mai tang fu mai zhe" (monologue; also called a "mime"), *Yazi*, pp. 43–46.

33. On Zhou Zuoren's translation and popularization of *kyōgen* for the Chinese audience, see Wolff, pp. 31, 69. Zhou's main contribution was *Kuangyan shifan*, published in 1926, the same year Shen Congwen had his *kyōgen* craze. In fact Shen was not the only one to write "Chinese *kyōgen*." For another example, see Wang Xiangchen's "Wei Shui hebin."

34. "Yazi"; "Guonian"; "Ye dian." Only "Yazi" is named a *kyōgen*, but the other plays are similar in style. So is another play, a battle of wits between a soldier and a peddler, "Yanggao."

35. *Shenwu zhi ai*, *WJ* 8: 251–63. *Fengzi*, ch. 10, *WJ* 4: 382–86. The new version of *Shenwu zhi ai* revises some of the information, making it consistent with the description in *Fengzi*. For a summary of local customs regarding the Nuo, see Kinkley, "Vision," pp. 297–306. A West Hunan Miao Nuo is described in Ling and Rui, pp. 178–93. A Han Nuo at Mayang, just a few miles south of Fenghuang, is described by Wei Juxian. Int. 1980.vi.21; 1980.vi.27 (confirmed masks were worn); 1981.i.16. Quotation from *Xiangxi*, *WJ* 9: 378. Corroborative information on the Nuo was given at the Fenghuang seminars, 1980.viii.14.

36. "Ganren yaoqu," *CF*, 25 Dec. 1926, p. 60. Int. 1980.vi.21.

37. Kinkley, "Vision," pp. 301–2. Int. 1980.vi.21; 1980.vi.27. The 1980.viii.14 Fenghuang seminar corroborated most of the details about Xiao gods, including their penchant for stealing household articles.

38. West Hunanese shamans, too, were thought to have the power to "steal" things by magic. The ritual expert lifted a bowl over his head and presented it to the four directions. When he lowered it, it would be filled with cooked food, wine, or whatever someone in the audience had called for. Precisely that amount would be found missing from someone else's rice bowl or wine crock in the vicinity. In 1930 it was reported that adepts supplied their food by this means, or performed the trick on demand, for a fee of 400–500 cash. One could be jailed by the authorities on the strength of such evidence of theft; Rev. Basil Bauer, C. P. (reporting from Gaocun, river port of Fenghuang), "Muan Joseph Tells a Story," *The Sign* 10, no. 4 (Nov. 1930): 251.

39. *Fengzi*, ch. 10, *WJ* 4: 384–85. Fenghuang seminars, 1980.viii.14.

40. "Xiaoshen," *Yazi* (1926), p. 47.

41. *Ibid.*, pp. 48–49.

42. "San shou sudupo"; explained in Shen's folkloric essay entitled "Guanyu san shou sudupo."

43. The flute story, told by the Shen family Miao nursemaid, does fit

one genre of Miao folklore: "Sheng zhi jilu," *WJ* 9: 42. Songs: "Ganren yaoqu."

44. "Ajin," *WJ* 8: 311–15. Interview with Yu Lihua and Ma Tingyun in Ala, Fenghuangxian, 1980.viii.15. I am intrigued by the fact that Shen started writing imaginative folkloric and quasi-folkloric fiction only after going to live in Shanghai. His mother and possibly his father lived with him there for a time. They might have supplied stories.

45. Lu Xun, letter to Qian Xuantong, in *Lu Xun shuxin ji*, vol. 1: 72. He Yubo, vol. 2: 129, criticizes Shen's dialect as being too obscure.

46. "Xue," *WJ* 1: 135–43. "Chuanshang anshang," *WJ* 1: 126–34. "Shizi chuan," *WJ* 3: 2–15. Another, even more explicit evocation of homesickness is "Liming" (June 1926), *WJ* 8: 107–15. The Younger Brother Mang whose death this piece is written in memory of (p. 115) was a younger brother of Huang Yushu; letter 1985.iii.9.

47. "Chuanshang anshang," *WJ* 1: 130.

48. *Ibid.*, pp. 129–30.

49. "Ganren yaoqu," *CF*, 25 Dec. 1926, p. 60.

50. "Huaihuazhen," *WJ* 1: 42.

51. "Qiebuzhe biji—Duanyang" (written the night of 12 June [1925]). Quotation from "Yi feng wei ceng fuyou de xin," *WJ* 10: 3. For more on Southern waters, see "Wo de xiezuo yu shui de guanxi," *WJ* 11: 323 26.

52. Li Zhenyi, p. 67. Int. 1980.vii.20.

53. "Tongxin." The town of Shiyangshao had been moved when I visited it in 1980, owing to the relocation of a reservoir. For a later celebration of barbarism, "of beauty and cruelty inextricably intertwined" in a brutal trial by ordeal, see *Xiangxi*, *WJ* 9: 407–8.

54. On the "childlike mind" in Chinese literary theory, see James J. Y. Liu, pp. 78–81. On Shen's use of terms like *dai* and *chi*, see Kinkley, "Vision," pp. 191–92. The simpleton of "Laoshi ren" is an alter ego of Shen Congwen named Zikuan. At the time, Shen was publishing "Yishu zatan" and "'Zijincheng qima' guilai" under the pen name Zikuan. The fanatical rowing is mentioned in "Qiebuzhe biji—Duanyang," and in *Xiang xing san ji*, *WJ* 9: 280–84; repeated in *Xiangxi*, *WJ* 9: 374–76.

55. Shen confirmed that the Gelaohui dominated the docksides in West Hunan. He was quick to add that that branch of the Gelaohui was relatively upstanding (*zhengpai*); int. 1980.vii.24. Uncle No. 4: letter 1985.iii.9.

56. *Xiangxi*, *WJ* 9: 345, 346, 348; on Mayang, pp. 346–47; on Chu, p. 359. In English, see Kinkley, "Vision," pp. 225–37. On Darwinism, see Pusey.

57. For more on Shen's aesthetic idealism and a comparison with Cai Yuanpei's, see Kinkley, "Vision," pp. 178–83.

58. Shen is said to have advised Wu Mi to seek sexual release; Sun Ling, p. 55. Sun and a few others say Shen pursued other women after marriage

(see Chapter 7, note 76), but I can't confirm this. I doubt that Shen experienced sex long before (if ever before) his marriage. In "Tan shi" (published June 1931), he bragged that though he'd never seen a naked woman, he'd written many stories as if he had.

59. *Chang xia. Jiu meng.* "Ye dian."
60. *Ahei xiaoshi*, *WJ* 5: 191–249.
61. The Academia Sinica report is Ling and Rui. Reservations about its accuracy were expressed at the Fenghuang seminars, and indeed, it relies heavily on gazetteers. A compendium of Chinese studies of the Guizhou Miao is Wu Zelin, Chen Guojun, et al. For a summary in English of Miao sexual customs relevant to Shen's works, based on the above sources and many others, see Kinkley, "Vision," pp. 312–70.
62. Kinkley, "Vision," pp. 312–70.
63. Granet. Quotation from Ma Shaoqiao, p. 8.
64. Ma Shaoqiao, p. 8.
65. Kinkley, "Vision," p. 322. There seems to be informal "chaperoning," for verification, not as parental control—since it is done by a little girl—in Shen's "Yu hou," *WJ* 2: 93.
66. Kinkley, "Vision," pp. 318–25. Abadie, p. 167, uses the term "marriage fairs." "Long Zhu," *WJ* 2: 366–67.
67. The 1926 work: "Ganren yaoqu." Example from Guizhou: Mickey, p. 50 (see also p. 74). Example from Guangxi: Xiao Ganniu, comp., pp. 59–60.

The West Hunan Miao songs translated are from "Ganren yaoqu," nos. 35, 2, 24; 19, 33; 3 (sung by Wuming to Ahei in "Qiu," *WJ* 5: 206), 4; 12; 38. Others are translated in Kinkley, "Vision," pp. 332–44. These songs are authentic. One turned up, with slightly altered lyrics, in the folklore collection by Wang Yiyun, p. 57. A recent collection of West Hunan *Miao* love songs, translated into Chinese and annotated, is "Miaozu qingge (Xiangxi)," collected by Wu Xuenao, *Minjian wenxue* 153 (20 Oct. 1982): 76–84, 102.

In Shen's Zhen'gan song no. 10, tung trees and yams are phalli:

> A five-foot tung tree, tall and thick,
> I eat bean curd, the yam's your lick:
> I get my bean curd from your sister,
> Out of yams? Then eat my prick.

68. "Yu hou." *WJ* 4: 90–95, follows the original version, in *XS*. More songs were added to a revised (but still not final) version, in *Ba jun tu* [1], pp. 119–31. The revision, however, deletes the following words: "She squeezed the thing of Fourth Dog's which he would not ordinarily suffer others to harm. What seemed angry was that piece of Fourth Dog." "Yu hou," *Yu hou ji qita*, p. 11.

Chapter Five

1. Hsia, *A History*, pp. 189–211, 359–66.
2. Su Xuelin, p. 127. Su Xuelin's essay mixes penetrating and original insights with peculiar misperceptions and non sequiturs. She, alone among Shen's critics, recognized that some of his works were partly aimed at a young audience (she may go too far in saying he wrote "children's stories"). Yet she puts *Alice's Adventures in China* in that category, though it is an adult (perhaps excessively obscure) satire, and criticizes Shen's Miao stories as unrealistic, though they, above all, are candidates for children's literature.

Typical of Communist criticism is Ting Yi, pp. 186–87: "The characters of [Shen's] works have no resemblance to real people—they have no class character. They are the products of his imagination—they are what he, with his bourgeois and landlord outlook, thought they should be." Wang Yao, vol. 1: 236–37, also criticizes Shen for using his imagination too much, though he is more sympathetic than other Communist critics. (It appears that much of the content of his remarks is copied directly from Su Xuelin's article cited above.) Li Helin, pp. 240–41, claims that Shen wouldn't or couldn't write realistically, and so opposed realistic content in the works of others. For more charges, see Liu Shousong, vol. 2: 62–63, 79, 289. Most PRC critics, however, slight Shen Congwen by simply leaving him out of their literary histories. This is true even in the post-Mao era. Shen is completely ignored in two compendia titled *Zhongguo xiandai wenxueshi*, both the one edited by Lin Zhihao et al. and the one edited by the "Nine Institutes and Schools." He gets a mention in a *Zhongguo xiandai wenxueshi* edited by Tang Tao (vol. 2: 279–80), which devotes one and one-half pages to Shen and is basically negative in summing up his achievement. Shen is also omitted from the *Zhongguo wenxuejia cidian*, vol. 1.

3. Taoism (Daoism) is among several lines of interpretation used by Hsia, *A History*, pp. 199–200, and MacDonald, pp. 5, 143–44. See also William L. MacDonald, "Shen Ts'ung-wen's Approach to Reality," paper presented to the annual meeting of the Association for Asian Studies, New York, 1972. Shen's "Countryman" is compared to Camus' "Stranger" in Nieh, pp. 67–69. The same book analyzes Shen's symbolism, pp. 67–110.
4. Brooks, p. 54.
5. Ibid., p. 6.
6. See Zhu Guangqian, "Cong Shen Congwen."
7. Examples of gentry writing are the various picture albums of the Miao—such as the *Miao Man tuce* (late seventeenth century)—and Yan Ruyi's *Miao fangbei lan* (1843). A whiff of the old gentry tradition is still conveyed by such pieces as Sheng Xiangzi's "Hunan zhi Miao Yao" and

"Hunan Miao shi shulue," and Yang Lixing's "Xiang xi'nan Miao Yao de yule."
8. Kinkley, "Vision," pp. 328–31. Int. 1980.vi.27.
9. "Under Moonlight" ("Yuexia xiaojing"), Ching and Payne, trans., p. 92.
10. Ibid.
11. Ibid.; quotations from pp. 92–93, 91, respectively.
12. Ibid., pp. 88, 91.
13. Bernatzik, p. 197.
14. Ching and Payne, trans., pp. 93, 96.
15. Fenghuang seminars, 1980.viii.14–18.
16. *Fengzi*, *WJ* 4: 356–57.
17. See Kinkley, "Vision," pp. 368–70.
18. "Long Zhu," *WJ* 2: 372.
19. *Fengzi*, ch. 10 (1937), *WJ* 4: 381.
20. Ching and Payne, trans., p. 88.
21. Ibid., p. 101.
22. Ibid., p. 88.
23. Kinkley, "Vision," p. 327. See Pan Dengchang. Tujia, too, have communal singing-match competitions and song masters. See Yuan Bingchang.
24. Frye, pp. 33–34.
25. Nuoyou of "Under Moonlight" (Ching and Payne, trans., p. 93) and many characters of *Shenwu zhi ai* sing Long Zhu's praises; the shaman of the latter work is said to have studied singing with Long Zhu's dwarf. *Shenwu zhi ai*, *WJ* 8: 245, 246, 248, 250, 257, 258, 264, 267, 273, 276, 282, 297, 299.
26. Ching and Payne, trans., p. 88.
27. "Yuexia xiaojing," *Yuexia xiaojing*, p. 22, bears the annotation that the story comes from Huangluozhai. Confirmed by Shen in int. 1980.vi.21. The recent information on Huangluozhai is from the August 1980 Fenghuang seminars.
28. Ching and Payne, trans., pp. 89–90.
29. Kinkley, "Vision," pp. 362–63.
30. "Yuexia xiaojing," *WJ* 5: 47.
31. Ching and Payne, trans., p. 97. Zhou Zuoren, "Chuyequan xuyan." Shen's tracing of the Huangluozhai legend to *jus primae noctis* seems to be his own speculation. Evidently a second West Hunanese legend, about *jus primae noctis* as enjoyed by the Baojing native head, led him to posit the *jus* as the missing link in his thematic chain. See *Xiangxi*, *WJ* 9: 367, and Li Zhenyi, p. 60.
32. Eberhard, *Local Cultures*, pp. 134–39. Kinkley, "Vision," pp. 364–65.
33. Kinkley, "Vision," pp. 367–77. One cannot say what the situation

was in Huangluozhai, but Rock attributes similar double love suicides among the Naxi (Na-khi; speaking a Tibeto-Burman language, like the Tujia) to the sudden new subordination of Southwestern young people's sexuality to adult authority during the passage from tribal to Chinese society. Rock, "The Life and Culture of the Na-khi Tribe," p. 32. "The Romance" (Rock, trans.) is a traditional alternating boy-girl song that star-crossed Naxi lovers are supposed to sing as a lead-up to their suicides.

34. Ching and Payne, trans., p. 101.
35. Fenghuang seminars, August 1980.
36. Int. 1980.vi.20. Shen thought "Meijin, Baozi, yu na yang" might be real folklore, but could not clearly remember.
37. Int. 1980.vi.20. "Meijin, Baozi, yu na yang," *WJ* 2: 394.
38. "Meijin, Baozi, yu na yang," *WJ* 2: 392.
39. *Ibid.*, p. 393.
40. *Ibid.*, pp. 395–96. Similar laments appear on pp. 397 and 404.
41. The original version, in *Renjian yuekan* 1 (20 Jan. 1929): 57, is reprinted in *WJ* 2. A revised version, with the paragraph deleted, is in *Shen Congwen xuan ji* [4] (1983), vol. 2: 145.
42. *WJ* 2: 397.
43. "Qi ge yeren yu zuihou yi ge yingchunjie," *WJ* 8: 316–26. Confirmed as authentic legend in int. 1980.vi.27. Analysis in Kinkley, "Vision," pp. 272–77.
44. See Redfield, vol. 1: 288. Shen Congwen also sees the countryside as economically less complicated than the city. Inflation comes from "the city," as in "Guisheng," *WJ* 6: 339.
45. Wright, *The Last Stand*, pp. 3–4.
46. "*Congwen xizuo xuanji* daixu," *ZZ*, p. 120. Shen also speaks of himself as a country person in *ZZ*, p. 73; in "*Lixia ji* tiji" (1933), *WJ* 11: 33–34; and in "Cong xianshi xuexi" (1946), *WJ* 10: 299–322.
47. See MacDonald, "Characters and Themes."
48. "Guisheng," *WJ* 6: 338–61. *Alisi Zhongguo youji*, *WJ* 1: 458–60. "Gengfu Ahan," *WJ* 8: 102–3. "Sansan," *WJ* 4: 120–48.
49. *Bing gao*: "Guisheng," *WJ* 6: 341; see also p. 344. Fears dirtying floor, p. 344. "Lords": "San-San," Ching and Payne, trans., p. 74. This translation actually uses the term "great lord." Castoffs: "Guisheng," p. 339. *Bianzi huo*: "Guisheng," p. 358; "Sansan," *WJ* 4: 132. In 1929, when he was living in Shanghai and writing his most conventionally leftist works, Shen showed particular interest in indicating class relations. In "Yi zhi chuan," *WJ* 8: 225–34, Shen notes that *soldiers* and boat trackers are in effect as far apart in status (meaning power?) as "commissioners and the masses." He also points out that boat owners are close to being gentry—able to be patronizing toward party (KMT) and government officials. Shen does not, however, make his captain character into an overbearing person; he is master on the waters, having earned it by virtue of his experience.

50. *Bian cheng, WJ* 6: 73–163. "Huiming," *WJ* 3: 269–81. "Xiang cheng," *WJ* 7: 211–18. "Niu," *WJ* 3: 282–97.
51. "Shangui," *WJ* 2: 147–48.
52. "Ajin," *WJ* 8: 311–15. "Lüdian," *WJ* 8: 302–10.
53. "Shangui," *WJ* 2: 147–48.
54. *ZZ*, p. 93.
55. *Bian cheng, WJ* 6: 75.
56. Yaoyao: *Chang he, WJ* 7: 1–172. She is evidently modeled in part on a girl who lived near Chenzhou. See *Xiangxi, WJ* 9: 360–61, but also *Xiang xing san ji, WJ* 9: 266–68. Cuicui is partly modeled on a girl Shen saw and had a crush on in Luqi when he first left home; "Laoban," *WJ* 9: 296–97. Cuicui also has traits of a girl Shen saw at Qingdao; Liu Yiyou, "Lun Shen Congwen," p. 6. Zhang Zhaohe was nicknamed "Heimao" (Black Cat) at the Woosung China Institute, where Shen first wooed her; Situ Liangyi. Zhang Zhaohe and Mrs. Frankel confirmed this. Shen went on to name the heroine of his "Lüdian" "Little Black Cat" (1929; *WJ* 8: 302–10). He wrote autobiographically of the one he loved, describing her as beautifully dark, in "Zao" (1931; *WJ* 8: 442–52). He spoke again of thinking often of a dark woman in a letter to Liu Tingwei, "Feiyou cundi," 2, *Wenyi yuekan* 2, no. 7 (July 1931): 45–51. He also named a character resembling his wife "Heifeng" (Black Phoenix) in "San ge nüxing" (1933), *WJ* 5: 281–99. Zhang Zhaohe's dark complexion (like her striking beauty) was quite evident in her youth; see 1935 photograph, *WJ* 5: frontispiece. Short, spry people: int. 1980.vi.21. See also "Huiming," *WJ* 3: 271.
57. "Guisheng," *WJ* 6: 340.
58. Shrimp: *ibid.*, p. 338. Pushi is mentioned in "Guisheng." On its decay, see *Xiangxi, WJ* 9: 373–74.
59. *Bian cheng, WJ* 6: 78.
60. "Huiming," *WJ* 3: 274, 281. "Hei ye," *WJ* 5: 389. "Niu," *WJ* 3: 282–97. "Zhishi," *WJ* 6: 292–97.
61. "Sansan," *WJ* 4: 137 (nurse); 139–40 (city).
62. *Ibid.*, p. 140.
63. "Yu," *WJ* 3: 41–54.
64. Shen sarcastically echoes the term "sanctity of labor" in *Xiangxi, WJ* 9: 384–85. On the hard lot of boatmen and trackers, see especially "Yi zhi chuan," *WJ* 8: 225–34.
65. "Sansan," *WJ* 4: 140.
66. *Bian cheng, WJ* 6: 116.
67. "Guisheng," *WJ* 6: 342.
68. *Ibid.*, p. 351.
69. *Ibid.*, p. 352.
70. *Ibid.*, pp. 359–60.
71. "Xiaoxiao," *WJ* 6: 224.
72. *Chang he, WJ* 7: 25–29.
73. "Nitu," *WJ* 5: 315–47, "Fulan," *WJ* 6: 2–17. *Chang he, WJ* 7: 89.
74. "Huiming," *WJ* 3: 271, 281.
75. *Xiangxi, WJ* 9: 346.
76. *Chang he, WJ* 7: 9–10.

77. See Kinkley, "Vision," pp. 281–83.
78. "Guisheng," *WJ* 6: 343.
79. "Niu," *WJ* 3: 294.
80. *Chang he, WJ* 7: 44–45.
81. "Gengfu Ahan," *WJ* 8: 103.
82. *ZZ*, p. 2.
83. An example is the interest in the peddler origins of the shopkeeper in "Guisheng," *WJ* 6: 340. Shen is equally intent on explaining the origins of the wharfmaster Shunshun in *Bian cheng, WJ* 6: 82. Country folk don't pry: *Fengzi, WJ* 4: 321. Strangers may question: *Fengzi, WJ* 4: 339.
84. *Bian cheng, WJ* 6: 79. Nieh, p. 71.
85. "Niu," *WJ* 3: 284–85.
86. "Sansan," *WJ* 4: 143.
87. "Xiaoxiao," *WJ* 6: 224.
88. *Chang he, WJ* 7: 40.
89. *Bian cheng, WJ* 6: 81–82. "Zhangfu," *WJ* 4: 2–22.
90. "Cai jue," *WJ* 8: 184–93.
91. *Xiangxi, WJ* 9: 333.
92. Int. 1980.vii.24.
93. "Fufu," *WJ* 8: 384–93. Besides the fact that the man in "Ox" is nicknamed Uncle Big Ox, the ox is humorously referred to as a person. "Niu" was first published in *Xinyue* 2, nos. 6–7 (Sept. 1929), while Shen was in Shanghai. Controversies about the proletariat were raging at the time; Shen had published "Da cheng zhong de xiao shiqing" just a month before and, in 1928, *Alisi Zhongguo youji*.
94. "*Congwen xiaoshuo xizuo xuanji* tiji," *ZZ*, p. 121.
95. "Gengfu Ahan," *WJ* 8: 101–3.

Chapter Six

1. Wang Zengqi. First class: int. 1980.vi.20; the Hans H. Frankels, in a 1975.i.21 New Haven interview, cited the same anecdote, adding that Zhang Zhaohe herself found Shen a boring teacher. Shen's dissatisfaction with himself as a teacher is revealed in stories such as "Deng" (1929, Wusong), *WJ* 4: 23–45, and "Chuntian" (no date, but written in Shanghai—hence 1929–30?), *Youmu ji* (1934), pp. 45–87.

Shen's residence alternated between Qingdao and Peking in the years 1931–34. In the summer of 1931 he left Shanghai for Peking. He was a sometime teacher at Qingdao University, fall 1931–summer 1933; then moved back to Peking after his marriage in September 1933; but returned to Qingdao for the summer of 1934, as the "Tiji" to *Yuexia xiaojing* attests, *WJ* 5: 43. He was back in Peking in 1935 and later taught at Peking University. His career path was not smooth. Wu Xiaoling says that Shen was still only an associate professor when he taught at Kunming in the 1940's.

2. Fascists: "Tan jinbu," p. 3. For criticisms of Shen, see, e.g., Fan Rong. Shen answered charges that he was not realistic in 1946, in his "Cong xianshi xuexi," *WJ* 10: 299–322. Counter-responses came from Xia Yan and Yang Hua.

3. The foreign theorists cited appear in two single articles of Shen's, "Tan baoshou" (June 1938), *WJ* 11: 236–42, and "Tan jinbu," pp. 2–6.

4. Shen and Ding Ling wrote works called *A Mother* and *Mother*, respectively. Shen's "Three Men and a Woman" recalls Gorky's "Twenty-six Men and a Girl"; Shen's "My Education" recalls Gorky's "My Universities" to Helmut Martin (forthcoming contribution to the European Project on Chinese Literature encyclopedia). Yüan and Payne, trans., p. 11, go so far as to say that "Shen Ts'ung-wen's early stories can be compared with Gorki's. A fierce exaltation flows through them."

5. Shen Congwen was apolitical by the standards of his times. He refused to join the League of Left-wing Writers, government groups, or Su Wen's "middle-of-the-road" "third force." He of course steered clear of all political parties and their front organizations. However, he did speak well of Hu Yepin's organizational activities, in *Ji Ding Ling xuji*, p. 34. "Behind in the ranks" (*luowu*): *Bu si riji*, p. 67 (entry for 13 Aug. 1928). This echoes Lu Xun, "Wentan de zhanggu" (10 Aug. 1928), *Lu Xun quanji* 4: 130. Then Shen wrote an autobiographical story entitled "Luowu" (published 10 May 1929; *WJ* 8: 194–208). In it he depicts himself as pitiable. Shen's remark about being "behind" might seem a response to leftist criticism, as in *Ji Hu Yepin*, *WJ* 9: 82. But this first impression does not entirely hold up. Not only does "*luowu*" have a broader meaning in the story "Luowu" and in *Ji Hu Yepin* ("bending with the wind"); in "Fengya yu suqi" (15 Feb. 1935), *Feiyou cundi*, p. 35, Shen satirizes a right-wing revolutionary fan of KMT militarism, finding him typical of those who wouldn't think of falling "behind in the ranks." Shen said he was "behind" (*luohou*) and middle-aged in "Chenmo" (8 Oct. 1936), *WJ* 10: 60–64; even middle-aged in 1930; "*Shengming de mo tiji*," *WJ* 11: 7. Note that *WJ*, vol. 11, purports to reprint *Feiyou cundi*, but leaves out some chapters, such as "Fengya yu suqi." My references stick to the earlier edition of the book.

6. For comparison, see Smith, pp. x–xiii.

7. Many readers feel that Ding Ling's *Yijiusanlingnian chun Shanghai*, pt. 1, caricatures Shen Congwen. Courtship of Zhang Zhaohe: "Zao," *WJ* 8: 442–52; "Xianxian." The eponymous heroine Xianxian is an alter ego of Shen's Little Sister No. 9. She is embarrassed when a classmate asks her if she has heard an amusing "story" about "some famous author's" hopeless pursuit of a student named Zhang. A June 1931 love letter to Zhaohe through which Shen tried to renew his courtship is reprinted in *WJ* 12: 2–8. Her sister, Mrs. Frankel, said in a 1975.i.21 interview that Zhaohe at first never contemplated marrying Shen. He was so much older; his big pack of love letters was a bore; and so were his rambling stories about his army life and such. The marriage: "Zhufu" (1936), *WJ* 6: 324–37 (not to be confused with a 1945 story by this title in *WJ* 7: 233–46).

8. On Shen's editing of the Tianjin *Dagongbao* column, see Chapter 3

above, note 39. *Xiaoshuo yuekan* (*The Story Monthly*), published by Cangshan Shudian of Hangzhou, was co-edited by Shen Congwen, Lin Geng, Cheng Yirong, and Gao Zhi. It began with vol. 1, no. 1 (15 Oct. 1932); I have also seen vol. 1, nos. 2–4 (Nov., Dec. 1932; Jan. 1933). Then there was a true "Peking Types" journal, *Shuixing*, published by Wenhua Shuju of Beiping, co-edited by Shen's protégé Bian Zhilin, Ba Jin, Shen Congwen, Li Jianwu, Jinyi (Zhang Fangxu), and Zheng Zhenduo. Beginning with vol. 1, no. 1 (10 Oct. 1934), it published at least through vol. 2, no. 3, in the summer of 1935. Shao Huaqiang also learned, and got Shen to confirm, that Shen was de facto editor of Zhonghua Shuju's *Xin wenyi congshu* (New Literature Series; from Jan. 1930) and Dadong Shuju's *Xin wenxue congshu* (New Literature Series; from Dec. 1930), both of which were titularly under Xu Zhimo. Shao further discovered that Shen edited an eight-book *Xiandai jiezuo xuan ji* (Selected Modern Masterpieces Series), published in Dec. 1933 by the Dongfang Wenxueshe, reprinted in Jan. 1936 by Dongfang Shuju. All these collectanea were published in Shanghai. During the war, Shen's journal editing was pushed aside by other duties. It picked up again once he was back in Peking. In the meantime, several protégés succeeded him, as he had Xu Zhimo.

9. Art education: "'Yishu zhoukan' de dansheng" (1934) and "Yishu jiaoyu" (1937), *WJ* 12: 212–22. Art history: "Tantan muke" (1939), "Du Zhan Ziqian 'You chun tu'" (1947), *WJ* 12: 243–45, 279–95. Preservation: "Shoushi canpo—wenwu baowei yizhong kanfa." "Wenwu baowei de yizhong kanfa."

10. "Chenmo," *WJ* 10: 60–61. A year earlier, on 10 Dec. 1935, Shen was already observing that he had been quiet for one year. See *"Ba jun tu tiji."* Shen's disappointment with Lu Xun, mentioned at the end of Chapter 3, is indicated in "Lu Xun de zhandou," as well as sprinkled through works like *Bu si riji* (p. 14) and *Yi ge tiancai de tongxin* (pp. 84–85).

11. "Gei mou jiaoshou," *Feiyou cundi*, refers both to Shen's idea of the author as healer (pp. 18–19) and to a professor who misread Shen's story "Zisha" (*WJ* 6: 310–19) as being about him (pp. 15–16). After Wu Mi's death (from neglect, during the Cultural Revolution), Shen identified Wu as the anonymous addressee of Shen's published denial ("Gei mou jiaoshou"). See Ling Yu, p. 27. Similarly, a Mr. Huang of Hengyang misunderstood one of Shen's published letters to be about *him*. Shen's denial is in the form of an editor's note in the Tianjin *DGB*, 21 July 1935. Stories in which Shen dissects himself are "Zhufu," *WJ* 6: 324–37, and "Mian Zhi xiansheng zhuan," *WJ* 8: 453–58.

12. Young folk: most stories in *Yuexia xiaojing* are dedicated to Zhang Zhaohe's little brother. See *WJ* 5: 78, 101, etc. Textbooks: in Peking (1937), and then in Kunming (ca. 1939–40), Shen edited secondary-school literature texts for the government. With him were his sister-in-law, Zhang

Chonghe (now Mrs. Ch'ung-ho Chang Frankel), the noted essayist Zhu Ziqing, and Shen's old friend, former Qingdao University president Yang Zhensheng. Interview with Mrs. Frankel, New Haven, 1975.i.21. See also Sun Ling, p. 52. Shen's group did not leave Peking until war had actually broken out. Travel south was dangerous; they took machine gun fire on the train to Tianjin. Int. 1980.vi.21. Shen's leading role during the Kunming exile as inspirer of young writers and poets (some of whom he even provided lodging for, besides informal literary get-togethers, editing, and critical advice) was warmly remembered by two poets now matured (and married to each other), Zhao Ruihong and Yang Yi (sister of the translator Yang Xianyi). Interviews in Nanking, where both taught college, 1980.viii.4. Others who have reminisced fondly about Shen in Kunming include the poet Kai-yu Hsu, *The Chinese Literary Scene*, pp. 131–39; Stanford University mathematician Zhong Kailai; and physicist Wang Hao. Writer Sun Ling, pp. 56–60, remembers Shen's nurture, beginning in Peking, of Xiao Qian and Liu Jin (Cheng Yingliu). Liu went on to Kunming. Shen's other major fiction-writing protégés at the time were Lin Pu (Paul Lin, now a professor of philosophy at Southern University) and Wang Zengqi, who wrote model operas for the Gang of Four, lay low after their fall, and has now reemerged as a fiction writer and commentator on Shen Congwen. In the 1940's, Shen thought Wang the most promising writer among his students; int. 1980.vii.17. Young people Shen had promoted earlier in the 1930's, by the war already making their own way in the world, included Bian Zhilin, He Qifang, Li Guangtian, and Zang Kejia. As late as 1950, Shen encouraged a young Peking University Communist from Guizhou, Yue Daiyun, to study under him; Yue and Wakeman, p. 87. In 1958 Yue was judged a Rightist, but in the 1980's she seemed headed for important work again. (Yue got her label partly because of her association with Shen—though Shen was never so labeled. Again, Shen's CCP friends often suffered more from the revolution than he.)

13. "Yi zhou jian gei wu ge ren de xin," letter 1, *Feiyou cundi*, p. 3.

14. Old systems: *ibid.*, letter 4, p. 5. Old poetry: "Gei mou jiaoshou," *Feiyou cundi*, p. 17. Malnutrition, national character: "Yuandanri zhi 'Wenyi' duzhe," *Feiyou cundi*, pp. 26–30.

15. Diction, technique, form: "Gei yi ge xie shi de," *Feiyou cundi*, pp. 7–9. "Tan chuangzuo," *Feiyou cundi*, pp. 20–22. "Gei yi ge duzhe," *Feiyou cundi*, pp. 51–57. "Tan shi"; "Lun jiqiao," *WJ* 12: 104–7. Against "genius": "Chuangzuo zalun," "Zhi 'Wenyi' duzhe," *Feiyou cundi*, pp. 23–25. More antiromanticism is expressed in "Gei yi ge xie shi de." Hard work: "Gei yi ge duzhe," *Feiyou cundi*, p. 56. Caution in publishing: "Lun chuangzuo de taidu" (1931), p. 1. Also "Gei yi ge xie xiaoshuo de," *Feiyou cundi*, pp. 10–12. Shen says the addressee of this letter may have been Ba Jin.

Ling Yu, p. 27. Ba Jin himself brought up the fact that he and Shen had different philosophies of how much effort to devote to polishing versus pouring out one's soul as it comes; interview at Ba Jin's home in Shanghai, 1981.vii.9. Interestingly, Ba Jin's son, Li Xiaotang, was just then doing research on Shen Congwen. For Shen's criticism of individual authors and texts, see *Momo ji*.

16. "Gei yi ge duzhe," *Feiyou cundi*, p. 55.
17. "Gei yi ge xie shi de," *Feiyou cundi*, p. 9.
18. "Gei yi ge daxuesheng," *Feiyou cundi*, pp. 13–14. Shen spoke against going with the times in "Ganxiang" (1933). Mass language: "Cong 'xiaoxue dujing' dao 'dazhongyu wenti' de ganxiang" (1934); "Shanghai tongxin fuji." For background, see Goldman, "Left-wing Criticism," pp. 85–94.
19. See Lu Xun, *Selected Works* 4: 19.
20. "Lun 'Hai Pai'" (pub. 10 Jan. 1934), *WJ* 12: 158. Shen had spoken of "Hai Pai artiness" (instead of "celebrity-scholar artiness") joining with the "auctioneering of merchants" in *Ji Ding Ling*, *GW* 10, no. 38 (25 Sept. 1933). He also wrote "Guanyu 'Hai Pai,'" (pub. 21 Feb. 1934), *WJ* 12: 163–65.
21. Shen's "Lun 'Hai Pai'" was a response to Dai Kechong (pseud. Su Wen), "Wenren zai Shanghai." (Shen calls Dai by the pseudonym Dai used when he wrote novels, Du Heng.) Some scholars have suggested that Su Wen was responding to Shen's article "Wenxuezhe de taidu" (pub. 18 Oct. 1933), *WJ* 12: 148–54, but Shen does not use the term "Hai Pai" there; in fact he scolds Peking's professors, though to be sure, he makes mincemeat of Shanghai meeting-goers. Probably Su Wen was reacting to Shen's outburst in *Ji Ding Ling*. Even that piece simply restated long-standing views Shen had expressed in, e.g., "Shanghai zuojia" (pub. 15 Dec. 1932), which seems to be blasting Shanghai writers as a whole. Then, however, Shen was not yet a major spokesperson. Su and Shen may have felt themselves to be rivals for leadership of the nonpartisans.

Shen used "*boxiang*" in his "Wenxuezhe de taidu" and "Gei yi ge xie xiaoshuo de," *Feiyou cundi*, p. 12. This might appear to echo Lu Xun, "Chi boxiang fan" (26 June 1933), *Lu Xun quanji* 5: 252–54. However, Shen had already spoken of a "*boxiang* literary attitude" in "Lun chuangzuo de taidu" (pub. June 1931), p. 113; in "Zhai er mei zhai xianhua" (*WJ* 12: 95); and in "*Xue* xu" (1932). He referred satirically to "Shanghai *boxiangren*" (loafers) in 1929, in *Yi ge tiancai de tongxin*, p. 73, and to "*boxiang* poets" (Guo Moruo?) in "*Liu Yu shi xuan* xu," *WJ* 11: 22. On the Shanghai response to Shen, see Lu Fen. See also note 23.

22. Jiang Guangci, Creationists: "Xiandai Zhongguo wenxue de xiao ganxiang" (1930), p. 161. Shen confirmed Lin Yutang as one of his 1930's targets in int. 1980.vi.21. Zhang Ziping: "Yu Dafu, Zhang Ziping jiqi yingxiang" (first pub. 10 Jan. 1931), *WJ* 11: 141–44.

23. In post-1949 China, belonging to a "school" brought extra danger to oneself and to one's friends, from guilt by association. Shen was criticized for leading a conservative Jing Pai, which included Zhu Guangqian and others he published with in the late 1930's and 1940's. Indeed, Shen's younger friends Liu Zuchun and Yan Wenjing were criticized as a Xiao Jing Pai or Lesser Peking School. That probably was during the Cultural Revolution. Int. 1980.vi.21. Lu Xun's arch responses to Shen, made back in the 1930's, may have engendered some of Shen's 1950's trouble. In China, it is often assumed—incorrectly, as I point out below—that Lu Xun assailed Shen Congwen over the Jing Pai issue. Lu Xun did add his own satirical observations about the Jing Pai (it is unclear whether or not he meant to include Shen) after Shen wrote about the Hai Pai, and he belittled Shen's incomplete conceptualization (not his basic anti-Shanghai thrust). The rift between Shen and Lu Xun here seems to have been mostly personal. The Lu Xun pieces are "'Jing Pai' yu 'Hai Pai'" and "Beiren yu Nanren," in *Lu Xun quanji* 5: 491–95, and "'Jing Pai' he 'Hai Pai,'" in *Lu Xun quanji* 6: 300–304. As time went on, mutual belittlement crept into Shen's and Lu Xun's writings. By rights, they should have been on the same side in, for instance, their attacks on "humor." See Long Haiqing, "Shen Congwen and Lu Xun," pp. 22–23. However, Shen Congwen ended up criticizing Lu Xun's *zawen* magazines, too, so Lu Xun counter-criticized, in his "Qi lun 'wenren xiangqing'—liang shang," *Lu Xun quanji* 6: 397–401. Small wonder that in int. 1980.vi.21, Shen at first wanted to backtrack: "There was no Jing Pai. Nor was there a Hai Pai. They didn't really exist. Not concretely. The people Lu Xun scolded were the same ones I was scolding. But when he scolded them it was reasonable, and when I scolded them, it was unreasonable." But see the interesting definitions of the Hai Pai Shen went on to give, quoted below.

24. "*Lunpan* de xu" (July 1929). Also *Yi ge tiancai de tongxin* (1929), p. 71. *Ji Ding Ling* (1933), uses "New Hai Pai" on p. 166 and "Hai Pai" on p. 165.

25. I have not seen Shen's published Wuhan University lectures, *Xin wenxue jiangyi*. Shen told Shao Huaqiang they were similar to "Lun Zhongguo chuangzuo xiaoshuo" and *Momo ji*; courtesy Shao, letter of 1985.xi.3.

26. *Ji Hu Yepin*, *WJ* 9: 78–83. *Ji Ding Ling*, pp. 152–53, 159–71. Before *Honghei*, the trio edited a "Hong yu hei" supplement for the *Zhongyang ribao*, Jul.–Oct. 1928.

27. Ibid. Collusion: *Ji Ding Ling*, *GW* 10, no. 39 (2 Oct. 1933): 176 (KMT censors excised this passage from book reprints of *Ji Ding Ling*). Officials out of power: "Jinshu wenti" (1934), *WJ* 12: 327.

28. *Yi ge tiancai de tongxin*, p. 71. This explains the "occasion" for this book and its facetious title. An ad referring to Shen's genius appears in the friendly journal *Xinyue* 1, no. 11 (Jan. 1929), following Shen's story "Ajin."

29. *Ji Ding Ling xuji,* p. 12 and following.

30. "Lun 'Hai Pai,'" *WJ* 12: 159–62; *Ji Ding Ling,* p. 166; "Xiandai Zhongguo wenxue de xiao ganxiang," p. 160; "Guanyu 'Hai Pai,'" *WJ* 12: 165; "*Lunpan* de xu." Gangsters: int. 1980.vi.21. Shen said, "My articles explained [the Hai Pai] very clearly. Mainly it was that they changed very fast; you couldn't pin them down. They threw in their lot with the commercial interests, while the people in Peking came from the academy, schools—they were of no use commercially. Peking [writers] had to rely on ads, like the theater did, because they filled no economic function. In Shanghai it was like this: you had to entertain the news media, and sometimes you had to have dealings with gangsters, too, otherwise they'd make trouble for you. There was nothing like that in Peking. Put abstractly, Peking amounted to the scholars' *pai* (school). They filled an academic function. They were conscientious in their work; they didn't try to finesse it. And maybe they were a little more conservative. In political thought, they were behind the others."

31. *Ji Ding Ling,* p. 163. List of authors excluded: "Lun 'Hai Pai,'" *WJ* 12: 159–60. Difficulties of fiction journals: "Duiyu zhe xin kan dansheng de songci," *WJ* 12: 190–93.

32. *Zagan,* minor critics: "*Lunpan* de xu." "Humor": "Fengya yu suqi" (1935), *Feiyou cundi,* pp. 35–40. Lao She had written "humor" and Shen was glad he gave it up; "*Xue* xu," Shanghai *Shishi xinbao,* 4 Dec. 1932. This is excised from *WJ* 11: 13. "Xin de wenxue yundong he xin de wenxueguan," *Zhu xu* (1941 ed.), p. 60. See also *Ji Ding Ling xuji,* p. 136. Shi Zhicun: "Tantan Shanghai de kanwu" (1935), *WJ* 12: 177.

33. Unprincipled changeability: "Lun 'Hai Pai,'" *WJ* 12: 158; "Xiandai Zhongguo wenxue de xiao ganxiang," p. 159; *Ji Hu Yepin, WJ* 9: 82. Liangyou and Zhang Ziping: "Yu Dafu, Zhang Ziping jiqi yingxiang," *WJ* 11: 143, 141–44. "Sentimental leftists": "Lun 'Hai Pai,'" *WJ* 12: 159. Fads: "Yu Dafu, Zhang Ziping jiqi yingxiang," *WJ* 11: 144; *Ji Ding Ling,* p. 181. Against amateurism: "Wenxuezhe de taidu." In "Lun chuangzuo de taidu," p. 1, Shen less self-servingly defines literature as a profession as opposed to a trade.

34. Su Xuelin, "Present Day Fiction and Drama in China," in Schyns, p. xvii.

35. In int. 1980.vi.21, Shen said: "Yes, it's like that in their operas. The Shanghai style is always changing. It has lots of gimmicks. In props and tradition, Peking kept the tradition, was conservative in some respects. But the Hai Pai frequently won out. You know why? Because they pleased the audience. The same was true of Shanghai publishing." ... In business, Shanghai Types could turn a profit on money exchanges of the lowest magnitude, whereas a Pekingese was likely to lose money (paraphrase).

36. In "Lun 'Hai Pai,'" *WJ* 12: 161, Shen says, "In China a literary jour-

nal should be like a school." "Wenyun de chongjian," *Zhu xu* (1941 ed.), p. 105, repeats that "As soon as the literary movement parts ways with the universities, then dissociation from education, lethargy, degeneration, and loss of vitality are predictable consequences."

37. New Saturday School: "Yu Dafu, Zhang Ziping jiqi yingxiang," *WJ* 11: 142–43; "Shanghai zuojia," p. 180. On the "old" Saturday School, see Link, pp. 21, 166. Also "Lun 'Hai Pai,'" *WJ* 12: 158. On the New Hai Pai, see note 24. "Haishang Taste": "Shanghai zuojia," p. 180. "Haishang merchants": *Ji Ding Ling*, p. 165.

38. "Yu Dafu, Zhang Ziping jiqi yingxiang," *WJ* 11: 141–43. *Ji Ding Ling xuji*, p. 136, speaks of Shen getting interested in literary history at this time.

39. "Zhai er mei zhai xianhua," *WJ* 12: 92–94. Lee, p. 303, n. 69, notes that Liu Bannong called Guo Moruo "the poet on the Shanghai beach who compares himself to Goethe." Lu Xun ridiculed Shanghai writing in "Shanghai wenyi zhi yi pie" (from a 12 Aug. 1931 talk), *Lu Xun quanji* 4: 276–92.

40. Rumors about Shen and Ding: *Ji Ding Ling xuji*, pp. 5–6. Later, Shen often fussed about newspapers that speculated about his love life. See "Ba jun tu," *WJ* 8: 172, 190. Celebrity writers: "Lun 'Hai Pai,'" *WJ* 12: 158; "Guanyu 'Hai Pai,'" *WJ* 12: 164. Payola: "Lun 'Hai Pai,'" *WJ* 12: 159. "Lewd American music": "Zhanzheng dao mou shi yihou," *WJ* 8: 459. Competition: "Xiandai Zhongguo wenxue de xiao ganxiang," p. 159.

41. Foreignized writing: "Xiandai Zhongguo wenxue de xiao ganxiang," p. 161. Japanese influence: *ibid.*, pp. 159, 160.

42. *Zagan*; climate of criticasters: "*Lunpan* de xu." Lu Xun: "Xiandai Zhongguo wenxue de xiao ganxiang," p. 161. Shen also wrote that his leftist friend Yao Pengzi was just playing with "isms" when he edited a magazine for Lu Xun. This passage has been excised from *WJ* 9: 83; see *Ji Hu Yepin* (1932 ed.), pp. 67–68.

43. Shen obliquely criticized the violence of Communist revolution in a letter to a friend interested "in the French revolution": "Gei mou zuojia," *Feiyou cundi*, pp. 46–50. Shen asked him to cool down. (This is another work missing from the *WJ*.) "Proletarian literature" as a capitalist gimmick: "Nan xing zaji," *CF*, 4 Feb. 1928. The same is implied in *Ji Hu Yepin*, *WJ* 9: 82, and was repeated in int. 1980.vi.20! Leftists of merit: "Shanghai zuojia," p. 181, and "Datou wenxue" (1933), *WJ* 12: 155–57. When Shen in 1946 restated his complaints against the prewar literary scene, he voiced his strongest objections ever against the politicization of literature, but again his heaviest salvos were against the Shanghai-Nanking axis. "Cong xianshi xuexi," *WJ* 10: 306–10.

44. Lu Xun's "Shanghai wenyi zhi yi pie" (1931) criticized Shanghai literature in much the same terms as Shen in 1933–34. (Actually, Shen had

been polemicizing against Shanghai since 1929, as I have said.) In fact, it seemed to me that Shen in 1934 may have felt himself to be echoing Lu Xun in this polemic. And Shen agreed with that, in int. 1980.vi.21. Cao Juren quotes Lu Xun as actually using the term "Hai Pai" in the 12 Aug. speech that led to "Shanghai wenyi zhi yi pie," although that phrase does not appear in the text printed in *Lu Xun quanji* (1973) 4: 278. See Cao Juren, p. 137. Anyway, Lu Xun shared with Shen (1) the term *boxiang* (see above, note 21); (2) ridicule of plagiarism and flip-flops ("Shanghai wenyi zhi yi pie"); (3) linkage of the old *fin de siècle* talented scholars (Shen's Old Hai Pai) with the 1910's and 1920's pulps (Shen's New Saturday School), the Creation Society, and pseudo-revolutionary 1930's works; (4) ridicule of literary trends without works (cf. Shen's "authors without works"); and (5) disgust with trivial "humor" writing (see above, note 23). Later, Shen criticized the essays of *Taibai* (though finding them better than those in Lin Yutang's magazines), while praising the seriousness of *Yiwen*. Both *Taibai* and *Yiwen* were run by people in Lu Xun's camp. It is interesting, politically, that Shen chose Lu Xun when Lin Yutang was the alternative. "Tantan Shanghai de kanwu" (1935), *WJ* 12: 175.

45. Tang Tao, pp. 250–51, as noted in Gunn, p. 53.

46. Dai Kechong, "Wenren zai Shanghai." On the Shanghai Contemporains, I'm much indebted to Leo Ou-fan Lee, "'Modernism' in Chinese Literature of the 1930's," paper presented to the 27th Annual Meeting of The American Association for Chinese Studies, 23 Nov. 1985, and to Harry A. Kaplan, "Dai Wangshu, *Les Contemporains*, and the Chinese Modernist Aesthetic," paper presented to the American Historical Association Annual Meeting, 29 Dec. 1985.

47. "Lun Mu Shiying," *WJ* 11: 203–5 (includes comments on Fei Ming). Kaplan, "Dai Wangshu..." (cited in n. 46), mentions the art gossip. Note, however, that Shen's *Xiaoshuo yuekan* printed literary "news," too.

48. *Yi ge tiancai de tongxin*, pp. 78–79.

49. On Lu Xun: int. 1981.i.16. Hunanese: "Xiangren duiyu xin wenxue yundong de gongxian," *WJ* 12: 194–95.

50. "Zhi 'Wenyi' duzhe," *Feiyou cundi*, p. 28. See also "Zhishijieji yu jinbu" (25 Oct. 1933), *WJ* 12: 322–26, and Shen's rebuttal of the fascist Chen Quan in "Du lun yingxiong chongbai" (1940), *WJ* 12: 374–84.

51. Politics ("tendency") in literature sanctioned by Shen: *Ji Hu Yepin*, *WJ* 9: 81; *Ji Ding Ling*, pp. 165–66. But make it literature: "Gei yi ge xie xiaoshuo de," *Feiyou cundi*, p. 11.

52. Change of clothes: int. 1981.i.16; *Ji Ding Ling xuji*, pp. 15–17. Cai Yuanpei ("Cai X X"): *Ji Ding Ling xuji*, pp. 53–55, 82–83. (Cai's daughter, Cai Weilian, knew Ding Ling and painted a famous portrait of her, now a frontispiece in *Ding Ling wenji*, vol. 2.) Money matters: int. 1981.vii.17,

with the Shens, Ling Yu, Shao Huaqiang, Wang Xu. Shen also went to see KMT notable Zhang Qun in Shanghai, after a second trip to Nanking to get a letter of introduction from Cai Yuanpei; *Ji Ding Ling xuji*, p. 58. Shao and Chen: Boorman, ed., 3: 274. Shen's third trip to Nanking, with Ding, and Shen's and an unnamed person's interview with Chen Lifu are described in *Ji Ding Ling xuji*, pp. 91–95. Communists Li Da and Shi Cuntong had asked Shen to go see Chen Lifu. But Hu Yepin was held by the Blue Shirts' Military Statistical Bureau, not the C.C. Clique's Central Statistical Bureau; int. 1981.vii.17. Among the many rumors about how Hu died, *Ji Ding Ling xuji*, pp. 95–99, gives one about Hu being shot with his comrades, as in Ding Ling's story, "Mouye." But soon this became a minority view. *China Forum* 2, no. 6 (29 May 1933) says Hu was buried alive. Shen, in "Ding Ling nüshi beibu" (25 May 1933; pub. 4 June), *WJ* 12: 314, says he doesn't know which rumor to believe—that Hu was dropped into the Huangpu River in a bag or buried alive. Feuerwerker, p. 161, n. 47, views Shen's account of his and Ding's visit to a prison where they caught a glimpse of Hu (*Ji Ding Ling xuji*, pp. 63–79) as "probably one of the most affecting narratives in modern Chinese literature." Bribery demands inflicted on Ding Ling herself: *Ji Ding Ling xuji*, p. 113.

53. *Ji Ding Ling xuji*, pp. 113–35. At some point after Hu's arrest, Ding Ling lived with an uncle of Shen's in Shanghai; int. 1981.vii.17. Ding Ling and *Ji Hu Yepin*: Peking interview of Shao Huaqiang, Ling Yu, Wang Xu, Wang Yarong, 1981.vii.18. See also *Ji Ding Ling xuji*, pp. 171–73.

54. Shen has never even answered Ding's criticisms of him, probably in order to preserve what he evidently feels is a moral advantage.

55. "Ding Ling nüshi beibu," *WJ* 12: 314–16, with the original *Duli pinglun* punctuation. Hu Shi added a disclaimer at the end (not reprinted in *WJ*), probably under pressure to pull the article. Shen's second piece was "Ding Ling nüshi shizong" (4 June 1933, pub. 12 June), *WJ* 12: 317–19. "Ting Ling Kidnapped!," *China Forum* 2, no. 6 (29 May 1933), says that the first printed word on Ding's arrest was a protest telegram from over 30 intellectuals. This was "Cai Yuanpei deng dian Jing yingjiu Ding Pan" (Cai Yuanpei et al. telegraph Nanking to save Ding and Pan), Shanghai *Shenbao*, 24 May 1933, p. 10 (reprinted with a new headline in the *China Forum*, 29 May, Chinese-language edition only). Shen Congwen was a signer.

56. Feng Da and KMT responsible: "Ting Ling Kidnapped!," *China Forum* 2, no. 6 (29 May 1933). The next issue of *China Forum*, no. 7 (19 June 1933), reported Ma Shaowu as the chief villain, in Li Chie-chen [Li Jucun, pseud.], "Ting Ling's Kidnappers Exposed by Witness." The same issue reported Ma's death, in "Ma Chao-wu Murdered By His Own Men:

Li Chie-chen's Story Confirmed," and the news about Chen Lifu, in "Ting Ling's Whereabouts Still Unknown." At this time Ding Ling was still thought to be alive.

57. Int. 1981.vii.17; much of this was already told in *Ji Ding Ling xuji*, pp. 137–38. For Shen's views on Feng Da (referred to not by name but as an American woman reporter's Cantonese interpreter), Feng's influence on Ding before the kidnapping, and doubts Shen expressed to Ding about her affair, see *Ji Ding Ling xuji*, pp. 138–46, 164–66, 177–78, 181, 186–88. Ding Ling, for her part, may have mocked Shen's pursuit of Zhang Zhaohe (p. 185). The book reveals that Shen's relationship with Ding was getting somewhat frayed toward the end. All this, and the letters Shen quotes from, give the book the ring of truth. Smedley's account is in *Battle Hymn of China*, pp. 115–20.

58. Literary evidence: "San ge nüxing," *WJ* 5: 290–91, 293, 297. This edition, more thoroughly than previous editions, deletes (1) Xuanruo as the name of the Shen persona, replacing it with "X X"; (2) Mengke as the name of the leftist (probably the X's at the bottom of *WJ* 5: 290—or "Mengke X X," in the Kaiming ed.—should be "Mengke *beibu*" [Mengke's arrest], or "Mengke *shizong*" [Mengke's disappearance]); and (3) references to "Shanghai, Nanjing" and to "Nanjing," which *WJ* replaces with "X X." *WJ* 5: 291 should read "Heifeng [Zhang Zhaohe] was probably thinking of events past, from two years ago at the seashore, and about her fiancé. On business in Shanghai and Nanking, he was going about everywhere, braving the heat. She fell silent." (The story later makes a connection between this and Mengke's predicament. The heat of Jiangnan contrasts with previous images of green coolness at Qingdao.) Another altered phrase, in *WJ* 5: 297, originally read: "The telegram was sent from Nanking...." *WJ* also deletes a passage that says Xuanruo invited Mengke to come to Wusong to meet Heifeng. The original text is in *Xin shehui banyuekan*. I analyze the story in more depth below.

The fact that Shen joined in the 24 May Shanghai protest telegram to Nanking (see note 55) might be further evidence that he was in Shanghai by the end of May, although he could have telegraphed his consent. Shen's 25 May article written for the *Duli pinglun* might have been written in Shanghai and mailed to Peking; that would explain why it was not printed until June. "Ting Ling Murdered!," *China Forum* 2, no. 8 (14 July 1933), says that popular convictions that Ding was dead "ripened into a virtual certainty when local [Shanghai] Chinese papers on June 28 reprinted a piece of anonymous correspondence published in the Tientsin *Ta Kung Pao* on June 25. This uncredited report stated that Ting Ling was killed sometime during the early morning of June 15, six hours after the murder of Ma Chao-wu in front of a Settlement brothel." That report is "Ding

Ling yi bei qiangju, Ma Shaowu bu Ding hou ji yu tongju," Tianjin *DGB*, 25 June 1933, p. (1) 3.

59. "*Ji Ding Ling nüshi* ba" (pub. 23 Sept. 1933), *WJ* 11: 28–32, implies that Ding Ling might very well have already been executed. It also mentions that the man who had been living with Ding Ling the last two years was reported to be the man who betrayed her.

60. *Ji Ding Ling* appeared in *GW* 10, nos. 29–39 (24 July–2 Oct. 1933). What later became *Ji Ding Ling xuji* was printed without pause as a continuation, in *GW* 10, nos. 40–50 (9 Oct.–18 Dec. 1933). The date-and-place line for the second volume, "Completed in Peking, 13 Dec. 1933," is in the reprint, *Ji Ding Ling xuji* (pub. 1940).

61. I raise these seemingly obvious points because some have evidently suggested that Shen wrote his reminiscences to profit from Ding Ling's disappearance. L. Insun (1938) spoke with Ding Ling in Yan'an about people who profited during Ding's captivity by putting out collections of her works. The editor says that a paragraph about Shen Congwen has been excised, since Shen has never done such a thing. Ding Ling has denounced *Ji Ding Ling* as "bad fiction" in recent years, as at a 1981.xi.16 Columbia University seminar, but I never heard her accuse Shen of having profited from her predicament.

62. The 25 June Tianjin article and Shanghai reprints said that Ding Ling went over to the government and became Ma Shaowu's lover. Continues the *China Forum*, without comment, in "Ting Ling Murdered!," "The [anonymous] writer avoids mentioning who killed Ting Ling or how she was killed but seeks to leave the inference that she was killed by Ma's fellow-gangsters in revenge." The author of the *DGB* piece may well have "dished the dirt" so heavily as to lessen his or her credibility. But at some point in 1933 someone—Zhang Tiesheng, Shen thinks, a KMT reporter for a Tianjin newspaper—reported the truth: that Ding Ling was alive and living under government auspices with Feng Da. Int. 1981.vii.17. Depending on whether it was implied that Ding was under house arrest or had submitted willingly, this might have made Ding Ling look equally villainous: wedded to a man who informed on leftists at a time when leftist writers were still disappearing.

63. Friends in China say they think pressure from Ding's attacks may have contributed to Shen's 1949 suicide attempt (not that she was the only one). From 1979 until her death in 1986, Ding Ling was again so powerful that fear that she *might* object caused official organs in China not only to deny permission for the reprinting of certain of Shen's works, but to deny Chinese scholars permission to include in their lists of Shen Congwen's works (as a tentative expression of personal opinion) any work of uncertain authorship that had been claimed by Ding Ling. At Columbia,

1981.xi.16, Ding Ling said that she had never read *Ji Ding Ling* until two years before, when a Japanese gave her a copy. So much for her credibility on this issue. I can suggest some possible reasons for why Ding Ling hated *Ji Ding Ling*, but I am not satisfied that they fully explain her vindictive attitude.

First, *Ji Ding Ling*, though the fullest and most sympathetic account of her written before Liberation, certainly does not show Ding Ling as she would have depicted herself. Shen shows Hu and Ding as having entered the revolution partly out of naïveté, and Ding as insensitive to Hu's danger on the eve of his arrest. The reminiscence talks of Ding Ling's love life, compares her to Mme. Bovary (*Xuji*, p. 164), and shows her going into leftist politics under the influence of her lovers. First came Hu Yepin; then came someone else (Feng Xuefeng?). (At least *Xuji*, p. 163, can be read this way, perhaps in the second case referring to her entry into Party activities.) Shen depicts Ding Ling just before her capture as fat, friendless, depressed, even a little demoralized. (And perhaps she was. In the less censored *GW* ed., Shen defends revolutionary activities of Hu and Ding he didn't agree with himself. *Ji Ding Ling*, pp. 177–78, even voices their argument against liberalism in literature.)

Second, in describing Ding's political activities with Hu Yepin, Shen may have unwittingly shown her as a partisan of Li Lisan and his line, thus making the reorganized Communist Party of 1931–35 (under the Russian-returned student faction) less likely to come to her rescue, or somehow bringing her trouble with the Maoist leadership later on. Shen cited this as a key factor in int. 1981.i.16, adding that "'Lisan! Lisan!' was always on her lips." Shen then knew nothing about divisions within the CCP; maybe Ding Ling wasn't too clear about them herself.

Third, experts on Shen in China say that Ding Ling may have chiefly disliked Shen's condescending passages about Feng Da. There Ding Ling was with Feng, feeling guilty to begin with, and Shen had written how much she needed Hu Yepin again (*Xuji*, pp. 181–82), implying that Ding happened on Feng Da out of fatigue, that Feng was a "hothouse" stifling her (pp. 165–66), etc.

Possibly Shen in his haste made some minor errors in names and places, or even changed some (e.g., addresses of safe houses) to "protect the innocent," as he implied he did when writing *Ji Hu Yepin* (*Ji Ding Ling xuji*, p. 172). Errors or cover-ups could have backfired and later given Ding Ling's enemies ammunition to attack her, but no more than the truths about Ding Ling he told, and certainly no more than Ding Ling's actions known directly to the CCP after 1936. Ding Ling's foes preferred juicier and more spurious "sources": her early fiction and the mosquito press.

64. After Ding Ling turned up in Yan'an, Shen felt free to mention having visited her at her Nanking place of captivity, "half a year" after her

arrest, as I read the slightly ambiguous "Ji Cai Weilian nüshi" (June 1939), *WJ* 10: 73. That would be Nov. or Dec. 1933, just when Shen was on his way south to Fenghuang. This article has not generally been known in China, and may be the only mention of the visit in print. I had a mutual friend ask Shen about this in Peking in the spring of 1985. Shen, as usual, did not admit to any 1933 visit. But his wife was present when my friend quizzed them, and it came out that Shen had visited Ding and Feng Da in the spring of 1935; Zhang Zhaohe had gone with him. Always trusting written evidence above all, I tentatively conclude, then, that Shen may have seen Ding Ling twice (or more)—at the turn of 1934, going to or from Hunan, *and* in the spring of 1935, when both Shens were traveling from Peking to Suzhou. All this opens up a whole new world of explanations for the Ding-Shen feud. Perhaps Ding Ling blamed Shen for not rescuing her, or even thought him a witting or unwitting co-conspirator in removing her from her dangerous revolutionary life, since he did not agree with her activities. For all anyone knows, Shen may have been involved in a deal having to do with Ding's life. Any conclusion not based on all the facts could be highly misleading. Shen and Ding were in such danger that it is hard to think of any act either of them might have perpetrated at the time that could not be forgiven. A minor charge against Shen made by Ding, which Shen does not refute, is that he did not visit her mother when he returned to Hunan (1933-34 and 1937). (Columbia seminar, 1981.xi.16; Insun, p. 42.) But Shen might have been too ashamed to face Ding's mother, either because he did not like the Ding Ling he saw in Nanking, or because he and Ding had deceived the old woman on their previous trip to Hunan; see *Ji Ding Ling xuji*, pp. 121-34. Also, it might have been dangerous. In late 1933, Hunanese local authorities were suspicious that Shen was a leftist. "*Sanwen xuanyi* xu," *WJ* 11: 85.

Shen also made a rare, not very charitable mention of Ding Ling right after she resurfaced in Yan'an. He concluded a whimsical sketch about "fatsos" in Chinese literature with a sudden and unexpected reference to Ding: "Lao She is the ideal imagined fatso for those who don't know him, but Ding Ling is a real fatso among the women writers." "Wenxue zuojia zhong de pangzi" (4 Dec. 1936), pub. 1 Jan. 1937. This may imply that she was living very well. It could indicate disappointment with Ding Ling's sudden rejoining of the Communist movement. Just as likely, though, Shen might have come to dislike Ding Ling personally for, e.g., not properly looking out for her family before seeking greener pastures. (Such a reason allegedly later estranged Shen from a close male friend.) In any case, Shen continued to praise Ding Ling's importance in modern literature, as in "Baihuawen wenti," *Zhu xu*, p. 80, and "Xin de wenxue yundong yu xin de wenxueguan," p. 61.

65. The last half of *Ji Ding Ling xuji* was likely written in Nov. and

Dec. 1933. Probably Shen had not yet visited Ding in Nanking, but by then he might well have heard that she was alive and with Feng Da. This might explain his moderate depiction of Feng Da, as a person not so very *evil* as to call into question Ding's judgment in falling in love with him, though not really worthy of her. If Shen wrote the final chapters to shock Ding Ling to her senses and wean her away from Feng Da, that might explain Ding Ling's anger about the book. Evidently Ding Ling was permitted to read, write, and even leave her house during her peculiar detainment, so she might well have been permitted to read Shen Congwen's reminiscences of her.

66. "Jinshu wenti" (28 Feb. 1934), *WJ* 12: 329; "Lun dujing" (7 Jan. 1935), *WJ* 12: 342.

67. "Lun dujing," *WJ* 12: 342. "Jinshu wenti," *WJ* 12: 332.

68. "Lun dujing." See also "Quan ren dujing" (Oct. 1933), *WJ* 12: 320–21; "Cong 'xiaoxue dujing' dao 'dazhongyu wenti' de ganxiang." Quotations from "Jin ze" (Apr. 1935), *WJ* 12: 345, 347. See also *Hunan sheng zhi*, 1: 691–92.

69. Shen alludes to "ruling the nation with Confucianism" in "Jin ze"; in "Lun dujing" he zeroes in on misuse of what happen to be the four virtues extolled in the New Life movement. See also his letter of 20 Mar. 1935, in *WJ* 12: 28–29. Subsequently Shen attacked the New Life movement in *Chang he*. Contemporaneous with the movement was "Xin yu jiu," *WJ* 6: 250–60; that it is not just about abstract morality is suggested by Shen's submission of it to *Duli pinglun* rather than a fiction magazine. Shen confirmed that the story was indeed a critique of the New Life movement in int. 1980.vi.20.

70. Executioner relative: int. 1981.i.16. Ritual beating of the executioner was a real custom, attested to by the magistrate of Yuanzhou. See Rev. Kevin Murray, C.P., "So This Is Yuanchow," *The Sign* 3, no. 1 (Aug. 1923): 42. Shen says so too, in "Ershi niandai de Zhongguo xin wenxue," *WJ* 10: 327. The schoolteachers in this story may be partly modeled after Fenghuang teachers executed during the KMT "Party purification." See *WJ* 9: 314–15.

71. Amulets: "Fengya yu suqi," *Feiyou cundi*, p. 39. Recording: "Duanpian xiaoshuo," *WJ* 12: 114. On Shen's idealism, see Kinkley, "Vision," pp. 179–83. Socrates, i.e. Plato, recommended: "Gei mou zuojia," *Feiyou cundi*, p. 50. Also "Sugeladi tan Beiping suoxu" (Socrates discusses what Peking needs; 1948). Writing from emotions "just like religious ones": "*Lixia ji* tiji," *WJ* 11: 34.

72. Logic textbook: Jin, "Lingling suisui." One KMT source remembers Shen as "absorbing himself" in the works of Plato; Jing Xin, "Shen Congwen qiren" (1968). Ironies of existence: The plot twists in many of Shen's 1930's stories seem not just Maupassantian, but representative of

"fate." E.g., "Shan dao zhong," *WJ* 6: 236–49; or "Guisheng." French Symbolism: Lee, p. 22. Some reprinted "Nightmares" are in *WJ* 10: 83–125.

73. "Exercises": "*Congwen xiaoshuo xizuo xuanji* daixu," *ZZ*, pp. 118–24. Lack of "thought": He Yubo, 2: 142.

74. "Ba jun tu," *WJ* 6: 168–94. In int. 1980.vi.27, Shen said his title was simply inspired by the eight fine horses of King Mu of Zhou, not by any of several historical "portraits" actually painted after the same subject. "Ba jun tu" was written at Qingdao in 1933, according to letter 1985.vi.14, and published in a Shanghai paper, according to "Shuiyun." That would be just before Shen's marriage. Yet "Ba jun tu" was first published in a major forum only two years later, in *Wenxue* 5, no. 2 (1 Aug. 1935): 293–307. These complications may explain the confusing statements in "Shuiyun," *WJ* 10: 275–76.

75. Shen speaks of authors as "healers of the personality" in "Gei mou jiaoshou," *Feiyou cundi*, pp. 18–19. Many of his letters in this book make seemingly probing analyses of the addressee's psychology.

76. Int. 1980.vi.21.

77. Confession: "Shuiyun," *WJ* 10: 275. Shen felt that Wen Yiduo was sexually frustrated because he had a countrified wife, so Professor A, though a physicist, might represent Wen. Cheng Yingliu reminisced to Shao Huaqiang that relations between Shen and Wen were tense during the war. Liang Shiqiu might be Professor E, or D, who admires self-control. (See Gálik, p. 298, on Liang's views about the need for internal checks in morality and literature.) The liberated woman is said to be modeled after Yu Shan, a Qingdao University social butterfly, wife of Zhao Taimou (who would be G). Xu Zhimo is said to have warned Ms. Yu, at Qingdao, to rein herself in, unaware that Wen Yiduo was already taken with her. So I think Dashi may have some of Wen in him, too. Identifications by Shao Huaqiang, letter of 1985.xi.3. "San ge nüxing," *WJ* 5: 281–99. Identifying these characters is easier in the original edition; see note 58, above. Pujing is only 23–24, but Ding Ling was originally thought to be younger (b. 1907–8) than she was (b. 1904). See Zhao Yansheng, in Schyns, p. 19 (says 1907). Ding Ling's real age was closer to that of Shen's character Rurui. See note 87 below.

78. In Kinkley, "Vision," pp. 358–59, and in my *Bian cheng* entry for the European Project on Chinese Literature encyclopedia, I argued that there is Freudian symbolism in *Bian cheng*. Confirmation of this came in int. 1980.vi.27, and I went on to question Shen about some specific passages. He confirmed Freudian symbolism in the passages quoted here and denied it in the case of the sparrows going into nests (hence deleted here); that was "just country folks' way of talking, which city people wouldn't understand." To continue Shao Huaqiang's account of how Shen learned

about Freud (letter of 1982.vii.1; see Chapter 4 for Shen's discovery of Freud): Shen remembers, after reading Zhang Dongsun in 1929–30, enthusiastically learning of psychological theories at Qingdao University (1931–34), through Zhu Guangqian and Gao Juefu. Zhu wrote a book called *Biantai xinlixue* (*Abnormal Psychology*). Gao translated Freud's first 27 lectures at Clark University as *Jingshen fenxi yinlun* (*Introduction to Psychoanalysis*; Shanghai: Shangwu, Nov. 1933); seven more lectures appeared as *Jingshen fenxixue xinbian* (*New Materials on Psychoanalysis*; Shanghai: Shangwu, 1936); and there also appeared *Shi meng* (*The Interpretation of Dreams*; 1934). Shen was hazy but generally remembered the books and particularly the authors and translators; of course he probably was influenced by *talking* to Zhu Guangqian at Qingdao (as often happened), and he might have read Gao's translations in periodicals, before the books were published. Certainly Shen read Freud's own works in Chinese translation before the war. He also remembers a translation by Dong Qiusi (his good friend) of R. Osborn, *Freud and Marx*, but that was only printed, under the title *Jingshen fenxi yu bianzheng weiwulun* (*Psychoanalysis and Dialectical Materialism*), in 1940, by Xin Zhongguo Shuju. It was also Shao who discovered Shen's friendship with Lu Zhiwei (see Chapter 4). During his early Qingdao years, Shen must have learned much from Lu. Perhaps it was Shen, a journal co-editor, who reported on Lu in *Xiaoshuo yuekan* 1, no. 3 (15 Dec. 1932): 210. (Lu Zhiwei was a poet during the May Fourth movement.) The *Bian cheng* quotations are from *WJ* 6: 105, 122–23. Wildflowers: the red saxifrage (*huercao*, "tiger's ear grass," pp. 133, 136, 138, 145) seems to be the "red grass with tiger stripes" in *Fengzi, WJ* 4: 335.

79. "Chun," *WJ* 4: 266–79; "Ruomo yisheng," *WJ* 4: 280–99; "Bohan," *WJ* 6: 298–309; "Disi," *WJ* 3: 92–113.

80. "Ruomo yisheng," *WJ* 4: 295, itself makes the connection to an incident in the narrator's life. But this is none other than an incident in Shen's own life, told in the autobiographical "Laike," *WJ* 6: 195–201.

81. "Zisha," *WJ* 6: 310–21. Shen explains his point about *jingya* to Wu Mi in "Gei mou jiaoshou," *Feiyou cundi*, p. 15. Talk of *jingya* is omnipresent in Shen's works. The parallels between Liu and Shen himself are (1) beautiful wife; (2) loss of attraction (see below); (3) one child, a baby; (4) professor; (5) holds forth on *jingya* and love; (6) writes late into the night, worrying his wife, as in the story "Zhufu" [1], below. A substantial set of coincidences.

82. "Zhufu" [1], *WJ* 6: 334.

83. On the need for control in one's life, see "Yi zhou jian gei wu ge ren de xin," *Feiyou cundi*, pp. 3–4; and a love letter that says people are slaves; some are slaves to a leader, but I am a slave to you, whether you love me or not (to Zhang Zhaohe?): "Feiyou cundi," 1 (June 1931). But when Professor D of "Ba jun tu" (the Liang Shiqiu persona) argues for self-control in the matter of sex, he is implicitly refuted.

84. "Zhufu," *WJ* 6: 331; "Zhu xu," *WJ* 11: 277.
85. "Wang Xie zidi" (1937), *WJ* 6: 381–404; "Pingfan gushi" (1930), *WJ* 6: 50–68; "Daxiao Ruan" (1935), *WJ* 6: 362–80. According to Dong Yi, p. 61, n. 28, Little Ruan is modeled after the leftist writer Pan Mohua. Prince, p. 379, instead sees a reference to the poet Ruan Ji (210–63) and his elder brother's son, Ruan Xian. The idea of the story is reminiscent of Lao She's "Black Li and White Li."
86. "Huchu" (1931), *WJ* 4: 149–75; "Laike" (1933), *WJ* 6: 195–201; "Deng" (1929; revised for Zhang Zhaohe in the 1931 ed.), *WJ* 4: 23–45. Even here, the lamp could be a Xu Zhimo or Tagorean symbol of the radiance of a life.
87. "Sheng" (1933), *WJ* 5: 304–10. "Jing" (1932), *WJ* 4: 256–65. Hsia, *A History*, pp. 208–11. "Rurui," *WJ* 5: 252–80, was written in June 1933, as was "San ge nüxing." "Rurui" ends: "He loved her, and felt that he truly had loved her."
88. Buddhist symbolism: "Qingse yan" (1946). Explicit pantheism: "Qianyuan" (1940?), *WJ* 11: 284. "Shuiyun," *WJ* 10: 287–88, 290. Int. 1980.xii.13: "Later on I became a pantheist. I believed in nature. God (*shen*) was not with the ghosts, but with beauty. [It's that which] gives people a feeling of solemnity. So it's all right to call me a theist." Jatakas: *Yuexia xiaojing*, *WJ* 5: 42–43, 58–190. See Prince, pp. 338–48. "Knowledge": "Zhishi" (1934), *WJ* 6: 292–97; Prince, pp. 383–84. On Life: "Xiaoshuo zuozhe he duzhe," *Zhu xu*, pp. 90–92. "Qianyuan," *WJ* 11: 282–87 (Life as a flame, p. 284). "Shengming," *WJ* 11: 294–96. Poems written under the pen name "Yongyu": "Shengming" (1940); "Kan hong" (1941).
89. "Xiaoshuo zuozhe he duzhe," pp. 90–94.
90. *Ibid.*, p. 84.
91. "Zhu xu," *WJ* 11: 277. Mathematics and music: "Zhu xu," *WJ* 11: 278. Kant says this in the *Critique of Judgment*. On Shen's love of music, see Chapter 1, note 51. "Xiang shang": "Xiaoshuo zuozhe he duzhe," p. 84.
92. *ZZ*, pp. 88, 104. "*Congwen xiaoshuo xizuo xuanji* daixu," *ZZ*, p. 121.
93. Bergson: int. 1980.xii.13. In *Fengzi*, *WJ* 4: 308–9, the "X X philosophy" the young man studies must be Buddhist philosophy, for it has taught him the maxim about the lotus. Shen on Xu: "Youqing" (1981), *WJ* 10: 253–58. See also "*Congwen xiaoshuo xizuo xuanji* daixu," *ZZ*, p. 123: "I have taken from him a fire...."
94. To Xu Zhimo (unlike Shen Congwen), the idea of life as a burning flame, for instance, might not just have had overtones of Tagore but of Walter Pater. Anglophile Xu was well read in the Decadents. His journal *Xinyue* was partly modeled after *The Yellow Book*.
95. This is not to imply that Proust influenced Shen. Shen says he had not read Proust (in translation) in the 1930's; letter 1985.vi.14.
96. "San ge nüxing," *WJ* 5: 290, would clearly identify Heifeng [Zhang

Zhaohe] as the Fengzi who spoke by the seashore in "a previous novel" written by Heifeng's fiancé, had not the *WJ* edition replaced the two characters "Fengzi" with "X X." The middle-aged Qingdao gentryman, however, is entirely made up, not patterned after any real person; letter 1985.vi.14.

97. *Fengzi, WJ* 4: 346, 347, 348. Ch. 10 of *Fengzi* speaks still more clearly of the presence of God everywhere, and the danger that people will try to make gods of political leaders, but this chapter was penned only in 1937. Stars are explained as symbols of human beings, whose souls are isolated by the vast "distances" between people.

98. Cited in Bloom, p. 8.

99. David Kidd, preface to his translation of "After Rain" (*East-West Review* 3, no. 2 [Summer 1967]): 183.

100. A charge leveled at Japanese autobiographical writers; see Chambers.

Chapter Seven

1. "*Sanwen xuanyi* xu," *WJ* 11: 84. Written slowly: int. 1980.xi.12. In int. 1980.vii.24 I asked Shen why the novel was so idyllic and he responded that it was set in the early Republic, before social divisions became so intense.

2. Old Zhen'gan: *Fengzi*, ch. 5, *WJ* 4: 329–31; also *ZZ*, pp. 1–3. The Miao lord: *Fengzi*, pp. 333, 341.

3. *Fengzi, WJ* 4: 340–44. Roots: int. 1980.vi.20.

4. *Fengzi, WJ* 4: 366–72.

5. Xiaozhai, *WJ* 7: 180–202. Map 38 in the *Xiangxi zizhizhou dituce*, printed by the Zhou Revolutionary Committee about 1979, shows a Xiaozhai up in the hills about 10–15 miles northeast of Wangcun (now Taiping). It is near the top of the tallest peak in the area, Dengzhanta (elev. 1034 m.), in Yongshun county.

6. Xiaozhai, *WJ* 7: 182.

7. Int. 1980.vi.27. "*Sanwen xuanyi* xu," *WJ* 11: 83–85.

8. "*Sanwen xuanyi* xu," *WJ* 11: 84–85. The omitted chapter, "Teng Huishengtang jinxi," is printed with the rest of *Xiang xing san ji* in *WJ* 9: 320–27.

9. *Xiang xing san ji, WJ* 9: 254.

10. Ibid., pp. 281–84.

11. "*Sanwen xuanyi* xu," *WJ* 11: 84–85. Hints and premonitions in *Xiang xing san ji* appear, for instance, in *WJ* 9: 240. Roads: *Hunan sheng zhi*, 1: 697–98. Railroad: Kirby, pp. 197–99. West Hunan's ores were one target of developers. For Chen Quzhen's battles against He Long, see *Hunan sheng zhi*, 1: 608–15, 702–6.

12. *Xiang xing san ji, WJ* 9: 277.

13. Ibid., pp. 326–27. The original text is inconsistent about the number

of opium paraphernalia shops. "Black merchandise" in the 1930's was a euphemism specifically for opium, not contraband in general.

14. *Jiaofei zhanshi*, 5: 851–52. Letter of V. Rev. Quentin Olwell, C.P., *The Sign* 14, no. 7 (Feb. 1935): 416; Olwell, "Communists at Our Gates," *The Sign* 14, no. 9 (Apr. 1935): 546–47; Rev. Raphael Vance, C.P., "Sidelights of Supu," *The Sign* 14, no. 10 (May 1935): 607–8. *Hunan sheng zhi*, 1: 702–4. Dai: int. 1980.xi.15. See *Xiangxi*, *WJ* 9: 412. I received a fivepage biography of Dai Jitao (1891–1976), taken from an early draft of an as-yet-unpublished Fenghuang gazetteer compiled in Fenghuang in the 1980's. It confirms these details and says that Dai wrote articles on Chen Quzhen and about the expeditions against He Long, plus a piece entitled "Recalling He Jian's Establishment in West Hunan of Factories for the Manufacture of Morphine."

15. *Jiaofei zhanshi*, 5: 852–53. Chen's retreat: Letters of Rev. Raphael Vance, C.P., to Rev. Theophane Maguire, C.P., 1934.xii.23, 1935.i.3 (Passionist Eastern Provincial Archives).

16. Roads: Rev. Gregory McEttrick, C.P., to Rev. Theophane Maguire, C.P., 1936.viii.3. Troop estimate: McEttrick (at Yongsui) to Maguire, 1935.iii.10.

17. McEttrick to Maguire, 1935.iii.10, reports "Talk galore that there is the making of a first-class civil war in our midst unless Chen knuckles down and falls in line with the regular government army program. But he is an old-time warlord and it is proving difficult for him to change over to this Min-Kuo [Republic of China] idea."

18. *Chang he*, *WJ* 7: 102. Li Zhenyi, p. 64, similarly praises Chen Quzhen's decision to step down.

19. Int. 1980.vi.20, 1980.xi.14. Confirmed during interviews with elders at the Shanjiang Miao commune, Fenghuang county, 1980.viii.17.

20. For details, see Kinkley, "Vision," pp. 377–87. In *Xiangxi*, *WJ* 9: 399, Shen blames the rebellions on "outside corruption getting together with local bullies." The revision replaces a veiled phrase about the rebellions being the aftermath of the local leader's retirement with an explicit reference to Chen Quzhen being "oppressed" into retiring "by He Jian." Shen also claimed (p. 415) that many gangs were really border people from neighboring provinces. See also "*Sanwen xuanyi* xu," *WJ* 11: 85–86. Xenophobia: Li Zhenyi, p. 32. Transfers blamed: *Chang he*, *WJ* 7: 102.

21. Kinkley, "Vision," pp. 374–77, 380. Also *Hunan sheng zhi*, 1: 714–15. Sheng Xiangzi, "Zuijin," p. 56, says, euphemistically, that Liu Jianxu overemphasized military administration.

22. Reorganization and disarming of Chen's troops: letter of Rev. Gregory McEttrick, C.P., to Rev. Theophane Maguire, C.P., 1935.iv.13. Troops sent to Zhejiang: *Jiaofei zhanshi*, 5: 853; *Chang he*, *WJ* 7: 103; int. 1980.xi.14.

23. Letter of Rev. Gregory McEttrick, C.P., to Rev. Theophane Maguire, C.P., 1935.iv.13. Chen Quzhen's post: Sheng Xiangzi, "Zuijin," p. 56.

24. Sheng Xiangzi, "Zuijin," p. 61; McEttrick to Maguire, 1936.viii.3. According to a 1980.viii.18 supplementary deposition prepared by Fenghuang seminar participants the day after my trip to Shanjiang (hereafter referred to as the "Extra Materials"), Song Yuncheng (Song Lianquan), the chief 1936 rebel, was a *tun* granary head (and former officer of Chen Quzhen with a score to settle, according to Sheng Xiangzi) who had no family (or other?) relationship with Long Yunfei, the rebel leader of 1937.

25. Interviews at Shanjiang, 1980.viii.17. Int. 1980.vi.21, 1980.xi.15.

26. Kinkley, "Vision," pp. 378–79. For tax statistics, see Sheng Xiangzi, *Xiangxi Miaoqu*, p. 6. The fact that the demise of the old Miao leaders was intended was confirmed in Shanjiang interviews.

27. Sheng Xiangzi, "Zuijin," p. 62.

28. *Ibid.*, pp. 63–64.

29. Rev. Basil Bauer, C.P., "Beatings and Bandits," *The Sign* 16, no. 12 (July 1937): 738–40.

30. Zuo Qi, pp. 263–70; *Jiaofei zhanshi*, 5: 966. See also missionary letters in *The Sign*, Feb. and Mar. 1936, and *Chang he*, *WJ* 7: 27 (see note 95 below on how this passage was altered). Rev. Basil Bauer, C.P., "Beatings and Bandits," *The Sign* 16, no. 12 (July 1937): 739. Desertions from the Communists: Rev. Raphael Vance, C.P. (at Xupu) to Rev. Theophane Maguire, C.P., 1935.i.3.

31. Sheng Xiangzi, "Zuijin," pp. 59, 60. Shi Honggui, *Xiangxi Miaozu kaocha jiyao*, pp. 23–27, reprints the program.

32. Sheng Xiangzi, *Xiangxi Miaoqu*, pp. 4–5; Li Zhenyi, p. 31.

33. Li Zhenyi, p. 32. Li says Mayang did not fall. An informant at Shanjiang, 1980.viii.17, Wu Wende, said it did. See also Rev. Nicholas Schneiders, C.P., "Observations Under Fire," *The Sign* 17, no. 6 (Jan. 1938): 354–55; "Letters from Hunan," *The Sign* 17, no. 8 (Mar. 1938): 479–80; Rev. Gregory McEttrick, C.P., "Beating Off the Bandits" [Long Yunfei's son, at Yongsui], *The Sign* 18, no. 3 (Oct. 1938): 161–63; Rev. Cyprian Frank, C.P., "Chinese Pinpoint Etchings," *The Sign* 18, no. 6 (Jan. 1939): 355.

34. *Hunan sheng zhi*, 1: 758. Li Zhenyi, p. 64.

35. Lüjiaping: Rev. Cyprian Frank, C.P., "With the Bandits," *The Sign* 17, no. 8 (Mar. 1938): 478–79; the bandits told Father Frank they joined up to save their homes and families from destruction. Shen was very familiar with the town; int. 1980.xi.14. Lüjiaping and Taiping Creek still appear as place names in the *Xiangxi zizhizhou dituce*, map 23. Yuanling attack: *Xiangxi*, *WJ* 9: 360–61. "The bandits are the people": Gao Shukang. Shen called a bandit: "Mo cuoguo zhe qianzainanfeng de baoguo jihui" (early 1938), *WJ* 12: 363. The friend with whom Shen dined

may have been Wang Luyan, Shen vaguely recalls in letter 1985.vi.14. Reasons for writing *Xiangxi*: Li Zhenyi, "Preface" by Shen Congwen, pp. 2–3; "*Sanwen xuanyi* xu," *WJ* 11: 87; *Xiangxi*, *WJ* 9: 332; "*Chang he tiji*," *ZZ*, pp. 128–34. In his preface for Li Zhenyi, Shen says he wrote *Xiangxi* after going to Kunming, which in turn followed three months (elsewhere he says four) in Yuanling (beginning in Dec. 1937 or Jan. 1938). That would be about right; the book was first published serially, in the Hong Kong *DGB*, beginning 25 Aug. 1938. It would mean that he finished the book some time between April and August 1938. "*Sanwen xuanyi* xu," p. 86, says he *began* the book in the winter of 1937 (that would be in Changsha); that could still square with p. 88, which says he finished the book after going to Kunming. Prior to his stay in Yuanling, Shen taught briefly at Wuhan University (int. 1980.vi.27) and in Changsha.

36. "*Sanwen xuanyi* xu," *WJ* 11: 87–88. The name of Shen Yunlu's estate was homophonous with, but not identical to, his own name. The place served as a conference center for regional and touring central officials, army officers, and scholars. Letter: "Mo cuoguo zhe qianzainanfeng de baoguo jihui," *WJ* 12: 361–69. Letter 1985.vi.14 indicates that "Mo cuoguo" was addressed to potential rebels in general, none in particular, and says that *WJ* 12: 369 is mistaken in dating the piece "winter 1938"; it should be "early 1938." Shen also says he wrote "Mo cuoguo" after his meeting with Xu Teli (see below), which may imply Xu encouraged Shen to convey this message.

37. Assemblyman: int. 1980.vi.27; letter 1985.vi.14. At the Fenghuang seminars, 1980.viii.16, people said that Governor Zhang Zhizhong selected Shen and confirmed that Shen refused. They said a daughter of Xiong Xiling was chosen instead. The *Hunan sheng zhi*, 1: 774–76, lists Shen Congwen and one Xiong Zhi as assemblypersons for an Aug. 1939 Provisional Hunan Assembly. That would have been under Governor Xue Yue. Clearly Shen was not there; he was in Kunming from mid-1938 to 1945. Persuading Long Yunfei: int. 1980.vi.21, 1980.xi.14. Long Yunfei's victories: Extra Materials prepared by the Fenghuang seminar participants on 1980.viii.19.

38. Long's background: Wu Wende at Shanjiang, 1980.viii.17, with Wu Deyun and Wu Sancong. (Shanjiang commune is seated in old Zongbingying ["Brigade General's Battalion"], which formerly was Long Yunfei's headquarters.) Shen on Tian and Long: *Xiangxi*, *WJ* 9: 409–12. Int. 1980.vi.27, 1980.xi.14. (Tian Sannu was indeed a Gelaohui. That he was no relation of the Tian Xingshu clan: Fenghuang seminars, 1980.viii.16.) Long and gambling: Wu Wende.

39. Tun Offices: Wu Wende, 1980.viii.17; Extra Materials, 1980.viii.19; *Hunan sheng zhi*, 1: 741. The gazetteer, p. 741, n. 2, gives further unconfirmed details: that Long was a platoon commander in the West Hunan

armies in 1914, a commander of a mobile regiment in 1924, garrison headquarters commander for Fenghuang and Mayang in 1925, and head of the Tun Affairs army after 1928. Shen and most other sources are content to call Long a bandit-warlord-hero-brother and let it go at that. Long's slogans: Wu Wende et al. at Shanjiang; *Hunan sheng zhi*, 1: 741. On Wu Hengliang and Long's and Wu's alienation from the KMT: Extra Materials. (The Extra Materials are revisionist—relatively sympathetic to Long. They gloss over his resistance to Communism, noting only that Communists tried repeatedly to convert him, without success, so he ran off and committed suicide. The 1979 gazetteer is moderately revisionist. It says that Long "usurped" leadership of the rebellion against He Jian, but glosses over his subsequent anti-Communism.) On Long's resistance to Communism, see below. For the onetime official Communist view of Long as pariah, see Alley, pp. 23–24. Long Yunfei a sworn brother of He Long, "having his reasons": int. 1980.xi.14.

40. During the war Chen Quzhen was given a textile factory to run in Chongqing (where he could be watched): Fenghuang seminars, 1980.viii.16; interview with Rev. Cormac Shanahan, C.P., 1975.ix.12. Pacification: Li Zhenyi, pp. 14–15. Gu: Boorman, ed., 2: 242–43. Yushuwan was made into the seat of a new county, Huaihua, in order to provide stronger governance. Yongsui: Li Zhenyi, pp. 14–15.

41. Peck, pp. 391–92.

42. Most notorious of the professional bandits was "Peng [Chunrong] the Braying Donkey," who ludicrously called himself Commander of the Hunan-Hubei-Sichuan-Guizhou Border Anti-Japanese Guerrilla Forces. *Hunan sheng zhi*, 1: 793–95, 800–802; Li Zhenyi, pp. 14–17. KMT troops set loose: int. 1980.xi.15. There was also a famine in West Hunan in 1946. *Hunan sheng zhi*, 1: 819.

43. *Xiang xing san ji*, *WJ* 9: 316–17. See also *Xiangxi*, *WJ* 9: 399.

44. "Yi ge chuanqi de benshi" (1947), *WJ* 10: 155–56. One version of the story of the keys is in Wilson, p. 46.

45. "Yi ge chuanqi de benshi," *WJ* 10: 155–59. Int. 1980.xi.15, 1981.i.16. Shen praises Gu Jiaqi in *Xiangxi*, *WJ* 9: 412. Casualties: "Mo cuoguo zhe qianzainanfeng de baoguo jihui," *WJ* 12: 365–66. Shen Dieyu's men: "Dongjing," p. 22; this passage is close enough to Shen's other accounts of Jiashan that I take it to be factual. Shen Dieyu's body was dragged from the battlefield by his valet, the ruffian "Tiger Cub" (subject of Shen Congwen's "Huchu"); Huang Cunsheng, p. 17. Dieyu was later put to death, perhaps in the Cultural Revolution. Information on Dai and Xue is from Dai's biography in the unpublished 1980's Fenghuang gazetteer.

46. Int. 1980.vi.20, 1980.xi.14, 1980.xi.15, 1981.i.16. "Yi ge chuanqi de benshi," *WJ* 9: 150–51, 156–58.

47. Hsia, *A History*, p. 360.

48. *Chang he, WJ* 7: 15.
49. Chu, p. 17.
50. *Chang he, WJ* 7: 102. Unique information in a unique preface to "Qiu," *Wenju* 1, no. 3 (10 June 1942): 4, precisely sets the novel in Sept. 1936.
51. Int. 1980.vii.20.
52. *Chang he, WJ* 7: 25–29.
53. Ibid., pp. 56–57.
54. Ibid., p. 26. Confirmed identity of Chiang Kaishek, int. 1980.vi.20.
55. Ibid., pp. 88–89.
56. "*Chang he* tiji," *ZZ*, pp. 128–34.
57. Ibid., pp. 132–33. See the indication of an excision, *WJ* 7: 103. My suspicion that Shen tampered with the placement of what is now *Long River*'s last chapter comes from the preface to "Qiu," *Wenju* 1, no. 3 (10 June 1942): 4.
58. Int. 1980.vi.20. Shen makes nearly the same accusation in "Yi ge chuanqi de benshi," *WJ* 10: 156–57.
59. *Chang he, WJ* 7: 103. See the last line of ch. 4 of *Chang he, WJ* 7: 78: "It's people like them [from downstream Hunan] who think that all of us West Hunanese are bandits (*tufei*)."
60. Letter from Shen Congwen to Hu Shi, 16 Sept. 1944, in Shen Yunlong, ed., pp. 33–34.
61. Quotation: "Yi ge chuanqi de benshi," *WJ* 10: 157–58. Tian Junjian (1909–47), son of a Fenghuang merchant, narrowly escaped execution for his KMT activities in Fenghuang in 1927. He served in the West Hunan army from 1929 to 1933, then sought schooling in Changsha and entered the Whampoa Academy in 1936. He died in the Feb. 1947 KMT offensive against Chen Yi's troops in Shandong. From a Tian Junjian biography in the unpublished 1980's Fenghuang gazetteer. Tian identified in letter 1985.vi.14.
62. The most "patriotic" part of *Yunlu jishi*, on the Jiashan sacrifice, is not reprinted in *WJ* (it belongs after 7: 326). This section ends with the thought that maybe China has kept its "faith in being able to turn over a new leaf (*fanshen*)." "Yunlu jishi," Tianjin *Yishibao*, 1 Mar. 1947.
63. "Xiang cheng," *WJ* 11: 211–18.
64. From another piece of *Yunlu jishi* omitted from *WJ*: "Yunlu jishi," Tianjin *Yishibao*, 15 Mar. 1947. Biographical authenticity: letter 1985.iii.9.
65. "Dongjing," *Wenju* 2, no. 1 (8 Dec. 1943): 22–23.
66. "*Chang he* tiji," *ZZ*, p. 131.
67. *Xue qing, WJ* 7: 350–403. My "Shen Congwen and the Uses of Regionalism," p. 171, unfortunately repeats Shen's mistaken notion that the second story in the series, "Xue qing," was not published until Ba Jin rediscovered it among the confiscated manuscripts Ba got back after the

fall of the Gang of Four. Ba Jin did discover a text of "Xue qing" in a late 1940's book ms. that he never got to publish. But Shao Huaqiang has since learned that the story had in fact already been printed once, in Oct. 1946. Factuality; the Mans: int. 1980.vi.21. Factuality of "Chi yan," in toto: int. 1980.vi.20.

68. "Qiaoxiu and Dongsheng," trans. Gladys Yang, *Recollections of West Hunan*, p. 155 (*WJ* 7: 374).

69. "Qiaoxiu he Dongsheng," *WJ* 7: 374–75. Shen spoke of "the slow decomposition of society," *shehui manman de fenjie*, in int. 1980.vii.24.

70. "Zhu xu," *WJ* 11: 269, reprints a letter from an unnamed friend, probably at Yan'an (int. 1980.vi.20), inviting Shen to Shaanxi. Xu Teli: "*Sanwen xuanyi* xu," *WJ* 11: 86–87. Int. 1980.vi.21, 1980.vi.27. See also *Hunan sheng zhi*, 1: 743. Mao Dun's reminiscence mentions only a private meeting with Xu Teli in Changsha, 11 Oct. 1937. Mao Dun, *Huiyilu*, no. 21, *Xin wenxue shiliao* 1983, no. 4 (22 Nov. 1983): 17–18. Shen says his meeting with Xu Teli was during a second trip to Changsha; he had been there a few months before, to meet Wang Luyan. See the following note. Letter 1985.vi.14.

71. Int. 1980.vi.21; 1980.vii.23; letter 1985.vi.14 On Wang (d. 1944), who wrote fiction and was an Esperanto enthusiast, see Fan Boqun and Zeng Huapeng. The articles Shen wrote for Wang have not been found.

72. Sniping: "*Chang he* tiji," *ZZ*, p. 133. Three books: letter 1985.iii.9. Though *WJ* 10: 288 excises the reference, "Shuiyun," *Wenxue chuangzuo* 1, no. 5 (15 Feb. 1943): 59 mentions that *Yunlu Chronicles* was banned. *WJ* 10: 296 mentions a work "held up" three times. Delay of (Kaiming edition of) collected works: Yao Qingxiang. Art school: "Ji Cai Weilian nüshi," *WJ* 10: 73–76.

73. "Wenxuejie lianhe zhanxian suoyou de yiyi" (1936); "Wentan de 'tuanjie' yu 'lianhe.'" *Chabuduo*: "Zuojia jian xuyao yi zhong xin yundong" (1936); "Zai tan chabuduo" (1937). Shen did not directly mention Hu Shi, but he criticized leftist "movements," going with "the times," and imitative occasional writing such as the pieces that appeared after "the death of Gorky." (Shen wrote this six days after the death of Lu Xun.) In a 1980.xi.2 letter to me, Guo Moruo's sometime secretary Sun Xizhen remembered Shen's "*fan chabuduozhuyi*" (Sun added the *zhuyi*, or "ism") as an attack on leftism that was "uniformly" counterattacked (e.g., by the Beiping Writers' Association) in a "Fan 'fan chabuduo' zhuanhao" (Anti-'anti-about-the-same-itis' special number) of the "Wenxue xunkan" supplement to the *Beiping xinbao*. Sun added that Shen later left North China for the KMT areas. (But so did Guo Moruo.) See also Shao Huaqiang, "Cong 'fan chabuduo' kan."

74. *Zhanguoce*: int. 1980.vi.21. Shen says that the magazine was funded by Long Yun's economic supporter Miao Yuntai and Miao's Fudian Bank.

The CCP's smear of Shen as part of a "*Zhanguoce* clique" is a good example not only of illogical guilt by association, but also of turning black into white. (Qinghua historian Lei Haizong, a major target of the 1957 anti-Rightist purge, was called antisocialist and profascist, along with his "*Zhanguoce* clique." Any connection at all with the magazine was therefore cause for suspicion. Actually, since the magazine also wrote about government corruption, its "viewpoint," if it had one, is unclear.) The facts are that Shen published eight pieces in *Zhanguoce*, most notably a *criticism* of the *Zhanguoce* fascist Chen Quan's advocacy of Leader worship. The poet Zang Kejia, whose career Shen did so much to promote before Liberation, in a 1980.vi.26 Peking interview still repeated the lies about Shen and *Zhanguoce*. He said that Shen "worked with Chen Quan." (Zang also denied having ever known Kai-yu Hsu—but see *The Chinese Literary Scene*, pp. 187–96.) Shen on third parties: int. 1980.vii.23. "Fourth Party": interview with Jin Di, Flushing, New York, 1982.ii.6. Shen looked down on people who got into politics, Jin says, including perhaps Luo Longji. Probably so. Cheng Yingliu remembers that Shen said to him (in the late 1940's, well after Shen wrote "Ba jun tu") that Wen Yiduo got active in politics as a result of "sexual frustration." Courtesy Shao Huaqiang, letter of 1985.xi.3. It sounds like Shen.

75. Influenced by Freud and Joyce: int. 1980.vi.27. See also "Wo de xuexi," Hong Kong *DGB*, 20 Nov. 1951. Exactly how Shen absorbed elements of Joyce's style is unclear. So far as I know, Bian Zhilin and others had translated only small extracts of Joyce's work by the 1940's. But Shen was quick to acquire new ideas just from hearing about them and from perusing teaching materials prepared by his professor colleagues. About recent battles on behalf of modernist poetry, see William Tay, and Pan Yuan and Pan Jie. Shen on Bian: "Guanyu kanbudong," *WJ* 12: 334–39. "Gazing" and "Plucking": interview with Jin Di, 1982.ii.5. Jin says it was Shen's critics who conflated "Kan hong lu" and "Zhai xing lu" into one title. Later though, there was in fact a book called *Kan hong zhai xing lu*, Cheng Yingliu recalled to Shao Huaqiang. Cheng thinks it was published about 1945; Shen gave him a copy. All quotations from "Gazing at a Rainbow" cite "The Rainbow," trans. Ching and Payne, pp. 179–80. (Ching is Jin Di.)

76. "Shuiyun," discussed below, tells about women Shen loved besides his wife, and how he used *imagination* to put them into his works. In fact I count at least four "chance encounters" in the work. *WJ* 10: 271–72 discusses a woman Shen resisted by writing "Ba jun tu," possibly Yu Shan; she is not referred to as an *ouran* until p. 276. The woman Shen met at Xiong Xiling's house is discussed on pp. 275–79. The second and third *ouran* are on pp. 283–85 and 285–86. Finally, on pp. 290–93, an *ouran* (probably Gao Qingzi at Kunming) leaves; is she one of the previously

mentioned women? The confusion of references is part of what leads me to speculate that perhaps all the "encounters" are with a single woman who keeps turning up.

Shen was already widely known to have a "girlfriend" at Kunming in the 1940's (it was rumored that it was a physical relationship, but there is no proof), a young poet named Gao Qingzi (Gao Yunxiu) who worked at the Southwestern Union University Library. Naturally it was assumed that Shen put her into "Gazing at a Rainbow." (Zhang Zhaohe knew about her and even raised the subject with me once.) Shao Huaqiang has interviewed one of Gao's former roommates and discovered that Shen tutored Gao in writing at the Xiong Xiling house in Peking in the 1930's, and that she was already infatuated with Shen as a man and as a writer, long before they came together in Kunming. So Gao fits the description of one of the *ouran* in "Shuiyun," pp. 275–79. There are some discrepancies, but the woman in "Gazing at a Rainbow" wears a green silk gown, like the Peking *ouran* in *WJ* 10: 275–79. (Green symbolizes life; see "Lü yan.") Seashells mentioned in "Gazing" also suggest a link to Qingdao, 1933. I agree with Shao that Gao Qingzi seems doubly implicated as the woman in "Gazing," though the character could be a composite. I wrote the Shens asking about the *ouran* in "Shuiyun" and was simply told, in letter 1985.iii.9, "such a person did exist."

Jin Di says the room described in "Gazing at a Rainbow" was very familiar to him; it was in Shen's Kunming home. Jin talked to the Shens about this in 1982. Zhang Zhaohe said Shen would not let her read "Gazing at a Rainbow"! Jin asked Shen about the truthfulness of the story. "He just smiled. But his smile indicated there must be some truth in the story." Jin speculates that Shen *imagined* the girl being in his Kunming room with him. Jin Di reassured Mrs. Shen that the story might represent an author's fancy. She said, hopefully, "Maybe it's half true and half imagination." My thoughts exactly. Interview with Jin Di, 1982.v.2.

77. Sun Ling, p. 56. Jin Di, 1982.v.2, recalled Kunming newspaper attacks.

78. "Shuiyun," *WJ* 10: 287.

79. Besides *Zhu xu*, see the "Nightmare" series, in *WJ* 10: 83–125.

80. Shen makes his pacifism explicit in "Ershi niandai de Zhongguo xin wenxue," *WJ* 10: 327. In int. 1980.xii.13, he said "I was always a pacifist (*yi ge fanzhande*)" and went on to talk about the hypocrisy of people who said he didn't support the war effort against Japan. Antiwar sentiments in his works: "Lü yan" (pre-1943?), *WJ* 10: 87–88; "Chi yan" (Mar. 1945), *WJ* 7: 350–55. During the Civil War: "Dinghe [brother of Zhang Zhaohe] shi ge yinyuemi" (1946); "Xin feiyou cundi," no. 101 (1946); "Wusi" (1947); "Huanying Weidemai" (1947; an article recovered by Shao Huaqiang).

81. "Zaoshang—yi dui tu yi ge bing" (22 Mar. 1933), *WJ* 5: 311–14, is

identified by Dong Yi, p. 52, as being about resistance to Japan in the 1932 "Shanghai Incident." "Hei ye" (24 Sept. 1932), *WJ* 5: 384–94. "Guolingzhe" (22 Aug. 1934), *WJ* 6: 202–8. Last-named story: "Zhanzheng dao mou shi yihou" (May 1932), *WJ* 8: 459–67. Shen also complains about the silence over the loss of national territory in "Quan ren dujing." In int. 1980.xii.13, he spoke of using "new literature and philosophy to replace war for settling problems; armed force is not a way to settle things."

82. Jin Di, interview, 1982.ii.6, said that he, Jin, did most of the work for Shen's *Pingming* supplement and Yang Zhensheng's *Jingshi ribao* supplement. There was also a *Xiandai wenlu* or Contemporary Literature Series, edited by Yang Zhensheng, Shen Congwen, Zhu Guangqian, Feng Zhi, and Xu Ying, published in Beiping by Xin Wenhua Chubanshe. Its first collection was dated Dec. 1946. Shen's views: "Huanying Weidemai"; "Xin zhu xu" (renamed "Beiping de yinxiang he ganxiang" in *WJ* 10: 126–28); "Wenxue zhoukan kaizhang" (1946). China's demoralization before the fall: "Bianbian zuofeng" (1941), *WJ* 12: 370–73; "'Zhongguo wang hechu qu'" (1948); "Cong xianshi xuexi" (1946), *WJ* 10: 299–322; "Xin feiyou cundi," no. 101; "Tan kumen" (1946).

83. See "Shuiyun," *WJ* 10: 293–94, and the end of "Xin zhai xing lu" (1942).

84. Fu: int. 1980.vii.14. Shen shows the moral decay of wartime Free China harming postwar Peking especially in "Cong xianshi xuexi," *WJ* 10: 312–20.

85. "Sugeladi tan Beiping suoxu," *Lunyu* 147 (16 Feb. 1948): 1322. My translation is from a text recently revised by Shen (supplied by Shao Huaqiang), in which Shen expanded the part about students reporting on each other.

86. Hu Guisheng, pp. 26–28. Hu's information about West Hunanese resistance to Communism appears mostly credible in the specifics, though his commitment to his lost cause results in some exaggerations, e.g., a claim that the Long Yunfei homestead was destroyed. (Its ramparts still stood in Shanjiang in 1980.) Hu glosses over how many of the anti-Communist "heroes" were bandits, and accounts for Li Moan's villainy by saying that he was doing the bidding of General Cheng Qian, the penultimate KMT governor of Hunan, who tried to deliver his province to the Communists peacefully instead of making a last stand. Hu considers Cheng a traitor.

87. Hu Guisheng, pp. 27–32; *Hunan sheng zhi*, 1: 868–70; Dai Jitao biography in the unpublished 1980's Fenghuang gazetteer. Dai represented Fenghuang in legislative assemblies at Nanking and Changsha during the late 1940's; he was already retired from the military when Li Moan recalled him to negotiate with the rebels at Yuanling. Because the rebels resisted both the KMT and the CCP, historians of those two sides tell similar stories.

88. Hu Guisheng, pp. 33–40, 48–52. Land reform: *ibid.*, p. 139.

89. *Ibid.*, pp. 33-36, 41-44; on Wu Hengliang, pp. 107-8. Extra Materials prepared for me by the Fenghuang seminar, 1980.viii.19. Dai Jitao, too, took up symbolic provincial government posts in 1954 and 1964, after being "reeducated"; Dai biography in the unpublished Fenghuang gazetteer.

90. Hu Guisheng, pp. 45, 79, 82. The Extra Materials of 1980.viii.19 similarly say that Long Yunfei committed suicide. *Hunan sheng zhi*, 1: 741, says instead that he was killed by the masses during bandit pacification. Long not influenced by the KMT: int. 1980.xi.14. Shen volunteered this.

91. Long Enpu (who also participated in the 1937 anti-KMT rebellion, as letters in *The Sign* attest): Hu Guisheng, pp. 118-46. Tan Guoqing, son of a bandit, headed a gang of 300 in 1950 and escaped with his wife and a few dozen others. He resurfaced in the Dayong-Sangzhi-Yongshun border hills, an old no-man's-land. Zeng Xianyin. About 30,000: int. 1980.vii.20. Mostly Miao: int. 1980.xi.14. Hu Guisheng, pp. 94-96, claims that 30,000 were killed for resisting in Longshan.

92. Ma Fenghua, "Huainian Shen Congwen jiaoshou" (1963). I did not ask him about it, but I imagine Ma published his article at that time as an answer to officials in Taiwan who hated Shen Congwen for "helping the Communists." I got an earful of that kind of talk when in Taiwan in 1973-74. Asked about Ma Fenghua's article, Shen said it was "not completely reliable," int. 1980.xi.14. However, the details I repeat here were confirmed by other sympathetic informants. Premature obituary: Jing Xin.

93. To my knowledge Shen's last piece of major fiction was "Chuanqi bu qi," *WJ* 7: 382-403, written in Oct. 1947 and published a month later. Against control: "Jinri wenxue de fangxiang," minutes of the first forum of the Fangxiangshe, 7 Nov. 1948. (Ma Fenghua, a young economics major, was at this forum.) When Yao Qingxiang interviewed Shen, Shen broke precedent and openly criticized his student He Qifang for taking the political road.

94. Famine scrolls: "Zhongguo wenhua" page, *Shanghai wenhua* 5 (1 June 1946): 11. Shen's calligraphy was still highly prized in the 1980's. He gave away scrolls of his poems as gifts, and magazines reproduced his letters in the original script. Several of Shen's students were underground Communists even at Kunming, e.g., Chen Bulei's daughter; int. 1981.i.16.

95. A rare direct revelation of Shen's distaste for Communism is a passage in *Chang he* (1949 ed., pp. 22-23), which shows Communists harming honest people of means. In *WJ* 7: 27-28, the passage has been altered so that the CCP harms only a *bad* rich person. Since Shen was so tight-lipped about Communism, though, it is at best misleading to call him "anti-Communist," particularly if that term is understood in its usual pro-KMT sense. Shen's attitude, like many liberal intellectuals', was closer to "a

plague on both your houses," as his former Kunming colleague Wu Xiaoling put it (interview, 1980.vii.11). The passage in *Chang he*, for instance, goes on to say that the KMT came in and harmed the same people the CCP harmed. Most political references in the novel are anti-KMT.
Guo Moruo, "Chi fandong wenyi" (pub. 1 Mar. 1948). Guo could not have read the works of Shen's he criticizes. He evidently confuses Shen's "Yunnan kan yun," which is not at all erotic, with "Kan hong lu." See also Xia Yan (1948) and Feng Naichao. Shen called for an investigation of Wen Yiduo's assassination in "Huai Kunming," *WJ* 10: 137. I could not get Shen to identify the several people who tried to talk him into retreating with the KMT. Shen's letter to a student: Ma Fenghua, "Huainian," p. 13.
96. Ma Fenghua, "Huainian," pp. 13–14.
97. *Ibid.*, p. 14. Zhang Zhaohe's disagreements with Shen about the revolution are understandable. Though well educated, she had long played the role of a traditional wife. There was even a Communist martyr in her family, Zhang Zhang; int. 1981.i.24. On the dark side, a former student of Shen's says that ca. 1945–49 Zhang Zhaohe was disappointed with her husband for not being a better provider. There is some literary confirmation of this marital tension in "Zhufu" [2], *WJ* 7: 234–35. One researcher says that after 1949 Zhang contemplated divorcing Shen. However, unlike so many others in her circumstances, she did not go through with it, even though she might have felt unsure of Shen's fidelity during the war.
Zhang Zhaohe published half a dozen short stories, mostly in the Tianjin and Hong Kong *DGB*, under the pen name of Shuwen (confirmed in int. 1980.vi.20, 1980.vii.23). Evidently she also wrote a book, *Hupan*, published in Guilin during the war, by Wenhua Shenghuo Chubanshe. Her sons, Shen Longzhu and Shen Huchu, became factory workers (as did many other intellectuals' children).
98. Suicide: Ma Fenghua, "Huainian," p. 14; interviews with Wu Xiaoling, 1980.vii.11, and others. Chronology from telephone talk with Ma Fenghua, 1985.vii.23. Some say that Shen was fired from Peking University, but the "iron ricebowl" was already in effect, making it difficult to fire state employees. Wu Xiaoling says that Shen left voluntarily, and so do Wang Yarong and Wang Xu, "Shen Congwen and His Book on Ancient Costume," p. 28. Above all, Huang Yongyu, "Taiyang xia de fengjing," in *ZZ*, pp. 144–64, says that (1) Shen still lived at Peking University and was on the staff while being "remolded" at the Revolutionary University, and (2) Shen left Peking University two years before Huang's 1953 trip to Peking. In Hsu, *The Chinese Literary Scene*, p. 135, Shen says that his contract was renewed by Furen after it was reorganized as People's University. Peking University is mentioned, but how he left is vague. In this account, Shen says he "started research" on the palace relics in 1950. On how Wang Xu met Shen, see Xiao Li, "Shen Congwen xian-

sheng ersan shi." Also int. 1980.vii.4. (Shen's two assistants named Wang are not related.)

99. "Wo de xuexi" (1951). Shen jokes about "retreating to the second line" in "The Heart of the Dragon." According to Jia Shumei, Shen at some time "not long after Liberation" was sent down with a brigade to carry out land reform in Sichuan. Shen's mention of Rudin and Don Quixote in his confession echoes Turgenev's famous 1860 essay "Hamlet and Don Quixote," in which Hamlet represents wavering and Quixote strength. *Rudin* (originally trans. Zhao Jingshen, 1928) was and still is extremely popular in China.

100. Spence, p. 325. See Ding Ling, "Ji yi ge zhenshi ren de yi sheng" (1950). This was reprinted in a preface to Hu Yepin's collected works and, without any softening of the passages about Shen, in Ding Ling, "Yepin yu geming" (1980). Ma Fenghua, "Huainian," p. 16, says Ding Ling solicited an article from Shen for *People's Literature*. But, for whatever reason, Shen did not publish in that magazine until after Ding Ling was purged. Kaiming: int. 1980.vi.27. On the silence about Shen, see Chapter 5, note 2, above.

101. My listing of Shen's post-1949 works is not complete. Some works are already lost. Only about ten wood-cut editions of *Zhanguo qiqi* were ever made; int. 1980.vii.4. This book, and *Ming jin*, may not be extant. Wang Yarong, interview 1980.vi.20, supplementing her "Shen Congwen xiao ji," p. 49, says that Shen took over the major work (mostly on porcelain) of *Zhongguo gongyi meishu shi* when its editors, Luo Shuzi and Chen Zhifo, died, the former in the Cultural Revolution. Shen also worked on *Zhongguo de ciqi* (Beijing: Zhongguo caizheng jingji chubanshe, 1963); he wrote the preface. For other projects Shen contributed to, mostly anonymously, see Xiao Li, "Shen Congwen he ta de *Zhongguo gudai fushi yanjiu*," p. 30. Being an expert on historical dress, Shen often advises on costumes for historical movies. A Japanese delegation sought him out to authenticate the portrait of the Tang-era Sinophile Shōtoku Taishi on Japan's currency; Mo Lingping.

PPCC: Shen's speech appeared in *Guangming ribao*, 8 Feb. 1956. He wrote about what he saw at home in "Xin Xiang xing ji." I believe he did not return to Fenghuang again until the summer of 1982; Zhang Linglin. Shen could have "selected" Miao nationality for himself (as his elder brother selected "Tujia"), so as to become a delegate at the National People's Congress. However, he thought it was enough to be a member of the PPCC, so he selected "Han"; int. 1980.vi.20. Being a PPCC delegate gave him yearly vacations and some protection for his work. Most of his trips— and they continued right up until his 1983 stroke—were to major archaeological sites.

"Paolongtao" and "Yi dian huiyi, yi dian ganxiang," originally in *Renmin wenxue*, are reprinted in *WJ* 10: 205–16.

102. For encomiums, see Shen's speech (which is, however, more filled with self-criticisms), *Guangming ribao*, 8 Feb. 1956, and "Yi dian huiyi." CCP invitation: int. 1981.ii. Shen has not been invited since. The Hundred Flowers reissue is *Shen Congwen xiaoshuo xuanji* (1957). Nieh, pp. 117–19, assumes that an editor made the changes, but I think that Shen was quite capable of having made them himself.

103. Int. 1980.vii.4; 1980.xi.14; 1980.xii.13.

104. Reams: int. 1980.vi.27. Shen does not publish most of his poems; he gives them to close friends. At int. 1980.vii.12, he gave me one about Tang Taizong which he called "satirical." Written in the early 1970's, it communicates Shen's suffering in the Cultural Revolution and, he says, criticizes "people like Feng Youlan" who spun around in order to stay in political good graces. The poem I've translated is in *WJ* 10: 350–51. Mao's poem, with a translation, is in *Mao Zedong shici*, pp. 74–75.

105. The alternative version is among 16 poems in a 1962 letter from the Shens to the Frankels. Shen mentions that the prefaces couldn't be published due to "some taboos." Wu Han Shen's student: int. 1980.vi.21; 1980.vii.23.

106. Witke, p. 62. Toilets (women's, at the Historical Museum), cadre school, Huang history: Huang Yongyu, *ZZ*, pp. 158–61. Shen did write the preface to his Huang history, about 1970. It is now with the Huangs, unpublished for fear of "consequences." Int. 1980.vii.4; 1980.vii.17. Hsu, *The Chinese Literary Scene*, p. 139. Hsu's more private first draft, *Our China Trip*, p. 117, says that Shen "didn't participate in any physical labor at all." Eight raids: Xiao Li, "Shen Congwen xiansheng ersan shi," p. 37; interview with Ling Yu, Shao Huaqiang, Wang Xu, Wang Yarong, 1981.vii.18. Wang Yarong, and the criticizing artists: interviews with Wang Yarong, 1980.vi.20; 1980.vii.6; 1980.vii.8. Persecutions, research from memory: Xiao Li and Wang Yarong articles, int. 1980.vii.4.

107. House: interview with Wang Yarong, 1980.vii.25. Shen lived in the tiniest house from about 1971 to 1977, then in an only slightly larger one. He moved into his three-room "luxury" apartment some time around 1980. Truth to tell, he was reluctant to make the move—had to be pushed by a son who wanted the old house himself. Quotations from Hsu, *The Chinese Literary Scene*, pp. 131–33. The big book on costumes is *Zhongguo gudai fushi yanjiu* (1981). A panel of specialists in Hong Kong judged it to be a major advance in its field, though with some lacunae suggestive of China's long scholarly isolation; Liang Zhonghao. Zhou Enlai: int. 1980.vii.4; Wang Yarong, p. 49. For hints about continued interference in publishing, see Shen's Mar. 1980 letter to Ma Fenghua, photocopied and transcribed in Ma, "Chongwu," pp. 38–41.

108. Meng Xue, p. 37; int. 1980.vii.5, vii.24. The first film, directed by Xu Changlin in Shanghai (partly filmed in West Hunan), was not released, so far as I know. It lacked feel for the locality and had extraneous stories,

Shen says. It also made the wharfside people into "bad guys." (The second film deals with this problem by virtually ignoring Shunshun.) The second film was made by Peking Studios and directed by Ling Zifeng. Shen carefully worked over its screenplay; a page of it, reproduced in Feng Weicai, p. 28, shows that he tried to correct tiny ethnographic details. These movies are not to be confused with a third, called *Cuicui* (Hong Kong, 1950's).

109. A list of the often partisan criticisms about Shen Congwen that began to reemerge is provided by Xiao Xing. See also the four-sided debate on *The Frontier City* in *Shulin* 26 (1 Jan. 1984), Zhong Jihua, pp. 22–23, and Lin Qing. Shen does have powerful friends; Shen is the unnamed writer in Ba Jin's *Tansuo ji*, pp. 42, 46–47. The book whose publication was rescinded was a Chinese translation of Kinkley, "Vision," which has, however, now found a new publisher. The supra-ideological pride in Shen Congwen that was obvious to me as I talked to people in West Hunan is evidenced in Liu Yiyou, "Tao li bu yan," and Long Haiqing (a Miao), "Lue lun Miaozu zuojia Shen Congwen jiqi chuangzuo." After, and evidently only after, the spiritual pollution campaign passed, local pride surfaced again, as in Liu Yiyou's 1983 piece, printed in 1985. Now Gu Hua says he was influenced by Shen. (The government is promoting Gu as "another" Shen Congwen, but without Shen's ideological faults.) Long Haiqing says that the West Hunanese Sun Jianzhong (Tujia) and Wu Xuenao (Miao) were influenced by Shen (letter to me). Liu Zuchun, Lin Pu, and Li Zhenyi, who, influenced by Shen Congwen, wrote about West Hunan in the 1940's, stopped writing long ago. "Liu Zuchun" and "Lin Pu" were at times thought to be pen names for Shen Congwen.

Shen Congwen is acknowledged as a pioneer of *xiangtu wenxue* in Zhao Xiaqiu and Zeng Qingrui, 1: 545–47, 581–84. The term *xiangtu wenxue* has for some years been applied to Taiwan's nativist rural literature, but it has not been a generally recognized category in PRC literary history (the use now may reflect the PRC desire to unify with Taiwan). Interestingly, one of the earliest references to Shen as a *xiangtu wenxue* writer was made in Taiwan (where Shen is still proscribed), by Cai Yizhong, pp. 202–5. In the category of rural writing, Shen himself believes that he has influenced the writers Sha Ting (Sha Ding) and He Qifang; int. 1980.vii.24.

110. The KMT press misrepresented Shen's tour of America as a private "trip to visit relatives." That was one of its purposes, and the Frankels did provide the utmost in financial and logistical help. But it was also an official trip funded by the Chinese government. Invitations to Shen from American universities arrived in the summer of 1980. Because of stumbling blocks having to do with who might accompany him, concern that he would be expected to talk politics if he went on government money, and health worries, Shen Congwen considered calling it off, or going later, using his own money (he had enough, interestingly enough). He told me

that the trip might not come off, since he wanted above all to maintain his dignity, as he put it; int. 1980.vii.23. But obstacles were cleared. During his trip, Shen mostly avoided the subject of politics. See *WJ* 10: 331–39. The KMT in America made an effort to persuade Shen during his visit to come to Taiwan. He was not interested. His book on costume was, however, pirated in Taiwan, with Shen's name excised from the cover.

In 1978, Shen Congwen left the Historical Museum to become an academician (or "professor") in the Institute of History of the newly founded Chinese Academy of Social Sciences, under his old friend Hu Qiaomu. See Wang Yarong, "Shen Congwen xiao ji." Shen organized a Working Group for Research on Ancient Costume under the Institute; space for work was found for him during two summers at the Friendship Guest House in northwest Peking. Usually he works at home. At the Fourth Congress of the Chinese Writers' Association, Shen and some other old writers were elected (Shen in absentia) as advisers to the Association: Foreign Broadcast Information Service, *Daily Report, China*, 9 Jan. 1985, monitoring Beijing Xinhua Domestic Service, 7 Jan. 1985.

Conclusion

1. "Xiaoshuo yu shehui" (1942), *WJ* 12: 133; "'Wenyi zhengce' tantao" (1943), p. 3; "Xiangren duiyu xin wenxue yundong de gongxian" (1945), *WJ* 12: 194–200. Shen stresses the literary importance of Liang Qichao, Wu Zhihui, Lin Shu, Yan Fu, and Hunanese 1895–98 reformers such as Xiong Xiling and Tan Sitong. He cites Liang as the first vernacularizer in "Wenxue yu qingnian qinggan jiaoyu" (1946, furnished by Shao Huaqiang). See also "Xindang zhong yi ge Hunan xiangxiaren" (1948).

2. Barlow, p. 125.

3. Letter from Shen Congwen to Hans H. and Ch'ung-ho Chang Frankel.

4. The *yan zhi/zai Dao* distinction, explicated in Pollard, pp. 1–29, was applied by Shen himself, to poetry, in "Tan xiandai shi" (1948), *WJ* 12: 79. *Yan zhi* meant "lyrical," he said, and *zai Dao* "political."

5. Fang Houshu, p. 7.

6. It should be added that before 1949 Shen read and liked the works of Sha Ting, Ai Wu, and Zhao Shuli; "Xin feiyou cundi," 273 (1947), *WJ* 12: 67. He acknowledged the poetry of Ai Qing in "Xin feiyou cundi" (1947), *WJ* 12: 50. About 1940–42, Shen praised Liu Baiyu and Yao Xueyin, in "Mingri de wenxue zuojia," p. 107.

7. "Xin feiyou cundi," 285 (1947; to a woman author named Xiao), *WJ* 12: 70–75.

8. "Duanpian xiaoshuo" (1941), *WJ* 12: 113–27.

9. Even in the Northern Expedition, peasant associations were established only in Mayang and Zhijiang. They were by far the smallest in

Hunan. (Small associations were also established around Dongting Lake, in Changde and Taoyuan, and in Xupu.) Organization in Fenghuang, Luqi, and even Yuanling was too negligible for the counties even to be listed. *Hunan sheng zhi*, 1: 568–69.

10. Interview in Hangzhou with Sun Xizhen (died 31 Dec. 1984), 1980.viii.9. Sun criticized Shen for putting literature above politics, for knowing Hu Shi and Chen Yuan, and for criticizing leftist literature as monotonous. "First you have to get your *sixiang* (thought, ideology) straight," he emphasized, then there can be improvement in literature.

11. A frank article is Zheng Fangkun's. Fenghuang's 1983 per-capita income was "just 108 yuan, only a third of that recorded elsewhere in the province. In some townships, the per-capita income was only 62 yuan, not even enough to buy food." Diversification (producing tobacco instead of grain) and the new economic policies had in 1984 already raised per-capita income to 169 yuan. A second railway line opened nearby, in 1983. Probably tourism lies in West Hunan's future.

Selected Bibliography

Abadie, Maurice. *Les races du Haut-Tonkin de Phong-Tho à Lang-Son.* Paris, 1924.
Acton, Harold, and Ch'en Shih-hsiang. *Modern Chinese Poetry.* London, 1936.
Alley, Rewi. *Travels in China, 1966-71.* Peking, 1973.
Analects of Confucius, The. Arthur Waley, trans. New York, 1938.
Anderson, E. N., Jr. "The Folksongs of the Hong Kong Boat People." *Journal of American Folklore* 80, no. 317 (July-Sept. 1967): 285-96.
Ba Jin 巴金. *Tansuo ji* 探索集 (Explorations). Hong Kong, 1981.
Bai Juyi. *Bai Juyi ji* 白居易集 (The works of Bai Juyi). Gu Xuejie 顧學頡, ed. Beijing, 1979.
Ball, J. Dyer. *Things Chinese.* 5th ed. Shanghai, 1925.
Barlow, Tani E. Review of Yi-tsi Mei Feuerwerker, *Ding Ling's Fiction,* in *Chinese Literature: Essays, Articles, Reviews* 5, no. 1/2 (July 1983): 125-28.
Beck, Karl H., Rev. "Memoirs of Hsiang-Si Mission." Unpubl. ms. Lancaster Central Archives, Evangelical and Reformed Historical Society. Foreword dated 15 May 1970.
Bernatzik, Hugo Adolf. *Akha and Miao: Problems of Applied Ethnography in Farther India.* Alois Nagler, trans. New Haven, Conn., 1970.
Billingsley, P. R. "Bandits, Bosses, and Bare Sticks." *Modern China* 7 (July 1981): 235-88.
Birch, Cyril, ed. *Anthology of Chinese Literature.* Vol. 2. New York, 1972.
Bland, J. O. P. *China, Japan and Korea.* New York, 1921.
———, and E. Backhouse. *China Under the Empress Dowager.* Philadelphia, 1910.
Bloom, Harold. "The Central Man." *The New York Review of Books* 31, no. 12 (19 July 1984).
Boorman, Howard L., ed. *Biographical Dictionary of Republican China.* 5 vols. New York, 1967-79.

Booth, Wayne C. *The Rhetoric of Fiction*. Chicago, 1961.
Brooks, Cleanth. *William Faulkner: The Yoknapatawpha Country*. New Haven, Conn., 1963.
Cai Yizhong 蔡義忠. *Cong Shi Naian dao Xu Zhimo* 從施耐庵到徐志摩 (From Shi Naian to Xu Zhimo). Taibei, 1975.
Cai Yuanpei. *Cai Yuanpei minzuxue lunzhu* 蔡元培民族學論著 (Works on ethnography by Cai Yuanpei). Taibei, 1962.
Cambridge History of China, The. Vol. 11. John K. Fairbank and Kwang-ching Liu, eds. Cambridge, Eng., 1980.
Cao Juren 曹聚仁. "Hai Pai" 海派 (The Shanghai School). In his *Shanshui, sixiang, renwu* 山水, 思想, 人物 (Landscapes, ideologies, personalities). Hong Kong, 1956.
Carlsberg, Gustav. *The Changing China Scene*. Hong Kong, 1958?
Casselman, Arthur Vale. "From Six to Sixty to Six." Unpubl. ms. Lancaster Central Archives, Evangelical and Reformed Historical Society. Foreword dated 1951.
Chai, Ch'u, and Winberg Chai, eds. *A Treasury of Chinese Literature*. New York, 1965.
Chambers, Anthony H. "Transcending the 'I-Novel.'" *New York Times Book Review*, 7 Oct. 1984.
Chen Mengjia 陳夢家, ed. *Xinyue shixuan* 新月詩選 (A selection of poetry from the *Crescent Monthly*). Shanghai, 1931.
Ch'en, Jerome. "Defining Chinese Warlords and Their Factions." *Bulletin of the School of Oriental and African Studies* 31, no. 3 (1968): 563–600.
———. *Yuan Shih-k'ai*. 2d ed. Stanford, Calif., 1972.
Cheng, Ching-mao. "The Impact of Japanese Literary Trends on Modern Chinese Writers." In Goldman, ed., *Modern Chinese Literature*.
Ch'i, Hsi-sheng. *Warlord Politics in China, 1916–1928*. Stanford, Calif., 1976.
China Forum. Shanghai. English and Chinese editions reprinted and bound together by the Center for Chinese Research Materials, Washington, D.C.
Chinese Communists Who's Who. Taipei, 1970.
Ching Ti [Jin Di] and Robert Payne, trans. *The Chinese Earth: Stories by Shen Tseng-wen*. London, 1947. (A new edition, cited in the notes, contains a new preface by the author and an afterword, "About the Author" [New York, 1982].)
Chow Tse-tsung. *The May Fourth Movement*. Cambridge, Mass., 1960.
Chu, Lillian Chen Ming. "*The Long River* by Shen Ts'ung-wen: Introduction and Partial Translation." M.A. thesis, Columbia Univ., 1966.
Clarke, Samuel R. *Among the Tribes in South-West China*. London, 1911.
Cohen, Paul A. *China and Christianity*. Cambridge, Mass., 1963.
Connolly, Cyril. *Enemies of Promise*. Rev. ed. New York, 1948.
Cowley, Malcolm, ed. *The Portable Faulkner*. Rev. ed. New York, 1967.

Dagongbao 大公報 ("L'Impartial"). Tianjin, Shanghai, Chongqing, Hong Kong. Simultaneous editions in different cities not necessarily identical.

Dai Kechong 戴克崇 (pseuds. Su Wen 蘇汶, Du Heng 杜衡). "Wenren zai Shanghai" 文人在上海 (Authors in Shanghai). *Xiandai* 4, no. 2 (1 Dec. 1933): 281–82.

Daiches, David, and John Flower. *Literary Landscapes of the British Isles: A Narrative Atlas.* New York, 1979.

de Beauclair, Inez. *Tribal Cultures of Southwest China.* Taipei, 1970.

Ding Ling. *Ding Ling wenji* 丁玲文集 (The works of Ding Ling). 5 vols. Changsha, 1982.

———. "Ji yi ge zhenshi ren de yi sheng" 記一個眞實人的一生 (Recalling the life of an honest man). *Renmin wenxue* 3, no. 2 (1 Dec. 1950): 17–25.

———. "Mouye" 某夜 (A certain night). *Wenxue yuebao* 1, no. 1 (June 1932): 93–100.

———. "Yepin yu geming" 也頻與革命 (Hu Yepin and the revolution). *Shikan* 130 (Mar. 1980): 30–31.

———. *Yijiusanlingnian chun Shanghai* 一九三〇年春上海 (Shanghai: Spring 1930). *XS* 21, no. 9 (Sept. 1930): 1297–1316; 21, no. 11 (Nov. 1930): 1603–15; 21, no. 12 (Dec. 1930): 1723–34.

Ding Xilin. "Oppression." Joseph S. M. Lau, trans. In Edward M. Gunn, ed., *Twentieth-Century Chinese Drama: An Anthology* (Bloomington, Ind., 1983). Supplementary materials in *Renditions* 3 (Autumn 1974): 117, 124.

Doležalová, Anna. *Yü Ta-fu: Specific Traits of His Literary Creation.* Bratislava, 1971.

Dong Yi 董易. "Shitan Shen Congwen bufen xiaoshuo sixiang qingxiang de fuzaxing" 試談沈從文部分小說思想傾向的複雜性 (Tentative thoughts on the ideological complexity of some of Shen Congwen's fiction). *Wenxue pinglun* 1983, no. 6 (15 Nov.): 48–61.

Dongfang zazhi 東方雜誌 ("The Eastern Miscellany"). Shanghai. Fortnightly chronologies of current events.

Duiker, William J. *Ts'ai Yüan-p'ei: Educator of Modern China.* University Park, Pa., 1977.

Eberhard, Wolfram. *China's Minorities: Yesterday and Today.* Belmont, Calif., 1982.

———. *The Local Cultures of South and East China.* Alide Eberhard, trans. Leiden, 1968.

Ebrey, Patricia Buckley, ed. *Chinese Civilization and Society.* New York, 1981.

Evangelical-Messenger, The. Cleveland. Daily newspaper of the Evangelical Church.

Evangelical Missionary World. Monthly magazine of the Evangelical Church.

Eyes East: Interesting Facts About China. Union City, N.J., 1930?

Fan Boqun 范伯群 and Zeng Huapeng 曾華鵬. *Wang Luyan lun* 王魯彥論 (On Wang Luyan). Shanghai, 1981.

Fan Rong 凡容. "Shen Congwen de 'Guisheng'" 沈從文的「貴生」(Shen Congwen's "Guisheng"). *Zhongliu* 2, no. 7 (20 June 1937): 390–94.

Fang Houshu. "Progress in the Publishing Industry." *China Reconstructs* 34, no. 4 (Apr. 1985): 5–7.

Fangxiangshe 方向社 (The Direction Society). "Jinri wenxue de fangxiang" 今日文學的方向 (The direction of contemporary literature). Tianjin *DGB*, "Wenyi" 107, 14 Nov. 1948.

Feng Naichao 馮乃超. "Lue lun Shen Congwen de Xiong gongguan" 略論沈從文的熊公館 (A brief discussion of Shen Congwen's Xiong mansion [article]). *Dazhong wenyi congkan* 1 (1 Mar. 1948).

Feng Weicai 馮偉才. "Fang Shen Congwen tan *Bian cheng*" 訪沈從文談「邊城」(Interviewing Shen Congwen about *The Frontier City* [film]). *Xianggang wenxue* 9 (5 Sept. 1985): 27–29. Reproduces a page of the screenplay with Shen Congwen's suggested revisions.

Fenghuang ting xu zhi 鳳凰廳續志 (Fenghuang gazetteer, continued). 1892.

Fenghuang ting zhi 鳳凰廳志 (Fenghuang gazetteer). 1875 (rev. of 1824 ed.).

Feuerwerker, Yi-tsi Mei. *Ding Ling's Fiction*. Cambridge, Mass., 1982.

Foreign Broadcast Information Service. *Daily Report, China*. Washington, D.C.

Forester, Lancelot. *The New Culture in China*. London, 1936.

Franck, Harry A. *Roving Through Southern China*. New York, 1925.

Frye, Northrop. *Anatomy of Criticism: Four Essays*. Princeton, N.J., 1957.

Fu Juejin 傅角今. *Hunan dili zhi* 湖南地理志 (Geographical gazetteer of Hunan). Wuchang, 1933.

Gaimushō Jōhōbu 外務省情報部 ([Japanese] Foreign Office, Intelligence Bureau). *Gendai Chūka Minkoku Manshūkoku jimmeikan* 現代中華民國滿洲國人名鑑 (Who's who in the Republic of China and Manchukuo). Tokyo, 1932.

———. *Gendai Shina jimmeikan* 現代支那人名鑑 (Who's who in modern China). Tokyo, 1916, 1928.

Gálik, Marián. *The Genesis of Modern Chinese Literary Criticism*. London, 1980.

Gao Shukang 高叔康. "Xi xing za ji" 西行雜記 (Random notes on a trip west). Chongqing *Zhongyang ribao*, 25 Sept.–30 Oct. (and beyond?) 1938.

Gao Zhi 高植. "Zhimo yu wo" 志摩與我 (Xu Zhimo and me). *Xiaoshuo yuekan* 1, no. 2 (15 Nov. 1932): 103–15.

Gay, Peter. *Freud, Jews and Other Germans: Masters and Victims in Modernist Culture*. New York, 1978.

Gillin, Donald G. *Warlord: Yen Hsi-shan in Shansi Province, 1911–1949*. Princeton, N.J., 1967.

Goldblatt, Howard. "The Rural Stories of Hwang Chun-ming." In Jeannette L. Faurot, ed., *Chinese Fiction from Taiwan* (Bloomington, Ind., 1980).
Goldman, Merle. "Left-Wing Criticism of the *Pai-hua* Movement." In Benjamin I. Schwartz, ed., *Reflections on the May Fourth Movement: A Symposium* (Cambridge, Mass., 1972).
———, ed. *Modern Chinese Literature in the May Fourth Era*. Cambridge, Mass., 1977.
Graham, David Crockett. "The Ceremonies of the Ch'uan Miao." *Journal of the West China Border Research Society* 9 (1937): 71–119.
———. "The Customs of the Ch'uan Miao." *Journal of the West China Border Research Society* 9 (1937): 13–70.
———. *Folk Religion in Southwest China*. Washington, D.C., 1961.
———. *Songs and Stories of the Ch'uan Miao*. Washington, D.C., 1954.
Granet, Marcel. *Fêtes et chansons anciennes de la Chine*. Paris, 1919.
Grieder, Jerome B. *Hu Shih and the Chinese Renaissance*. Cambridge, Mass., 1970.
Gu Zhibiao 谷志標. "Hongjiaguan juyi" 洪家關聚義 (The righteous gathering at Hongjiaguan). In *Xinghuo liaoyuan*, vol. 1B: 618–26.
Gunn, Edward M. *Unwelcome Muse: Chinese Literature in Shanghai and Peking, 1937–1945*. New York, 1980.
Guo Moruo 郭沫若. "Chi fandong wenyi" 斥反動文藝 (Castigate reactionary literature and art). *Dazhong wenyi congkan* 1 (1 Mar. 1948).
Hall, John C. *The Yunnan Provincial Faction, 1927–1937*. Canberra, 1976.
Hanan, Patrick. *The Chinese Vernacular Story*. Cambridge, Mass., 1981.
Hawkes, David. "Introduction." In Cao Xueqin, *The Story of the Stone*. David Hawkes, trans. Vol. 1. Baltimore, 1973.
He Long 賀龍. "Xiang E xi chuqi de geming douzheng" 湘鄂西初期的革命鬥爭 (Initial revolutionary struggles in western Hunan and Hubei). In *Xinghuo liaoyuan*, vol. 1B: 603–17.
He Qifang 何其芳, Li Guangtian 李廣田, and Bian Zhilin 卞之琳. *Hanyuan ji* 漢園集 (Han Gardens collection). Shanghai, 1936.
He Xunchen 賀勳臣. "Huoyue zai Xiang E bianjing" 活躍在湘鄂邊境 (Coming alive in the Hunan-Hubei borderlands). In *Xinghuo liaoyuan*, vol. 1B: 646–52.
He Yubo 賀玉波. "Shen Congwen de zuopin pingpan" 沈從文的作品評判 (Criticism of works by Shen Congwen). In her *Xiandai Zhongguo zuojia lun* 現代中國作家論 (On modern Chinese authors). 2 vols. Shanghai, 1932.
"Heart of the Dragon, The." Television series by Antelope-Sino-Hawkshead, U.K. Alasdair Clayre, executive producer. 1984.
Ho, Ping-ti. *Studies on the Population of China, 1368–1953*. Cambridge, Mass., 1959.

Howe, Irving. *The Idea of the Modern in Literature and the Arts.* New York, 1967.

Hsia, C. T. *A History of Modern Chinese Fiction.* 2d ed. New Haven, Conn., 1971.

———. "*The Korchin Banner Plains*: A Biographical and Critical Study." In *La littérature chinoise au temps de la guerre de résistance contre le Japon (de 1937 à 1945)* (Paris, 1982).

———, ed., with the assistance of Joseph S. M. Lau. *Twentieth-Century Chinese Stories.* New York, 1971.

Hsu, Kai-yu. *The Chinese Literary Scene.* New York, 1975.

———. *Our China Trip.* Privately published, 1974.

———. *Wen I-to.* New York, 1980.

Hu Guisheng 胡貴生. *Miaomin lei* 苗民淚 (Tears of the Miao people). Hong Kong, 1956.

Hu Naian 胡耐安. *Xin Xiang jun zhi* 新湘軍志 (A treatise on the new Hunan army). Muzha, Taibei County, 1969.

Hu Yepin 胡也頻. "Gei Maolin" 給懋琳 (To Maolin [Shen Congwen]; poem). *CF* 1468 (3 Nov. 1926): 7.

———. "San ge bu tongyi de renwu" 三個不統一的人物 (Three people at odds). *Honghei* 3 (10 Mar. 1929): 135–51.

Hu Zili 胡自立. *Dangdai Zhongguo mingren zhi* 當代中國名人誌 (Who's who in China today). Shanghai, 1939.

Huang Bofei 黃伯飛 (Parker Huang). "Que shi you yuan" 確是有緣 (Fated, indeed). *Haineiwai* 28 (Nov.–Dec. 1980): 27–28.

Huang Cunsheng 黃村生. "Shen Congwen de xiong yu di" 沈從文的兄與弟 (Shen Congwen's brothers). *Biduan banyuekan* 2 (15 Jan. 1968): 15–17.

Huang Muru 黃穆如. "Xinhai Xiangxi guangfu jingguo" 辛亥湘西光復經過 (The recovery of West Hunan in the 1911 revolution). In *Hunan wenshi ziliao xuanji* 湖南文史資料選輯 (Selected historical accounts of past events in Hunan). Changsha, 1981.

Huang Yongyu 黃永玉. "Dongwu pian" 動物篇 (Animal crackers). *Jintian* 1 (Dec. 1978): 23. Trans. David S. G. Goodman, *Beijing Street Voices* (London, 1981), pp. 21–25.

———. "Taiyang xia de fengjing" 太陽下的風景 (A sunlit landscape). In *ZZ*, pp. 144–64.

Hunan Province Gazetteer. Vol. 2. Changsha, 1961. Trans. Joint Publications Research Service, no. 16,387. Washington, D.C., 1962.

Hunan sheng zhi 湖南省志 (Gazetteer of Hunan province). Vol. 1: Chronology of the Last Hundred Years in Hunan. Changsha, 1979 (rev. of 1959 ed.).

Insun, L. *Ding Ling zai Shaanbei* 丁玲在陝北 (Ding Ling in northern Shaanxi). Hong Kong, 1938.

Jia Shumei 賈樹枚. "Yongyuan de yongbao ziji de gongzuo bufang" 永遠地擁抱自己的工作不放 (Forever keeping at his own work, no matter what). *Guangming ribao*, 7 Nov. 1980.
Jiaofei zhanshi 剿匪戰史 (The military history of our Bandit [i.e., Communist] exterminations). Guofangbu Shizhengju 國防部史政局 (Ministry of Defense, Bureau of Military History), ed. 6 vols. Taibei, 1967.
Jiekai shizong de mimi 揭開失踪的秘密 (Uncovering the mystery of the missing person). Hunan Gongan Bianweihui「湖南公安」編委會 (The Editorial Committee of *Hunan Public Security*), ed. Changsha, 1980.
Jin 槿. "Lingling suisui" 零零碎碎 (Miscellanea). *Shijie ribao*, 3 Oct. 1946.
Jing Shan 景山. "Lu Xun shuxin bufen renwu shijian kaoshi" 魯迅書信部分人物事件考釋 (Identifications of some persons and events mentioned in Lu Xun's correspondence). *Xin wenxue shiliao* 4 (Aug. 1979): 292–301.
Jing Xin 井心. "Shen Congwen qiren" 沈從文其人 ([Obituary of] Shen Congwen). Taibei *Zhongyang ribao*, 9 June 1968.
Jun 菌 (pseud.). "Gei Xuanruo" 給璇若 (To Xuanruo [pen name of Shen Congwen]). *XP* 6, no. 139 (6 Aug. 1927): 702–4.
Kapp, Robert A. *Szechwan and the Chinese Republic: Provincial Militarism and Central Power, 1911–1938*. New Haven, Conn., 1973.
Karl, Frederick R. *Modern and Modernism: The Sovereignty of the Artist, 1885–1925*. New York, 1985.
Kinkley, Jeffrey C. "Shen Congwen and the Uses of Regionalism in Modern Chinese Literature." *Modern Chinese Literature* 1, no. 2 (Spring 1985): 157–83.
———. "Shen Ts'ung-wen's Vision of Republican China." Ph.D. diss., Harvard Univ., 1977. Trans. Shao Huaqiang 邵華強, Yu Jianhua 虞建華, and Tong Shijun 童世駿 as *Shen Congwen bixia de Zhongguo* 沈從文筆下的中國. Shanghai, forthcoming.
———, ed. *After Mao: Chinese Literature and Society, 1978–1981*. Cambridge, Mass., 1985.
Kirby, William C. *Germany and Republican China*. Stanford, Calif., 1984.
Klein, Donald W., and Anne B. Clark, eds. *Biographic Dictionary of Chinese Communism, 1921–1965*. 2 vols. Cambridge, Mass., 1971.
Klöpsch, Volker, and Roderich Ptak, eds. *Hoffnung auf Frühling: Moderne Chinesische Erzählungen*. Frankfurt am Main, 1980.
Lary, Diana. *Region and Nation: The Kwangsi Clique in Chinese Politics, 1925–1937*. Cambridge, Eng., 1974.
Lau, Joseph S. M., C. T. Hsia, and Leo Ou-fan Lee, eds. *Modern Chinese Stories and Novellas: 1919–1949*. New York, 1981.
LeBar, Frank M., Gerald C. Hickey, and John K. Musgrave. *Ethnic Groups of Mainland Southeast Asia*. New Haven, Conn., 1964.
Lee, Leo Ou-fan. *The Romantic Generation of Modern Chinese Writers*. Cambridge, Mass., 1973.

Lemoine, Jacques. *Un village Hmong Vert du Haut Laos*. Paris, 1972.

Li Helin 李何林. *Jin ershi nian Zhongguo wenyi sichao lun* 近二十年中國文藝思潮論 (On the ideological tides in Chinese literature and art during the last 20 years). Shanghai, 1939.

Li Zhenyi 李震一. *Hunan de xibeijiao* 湖南的西北角 (The northwest corner of Hunan). Changsha, 1947.

Liang Shiqiu 梁實秋. *Tan Xu Zhimo* 談徐志摩 (About Xu Zhimo). Taibei, 1958.

Liang Zhonghao 梁仲豪, rapporteur. "Shen Congwen *Zhongguo gudai fushi yanjiu* zuotanhui" 沈從文「中國古代服飾研究」座談會 (Colloquium on Shen Congwen's *Researches into Ancient Chinese Costume*). *Baixing* 1981, no. 11 (1 Nov.): 38–40.

Liao Hansheng 廖漢生. "Hongse de 'shenbing'" 紅色的「神兵」 (Red "spirit soldiers"). In *Xinghuo liaoyuan*, vol. 1B: 653–56.

Lin Pu 林蒲. "Xiangxi xing" 湘西行 (Marching through West Hunan). Hong Kong *DGB*, 26 Apr.–10 June 1940.

Lin Qing 林青. "*Furongzhen* he *Bian cheng* yishu fengge de bijiao yanjiu" 「芙蓉鎮」和「邊城」藝術風格的比較研究 (A comparative study of the literary styles of [Gu Hua's] *A Small Town Called Hibiscus* and *The Frontier City*). *Wenyi luncong*, vol. 20. Shanghai, 1984.

Ling Chunsheng 凌純聲 and Rui Yifu 芮逸夫 [authors prefer Ling Shunsheng and Ruey Yih-fu]. *Xiangxi Miaozu diaocha baogao* 湘西苗族調查報告 (Report on a survey of the West Hunan Miao). Shanghai, 1947.

Ling Yu 凌宇. "Shen Congwen tan ziji de chuangzuo" 沈從文談自己的創作 (Shen Congwen talks about his own writing). *Wenjiao ziliao jianbao* 112 (Apr. 1981): 26–31.

Link, Perry. *Mandarin Ducks and Butterflies: Popular Fiction in Early Twentieth-Century Chinese Cities*. Berkeley, Calif., 1981.

Liu, James J. Y. *Chinese Theories of Literature*. Chicago, 1975.

Liu Shousong 劉綬松. *Zhongguo xin wenxueshi chugao* 中國新文學史初稿 (First draft of a history of China's new literature). Beijing, 1956.

Liu Yiyou 劉一友. "Lun Shen Congwen de xiangqing jiqi *Bian cheng* chuangzuo" 論沈從文的鄉情及其「邊城」創作 (On Shen Congwen's feelings for his home and the writing of *The Frontier City*). *Jishou Daxue xuebao*. Social Sciences Edition 1985, no. 3 (25 Aug.): 6–13.

———. "Tao li bu yan, xia zi cheng xi" 桃李不言下自成蹊 (Quiet but resplendent; blazing his own trail). *Jishou Daxue xuebao*. Social Sciences Edition 1982, no. 2 (1982): 6–13, 18.

Liu Zuchun 劉祖春. "Wo de jiaoyu" 我的教育 (My education). Shanghai *DGB*, 6, 9 Aug. 1937.

Loeb, E. M. "Courtship and the Love Song." *Anthropos* 45 (1950): 821–51.

Long Haiqing 龍海清. "Bu shou suiyue jiban de ren—fang lao zuojia Shen Congwen xiansheng" 不受歲月羈絆的人—訪老作家沈從文先生 (A man who doesn't feel the effects of his age—interviewing veteran writer Mr. Shen Congwen). *Xiangjiang wenyi* 3 (Mar. 1980): 43–46.

———. "Lue lun Miaozu zuojia Shen Congwen jiqi chuangzuo" 略論苗族作家沈從文及其創作 (A brief discussion of the Miao author Shen Congwen and his creative writings). *Qiusuo* 1983, no. 2 (13 April): 101–6.

———. "Shen Congwen and Lu Xun." Jeffrey C. Kinkley, trans. *Haineiwai* 30 (Mar.–Apr. 1981): 20–25.

Lu Fen 蘆焚 (pseud. of Wang Changjian 王長簡). "'Jing Pai' yu 'Hai Pai'" 「京派」與「海派」 (The "Peking School" and the "Shanghai School"). Tianjin *DGB*, 10 Feb. 1934.

Lu Xun. *Lu Xun quanji* 魯迅全集 (The complete works of Lu Xun). 20 vols. Beijing, 1973.

———. *Lu Xun shuxin ji* 魯迅書信集 (Correspondence of Lu Xun). 2 vols. Beijing, 1976.

———. *Selected Works.* Yang Xianyi and Gladys Yang, trans. 4 vols. Beijing, 1980.

Lunn, Eugene. *Marxism and Modernism: An Historical Study of Lukács, Brecht, Benjamin, and Adorno.* Berkeley, Calif., 1982.

Luo Ergang 羅爾綱. *Xiangjun xin zhi* 湘軍新志 (A new treatise on the Hunan Army). Changsha, 1939.

Ma Fenghua 馬逢華. "Chongwu Shen Congwen jiaoshou" 重晤沈從文教授 (Reencounter with Professor Shen Congwen). *Zhuanji wenxue* 42, no. 2 (Feb. 1983): 38–46.

———. "Huainian Shen Congwen jiaoshou" 懷念沈從文教授 (Fondly remembering Professor Shen Congwen). *Zhuanji wenxue* 2, no. 1 (Jan. 1963): 13–16, 6.

Ma Shaoqiao 馬少僑. *Qingdai Miaomin qiyi* 清代苗民起義 (The righteous risings of the Miao people in the Qing dynasty). Wuhan, 1956.

MacDonald, William Lewis. "Characters and Themes in Shen Ts'ung-wen's Fiction." Ph.D. diss., Univ. of Washington, 1970.

Mackerras, Colin. "Folksongs and Dances of China's Minority Nationalities." *Modern China* 10, no. 2 (Apr. 1984): 187–226.

Maguire, Theophane, Rev. *Hunan Harvest.* Milwaukee, 1946.

Mair, Victor H. "Li Po's Letters in Pursuit of Political Patronage." *Harvard Journal of Asiatic Studies* 44, no. 1 (June 1984): 123–53.

Mao Dun 茅盾. *Huiyilu* 回憶錄 (Reminiscences). *Xin wenxue shiliao.* 1983–85.

Mao Zedong. *Mao Zedong shici* 毛澤東詩詞 (Mao Zedong poems [in Chinese and English]). Beijing, 1976.

Maruyama, Masao. "Patterns of Individuation and the Case of Japan: A Conceptual Scheme." In Marius B. Jansen, ed., *Changing Japanese Attitudes Toward Modernization* (Princeton, N.J., 1965).

McCormack, Gavan. *Chang Tso-lin in Northeast China, 1911–1928*. Stanford, Calif., 1977.
McDougall, Bonnie S. *The Introduction of Western Literary Theories into Modern China*. Tokyo, 1971.
Meng Xue 夢學. "Lao zuojia Shen Congwen yu dianying jieyuan" 老作家沈從文與電影結緣 (Veteran author Shen Congwen's date with the movies). *Haineiwai* 49 (Apr.–Sept. 1985): 37.
Miao Man tuce 苗蠻[蠻]圖冊 (Picture album of the Miao and Man tribes). Rui Yifu 芮逸夫 [Ruey Yih-fu], ed. With the Institute of History and Philology, Academia Sinica. Taibei, 1973.
Mickey, Margaret Portia. *The Cowrie Shell Miao of Kweichow*. Cambridge, Mass., 1947.
Mills, Harriet C. "Lu Xun: Literature and Revolution—From Mara to Marx." In Goldman, ed., *Modern Chinese Literature*.
Minutes of the Annual Mission Meeting of the Reformed Church of the U. S. Hankow, 1918–35.
Mo Lingping 莫靈平. "Zai Beijing fang Shen Congwen ji Huang Yongyu" 在北京訪沈從文及黃永玉 (Visiting Shen Congwen and Huang Yongyu in Peking). *Jiushi niandai* 180 (Jan. 1985): 83–86.
Moréchand, Guy. "Le chamanisme des Hmong." *Bulletin de l'École française d'Extrême-Orient* 54 (1968): 53–294.
Munro, Stanley R. *Genesis of a Revolution*. Singapore, 1979.
New China's First Quarter-Century. Peking, 1975.
Nieh, Hua-ling. *Shen Ts'ung-wen*. New York, 1972.
Nivison, David S. *The Life and Thought of Chang Hsüeh-ch'eng (1738–1801)*. Stanford, Calif., 1966.
Olney, Douglas P. *A Bibliography of the Hmong (Miao)*. Minneapolis, 1981.
Outlook of Missions, The. Philadelphia. Monthly magazine of the Reformed Church.
Pan Dengchang 潘登常, singer; Wang Tianruo 王天若, recorder. "Shiniu" 世牛 (Miao: "Festivity"). *Minjian wenxue* 154 (20 Nov. 1982): 73–81.
Pan Yuan and Pan Jie. "The Non-Official Magazine *Today* and the Younger Generation's Ideals for a New Literature." In Kinkley, ed., *After Mao*.
Payne, Robert. *Chinese Diaries, 1941–1946*. New York, 1970.
Peck, Graham. *Two Kinds of Time*. Boston, 1950.
Pollard, David E. *A Chinese Look at Literature: The Literary Values of Chou Tso-jen in Relation to the Tradition*. Berkeley, Calif., 1973.
Powell, Irena. *Writers and Society in Modern Japan*. Tokyo, 1983.
Powell, Ralph L. *The Rise of Chinese Military Power, 1895–1912*. Princeton, N.J., 1955.
Prince, Anthony John. "The Life and Works of Shen Ts'ung-wen." Ph.D. diss., Univ. of Sydney, 1968.

Průšek, Jaroslav. "Subjectivism and Individualism in Modern Chinese Literature." In Leo Ou-fan Lee, ed., *The Lyrical and the Epic* (Bloomington, Ind., 1980).
———. *Three Sketches of Chinese Literature*. Prague, 1969.
———, ed. *Dictionary of Oriental Literatures*. 3 vols. New York, 1974.
Pusey, James Reeve. *China and Charles Darwin*. Cambridge, Mass., 1983.
Qian Zhongshu 錢鍾書. "Mao" 貓 (Cat). In his *Ren shou gui* 人獸鬼 (Men, beasts, ghosts). Shanghai, 1946.
Qing shi 清史 (History of the Qing dynasty). Reprint ed., Taibei, 1961.
Redfield, Robert. "Tribe, Peasant, and City." In his *Human Nature and the Study of Society*. Margaret Park Redfield, ed. Vol. 1. Chicago, 1962.
Rock, Joseph F. "The Life and Culture of the Na-khi Tribe of the China-Tibet Borderland." *Verzeichnis der Orientalischen Handschriften in Deutschland*. Supplement vol. 2. Wiesbaden, 1963.
———, trans. "The Romance of ^{2}K'a-^{2}mä-^{1}gyu-^{3}mi-^{2}gkyi." *Bulletin de l'École française d'Extrême-Orient* 39, fasc. 1 (1939): 1–152.
Rozman, Gilbert, ed. *The Modernization of China*. New York, 1981.
Ruhlen, Merritt. *A Guide to the Languages of the World*. Stanford, Calif., 1975.
Russell, Bertrand. *The Problem of China*. New York, 1922.
Schafer, Edward. *The Golden Peaches of Samarkand: A Study of T'ang Exotics*. Berkeley, Calif., 1963.
———. *The Vermilion Bird: T'ang Images of the South*. Berkeley, 1967.
Schneider, Laurence A. *Ku Chieh-kang and China's New History*. Berkeley, Calif., 1971.
Schoppa, R. Keith. *Chinese Elites and Political Change: Zhejiang Province in the Early Twentieth Century*. Cambridge, Mass., 1982.
Schram, Stuart. *Mao Tse-tung*. New York, 1966.
Schyns, Joseph. *1500 Modern Chinese Novels and Plays*. Hong Kong, 1966 (reprint of 1948 ed.).
Shanghai wenhua 上海文化 (Shanghai culture). Shanghai. "Zhongguo wenhua" 中國文化 (Chinese Culture page).
Shao Huaqiang 邵華強. "Cong 'fan chabuduo' kan Shen Congwen de wenyiguan" 從「反差不多」看沈從文的文藝觀 (Looking at Shen Congwen's view of literature from his opposition to "about-the-same-itis"). *Shanghai Shifan Xueyuan xuebao*. Social Sciences Edition 1981, no. 1 (25 Mar.): 66–68.
——— and Ling Yu 凌宇, eds. *Shen Congwen wenji* 沈從文文集 (The works of Shen Congwen). 12 vols. Guangzhou and Hong Kong, 1982–85.
———. *Shen Congwen yanjiu* 沈從文研究 (Research on Shen Congwen). Guangzhou and Hong Kong, forthcoming.

Shen Congwen zhuzuo ji yanjiu ziliao, Diyi ji 沈從文著作及研究資料第一輯 (Works by Shen Congwen and research materials on him, First collection). Hong Kong, 1978.

Shen Congwen ziliao ji 沈從文資料集 (Research materials on Shen Congwen). Hong Kong, 1972?

Shen Congwen ziliao ji, Di'er ji 沈從文資料集第二輯 (Research materials on Shen Congwen, Second collection). Hong Kong, 1976?

Shen Yuemeng 沈岳萌 [following Zhang Zhaohe, I attribute this piece to Shen Congwen]. "Wo de Erge" 我的二哥 (My Elder Brother No. 2). In Shen Congwen, *Momo ji* (Shanghai, Apr. 1934).

Shen Yunlong 沈雲龍, ed. and annot. "Shen Congwen yu Hu Shi laiwang shuxin" 沈從文與胡適來往書信 (Correspondence between Shen Congwen and Hu Shi). *Zhuanji wenxue* 43, no. 6 (Dec. 1983): 31–35.

Shenbao 申報 ("Shun pao"). Shanghai. Daily newspaper.

Sheng Xiangzi 盛襄子. "Hunan Miao shi shulue" 湖南苗史述略 (Brief account of the history of the Miao in Hunan). *Xin Yaxiya* 13, no. 4 (1 Apr. 1937): 61–80.

———. "Hunan Miao Yao wenti kaoshu" 湖南苗猺問題考述 (Findings on problems of the Miao and Yao of Hunan). *Xin Yaxiya* 10, no. 5 (1 Nov. 1935): 11–23.

———. "Hunan zhi Miao Yao" 湖南之苗猺 (The Miao and Yao of Hunan). *Xin Yaxiya* 8, no. 4 (1 Oct. 1934): 57–67.

———. *Xiangxi Miaoqu zhi shezhi jiqi xianzhuang* 湘西苗區之設治及其現狀 (Administration and current conditions in the Miao areas of West Hunan). Chongqing, 1943.

———. "Zuijin Hunan de Miaomin kaihua yundong" 最近湖南的苗民開化運動 (The recent campaign to civilize the Hunan Miao people). *Xin Yaxiya* 13, no. 1 (1 Jan. 1937): 51–66.

Sheridan, James E. *China in Disintegration: The Republican Era in Chinese History, 1912–1949.* New York, 1975.

———. *Chinese Warlord: The Career of Feng Yü-hsiang.* Stanford, Calif., 1966.

Shi Honggui 石宏規. *Xiangxi Miaozu kaocha jiyao* 湘西苗族考察紀要 (Essentials of an investigation into the West Hunan Miao). Changsha [?], preface dated 1936.

Shina shōbetsu zenshi 支那省別全誌 (Complete gazetteer of China, by province). Tōa Dōbunkai 東亞同文會, ed. Vol. 10: Hunan. Tokyo, 1918.

Sign, The. Union City, N.J. Monthly magazine of The Passionist Missions, Inc.

Sima Changfeng 司馬長風. "Lu Xun bu xuan Shen Congwen" 魯迅不選沈從文 (Lu Xun's nonselection of works by Shen Congwen). In his *Xin wenxue congtan* 新文學叢談 (Collected talks on the new literature). Hong Kong, 1975.

———. *Zhongguo xin wenxue shi* 中國新文學史 (History of the new Chinese literature). Hong Kong, 1975.

Singal, Daniel Joseph. *The War Within: From Victorian to Modernist Thought in the South, 1919–1945*. Chapel Hill, N.C., 1982.

Situ Liangyi 司徒良裔. "Ji Shen Congwen" 記沈從文 (Remembering Shen Congwen). Shanghai *DGB*, "Wenyi" 106, 28 Jan. 1947.

Skinner, G. William, ed. *The City in Late Imperial China*. Stanford, Calif., 1977.

Smedley, Agnes. *Battle Hymn of China*. New York, 1943.

———. *The Great Road: The Life and Times of Chu Te*. New York, 1956.

Smith, Henry Dewitt, II. *Japan's First Student Radicals*. Cambridge, Mass., 1972.

Snow, Edgar. *Red Star Over China*. New York, 1938.

———, ed. *Living China*. New York, 1936.

Snyder, George Randolf. *Ward Hartman: Pioneer Midst Change*. Piqua, Ohio, n.d. [post-1967].

Solinger, Dorothy J. *Regional Government and Political Integration in Southwest China, 1949–1954: A Case Study*. Berkeley, Calif., 1977.

Spence, Jonathan D. *The Gate of Heavenly Peace*. New York, 1981.

Su Xuelin 蘇雪林. "Shen Congwen lun" 沈從文論 (On Shen Congwen). In her *Su Xuelin xuan ji* 蘇雪林選集 (Selected works of Su Xuelin). Taibei, 1961.

Sun Ching-chih (Sun Jingzhi 孫敬之), ed. *The Economic Geography of Central China*. Joint Publications Research Service, trans. 2227-N. Washington, D.C., 1960.

Sun Ling 孫陵. *Fushi xiaopin* 浮世小品 (Little essays about the floating life). Taibei, 1961.

Sutton, Donald S. *Provincial Militarism and the Chinese Republic: The Yunnan Army, 1905–1925*. Ann Arbor, Mich., 1980.

Tandangdang zhaizhu (pseud.) 坦蕩蕩齋主. *Xiandai Zhongguo mingren waishi* 現代中國名人外史 (Who's who in modern China: An unauthorized version). Beiping, 1935.

Tang Tao 唐弢. "'Mingshi caiqing' yu 'shangren jingmai'" 「名士才情」與「商業競賣」 ("Arty celebrity scholars" and "merchant auctioneers"). In *Tang Tao zawen xuan* 唐弢雜文選 (Selected essays of Tang Tao). Beijing, 1955.

Tang Yi 唐夷. "Miaoren de zhenshi xianzhuang" 苗人的真實現狀 (The true circumstances of the Miao). *Yuzhoufeng* 41 (16 May 1937): 229–31.

Tay, William. "'Obscure Poetry': A Controversy in Post-Mao China." In Kinkley, ed., *After Mao*.

Tian Maozhong 田茂忠, comp. "Tujiazu qingge" 土家族情歌 (Love songs of the Tujia folk). *Minjian wenxue* 170 (20 Mar. 1984): 31.

Ting Yi [Ding Yi]. *A Short History of Modern Chinese Literature*. Peking, 1959.
Trilling, Lionel. *Beyond Culture: Essays on Literature and Learning*. New York, 1965.
Wade, T. F. "The Army of the Chinese Empire." *The Chinese Repository* 20, nos. 5, 6, 7 (1851).
Wang, Chi-chen. *Contemporary Chinese Stories*. New York, 1944.
Wang Hao 王浩. "Chongfeng Shen Congwen xiansheng" 重逢沈從文先生 (Reencounter with Mr. Shen Congwen). *Haineiwai* 28 (Nov.–Dec. 1980): 25–26.
Wang Xiangchen 王向辰 (pseud. Lao Xiang 老向). "Wei Shui hebin" 渭水河濱 (On the banks of the Wei River). *XP* 7, no. 161 (7 Jan. 1928): 93–96.
Wang Yao 王瑤. *Zhongguo xin wenxue shigao* 中國新文學史稿 (Draft history of China's new literature). Shanghai, 1954.
Wang Yarong 王亞蓉. "Shen Congwen xiao ji" 沈從文小記 (A sketch of Shen Congwen). *Zhandi* 1980, no. 4: 34–36.
——— and Wang Xu 王㐓. "Shen Congwen and His Book on Ancient Costume." *China Reconstructs* 29, no. 11 (Nov. 1980): 28–32.
Wang Yiyun 王挹雲, comp. "Xiangxi min'ge" 湘西民歌 (West Hunanese folk songs). *Minjian wenyi xuan ji* 9 (Aug. 1955): 56–62.
Wang Zengqi 汪曾祺. "Shen Congwen jiao chuangzuo" 沈從文教創作 (Creative writing as taught by Shen Congwen). *Renmin ribao* [overseas ed.], 22 June 1986.
Wang Zhefu 王哲夫. *Zhongguo xin wenxue yundong shi* 中國新文學運動史 (A history of China's new literature movement). Beiping, 1933.
Wei Juxian 衛聚賢. "Nuo" 儺 (The Nuo rite). *Shuowen yuekan* 1, no. 12 (15 Dec. 1939): 1–12.
Wen Gongzhi 文公直. *Zuijin sanshi nian Zhongguo junshi shi* 最近三十年中國軍事史 (A military history of China during the last 30 years). Taibei, 1962 (reprint of 1930 ed.).
Wen Yiduo. *Wen Yiduo quanji* 聞一多全集 (The complete works of Wen Yiduo). Hong Kong, n.d. [1970's] (reprint of 1948 ed.).
Wenxuejia de qingshu 文學家的情書 (Authors' love letters). Hong Kong, n.d. [1970's].
Wiens, Herold J. *China's March Toward the Tropics*. Hamden, Conn., 1954.
Williams, Robert C. *Artists in Revolution: Portraits of the Russian Avant-garde, 1905–1925*. Bloomington, Ind., 1977.
Wilson, Dick. *When Tigers Fight*. New York, 1982.
Witke, Roxane. *Comrade Chiang Ch'ing*. Boston, 1977.
Wolff, Ernst. *Chou Tso-jen*. New York, 1971.

Woodcock, George. "The Lure of the Primitive." *The American Scholar* 45, no. 3 (Summer 1976): 387–402.

Wright, Mary Clabaugh. *The Last Stand of Chinese Conservatism: The T'ung-Chih Restoration, 1862–1874*. New York, 1967.

———, ed. *China in Revolution: The First Phase, 1900–1913*. New Haven, Conn., 1968.

Wu Xuenao 吳雪惱, trans. and comp. "Miaozu qingge (Xiangxi)" 苗族情歌(湘西) (Miao folk songs from West Hunan). *Minjian wenxue* 153 (20 Oct. 1982): 76–84, 102.

Wu Zelin 吳澤霖, Chen Guojun 陳國鈞, et al. *Guizhou Miao Yi shehui yanjiu* 貴州苗夷社會研究 (Research on Miao and Yi society). Guiyang, 1942.

Xia Yan 夏衍. "Guan de zhu ma? Guan bu zhu le!" 關得住嗎?關不住了! (Can you shut it out? No you can't!). In his *Jieyu suibi* 劫餘隨筆 (Rambling thoughts after the calamity). Hong Kong, 1948.

Xiangxi zizhizhou dituce 湘西自治州地圖册 (Atlas of the West Hunan Autonomous Prefecture). Jishou? Printed by the Zhou Revolutionary Committee, ca. 1979.

Xiao Ganniu 蕭甘牛, comp. "Da Miao Shan qingge" 大苗山情歌 (Love songs from Da Miao Shan). *Minjian wenxue* 21 (Dec. 1956): 52–65.

Xiao Li 蕭離. "Shen Congwen he ta de *Zhongguo gudai fushi yanjiu*" 沈從文和他的「中國古代服飾研究」(Shen Congwen and his *Researches into Ancient Chinese Costume*). *Xin guancha* 265 (10 Sept. 1981): 29–30.

———. "Shen Congwen xiansheng ersan shi" 沈從文先生二三事 (A few things about Mr. Shen Congwen). *Wenhui zengkan* 1980, no. 7 (10 Nov.): 36–39.

Xiao Xing 曉行. "Guanyu ji wei Zhongguo xiandai zuojia yanjiu zongshu" 關於幾位中國現代作家研究綜述 (Summary of [recent] research on some modern Chinese authors). *Zuopin yu zhengming* 41 (17 May 1984): 78–80.

Xiaoshuo yuekan 小說月刊 (The story monthly) Hangzhou.

Xinghuo liaoyuan 星火燎原 (A single spark can start a prairie fire). 10 vols. to date. Beijing, 1958 and continuing to the present.

Yan Ruyi 嚴如熤. *Miao fangbei lan* 苗防備覽 (Defense against the Miao). 1843.

Yang, Gladys, trans. *The Border Town and Other Stories*. Beijing, 1981.

———. *Recollections of West Hunan*. Beijing, 1982.

Yang Hua 楊華. "Lun Shen Congwen de 'Cong xianshi xuexi'" 論沈從文的「從現實學習」(On Shen Congwen's "Learning from Reality"). *Wencui* 2, no. 12/13 (1 Jan. 1947): 38–41.

Yang Jialuo 楊家駱. *Minguo mingren tujian* 民國名人圖鑑 (Who's who in the Republic). Nanjing, 1937.

Yang Lixing 楊力行. "Xiang xi'nan Miao Yao de yule jihui ji jieling" 湘西南苗傜的娛樂集會及節令 (Amusements, assemblies, and festivals of the Miao and Yao of southwestern Hunan). *Hunan wenxian* 2 (Apr. 1969): 28–33.

Yao Nailin 姚乃麟. *Xiandai zuojia lun* 現代作家論 (On modern writers). Shanghai, 1937.

Yao Qingxiang 姚卿詳. "Shen Congwen." Tianjin *Yishibao*, 23 Oct. 1946.

[Yin] Yuangui [印] 遠桂, recorder. "Ganren yaoqu xuan" 竿人謠曲選 (Selected songs from the Zhen'gan folk). *CF* 2037, 2039–42 (20, 22–25 Aug. 1927): 35, 37, 39, 41, 43.

Yu Dafu 郁達夫. "Gei yi wei wenxue qingnian de gongkai zhuang" 給一位文學青年的公開狀 (Open letter to a young man in literature). In *Dafu quanji* 達夫全集 (The complete works of Yu Dafu). Beijing, 1930.

Yuan Bingchang 袁丙昌. "Ting Tujiazu saigehui" 聽土家族賽歌會 (Listening in on a Tujia singing competition festival). *Minjian wenxue* 163 (20 Aug. 1983): 96–101.

Yüan Chia-hua and Robert Payne, eds. and trans. *Contemporary Chinese Stories*. London, 1946.

Yue Daiyun and Carolyn Wakeman. *To the Storm: The Odyssey of a Revolutionary Chinese Woman*. Berkeley, Calif., 1985.

Zeng Xianyin 曾憲蔭. "Shen shan jian feishou" 深山殲匪首 (Wiping out the bandit chief deep in the mountains). In *Jiekai shizong de mimi*.

Zhang Dongsun 張東蓀. *Jingshen fenxixue ABC* 精神分析學 ABC (The ABCs of psychoanalysis). Shanghai, 1929.

Zhang Linglin 張玲麟. "Shen Congwen huanxiang ji" 沈從文還鄉記 (Shen Congwen's return home). *Zhuanji wenxue* 42, no. 2 (Feb. 1983): 47–48.

Zhang Pengyuan [author prefers Chang P'eng-yuan] 張朋園. *Zhongguo xiandaihua de quyu yanjiu: Hunan sheng, 1860–1916* 中國現代化的區域研究:湖南省 1860-1916 (Regional studies of modernization in China: Hunan, 1860–1916). Taibei, 1983.

Zhang Zhaohe 張兆和. *Hupan* 湖畔 (By the lake). Guilin, n.d. [early 1940's?].

Zhao Xiaqiu 趙遐秋 and Zeng Qingrui 曾慶瑞. *Zhongguo xiandai xiaoshuo shi* 中國現代小說史 (A history of modern Chinese fiction). 2 vols. Beijing, 1984.

Zheng Fangkun. "Hunan: Agriculture Enjoys Priority. West Hunan: Getting Rid of Poverty." *Beijing Review* 28, no. 37 (16 Sept. 1985): 24–26.

Zhong Jihua. "My Views on the Study of Modern Literature." *Beijing Review* 27, no. 20 (14 May 1984): 22–24. Rejoinder by Jeffrey C. Kinkley in 27, no. 36 (3 Sept. 1984): 5.

Zhong Jingwen 鍾敬文, ed. *Minjian wenyi xin lunji* 民間文藝新論集 (New collection of writings on folk literature and art). N.p., 1950.

Zhong Kailai 鍾開萊. "Zhong Kailai jiaoshou tan Shen Congwen xiansheng" 鍾開萊教授談沈從文先生 (Professor K. L. Chung talks about Mr. Shen Congwen). *Haineiwai* 27 (Sept.–Oct. 1980): 24–26.

Zhongguo wenxuejia cidian 中國文學家辭典 (Dictionary of Chinese authors). 1 vol. to date. Chengdu, 1979.

Zhongguo xiandai wenxueshi 中國現代文學史 (A history of modern Chinese literature). Lin Zhihao 林志浩 and the People's Univ. Dept. of Languages and Literatures, eds. 2 vols. Beijing, 1980.

Zhongguo xiandai wenxueshi. "Nine Institutes and Schools" [headed by Beijing, Nanjing, and Xiamen universities], eds. Nanjing, 1979.

Zhongguo xiandai wenxueshi. Tang Tao 唐弢, ed. 2 vols. Beijing, 1979.

Zhou Fennuo 周芬娜. "Ding Ling, Hu Yepin, Shen Congwen" 丁玲, 胡也頻, 沈從文. *Zhongguoren yuekan* 2, no. 8 (Sept. 1980): 96–100.

Zhou Zuoren 周作人. "Chuyequan xuyan" 初夜權序言 (Preface on the *jus primae noctis*). *Yusi* 103 (30 Oct. 1926): 491–93.

———, trans. *Kuangyan shifan* 狂言十番 (Ten *kyōgen*). Beijing, 1926.

Zhu Guangqian 朱光潛. "Cong Shen Congwen xiansheng de renge kan ta de wenyi fengge" 從沈從文先生的人格看他的文藝風格 (Looking at Mr. Shen Congwen's literary style in view of his character). *Hua cheng* 5 (May 1980): 119.

Zhuangshi 裝飾 (Decoration). Beijing. Bimonthly illustrated journal.

Zuo Qi 左齊. "Ba qian li lu yun he yue" 八千里路雲和月 (A several-thousand-mile trek). In *Xinghuo liaoyuan*, vol. 1A: 263–70.

Zuojia nishi 作家膩事 (Intimate affairs of the authors). Qianqiu chubanshe 千秋出版社, ed. Hong Kong, 1971 (reprint of 1931 ed.).

A Chronological Listing of Shen Congwen's Works, by Date of Publication

This list, compiled with much assistance from Shao Huaqiang, highlights first editions. Reprints are noted if they gained wide currency or show significant revision. (Texts altered in content as well as style bear a "*".) Readers most interested in final versions will want to refer to *WJ*. Shen revised all his works one last time for it, regrouping odd pieces into new collections. Censors barred many of his articles about literary policy and reminiscences of Ding Ling from *WJ*. Two whole volumes of coordinate "research materials" were killed by the 1983 campaign against "spiritual pollution." Still, many of *WJ*'s omissions reflect the author's judgment, over the protests of project editors who preferred inclusiveness. Readers may of course disagree with some of Shen's choices. For instance, the 1935 text of "Yu hou," from which David Kidd made his delightful translation, has folk songs lacking in both the original and *WJ* versions. Yet the songs appear in another "final," authorized edition, Ling Yu's choice 1983 five-volume *Shen Congwen xuan ji*. Critics must choose their own best texts.

My sense is that ten to fifteen percent of Shen's oeuvre is still missing. That includes stories and poems from the 1920's, miscellaneous pieces published in short-lived 1930's magazines, and essays and letters printed in early-1940's Kunming and late-1940's Peking newspapers. Literarily, the major lost items may be early 1940's fiction, including "Zhai xing lu" and the Chinese text of "Kan hong lu." Shao Huaqiang has leads for dozens more unrecovered works, but since he and I have come across pre-advertised pieces of Shen's that were never printed, or perhaps even written, we are reluctant to list unverified works. If I have not personally seen an item in its original publication, I have marked it with " + "; " ++ " indicates items I have never seen, even in reprint. Nonextant short-story collections (all marked " ++ ") were included below if Shen recalled to Shao or me that they did in fact exist.

I have listed Shen's works year by year, with articles first and whole books second. Books first published serially appear in both categories. An entry for a work in a journal states: (1) the title of the work; (2) an English translation of the title, with an indication of the genre, if not prose; (3) the first date of publication and (4) the place of it; (5) alternative titles for the work; (6) the volume and page numbers of the work in *WJ*, if it is reprinted there; (7) the names of translators of the work, keyed to fuller entries in the Selected Bibliography; and (8) in parentheses, the date of writing, but only if the author supplied it soon after the fact. Shen did not always record when he finished a work, or necessarily exclusively use the Western calendar. Inferences are enclosed in brackets; educated guesses are followed by question marks. They reflect my opinion alone. Years and days are given in Arabic numerals; months, in Roman numerals.

Example:
"Deng" 燈 (Lamp). 1930.ii.10. *Xinyue* 2.12: 24 p. *WJ* 4: 23–45.* Tr. by Ching and Payne as "The Lamp." Tr. by Kai-yu Hsu as "The Lamp." In Lau et al. Tr. by Yüan and Payne as "The Lamp." ([1929].v.24).

The short story "Deng," which I render as "Lamp," first appeared on 10 February 1930, in volume 2, number 12 of *Xinyue*. *Xinyue* had no cover-to-cover page numbers, but devoted 24 internally numbered pages to "Deng." The story is reprinted in the *Shen Congwen wenji*, volume 4, pages 23 to 45, and has been translated three times. See the Selected Bibliography, under (1) Ching and Payne, (2) Lau et al., and (3) Yüan and Payne. The asterisk indicates that reprintings of the work, including the final one, in *Wenji*, differ from the earliest version. (Shen gave the story a new ending. This is one reason why translations of the story vary so much: they were made from different texts.) Shen's original date-and-place line, in *Xinyue*, says "May 24." It also gives "Wusong" as the place. I have not burdened these entries with place name data, but from it I was able to deduce the year in this case. "Deng" must have been completed on 24 May 1929.

1924

"Yi feng wei ceng fuyou de xin" 一封未曾付郵的信 (A letter never mailed). 1924.xii.22. *CF* 306: 3–4. *WJ* 10: 2–5.
"Wo hen ta de shi..." 我恨他的是... (I hate him because...). 1924.xii.28. *CF* 311: 4. ([1924].xii.20).

1925

"Pingfan gushi" [1] 平凡故事 (An ordinary story; Shen's first piece by this title). 1925.i.13. *Jingbao*, "Minzhong wenyi" 5. ++
"Yaoye," 1, 2 遙夜 (Long nights, nos. 1 and 2). 1925.i.19. *CF* 13: 2–3. *WJ* 9: 18–22. (1924.xii.26, "one day after Christmas").
"Gongyu zhong" 公寓中 (In a lodging house). 1925.i.30, 31. *CF* 18, 19: 3;

3–4. (First entries dated [1924].xi.16–28; second installment, [1924], "Christmas, at the Qinghua Hostel").

"Yaoye," 3 遙夜 (Long nights, no. 3). 1925.ii.3. *CF* 22: 4. (Ch. cal. 1924, New Year's Eve; W. cal. [1925].i.23]).

"Yaoye," 4 遙夜 (Long nights, no. 4). 1925.ii.12. *CF* 30: 4. ([1925].i.30).

"San Bei xiansheng jiaxun" 三貝先生家訓 (The family precepts of Mr. San Bei). 1925.ii.20. *CF* 37: 4. *WJ* 8: 2–5.

"Yaoye," 5 遙夜 (Long nights, no. 5). 1925.iii.9. *CF* 52: 4. ([1925].ii.22).

"Kuangren shujian—Yu X" 狂人書簡—與X (A madman's correspondence—To X). 1925.iii.10. *Jingbao*, "Minzhong wenyi" 12. ++ (1925.iii.1).

"Liuguang" 流光 (The swift flow of time). 1925.iii.21. *CF* 63: 4. *WJ* 10: 6–9.

"'Ni yao zhidao'" 「你要知道」 ("You must know"). 1925.iv.18. *Jingbao fukan* 122: 134–35. ([1925].iv.15).

"'Wo xin li' ye 'changchang xiang'" 「我心裏」也「常常想」 (I, too, "often think," "in my heart"). 1925.iv.26. *Jingbao fukan* 130: 199–200.

"Kuangren shujian—Gei dao X Daxue diyi jiaoshi jiao naozhi de kelian pengyou" 狂人書簡—給到X大學第一教室絞腦汁的可憐朋友 (A madman's correspondence—To my pathetic friends who go to X University to cudgel their brains in classroom no. 1). 1925.iv.28. *Jingbao*, "Minzhong wenyi" 19. + *WJ* 10: 16–19. (1925.iv.15).

"Kuangren shujian—Gei dizhe tou de kui" 狂人書簡—給低着頭的葵 (A madman's correspondence—To sunflowers that have bowed their heads). 1925.iv.28. *Jingbao*, "Minzhong wenyi" 19. ++ (1925.iv.10).

"Chun yue" 春月 (Spring moon; poem). 1925.v.9. *CF* 103: 64.

"Kuangren shujian—Gei shifu de xin" 狂人書簡—給師傅的信 (A madman's correspondence—A letter to Teacher). 1925.v.12. *Jingbao*, "Minzhong wenyi" 21. ++ (1925.iv.13).

"Zhi Wei Gang xiansheng" 致唯剛先生 (To Mr. Wei Gang; actual letter to Lin Zaiping). 1925.v.12. *CF* 105: 79–80. *WJ* 10: 260–62. ([1925].v.8).

"Shilu de xiao gaoyang" 失路的小羔羊 (The little lost lamb; poem). 1925.v.14. *CF* 107: 96.

"Daigou" 代狗 (Daigou; Miao: "Young fella"). 1925.v.16. *Jingbao*, 6th supp., *Wenxue zhoukan* 20: 154–56. *WJ* 1: 19–22. ([1925].iv.30).

"Tuzhuobian" 屠桌邊 (At the butcher's block). 1925.v.21. *CF* 112: 133–35. *WJ* 2: 60–66. ([1925].iv.16).

"Kuangren shujian—Gei wo jiang bian lao yang de Dage" 狂人書簡—給我將變老樣的大哥 (A madman's correspondence—To my Elder Brother, who is about to change). 1925.v.26. *Jingbao*, "Minzhong wenyi" 22. ++ (1925.v.2).

"Henji" 痕跡 (Traces; poem). 1925.vi.13. *Jingbao*, 6th supp., *Wenxue zhoukan* 24: 188–89. ([1925].v.17).

"Fusheng" 福生 (Fusheng [name]). 1925.vi.29. *Yusi* 33: 275–78. *WJ* 8: 6–11.

"Xiang jian de xia (Zhen'gan tuhua)" 鄉間的夏(鎮筸土話) (Summer in the countryside [Rustic dialect from Zhen'gan]; poems with annotations). 1925.vii.12. *Guoyu zhoukan* 5: 5–6. ([1925].vi.20).

"Qiebuzhe biji—Duanyang" 怯步者筆記—端陽 (Jottings of a timorous man—On the Duanyang Festival). 1925.vii.16. *CF* 1226: 79–80. No. 4 of "Sheng zhi jilu." *WJ* 9: 45–48. ([1925].vi.12, night).

"Dao fenmu de lu" 到坟墓的路 (Roads to the grave; poems). 1925.vii.22. *CF* 1230: 109–10. (1925.vii.18).

"Dao fenmu qu" 到坟墓去 (To the grave; poem). 1925.vii.23. *CF* 1231: 120. (1925.vii).

"Chang he xiao qiao" 長河小橋 (A little bridge over a long river). 1925.vii.31. *CF* 1236: 160. (Ch.cal. [1925].v.5; W. cal. [1925].vi.25]).

"Jueshi yihou" 絕食以後 (After fasting; one section is a letter to Lin Zaiping). 1925.viii.4, 6. *CF* 1240, 1242: 31–32, 43–44. ([1925].vii.23).

"Yujin" 餘燼 (Embers; poem). 1925.viii.15. *Chenbao*, "Wenxue xunkan" 78: 12. ([1925].vii.24).

"Yaoye," 9 遙夜 (Long nights, no. 9; poem). 1925.viii.21. *CF* 1254: 132.

"Di'er ge Feifei" 第二個狒狒 (The second Feifei; "Feifei," after the Chinese rendering of "Tartarin"). 1925.viii.22. *CF* 1255: 138–40. *WJ* 8: 12–16. ([1925].viii.16).

"Qiren qiye 其人其夜 (The fellow and his nights; poem). 1925.viii.22. *Jingbao*, 6th supp., *Wenxue zhoukan*, p. 51. ([1925].viii).

"Dao Beihai qu" 到北海去 (Going to Beihai). 1925.viii.25. *Chenbao*, "Wenxue xunkan" 79: 16–18. *WJ* 9: 12–17. ([1925].viii.5).

"Yaxia shiren" 崖下詩人 (Poet beneath the cliffs). 1925.viii.27, 29. *CF* 1259, 1260: 170–71, 180. *WJ* 8: 17–21. ([1925].viii.22).

"Qiebuzhe biji—jisheng" 怯步者筆記—雞聲 (Jottings of a timorous man—cock crows). 1925.viii.29. *XP* 2.38: 237–38. No. 3 of "Sheng zhi jilu." *WJ* 9: 43–45; 10: 20–21. ([1925].vi.14).

"Huashi jia xiong" 畫師家兄 (Our elder brother, the artist; epistolary narrative). 1925.viii.31. *CF* 1261: 187–88. *WJ* 8: 22–25. ([1925].viii.25).

"Yong 'A' zi jixialai de shi" 用 A 字記下來的事 (Events to be filed under 'A'). 1925.ix.5. *Chenbao*, "Wenxue xunkan" 80: 4–6. ([1925].viii.14, morning).

"Xishan de yue" 西山的月 (Moon over the Western Hills). 1925.ix.7. *CF* 1267: 47–48. *WJ* 10: 22–26. ([1925].ix.1).

"Jiuyue jiju" 舊約集句 (Words from the Old Testament). 1925.ix.12. *CF* 1270: 72.

"Chulian" 初戀 (First love; poem). 1925.ix.20. *Guoyu zhoukan* 15: 6. (1925.vii).

"Zhen'gan de ge" 鎮筸的歌 (Zhen'gan songs; poems). 1925.ix.20. *Guoyu zhoukan* 15: 5–6. (1925.vii).

"Mian xie" 棉鞋 (Cotton shoes). 1925.ix.21. *CF* 1276: 115–18. *WJ* 8: 26–33. ([1925].ix.5).

"Xiwang" 希望 (A wish; poem). 1925.ix.27. *CF* 1281: 160 ([1925].ix.23).
"Fuguan" 副官 (Adjutant). 1925.x.17. *XP* 2.45: 307–8. *WJ* 8: 34–37. ([1925].ix.28).
"Chahui yihou" 茶會以後 (After the tea party). 1925.x.19. *CF* 1292: 38–39. Authorship uncertain; Shen does not remember it as his story. Courtesy Shao. (1925.i.6).
"Yi tian shi zhe yang guo de" 一天是這樣過的 (Thus passes a day). 1925.x.21. *CF* 1293: 42–44. In *Yazi*, retitled "Yi tian" 一天 (A day). *WJ* 8: 38–49; 9: 27–37. (1925.x.10 Holiday).
"Menshi" [1] 捫蝨 (Nit-picking; Shen's first piece by this title). 1925.x.24. *CF* 1295: 51–52. ([1925].ix?.24).
"Ye yu" [1] 夜漁 (Night fishing; Shen's first piece by this title). 1925.x.26. *CF* 1296: 54–55. *WJ* 1: 14–18. ([1925].iii.21).
"Mai tang fu mai zhe" 賣糖復賣蔗 (The sugar peddler sells cane; dramatic monologue—"mime"). 1925.x.29. *CF* 1298: 63–64. ([1925].x.19).
"Shiji" 市集 (At market). 1925.xi.11. *CF* 1305: 24. *WJ* 10: 10–15. ([1925].iii.20; afterword by Xu Zhimo, 1925.iv.15).
"Dutu" 賭徒 (Gamblers; play—"mime"). 1925.xi.12. *CF* 1306: 28. (Rev. [1925].x.27).
"Shuiche" 水車 (The water wheel). 1925.xi.14. *CF* 1307: 32. *WJ* 9: 23–26. ([1925].xi.6).
"Gengfu Ahan" 更夫阿韓 (Ahan the night watch). 1925.xi.16. *CF* 1308: 35–36. *WJ* 8: 99–106. ([1925].v.4).
"Guanyu 'Shiji' de shengming" 關于「市集」的聲明 (Statement about "At Market"). 1925.xi.16. *CF* 1308: 36. With a reply by Xu Zhimo.
"Meigui yu Jiumei" 玫瑰與九妹 (Roses and Little Sister No. 9). 1925.xi.19. *CF* 1400: 44. *WJ* 1: 10–13.
"Menshi" [2] 捫蝨 (Nit-picking; second piece by this title). 1925.xi.23. *CF* 1402: 52. ([1925].xi.8).
"Ruilong" 瑞龍 (Ruilong [name]). 1925.xi.26. *CF* 1404: 58–60. *WJ* 8: 57–66.
"Ye dian" 野店 (Inn of the wilds; play—"mime"). 1925.xi.28. *CF* 1405: 64. (Rev. [1925].xi.15).
"Laba zhou" 臘八粥 (Holiday fruit congee). 1925.xii.1. *Chenbao* 7th Anniv. Extra Edition, pp. 370–73. *WJ* 1: 23–27. (1924?.xii.26).
"Yifang" 移防 (Transfer). 1925.xii.7. *CF* 1406: 3–4. In *Yazi*, retitled "Chuanshang" 船上 (On board the boats). *WJ* 1: 28–33. ([1925].ix.21).
"Panbing" 叛兵 (Mutineers; poem). 1925.xii.19. *CF* 1413: 32. ([1925].xi).

1926

"Du dao" 賭道 (Gambling). 1926.i.23, 25. *CF* 1429, 1430: 43–44, 47–48. *WJ* 8: 67–73. ([1925].xii.27).
"Song daibiao" 宋代表 (Representative Song). 1926.i.25. *DF* 23.2: 111–15. *WJ* 8: 50–56. ([1925].x.16).

"'Feifei' de beiai"「狒狒」的悲哀 (Feifei's sadness; poem). 1926.ii.6. *XP* 3.61: 170–71. (1926?.i?.12).
"Tongxin" 通信 (Letter). 1926.iii.6. *CF* 1449: 16. (Ch. cal. [1926].i.10; W. cal. [1926.ii.22]).
"Muqin" [1] 母親 (The mother; first of two plays by this title). 1926.iii.10. *CF* 1451: 22–23. ([1926].ii).
"Wo xihuan ni" 我喜歡你 (I love you; poem). 1926.iii.10. *CF* 1451: 24. ([1926].ii).
"Zhanling Weicheng" 佔領渭城 (Occupying Weicheng). 1926.iii.11. *CF* 1361: 25–27. In *Yazi*, retitled "Zhanling" 佔領 (Occupying a new town). *WJ* 1: 34–41. (1926).
"Candong" 殘冬 (The last days of winter; poem). 1926.iii.13. *CF* 1362: 32. (Ch. cal. 1926, New Year; W. cal. [1926.ii.13]).
"Ai" 愛 (Love; poem). 1926.iii.18. *CF* 1365: 44. ([1926].iii.7).
"Tangxiong" 堂兄 (Cousin [male first cousin on the father's side]). 1926.iii.20. *CF* 1366: 46–48. *WJ* 8: 74–84. (Ch. cal. [1926], day before i.15; W. cal. [1926.ii.26]).
"Sheng zhi jilu," 1, 2 生之記錄 (Record of living, nos. one and two). 1926.iii.27, 29. *CF* 1370, 1371: 63, 68. No. 3 (included in this series retrospectively) is "Qiebuzhe biji—jisheng"; no. 4, "Qiebuzhe biji—Duanyang"; no. 5, "Lü de huaping." 1–5 in *WJ* 9: 38–50.
"Hui" 悔 (Regrets; poem). 1926.iii.31. *CF* 1372: 72. ([1926].iii).
"Muqin" [2] 母親 (The mother; second of two plays by this title). 1926.iii.31; iv.5. *CF* 1372, 1374: 70–72; 12. (1926.iii).
"Wuti" 無題 (Untitled; poem). 1926.iv.3. *XP* 3.69: 335. ([1926].iii).
"Zhong jun" 重君 (Master Zhong). 1926.iv.7. *CF* 1375: 14–15. ([1925].x).
"Meng" 夢 (Dream; poem). 1926.iv.8. *CF, shi juan* 2: 20. ([1926].iii.28).
"Mangren" 盲人 (The blind one; play). 1926.iv.14, 17, 19. *CF* 1378–1380: 31–32, 38–39, 44. ([1926], end of March).
"Yun qu" 雲曲 (Cloud song; poem). 1926.iv.14. *CF* 1378: 32.
"Cheng Xiao Sha" 呈小莎 (Humbly offered to Sophie; poem). 1926.iv.17. *CF* 1379: 40 ([1926].iii.13).
"Zai bie yi ge guodu li" 在別一個國度裏 (In a separate realm). 1926.iv.24; v.1; v.8; v.15. *XP* 3.72–75: 394–99, 416–18, 428–33, 451–55. In *Nanzi xuzhi*, retitled "Nanzi xuzhi" 男子須知 (What a man must know). *WJ* 8: 146–72. (1926.iii.24).
"Lü de huaping" 綠的花瓶 (A green vase). 1926.v.3. *CF* 1386: 7–8. No. 5 of "Sheng zhi jilu." *WJ* 9: 48–50. ([1926], end of April).
"Huaihuazhen" 槐化鎮 (Huaihua town). 1926.v.5. *CF* 1387: 11–12. *WJ* 1: 42–46. ([1926].iv.30).
"Huan yuan" 還愿 (Returning thanks to the gods; poem). 1926.v.6. *CF, shi juan* 6: 16. ([1926].iii.28).
"Yue qu" 月曲 (Moon song; poem). 1926.v.6. *CF, shi juan* 6: 15–16. ([1926].iii).

"X" X (X [the Roman letter]; poem). 1926.v.19. *CF* 1393: 43. ("One dreamy evening, [1926].v.10").
"Qiuren" 囚人 (Prisoner; poem). 1926.v.22. *XP* 3.76: 478–79. ([1926].iii).
"Ji Bai Di" 寄柏弟 (Sent to Younger Brother Bai; poem). 1926.v.31. *CF* 1398: 71. ([1926].v.25).
"Junzi" 菌子 (Junzi [name]). 1926.vi.14, 16, 21, 23; vii.3. *CF* 1404, 1405, 1407, 1408, 1412: 30–31, 35–36, 44, 48; 2–3. *WJ* 8: 85–98. ([1926].iii).
"Bomu" 薄暮 (Dusk; poem). 1926.vi.28. *CF* 1410: 55. ([1926].vi).
"Liming" 黎明 (Daybreak). 1926.vi.28, 30. *CF* 1410, 1411: 53–54, 59–60. *WJ* 8: 107–15. (Ch. cal. [1926], 3 days before v.5 Festival; W. cal. [1926.vi.11]).
"Yazi" 鴨子 (Duck; play). 1926.vii.17. *XP* 4.84: 111–14. ([1926].vi.28).
"Shaobing" 哨兵 (Sentry). 1926.vii.26, 28. *CF* 1422, 1423: 42–44, 45–47. *WJ* 8: 116–29. ([1926].vi.20).
"San shou sudupo" 三獸窣堵波 (The stupa of the three animals; play). 1926.vii.31. *CF* 1424: 49–50.
"Yu" [1] 雨 (Rain; Shen's first piece by this title). 1926.vii. *Shijie ribao*, bound vol. 1. + In *Yazi*. *WJ* 1: 2–4. ([1926].v.13).
"Di'er ge Feifei yin" 第二個狒狒引 (Preface to *The Second Feifei*). 1926.viii.2. *CF* 1425: 3. *WJ* 11: 2–3. (1926.vii.15).
"Lubian" 爐邊 (Hearthside). 1926.viii.10. *XS* 17.8: 6–10. *WJ* 2: 67–73. ([1926].vi).
"Yanggao" 羊羔 (Lamb; play). 1926.viii.14. *XP* 4.88: 192–95. ([1926].vii.18).
"Wo de xiaoxue jiaoyu" 我的小學教育 (My primary school education). 1926.viii.18. *CF* 1432: 29–31. *WJ* 2: 20–30. ([1926].viii.10).
"Láo mei, zuohen!" (Title in Romanized Miao, misprints corrected acc. *WJ*: "Maiden, How Beautiful You Are!"). 1926.viii.30. *CF* 1437: 49–50. *WJ* 10: 27–33. ([1926].viii.21, late at night).
"Chuanshibing" 傳事兵 (Camp messenger). 1926.ix.11, 13. *CF* 1442, 1443: 19–20, 21 22. *WJ* 2: 80–87. ([1926].viii.27).
"Yi ge wanhui" 一個晚會 (A soiree). 1926.ix.29, 30; x.2. *CF* 1449, 1450, 1451: 45–46, 51–52; 3–4. *WJ* 8: 130–43. ([1926].viii.20).
"Ji Lu Tao" 記陸弢 (Remembering Lu Tao). 1926.x.22. *Shijie ribao*, "Wenxue" 1. + *WJ* 2: 74–79. ([1926].ix).
"Guonian" [1] 過年 (New Year's; Shen's first piece by this title, a play). 1926.x.25. *CF* 1463: 50–51.
"Du Mengwei de shi xiangqi nei ge 'ai' zi" 讀夢葦的詩想起那個「愛」字 (Thinking about that word, "love," after reading [Liu] Mengwei's poetry). 1926.x.29. *Shijie ribao*, "Wenxue" 2. ++ ([1926].x).
"Songzi jun" 松子君 (Master Songzi). 1926.xi.22, 24. *CF* 1479, 1480: 50–52, 54–56. *WJ* 2: 40–59. ([1926].xi.10).
"Guanyu san shou sudupo" 關於三獸窣堵波 (About "The Stupa of the Three Animals"). 1926.xi. *Yazi*. (1926?.vii.20).

"Wangshi" 往事 (Events gone by). 1926.xi. *Yazi*. *WJ* 1: 5–9.
"Xiaocao yu fuping" 小草與浮萍 (The little grass and the duckweed). 1926.xi. *Yazi*. *WJ* 9: 6–11. (1926?.ii.14).
"Xiaoshen" 宵神 (The Xiao god; play). 1926.xi. *Yazi*.
"Xishuai" 蟋蟀 (Cricket; play). 1926.xi. *Yazi*. (1925?.viii.13).
"Yinghuo" 螢火 (Firefly; poem). 1926.xi. *Yazi*.
"Yuexia" 月下 (Under the moon). 1926.xi. *Yazi*. *WJ* 9: 2–5.
"Tushushi" 圖書室 (The reading room). 1926.xii.4. *CF* 1486: 12. Authorship uncertain. Shen considers it his. Courtesy Shao. ([1926].xi.7).
"Lansheng tong Lansheng taitai" 嵐生同嵐生太太 (Lansheng and his Mrs.). 1926.xii.11. *XP* 5.105: 16–20. *WJ* 2: 31–39. ([1926].xii).
"Ganren yaoqu" 竿人謠曲 (Songs of the Zhen'gan folk; folk songs, with introduction and commentary). 1926.xii.25, 27, 29. *CF* 1498, 1499, 1500: 59–60, 63–64, 67–68. (Completed 1926.xi).

Yazi 鴨子 (Duck). Beijing: Beixin. Nov. 1926. *WJ* 1: 1–46; 9: 1–50 (abridged).
Di'er ge Feifei 第二個狒狒 (The second Feifei). Beijing: Chenbaoshe. 1926? ++
Shiji 市集 (At market). Beijing: Chenbaoshe. 1926? ++

1927

"Meng'en de haizi" 蒙恩的孩子 (The child of Meng'en; play). 1927.i. *XP*, 2nd Anniv. Extra Edition, pp. 250–59.
"Ruwuhou" 入伍後 (After entering the ranks). 1927.i. *XP*, 2nd Anniv. Extra Edition, pp. 205–217. *WJ* 2: 2–19. ([1926].xi.7).
"Shu" 曙 (Dawn; poem). 1927.i. *XP*, 2nd Anniv. Extra Edition, pp. 240–49. (Ch. cal. 1926, 5 days before the viii.15 Festival; W. cal. [1926].ix.16]).
"Shisi ye jian" 十四夜間 (Night of the fourteenth). 1927.iv.10. *XS* 18.4: 4 p. *WJ* 2: 176–84. Tr. by Ching and Payne as "The Fourteenth Moon."
"Fengfu zhi ge" 瘋婦之歌 (Song of the crazy woman; poem). 1927.iv.16. *XP* 5.123: 376–78. ([1927].iii.26).
"Chen" 晨 (Morning). 1927.v.7. *XP* 5.126: 426–32. *WJ* 1: 56–66. (1927.iii).
"Guizishou" 劊子手 (The executioner). 1927.v.10. *DF* 24.9: 71–75.
"Migan" 蜜柑 (Sweet mandarins). 1927.v.28. *XP* 5.129: 490–93. *WJ* 1: 67–72.
"Zaocan" 早餐 (Breakfast). 1927.vi.17, 18, 20. *CF* 1974, 1975, 1977: 30, 32, 34.
"Chuba na ri" 初八那日 (The first eighth of the month). 1927.vi.18. *XP* 6.132: 550–54. *WJ* 1: 48–55.
"Caosheng" 草繩 (Grass rope). 1927.vi.21, 22. *CF* 1978, 1979: 36, 38. *WJ* 1: 73–79. (Completed [1927].iii.28).

"Qian Sheng de ai" 乾生的愛 (Qian Sheng's love). 1927.vi.23, 24, 25. *CF* 1980, 1981, 1982: 40, 42, 44. (1927.v).

"Lie yezhu de ren" 獵野猪的人 (The wild pig hunter). 1927.vi.25. *XP* 6.133: 573–79. In *Migan*, retitled "Lie yezhu de gushi" 獵野猪的故事 (A story about hunting wild pigs). *WJ* 1: 80–89. ([1927].iv).

"Qie han" 怯漢 (A fainthearted man). 1927.vi.27, 28. *CF* 1984, 1985: 46, 48. (1927, late spring).

"Chun" [1] 春 (Spring; Shen's first piece by this title; alternating boy-girl song). 1927.vi.29, 30. *CF* 1986, 1987: 50, 52. (Completed [1927].vi.10).

"Huoren de jiating" 或人的家庭 (Someone's family). 1927.vii.1. *CF* 1988: 1–2. *WJ* 2: 168–75. ([1927].vi.20).

"Huang jun riji" 篁君日記 (The diary of Master Huang). 1927.vii.13–16, 18–21, 30; ix.22–24. *CF* 1999–2002, 2004–2007, 2016, 2069–2071: 20, 22, 24, 26, 28, 30, 32, 34, 49–50; 38, 40, 42. *WJ* 2: 185–249. (Interior preface "by Huang jun" is dated 1926.xii.27; author's preface is dated [1927].vi.24).

"Shangui" 山鬼 (Mountain spirit). 1927.vii.16, 23. *XP* 6.136, 137: 630–37, 655–58. In *Congwen xiaoshuo ji*, retitled "Yi ge shenmi de dianzi" 一個神秘的顛子 (A mysterious madman). *WJ* 2: 135–66.

"Chang xia" 長夏 (Long summer). 1927.viii.1–6. *CF* 2018–2023: 2, 4, 6, 8, 10, 12.

"Wo de lin" 我的隣 (My neighbors). 1927.viii.10. *XS* 18.8: 84–88. *WJ* 1: 156–62.

"Lao Wei de meng" 老魏的夢 (Friend Wei's dream). 1927.viii.18–20, viii.22–23. *CF* 2035–2037, 2039–2040: 32, 34, 36, 38, 40. In *Laoshi ren*, main body (without the preface) excerpted, under the original interior title of "Yi ge furen de riji" 一個婦人的日記 (A woman's diary). *WJ* 1: 186–200. (Completed 1927.vii; diary entries run from [1927].iv.13 to v.7).

"Qiu" [1] 秋 (Autumn; Shen's first work by this title, a poem). 1927.viii.26. *CF* 2043: 45. (Ch. cal. vii.15 Festival, night; W. cal. [1927.viii.12]).

"Louluo" 嘍囉 (Outlaws). 1927.ix.5 8. *CF* 2053–2056. 8, 10, 12, 14. *WJ* 2: 308–16.

"You Erzha" 遊二閘 (Touring Two Locks). 1927.ix.28–30. *CF* 2075–2077: 48, 50, 52. *WJ* 10: 34–41. ([1927].ix.22, late at night).

"Kan airen qu" 看愛人去 (Going to see someone else's lover). 1927.ix. *Migan*. (1927?.v).

"Qu—piao" 覷 — 瞟 (Peering—ogling; poem). 1927.x.8. *CF* 2085: 13. ([1927].ix).

"Lianzhang" 連長 (The captain). 1927.x.24–26. *CF* 2100–2102: 38, 40, 42. *WJ* 1: 144–55. (Ch. cal. [1927], 5 days after the ix.9 Festival; W. cal. [1927.x.9]).

"Dao shijie shang zixu" 到世界上自序 (Author's preface to *Into the World*). 1927.x.26, 27. *CF* 2102, 2103: 41, 43.

"Xue" 雪 (Snow). 1927.x.27–29, 31. *CF* 2103–2105, 2107: 44, 46, 48, 50. *WJ* 1: 135–43.

"Zhe ge nanren he nei ge nüren" 這個男人和那個女人 (This man and that woman). 1927.xi.21–26. *CF* 2128–2133: 36, 38, 40, 42, 44, 46. In *Laoshi ren*, retitled "Yi jian xin de zuinie" 一件心的罪孽 (A crime of the heart); lacks the preface. ([1927].xi.4).

"Laoshi ren" 老實人 (The simpleton). 1927.xii.7–10, 12–17. *CF* 2144–2147, 2149–2154: 12, 14, 16, 18, 20, 22, 24, 26, 28, 30. *WJ* 1: 92–125. (1927, winter).

"Yishu zatan" 藝術雜談 (A rambling talk about art). 1927.xii.12. *CF* 2149: 19–20.

"Haoguan xianshi de ren" 好管閒事的人 (The busybody). 1927.xii.19–24. *CF* 2156–2161: 32, 34, 36, 38, 40, 42. *WJ* 2: 252–69. ([1927].xi.20).

"Chuanshang anshang" 船上岸上 (Aboard and on shore). 1927.xii.29, 30, 31. *CF* 2165, 2166, 2167: 48, 50, 52. *WJ* 1: 126–34. ([1927].xii).

Migan 蜜柑 (Sweet mandarins). Shanghai: Xinyue. Sept. 1927. May 1928. *WJ* 1: 47–89 (abridged).

Yazhai furen 押寨夫人 (Captive mistress of the stockade; after the title story, which is "Zai bie yi ge guodu li" under a new title). Shanghai: Shangwu. 1927. ++

Dao shijie shang 到世界上 (Into the world). Shanghai? 1927? ++ Publication recollected by Shen Congwen.

1928

"Zai sishu" 在私塾 (In a private school). 1928.i.10. *XS* 19.1: 87–99. *WJ* 1: 163–85. ([1927].xi).

"Nan xing zaji" 南行雜記 (Discursive notes on a trip south). 1928.ii.1–4. *CF* 2189–2192: 2, 4, 6, 7–8. (Diary entries for [1928].i.9, 10, 11, 13).

"Laoshi ren xu" 老實人序 (Preface to *The Simpleton*). 1928.ii.4. *XP* 7.165: 178–79. Entitled "Zixu" 自序 (Author's preface) in *Laoshi ren*. This piece is also the preface to *Yi ge furen de riji*. ([1927].xii).

"Diedie" 爹爹 (Daddy). 1928.ii.23, 26?, 28, cont.? *Zhongyang ribao*, "Modeng" 13, 15, 16, cont.? *WJ* 2: 341–59.

"Jiu meng" 舊夢 (Past dreams). 1928.ii.25–ix.29. *XP* 7.168 to 8.199, in 28 installments, continuous but for 8.184–186 (1928.vi.16, 23, 30) and 8.195 (1928.ix.1). (Completed 1928.vii).

"Alisi Zhongguo youji" 阿麗思中國遊記 (Alice's adventures in China). 1928.iii.10–vi.10 (vol. 1); 1928.vii.10–x.10 (vol. 2). *Xinyue* 1.1–8. *WJ* 1: 207–466.

"Houxu" 後序 (Retrospective preface [to the first volume of *Alice's Adventures in China*]). 1928.iii.10. *Xinyue* 1.1. *WJ* 1: 202–206.

"Huoren de taitai" 或人的太太 (Someone's wife). 1928.iii.10. XS 19.3: 324–29. WJ 2: 270–79. ([1927].xii).
"Zuwu" 卒伍 (To the ranks). 1928.iii.12, cont. not seen. Zhongyang ribao, "Yishu yundong" 4, cont. not seen. WJ 2: 317–40.
"Xiang" 想 (Thinking; poem). 1928.iv.10. XS 19.4: 466.
"Xin meng" 新夢 (New dreams). 1928.v.1–5, 7–10. CF 2279–2283, 2285–2288. In Haoguan xianshi de ren, retitled "Huanhu xiansheng" 煥乎先生 (Mr. Huanhu). WJ 2: 280–307.
"'Zijincheng qima' guilai" 「紫禁城騎馬」歸來 (Coming back from 'horseback riding in the Forbidden City'). 1928.v.18. CF 2296: 31–32. ([1928].v.5, night).
"Xuxu" 絮絮 (Talking on and on; poem). 1928.vi. XP Third Anniv. Extra Edition, pp. 104–119. (1928.i).
"Di'er juan de xu" 第二卷的序 (Preface to the second volume [of Alice's Adventures in China]). 1928.vii.10. Xinyue 1.5. WJ 1: 344–46. (1928.v.20).
"Baizi" 柏子 (Baizi [name]). 1928.viii.10. XS 19.8: 933–37. WJ 2: 96–103. Tr. by Ching and Payne as "Pai Tzu." Tr. by Kai-yu Hsu as "Pai-tzu." In Lau et al., pp. 222–26. Tr. under Edgar Snow as "Pai Tzu." In Living China. (1928.v.25).
"Shang cheng li lai de ren" 上城裏來的人 (Refugees in the city). 1928.viii.15. Zhongyang ribao, "Hong yu hei" 10. WJ 5: 300–303. (1928.viii).
"Bu si riji" 不死日記 (A pre-posthumous diary). 1928.viii.28, 30 (other parts not available except in Bu si riji). Zhongyang ribao, "Hong yu hei" 15, 17, and possibly following issues. (Diary entries in the book run from [1928].vii.1 to vii.29).
"Yu hou" 雨後 (After rain). 1928.ix.10. XS 19.9: 1056–59. 1935 rev. in Ba jun tu [1]. WJ 2: 90–95. Tr. by David Kidd as "After Rain." East-West Review 3.2 (Summer 1967): 183–89. (1935 ed. says "written in 1928").
"Tuhu" 屠戶 (The butcher). 1928.ix.21–26. Zhongyang ribao, "Hong yu hei." ++
"You xuewen de ren" 有學問的人 (A man with education). 1928.ix.22. Zhongyang ribao, "Hong yu hei." + WJ 2: 118–27. (1928).
"Mou fufu" 某夫婦 (A certain couple). 1928.ix.28. Zhongyang ribao, "Hong yu hei" 34. WJ 2: 128–33. (1927).
"Cai jue" 採蕨 (Gathering bracken). 1928.x.9. Zhongyang ribao, "Hong yu hei." + WJ 8: 184–93.
"You—ju" 誘—拒 (Enticement—rebuff). 1928.x.10. XS 19.10: 1147–56. ([1928].vii).
"Honghei chuangzuo yugao" 「紅黑」創作預告 (An advance notice of the creation of Red and Black [Monthly]). 1928.x.26. Zhongyang ribao, "Hong yu hei" 47. Claimed by Shen as his work.
"Diyici zuo nanren de neige ren" 第一次作男人的那個人 (The one who was a man for the first time). 1928.xi.10. XS 19.11: 1279–86. WJ 2: 104–17. ([1928].viii.10).

"Song" 頌 (Ode; poem). 1928.xi.10. *Xinyue* 1.9: poetry, p. 4. Tr. by Acton and Ch'en as "Ode."
"Yu" [2] 雨 (Rain; Shen's second piece by this title). 1928.xi.10. *Xinyue* 1.9: 14 p. *WJ* 5: 238–49.
"Ta tong ta de huoban zhi yi" 他同他的夥伴之一 (He and his companions, no. 1). 1928.xii.1. *Ronglu* 1. + In *Long Zhu*, entitled "Queming gushi" 闕名故事 (Story without a name). *WJ* 2: 405–18. (1928.x).
"Zhongnian" [1] 中年 (Middle age; Shen's first piece by this title). 1928.xii. *Bu si riji*. (Continuation of "Bu si riji," with diary entries from [1928].viii.11 to viii.26).
"Shanzhongli de shenghuo" 善鐘里的生活 (Life in Shanzhongli [Shanghai]). 1928.xii. *Bu si riji*. (Continuation of "Bu si riji" and "Zhongnian" [1], with diary entries from [1928].viii.27 to viii.30).

Ruwuhou 入伍後 (After entering the ranks). Shanghai: Beixin. Feb. 1928. Feb. 1929. *WJ* 2: 1–87.

Laoshi ren 老實人 (The simpleton). Shanghai: Xiandai shuju. 1 July 1928. 1 May 1933. Also reprinted as *Yi ge furen de riji*. *WJ* 1: 91–200 (lacks preface).

Alisi Zhongguo youji 阿麗思中國遊記 (Alice's adventures in China). Shanghai: Xinyue. 2 vols.: vol. 1, July 1928; vol. 2, Dec. 1928. *WJ* 1: 201–466.

Haoguan xianshi de ren 好管閒事的人 (The busybody). Shanghai: Xinyue. July 1928. June 1930. Cover drawn by Shen Congwen. *WJ* 2: 251–359 (abridged).

Huang jun riji 篁君日記 (The diary of Master Huang). Beiping: Beiping wenhua xueshe. Sept. 1928. *WJ* 2: 185–249.

Yu hou ji qita 雨後及其他 (After rain, and other stories). Shanghai: Chunchao shuju. 1 Oct. 1928. *WJ* 2: 89–133 (abridged).

Chang xia 長夏 (Long summer). Shanghai: Guanghua. Oct. 1928. May 1932.

Guizishou 劊子手 (The executioner). Shanghai: Guanghua. Oct. 1928. ++

Shangui 山鬼 (Mountain spirit). Shanghai: Guanghua. Oct. 1928. *WJ* 2: 135–66 (abridged).

Bu si riji 不死日記 (A pre-posthumous diary). Shanghai: Renjian shudian. Dec. 1928.

Yi ge wunü de tongxin 一個舞女的通信 (Correspondence from a danseuse; later entitled "Xin," or "Letters"). Shanghai. 1928–29? ++ As remembered by Shen Congwen.

1929

"Ajin" 阿金 (Ajin [name]). 1929.i.10. *Xinyue* 1.11: 5 p. *WJ* 8: 311–15. * ([1928].xii.26, evening).

"Long Zhu" 龍朱 (Long Zhu [name]). 1929.i.10. *Honghei* 1: 13–35. *WJ* 2:

362–83. Tr. by Chai and Chai as "Lung Chu." Tr. by Ching and Payne as "Lung Chu." (1929).

"Shi ming" 釋名 (Explanation of our name ["Honghei"; West Hunanese dialect: "One way or another"]). 1929.i.10. *Honghei* 1: 1–2. ([1928].xii.20).

"Meijin, Baozi, yu na yang" 媚金, 豹子, 與那羊 (Meijin, Baozi, and the white kid). 1929.i.20. *Renjian yuekan* 1: 54–62. *WJ* 2: 392–404. Tr. by Ching and Payne as "The White Kid."

"Canjun" 參軍 (Staff officer). 1929.ii.10. *Honghei* 2: 81–89. *WJ* 2: 384–91. (1928, winter solstice).

"Lüdian" 旅店 (The inn). 1929.ii.10. *Xinyue* 1.12: 10 p. *WJ* 8: 302–10. ([1929].i.10, "while sick").

"Shuo gushi ren de gushi" 說故事人的故事 (A tale of a storyteller). 1929.ii.10. *XS* 20.2: 395–400. *WJ* 2: 419–28.

"Shi nian zhi hou" 十年之後 (Ten years later). 1929.ii.20. *Renjian yuekan* 2. ++

"Chuxi" 除夕 (Chinese New Year's Eve). 1929.ii. *Nanzi xuzhi*. *WJ* 8: 173–82.

"Jiehun yiqian" 結婚以前 (Before the marriage). 1929.iii.10. *Xinyue* 2.1: 13 p. In *Lüdian ji qita*, retitled "Jiehun zhi 之 qian." In *Xin shidai yuekan* 3.4 (1 Dec. 1932): 1–16, retitled "Hun qian" 婚前. *WJ* 5: 227–37. ([1928].xii.3).

"Shenwu gushi" 神巫故事 (The story of a shaman). 1929.iii.10. *Honghei* 3: 121–31. Ch. 4 of *Shenwu zhi ai*. *WJ* 8: 275–84.

"Liang ge malu shang de zuojia" 兩個馬路上的作家 (Two writers on the street). 1929.iii.20. *Renjian yuekan* 3. ++

"Guonian" [2] 過年 (New Year's; Shen's second piece by this title, a story). 1929.iii. *Banlü* 12. ++

"Zhiwu" 支吾 (Beating around the bush; play). 1929.iii. *Shisi ye jian*. (1926.iii; rev. 1927.viii).

"Ri yu ye" [1] 日與夜 (Day and night; Shen's first piece by this title). 1929.iv.10. *Honghei* 4: 197–213. Ch. 5 of *Shenwu zhi ai*. *WJ* 8: 285–95.

"Nuo" 儺 (The Nuo). 1929.iv.20. *Renjian yuekan* 4. ++

"Luowu" 落伍 (Behind in the ranks). 1929.v.10. *Xinyue* 2.3: 18 p. *WJ* 8: 194–208. (1929, spring, acc. *WJ*).

"Qi ge yeren yu zuihou yi ge yingchunjie" 七個野人與最後一個迎春節 (Seven barbarians and the last rite of spring). 1929.v.10. *Honghei* 5: 225–35. *WJ* 8: 316–26. Tr. by Stanley R. Munro as "Seven Barbarians and the Last Spring Festival." ([1929].iii.1).

"Shenwu zhi ai" 神巫之愛 (The shaman's love; parts printed previously as "Shenwu gushi"). 1929.v. *Shenwu zhi ai*. *WJ* 8: 242–300.

"Daoshi yu Daochang" 道師與道場 (Taoist priests and Taoist rites). 1929.vi.10. *Honghei* 6: 267–82. *WJ* 3: 55–68.

"Yi ge tiancai de tongxin" 一個天才的通信 (Correspondence from a born talent). 1929.vi.10. *Honghei* 6: 295–311. One part only; location of other parts unknown. (Preface, to the whole book: [1929].vi.30).

"Yuanxiao" 元宵 (The lantern festival). 1929.vi.10, 25. *DF* 26.11: 91–100; 26.12: 109–120. *WJ* 8: 327–64. (1929, spring, acc. *WJ*).

"Ji gei mou bianji xiansheng" 寄給某編輯先生 (To you, mister editor). 1929.vii.10. *Honghei* 7: 351–66. *WJ* 8: 209–24.

"Yi ge muqin" 一個母親 (A mother). 1929.vii.10. *Xinyue* 2.5: 41 p. *WJ* 5: 5–39.

"Da cheng zhong de xiao shiqing" 大城中的小事情 (A small matter in a big city). 1929.viii.10. *Honghei* 8: 407–12. *WJ* 8: 235–40.

"Yi zhi chuan" 一隻船 (A boat). 1929.viii.10. *Honghei* 8: 367–78. *WJ* 8: 225–34.

"Huiming" 會明 (Huiming [name]). 1929.ix.10. *XS* 20.9: 1459–65. *WJ* 3: 269–81. * Tr. by Ching and Payne as "The Yellow Chickens." (1929).

"Niu" 牛 (Ox). 1929.ix.10. *Xinyue* 2.6/7: 18 p. *WJ* 3: 282–97. (1929, summer, acc. *WJ*).

"Wo de jiaoyu" 我的教育 (My education). 1929.ix.10. *Xinyue* 2.6/7: 35 p. *WJ* 3: 114–42. Tr. by Helmut Martin and Volker Klöpsch as "Meine Erziehung." In Klöpsch.

"Caiyuan" 菜園 (Vegetable garden). 1929.x.10. *XS* 20.10: 1615–20. *WJ* 6: 261–71.

"Fufu" 夫婦 (The lovers; with postscript on Fei Ming). 1929.xi.10. *XS* 20.11: 1729–34. *WJ* 8: 384–93. Tr. by Ching and Payne as "The Lovers." (1929.vii.14).

"Tongzhi de yandou gushi" 同志的煙斗故事 (A tale about a comrade's pipe). 1929.xii.10. *XS* 20.12: 1897–1902. * In *Xin yu jiu*, retitled "Yandou" (The pipe). *WJ* 6: 272–83.

Dai guan riji 獃官日記 (Diary of a dumb bureaucrat). Shanghai: Yuandong. 20 Jan. 1929. Given to the printers 20 Dec. 1928. (Diary entries go from 1928?.iii.8 to v.31).

Nanzi xuzhi 男子須知 (What a man must know). Shanghai: Honghei chubanshe. Feb. 1929. *WJ* 8: 145–82 (under "Zai bie yi ge guodu li").

Shisi ye jian 十四夜間 (Night of the fourteenth). Shanghai: Guanghua. March 1929. *WJ* 2: 167–84 (abridged).

Shenwu zhi ai 神巫之愛 (The shaman's love). Shanghai: Guanghua. May 1929. Rev. ed., [Guilin]: Kaiming. Sept. 1943. Shanghai: Kaiming. Jan. 1949. Guangzhou: Huacheng. March 1983. *WJ* 8: 241–300.

Diyici lian'ai 第一次戀愛 (The first love). Shanghai: Honghei. 1929? ++

Gemingzhe 革命者 (The revolutionary). Shanghai: Honghei. 1929? ++

1930

"Xiaoxiao" 蕭蕭 (Xiaoxiao [name]). 1930.i.10. *XS* 21.1: 139–45. *WJ* 6: 220–35. Tr. by Eugene Eoyang as "Hsiao-hsiao." In Lau et al. Tr. by

Lee Yi-hsieh as "Hsiao-hsiao." *T'ien Hsia Monthly* 7.3 (Oct. 1938): 295–309. Tr. by Li Ru-mien as "Little Flute." *Life and Letters* 60.137 (1949): 20–29. Tr. by Gladys Yang as "Xiaoxiao" in *The Border Town and Other Stories*. (1929, winter, acc. *WJ*).

"Deng" 燈 (Lamp). 1930.ii.10. *Xinyue* 2.12: 24 p. *WJ* 4: 23–45. * Tr. by Ching and Payne as "The Lamp." Tr. by Kai-yu Hsu as "The Lamp." In Lau et al. Tr. by Yüan and Payne as "The Lamp." ([1929].v.24).

"Xue" 血 (Blood). 1930.ii.10. *XS* 21.2: 369–72. *WJ* 8: 394–400.

"*Chen* de xu"「沉」的序 (Preface to *Sinking*). 1930.iii.3. *Yishibao*. + In *Momo ji*. ([1929].xii).

"Louju" 樓居 (Living in a loft). 1930.iii.10. *XS* 21.3: 581–86. *WJ* 8: 401–12.

"Zhangfu" 丈夫 (The husband). 1930.iv.10. *XS* 21.4: 669–79. *WJ* 4: 2–22. Tr. by Ching and Payne as "The Husband." Partial tr. by Shih Ming as "Husband." *Asia* 37 (July 1937): 524–25. Tr. by Gladys Yang as "The Husband" in *The Border Town and Other Stories*. (1930.iv).

"Ji yi daxuesheng" 記一大學生 (Remembering a college student). 1930.iv. *Lüdian ji qita*.

"Lunpan de xu"「輪盤」的序 (Preface to *Roulette*). 1930.iv. In Xu Zhimo 徐志摩. *Lunpan*. Shanghai, Zhonghua. ([1929].vii).

"*Shengming de mo* tiji"「生命的沫」題記 (Preface to *The Froth of Life*). 1930.vi.1. *Xiandai wenxue* 1.1. + *WJ* 11: 7–9. (1930.iv.30).

"Weibo" 微波 (Ripples). 1930.vi.10. *XS* 21.6: 939–51. ([1930].iv).

"Disi" 第四 (No. 4). 1930.vi. *Shen Congwen jia ji*. *WJ* 3: 92–113.

"Dong de kongjian" 冬的空間 (In the emptiness of winter). 1930.vi. *Shen Congwen jia ji*. *WJ* 3: 143–268.

"Ye" [1] 夜 (Night; Shen's first story by this title). 1930.vi. *Shen Congwen jia ji*. Tr. by Chi-chen Wang as "Night March."

"Zisha de gushi" 自殺的故事 (The story of a suicide). 1930.vi. *Shen Congwen jia ji*. (1929.xii).

"Tao de qian yi tian" 逃的前一天 (The day before he deserted). 1930.vii.10. *XS* 21.7: 1075–84. *WJ* 8: 366–83. (1929.iv).

"Yi ge nüren" 一個女人 (A woman). 1930.ix.1. *Funü zazhi* 16.9: 31–38. *WJ* 8: 413–26.

"Bohan" 薄寒 (Chill). 1930.ix.10. *XS* 21.9: 1317–22. *WJ* 6: 298–309.

"Pingfan gushi" [2] 平凡故事 (An ordinary story; Shen's second piece by this title). 1930.ix.15. *Wenyi yuekan* 1.2: 19–32. *WJ* 6: 50–68. (1930.vii).

"San ge nanzi he yi ge nüren" 三個男子和一個女人 (Three men and a woman). 1930.x. *Wenyi yuekan* 1.3: 15–33. Retitled "San ge nanren 男人 he yi ge nüren." *WJ* 6: 25–49. Tr. by Ching and Payne as "Three Men and a Girl." Tr. by Kai-yu Hsu as "Three Men and One Woman." In Lau et al. (1930.viii.24).

"Women zenme yang qu du xin shi" 我們怎麼樣去讀新詩 (How ought

we to read new poetry?). 1930.x. *Xiandai xuesheng* 1.1: 9 p. *WJ* 12: 97–103. ([1930].vii.26).

"Yi ge nü juyuan de shenghuo" 一個女劇員的生活 (The life of an actress). 1930.x–xi; 1931.i, etc. *Xiandai xuesheng* 1.1; 1.2; 1.4; further copies not available. Goes through ch. 4. *WJ* 3: 299–426.

"Lun Jiao Juyin de shi" 論蕉菊隱的詩 (On Jiao Juyin's poetry). 1930.xi.30. *Zhongyang ribao*, "Wenyi zhoukan" 5. + In *Momo ji*, retitled "Lun Jiao Juyin de yeku" 論蕉菊隱的夜哭 (On Jiao Juyin's *Crying at Night*). *WJ* 11: 125–130.

"Lun Shi Zhicun yu Luo Heizhi" 論施蟄存與羅黑芷 (On Shi Zhicun and Luo Heizhi). 1930.xi. *Xiandai xuesheng* 1.2: 8 p. *WJ* 11: 107–112.

"Lun Wang Jingzhi de hui de feng" 論汪靜之的蕙的風 (On Wang Jingzhi's *Fragrant Breezes*). 1930.xi. *Wenyi yuekan* 1.4: 133–40. *WJ* 11: 152–60.

"Shan dao zhong" 山道中 (On a mountain path). 1930.xii.10. *XS* 21.12: 1706–12. *WJ* 6: 236–49.

"Zhiji pengyou" 知己朋友 (Bosom buddy). 1930.xii.16. *Xiandai wenxue* 1.6. ++ (1930.viii.24).

"Xiandai Zhongguo wenxue de xiao ganxiang" 現代中國文學的小感想 (Some thoughts on modern Chinese literature). 1930.xii. *Wenyi yuekan* 1.5: 159–62.

"Haishang tongxun" 海上通訊 (Correspondence from Shanghai). 1930. *Yan Da yuekan* 6.2. + *WJ* 10: 42–45. (Identified in *WJ* as a letter to Xia Fuxin).

"Lun Guo Moruo" 論郭沫若 (On Guo Moruo). 1930. *Richu* 1.1 + In *Momo ji*.

Yi ge tiancai de tongxin 一個天才的通信 (Correspondence from a born talent). Shanghai: Guanghua. Feb. 1930. Shanghai: Daguang. Aug. 1935. June 1936. Cover shows a page from Shen Congwen's draft ms.

Lüdian ji qita 旅店及其他 (The inn, and other stories). Shanghai: Zhonghua. April 1930 (says publication page; title page says 1929). Kunming: Zhonghua. 1940. *WJ* 8: 301–64 (abridged).

Shen Congwen jia ji 沈從文甲集 (Shen Congwen's "A" collection). Shanghai: Shenzhou guoguang she. June 1930. *WJ* 3: 91–297 (abridged).

Jiu meng 舊夢 (Past dreams). Shanghai: Shangwu. Dec. 1930.

Zhongguo xiaoshuo shi jiangyi 中國小說史講義 (Lectures on the history of Chinese fiction). Shen Congwen and Sun Lianggong 孫俍工, eds. N. p. [Shanghai]: Jinan Daxue chubanshe. N. d. 1930?

Chen 沉 (Sinking). Shanghai? 1930? ++ Recollected by Shen Congwen.

1931

"Shenshi de taitai" 紳士的太太 (The gentry wife). 1931.i.10. *Xinyue* 3.1: 35 p. *WJ* 4: 88–118 (1929; "to be continued"—but without continuation).

"Yu Dafu, Zhang Ziping jiqi yingxiang" 郁達夫張資平及其影響 (Yu Dafu, Zhang Ziping, and their influence). 1931.i.10. *Xinyue* 3.1: 8 p. *WJ* 11: 139–45.
"Huanxiang" 還鄉 (Homecoming). 1931.i. *Shizi chuan*. *WJ* 3: 26–40. (1929, acc. *WJ*).
"Lun Zhu Xiang de shi" 論朱湘的詩 (On Zhu Xiang's poetry). 1931.i. *Wenyi yuekan* 2.1: 47–55. *WJ* 11: 113–24.
"Shizi chuan" 石子船 (The marble carrying boat). 1931.i. *Shizi chuan*. *WJ* 3: 2–15.
"[*Shizi chuan*] Houji" 後記 (Afterword to *The Marble Carrying Boat*). 1931.i. *Shizi chuan*. *WJ* 3: 89–90.
"Ye" [2] 夜 (Night; Shen's second story by this title). 1931.i. *Shizi chuan*. *WJ* 3: 16–25.
"Yi ri de gushi" 一日的故事 (The story of one day). 1931.i. *Shizi chuan*. *WJ* 3: 69–88.
"Yu" 漁 (Fishing). 1931.i. *Shizi chuan*. *WJ* 3: 41–54. (1929, acc. *WJ*).
"Lun Wen Yiduo de sishui" 論聞一多的死水 (On Wen Yiduo's *Stagnant Water*). 1931.ii.10. *Xinyue* 3.2: 7 p. *WJ* 11: 146–51.
"Lun Liu Bannong yangbian ji" 論劉半農揚鞭集 (On Liu Bannong's *Raising the Whip [Poetry] Collection*). 1931.ii. *Wenyi yuekan* 2.2: 103–108. *WJ* 11: 131–38.
"Lun Zhongguo chuangzuo xiaoshuo" 論中國創作小說 (On the creation of Chinese fiction). 1931.iv; vi.30. *Wenyi yuekan* 2.4: 1–11; 2.5/6: 215–24. *WJ* 11: 161–86. Excerpt entitled "Lun Bing Xin de chuangzuo" 論冰心的創作 (On Bing Xin's creative writing).
"Liancui chuangzuo yi ji xu" 連萃創作一集序 (Preface to the first collection of creative writing by [Li] Liancui). 1931.v.21. *Wenyi zhoukan* 31. ++
"Chuntian" 春天 (Springtime). 1931.v. *Shen Congwen zi ji*. (1930?.iii).
"Jianshe" 建設 (Construction). 1931.v. *Shen Congwen zi ji*. *WJ* 4: 46–87. (1929, acc. *WJ*).
"Qunya ji fuji" 羣鴉集附記 (Afterword to *Flock of Crows Collection* [never-published poetry collection by Bian Zhilin]). 1931.v. *Chuangzuo yuekan* 1.1: 151–56. *WJ* 11: 16–21. (1931.iv.20).
"Ye yu" [2] 夜漁 (Night fishing; Shen's second piece by this title). 1931.v. *Chuangzuo yuekan* 1.1: 31–46.
"Ganxiang" 感想 (Thoughts). 1931.vi.1. *Chuangzuo yuekan* 1.2: 121–23. ([1931].iv.20).
"Lun chuangzuo de taidu" 論創作的態度 (On attitudes toward creative writing). 1931.vi.1. *Chuangzuo yuekan* 1.2: 111–13. ([1931].v?.19).
"Tan shi" 談詩 (About poetry). 1931.vi.1. *Chuangzuo yuekan* 1.2: 115–16.
"Feiyou cundi," 1 [outside the reprinted series] 廢郵存底(一) (Letters never mailed, no. 1; not reprinted in *Feiyou cundi*; evidently written to Zhang Zhaohe). 1931.vi.30. *Wenyi yuekan* 2.5/6: 119–23. *WJ* 12: 2–8. (1931.vi).

"Gao Zhi xiaoshuo ji xu" 高植小說集序 (Preface to *Fiction by Gao Zhi*). 1931.vii.1. *Chuangzuo yuekan* 1.3: 133–35. (1931.vi.8).

"Jiachen xianhua," 1 甲辰閒話 (Chat from Jiachen [Shen Congwen], no. 1). 1931.vii.1. *Chuangzuo yuekan* 1.3: 129–31. *WJ* 12: 86–88. ([1931].vi.10).

"Yi ge timian de junren" 一個體面的軍人 (A handsome soldier; unfinished). 1931.vii.1. *Chuangzuo yuekan* 1.3: 163–80.

"Feiyou cundi," 2 [outside the reprinted series] 廢郵存底(二) (Letters never mailed, no. 2; not reprinted in *Feiyou cundi*; written to Liu Tingwei). 1931.vii.31. *Wenyi yuekan* 2.7: 45–48. *WJ* 12: 9–13. ([1931].vi.19).

"Feiyou cundi," 3 [outside the reprinted series] 廢郵存底(三) (Letters never mailed, no. 3; consists of two letters). 1931.vii.31. *Wenyi yuekan* 2.7: 48–51. *WJ* 12: 14–15 prints the first letter only. (First letter, [1931].vi.19; second undated).

"Jie" 街 (The street). 1931.vii.31. *Wenyi yuekan* 2.7: 53–55. *WJ* 10: 46–49. ([1931].v.10).

"*Shanhua ji* jieshao" 「山花集」介紹 (Introduction to *Mountain Flowers Collection* [of poetry by Liu Tingwei]). 1931.vii.31. *Wenyi yuekan* 2.7: 125–26. *WJ* 11: 187–88. (1931.vi).

"Jiachen xianhua," 2 甲辰閒話 (Chat from Jiachen, no. 2). 1931.viii.1. *Chuangzuo yuekan* 1.4: 121–23. *WJ* 12: 89–91.

"Yisheng" [1] 醫生 (Doctor; Shen's first story by this title). 1931.viii.10. *XS* 22.8: 1017–30. *WJ* 4: 176–201. (Finished 1931.iv.24).

"Zhai er mei zhai xianhua" 窄而霉齋閒話 (Chat from The Cramped and Moldy Studio). 1931.viii.31. *Wenyi yuekan* 2.8: 157–60. *WJ* 12: 92–96. ([1931].vi.10).

"Daode yu zhihui" 道德與知慧 (Morality and wisdom). 1931.viii. *Xinyue* 3.8: 16 p. *WJ* 8: 427–41. (Completed 1931.iv.27).

"Xie zai 'Long Zhu' yi wen zhi qian" 寫在「龍朱」一文之前 (Preface to the tale "Long Zhu"). 1931.viii. *Long Zhu*. *WJ* 2: 362–63.

"Sansan" 三三 (Sansan [name]). 1931.ix.30. *Wenyi yuekan* 2.9: 41–62. *WJ* 4: 120–48. Tr. by Ching and Payne as "San-San." ([1931].viii.5 to ix.17).

"Duihua" 對話 (Dialogue; poem). 1931.ix. In Chen Mengjia.

"Qiu zhi lunluo xu" 秋之淪洛序 (Preface to [Li Liancui's poetry collection] *Ruin in Autumn*). 1931.x.1. *Xin shidai yuekan* 1.3: 4 p. *WJ* 11: 10–12. (1930.x).

"Shiren he xiaoshuojia" 詩人和小說家 (A poet and a fiction writer [i.e., Hu Yepin and Ding Ling]). 1931.x.4–xi.29? [last issue unavailable to me]. *Shibao*. Beginning with installment 11, 1931.x.15, the title changes to "Ji Hu Yepin" 記胡也頻 (Remembering Hu Yepin). *WJ* 9: 51–98. * (1931.ix.5).

"Huchu" 虎雛 (Tiger cub). 1931.x.10. *XS* 22.10: 1249–63. *WJ* 4: 149–75. (Finished 1931.v.15).

"Zao" 燥 (Restless). 1931.x.10. *Wenyi yuekan* 2.10: 85–92. *WJ* 8: 442–52.
"Zhongnian" [2] 中年 (Middle age; Shen's second piece by this title). 1931.x. *Xinyue* 3.10: 13 p. (1931.vi.21).
"Qian xiaojing" 黔小景 (Little scene in Guizhou). 1931.xi.20. *Beidou* 1.3: 1–7. *WJ* 4: 202–11. ([1931].x.10).
"Zhi 'Wenyi' duzhe" 致「文藝」讀者 (To the readers of the "Literature" supplement). 1931.xii.26? Tianjin *DGB*, "Wenyi" (unverified). + Ch. 7 of *Feiyou cundi*. (Date-and-place line provides the dubious date of publication cited).

Shizi chuan 石子船 (The marble carrying boat). Shanghai: Zhonghua. Jan. 1931 (1930, acc. title page). Sept. 1932. March 1936. *WJ* 3: 1–90.
Congwen xin zhu 從文新著 (New works by Congwen). Shanghai: Dadong shuju. April 1931. ++
Shen Congwen zi ji 沈從文子集 (Shen Congwen's "AA" collection). Shanghai: Xinyue. May 1931. *WJ* 4: 1–118 (abridged).
Long Zhu 龍朱 (Long Zhu [name]). Shanghai: Xiaoxing shudian. Aug. 1931. *WJ* 2: 361–428.
Yi ge nü juyuan de shenghuo 一個女劇員的生活 (The life of an actress). Shanghai: Dadong. Aug. 1931. *WJ* 3: 299–426.
Xin wenxue jiangyi 新文學講義 (Lectures on the new literature). Wuhan: Wuhan Daxue. 1931? ++ Shen Congwen's lectures at Wuhan University.

1932

"Liu Yu shi xuan xu" 「劉宇詩選」序 (Preface to *Poetry by Liu Yu*). 1932.i. *Liu Yu shi xuan*. + Shanghai: Beixin. *WJ* 11: 22–25. (1931.x.20).
"Chuzi" 廚子 (The cook). 1932.ii.28. *Wenyi yuekan* 3.2: 131–43. *WJ* 4: 239–55.
"Nitu" 泥塗 (Mud). 1932.iii.16–iv.15. *Shibao*. *WJ* 5: 315–47. (1932.i.25).
"Xianxian" 賢賢 (Xianxian [name]). 1932.iii.31. *Wenyi yuekan* 3.3: 279–84. (1931.iii.27).
"Huanghun" [1] 黃昏 (Twilight; poem; Shen's first piece by this title). 1932.iv.30. *Wenyi yuekan* 3.4: 440.
"Jiju moudi de shenghuo" 寄居某地的生活 (Putting up in a certain place). 1932.iv.30. *Wenyi yuekan*. 3.4: 403–407. Ch. 1 of *Fengzi*. *WJ* 4: 304–309.
"Yi ge huanghun" 一個黃昏 (One day at twilight). 1932.iv.30. *Wenyi yuekan* 3.4: 407–12. Ch. 2 of *Fengzi*. *WJ* 4: 309–16.
"Yinzhe pengyou" 隱者朋友 (The reclusive friend). 1932.iv.30. *Wenyi yuekan* 3.4: 412–15. Ch. 3 of *Fengzi*. *WJ* 4: 316–21.
"Mou yi ge wanshang shenshi de keting li" 某一個晚上紳士的客廳裏 (One evening in a gentry parlor). 1932.iv.30. *Wenyi yuekan* 3.4: 415–21. Ch. 4 of *Fengzi*. *WJ* 4: 321–29.

"Yi ge bei ditu suo yiwang de yi chu bei lishi suo yiwang de yi tian" 一個被地圖所遺忘的一處被歷史所遺忘的一天 (On a day forgotten by history, in a place not on the map). 1932.iv.30. *Wenyi yuekan* 3.4: 422–30. Ch. 5 of *Fengzi*. *WJ* 4: 329–40 (with title slightly rev.).

"Jing" 靜 (Quiet). 1932.v.1. *Chuanghua* 1.1: 77–84. *WJ* 4: 256–65. Tr. by William L. MacDonald as "Quiet." *Triquarterly* 31 (fall 1974): 14–24. Tr. by Wai-lim Yip and C. T. Hsia as "Quiet." In Hsia and Lau. (1932.iii.30).

"Lingling" 玲玲 (Lingling [name]). 1932.vi.30. *Wenyi yuekan* 3.5/6: 593–604. In *Rurui ji*, retitled "Bairi" 白日 (Daytime). *WJ* 5: 358–73. Tr. by Wai-lim Yip and C. T. Hsia as "Daytime." In Hsia and Lau.

"Wanqing" 晚晴 (Evening clearing). 1932.vi.30. *Wenyi yuekan* 3.5/6: 577–83. In *Rurui ji*, retitled "Huanghun" [2] 黃昏 (Twilight; Shen's second piece by this title). *WJ* 5: 374–83.

"Kuangchang" 礦場 (The mines). 1932.vi.30. *Wenyi yuekan* 3.5/6: 617–42. Ch. 6 of *Fengzi*. *WJ* 4: 340–44.

"Qu kuangshan de lu shang" 去礦山的路上 (On the road to the mines). 1932.vi.30. *Wenyi yuekan* 3.5/6: 620–24. Ch. 7 of *Fengzi*. *WJ* 4: 344–49.

"Zai lilin zhong" 在栗林中 (In a chestnut forest). 1932.vi.30. *Wenyi yuekan* 3.5/6: 624–32. Ch. 8 of *Fengzi*. *WJ* 4: 350–61.

"Ri yu ye" [2] 日與夜 (Day and night; Shen's second piece by this title). 1932.vi.30. *Wenyi yuekan* 3.5/6: 632–42. Ch. 9 of *Fengzi*. *WJ* 4: 361–74.

"Dushi yi furen" 都市一婦人 (A lady of the city). 1932.vii.1. *Chuanghua* 1.3: 328–45. *WJ* 4: 214–38.

"Chun" [2] 春 (Spring; Shen's second work by this title). 1932.vii. *Xiandai* 1.3: 386–95. *WJ* 4: 266–79. (1932.vi).

"Nuofu" 懦夫 (The coward). 1932.viii.4–ix.9 (37 consecutive daily installments). *Shibao*.

"Lun Xu Zhimo de shi" 論徐志摩的詩 (On Xu Zhimo's poetry). 1932.viii. *Xiandai xuesheng* 2.2. + *WJ* 11: 189–202.

"Qiu" [2] 秋 (Autumn; Shen's second work by this title). 1932.ix.1. *Xin shidai yuekan* 3.1: 33–46. *WJ* 5: 205–17.

"Yi zhou jian gei wu ge ren de xin" 一週間給五個人的信 (Letters to five people from a given week). 1932.ix. *Xiandai* 1.5: 640–42. Ch. 1 of *Feiyou cundi*. *WJ* 11: 298–300 (title rev.). ([1932].vii.13).

"Ruomo yisheng" 若墨醫生 (Dr. Ruomo). 1932.x.1. *Xinyue* 4.3: 22 p. *WJ* 4: 280–99. (1931.vii.15).

"Bianhou" 編後 (Editor's afterword). 1932.x.15. *Xiaoshuo yuekan* 1.1: 96. ([1932].x.13, night).

"Fakanci" 發刊辭 (Editor's foreword). 1932.x.15. *Xiaoshuo yuekan* 1.1: 1–2.

"Bing" 病 (Sickness). 1932.xi.1. *Xin shidai yuekan* 3.3: 23–34. Retitled "Zhuogui" in 1946 rev. *WJ* 5: 218–26.

"Yisheng" [2] 醫生 (The doctor; Shen's second story by this title). 1932.xi.1. *Xinyue* 4.5: 8 p. Also *Yuexia xiaojing*. *WJ* 5: 156–62. (1932.x).
"Bianjiao hou" 編校後 (Editor's afterword). 1932.xi.15. *Xiaoshuo yuekan* 1.2: 175–76.
"Heian chongmanle kongjian de mouye" 黑暗充滿了空間的某夜 (A night filled with darkness). 1932.xi.15. *Shenbao yuekan* 1.5: 121–26. In *Rurui ji*, retitled "Hei ye" 黑夜 (Dark night). *WJ* 5: 384–94. Tr. by Yüan and Payne as "Under Cover of Darkness." ([1932].ix.24).
"Mian Zhi xiansheng zhuan" 倪之先生傳 (The biography of Mr. Mian Zhi; unfinished). 1932.xi.15. *Xiaoshuo yuekan* 1.2: 117–22. *WJ* 8: 453–58.
"Jieri" 節日 (Festival). 1932.xi.16. *DF* 29.6: 9–14. *WJ* 5: 348–57.
"*Xue* xu" 「雪」序 (Preface to *Snow* [by Gao Zhi 高植]). 1932.xii.4, 11. *Shishi xinbao*. First part in "Xingqi xuedeng" 7. * *WJ* 11: 13–15.
"Zhanzheng dao mou shi yihou" 戰爭到某市以後 (After the war came home). 1932.xii.5. *Weiyin* 1.7/8. + *WJ* 8: 459–67. (1932.v).
"Duiyu shiren de ganxiang" 對於詩人的感想 (My feelings about poets). 1932.xii.15. *Xiaoshuo yuekan* 1.3: 178.
"Guanyu Beifang shiren zhi zhongzhong" 關於北方詩人之種種 (All about the Northern poets). 1932.xii.15. *Xiaoshuo yuekan* 1.3: 210, 220.
"Jiachen xianhua" [3] 甲辰閒話 (Chat from Jiachen; third item by this title). 1932.xii.15. *Xiaoshuo yuekan* 1.3: 181.
"Juantou yu" 卷頭語 (Opening words). 1932.xii.15. *Xiaoshuo yuekan* 1.3: 177. *WJ* 11: 26–27.
"Shanghai zuojia" 上海作家 (Shanghai writers). 1932.xii.15. *Xiaoshuo yuekan* 1.3: 179–81. (1932.xii.8).

Huchu 虎雛 (Tiger cub). Shanghai: Xin Zhongguo shuju. Jan. 1932. Jan. 1933. *WJ* 4: 119–211 (abridged).
Liu Yu shi xuan 劉宇詩選 (Poetry by Liu Yu). Shen Congwen, ed. Shanghai: Beixin. Jan. 1932. ++
Ji Hu Yepin 記胡也頻 (Remembering Hu Yepin). Shanghai: Guanghua. June 1932. Shanghai: Daguang. 1935. *WJ* 9: 51–98.
Nitu 泥塗 (Mud). Beiping: Xingyuntang shudian. 1 July 1932.
Dushi yi furen 都市一婦人 (A lady of the city). Shanghai: Xin Zhongguo shuju. Nov. 1932. June 1933. *WJ* 4: 213–99 (abridged).
Yilin ji 一鱗集 (Fragments). Hangzhou: Cangshan. ++ Nov. 1932? Actual printing and date unverified.
Xiandai shi jiezuo xuan 現代詩傑作選 (Masterpieces of modern poetry). Shen Congwen, ed. Shanghai: Qingnian shudian. Dec. 1932. Works by 39 poets, from Hu Shi to Dai Wangshu.
Yi ge furen de riji 一個婦人的日記 (A woman's diary). Shanghai: Xinguang. 1932. 1937. This book is *Laoshi ren* under a different title.

1933

"Youfang" 油坊 (The oil press). 1933.i.1. *Xin shidai yuekan* 3.5/6: 43–58. *WJ* 5: 194–204.

"Shantuo" 扇陀 (Sāntā [name, Indian]). 1933.i. *Xiandai* 2.3: 382–98. *WJ* 5: 79–101. (1932.x).

"Yuexia xiaojing" 月下小景 (Under moonlight). 1933.ii.1. *DF* 30.3: 1–8. *WJ* 5: 44–57. Tr. by Ching and Payne as "Under Moonlight." (Finished 1932.ix.22).

"Lieren gushi" 獵人故事 (The birdcatcher's story). 1933.iii. *Xinyue* 4.6: 16 p. *WJ* 5: 125–39. (1933).

"Zaoshang—yi dui tu yi ge bing" 早上——一堆土一個兵 (Morning: A soldier on a mound of earth). 1933.v.1. *DF* 30.9: 6–8. *WJ* 5: 311–14. ([1933].iii.22).

"Weijuan" 微倦 (Listless; poem). 1933.v. *Xihu wenyuan* 1. ++ (1933.iii.7).

"Ding Ling nüshi beibu" 丁玲女士被捕 (Ms. Ding Ling arrested). 1933.vi.4. *Duli pinglun* 52/53: 12–13. *WJ* 12: 314–16. ([1933].v.25).

"Ding Ling nüshi shizong" 丁玲女士失蹤 (Ms. Ding Ling has disappeared). 1933.vi.12. Tianjin *DGB*, "Wenxue fukan" 284. *WJ* 12: 317–19. (1933.vi.4).

"Yi ge nongfu de gushi" 一個農夫的故事 (A plowman's story). 1933.vi.16. *DF* 30.12: 1–9. *WJ* 5: 140–55. (Completed 1933.iv.10).

"Laike" 來客 (The visitor). 1933.vii.15. *Shenbao yuekan* 2.7: 117–20. *WJ* 6: 195–201. (1933.iv).

"Ji Ding Ling nüshi" 記丁玲女士 (Remembering Ms. Ding Ling). 1933.vii.24–x.2 (later reprinted as *Ji Ding Ling*); 1933.x.9–xii.18 (later printed as *Ji Ding Ling xuji*). *GW* 10.29–50.

"Lue zhuan" 略傳 (Brief biography). 1933.vii. In Wang Zhefu. (1930.iii.2).

"Nüren" [1] 女人 (Woman; Shen's first story by this title). 1933.vii. *Xiandai* 3.3: 342–46. *WJ* 5: 72–78. (1933.iv.22).

"San ge nüxing" 三個女性 (Three women). 1933.viii.1; viii.16; ix.1; ix.16. *Xin shehui banyuekan* 5.3–6: 75–77, 100–103, 123–26, 149–52. *WJ* 5: 281–99. (1933.vi).

"Nüren" [2] 女人 (Woman; Shen's second story by this title). 1933.viii.25–ix.10. *Shenbao*, "Ziyou tan" (17 consecutive issues). In *Rurui ji*, retitled "Rurui" 如蕤 (Rurui [name]). *WJ* 5: 252–80. (1933.vi).

"Sheng" 生 (Living). 1933.ix.10. *Renmin pinglun* 1.17: 23–27. *WJ* 5: 304–10. ([1933].ix.3).

"*Ji Ding Ling nüshi* ba" 「記丁玲女士」跋 (Postscript to *Remembering Ms. Ding Ling*). 1933.ix.23. Tianjin *DGB*, "Wenyi" 1. *WJ* 11: 28–32. (1933.vi).

"Aiyu" 愛慾 (Love and desire). 1933.ix. *Xiandai* 3.5: 588–604. *WJ* 5: 102–24. (1933.vii.18).

"Yi ge muqin xu" 一個母親序 (Preface to *A Mother*). 1933.x.1. *Yi ge muqin. WJ* 5: 2–4.

"Quan ren dujing" 勸人讀經 (Exhorting people to read the classics). 1933.x.5. *Shenbao*, "Ziyou tan." *WJ* 12: 320–21.

"Lüzi gushi" 驢子故事 (The story of the donkey). 1933.x.14. Tianjin *DGB*, "Wenyi" 7.

"Wenxuezhe de taidu" 文學者的態度 (The proper attitude for a litterateur). 1933.x.18. Tianjin *DGB*, "Wenyi" 9. *WJ* 12: 148–54. (1933.x.13).

"Zhishijieji yu jinbu" 知識階級與進步 (The intelligentsia and progress). 1933.x.28. Tianjin *DGB*, "Wenyi" 11. *WJ* 12: 322–26. ([1933].x.25).

"Datou wenxue" 打頭文學 ("Spear-head" literature). 1933.xi.1. Tianjin *DGB*, "Wenyi" 12. *WJ* 12: 155–57.

"Kangkai de wangzi" 慷慨的王子 (The generous prince). 1933.xi.15. *Yuexia xiaojing. WJ* 5: 163–90. (1933.i.20).

"Xunmi" 尋覓 (The quest). 1933.xi.15. *Yuexia xiaojing. WJ* 5: 58–71. (1933.iv.17).

"*Yuexia xiaojing* tiji" 「月下小景」題記 (Preface to *Under Moonlight*). 1933.xi.15. *Yuexia xiaojing. WJ* 5: 42–43. (Rev. 1934.vii.25; rev. again and enlarged for the 1943 *Yuexia xiaojing*, which gives the dates 1935.xi.27, with rev. completed 1941.i.12).

"Chuangzuo zalun" 創作雜論 (A discursive talk about creative writing). 1933.xii.30. Tianjin *DGB*, "Wenyi" 28.

"Xin (ji yi ge wunü de tongxin)" 信(即一個舞女的通信)(Letters [namely, correspondence from a danseuse]). 1933.xii. In Dai Yihe 戴一鶴, ed. *Mingjia duanpian chuangzuo xuan* 名家短篇創作選 (A selection of short creative works by famous authors). Shanghai: Dazhong, vol. 2, 431–555. The secondary title was used in a previous publication of this item, as a book. (1928.v.9, "on National Humiliation Day").

Ahei xiaoshi 阿黑小史 (The story of Ahei). Shanghai: Xin shidai. 1 March 1933. (Note: *Momo ji*, but not this book, contains the "Preface to *The Story of Ahei*"). *WJ* 5: 191–249.

Kangkai de wangzi 慷慨的王子 (The generous prince). Shanghai: Liangyou. 27 March 1933.

Fengzi 鳳子 (Fengzi [name]). Hangzhou: Cangshan. July 1933. Beiping: Lida. Summer 1934? Existence of this ed. unverified. What became ch. 10 of *Fengzi* was written only in 1937. *WJ* 4: 301–74.

Yi ge muqin 一個母親 (A mother). Shanghai: Hecheng shuju. 1 Oct. 1933. Shanghai: Fuxing. Oct. 1936. *WJ* 5: 1–39.

Yuexia xiaojing 月下小景 (Under moonlight). Shanghai: Xiandai shuju. 15 Nov. 1933. 20 Oct. 1934. Rev. ed., [Guilin]: Kaiming. Dec. 1943. Shanghai: Kaiming. Oct. 1946. March 1948. Jan. 1949. The 1946 and 1948 editions differ from the 1943 and 1949 editions in pagination. *WJ* 5: 41–190.

Nuofu 懦夫 (The coward). Shanghai: Xin shidai shuju. 1933? ++ Advertised in 1933; existence unverified.

Shenshi de taitai 紳士的太太 (The gentry wife). Shanghai: Santong shuju. N.d. 1933? Nov. 1940.

1934

"Bian cheng" 邊城 (The frontier city). 1934.i.1 (double issue); i.15; iii.12; iii.19; iii.26; iv.2; iv.9; iv.16; iv.23. *GW* 11.1/2, 4, 10–16. *WJ* 6: 73–163. Tr. by Ching and Payne as "The Frontier City." Tr. by Emily Hahn and Shing Mo-lei as "Green Jade and Green Jade." *T'ien Hsia Monthly* 2.1–4 (Jan.–April 1936). Tr. by Gladys Yang in *The Border Town and Other Stories*. Tr. anonymously into French as "Une bourgade à l'écart." *Littérature chinoise* 1980.8, 9 (Aug.–Sept. 1980). (Completed 1934.iv.19).

"Xinnian shibi" 新年試筆 (Trying out my pen on the New Year). 1934.i.1. *Wenxue* 2.1: 24–25. Ch. 6 of *Feiyou cundi*, retitled "Tan chuangzuo" 談創作 (About creative writing). *WJ* 11: 313–15.

"Yuanri shibi" 元日試筆 (Trying out my pen at the New Year). 1934.i.3. Tianjin *DGB*, "Wenyi" 30. Ch. 8 of *Feiyou cundi*, retitled "Yuandanri zhi 'Wenyi' duzhe" 元旦日致「文藝」讀者 (To the readers of the "Literature" Supplement, on the New Year). *WJ* 11: 319–22.

"Lun 'Hai Pai'" 論「海派」 (On the "Shanghai School"). 1934.i.10. Tianjin *DGB*, "Wenyi" 32. *WJ* 12: 158–62. (1934.i.7).

"Guanyu 'Hai Pai'" 關於「海派」 (About the "Shanghai School"). 1934.ii.21. Tianjin *DGB*, "Wenyi" 43. *WJ* 12: 163–65. ([1934].ii.17).

"Jinshu wenti" 禁書問題 (The problem of book banning). 1934.iii.5. *GW* 11.9: 4 p. *WJ* 12: 327–33. (1934.ii.28).

"Yakewei de ye" 鴨窠圍的夜 (A night at Mallard-nest Village). 1934.iv.1. *Wenxue* 2.4: 618–21. Ch. 3 of *Xiang xing san ji*. *WJ* 9: 242–49. Tr. by Gladys Yang as "A Night at Mallard-Nest Village" in *Recollections of West Hunan*.

"Yi ge tong wo guo Taoyuan de pengyou" 一個同我過桃源的朋友 (A friend who went with me to Taoyuan). 1934.iv.18. Tianjin *DGB*, "Wenyi" 59. Ch. 1 of *Xiang xing san ji*, retitled "Yi ge dai shuitapi maozi de pengyou" 一個戴水獺皮帽子的朋友 (A friend in an otterskin hat). *WJ* 9: 226–33.

"*Bian cheng* tiji" 「邊城」題記 (Preface to *The Frontier City*). 1934.iv.25. Tianjin *DGB*, "Wenyi" 61. Ch. 13 of *Feiyou cundi*. *WJ* 6: 70–72. (1934.iv.24).

"*Ahei xiaoshi* xu" 阿黑小史序 (Preface to *The Story of Ahei*). 1934.iv. *Momo ji*. *WJ* 5: 192–93. (1928.x).

"Fulan" 腐爛 (Rot). 1934.iv. *Youmu ji*. *WJ* 6: 2–17. (1929.vii.20).

"Lu Xun de zhandou" 魯迅的戰鬥 (Lu Xun's combat actions). 1934.iv. *Momo ji*.

"Lun Feng Wenbing" 論馮文炳 (On Feng Wenbing). 1934.iv. *Momo ji.* *WJ* 11: 96–102. ([193-].vii.21).

"Lun Luo Huasheng" 論落華生 (On Luo Huasheng). 1934.iv. *Momo ji.* *WJ* 11: 103–106.

"Wo de Erge" 我的二哥 (My Elder Brother No. 2; short biography of Shen Congwen, written in the voice of his Little Sister No. 9, Yuemeng). 1934.iv. *Momo ji.* (1930.iii).

"Ye de kongjian" 夜的空間 (In the void of night). 1934.iv. *Youmu ji. WJ* 6: 18–24. (Rev. 1930.viii).

"*Fengzi* tiji" 「鳳子」題記 (Preface to *Fengzi*). 1934.v.30. Tianjin *DGB,* "Wenyi" 71. *WJ* 4: 302–3. (1934.v.27).

"Yijiusansi nian Yiyue shiba" 一九三四年一月十八 (January 18, 1934). 1934.vi.13. Tianjin *DGB,* "Wenyi" 74. Ch. 4 of *Xiang xing san ji. WJ* 9: 250–57. An excerpt is printed in *Zhongguo xin wenxue daxi xubian,* 6: 273–74, retitled "Chenzhou tuzhong" 辰州途中 (On the way to Chenzhou).

"Chen He xiao chuan shang de shuishou" 辰河小船上的水手 (The deck hands of a little Chen River boat). 1934.vii.1. *Wenxue* 3.1: 269–74. Ch. 6 of *Xiang xing san ji. WJ* 9: 270–79.

"Sun Dayu" 孫大雨 (Sun Dayu [person]). 1934.vii.5. *Renjianshi* 7: 41–43.

"Yi ge duoqing shuishou yu yi ge duoqing furen" 一個多情水手與一個多情婦人 (A hot-blooded boatman and an amorous woman). 1934.vii.7. Tianjin *DGB,* "Wenyi" 82. Ch. 5 of *Xiang xing san ji. WJ* 9: 258–69. Tr. by Gladys Yang as "An Amorous Boatman and an Amorous Woman" in *Recollections of West Hunan.*

"Wu ge junguan yu yi ge meikuang gongren" 五個軍官與一個煤礦工人 (Five army officers and a coal miner). 1934.vii.23. *GW* 11.29: 4 p. Ch. 8 of *Xiang xing san ji. WJ* 9: 287–93. Tr. by Gladys Yang as "Five Army Officers and a Miner" in *Recollections of West Hunan.*

"Wo de xiezuo yu shui de guanxi" 我的寫作與水的關係 (The relation of my works to water). 1934.vii. In Zheng Zhenduo 鄭振鐸 and Fu Donghua 傅東華, eds. *Wo yu wenxue* 我與文學 (Literature and me). Shanghai: Shenghuo shuju, pp. 281–85. Ch. 9 of *Feiyou cundi. WJ* 11: 323–26.

"Cong 'xiaoxue dujing' dao 'dazhongyu wenti' de ganxiang" 從「小學讀經」到「大眾語問題」的感想 (My thoughts, from "studying the classics in primary school" to "the question of a mass language"). 1934.viii.1. Tianjin *DGB,* "Wenji" 89.

"Shanghai tongxin fuji" 上海通信附記 (Postscript to a letter from Shanghai [by Cao Juren]). 1934.viii.11. Tianjin *DGB,* "Wenyi" 92. (1934.viii.7).

"Guolingzhe" 過嶺者 (The one who crossed over the mountains). 1934.viii.22. Tianjin *DGB,* "Wenyi" 95. *WJ* 6: 202–208.

"Laoban" 老伴 (Companion till death do us part). 1934.viii. *Xuewen* 1.4: 15–23. Ch. 9 of *Xiang xing san ji. WJ* 9: 294–301.

"Ben kan yibai qi" 本刊一百期 (On the hundredth issue of this publication). 1934.ix.8. Tianjin *DGB*, "Wenyi" 100. ([1934].ix.6).

Editor's Addendum to "Lun Lao She *Lihun*" 論老舍「離婚」(On Lao She's *Divorce*). 1934.ix.12. Tianjin *DGB*, "Wenyi" 101.

"Shen Congwen xiansheng de fuxin" 沈從文先生的復信 (Mr. Shen Congwen's letter in reply [opinion solicited on the Mass Language controversy]). 1934.ix.15. *Shehui yuebao* 1.4: 2–3.

"'Yishu zhoukan' de dansheng"「藝術周刊」的誕生 (On the birth of "Art Weekly"). 1934.x.7. Tianjin *DGB*, "Yishu zhoukan" 1. *WJ* 12: 212–17.

"Huchu zai yu ji" 虎雛再遇記 (Reencounter with the Tiger Cub). 1934.x.10. *Shuixing* 1.1: 65–71. Ch. 10 of *Xiang xing san ji*. *WJ* 9: 302–309.

"Bianzhe fuji" 編者附記 (Editor's addendum [about Pearl Buck]). 1934.x.27. Tianjin *DGB*, "Wenyi" 114.

"Qingxu de ticao" 情緒的體操 (Calisthenics for the feelings). 1934.xi.10. *Shuixing* 1.2: 207–10. Ch. 11 of *Feiyou cundi*. *WJ* 11: 327–30.

"San nian qian de Shiyiyue, ershier ri" 三年前的十一月,二十二日 (The twenty-second of November, three years ago [Xu Zhimo's funeral]). 1934.xi.21. Tianjin *DGB*, "Wenyi" 121. *WJ* 10: 50–56.

Untitled editor's postscript to Sun Dayu's translation, "Liye Wang beiju" 黎琊王悲劇 (The tragedy of King Lear). 1934.xi.24. Tianjin *DGB*, "Wenyi" 122.

"Bian Zhilin fudiao" 卞之琳浮雕 (Bian Zhilin in relief; poem). 1934.xii.1. Tianjin *DGB*, "Wenyi" 124.

"Zhishi" 知識 (Knowledge). 1934.xii.10. *Shuixing* 1.3: 315–19. *WJ* 6: 292–97.

"Xiao Qian xiaoshuo ji tiji" 蕭乾小說集題記 (Preface to *Fiction by Xiao Qian*). 1934.xii.15. Tianjin *DGB*, "Wenyi" 128. Retitled "*Lixia ji* tiji" 「籬下集」題記 (Preface to *Under the Eaves of Others*). *WJ* 11: 33–34. (1933.xii.13).

"Xiandai Zhongguo zuojia pinglun xuan tiji" 現代中國作家評論選題記 (Preface to *Selected Essays on Modern Chinese Authors* [Shen Congwen, ed.]). 1934.xii.22. Tianjin *DGB*, "Wenyi" 130. *WJ* 11: 35–37. ([1934].xii.17).

"Zhi yi ge zuozhe de gongkai xin" 致一個作者的公開信 (Open letter to a writer). 1934.xii.26. Tianjin *DGB*, "Wenyi" 131. *WJ* 12: 20–22. ([1934].xii.20).

Momo ji 沫沫集 (Froth). Shanghai: Dadong. April 1934. *WJ* 11: 95–234. *

Youmu ji 遊目集 (The roving eye). Shanghai: Dadong. April 1934. *WJ* 6: 1–68 (abridged).

Rurui ji 如蕤集 (Rurui collection; not to be confused with *Rurui*). Shanghai: Shenghuo. May 1934. Oct. 1934. May 1935. *WJ* 5: 251–394.

Congwen zizhuan 從文自傳 (Congwen's autobiography). Shanghai: Diyi chubanshe. 15 July 1934. 25 Aug. 1936. Shanghai: Zhongyang shudian. Jan. 1943. (This edition, supertitled *Wo de shenghuo* 我的生活 [My life], edits out some of the dialect; the Ching and Payne translation seems to be from this text.) Rev. ed. (not reflecting the Shanghai 1943 changes, which probably were not made by Shen himself), [Guilin]: Kaiming. Sept. 1943. Shanghai: 1948, with variant pagination. Jan. 1949, with 1943 pagination. Taiwan pirate of 1949 ed., entitled *Shen Congwen zizhuan*. Taibei: Shiyue. Oct. 1969. Hong Kong pirate of 1949 ed., entitled *Congwen zagan xuan ji* 從文雜感選集 (Selection of Congwen's random thoughts). Hong Kong: Huitong. June 1970. [1980] rev. ed. *: Hong Kong: Shidai. Dec. 1980. Beijing: Renmin wenxue chubanshe. Dec. 1981. (The last is bound with other essays by Shen Congwen, and one by Huang Yongyu.) *WJ* 9: 99–224. Ch. 3 and 5 tr. by Gladys Yang in *Recollections of West Hunan*. Ch. 16 tr. by Ching and Payne as "Ta Wang." Ch. 16 tr. by William L. MacDonald as "A Bandit Chief." In Cyril Birch. (An author's note, added only in 1980, says "Written August 1931, in Qingdao," but Shen in interview, and in his 17 May 1980 afterword, says he wrote the book in the autumn of 1932. I opt for 1932.)

Ji Ding Ling 記丁玲 (Remembering Ding Ling; reprint of the first half of "Ji Ding Ling nüshi"). Shanghai: Liangyou. 1 Sept. 1934 (given to the printers 10 Jan. 1934). 20 June 1935. (This is the most heavily censored of all editions, though it happens to contain some lines missing from the *GW* original, which otherwise is by far the version most fully intact. Only this edition has photographs.) Shanghai: Liangyou. Sept. 1939. May 1940. (More complete than the 1935 ed., but inferior to the *GW* printing. 1940 version is bound with the sequel.)

Bian cheng 邊城 (The frontier city). Shanghai: Shenghuo shudian. Oct. 1934. June 1935. May 1937. Rev. ed., [Guilin]: Kaiming. Sept. 1943. Shanghai: Kaiming. Oct. 1946. 1949. Numerous unauthorized reprints in Hong Kong and even Taibei. Retitled *Cuicui* 翠翠, after the Hong Kong film version (which takes the name of the heroine), the book was published in Hong Kong by Lili chubanshe in an edition with photographs of scenes from the movie. N.d. Late 1950s? *WJ* 6: 69–163. For translations, see listing under "Bian cheng," 1934.i.1.

Baoban 豹斑 (Leopard spots). Beiping: Lida. 1934? ++

1935

"Zhi yi ge dushuren de gongkai xin" 致一個讀書人的公開信 (Open letter to a scholar). 1935.i.6. Tianjin *DGB*, "Wenyi" 133. *WJ* 12: 23–27. (1935.i.1).

"Teng Huishengtang de jinxi" 滕回生堂的今昔 (The past and present of Teng's Health Restorative Shop). 1935.i.7. *GW* 12.2: 4 p. Titularly a chapter of *Xiang xing san ji*, but never printed in that book until 1984, when it appeared as ch. 12 (the final chapter, with the "de" omitted from the title), in *WJ* 9: 320–27.

"Beijing" 北京 (Peking; poem). 1935.i.10. *Shuixing* 1.4: 410–11.

"Lun dujing" 論讀經 (On reading the classics). 1935.i.21. *GW* 12.4: 3 p. *WJ* 12: 340–44. (1935.i.7).

"Xin wenren yu xin wenxue" 新文人與新文學 (New litterateurs and new literature). 1935.ii.3. Tianjin *DGB*, "Wenyi" 137. *WJ* 12: 166–71. ([1935].i.3).

"He Qifang fudiao" 何其芳浮雕 (He Qifang in relief; poem).1935.ii.17. Tianjin *DGB*, "Wenyi" 139. ([1935].ii.12).

"Bianzhe bai" 編者白 (From the editor). 1935.iii.3. Tianjin *DGB*, "Wenyi" 141.

"Fengya yu suqi" 風雅與俗氣 (Elegance and vulgarity). 1935.iii.10. *Shuixing* 1.6: 574–78. Ch. 10 of *Feiyou cundi*. ([1935].ii.15).

"'Xiaoxi'" 「消息」 ("News"). 1935.iii.10. Tianjin *DGB*, "Wenyi" 142.

"Youpi de Chenzhuang tiji" 幽僻的陳莊題記 (Preface to *Remote Chen Village* [by Wang Xianglin 王相林]). 1935.iii.10. *Shuixing* 1.6: 670–72. *WJ* 11: 38–40. (1935.ii.18).

"Yi feng gongkai xin" 一封公開信 (An open letter). 1935.iii.24. Tianjin *DGB*, "Wenyi" 144. *WJ* 12: 28–29. ([1935].iii.20).

"Taoyuan yu Yuanzhou" 桃源與沅州 (Taoyuan and Yuanzhou). 1935.iii.25. *GW* 12.11: 5 p. Ch. 2 of *Xiang xing san ji*. *WJ* 9: 234–41. ([1935].iii).

"Xiangziyan" 箱子巖 (Chest Precipice [place name]). 1935.iv.10. *Shuixing* 2.1: 62–67. Ch. 7 of *Xiang xing san ji*. *WJ* 9: 280–86. Tr. by Gladys Yang as "Chest Precipice" in *Recollections of West Hunan*.

"Jin ze" 盡責 (Fulfilling one's responsibility). 1935.iv.29. *GW* 12.16: 2 p. *WJ* 12: 345–48.

"Jieshao *[Zhongguo] xin wenxue daxi*" 介紹「[中國]新文學大系」 (Introducing the *Great Compendium of the New Chinese Literature*). 1935.v.5. Tianjin *DGB*, "Wenyi" 150. Original title omits "Zhongguo." *WJ* 12: 172–73.

"Zhang Daxiang" 張大相 (Zhang Daxiang [name]). 1935.v.5. Tianjin *DGB*, "Wenyi" 150. *WJ* 7: 174–79.

"Feiyou cundi" [outside the reprinted series] 廢郵存底 (Letters never mailed; not reprinted in *Feiyou cundi*). 1935.v.10. *Wuhan ribao*. + *WJ* 12: 30–31. (1935.iv.14).

"Yi ge jinshiyan pengyou" 一個近視眼朋友 (A nearsighted friend). 1935.v.10. *Shuixing* 2.2: 198–206. Ch. 11 of *Xiang xing san ji*, retitled "Yi ge aixi bizi de pengyou" 一個愛惜鼻子的朋友 (A friend who treasures his nose). *WJ* 9: 310–19.

"Xin he jiu" 新和舊 (The new and the old). 1935.v.19. *Duli pinglun* 151: 17–23. Retitled "Xin yu 與 jiu." *WJ* 6: 250–60.

"Yi feng xin" 一封信 (A letter). 1935.vi.1. *Zhongxuesheng* 56: 31–35. ([1935].iv.10).

"Shiye" 失業 (Unemployment). 1935.vi.10. *Shuixing* 2.3: 227–33. *WJ* 6: 284–91.

"Zhongguoren de bing" 中國人的病 (The Chinese illness). 1935.vi.10. *Shuixing* 2.3: 321–24. *WJ* 12: 349–52.

"Feiyou cundi" [outside the reprinted series] 廢郵存底 (Letters never mailed; not reprinted in *Feiyou cundi*). 1935.vi.23. Tianjin *DGB*, "Wenyi" 157. *WJ* 12: 32–35. ([1935].vi.21).

"Feiyou cundi" [outside the reprinted series] 廢郵存底 (Letters never mailed; not reprinted in *Feiyou cundi*). 1935.vi.30. Tianjin *DGB*, "Wenyi" 158. ([1935].vi.24).

"Guwenguan" 顧問官 (Staff adviser). 1935.vii.1. *Wenxue* 5.1: 96–101. *WJ* 6: 209–18. (1935.iv.26).

"Gei yi ge daxuesheng" [1] 給一個大學生 (To a college student; Shen's first letter by this title; originally entitled only "Feiyou cundi"). 1935.vii.14. Tianjin *DGB*, "Xiao gongyuan" 1734. Ch. 4 of *Feiyou cundi*. *WJ* 11: 307–308.

Editor's Note to a Mr. Huang of Hengyang. 1935.vii.21. Tianjin *DGB*, "Wenyi" 161.

"Feiyou cundi: Guanyu 'piping' yidian taolun" [outside the reprinted series] 廢郵存底——關於「批評」一點討論(Letters never mailed: A short discussion of "criticism"; not reprinted in *Feiyou cundi*). 1935.vii.28. Tianjin *DGB*, "Xiao gongyuan" 1748. *WJ* 12: 36–38. ([1935].vii.20).

"Ba jun tu" 八駿圖 (Portrait of eight steeds). 1935.viii.1. *Wenxue* 5.2: 293–307. *WJ* 6: 168–194. (Written and first published in 1933?)

"Tantan Shanghai de kanwu" 談談上海的刊物 (Chatting about Shanghai periodicals). 1935.viii.18. Tianjin *DGB*, "Xiao gongyuan" 1769. *WJ* 12: 174–78.

"Lun jiqiao" 論技巧 (On technique). 1935.viii.31. Tianjin *DGB*, "Xiao gongyuan" 1782. *WJ* 12: 104–107. (1935.viii.27).

"Zisha" 自殺 (Suicide; not to be confused with "Zisha de gushi"). 1935.ix.1. Tianjin *DGB*, "Wenyi" 1. *WJ* 6: 310–21. ([1935].viii.7).

"Lun Mu Shiying" 論穆時英 (On Mu Shiying). 1935.ix.9. Tianjin *DGB*, "Wenyi" 6. *WJ* 11: 203–205.

"Gei mou jiaoshou" 給某教授 (To a particular professor). 1935.ix.15. Tianjin *DGB*, "Wenyi" 9. Ch. 5 of *Feiyou cundi*. *WJ* 11: 309–12. ([1935].ix.13).

"Feiyou cundi" [outside the reprinted series] 廢郵存底 (Letters never mailed; not reprinted in *Feiyou cundi*). 1935.x.13. Tianjin *DGB*, "Wenyi" 24. *WJ* 12: 39–41. ([1935].x.10).

"Shijian" 時間 (Time). 1935.x.28. Tianjin *DGB*, "Wenyi" 33. *WJ* 10: 57–59. (1935.x).

"Xin shi de jiu zhang" 新詩的舊賬 (The old debts of new poetry). 1935.xi.10. Tianjin *DGB*, "Wenyi" 40. *WJ* 12: 179–85. ([1935].xi.3).
"Du [Zhongguo] xin wenxue daxi" 讀「[中國]新文學大系」(Reading the Great Compendium of the New Chinese Literature). 1935.xi.29. Tianjin *DGB*, "Wenyi" 51. Original title omits "Zhongguo." *WJ* 12: 186–89.
"Bingji tong wo" 冰季同我 ([Xie] Bingji and me). 1935.xi. In Xie Bingji. *Wenrou* 溫柔 (Soft and gentle). Shanghai, Daguang. *WJ* 11: 4–6. (1929, end of autumn).
"Fuji" 附記 (Addendum [to special memorial issue on Xu Zhimo]). 1935.xii.8. Tianjin *DGB*, "Wenyi" 56. (1935.xi.19).
"Gei mou zuojia" 給某作家 (To a certain author). 1935.xii.16. *Wenxue jikan* 2.4: 1067–69. Ch. 12 of *Feiyou cundi*.
"Ba jun tu tiji" 「八駿圖」題記 (Preface to *Portrait of Eight Steeds*). 1935.xii.20. Tianjin *DGB*, "Wenyi" 63. *WJ* 6: 166–67. (1935.xii.10).

Fushi ji 浮世輯 ("Floating world" collection). [Yao] Pengzi [姚]蓬子, Shen Congwen, et al., eds. Shanghai: Liangyou. 10 Sept. 1935. 15 Nov. 1935. Reprinted under the title *Fushi hua ji qita* 浮世畫及其他 ("Portrait of the Floating World" [title of a story by Yao Pengzi] and other stories). Shanghai: Liangyou. March 1940.

Ba jun tu [1] 八駿圖 (Portrait of eight steeds). Shanghai: Wenhua shenghuo. Dec. 1935. Preface and nine stories. *WJ* 6: 165–218 (abridged).

Ba jun tu [2]. Shanghai: Xingguang. N. d. 1935? Four stories.

1936

"Xizuo xuanji dai xu" 習作選集代序 (In lieu of a preface for my *Selected Exercises*). 1936.i.1. *GW* 13.1: 4 p. In *Congwen xiaoshuo xizuo xuan* and *Ajin*, retitled "Xiti" 習題 (Preface to my exercises). *WJ* 11: 41–47.
"Daci, 6—Cong jiannan zhong qu shiyan" 答辭六—從艱難中去試驗 (Reply, no. 6—Experiment despite hardship). 1936.i.8. Tianjin *DGB*, "Wenyi" 74. *WJ* 12: 42–43.
"Daci, 8" 答辭八 (Reply, no. 8). 1936.i.15. Tianjin *DGB*, "Wenyi" 78. *WJ* 12: 44–45.
"Daci, 10—Tiancai yu naixing" 答辭十—天才與耐性 (Reply, no. 10—Genius and perseverance). 1936.i.22. Tianjin *DGB*, "Wenyi" 82. *WJ* 12: 46–47.
"Daci, 13" 答辭十三 (Reply, no. 13). 1936.ii.5. Tianjin *DGB*, "Wenyi" 88. *WJ* 12: 48–49.
"Qishi" 啓事 (Postscript). 1936.ii.19. Tianjin *DGB*, "Wenyi" 96.
"Gei zhi zai xiezuo zhe" 給志在寫作者 (To one who intends to write). 1936.iii.29. Tianjin *DGB*, "Wenyi" 118. *WJ* 12: 108–12. (1936.iii.27).
Editor's Note announcing transfer of editorship to Xiao Qian. 1936.iii.29. Tianjin *DGB*, "Wenyi" 118.
"Zhi Shi Zhicun han si tong" 致施蟄存函四通 (Four letters to Shi Zhicun.

1936.v. In Kong Lingjing 孔另境, ed. *Xiandai zuojia shujian* 現代作家書簡 (Letters by modern Chinese authors). Shanghai: Shenghuo shudian. May 1936. *WJ* 12: 16–19 (two letters only). (Four letters dated 1933–35).
"Zhi Zhao Jiabi han er tong" 致趙家璧函二通 (Two letters to Zhao Jiabi). 1936.v. In Kong Lingjing, ibid. (Letters dated 1934, 1935).
"Zhi Zhao Jingshen han yi tong" 致趙景深函一通 (A letter to Zhao Jingshen). 1936.v. In Kong Lingjing, ibid.
"Shi he kong" 時和空 (Time and space; poem). 1936.viii.30. Tianjin *DGB*, "Wenyi" 206. ([1936].vii.1).
"Youyu de xinshang" 憂鬱的欣賞 (An appreciation of melancholy; poem). 1936.x.18. Tianjin *DGB*, "Wenyi" 230. (Ch. cal. [1936].vii, in the Big Heat; W. cal. [1936].ix.8/9]).
"Zuojia jian xuyao yi zhong xin yundong" 作家間需要一種新運動 (Authors need a new movement). 1936.x.25. Tianjin *DGB*, "Wenyi" 237.
"Chenmo" 沉默 (Silence). 1936.xi.1. *Wen ji yuekan* 1.6: 1132–34. *WJ* 10: 60–64. ([1936].x.8).
"Wentan de 'tuanjie' yu 'lianhe'" 文壇的「團結」與「聯合」("Pulling together" and "uniting" the literary scene). 1936.xi.16. *GW* 13.45: 3 p. Abstracted 1937.i.1. in *Wenzhai* 1.1: 124–25.
"Wenxuejie lianhe zhanxian suoyou de yiyi" 文學界聯合戰綫所有的意義 (The full significance of a united front in the literary world). 1936.xi.20. *Dazhong zhishi* 1.3: 44–46. Abstracted 1937.i.1 in *Wenzhai* 1.1: 124.
"Duiyu zhe xin kan dansheng de songci" 對於這新刊誕生的頌辭 (Compliments on the birth of this new journal). 1936.xii.1. *Qingnian zuojia* 1.1. + *WJ* 12: 190–93. ([1936].xi.18).

Congwen xiaoshuo ji 從文小說集 (Fiction by Congwen). Shanghai: Daguang. Jan. 1936. Contains "Chang xia."
Xiandai riji wenxuan 現代日記文選 (A selection of modern diary literature). Shen Congwen, ed. Shanghai: Dongfang shuju. Reprint Jan. 1936.
Xiang xing san ji 湘行散記 (Discursive notes on a trip through Hunan). Shanghai: Shangwu. March 1936. Aug. 1936. Changsha: Shangwu. 1938. Rev. ed., [Guilin]: Kaiming. Dec. 1943. Shanghai: Kaiming. 1946. March 1948. Jan. 1949. Pagination varies. *WJ* 9: 225–319. Ch. 3, 5, 7, 8 tr. by Gladys Yang in *Recollections of West Hunan.*
Shen Congwen xuan ji [1] 沈從文選集 (Selected works by Shen Congwen; first collection by this title). Xu Chensi 徐沉泗 and Ye Wangyou 葉忘憂, eds. Shanghai: Wanxiang shuwu. April 1936. Sept. 1947. Pirate reprint, without the preface, entitled *Shen Congwen daibiao zuo xuan* 沈從文代表作選 (A selection of representative works by Shen Congwen). Hong Kong: Bailing. N. d. 1976?
Congwen xiaoshuo xizuo xuan 從文小說習作選 (Selected exercises from

Congwen's fiction writing). Shanghai: Liangyou. 1 May 1936. Given to the printers 20 Jan. 1936.

Shen Congwen xiaoshuo xuan [1] 沈從文小説選 (A selection of fiction by Shen Congwen; first collection by this title). [Tang] Shaohou [唐] 少侯, ed. Shanghai: Fanggu shudian. June 1936. Pirated in Hong Kong, about 1976, under the inappropriate title *Shen Congwen zixuan xiaoshuo ji* 沈從文自選小説集 (Shen Congwen's own selection of his stories). No publishing information.

Shen Congwen jiezuo xuan 沈從文傑作選 (Selected masterpieces by Shen Congwen). Shanghai: Xinxiang shudian. Oct. 1936. + March 1947.

Xin yu jiu 新與舊 (The new and the old). Shanghai: Liangyou. 1 Nov. 1936. Nov. 1940. July 1944. Feb. 1945. May 1945. Pagination varies. *WJ* 6: 219–321.

Xiandai Zhongguo zuojia pinglun xuan 現代中國作家評論選 (Selected essays on modern Chinese authors). Beiping: Publisher unknown. 1936? ++

1937

"Weida de shouhuo" 偉大的收穫 (A great harvest [on Cao Yu's *Sunrise*]). 1937.i.1. Tianjin *DGB*, "Wenyi" 276. *WJ* 11: 206–208. ([1936].xii.10).

"Wenxue zuojia zhong de pangzi" 文學作家中的胖子 (Fatsos among the authors). 1937.i.1. *Yuzhoufeng* 32: 400–402. ([1936].xii.4).

"Wo duiyu shuping de ganxiang" 我對於書評的感想 (My thoughts on book reviewing). 1937.i.17. Tianjin *DGB*, "Wenyi" 285. ([1936].xi.29).

"Yishu jiaoyu" 藝術教育 (Art education). 1937.i.25. *GW* 14.5: 15–18. *WJ* 12: 218–22. ([1937].i.7).

"Gei yi ge xie shi de" 給一個寫詩的 (To a writer of poetry). 1937.i. Ch. 2 of *Feiyou cundi*. *WJ* 11: 301–303.

"Gei yi ge xie xiaoshuo de" 給一個寫小説的 (To a writer of fiction). 1937.i. Ch. 3 of *Feiyou cundi*. *WJ* 11: 304–306.

"Zhi 'Wenyi' duzhe" 致「文藝」讀者 (To the readers of the "Literature" Supplement). 1937.i. Ch. 7 of *Feiyou cundi*. *WJ* 11: 316–18. (1931.xii.26).

"Gei yi ge duzhe" 給一個讀者 (To a reader). 1937.i. Ch. 13 of *Feiyou cundi*. *WJ* 11: 331–36.

"Chuang" 窗 (Window; poem). 1937.ii.10. *Xin shi* 5. ++

"Du *Xibanya youji*" 讀「西班牙遊記」(Reading *Notes on a Trip Through Spain* [by Deng Yizhi 鄧以蟄]). 1937.ii.26. Tianjin *DGB*, "Wenyi" 303. (1937.i.20).

"Tan xiezi" [1] 談寫字 (About calligraphy; Shen's first piece by this title). 1937.iv.4. Tianjin *DGB*, "Wenyi" 319. *WJ* 12: 223–28.

"Guisheng" 貴生 (Guisheng [name]). 1937.v.1. *Wenxue zazhi* 1.1: 41–67. *WJ* 6: 338–61. Tr. by Gladys Yang in *The Border Town and Other Stories*. (1937.iii).

"Wang Xie zidi" 王謝子弟 (Sons of the rich). 1937.v.17. *GW* 14.19: 65–72. *WJ* 6: 381–403.

"Daxiao Ruan" 大小阮 (Big Ruan and Little Ruan). 1937.vi.1 *Wenxue zazhi* 1.2: 88–110. *WJ* 6: 362–80. (1935.iv.14).

"Shengcun" 生存 (Existence). 1937.vi.15. *Wencong* 1.4: 637–45. *WJ* 6: 404–12. ([1937].v.15).

"Lanyong mingci de shangque" 濫用名詞的商榷 (A discussion of terminological overkill). 1937.vi.30. Tianjin *DGB*, "Wenyi" 355. *WJ* 12: 236–42. ([1937].vi.5).

"Shen zhi zai xian" 神之再現 (The reappearance of the gods). 1937.vii.1. *Wenxue zazhi* 1.3: 128–47. Ch. 10 of *Fengzi*. *WJ* 4: 374–90.

"Guanyu kanbudong" 關於看不懂 (About finding works to be incomprehensible; letter to Hu Shi). 1937.vii.4. *Duli pinglun* 241: 16–19. *WJ* 12: 334–39. ([1937].vi.18).

"Xiaozhai" 小砦 (Xiaozhai [place name, lit. "Little Stockade"]). 1937.vii.5; vii.19; vii.26; viii.2; viii.9. *GW* 14.26, 28–31. *WJ* 7: 180–202. (Unfinished when the war broke out).

"Zai tan chabuduo" 再談差不多 (More on about-the-same-itis). 1937.viii.1. *Wenxue zazhi* 1.4: 34–40.

Feiyou cundi 廢郵存底 (Letters never mailed). Xiao Qian 蕭乾, author of the second half of the book. Shanghai: Wenhua shenghuo. Jan. 1937. Dec. 1939. Rev. ed., [Guilin]: Kaiming. 1943. Shanghai: Kaiming. 1949. All but the last chapter reprinted in *Yunnan kan yun ji*. 1943. *WJ* 11: 297–336. * *WJ* omits the relatively political chapters 10 and 12 ("Fengya yu suqi"; "Gei mou zuojia").

Ershi ren suoxuan duanpian jiazuo ji 二十人所選短篇佳作集 (A book of outstanding short stories as recommended by twenty guest editors). Zhao Jiabi 趙家璧, ed. Shanghai: Liangyou. 15 Feb. 1937. Shen Congwen, for his part, selected stories by Liu Zuchun, Li Xin, and Tian Tao to be printed in this volume.

1938

"Tan baoshou" 談保守 (About conservatism). 1938.vii.1. *Xin dongxiang* 1.2: 52–55. *WJ* 11: 236–42. ([1938].vi.14).

"Xiangxi" 湘西 (West Hunan). 1938.viii.25–xi.17. Hong Kong *DGB*, "Wenyi," 1st refounding issue to no. 442. (Only this edition has photographs, of West Hunan.) *WJ* 9: 336–415. * 2 ch. tr. by Gladys Yang in *Recollections of West Hunan*.

"Tan jinbu" 談進步 (About progress). 1938.ix. *Wenyi jikan* 1.3: 2–6.

"Tan langsong shi" 談朗誦詩 (About intoning poetry). 1938.x.1–x.5? Hong Kong *Xingdao ribao*. Unverified. + In *Kunming dong jing*. *WJ* 11: 243–55.

"Gei qingnian pengyou" 給青年朋友 (To a young friend). 1938.xi.15. *Xin dongxiang* 1.10: 319–21. *WJ* 12: 353–57.

"Mo cuoguo zhe qianzainanfeng de baoguo jihui—Gei Xiangxi ji ge zai-xiang junren" 莫錯過這千載難逢的報國機會——給湘西幾個在鄉軍人 (Do not scorn this once-in-a-lifetime opportunity to repay your country: To some officers in the West Hunan countryside; letter). 1938? + Ms. in Shen Congwen's private collection. *WJ* 12: 361–69. (1938, winter, acc. *WJ*, but location is given as Changsha, suggesting a date in late 1937, as Shen subsequently agreed).

1939

"Xiangxi tiji" 湘西題記 (Preface to *West Hunan*). 1939.i.8. *Jinri pinglun* 1.2: 12–14. *WJ* 9: 330–35.

"Yiban huo teshu" 一般或特殊 (Ordinary or special). 1939.i.22. *Jinri pinglun* 1.4: 5–7.

"Kunming dong jing" 昆明冬景 (Winter scenes in Kunming). 1939.ii.6. Hong Kong *DGB*, "Wenyi" 522. Alternate title "Zai Kunming de shihou" 在昆明的時候 (While in Kunming). *WJ* 10: 66–71. Tr. by Wong Kam-ming and Jeffrey C. Kinkley as "While in Kunming." *Haineiwai* 28 (Nov.–Dec. 1980): 5–9.

"Zhen suren he jia daoxue" 真俗人和假道學 (Authentic yahoos vs. phony moralists). 1939.v.15. Kunming *Zhongyang ribao*, "Pingming" 1. + In *Kunming dong jing*.

"Tantan muke" 談談木刻 (About woodcut art). 1939.vi.2. *Dawanbao*, "Dushujie." + *WJ* 12: 243–45.

"Yi zhong taidu" 一種態度 (One kind of attitude). 1939.vi.25. *Jinri pinglun* 2.1: 13. *WJ* 12: 358–60.

"Ji Cai Weilian nüshi" 記蔡威廉女士 (Remembering Ms. Cai Weilian). "1939.vi.31" (date does not exist in Ch. or W. calendar; misprint for vi.30?). *Xin dongxiang* 2.10: 733–34. *WJ* 10: 72–76.

"Zhufu" [1] 主婦 (Housewife; Shen's first story by this title). 1939.xii. *Zhufu ji*. *WJ* 6: 324–37. (Written 1936, rev. 1937.v).

Xiangxi 湘西 (West Hunan). Changsha: Shangwu. Aug. 1939. Rev. ed., Shanghai: Kaiming. April 1944. 1946. *WJ* 9: 329–415. * 2 ch. tr. by Gladys Yang in *Recollections of West Hunan*.

Ji Ding Ling xuji 記丁玲續集 (Sequel to *Remembering Ding Ling*). Shanghai: Liangyou. Sept. 1939. May 1940. (Author's note: "Completed in Peking, 13 Dec. 1933; revised in Kunming, 26 July 1939"). There were no printings of this ms. between its debut as a serial, in 1933, and its first publication as a book, in 1939.

Kunming dong jing 昆明冬景 (Winter scenes in Kunming). Shanghai: Wenhua shenghuo. Sept. 1939. Guilin: Wenhua shenghuo. Dec. 1941. Aug. 1942. Note: The newly constituted collection called *Kunming dong jing* in *WJ* 11: 235–55 bears little resemblance to the book originally so entitled.

Zhufu ji 主婦集 (Housewife). Shanghai: Shangwu. Dec. 1939. Changsha: Shangwu. July 1940. Shanghai: Shangwu. March 1947. June 1948. *WJ* 6: 323–412.

1940

"Tan ren" 談人 (About mankind). 1940.i.1. Hong Kong *DGB*, "Wenyi" 763.

"Zhu xu," 1, 2 燭虛 (The candle extinguished). 1940.iv.1. *Zhanguoce* 1: 17–24. Part 2 in this version lacks a final paragraph printed in *Zhu xu*. *WJ* 11: 258–68.

"Baihuawen wenti" 白話文問題 (The question of the vernacular). 1940.iv.15. *Zhanguoce* 2: 13–21. Slightly rev. in *Zhu xu*.

"Gei yi ge daxuesheng" [2] 給一個大學生 (To a university student; Shen's second letter by this title). 1940.v.1. *Zhanguoce* 3: 38–39. Ch. 3 of *XFC*. *WJ* 11: 343–44. (1940.ii.3).

"Gei yi ge qingnian zuojia" 給一個青年作家 (To a young writer). 1940.v.1. *Zhanguoce* 3: 39. Ch. 4 of *XFC*. *WJ* 11: 345–46. (1940.ii.3).

"Gei yi ge shiren" 給一個詩人 (To a poet). 1940.v.1. *Zhanguoce* 3: 40. Ch. 5 of *XFC*. *WJ* 11: 347–48. ([1940].ii.30. Either a misprint, or Ch. cal., in which case W. cal. date is [1940.iv.7]).

"Gei yi ge zhongxue jiaoyuan" 給一個中學教員 (To a secondary school teacher). 1940.v.1. *Zhanguoce* 3: 40–42. Ch. 6 of *XFC*. *WJ* 11: 349–51. (1940.iv.15).

"Xu feiyou cundi" 續廢郵存底 (Continuing letters never mailed; not to be confused with a newly constituted book of the same title printed in *WJ* 11, which is a slightly altered version of *XFC*). 1940.v.1. This is the collective name for "Gei yi ge qingnian zuojia," "Gei yi ge daxuesheng," "Gei yi ge shiren," "Gei yi ge zhongxue jiaoyuan." *Zhanguoce* 3: 38–42.

"'Wusi' ershi nian" 「五四」二十年 (Twenty years after "May Fourth"). 1940.v.4. Hong Kong *DGB*, "Wenyi" 830. (1940, end of April).

"Wenyun de chongjian" 文運的重建 (Reconstructing the literary movement). 1940.v.5. Kunming *Zhongyang ribao*. + In *Zhu xu*. (1940.v.1).

"Wang sao" 王嫂 ("Sister Wang" [a Shen family servant]). 1940.v.29. Hong Kong *DGB*, "Wenyi" 848. Rev. ed. in *Wenju* 1.2 (20 April 1942): 1–4. *WJ* 7: 203–10.

"Du [lun] yingxiong chongbai" 讀「[論]英雄崇拜」(My reaction to "On Hero Worship" [by Chen Quan]). 1940.vi.1. *Zhanguoce* 5: 16–25. Original version omits "lun." *WJ* 12: 374–84.

"*Qian Dian dao shang*" 「黔滇道上」([Review of] *On the Road to Guizhou and Yunnan* [by Li Lincan 李霖燦]). 1940.vi.1. Kunming *Zhongyang ribao*, "Pingming." + *WJ* 11: 209–10.

"Xizuo juli: (1) Cong Xu Zhimo zuopin xuexi 'shuqing'" 習作舉例(一) 從徐志摩作品學習「抒情」(One of my exercises: [1] Studying "lyricism" from Xu Zhimo's works). 1940.vi.16. *Guowen yuekan* 1.1: 16–20. *WJ* 11: 211–18.

"Xiang cheng" 鄉城 (A country town). 1940.vi.24. Hong Kong *DGB*, "Wenyi" 867. *WJ* 7: 211–18. Tr. by Shih Ming as "Old Mrs. Wang's Chickens." *T'ien Hsia Monthly* 11.3 (Dec.–Jan. 1940–41): 274–80.

"Zhu xu," 4 燭虛 (The candle extinguished). 1940.vii.15. *Zhanguoce* 8: 15–19. Has an opening paragraph lacking in the *Zhu xu* version; omits a closing paragraph of the *Zhu xu* version. Version identical to *Zhu xu*'s was printed 1940.viii.19 in Hong Kong *DGB*, "Wenyi" 907. *WJ* 11: 270–75.

"Xin de wenxue yundong yu xin de wenxueguan" 新的文學運動與新的文學觀 (A new literary movement and a new view of literature). 1940.viii.5. *Zhanguoce* 9: 1–5. Version in *Zhu xu* is slightly revised.

"Xiaoshuo zuozhe he duzhe" 小說作者和讀者 (Fiction's writers and readers). 1940.viii.15. *Zhanguoce* 10: 13–24. ([1940].viii.3 lecture).

"Shengming" [1] 生命 (Life; one of two pieces Shen wrote by this title, tentatively assigned as the first; poem). 1940.viii.17. Hong Kong *DGB*, "Wenyi" 905.

"Lianhua" 蓮花 (Lotus flower). 1940.viii.19. Hong Kong *DGB*, "Wenyi" 907.

"Zhu xu," 5 燭虛 (The candle extinguished). 1940.ix.14. Hong Kong *DGB*, "Wenyi" 925. *WJ* 11: 275–81. (1939.v.5; v.10; vi.1; viii.3).

"Xizuo juli: (2) Cong Zhou Zuoren Lu Xun zuopin xuexi shuqing" 習作舉例(二)從周作人魯迅作品學習抒情 (One of my exercises: [2] Studying lyricism from Zhou Zuoren's and Lu Xun's works). 1940.ix.16. *Guowen yuekan* 1.2: 26–30.

"Tan jiating" 談家庭 (About the family). 1940.x.1. *Zhanguoce* 13: 9–13.

"Xizuo juli: (3) You Bing Xin dao Fei Ming" 習作舉例(三)由冰心到廢名 (One of my exercises: [3] From Bing Xin to Fei Ming). 1940.x.16. *Guowen yuekan* 1.3: 25–29. *WJ* 11: 219–31.

"Nan nü pingdeng" 男女平等 (Equality between the sexes). 1940.x.27. Kunming *Zhongyang ribao*. ++

"Kan yun" 看雲 (Gazing at clouds). 1940.xii.12. Hong Kong *DGB*, "Wenyi" 987. In *Yunnan kan yun ji*, retitled "Yunnan kan yun" 雲南看雲 (Gazing at clouds in Yunnan). Ch. 1 of *XFC*. *WJ* 10: 77–82.

"Gei yi ge Guangdong pengyou" 給一個廣東朋友 (To a friend in Guangdong). 1940.xii.30. Hong Kong *DGB*, "Wenyi" 1000. Ch. 2 of *XFC*. *WJ* 11: 338–42. (1940).

"Kan hong lu" 看虹錄 (Gazing at a rainbow). 1940? ++ Chinese text not extant? Tr. by Ching and Payne as "The Rainbow."

"Zhai xing lu" 摘星錄 (Plucking a star). 1940? ++ Not extant?

Wo de jiaoyu 我的教育 (My education). Shanghai: Santong. Oct. 1940. ++
Guolingzhe 過嶺者 (The one who crossed over the mountains). Shanghai: Xingguang. N.d. 1940?

1941

"Bianbian zuofeng" 變變作風 (Always shifting with the times). 1941.iii.15. Hong Kong *DGB*, "Wenyi" 1051. *WJ* 12: 370–73.

"Changgeng" 長庚 (Venus). 1941.viii. *Zhu xu. WJ* 11: 288–93.

"Qianyuan" 潛淵 (The profound). 1941.viii. *Zhu xu. WJ* 11: 282–87. (19––.x.16).

"Shengming" [2] 生命 (Life; one of two pieces Shen wrote by this title). 1941.viii. *Zhu xu. WJ* 11: 294–96.

"Zhu xu," 3 燭虛 (The candle extinguished). 1941.viii. *Zhu xu. WJ* 11: 268–69.

"Kan hong" 看虹 (Gazing at rainbows; poem). 1941.xi.5. Hong Kong *DGB*, "Wenyi" 1219. (1941.iii.31).

Rurui 如蕤 (Rurui). Shanghai: Yiliu shudian. Jan. 1941. Contents similar to *Shen Congwen jiezuo xuan*.

Zhu xu 燭虛 (The candle extinguished). Shanghai: Wenhua shenghuo. Aug. 1941. *WJ* 11: 257–96 (abridged).

1942

"Gei yi ge zai Mangshi fuwu de xiaoxue jiaoyuan" 給一個在芒市服務的小學教員 (To a primary school teacher serving in Mangshi [Yunnan]). 1942.ii.16. *Wenju* 1.1: 19–21. Ch. 10 of *XFC. WJ* 11: 363–67. (1941.xii).

"Duanpian xiaoshuo" 短篇小說 (The short story). 1942.iv.16. *Guowen yuekan* 18. + *WJ* 12: 113–27. (Speech of 1941.v.2; rev. v.20).

"Qiushou he shexi" 秋收和社戲 (Autumn harvest and village opera). 1942.v.1. *Ziyou Zhongguo* New Series 2.1/2: 23–31. Ch. 11 of *Chang he*, where the title is shortened to "Shexi." *WJ* 7: 162–72.

"Qiu" [3] 秋 (Autumn; Shen's third item by this title). 1942.vi.10. *Wenju* 1.3: 4–10. Ch. 2 of *Chang he. WJ* 7: 22–38.

"Shiye he zhiye: Gei yi ge gaiye ru yinhang de nianqing zuojia" [*Xin feiyou cundi*, outside the reprinted series] 事業和職業：給一個改業入銀行的年青作家 (A trade vs. a profession: To a young author who's changing over to banking; not to be confused with "Zhiye yu shiye"). 1942.vii.7. Chongqing *DGB*. Titularly ch. 22 of *Xin feiyou cundi*, but not in fact bound with *XFC* in *Yunnan kan yun ji*.

"Da bang chuan long matou shi" 大幫船攏碼頭時 (When the boat convoy comes to town). 1942.ix.15. *Wenxue chuangzuo* 1.1: 13–17. Rev. 1947.v and printed in *Zhishi yu shenghuo* 5 (16 June 1947): 21–25. Ch. 6 of *Chang he. WJ* 7: 95–108.

"Wenxue yundong de chongzao" 文學運動的重造 (Rebuilding the literary movement). 1942.x.10. *Wenyi xianfeng* 1.2: 3–6. (1942.ix.1; rewritten [1942].xii, as in *Yunnan kan yun ji*.

"Wei shenme xie, you shenme yiyi: Gei yi ge zuojia" 爲甚麼寫, 有甚麼意義 (給一個作家) (Why write? What's the significance of it? To an author). 1942.x.15. *Wenxue chuangzuo* 1.2: 61–62. Ch. 11 of *XFC*. *WJ* 11: 368–70.

"Xin Hunan jingshen" 新湖南精神 (The new Hunanese spirit). 1942.x.15. *Wenxue chuangzuo* 1.2: 62–64. Ch. 12 of *XFC*, retitled "Gei zhu Changsha yi ge paodui xiao junguan" 給駐長沙一個砲隊小軍官 (To a young artillery officer in Changsha). *WJ* 11: 371–75. (1942.ix).

"Zhai juzi" 摘橘子 (Picking tangerines). 1942.x.15. *Chuangzuo yuekan* 1.4/5: 19–24. Ch. 5 of *Chang he*. *WJ* 7: 79–94. Tr. by Lillian Chu. (Rev. 1942.vi).

"Xiaoshuo yu shehui" 小說與社會 (Fiction and society). 1942.x.25. *Shijie xuesheng* 1.10. (1942.ix.29).

"Xin zhai xing lu" 新摘星錄 (Plucking stars again). 1942.xi.22; xi.29; xii.6; xii.13; xii.20. *Dangdai pinglun* 3.2–6. *WJ* 7: 259–300. (1940.vii.18; rev. 1942.x).

1943

"Shuiyun: Wo zenme chuangzao gushi, gushi zenme chuangzao wo" 水雲—我怎麼創造故事, 故事怎麼創造我 (Water and clouds: How I create stories, and how they create me). 1943.i.15; ii.15. *Wenxue chuangzuo* 1.4, 5. *WJ* 10: 263–98. (1942).

"'Wenyi zhengce' tantao" ["jiantao," in *Yunnan kan yun ji*]「文藝政策」探討[檢討] (An inquiry into "policy for literature"). 1943.i.20. *Wenyi xianfeng* 2.1: 3–8.

"Chang he tiji" 長河題記 (Preface to *Long River*). 1943.iv.21. Chongqing *DGB*, "Zhanxian" 971. *WJ* 7: 2–8. (Rev. 1943.ii.23).

"Kan hong zhai xing lu houji" 看虹摘星錄後記 (Afterword to *Accounts of Gazing at Rainbows and Plucking Stars*). 1943.v.24. Chongqing *DGB*, "Wenyi" 29. *WJ* 11: 48–53.

"Jianweizhai bitan" 見微齋筆談 (Notes from the Studio of Small Beginnings; an essay on cannibalism). 1943.vi.1. *Wenxue chuangzuo* 2.2: 65–66, 64.

"Gei yi ge junren" 給一個軍人 (To a soldier). 1943.vi. *Yunnan kan yun ji*. Ch. 7 of *XFC*. *WJ* 11: 352–54. (194–.v.23).

"Xuexi xiezuo" 學習寫作 (Learning to write). 1943.vi. *Yunnan kan yun ji*. Ch. 8 of *XFC*. *WJ* 11: 355–57. (1942.vi.3).

"Zhiye yu shiye" 職業與事業 (A profession vs. a trade). 1943.vi. *Yunnan kan yun ji*. Ch. 9 of *XFC*. *WJ* 11: 358–62.

"Mingri de wenxue zuojia" 明日的文學作家 (The authors of tomorrow). 1943.vi. *Yunnan kan yun ji*. Ch. 13 of *XFC*. (194–.iii.21).

"Mei yu ai" 美與愛 (Beauty and love). 1943.vi. *Yunnan kan yun ji*. Ch. 14 of *XFC*. *WJ* 11: 376–79.

"Lun touzi" 論投資 (On investing). 1943.vi. *Yunnan kan yun ji*. Ch. 15 of *XFC*.

"Dushuren dubo" 讀書人賭博 (The gambles of learned folk). 1943.vi. *Yunnan kan yun ji*. Ch. 16 of *XFC*. (Rev. 1943.iv.20).

"Xiang ju" 鄉居 (Living in the country). 1943.x.1. *Wenxue chuangzuo* 2.4: 48–51. (Rewritten 1943.vi.3).

"Dongjing" 動靜 (Stirrings). 1943.xii.8. *Wenju* 2.1: 20–27.

"Women xuyao yi ge disi dang" 我們需要一個第四黨 (What we need is a *fourth* party). 1941–45? Jin Di recalls that this title was published in a Kunming newspaper. The entire text of the article was excised by the censors.

Yunnan kan yun ji 雲南看雲集 (Gazing at clouds in Yunnan). Chongqing: Guomin tushu chubanshe. June 1943.

Ajin 阿金 (Ajin [name]). [Guilin]: Kaiming. July 1943. Rev. ed., Shanghai: Kaiming. 1949.

Heifeng ji 黑鳳集 (Black phoenix). [Guilin]: Kaiming. July 1943. Shanghai: Kaiming. March 1948. March 1949.

Chang he 長河 (Long river). [Guilin]: Kaiming. Sept. 1943? Rev. ed., Kunming: Chongwen yinshuguan. 1945. Shanghai: Kaiming. Aug. 1948, with variant pagination. Jan. 1949, with original pagination. *WJ* 7: 1–172. Ch. 1, 3, 5 tr. by Lillian Chu. Ch. 3 tr. by Nancy Gibbs. In Ebrey.

Chun Deng ji 春燈集 ("Spring" and "Lamp" collection). [Guilin]: Kaiming. Sept. 1943. Shanghai: Kaiming. Jan. 1949.

Hei ye 黑夜 (Dark night). [Guilin]: Kaiming. Sept. 1943. Shanghai: Kaiming. Jan. 1949.

Chun 春 (Spring). [Guilin]: Kaiming. Dec. 1943. Rev. ed., Shanghai: Kaiming. Jan. 1949.

Xin feiyou cundi [1] 新廢郵存底 (New letters never mailed). 1943? Not seen, except in *Yunnan kan yun ji*; possibly never a separate book. Note: This collection is retitled *Xu* 續 *feiyou cundi* in *WJ* 11: 337–79. However, it lacks ch. 1, 13, 15, and 16 ("Yunnan kan yun"; "Mingri de wenxue zuojia"; "Lun touzi"; "Dushuren dubo"). Also note: *WJ* 12 opens with a *Xin feiyou cundi* [2]. It is a different work.

1944

"Lü yan" 綠魘 (Green nightmare). 1944.ii.1. *Dangdai wenyi* 1.2: 41–49. *WJ* 10: 83–106. (Rewritten 1943.xii.10; rev. 1946.iii.26 and reprinted 1946.xii in *Xiandai wenlu* 1: 77–96).

"Zuojia shenghuo zishu—Shen Congwen" 作家生活自述—沈從文 (Authors on their own lives—Shen Congwen). 1944.iv. *Dangdai wenyi* 1.4. ++

1945

"Chi yan" 赤魘 (Red nightmare). 1945.iii.20. Kunming *Guanchabao*, "Shenghuofeng" 20. + *WJ* 7: 350–55.

"*Duan hong* yinyan" 「斷虹」引言 (Preface to *Broken Rainbow*). 1945.iv.1. *Chunqiu* 3.1. + *WJ* 11: 54–61.

Yan 魘 (Nightmares). 1945? ++ The existence of this book is not verified. Shao Huaqiang has seen it advertised.

Kan hong zhai xing lu 看虹摘星錄 (Accounts of gazing at rainbows and plucking stars). Jiangxi province? 1945? ++ The existence of this book is not verified, but Cheng Yingliu says he recollects it.

1946

"Chi dabing" 吃大餅 (Eating flatbread). 1946.i.5. *Yuekan* 1.3. ++

"Shuping de ziyou jiefang yundong" 書評的自由解放運動 (The movement for freedom of expression in book reviews). 1946.v.1. *Shanghai wenhua* 4: 18. *WJ* 12: 206–10. Excerpted from 1937.i.17 piece, "Wo duiyu shuping de ganxiang."

"Yunnan de meishu jiaoyu" 雲南的美術教育 (Art education in Yunnan). 1946.v.25. *Mintan zhoukan* 2/3. ++

"Hongqiao" 虹橋 (Rainbow). 1946.vi.1. *Wenyi fuxing* 1.5: 520–26. *WJ* 7: 219–32.

"Xiangren duiyu xin wenxue yundong de gongxian" 湘人對於新文學運動的貢獻 (The contributions of Hunanese to the new literature movement). 1946.vii.30. Shanghai *DGB*, "Wenyi" 43. *WJ* 12: 194–200. (1945.viii.15, acc. *WJ*).

"Cheng yan" 橙魘 (Orange nightmare). 1946.viii.1. *Chunqiu* 3.2. ++ (1945.vi).

"Yingshengchong" 應聲蟲 (Yesmen). 1946.viii.11, 12. Shanghai *DGB*.

"Huai Kunming" 懷昆明 (Yearning for Kunming). 1946.viii.13. Shanghai *DGB*, "Wenyi" 47. *WJ* 10: 133–38. ([1946].viii.9).

"Dinghe shi ge yinyuemi" 定和是個音樂迷 (Dinghe is a music addict; referring to Shen's brother-in-law, Zhang Dinghe). 1946.viii.20. Shanghai *DGB*, "Wenyi" 49.

"Wenxue yu qingnian qinggan jiaoyu" 文學與青年情感教育 (Literature and educating the feelings of youth). 1946.ix.1. *Jingshi ribao*, "Wenyi zhoukan" 3.

"Yi zhong xin de wenxueguan" 一種新的文學觀 (A new view of literature). 1946.ix.1. *Wenchao yuekan* 1.5: 285–88.

"Zenyang ban yi fen hao baozhi" 怎樣辦一份好報紙 (How to run a good newspaper). 1946.ix.1. *Shanghai wenhua* 8: 22–24. *WJ* 12: 201–205 (retitled "Zenyang banhao yifen baozhi").

"Xin zhu xu" 新燭虛 (The candle extinguished, sequel). 1946.ix.22. *Jingshi ribao*, "Wenyi zhoukan" 6. Retitled "Beiping de yinxiang he ganxiang" 北平的印象和感想 (My impressions and thoughts about Peking). *Shanghai wenhua* 9 (1 Oct. 1946): 50–53. *WJ* 10: 126–32. (1946.viii.9, acc. *WJ*).

"Qiong yu yu" 窮與愚 (Poor and ignorant). 1946.x.10. *Yishibao*. *WJ* 12: 385–90. Rev. and retitled "Cong kaifa tounao shuoqi" 從開發頭腦說起 (Proceeding from the idea of opening up people's minds). 1946.xii.1. *Shanghai wenhua* 11: 18–20. ([1946].x.8).

"Tan kumen—Nie Qing yiwen yinyan" 談苦悶—聶清遺文引言 (About feeling dejected—Preface to the posthumously published writings of Nie Qing). 1946.x.10. Shanghai *DGB*. Also Tianjin *DGB*, 2 Feb. 1947.

"Wenxue zhoukan kaizhang" 文學周刊開張 (On starting up the "Literature Weekly" Supplement). 1946.x.13. *Yishibao*, "Wenxue zhoukan" 10. ([1946].x.7).

"Zhufu" [2] 主婦 (Housewife; Shen's second story by this title). 1946.x.13. Tianjin and Shanghai *DGB*, "Wenyi" 1. *WJ* 7: 233–46. (1945.ix.9).

"Bianzhe yan" 編者言 (Words from the editor). 1946.x.20. *Yishibao*, "Wenxue zhoukan" 11. ([1946].x.17).

"Xue qing" 雪晴 (After snow). 1946.x.20. *Jingshi ribao*, "Wenyi." + *WJ* 7: 356–62. Tr. by Gladys Yang as "After Snow" in *Recollections of West Hunan*. (Rewritten 1946.x.12).

"Cong xianshi xuexi" 從現實學習 (Learning from reality). 1946.xi.3; xi.10. Tianjin and Shanghai *DGB*, "Wenyi" 4, 5. *WJ* 10: 299–322. ([1946].x.20).

"Shen Congwen lun zuojia" 沈從文論作家 (Shen Congwen on writers). 1946.xi.13. Shanghai *Qiaoshengbao*. ++

"Xin feiyou cundi," 101 [outside the reprinted series] 新廢郵存底 (New letters never mailed, no. 101; not bound with *XFC*). 1946.xi.16. *Yishibao*, "Wenxue zhoukan" 15. ([1946].xi.11).

"Qingse yan" 青色魘 (Blue nightmare). 1946.xi.24. *Yishibao*, "Wenxue zhoukan" 16. *WJ* 7: 247–58.

"Zhuogui" 捉鬼 (Catching the spirit). 1946.xii.21. *Yishibao*, "Wenxue zhoukan" 20. (A revision of the 1932.xi.1 story, "Bing").

Zai Kunming de shihou 在昆明的時候 (While in Kunming). Chongqing: Zhongwai shudian. Feb. 1946. Guangzhou: March 1946. Beiping: May 1946. Contains works by Shen, He Qifang, Tian Han, Ba Jin, and others.

1947

"Songren xiequ" 宋人諧趣 (Humor in the Song dynasty). 1947.i.1; i.16? *Lunyu* 120: 96–99; 121? (issue unavailable). *WJ* 12: 246–65.

"Xin shuye he zuojia" 新書業和作家 (The new book industry and writers). 1947.i.16? *Lunyu* 121? ++
"Yunlu jishi" 芸廬紀事 (Yunlu chronicles [Yunlu was the Yuanling residence of Shen Yunlu 沈雲麓]). 1947.ii.1; ii.16; iii.1; iii.15, iii.29. *Yishibao*, "Wenxue zhoukan" 26, 28, 30, 32, 34. * *WJ* 7: 301–47. *WJ* edition has extensive changes; whole chapters are cut out.
"Xin feiyou cundi" [outside the reprinted series] 新廢郵存底 (New letters never mailed). 1947.iii.22. *Yishibao*, "Wenxue zhoukan" 33. *WJ* 12: 50–51.
"Yi ge chuanqi de benshi" 一個傳奇的本事 (Material for a fairy tale). 1947.iii.23. Tianjin *DGB*, "Wenyi" 24. Shanghai *DGB* of the same day has the same text but different illustrative woodcuts (by Huang Yongyu, in both editions). *WJ* 10: 139–65, with 1979.x.14 postscript. ([1947].iii.11).
"Xue he wu" 雪和霧 (Snow and mist). 1947.iv.12. *Yishibao*, "Wenxue zhoukan," 36. Written under the pen name "Shantuo," likely Shen Congwen, although he could not remember for certain.
"Xin feiyou cundi," 253, 254 [outside the reprinted series] 新廢郵存底 (New letters never mailed, nos. 253 and 254). 1947.iv.12. *Yishibao*, "Wenxue zhoukan" 36. *WJ* 12: 55–59.
"Xing yu zhengzhi" 性與政治 (Sex and politics). 1947.iv.16. *Zhishi yu shenghuo* 1: 10–13. Also *Lunyu* 129 (16 May 1947): 493–500.
"Zhi Zhuoren" 致灼人 (To Zhuoren; letter). 1947.iv.21. *Qinghua zhoukan* 685 (new ser. 9). + *WJ* 12: 52–54. (1947.iii.25).
"Wusi" 五四 (May Fourth). 1947.v.4. *Yishibao*, "Wenxue zhoukan" 39.
"Xin feiyou cundi," 256 [outside the reprinted series] 新廢郵存底 (New letters never mailed, no. 256). 1947.v.10. *Yishibao*, "Wenxue zhoukan" 40.
"Qiaoxiu he Dongsheng" 巧秀和冬生 (Qiaoxiu and Dongsheng [names]). 1947.vi.1. *Wenxue zazhi* 2.1: 103–23. *WJ* 7: 363–81. Tr. by Gladys Yang as "Qiaoxiu and Dongsheng" in *Recollections of West Hunan*. (1947, end of March).
"Songren yanju de fengcixing" 宋人演劇的諷刺性 (Satire in Song drama). 1947.vi.1. *Lunyu* 130: 536–41. *WJ* 12: 266–78.
"Ren yu di" 人與地 (The people and the land). 1947.vi.28. *Yishibao*, "Wenxue zhoukan" 46. Ch. 1 of *Chang he*. *WJ* 7: 9–21. Tr. by Lillian Chu.
"Xin feiyou cundi," 258, 259 [outside the reprinted series] 新廢郵存底 (New letters never mailed, nos. 258 and 259). 1947.vii.20. *Pingming ribao*, "Xingqi yiwen." + *WJ* 12: 60–62 (259 only).
"Hei yan" 黑魘 (Black nightmare). 1947.viii.1. *Zhishi yu shenghuo* 8: 22–24. *WJ* 10: 107–17. (1943.xii.31).
"Huanying Weidemai" 歡迎魏德邁 (Welcome to [U.S. Gen. Albert C.] Wedemeyer). 1947.viii.1. Tianjin *DGB*.

"Hunan de xibei jiao xuyan" 「湖南的西北角」序言 (Preface to *The Northwest Corner of Hunan* [by Li Zhenyi]). 1947.viii.2. *Yishibao*, "Wenxue zhoukan" 51. *WJ* 11: 62–66. (1947.vii).
"Bai yan" 白魘 (White nightmare). 1947.viii.16. *Zhishi yu shenghuo* 9: 22–25. *WJ* 10: 118–25. (1944; rev. 1947).
"Qishi" 啟事 (Postscript). 1947.ix.20. *Yishibao*, "Wenxue zhoukan" 58. *WJ* 12: 69.
"Xin feiyou cundi, 273: Yi shou shi de taolun" [outside the reprinted series] 新廢郵存底——一首詩的討論 (New letters never mailed, no. 273: A discussion of a poem [by Zhang Bai]). 1947.ix.20. *Yishibao*, "Wenxue zhoukan" 58. *WJ* 12: 67–68. ([1947].ix.10).
"Xin feiyou cundi, 281: Guanyu xuexi" [outside the reprinted series] 新廢郵存——關于學習 (No. 281: About study). 1947.ix.20. *Yishibao*, "Wenxue zhoukan" 58.
"Xin feiyou cundi, 285: Yi ge bianjiang gushi de taolun" [outside the reprinted series] 新廢郵存底——一個邊疆故事的討論 (No. 285: Discussion of a story about the frontier). 1947.ix.20. *Yishibao*, "Wenxue zhoukan" 58. *WJ* 12: 70–75.
"Zhai er mei zhai feiyou (Xin 19)" 窄而霉齋廢郵(新十九) (Letters never mailed from the Cramped and Moldy Studio, new series, no. 19). 1947.ix.28. *Pingming ribao*, "Xingqi yiwen." + *WJ* 12: 63–66.
"Benkan yi nian" 本刊一年 (After one year of our supplement). 1947.x.18. *Yishibao*, "Wenxue zhoukan" 62.
"Yi zhong xin xiwang" 一種新希望 (A new hope). 1947.x.21. *Yishibao*. ++
"Xin feiyou cundi," 324 [outside the reprinted series] 新廢郵存底 (New letters never mailed, no. 324). 1947.x.25. *Yishibao*, "Wenxue zhoukan" 63. *WJ* 12: 76–77.
"Xue Lu Xun" 學魯迅 (Study Lu Xun). 1947.xi.1. *Zhishi yu shenghuo* 14: 16. *WJ* 11: 232–34.
"Yi ge fukan neng jituo xie shenme xiwang" 一個副刊能寄托些什麼希望 (What kind of hopes can be entrusted to a supplement?). 1947.xi.1. *Yishibao*, "Wenxue zhoukan" 64. Excerpted from the 1946.x.20 piece, "Bianzhe yan."
"Chuanqi bu qi" 傳奇不奇 (Truth is stranger than fiction). 1947.xi. *Wenxue zazhi* 2.6: 89–109. *WJ* 7: 382–403. Tr. by Gladys Yang as "Truth Is Stranger than Fiction" in *Recollections of West Hunan*. (1947.x, acc. *WJ*. 1980 Hong Kong *Congwen sanwen xuan* says: "Beiping, the last day of 1947. Reread the last day of 1948; I think this story already has no hope of being completed.").
"Beiping tongxin, Diyi" 北平通信,第一 (Correspondence from Peking, No. 1). 1947.xii.1. *Lunyu* 142: 1078–81.
"Yingjie qiutian—Beiping tongxin" 迎接秋天——北平通信 (Greeting the autumn—Correspondence from Peking). 1947.xii.15. *Zhishi yu shenghuo* 16. + Also *Lunyu* 163 (16 Oct. 1948): 1972–75. (1947?.ix.21).

Shen Congwen xuan ji [2] 沈從文選集 (Selected works by Shen Congwen; second collection by this title). Chen Lei 陳磊, ed. Shanghai: Lüyang shuwu. N. d., ca. 1947-49.

1948

"Huai Tatamulin—Beiping tongxin" 懷塔塔木林—北平通信 (Remembering Tatamulin—Correspondence from Peking). 1948.i.1. *Zhishi yu shenghuo* 17/18. + Also in *Lunyu* +, and in Tatamulin [Xiao Qian], *Hongmao changtan* 紅毛長談 (Lengthy discourse by a red-haired barbarian). Shanghai. Aug. 1948. Pp. 78-82.

"Zhijiangxian de Xiong gongguan" 芷江縣的熊公館 (The Xiong family mansion in Zhijiang). 1948.i.3. Tianjin *DGB*. *WJ* 10: 166-73. (1947.xii.19).

"Xin feiyou cundi," 357 [outside the reprinted series] 新廢郵存底 (New letters never mailed, no. 357). 1948.i.17. *Yishibao*, "Wenxue zhoukan" 74. Also called "Tan xiandai shi" 談現代詩 (About modern poetry). *WJ* 12: 78-80. (1947.xii).

"Lun texie" 論特寫 (On reportage about feature subjects). 1948.i.31. *Yishibao*, "Wenxue zhoukan" 76. *WJ* 12: 136-42. (1948.i.7; rev. [1948].i.24).

"Gudu xinyang—Beiping tongxin" 故都新樣—北平通信 (The new look of the old capital—Correspondence from Peking). 1948.ii.16. *Zhishi yu shenghuo* 21: 14-15.

"Sugeladi tan Beiping suoxu [Beiping tongxin zhi 3]" 蘇格拉底談北平所需(北平通信之三) (Socrates discusses what Peking needs [correspondence from Peking, no. 3]). 1948.ii.16; iii.1. *Lunyu* 147, 148: 1320-22, 1352-54.

"[Xin] feiyou cundi, 358: Fu yi ge muke gongzuozhe" [outside the reprinted series] [新]廢郵存底—覆一個木刻工作者 ([New] letters never mailed, no. 358: Reply to a woodcut art worker). 1948.ii.21. *Yishibao*, "Wenxue zhoukan" 79.

"Xindang zhong yi ge Hunan xiangxiaren he yi ge Hunanren de pengyou" 新黨中一個湖南鄉下人和一個湖南人的朋友 (A Hunan country fellow of the reform party and a friend of the Hunanese [i.e., Xiong Xiling and Liang Qichao]). 1948.ii.21. *Yishibao*, "Wenxue zhoukan" 79. (1948.i.13, midnight).

"Shitan yishu yu wenhua—Beiping tongxun, 4" 試談藝術與文化(北平通訊之四) (Tentative thoughts on art and culture—Correspondence from Peking, No. 4). 1948.iii.1. *Zhishi yu shenghuo* 22: 11-13. Also *Lunyu* 150 (1 April 1948): 1428-31.

"[Xin] feiyou cundi, 391—Fu shi zhong laobaixingshe zhu tongxue" [outside the reprinted series] [新]廢郵存底—復市中老百姓社諸同學 ([New] letters never mailed, no. 391—Reply to the students of the Common People's Society in a municipal middle school). 1948.iv.25. *Pingming ribao*, "Xingqi yiwen." + *WJ* 12: 81-82. (1948.iii.21).

"Jinian Wusi" 紀念五四 (Commemorating May Fourth). 1948.v.4. *Yishibao*, "Wenxue zhoukan" 90.

"[Xin] feiyou cundi" [outside the reprinted series] [新]廢郵存底 ([New] letters never mailed). 1948.vi.12. *Yishibao*, "Wenxue zhoukan" 96. *WJ* 12: 83–84.

"Tan xiezi" [2] 談寫字 (About calligraphy; Shen's second piece by this title). 1948.vii.1. *Lunyu* 156: 1692–95. Reprinted 1948.ix in *Wenxue zazhi* 3.4: 64–68. *WJ* 12: 229–35.

"'Zhongguo wang hechu qu'"「中國往何處去」("Where is China headed?"). 1948.ix.1. *Lunyu* 160: 1852–54.

"Shoushi canpo—wenwu baowei yizhong kanfa" 收拾殘破——文物保衛一種看法 (Restore things that are decaying—an opinion about protecting artifacts). 1948.x.1, x.16. *Lunyu* 162, 163: 1936–37, 1986–87. *WJ* 12: 296–304.

"Guanyu Beiping tezhong shougongyi zhanlanhui yi dian yijian" 關于北平特種手工藝展覽會一點意見 (My humble opinion of the Peking exhibition of special handicrafts). 1948.x.9. Tianjin *DGB*. *WJ* 12: 305–12. (1948.x.7).

"Wenwu baowei de yizhong kanfa" 文物保衛的一種看法 (An opinion about protecting artifacts). 1948.x.9. Tianjin *DGB*.

1949

"Du 'You chun tu' yougan" 讀「游春圖」有感 (My reaction to the "Painting of a Spring Outing"). 1949.iv.1. *Zi yue* 6, appendix, "Yizhou" 1. Retitled "Du Zhan Ziqian 'You chun tu'" 讀展子虔「游春圖」(Appraising the "Painting of a Spring Outing" attributed to Zhan Ziqian). + *WJ* 12: 279–95. (1947.vii).

1951

"Wo de xuexi" 我的學習 (My study; Shen Congwen's "confession"). 1951.xi.19–22. Hong Kong *DGB*.

1953

"Zhongguo zhijin jinduan de lishi fazhan" 中國織金錦緞的歷史發展 (The historical development of gold brocade in China). 1953.ix.3. *Xin jianshe* 60: 16–22. In *Longfeng yishu*, retitled "Zhijinjin" 織金錦 (Gold brocade).

"Zhongguo gudai taoci" 中國古代陶瓷 (Ancient Chinese ceramics). 1953.x.1. *Xin guancha* 19: 24–26. (Rev. 1953.vii).

1954

"Luetan kaozheng gongzuo bixu wenxian yu shiwu xiangjiehe" 略談考証工作必須文獻與實物相結合 (A brief talk about the need of textual research to combine study of documents with that of artifacts). 1954.x.3. *Guangming ribao*.

Zhanguo qiqi 戰國漆器 (Lacquerware of the Warring States period). Beijing: Publisher unknown. 1953–54? ++

1956

"Shen Congwen de fayan" 沈從文的發言 (Speech by Shen Congwen [at the Second People's Political Consultative Conference]). 1956.ii.8. *Guangming ribao.*

"Tiananmen qian" 天安門前 (In front of the Gate of Heavenly Peace). 1956.vii.9. *Renmin ribao. WJ* 10: 176–79.

"Chun you Yiheyuan" 春遊頤和園 (Touring the Summer Palace in the spring). 1956.viii. *Meili de Beijing. WJ* 10: 197–204.

"Beijing you xuduo bowuguan, tongshi you shi ge daxing jianzhu bowuguan" 北京有許多博物館,同時又是個大型建築博物館 (Peking has many museums, and is itself a giant museum of architecture). 1956.x.15. *Wenhuibao. WJ* 10: 180–84. (1956.ix).

Meili de Beijing 美麗的北京 (Beautiful Peking). Cao Yu 曹禺 and Shen Congwen, eds. Hong Kong: Sanlian. Aug. 1956.

1957

"Cong yi ben shu tantan minzu yishu" 從一本書談談民族藝術 (A chat about ethnic art, proceeding from a book [*Artistic Designs of the Minority Peoples of Guangxi*]). 1957.v.22. *Lüxingjia* 1957.5: 26, 45. *WJ* 10: 185–88.

"Liang feng xin" 兩封信 (Two letters; two previously unpublished letters, one to Hu Yepin and Jiang Bingzhi [Ding Ling], the other to Zhu Wen). 1957.vi.1. *Shen Congwen xiaoshuo sanwen xuan.* (First letter, 1928?.i.11; second letter, early 1930's).

"Xin Xiang xing ji" 新湘行記 (A trip through New Hunan). 1957.vi.22. *Lüxingjia* 1957.6: 3–5. *WJ* 10: 189–96. (1957.v).

"Paolongtao" 跑龍套 (Supporting actors). 1957.vii.8. *Renmin wenxue* 92: 136–37. *WJ* 10: 205–209.

"Tan 'Xie you ji'" 談「寫游記」(About "Writing Travel Accounts"). 1957.vii.22. *Lüxingjia* 1957.7: 34–35. *WJ* 12: 143–46. (1957.vi.20).

"Yi dian huiyi, yi dian ganxiang" 一點回憶,一點感想 (A few memories, a few thoughts). 1957.viii.8. *Renmin wenxue* 93: 2–5. *WJ* 10: 210–16. (1957.vii).

"Xuan ji tiji" 選集題記 (Preface to the *Selected Fiction*). 1957.x. *Shen Congwen xiaoshuo xuan ji. WJ* 11: 67–72. (1957, March to July; rev. 1981.xii.1 and given postscript, in *Shen Congwen xiaoshuo xuan* [3], 1: 1–7.)

Shen Congwen xiaoshuo sanwen xuan 沈從文小説散文選 (A selection of Shen Congwen's fiction and essays). Hong Kong: Xinxue shudian. 1 June 1957. Preface by Wen Zichuan 溫梓川.

Shen Congwen xiaoshuo xuan ji 沈從文小說選集 (A collection of Shen Congwen's selected fiction). * Beijing: Renmin wenxue chubanshe. Oct. 1957. Pirate ed. entitled *Shen Congwen duanpian xiaoshuo xuan* 沈從文短篇小說選 (Selected short stories by Shen Congwen). Hong Kong: Wenjiao chubanshe. April 1978.

Zhongguo sichou tu'an 中國絲綢圖案 (Patterns on Chinese fabrics). Shen Congwen and Wang Jiashu 王家樹, eds. Beijing: Zhongguo gudian yishu chubanshe. Dec. 1957.

Shen Congwen xuan ji [3] 沈從文選集 (Selected works by Shen Congwen; third collection by this title). Hong Kong: Wenxue chubanshe. 1957. 1973. Has anonymous preface.

1958

"Longfeng tu'an de yingyong he fazhan" 龍鳳圖案的應用和發展 (The use and development of dragon and phoenix designs). 1958.vii.17. *Zhuangshi* 1: 9–13. In *Longfeng yishu*, retitled "Longfeng yishu" 龍鳳藝術 (The art of dragons and phoenixes). (1958.vi).

"Tan ranxie" 談染纈 (About dyed silks). 1958.ix.8. *Wenwu cankao ziliao* 97: 13–15.

"Yu de yishu" 魚的藝術 (The fish in art history). 1958.xi.5. *Zhuangshi* 2: 10–15. Tr. anonymously as "The Fish Motif in Chinese Art." *Chinese Literature* (Feb. 1962): 93–97. (1958.xi).

"Gudai jingzi de yishu" 古代鏡子的藝術 (The art of ancient mirrors). 1958.xi. *Tang Song tong jing* (preface). Reprinted in *Longfeng yishu*. (1956.v.1 Festival).

Tang Song tong jing 唐宋銅鏡 (Bronze mirrors of the Tang and Song dynasties). Beijing: Zhongguo gudian yishu chubanshe. Nov. 1958.

1959

"Rang women youyi chang qing" 讓我們友誼長青 (Let our friendship long remain fresh). 1959.i.1. *Xiangtu* 3.1: 7.

"Tan tiaohua" 談挑花 (About embroidery). 1959.i.5. *Zhuangshi* 3: 8–9.

"Jinhua zhi" 金花紙 (Decorated stationery). 1959.ii.8. *Wenwu* 102: 10–12. Retitled "Tan 談 Jinhua zhi" (About decorated stationery).

"Jieshao ji pian Qingchu huajin" 介紹幾片清初花錦 (Introducing some pieces of Early Qing brocade). 1959.iii.5. *Zhuangshi* 4: 11.

"Piqiuhua" 皮球花 ("Rubber Ball" designs). 1959.v.5. *Zhuangshi* 5: 47–49. Retitled "Tan 談 piqiuhua." (About "rubber ball" designs).

"Tantan 'Wenji gui Han tu'" 談談「文姬歸漢圖」(A chat about paintings depicting Cai Wenji's return to China). 1959.vi.8. *Wenwu* 106: 32–35. (1955; rev. 1959.iv).

"Shu zhong jin" 蜀中錦 (Central Sichuan brocades). 1959.vii.5. *Zhuangshi* 6: 43–45.

"Tan ciqi yishu" 談磁器藝術 (About the art of porcelain). 1959.xi.8. *Guangming ribao.* (1959.x).

"Dao Jinyi" 悼靳以 (Mourning Jinyi). 1959.xii.8. *Renmin wenxue* 121: 127–28. *WJ* 10: 217–20. ([1959].x.8, night).

Xiaoxiao 蕭蕭 (Xiaoxiao [name]). Hong Kong: Xinyue. Oct. 1959. Not to be confused with another Hong Kong book of the same title, published by Guoguang in April 1961. The latter is entirely excerpted from the 1957 Peking *Shen Congwen xiaoshuo xuan ji.* Both editions of *Xiaoxiao* are, strictly speaking, pirated.

Ming jin 明錦 (Ming dynasty brocades). Beijing: Wenwu chubanshe. 1959. ++

1960

"Boli gongyi de lishi tantao" 玻璃工藝的歷史探討 (An inquiry into the history of glass handicrafts). 1960.i. *Meishu yanjiu* 13: 35–38.

"Hua bian" 花邊 (Embroidered hems). 1960.v. *Zhuangshi* 11: 54–55.

"*Ming jin* tiji" 「明錦」題記 (Preface to *Ming Brocades*). 1960. *Longfeng yishu*, pp. 34–40. (1954).

"Tahu jianzhi" 塔戶剪紙 (Paper cuts from Tahu [Luqi, West Hunan]). 1960. *Longfeng yishu*, pp. 52–55.

"Tiji" 題記 (Preface). 1960. *Longfeng yishu*, pp. 1–2. (1959.xii).

"Xiangxi Miaozu de yishu" 湘西苗族的藝術 (The art of the West Hunan Miao people). 1960. *Longfeng yishu. WJ* 10: 221–26.

Ba jun tu [3] 八駿圖 (Portrait of eight steeds). Hong Kong: Rixin. Jan. 1960. This pirated edition has four stories and is different in content from other volumes published under this title.

Longfeng yishu 龍鳳藝術 (The art of dragons and phoenixes). Beijing: Zuojia chubanshe. 1960.

1961

"Cong 'bu pa gui de gushi' zhu tan dao wenxian yu wenwu xiangjiehe wenti" 從「不怕鬼的故事」注談到文獻與文物相結合問題 (Turning from the commentary to "Stories About Not Fearing Ghosts" to the problem of combining study of documents with that of artifacts). 1961.vi.18. *Guangming ribao.*

"'Banpiaojia' he 'dianxiqiao'" 「分瓟斝」和「點犀盃」 (The terms "*banpiaojia*" and "*dianxiqiao*" [in *The Dream of the Red Chamber*]). 1961.viii.6. *Guangming ribao.*

"Cong wenwu tantan guren de huzi wenti" 從文物談談古人的鬍子問題 (A chat about ancient people's beards, proceeding from artifact evidence). 1961.x.21, 24. *Guangming ribao.*

"'Xingxiqiao' zhiyi" 「杏犀盃」質疑 (A query about the term "*xingxiqiao*"). 1961.xi.12. *Guangming ribao.*

1962

"Jinggangshan qingchen" 井岡山清晨 (A clear morning on Mt. Jinggang; poem). 1962.ii.12. *Renmin wenxue* 147: 13–14. *WJ* 10: 342–45. (1961.xii.22).

"Jianshe xin shan cun, ganbu xiafang shang Jinggangshan si zhou nian jieri" 建設新山村, 幹部下放上井岡山四周年節日 (Constructing a new mountain village, on the fourth anniversary of the sent-down cadres' ascent of Mt. Jinggang; poem). 1962.ii.12. *Renmin wenxue* 147: 14–15. *WJ* 10: 346–47.

"Xiashan hui Nanchang tuzhong" 下山回南昌途中 (While descending the mountain, on the way back to Nanchang; poem). 1962.ii.12. *Renmin wenxue* 147: 15–16. *WJ* 10: 348–49. (1961.xii.30).

"Lushan 'Huajing' Bai Juyi zuoshi chu" 廬山「花徑」白居易作詩處 (In the "Path of Flowers" on Mt. Lu, where Bai Juyi once wrote poetry; poem). 1962.ii.12. *Renmin wenxue* 147: 16. *WJ* 10: 350–51. (1961.xii.12).

"Lushan Hanpokou Wangpoting" 廬山含鄱口望鄱亭 (The Mt. Lu vistas, Mouth Enclosing Poyang Lake, and Pavilion for Looking at Poyang Lake; poem). 1962.ii.12. *Renmin wenxue* 147: 16. Rev. and retitled "Lushan Hanpokou." *Haineiwai* 28 (Nov./Dec. 1980): 9–10. *WJ* 10: 352. (1961.xii.12).

"Tan Guang xiu" 談廣繡 (About Cantonese embroidery). 1962.viii.9. *Yangcheng wanbao.* ++

"Xuexi gudian wenxue yu lishi shiwu wenti" 學習古典文學與歷史實物問題 (Problems in the study of ancient literature and historical objects; private letter). 1962.x.21. *Guangming ribao.*

1963

"Guojie he guandeng" 過節和觀燈 (Festivals and lanterns). 1963.iv.12. *Renmin wenxue* 161: 42–47. *WJ* 10: 227–40. (1963.iii).

"Xuyan" 序言 (Preface). 1963. *Zhongguo de ciqi* 中國的瓷器 (Chinese porcelain). Ed. Jingdezhen Research Institute, Jiangxi Province Office of Light Industry. Beijing: Zhongguo caizheng jingji chubanshe. (1962.vi).

1975

"Gugong de jianzhu" 故宮的建築 (The architecture of the imperial palace). 1975.vi. In Cao Yu 曹禺, Lao She 老舍, eds. *Beijing de huiyi* 北京的回憶 (Memories of Peking). Hong Kong: Wenhua/Shenghuo, pp. 62–64.

1980

"Xi xin qing" 喜新晴 (Happiness at the clearing in the weather; poem). 1980.iii.10. *Haiyang wenyi* 7.3: 45. *WJ* 10: 357–58. (1970.x, acc. *WJ*; rev. 1980.i.9).

"Fuji" 附記 (Postscript [to 1947 work "Yi ge chuanqi de benshi"]). 1980.v.10. *Haiyang wenyi* 7.5: 20–22. (1979.x.14).

"Congwen xizuo jianmu" 從文習作簡目 (Congwen's brief list of his exercises). 1980.v. *Hua cheng* 5: 140.

"Ni yong huai shi" 拟咏懷詩 (Verse by way of an elegy). 1980.v. *Hua cheng* 5: 120–21. *WJ* 10: 359–62. (1971, acc. *WJ*).

"*Congwen sanwen xuan* tiji" 「從文散文選」題記 (Preface to *Selection of Congwen's Essays* [Hong Kong]). 1980.vi. *Dipingxian* 11: 4–6. *WJ* 11: 73–75. (1980.iii.25).

"Congwen zizhuan" 從文自傳 (Congwen's autobiography, 1980 ed.). * 1980.viii.22; xi.22; 1981.ii.22. *Xin wenxue shiliao* 8–10. (1980.v).

"Wo suo liaojie de Situ Qiao xiansheng" 我所瞭解的司徒喬先生 (The Situ Qiao I knew). 1980.x. *Zhongguo jianshe* 29.10: 68–73. Retitled "Wo suo jiandao 見到 de Situ Qiao xiansheng." *WJ* 10: 249–52.

"Shuangxi daxue" 雙溪大雪 (The big snows of Shuangxi [Hubei]; poem). 1980.xi.10. *Wenhui zengkan* 1980.7: 40. *WJ* 10: 365–68. (1970).

"Yi ge wufa toudi de youjian" 一個無法投遞的郵件 (An undeliverable letter). 1980.xi.16. *Guangjiaojing* 98: 32–33. Reprinted 1981.iv in internal Nanking magazine *Wenjiao ziliao jianbao*.

"Yi Xianghe" 憶翔鶴 (Remembering [Chen] Xianghe). 1980.xi.22. *Xin wenxue shiliao* 9: 147–50. *WJ* 10: 241–48. (1980.viii.10).

"Ganzhou Bajingtai" 贛州八境台 (The Eight-boundary Platform of Ganzhou; poem). 1980.xi/xii. *Haineiwai* 28: 9.

"Ershi niandai de Zhongguo xin wenxue" 二十年代的中國新文學 (The new Chinese literature of the 1920's; talk at Columbia Univ.). 1980.xi/xii. *Haineiwai* 28: 11–13. *WJ* 10: 323–30. (1980.xi.7).

"Shen Congwen tan ziji de chuangzuo" 沈從文談自己的創作 (Shen Congwen talks about his own writing). 1980.xii. In Ling Yu.

"Guanyu zenyang yanjiu Zhongguo wudaoshi de yi feng xin" 關于怎樣研究中國舞蹈史的一封信 (A letter about how to do research on the history of Chinese dance). 1980. *Wudao luncong* 1: 19–23.

"Renjian zhong wanqing" 人間重晚晴 (The world will take note of a late blooming). 1980? + *WJ* 11: 90–93.

Congwen sanwen xuan 從文散文選 (A selection of Congwen's essays). Hong Kong: Shidai. Dec. 1980. Authorized edition, with author's preface.

1981

Calligraphy on 1981 "China Image" Calendar. 1981.i.1. Hong Kong: Manshih Yonfan. Photography by Yang Fan 楊凡.

"Shen Congwen xiansheng shizuo" 沈從文先生詩作 (Poetry by Mr. Shen Congwen). 1981.i.16. *Guangjiaojing* 100: 86–87, and back cover.

"Cong xin wenxue zhuan dao lishi wenwu" 從新文學轉到歷史文物 (Turning from new literature to historical artifacts; speech at St. John's Univ.). 1981.i/ii. *Haineiwai* 29: 23–25. *WJ* 10: 331–39. (1980.xi.24).

"Shen Congwen xiansheng de laixin" 沈從文先生的來信 (A letter from Mr. Shen Congwen). 1981.iii.16. *Guangjiaojing* 102: 57. Previously unpublished letter to Zhao Jingshen. 1981.iv. *Zhongguo xiandai wenyi ziliao congkan*, 6: 224. Shanghai: Shanghai wenyi chubanshe. ([1930.iv]).

"Youqing" 友情 (Friendship). 1981.xi.22. *Xin wenxue shiliao* 1981.4: 111–13. *WJ* 10: 253–58. (1981.viii).

"Tiji" 題記 (Preface). 1981.xi. *Shen Congwen sanwen xuan* and *Shen Congwen xiaoshuo xuan*. Changsha: Hunan renmin. *WJ* 11: 79–81. (1981.vi.1).

"Fuji" 附記 (Postscript). 1981.xii. *Congwen zizhuan*. *WJ* 11: 76–78. (1980.v.17).

Zhongguo gudai fushi yanjiu 中國古代服飾研究 (Researches into ancient Chinese costume). Hong Kong: Shangwu. Sept. 1981.

Shen Congwen sanwen xuan [1] 沈從文散文選 (A selection of essays by Shen Congwen; first collection by this title). Changsha: Hunan renmin. Nov. 1981.

Congwen zizhuan 從文自傳 (Congwen's autobiography; rev. ed.). * Beijing: Renmin wenxue chubanshe. Dec. 1981. Bound with some essays by Shen and one by Huang Yongyu.

Shen Congwen xiaoshuo xuan [2] 沈從文小說選 (A selection of fiction by Shen Congwen; second collection by this title). Changsha: Hunan renmin. Dec. 1981.

1982

"Xiangxi sanji xu" 「湘西散記」序 (Preface to *Recollections of West Hunan*). 1982.ii.10. Chinese publication under the title "*Sanwen xuanyi* xu" 「散文選譯」序 (Preface to *Selected Essays [by Shen Congwen] in Translation*). *Dushu* 1982.2: 112–18. *WJ* 11: 82–89. Tr. by Gladys Yang as "Author's Preface" in *Recollections of West Hunan*. (1981.ix).

"Preface to the Morningside Edition" and, assisting Hans H. Frankel, "About the Author" (in English). 1982. *The Chinese Earth*. Ching Ti and Robert Payne, tr.

Shen Congwen wenji 沈從文文集 (The works of Shen Congwen). Shao Huaqiang 邵華強 and Ling Yu 凌宇, eds. 12 vols. International edition, Hong Kong: Sanlian. National edition, Guangzhou: Huacheng. Jan. 1982–Jan. 1985.

Shen Congwen xiaoshuo xuan [3] 沈從文小說選 (A selection of fiction by Shen Congwen; third collection by this title). Ling Yu, ed. 2 vols. Beijing: Renmin wenxue chubanshe. Oct. 1982.

Shen Congwen sanwen xuan [2] 沈從文散文選 (A selection of essays by

Shen Congwen; second collection by this title). Ling Yu, ed. Beijing: Renmin wenxue chubanshe. Dec. 1982.

1983

"Xu Zhimo quan ji xu"「徐志摩全集」序 (Preface to *The Complete Works of Xu Zhimo*). 1983.v.10. *Dushu* 1983.5: 96–97. (1983.ii.2).

"Xu" 序 (Preface). 1983.v. *Shen Congwen xuan ji* [4]. Chengdu. (1982.iii.20).

"Jiangling Chu mu chutu de sizhipin" 江陵楚墓出土的絲織品 (Silks unearthed in the Chu Kingdom graves at Jiangling). 1983.vi. *Zhongguo huabao* 420: 30–33. Teng Rensheng 滕壬生 and Wu Shunqing 吳順清, co-authors.

Three previously unpublished letters from Shen Congwen to Hu Shi. 1983.xii. In Shen Yunlong. (1934.vi.25; 1936.iv.9; 1944.ix.16).

Shen Congwen xuan ji [4] 沈從文選集 (Selected works by Shen Congwen; fourth collection by this title). Ling Yu, ed. 5 vols. Chengdu: Sichuan renmin. May–June 1983.

1984

"Jingmen zayong" 京門雜詠 (Miscellaneous poems from the gates of the capital). 1984.xii. *WJ* 10: 363–64. (1973).

"Yulin shicao" 郁林詩草 (Rough poems from a land of fragrant woods). 1984.xii. *WJ* 10: 353–56. ("Old works of 1963, winter").

Xiangxi fengcai 湘西風采 (West Hunan beauty). Changsha: Hunan renmin. 1984. ++

1985

"Shen Congwen zai Jishou Daxue de jianghua" 沈從文在吉首大學的講話 (Shen Congwen's talk at Jishou University). 1985.viii.25. *Jishou Daxue xuebao* (Social Sciences Edition) 12 [1985.3]: 1–5. (1982.v.27 informal speech; journal title is in Shen's calligraphy).

Character List

This list omits authors, books, and journals that have their own entries in the Selected Bibliography, and internationally known people and places.

Ahei 阿黑
Ai Qing 艾青
Ai Wu 艾蕪
Ajin 阿金
Ala (Yala) 阿拉
amei 阿妹
Arisaka 有坂
aya 阿姈
baba 粑粑
bagong (-sheng) 拔貢(生)
Bai Chongxi 白崇禧
Bailin 柏林
Baixing 百姓
Bamian 八面
Ban Gu 班固
Banlü 伴侶
bao 堡
Baoding 保定
baojia 保甲
Baojing 保靖
baozhai 堡寨
Baozi 豹子
beibu 被捕
Beidou 北斗
Beiping xinbao 北平新報
Beiyang 北洋
Bian Zhilin 卞之琳
bianzi huo 辮子貨

Biduan banyuekan 筆端半月刊
bing gao 稟告
Bing Xin 冰心
boxiang (-ren) 白相(人)
buchongbing 補充兵
buxizu 補習組
Cai E 蔡鍔
Cai Juyou 蔡鉅猷
Cai Weilian 蔡威廉
Cangshan 蒼山
Cao Xueqin 曹雪芹
Cao Yu 曹禺
Cao Zhenya 曹振亞
chabuduo 差不多
Chadong (std. orth.) 茶洞
Chadong (Shen's orth.) 茶峒
Changde 常德
Chen (River) 辰
Chen Bulei 陳布雷
Chen Duxiu 陳獨秀
Chen Hanzhang 陳漢章
Chen Jiying 陳紀瀅
Chen Lifu 陳立夫
Chen Mengxiong 陳夢熊
Chen Quan 陳銓
Chen Quzhen (Xiangxiwang) 陳渠珍(湘西王)
Chen Weimo 陳煒謨

Chen Xianghe 陳翔鶴
Chen Yi 陳毅
Chen Yuan 陳源
Chen-Yuan (-Yong-Jing) 辰沅
　（永靖）
Chen Zhifo 陳之佛
Chenbao 晨報
Chenbao fukan 晨報副刊
Cheng Qian 程潛
Cheng Yingliu (Liu Jin) 程應鏐
　（流金）
Cheng Yirong 程一戎
Chenqi 辰谿
Chenzhou 辰州
chi 癡
Chiyou 蚩尤
Chongwen 崇文
Chu (kingdom) 楚
Chu ci 楚辭
Chu Yupu 褚玉璞
Chuanghua 創化
Chuangzao zhoubao 創造週報
Chuangzuo yuekan 創作月刊
chuanqi 傳奇
Chunqiu 春秋
Chunxiu 春秀
ci 詞
Cili 慈利
Ciyuan 辭源
Cuicui 翠翠
Dagu 大沽
dai 呆
Dai (nationality) 傣
Dai Jitao 戴季韜
Dai Wangshu 戴望舒
daipa 代帕
Dangdai pinglun 當代評論
Dangdai wenyi 當代文藝
Dashi (Zhou Dashi) 達士（周達士）
Dawanbao 大晚報
Dayong 大庸
Dazhong wenyi congkan 大衆文藝
　叢刊

Dazhong zhishi 大衆知識
dazhongyu 大衆語
Dengzhanta 燈盞它
diaobao 碉堡
Dieyu 叠餘
Ding Xilin 丁西林
Dipingxian 地平線
Dong (nationality) 侗
Dong (River) 洞（峒）
Dong Qiusi 董秋斯
Dongting 洞庭
Du Fu 杜甫
Duanmu Hongliang 端木蕻良
Duanwu (Duanyang) 端午（端陽）
dudu 都督
Duli pinglun 獨立評論
Dushu 讀書
"Dushujie" 讀書界
Erge 二哥
fanshen 翻身
Fei Ming (Feng Wenbing) 廢名
Feng Da 馮達
Feng Wenbing 馮文炳
Feng Xuefeng 馮雪峯
Feng Youlan 馮友蘭
Feng Yuxiang 馮玉祥
Feng Zhi 馮至
Fenghua 奉化
Fenghuang 鳳凰
fengkuang 瘋狂
Fengtian 奉天
Fu Zuoyi 傅作義
fubing 副兵
fukan 副刊
Funü zazhi 婦女雜誌
Furen 輔仁
fuye 副爺
gai yi ge xian 改一個縣
Gaizao 改造
Gan 苷
Ganziping 草子坪
Gao Juefu 高覺敷
Gao Peng 高鵬

Gao Qingzi (Yunxiu) 高青子（韻琇）
Gaocun 高村
Gelao 仡佬
Gelaohui 哥老會
Gongxian 鞏縣
gu 蠱
Gu Hongming 辜鴻銘
Gu Hua 古華
Gu Jiaqi (Xiuzhi) 顧家齊（修之）
Gu Jiegang 顧頡剛
Gu Qianli 顧千里
Gu Zhenglun 谷正倫
Guanchabao 觀察報
Guangjiaojing 廣角鏡
Guangming ribao 光明日報
guanxi 關係
Guisheng 貴生
Guowen yuekan 國文月刊
Guowen zhoubao 國聞週報
Guoyu zhoukan 國語週刊
Guzhang 古丈
Hai Pai 海派
Haineiwai 海內外
Haishang 海上
Haiyang wenyi 海洋文藝
"Hama" 蝦蟆
Han (nationality) 漢
Hanhuayuan 漢花園
Hanlin 翰林
Hanyang 漢陽
Hanyuan (Gongyu) 漢園（公寓）
Hao Ran 浩然
He Jian 何鍵
He Lin 賀麟
Heifeng 黑鳳
Heimao 黑貓
Hong Shen 洪深
"Hong yu hei" 紅與黑
Honghei 紅黑
Hongjiang 洪江
Hsia, C. T. (Xia Zhiqing) 夏志清
Hsu, Kai-yu (Xu Jicyu) 許芥昱

Hu Qiaomu 胡喬木
Hu Shi 胡適
Hua cheng 花城
Huaihua 懷化
Huang 黃
Huang Heqing 黃河清
Huang Jingming 黃鏡銘
Huang Juchuan 黃巨川
Huang Suying 黃素英
Huang Xinyu 黃信餘
Huang Yingpei 黃應培
Huang Yuan 黃源
Huang Yushu 黃玉書
Huangluozhai 黃羅寨
Huangxian 晃縣
huanhu qi you wenzhang 煥乎其有文章
huanxiang 幻想
Huayuan 花垣
huercao 虎耳草
huiguan 會館
Huiming 會明
Hunan wenxian 湖南文獻
huoguan 火罐
ji (self) 己
Jia Baoyu 賈寶玉
jiabianren 家邊人
Jiachen 甲辰
Jiang Guangci 蔣光慈
Jiangkou 江口
Jiangnan 江南
Jiao Juyin 焦菊隱
jiaodaodui 教導隊
jiaotou 𦥑頭
Jiashan 嘉善
Jin (River) 錦
Jin Di (Ching Ti) 金隄
Jin Yuelin 金岳霖
Jinan (Univ.) 暨南
Jing Pai 京派
Jing Yang 京樣
Jingbao 京報
Jinggangshan 井岡山

Jingguo Lianjun 靖國聯軍
Jingshi ribao 經世日報
Jingu qiguan 今古奇觀
jingya 驚訝
Jingzhou 京州
Jinri pinglun 今日評論
jinshi 進士
Jinyi (Zhang Fangxu) 靳以
　（章方叙）
Jinzhou 錦州
Jishou Daxue xuebao 吉首大學學報
jishuban 技術班
jiu 舅
Jiujiu (Jiumei) 九九（九妹）
jiushi 就食
Jiushi niandai 九十年代
Junzi 菌子
Kaiming 開明
Kang Chuchu 康楚楚
kang Ri dao He 抗日倒何
Kunqu 昆曲
kyōgen 狂言
laba zhou 臘八粥
Laifeng 來鳳
Lao Han Ren 老漢人
Lao She 老舍
laogeng 老庚
laoshi 老實
Lee, Leo Ou-fan (Li Oufan)
　李歐梵
Lei Haizong 雷海宗
Li (River) 澧
Li Bai 李白
Li Da 李達
Li Daren 李大任
Li Dazhao 李大釗
Li Guangtian 李廣田
Li Huiying (Liancui) 李輝英
　（連萃）
Li Jianwu 李健吾
Li Jinming 黎錦明
Li Jucun 李菊村
Li Lisan 李立三
Li Moan 李黙庵

Li Shangyin 李商隱
Li Xiaotang 李小棠
Li Xin 李欣
Li Yannian 李延年
Li Yunhang 李雲杭
liang 兩
Liang Qichao 梁啓超
Liang Sicheng 梁思成
Liangyou 良友
Lili 栗里
Lin Biao 林彪
Lin Geng 林庚
Lin Huiyin 林徽音
Lin Shu 林紓
Lin Yutang 林語堂
Lin Zaiping 林宰平
Ling Shuhua 凌淑華
Ling Zifeng 凌子風
Lingling 玲玲
Linli 臨澧
Liu Baiyu 劉白羽
Liu Bannong 劉半農
Liu Bocheng 劉伯承
Liu Jianxu 劉建緒
Liu Mengwei 劉夢葦
Liu Mianji 劉勉己
Liu Naou 劉吶鷗
Liu Shiqi 劉士奇
Liu Tingfang 劉廷芳
Liu Tingwei 劉廷蔚
Liu Xiang 劉湘
Liu Yunting 劉雲亭
Liulichang 琉璃廠
Lixian 澧縣
Liye 里耶
Long Enpu 龍恩普
Long Liangwei 龍良爲
Long Yun 龍雲
Long Yunfei 龍雲飛
Long Zhian 龍治安
Long Zhu 龍朱
Longshan 龍山
Longtan 龍潭
Lu Tao (of Guizhou) 盧燾

Character List

Lu Tao (Shen's friend) 陸弢
Lu Zhiwei 陸志韋
luguan 蘆管
Lunyu 論語
Luo Longji 羅隆基
Luo Rongguang 羅榮光
Luo Shuzi 羅卡子
Luo Wenjie 羅文杰
luohou 落後
luowu 落伍
Luqi 瀘溪
Lushan 廬山
lusheng 蘆笙
Luyang 瀘陽
Lüjiaping 呂家坪
Lüxingjia 旅行家
Ma Pizhai 麻皮齊
Ma Shaowu 馬紹武
Ma Tingyun 麻庭雲
Ma Yuan 馬援
Ma Zehui 馬澤蕙
malang 馬郎
Man (tribes) 蠻
Man Shuyuan 滿叔遠
Mang 莽
Manman 滿滿
Maodi 毛弟
maodun 矛盾
Maolin 茂林 (懋琳)
Mayang 麻陽
Mei Yiqi 梅貽琦
Meijin 媚金
Meishu yanjiu 美術研究
Meng Jiang 孟姜
Meng Muqiu 蒙慕秋
Mengke 夢珂
Miao 苗
Miao Yuntai 繆雲台
Miaozi 苗子
Minjian wenxue 民間文學
Minjian wenyi xuan ji 民間文藝選輯
Mintan zhoukan 民壇週刊
minxing 民性

"*Minzhong wenyi*" 民眾文藝
minzuxing 民族性
"*Modeng*" 摩登
mou 畝
Mu Shiying 穆時英
mufu 幕府
Mujiangping 木江坪
na dou shi yuan ziliao, bushi zuopin 那都是原資料,不是作品
nanxia 南下
Naxi 納西
Nie 聶
Nie Rende (Jiantang) 聶仁德 (儉堂)
Nieh, Hua-ling (Nie Hualing) 聶華苓
Nihon Rikugun Shikan Gakkō 日本陸軍士官学校
Ningguo 寧國
Nunu A-wen 孥孥阿文
Nuo 儺
Nuosong 儺送
Nuoxi 儺喜
Nuoyou 儺佑
ouran 偶然
pai (school) 派
paizhang 排長
Pan Guangdan 潘光旦
Pan Mohua 潘漠華
Panhu 槃瓠
Peng Chunrong (Jiao Lüzi) 彭春榮 (叫驢子)
"*Pingming*" 平明
Pingming ribao 平明日報
pipa 琵琶
Pujing 蒲靜
Pushi 浦市
Qi xia wu yi 七俠五義
Qian Men 前門
Qian Xuantong 錢玄同
Qiancheng 乾城
Qianyang 黔陽
Qianzhou 乾州
qianzong 千總

Character List

Qiaoshengbao 僑聲報
qie shuo 且說
Qilin 倚琳
qin jiu 親舅
Qingdao 青島
Qinghua 清華
Qinghua zhoukan 清華週刊
Qingming 清明
Qingnian zuojia 青年作家
Qiushui xuan chidu 秋水軒尺牘
Qiusuo 求索
qiwen congwu 稾文從武
Qu Shiying 瞿世英
Qu Yuan 屈原
Rao Mengkan 饒孟侃
re ai ni 熱愛你
Renjian yuekan 人間月刊
Renjianshi 人間世
Renmin pinglun 人民評論
Renmin ribao 人民日報
Renmin wenxue 人民文學
Richu 日出
Ronglu 鎔爐
Ruan Ji 阮籍
Ruan Xian 阮咸
Ruomo 若墨
Rurui 如蕤
Sangzhi 桑植
Sansan 三三
Sha Ting 沙汀
Shang Hunan 上湖南
Shang Xiangxi 上湘西
Shangguan Bi 上官碧
Shanghai Shifan Xueyuan xuebao 上海師範學院學報
Shanjiang 山江
Shantuo 扇陀
Shao Lizi 邵力子
Shao Xunmei 邵洵美
Shaoxing 紹興
shehui manman de fenjie 社會慢慢地分解
Shehui yuebao 社會月報

shen 神
Shen Hongfang 沈洪芳
Shen Hongfu (Maogou) 沈洪福（毛狗）
Shen Huchu 沈虎雛
Shen Longzhu 沈龍朱
Shen Wanlin 沈萬林
Shen Yuehuan (Congwen) 沈岳煥（從文）
Shen Yuepu (Yunlu, Yunliu) 沈岳扑（雲麓，雲六）
Shen Yuequan (Dieyu, Deyu) 沈岳荃（叠餘，得魚）
Shen Zongsi (Shaoxian) 沈宗嗣（少仙）
Shenbao yuekan 申報月刊
shenbing 神兵
sheng 生
shenghuo 生活
"Shenghuofeng" 生活風
shengming 生命
Shi Cuntong 施存統
Shi ji 史記
Shi juan 詩鐫
Shi meng 釋夢
Shi Zhicun 施蟄存
Shibao 時報
Shijie ribao 世界日報
Shijie xuesheng 世界學生
Shikan 詩刊
Shimen 石門
Shishi xinbao 時事新報
Shiwai Taoyuan 世外桃源
Shiwu Xuetang 時務學堂
Shiyangshao 石羊哨
shizong 失踪
Shōtoku Taishi 聖德太子
Shuangqing 雙清
Shuixing 水星
shuji 書記
Shulin 書林
Shunshun 順順
Shuowen yuekan 説文月刊

Shuwen 叔文
Sima Qian 司馬遷
sishu 私塾
Situ Qiao 司徒喬
sixiang 思想
Song Xilian 宋希濂
Song Yuncheng (Lianquan) 宋運澂（廉泉）
Songtao 松桃
Songzi 松子
Su Wen (Dai Kechong) 蘇汶（戴克崇）
sui 歲
Sun Fuyuan 孫伏園
Sun Jianzhong 孫健忠
Sun Junquan 孫均銓
Sun Xizhen 孫席珍
suona 嗩吶
Szeto, Paul (Situ Juxun) 司徒鉅勳
Taibai 太白
Taiping (rebels, creek) 太平
Taiping (city) 太坪
Tan Guoqing 覃國卿
Tan Sitong 譚嗣同
Tan Yankai 譚延闓
tang 糖
Tang Lichen 唐力臣
Tang Yongtong 湯用彤
Tang Zimo 湯子模
tangyuan 湯圓
Tao Guang 陶廣
Tao Qian 陶潛
Taoyuan 桃源
Teng 滕
Teng Lenghan 滕夘韓
Tian Han 田漢
Tian Jingyang 田景陽
Tian Junjian 田君健
Tian Sannu 田三怒
Tian Tao 田濤
Tian Wang 天王
Tian Xingliu 田星六
Tian Xingshu 田興恕

Tian Yingbi 田應弼
Tian Yingquan 田應全
Tian Yingzhao 田應詔
Tian Yiqing 田義卿
Tian Zhenyi 田真一
Tianbao 天保
tianzhen 天真
tidu 提督
ting 廳
Tongcheng 桐城
Tongren 銅仁
tongxin 童心
tongyangxi 童養媳
Tu Man 土蠻
Tu Miao 土苗
tudi 土地
tufei 土匪
Tuhua 土話
Tujia 土家
tun (fort) 堃
tun, Tun (colony) 屯
tuntian 屯田
Tuo (River) 沱
tusi 土司
Wang 王
Wang Dianlun 王殿輪
Wang Jialie 王家烈
Wang Jizhen 王際真
Wang Luyan 王魯彥
Wang Sanxin 王三辛
Wang Xiaoshan 王曉珊
Wang Xizhi 王羲之
Wang Xu 王朽
Wang Yangming 王陽明
Wang Yanhong 王彥泓
Wang Yuanhua 汪援華
Wang Zhengya 王正雅
Wangcun 王村
Weiyin 微音
Wen 文
Wen ji yuekan 文季月刊
Wenchangge 文昌閣
Wenchao yuekan 文潮月刊

Wencong 文叢
Wencui 文萃
Wenhui zengkan 文滙增刊
Wenhuibao 文滙報
Wenjiao ziliao jianbao 文教資料簡報
Wenju 文聚
Wenwu 文物
Wenwu cankao ziliao 文物參考資料
Wenxue 文學
Wenxue chuangzuo 文學創作
"Wenxue fukan" 文學副刊
Wenxue jikan 文學季刊
Wenxue pinglun 文學評論
"Wenxue xunkan" 文學旬刊
Wenxue zazhi 文學雜誌
Wenxue zhoukan 文學週刊
"Wenyi" 文藝
Wenyi fuxing 文藝復興
Wenyi jikan 文藝季刊
Wenyi luncong 文藝論叢
Wenyi xianfeng 文藝先鋒
Wenyi yuekan 文藝月刊
Wenyi zhoukan 文藝週刊
Wenzhai 文摘
Wu (Gate) 午
Wu Deyun 吳德雲
Wu Guangshi 吳光仕
Wu Han 吳晗
Wu Hengliang 吳恒良
Wu Mi 吳宓
Wu Rongzhen 吳榮臻
Wu Rou 吳柔
Wu Sancong 吳三淙
Wu Wende 吳文德
Wu Xiaoling 吳曉鈴
Wu Zhihui 吳稚輝
Wudao luncong 舞蹈論叢
wuduan shencai 五短身材
Wuhan ribao 武漢日報
Wuming 五明
Wusong 吳淞

Xia Fuxin 夏斧心
Xia Yun 夏雲
Xiandai 現代
Xiandai pinglun 現代評論
Xiandai wenlu 現代文錄
Xiandai wenxue 現代文學
Xiandai xuesheng 現代學生
Xiang (River) 湘
Xiang Kairan 向愷然
xiang shang 向上
Xiang Yingsheng 向膺生
Xiang Zhuo 項拙
Xiang Ziyun 向子雲
Xianggang wenxue 香港文學
Xiangjiang wenyi 湘江文藝
Xiangshan 香山
Xiangshan Ciyouyuan 香山慈幼院
Xiangshan Si 香山寺
Xiangtu 鄉土
xiangtu wenxue 鄉土文學
Xiangxi 湘西
Xiangxi Suijingchu 湘西綏靖處
xiangxiaren 鄉下人
Xiao (woman author) 蕭
"Xiao gongyuan" 小公園
Xiao Jing Pai 小京派
Xiao Ke 蕭克
Xiao Qian 蕭乾
Xiao wu yi 小五義
Xiao Xuanqing 蕭選青
Xiaoshen 霄神(小神)
Xiaoshuo yuebao 小説月報
Xiaoxiao 蕭蕭
Xiaozhai 小砦(小寨)
Xie Bingying 謝冰瑩
xiepi 邪僻
Xihu wenyuan 西湖文苑
Xin chao 新潮
Xin dongxiang 新動向
Xin guancha 新觀察
Xin Hai Pai 新海派
Xin jianshe 新建設

Xin shehui banyuekan 新社會半月刊
Xin shi 新詩
Xin shidai yuekan 新時代月刊
Xin wenxue shiliao 新文學史料
Xin Yaxiya 新亞細亞
Xingdao ribao 星島日報
"Xingqi xuedeng" 星期學燈
"Xingqi yiwen" 星期藝文
Xinyue 新月
Xiong 熊
Xiong Fenghuang 熊(雄)鳳凰
Xiong Kewu 熊克武
Xiong Xijing 熊希靜
Xiong Xiling 熊希齡
Xiong Zhi 熊芷
Xiushan 秀山
Xu Changlin 徐昌霖
Xu Dishan 許地山
Xu Simei 許思湄
Xu Teli 徐特立
Xu Ying 徐盈
Xu Zhimo 徐志摩
Xuanbo 旋玻
Xuanruo 璇若
"Xue deng" 學燈
Xue Yue 薛岳
Xuefengshan 雪峯山
Xuewen 學文
Xupu 漵浦
Yala (Ala) 雅拉
Yan Da yuekan 燕大月刊
Yan Fu 嚴復
Yan Wenjing 嚴文井
Yan Xishan 閻錫山
yan zhi 言志
Yang Changxiong 楊昌雄
Yang Daicheng 楊代誠
Yang Gang 楊剛
Yang Jinbiao 楊金標
Yang Kaihui 楊開慧
Yang Xianyi 楊憲義
Yang Yi 楊苡

Yang Zhensheng 揚振聲
Yangcheng wanbao 羊城晚報
Yangxi 陽戲
Yanjing 燕京
Yao 瑤(猺)
yao malang 搖馬郎
Yao Pengzi 姚蓬子
Yao Xueyin 姚雪垠
Yaoyao 夭夭
Ye Gongchao 葉公超
Ye Shaojun 葉紹鈞
yi 伊
Yi (Luoluo) 彝(羅羅)
yi ge fanzhande 一個反戰的
Yin Menglong 尹夢龍
yingxun 營汛
Yinzha 銀閘
Yiqing 儀青
Yishibao 益世報
"Yishu yundong" 藝術運動
Yiwen 譯文
"Yizhou" 藝舟
Yongshun 永順
Yongsui 永綏
Yongyu 雍羽
You (River) 酉
Youxi Huiguan 西西會館
Yu Guanghao 喻廣浩
Yu Lihua 喻理華
Yu Shan 俞珊
Yuan (River) 沅
Yuan Kejia 袁可嘉
Yuan Mei 袁枚
Yuan Shikai 袁世凱
Yuan Tongli 袁同禮
Yuanling 沅陵
Yuanyuan 瑗瑗
Yuanzhou 沅州
yubeibing 預備兵
Yue Daiyun 樂黛雲
Yuekan 月刊
Yuner 芸兒
Yunjiwei 雲騎尉

Yunlu (brother) 雲麓
Yunlu (Estate) 芸廬
Yushuwan 榆樹灣
Yusi 語絲
Yuzhoufeng 宇宙風
zagan 雜感
zai Dao 載道
Zang Kejia 臧克家
Zaowu 造物
zapai 雜牌
zawen 雜文
Zeng Guofan 曾國藩
Zeng Qinxuan 曾芹軒
zhai 寨
Zhandi 戰地
Zhang 張
Zhang Bai 張白
Zhang Boliang 張伯良
Zhang Caizhen 張采真
Zhang Chonghe 張充和
Zhang Jingsheng 張競生
Zhang Qun 張羣
Zhang Shenglin 張勝林
Zhang Shizhao 章士釗
Zhang Tianyi 張天翼
Zhang Tiesheng 張鐵生
Zhang Wende 張文德
Zhang Xiruo 張奚若
Zhang Xueji 張學濟
Zhang Yiping 章衣萍
Zhang Zhang 張璋
Zhang Zhizhong 張治中
Zhang Ziping 張資平
Zhang Ziqing 張子卿
Zhanguoce 戰國策
"Zhanxian" 戰線
Zhao Guiwu 趙龜武
Zhao Hengti 趙恒惕
Zhao Jingshen 趙景深
Zhao Kaiming 趙開明
Zhao Qiwen 趙其文
Zhao Ruihong 趙瑞蕻

Zhao Shuli 趙樹理
Zhao Taimou 趙太牟
Zhao Yansheng 趙燕聲
Zhaotong 昭通
Zhen Guanxi 鎮關西
Zheng Shufang 鄭叔方
Zheng Xidi 鄭西諦
Zheng Zhenduo 鄭振鐸
Zhen'gan 鎮筸
zhengpai 正派
Zhenqi 鎮溪
Zhijiang 芷江
Zhili 直隸
zhipei 支配
Zhishi yu shenghuo 知識與生活
Zhong 重
Zhongguo de ciqi 中國的瓷器
Zhongguo gongyi meishu shi 中國工藝美術史
Zhongguo huabao 中國畫報
Zhongguo jianshe 中國建設
Zhongguo xiandai wenyi ziliao congkan 中國現代文藝資料叢刊
Zhongguoren yuekan 中國人月刊
Zhongjia 仲家
Zhongliu 中流
Zhongxuesheng 中學生
Zhongyang ribao 中央日報
zhou, Zhou (prefecture) 州
Zhou (name) 周
Zhou Binchen 周彬臣
Zhou Ruilong 周瑞龍
Zhou Xicheng 周西成
Zhou Xieqing 周燮卿
Zhou Zefan 周則范
Zhou Zhaowu 周朝武
Zhu Wen 朱雯
Zhu Xiang 朱湘
Zhu Xiangqi 朱湘溪
Zhu Ziqing 朱自清
Zhuang (nationality) 壯

Zhuangzi 莊子	"Ziyou tan" 自由談
Zhuanji wenxue 傳記文學	Ziyou Zhongguo 自由中國
zhui niu 椎牛	Zongbingying 總兵營
Zi yue 子曰	Zongye 總爺
Zikuan 自寬	Zuopin yu zhengming 作品與爭鳴

Index

Ai Qing, 367
Ai Wu, 84, 367
America, 82–83f, 136, 187, 199, 243, 248, 258–59, 274, 280
Anarchism, 55, 275
Armies: Qing, 6, 28–29, 230, 276; old Gan, 13–14, 16–19, 28–31; warlord, 33–58, 61–66, 71, 133ff, 234–45 *passim*, 249; Red, 39, 53; Nationalist, 174, 231, 233, 235–50 *passim*, 260n, 262–63; PLA, 263–65, 267, 280
Army life, 33–39 *passim*, 43–55, 57, 61–66, 97, 118, 164, 217, 229; as source of stock characters, 126, 128
Art and beauty (Shen on), 137, 189–90, 215, 220–24, 260–61, 275, 277–78
Autobiographical writing, 111, 119; about Shen's childhood, 21–26 *passim*, 31f, 107f, 117, 131–33; about his early manhood, 43–55 *passim*, 74ff, 88, 94–104, 109, 122, 225–27, 328; about his middle age, 189, 191, 214, 217–22, 248ff, 254–57

Ba Jin, 21, 83f, 227, 269f, 336ff
Bai Chongxi, 263
Bai Juyi, 90, 271–72
Bandits, 28, 37–41 *passim*, 47, 51f, 55, 59, 61–65 *passim*, 231f, 234; in fiction, 43, 134, 157, 251; under KMT rule, 237–43, 263–64. *See also* Spirit soldiers
Baojing, 46, 61, 63ff, 71, 77f, 234, 263

Bian Zhilin, 75, 254, 336, 359, 403
Bible, 8of, 96, 99, 106, 119f, 121, 151
Bing Xin, 119
Blue Shirts, 202, 204f, 208, 252
Boating, 28, 61, 131–32, 233, 264, 280; Shen on, 135–37, 160, 166, 181f, 246
Bourgeoisie, 48, 87, 101–2, 106, 132, 161f, 175, 193
Brothers of Shen, *see* Shen Dieyu, Shen Yunlu
Buddhism, 64, 192, 210, 222, 224, 259, 277

Cai E, 33, 174, 183, 299
Cai Juyou, 308
Cai Yuanpei, 79, 112, 201, 203, 221, 261
Calligraphy and painting, 50, 55, 58f, 64, 190, 192, 265, 302
Cao Juren, 84
Cao Yu, 252
Cao Zhenya, 262–64
Capitalism (as criticized by Shen), 86, 105, 173, 195f, 199
Censorship, 104, 190f, 207, 246ff, 252, 270, 273f, 279, 387
Chabuduo ("about the same"), 253, 358
Chadong, 16, 148, 231
Changde, 41, 57, 59, 61, 69, 136, 234f, 243, 245, 262
Changsha, 17, 63, 65f, 136, 202, 240–45 *passim*, 252, 264
Character, national and local, 54, 133–37, 165, 193, 198, 225

Characters: mythic, 5, 9–11, 92, 148–58; taken from life, 21–27, 34n, 42–55, 86–109, 114–18, 191; urban, 86–109, 190f, 211–27, 254–57; rural, 114–84, 208–9, 216, 226, 229–34, 243–52
Chekhov, Anton, 2, 80, 187
Chen Duxiu, 80, 277
Chen Jiying, 319
Chen Lifu, 77, 203, 205
Chen Mengjia, 85
Chen Quan, 359
Chen Quzhen, 39f, 56, 61–66, 68, 71, 78, 232–44 *passim*, 262–64
Chen Yuan, 70, 82
Chenbao (Morning Post), 71f, 81f, 94, 97
Cheng Qian, 263
Cheng Yingliu (Liu Jin), 318, 337
Chenzhou (Yuanling), 17, 62, 234f, 238, 240, 248, 262–64; Shen in, 34, 36–41 *passim*, 45, 47, 56f, 232, 241, 250
Chiang Kaishek, 201ff, 208, 236ff, 244–47 *passim*, 268, 277
Children of Shen, 155, 267, 363
Ching Ti (Jin Di), 162, 265, 361
Christianity, 208f; in West Hunan and Guizhou, 19, 29, 38, 47, 57, 65, 218, 295–96, 307; Shen and, 81, 121, 224, 259, 277. *See also* Bible
Chu, 5, 10, 12, 133, 136, 168, 230
Cities: Shen's critique of, 81, 105, 137, 185, 194–200 *passim*, 223; through young-man persona, 102–3, 118, 131–33; through fictional "country folk," 147, 158–69 *passim*, 173, 181, 226, 245
Class, social (in Shen's works), 10, 147, 161–62f, 181, 184, 249; and class conflict, 55, 105, 183, 251, 258
Communism, 55, 189, 204, 206; Shen and, 43, 77–78, 227, 252f, 265–74, 276; Shen on, 104, 201, 265, 362–63; in fiction, 105, 209, 218, 221, 246, 250; after 1949, 113, 140, 228; historiography of, 134, 241f, 356; in West Hunan, 234–39, 242, 263–65, 280–81. *See also* He Long; Leftist writers

Confucian tradition: West Hunan as antithesis of, 7, 10–11, 133, 148; Shen's revolt against, 24, 32, 66, 87, 113f, 192, 207ff; opposition to, in fiction, 106, 108, 131. *See also* Gentry
Country folk, 114, 120, 124, 130, 144–84, 202, 229f; Shen as, 14, 27, 102–3, 159, 218; moral superiority of, 111, 131–37; definitions of, 14, 159; Shen's estrangement from, 133, 233
Creation Society, 66, 109, 195, 199
Crescent Monthly, 83
Cuicui, 37, 115, 164–66, 168, 171, 180, 216, 224, 234
Cultural Revolution, 81, 147, 153, 272

Dagongbao (L'Impartial), 84, 188, 258, 319
Dai Jitao, 235, 244, 262–63, 353, 361f
Dai Kechong (Su Wen), 197, 200–201
Dai Wangshu, 407
Darwinism, 6, 32, 64, 87, 113f, 166, 182; Shen and, 100–101f, 131–36 *passim*, 160, 162, 170, 233, 251, 277
Daudet, Alphonse, 2, 80, 88, 326
Dazhongyu ("mass language"), 194
Death: of Shen's intimates, 20f, 37, 78, 189, 232, 234, 280; Chinese attitudes toward, 137, 155, 168, 180f; as a literary theme, 165, 168, 171, 190, 210, 213, 216, 223. *See also* Suicide
Democratic parties (third party movement), 84, 253, 259, 266, 276
Dewey, John, 80, 187
Diary form, 22, 44–45, 91–92, 94, 96, 99, 108, 196
Dickens, Charles, 60, 187
Didacticism, 144–45, 154–58 *passim*, 164, 179, 228–29, 231, 246–48, 252; Shen's opposition to, 60, 80, 278; Shen's own, 102, 130–38, 167, 234
Ding Ling, 73–79 *passim*, 85, 95f, 98, 106, 138, 187f; after break with Shen, 189, 196f, 200, 203–7, 270, 272, 277, 335, 345–48; in Shen's fiction, 214–15, 222
Ding Xilin, 70, 82, 85, 92, 270

Dong Qiusi, 76ff, 350
Dragon boats, see Festivals
Drama: puppet plays, 24f, 126; West Hunan local operas, 28, 169, 178; Peking opera, 28, 198, 270. See also Nuo
Drama, life as (in Shen's works), 35, 54, 99, 144, 170, 176, 208
Dream of the Red Chamber, The, 3, 21, 32, 60, 98, 135, 273
Dreams, 108–9, 118, 162, 166, 171, 180, 209, 216
Dueling, 8, 25f, 133f, 137
Dumas, Alexandre and son, 80, 101; Shen as the "Dumas of China," 111, 187, 324

Eroticism, see Romance
Essays, 94, 96, 98, 108–9, 121–23; Shen's opposition to *zagan* and "humor," 108, 190, 197, 199; Shen's late, 185, 190, 210, 222, 257–61
Executions, 23, 30, 46–53 *passim*, 78, 105, 203f, 208–9, 243, 262–65 *passim*

Famine and pestilence, 65, 161, 170, 234, 243, 265, 308
Fascism, 186, 202, 208, 253, 359
Fate, 54, 58, 91, 156, 175, 178, 183, 233, 245, 257. See also Gambling; *Ouran*
Father figures, 50, 180, 225
Father of Shen, see Shen Zongsi
Faulkner, William, 4f, 114, 118, 227f
Fei Ming (Feng Wenbing), 112, 123, 201, 265, 269, 411
Feng Da, 197, 205f
Feng Xuefeng, 346
Feng Youlan, 70, 365
Feng Yuxiang, 41, 174
Feng Zhi, 85, 265, 361
Fenghuang (Zhen'gan), 13–19 *passim*, 29–34 *passim*, 62, 78, 136–37, 208, 230–45 *passim*, 263f, 289
Festivals, 10, 23, 25, 115–16, 141–42, 168, 176–77; Dragon Boat (Duanyang), 5, 133ff, 141, 167f, 176f, 216, 233

Fiction: Chinese traditional, 43–44, 50, 60, 80, 88, 92f, 305, 316; Western, 60, 80, 93–95, 114, 187; psychological, 144, 147, 160, 211–20, 227, 254–57; Shen on curative powers of, 191, 212, 217–19, 257. See also *Dream of the Red Chamber, The*
Folk songs, 76, 114, 124, 129, 169; alternating, 120, 142–45, 150–53, 156f, 216
Folklore, 121, 126, 153–55; in Shen's fiction, 8, 125f, 129–30, 147, 152–58; Shen's interest in, 72, 83–84, 111f, 123–30
Foods, 23, 27, 45, 115–17, 166, 176–77; of the poor, 10, 14, 25, 161, 163
Fortifications, 13–14, 18, 151, 162, 230, 239, 244
France, Anatole, 2, 80, 109
Freud, Sigmund, 113, 278, 350; influence of, on Shen, 131, 187, 201, 213, 215–19, 222f, 227, 254, 269; symbolism of, 144, 171, 216. See also Psychology
Friends from home, 33, 75–78, 116f, 234, 315; Xiao Xuanqing, 51, 57ff, 304; Zeng Qinxuan, 61; Man Shuyuan and family, 76, 131–32, 250–51; Yin Yuangui, 76
Frontier, 9–20 *passim*, 29, 43, 62, 114, 136, 139, 142, 174
Fu Zuoyi, 192, 260n

Gambling, 25, 38, 96, 125, 241; in Shen's childhood, 23, 27, 108; in the army, 46, 48f; deeper meanings of, in literature, 127f, 130, 175f, 178
Gan Army, see Armies
Gelaohui (Elder Brothers Society), 29–30, 37, 40n, 64, 135, 241, 305–6, 328
Gentry, 45, 50ff, 280; culture and manners of, 57ff, 71, 81, 137, 140, 175; Shen's dislike of, 68, 74, 100, 103; in fiction, 106, 108, 162, 179, 221, 225, 230, 250–51; tribespeople's view of, 149; peasants' view of, 159f
Gorky, Maxim, 80, 187

Grandfathers of Shen, *see* Huang family; Shen Hongfu
Greece and Rome, 93, 112, 119f, 122, 205, 212; mime in, 125; philosophers of, 209, 220, 259–61
Gu Hongming, 79
Gu Hua, 274
Gu Jiaqi (Xiuzhi), 244, 262
Gu Jiegang, 70, 112, 187
Gu Zhenglun, 242
Guizhou province: and the Shen family, 19, 21, 23, 117; army of, 33, 41, 51, 62, 64, 234, 242; Miao of, 139, 142, 154; opium of, 235
Guo Moruo, 66, 119, 192, 199, 266, 402

Hai Pai, *see* Shanghai School
Hanyuan Lodging House, 75, 77
He Jian, 207f, 233–38, 240, 242, 246
He Long, 39, 61, 65, 165, 233ff, 238f, 242, 280, 305–7
He Qifang, 75, 252, 254, 362
Heavenly King, 30, 170, 243
Hong Shen, 83
Honghei (Red and Black), 196
Hsia, C. T., 137, 146, 222, 245
Hu Shi, 24, 65, 80, 83, 202, 253, 261, 269, 277
Hu Yepin, 73f, 76f, 79, 106, 187ff, 196, 199f, 205; writing career of, 82, 85f, 98, 119; arrest of, 203
Huaihua, 41f, 45–55 *passim*, 263
Huang family of Fenghuang, 40n, 56, 59ff, 68f, 273, 278, 313; Huang Suying (mother), 18, 20, 22, 34, 77, 115, 117; Huang Heqing (grandfather), 20; Huang Yongyu, 20n, 81, 106, 289; Huang Cunsheng, 75, 79, 89, 97
Huangluozhai, 14, 153, 155
Huan province (central), 9, 17, 37, 40, 62–63, 75, 233–40, 262; as oppressor of West Hunan, 135, 174, 231, 246, 269; and Young China, 202
Hubei province, 9, 17, 39, 57, 117
Huiguan ("fellow-townsman hostel"), 75f, 78, 81
Humor, 48–54 *passim*, 80, 88–94 *passim*, 98f, 115, 172, 228, 245, 250, 427; country, 109, 124–29, 138, 143–44, 166, 179f. *See also* Essays; Satire

Industry, 63, 66, 105, 166, 173, 247, 281
Irony, 54, 99–106 *passim*, 188, 190, 212; linguistic, 88; structural, 169, 178, 208, 221–22

Japan, 12, 37, 40n, 61, 79, 188; military influences from, 33, 39, 40n, 42, 47, 49; literary influences from, 80, 95, 100, 125, 129, 199
Jiang Guangci, 195
Jiang Qing, 272
Jiangnan, 81f, 201–2, 238, 244
Jiao Juyin, 76, 402
Jiashan (city and battle), 243–45, 247, 249, 262
Jin Di (Ching Ti), 162, 265, 361
Jin Yuelin, 85, 265, 267
Jing Pai (Peking School), 194, 198–99, 336
Jingbao (Capital News), 76, 123–24
Jingya ("wonderment"), 219, 221, 224, 226
Jinyi (Zhang Fangxu), 84, 336
Joyce, James, 2, 114, 201, 269, 359

Kant, Immanuel, 137, 223, 261
"King of the Miao," *see* Long Yunfei
"King of West Hunan," *see* Chen Quzhen
Knight-errantry, 5, 25, 54, 60, 133–37, 158, 160, 202, 241
Kunming, 191, 240, 253, 256f, 337
Kuomintang (KMT), 39, 242; and Northern Expedition, 63, 72, 77f, 201, 242; "party purification" by, 78, 280. *See also* Nationalist regime
Kyōgen, 125, 129, 327

Language: Shen and the vernacular, 2n, 6, 65–66, 111, 118; Shen and the Classical, 60, 68, 88, 93, 106, 120, 132, 198, 272, 277; Shen's diction and grammar, 87–88, 93, 99, 119; dialect, 111, 115ff, 120–25, 130f, 138, 228, 245, 278; Shen on, 191f, 194, 201

Lao She, 84, 214, 252, 340, 351
Lee, Leo Ou-fan, 95, 100, 200
Leftist writers, 105–6, 199–200; Shen's disagreements with, 56, 70, 77, 113, 186–89, 193, 207, 274, 341; Shen's affinities with, 79, 104–8, 187, 196, 232f, 258–59; criticism of Shen by, 161, 186–88, 191, 200, 228, 252–53; Shen's comments on, 170, 188, 195–200 *passim*, 253
Letters (of Shen), 94f, 97f, 232; love, 59, 75, 138
Li Da, 77, 343
Li Dazhao, 80
Li Guangtian, 75
Li Huiying (Liancui), 84, 403
Li Jianwu, 269, 336
Li Jinming, 76
Li Lisan, 346
Li Moan, 262f
Li Shangyin, 59
Li Xin, 419
Li Yannian, 242
Liang Qichao, 72, 88, 186, 277
Liang Shiqiu, 83, 214, 349
Liang Sicheng, 18, 84, 98, 259
Libraries, 79, 97; Shen's career in, 64, 66, 71ff
Lin Geng, 84, 336
Lin Huiyin, 84, 107
Lin Pu (Ling Pu, Paul Lin), 337
Lin Shu, 60, 367
Lin Yutang, 108f, 195, 197, 201
Lin Zaiping, 72, 84f, 97f, 224
Ling Shuhua, 83, 318
Literary criticism (by Shen), 186, 190–202, 203
Literary revolution, 6, 60, 63, 65–68 *passim*, 80, 111, 123, 186, 276
Liu Baiyu, 367
Liu Bannong, 112, 199, 403
Liu Jianxu, 235, 244
Liu Jin (Cheng Yingliu), 318, 337
Liu Mengwei, 76, 82
Liu Naou, 200
Liu Tingfang, 70
Liu Tingwei, 76
Liu Xiang, 39

Liu Yunting, 37, 65
Liu Zuchun, 84, 339, 419
Local self-rule, 6, 63, 277
Long Yun, 253–54
Long Yunfei, 62, 162, 237, 239–42, 262–64
Lu Tao (of Guizhou), 41, 308
Lu Xun, 1ff, 82, 85, 130, 188, 197–201 *passim*; Shen compared to, 2, 6, 28, 110, 190, 195, 211, 219; satirized by Shen, 108–9
Lu Zhiwei, 112, 216, 350
Lüjiaping, 240, 245
Luo Huasheng (Xu Dishan), 85, 411
Luo Longji, 359
Luowu ("behind in the ranks"), 188, 199, 207
Lyricism, 67, 84, 88, 94, 109, 111, 118–23, 228, 269

Ma Fenghua (Feng-hwa Mah), 265, 267, 362f
Madness and emotional ill health, 96f, 101ff, 135, 165, 176, 212, 223; Shen on, 95–97, 102–3, 105, 109, 139; among the Shens, 292
Mandarin Duck and Butterfly writing, 107, 110, 198, 200
Manufacture (traditional), 27–28, 46, 48, 135f, 161, 171, 173, 176, 325–26
Mao Dun, 192, 197, 200, 252
Mao Zedong, 234f, 252, 277f; compared with Shen, 28, 147, 160; Shen on, 201f, 268, 270–71
Marketing, 45, 48, 52, 78, 116f, 132, 135; rural, 24–25, 181, 245
Marxism, *see* Communism; Leftist writers
May Fourth movement, 6, 56, 63–66, 79f, 188, 198f, 210
May Thirtieth movement, 105
Mayang, 33, 136–37, 238ff, 263
Miao (Hmong), 8–30 *passim*, 35, 72, 111, 116–63 *passim*, 169–82 *passim*, 225–31 *passim*, 237–45, 261–65; under warlordism, 38, 54; prejudice against, 107, 229, 269, 325. *See also* Nuo

Militia, 38, 45, 49, 51, 239, 250–51, 262–64, 299
Mining, 18, 63, 230, 250, 281
Modernism, 86f, 91, 111–14, 195, 200f, 211, 228, 231, 254–58f, 278
Moral degeneracy, 207–9, 257–60, 265; of tribespeople, 10–11, 144, 154, 157f; of country folk, 136, 231–32, 234, 246f, 251; of city people, 165, 190, 243
Mother of Shen, *see* Huang family
Movies, 197, 199, 259, 273, 299, 364, 365–66
Mu Shiying, 200–201

Narrative: in storytelling, 43–44; discursive, 67, 88–99, 104, 108–9, 115, 117, 123; verse in, 80, 142; folkloric, 153–58; Northrop Frye's modes of, 149, 152–53; well made, 179, 190, 213, 219, 225, 232, 247f, 250; experimental, 254–57
Nationalism: in West Hunan, 29; and Shen, 66, 108, 191, 241, 252, 258, 270, 274; in fiction, 103, 174; versus regionalism, 114, 123, 278
Nationalist (KMT) regime, 104–8, 183, 186f, 197, 202–9, 235–53 *passim*, 260–66, 269, 280; and Shanghai-Nanking axis, 84, 196, 201, 204–5; literature of, 199. *See also* Censorship; Kuomintang
Nature, 87, 113, 120, 136, 153, 162–68, 182
New Life movement, 172–73, 208–9, 246–47
Nie Rende, 40n, 56, 59, 64, 66, 224, 277, 308
Nieh, Hua-ling, 147, 180, 271
Nietzsche, Friedrich, 107, 113, 168, 197
Nostalgia, 23, 44, 102, 115–18, 123, 166, 186, 229, 231, 281
Nuo rites and dramas, 72, 120–21, 125–27, 177

Opium, 48ff, 57, 64, 136, 162f, 207, 269; smuggling and taxation of, 16, 62, 65, 232, 234f, 250f

Ouran ("by chance"), 220, 224ff, 256–57

Pacifism, 43, 64f, 69, 250, 258, 261, 277
Pan Guangdan, 83
Pantheism, 81, 85, 147, 153, 166, 193, 222–26, 255
Pastoral, 120, 148, 153, 169, 208, 232, 245, 275, 281
Peasants, *see* Country folk
Peking, 59, 66–83 *passim*, 100, 105, 185, 265f, 273; as literary capital, 56, 86; Shen on, 78–79, 133, 259–61, 270
Peking School (Jing Pai), 194, 198–99, 336
Personae (of Shen), 43–44, 94, 95–104f, 107ff, 118, 122, 165, 220
Pingming ribao (*The Dawn*), 258
Plot: adventure, 43, 60, 80; episodic, 67, 87f, 91, 93, 115f, 123; folk, 125, 127, 130; formal development of, 130, 147, 193, 211, 324; lack of, 166; disjointed, 248–50. *See also* Narrative
Poetry (Shen on), 107, 124, 144, 192, 254
Police, 58, 103, 105, 135, 196, 203, 260; Shen's career in, 58, 71
Poverty, 116, 161, 170, 173, 187, 194, 231. *See also* Famine
Primitivism, 9–10, 112–14, 133, 145, 148, 168, 174, 223, 275
Printing, 49f, 57, 68; Shen's career in, 65, 71
Prisons, 19f, 46, 58; in Shen's works, 98, 101ff, 120
"Proletarian literature," 105–6, 170, 199–200
Proletariat, 105–8, 170, 280
Prose poems, 93f, 108, 118, 122–23
Prostitutes, 48, 61, 175, 221; as objects of pity, 101, 158, 231–34; as passionate country folk, 160, 164, 167, 170, 179, 181, 229
Protect the Nation, War to, 33, 38, 40
Proust, Marcel, 3, 211, 214, 220, 225
Průšek, Jaroslav, 80, 94f
Psychology, 80, 85, 109, 112, 122, 131, 138. *See also* Fiction; Freud; Madness

Publishers, 72, 86, 104, 109, 185, 195–97; Kaiming, 270, 358
Pushi, 126, 166, 234

Qian Xuantong, 80, 85
Qian Zhongshu, 85, 319
Qing dynasty, 8–9, 13–19 *passim*, 28–35 *passim*, 42, 60, 78–79, 208
Qingdao, 83, 185, 204f, 215f, 218, 224f, 231, 256
Qu Yuan, 10, 121, 126, 133, 168, 233

Rao Mengkan, 82
Readers, 96–99, 104, 111, 122, 127, 129, 185, 210, 227
Realism: in Shen's early works, 44, 80, 104, 146–49, 152; doctrine of, 86, 191, 193, 209, 269; in Shen's mature works, 183–84, 187, 227f, 231, 246, 278f
Regional identification, 4, 75ff, 81, 242, 251, 261–62; Shen's own, 4, 44, 97, 107, 124, 133, 136–37, 148, 166, 184, 201–2, 228–29, 240, 247; and Southern versus Northern Chinese, 10, 33, 37, 55, 90, 130–31, 133, 158, 262; in the army, 19, 41, 55; versus nationalism, 114, 123f; and regional prejudices, 133, 228–29, 237, 240, 242, 245, 247f, 280; and literary polemics, 194–202
Regionalism (literary), 4–6, 23, 102–3, 107, 111–84, 225–35, 245–52, 274, 278–79; as vehicle for critique, 5–6, 111, 130–34, 137, 148, 158, 184, 195, 231
Relatives (of Shen Congwen), 20–33 *passim*, 56–61 *passim*, 75, 106, 117, 135, 165, 323; Fourth Uncle Teng, 23, 34–35, 234–35. *See also individual relatives, families, and relationships by name*
Religion: local, 23, 30, 108, 111–12, 117, 126ff, 176–77; organized, 81, 96f, 183, 190, 208, 222–26, 275, 279; and superstition, 175, 178, 207, 306, 327. *See also* Buddhism; Christianity; Pantheism

Renjian yuekan (*The World of Man*), 196
Revolution of 1911, 6, 19, 29–31, 39, 225, 230
Romance and sexuality: urban, 22, 91–93, 98–101, 107, 122, 211–22, 226, 254–57, 266; rural, 43, 167, 171–72, 180–82, 250; in Shen's love letters and poems, 59, 75, 77, 138; and eroticism, 59, 95, 118–20, 138–39, 151, 156, 228, 275, 278; and unrequited desire, 87, 95–98, 101–4, 109, 123; upper-class abuse of, 101–2, 162, 172, 175, 178; tribal, 112, 122, 124–27, 137–45, 149–58, 230; Shen's advocacy of, 137–38, 140, 144–45, 181f, 188f, 212f, 220, 256; and love suicides, 155f
Romanticism, 74, 80, 86–104 *passim*, 118, 120f, 164f, 249; opposition to, 168, 193, 250, 277
Russell, Bertrand, 80, 108

Satire, 88–94, 99, 106–9, 120f, 127, 187, 221, 246–47, 270–72; tempered with humor and compassion, 44, 55, 80, 91ff, 108; aimed at Shen, 69–70, 319, 335; of intellectuals, 107–9, 190–91, 212, 217–18, 324
Sexuality, *see* Romance
Sha Ting, 367
Shakespeare, William, 2, 126, 153
Shanghai, 66, 244; Shen in, 77, 83, 104–9, 187, 195–96, 203, 205; Shen's dislike of, 79, 84, 86, 158, 179, 194–202, 205
Shanghai School (Hai Pai): of literature, 194–202, 221; of opera, 197–98
Shao Huaqiang, 310, 324, 336, 349f, 359f, 387
Shao Lizi, 203
Shao Xunmei, 83
Shen Congwen (*see also* Shen Congwen, works):
—extraliterary life: names, 18, 34, 43, 57f, 98, 117, 205, 428; family, 18–24, 27, 31f, 39–40, 97, 115, 187; childhood, 18–36, 115–18; family economic status, 19f, 22, 58f, 269; ances-

try and tribal blood, 19–21, 71, 230; education, 22–24, 31–33, 55, 57–60, 70, 187, 189; personality, 24–28, 32, 59, 65, 71, 85, 114, 187f, 192, 220, 268–69, 273f, 276; foreign languages, 25, 67, 70, 72, 79, 93, 107; health and physique, 26–27, 34, 66, 74, 96, 102, 104, 273f; musical interests, 28, 261, 267, 278f; classical learning, 32, 50, 55, 57f, 59, 64, 66; Western learning, 32–33, 55f, 60, 112–14; army career, 32–36, 39–58, 61–66, 71; romances (real and alleged), 37, 58–59, 68, 74, 76–77, 98, 138, 188–89, 204, 218f, 229, 250, 256–57; relations with West Hunan leaders, 39–41, 56–59, 61, 234f, 241, 243–44; pre-1949 art interests, 48, 64, 78–79, 189, 220, 265; early poverty, 59, 70–75, 89, 97, 100–104; favorite reading, 60, 80; quasi-student life, 67–83; teaching career, 68, 70–71, 83, 123, 185f, 189, 192, 195; political difficulties, 77, 203–7, 232, 252–53; periods of low spirits, 81, 96, 99–105, 185–86, 189, 219, 224f, 233, 265–67, 268, 276; concern with aging, 102, 188–90, 192, 210, 226, 233; sexual experience, 138, 188–89; marital life, 189, 214, 219–20, 229, 363; late art history career, 189–90, 265–67, 270, 272–74, 278, 364; wartime activities, 191, 210f, 231, 240–41, 248, 252–54, 257–58; trips home, 206, 228–35 *passim*, 240–41, 252–53, 270, 364; suicide attempt, 265, 267, 276, 345; post-1949 eclipse, 265, 269–71, 273–74; CCP accusations and self-criticism, 266, 268–69, 339, 359; cadre school life, 271–73; trip abroad, 274. *See also* Libraries; Police; Printing
—literary life: experimentalism, 3–4, 67, 91, 120, 190, 193, 201, 210, 228, 254–58, 275; use of family, 21–23, 97f, 104, 115–17, 184; first writings, 57–59 *passim*, 71f, 82, 86–95; well-made works, 67, 109, 185, 201, 211; anti-formalism, 67, 87, 93–94, 193–94; letters to literary lions, 69, 72, 81, 85; remuneration, 72, 81, 104; editing activities, 73, 76f, 84, 187, 190, 196, 270, 336, 361; social protest works, 73–74, 84–86, 95–110, 131–33, 186, 196; literary successors, 75, 83–86 *passim*, 191, 318f, 337; traditional Chinese influences, 80, 88–95 *passim*, 115, 132, 164, 166f, 179, 189f, 193, 275, 305, 316; mentors, 82–85; avoidance of groups, 82–86, 186, 191–92, 194–202, 253, 268, 276; stylistic eclecticism, 86–95; genres, 86, 92–98 *passim*, 104, 106–9, 280; opposition to low culture, 95, 104, 110, 138, 199–200, 259; *romans à clef*, 98, 191, 214–15; formalism, 114, 186, 193–94, 196, 210, 275; "obscurity," 119, 186, 228, 254, 256; sense of history, 179, 228–31, 233–35, 236f, 245–52, 259, 279; philosophic fiction, 190–91, 209–27, 228, 230, 256–57; polemics, 194–202, 204–5, 207–8; engagement, 202, 208–9, 228–29, 231–35, 236, 240–41, 244–52, 257–61; nonengagement, 223, 252–54, 258f, 276; withdrawal from fiction, 265–66, 269–71, 276–79; post-1949 narrative writing, 271, 273, 278
—thought of: love of vitality, 7, 10–11, 114, 133–37, 144–45, 165, 171, 207, 277; anti-authoritarianism, 6, 22ff, 68, 70, 73, 85f, 249, 253, 265; avantgarde, 3–4, 86–87, 95, 210, 228, 254–58, 275, 279; optimistic humanism, 6, 56, 60, 173, 209ff, 221, 277; Young China ideas, 6–7, 56, 186; views on China, 6–7, 10–11, 68f, 74, 78–86 *passim*, 93–95, 100–109 *passim*, 158, 192–93, 207, 209; personal religious beliefs, 6, 11, 27, 81, 97, 103, 112, 135, 178, 185, 187, 209f, 221–26, 257–58, 351; noninvolvement with revolution, 6–7, 56, 70, 77, 113, 186, 188, 193, 226; eclecticism, 7, 56, 60, 79, 87f, 220; unconcern with imperialism, 7, 173, 207;

ethics, 25, 68, 96, 131–38, 174, 197, 208–9, 211–14; love of competition, 27, 100–101; military heroes, 28, 61–62, 64; defense of the army, 33f, 43f, 51, 55; idealism, 56, 68f, 73, 85, 148, 153, 191, 223f, 274, 276f; philosophy, 64, 73, 79f, 94, 121, 147, 190–91, 209–12, 220, 256–61, 275, 277, 326; advocacy of cultural revolution, 68, 86, 95, 108, 113–14, 192–93; antipathy toward politics, 68, 186, 188, 191–92, 252f, 259, 261, 269, 277, 362; academicism, 68, 85, 188, 194, 198; liberalism, 79, 83, 249, 269, 275; interest in psychology and social sciences, 80, 85, 112, 122, 138f, 154, 157, 186–87; anti-imperialism, 93, 104, 106, 108f, 195, 200, 207; political views, 105–9 *passim*, 186–88, 192, 199–209 *passim*, 218, 221, 226, 237, 249, 258–59, 276f, 335; aesthetic idealism, 112, 137, 173, 209f, 220–23, 261, 275–78; views on creativity, 193, 223

Shen Congwen, works:

—diaries, essays, letters, prose poems: *Bu si riji* (*A Pre-posthumous Diary*), 94, 104, 109, 397; "Gongyu zhong" ("In a Lodging House"), 91–92, 101, 388; "Huaihuazhen" ("Huaihua Town"), 92–93, 133, 392; "Huang jun riji" ("The Diary of Master Huang"), 106, 395; "Jiuyue jiju" ("Words from the Old Testament"), 106, 390; "Lü de huaping" ("A Green Vase"), 122–23, 392; "Mo cuoguo zhe qianzainanfeng de baoguo jihui" ("Do Not Scorn This Once-in-a-Lifetime Opportunity to Repay Your Country"), 241, 419–20; "Paolongtao" ("Supporting Actors"), 270, 432; "Sugeladi tan Beiping suoxu" ("Socrates Discusses What Peking Needs"), 259–61, 430; "Tongxin" ("Letter"), 134, 392; "Wo de jiaoyu" ("My Education"), 44–55 *passim*, 187, 400; "Women xuyao yi ge disi dang" ("What We Need Is a *Fourth* Party"), 253–54, 425; *Xin* (*Letters*), 93, 398, 409; "Xishan de yue" ("Moon Over the Western Hills"), 121, 390; "Xiti" ("Preface to My Exercises"), 159, 416; "Yaoye" ("Long Nights"), 98, 100, 121, 388ff; "Yi feng wei ceng fuyou de xin" ("A Letter Never Mailed"), 94, 388; "Yi ge chuanqi de benshi" ("Material for a Fairy Tale"), 244, 428; "Yi ge furen de riji" ("A Woman's Diary"), 22, 395; *Yi ge tiancai de tongxin* (*Correspondence from a Born Talent*), 94, 104, 108–9, 399; *Zhu xu* (*The Candle Extinguished*), 258, 421ff

—literary criticism: *Momo ji* (*Froth*), 192, 412; *Yunnan kan yun ji* (*Gazing at Clouds in Yunnan*), 252, 425

—nonfiction books: art history books, 270, 272f; *Congwen zizhuan* (*Congwen's Autobiography*), 21, 31, 37, 44, 178–79, 187, 190, 224, 412; Huang family history, 273; *Ji Ding Ling* [*xuji*] (*Remembering Ding Ling*) [and *Sequel*]), 190, 205–6, 252, 408, 413, 420; *Ji Hu Yepin* (*Remembering Hu Yepin*), 190, 404, 407; *Xiang xing san ji* (*Discursive Notes on a Trip Through Hunan*), 130, 190, 232–35, 417; *Xiangxi* (*West Hunan*), 130, 183, 240, 251, 419

—novels: *Alisi Zhongguo youji* (*Alice's Adventures in China*), 93–94, 107–8, 161, 396; *Bian cheng* (*The Frontier City*), 3, 21, 37, 115, 130, 134f, 148, 160–84 *passim*, 216, 224, 229–32 *passim*, 257, 273, 410; *Chang he* (*Long River*), 27, 109, 130, 135, 165, 172–80 *passim*, 190, 230, 236, 240, 245–48, 250ff, 258, 425; *Chang xia* (*Long Summer*), 138f, 395; *Dai guan riji* (*Diary of a Dumb Bureaucrat*), 107, 400; *Fengzi*, 126f, 134, 151–52, 176, 179, 216, 224–26, 230–31, 405–6, 419; *Jiu meng* (*Past Dreams*), 138f, 396; *Shenwu zhi ai* (*The Shaman's Love*), 126, 399; *Xiaozhai*, 231–232, 419; *Xue qing* (*After Snow*), 250–51, 427ff; *Yi ge nü*

juyuan de shenghuo (*The Life of an Actress*), 107, 402; *Yunlu jishi* (*Yunlu Chronicles*), 248–50, 253, 428
—plays: "Dutu" ("Gamblers"), 125, 391; "Guonian" ("New Year's"), 126, 393; "Mai tang fu mai zhe" ("The Sugar Peddler Sells Cane"), 125, 391; "Muqin" [1] ("Mother"), 92, 392; "Xiaoshen" ("The Xiao God"), 126–29f, 394; "Xishuai" ("Cricket"), 115, 394; "Yazi" ("Duck"), 125–26, 130, 393; "Ye dian" ("Inn of the Wilds"), 126, 138, 391
—poem in Classical Chinese: "Lushan 'Huajing' Bai Juyi zuoshi chu" ("In the 'Path of Flowers' on Mt. Lu"), 271–72, 435
—poems in vernacular Chinese: "Bomu" ("Dusk"), 120, 393; "Candong" ("The Last Days of Winter"), 122, 392; "Chun" [1] ("Spring"), 120, 395; "Chun yue" ("Spring Moon"), 120, 389; "Duihua" ("Dialogue"), 119, 404; "Ganren yaoqu" ("Songs of the Zhen'gan Folk"), 143–44, 394; "Huan yuan" ("Returning Thanks to the Gods"), 120–21, 126, 392; "Panbing" ("Mutineers"), 43, 391; "Shilu de xiao gaoyang" ("The Little Lost Lamb"), 120, 389; "Shu" ("Dawn"), 80, 394; "Song" ("Ode"), 118–19, 138, 398; "Wo xihuan ni" ("I Love You"), 118, 120, 392; "Xiang jian de xia" ("Summer in the Countryside"), 124–25, 390; "Yujin" ("Embers"), 119, 390; "Zhen'gan de ge" ("Zhen'gan Songs"), 124, 390
—short stories: Ahei cycle, 139, 182; "Ajin," 130, 176, 182, 398; "Ba jun tu" ("Portrait of Eight Steeds"), 109, 211–16, 218f, 257, 415; "Baizi," 181, 397; "Bohan" ("Chill"), 216–17, 401; "Cai jue" ("Gathering Bracken"), 182, 397; "Canjun" ("Staff Officer"), 43, 399; "Chuanqi bu qi" ("Truth Is Stranger Than Fiction"), 258, 429; "Chuanshang" ("On Board the Boats"), 43, 391; "Chuanshang anshang" ("Aboard and on Shore"), 131–32, 396; "Chuanshibing" ("Camp Messenger"), 44, 393; "Chun" [2] ("Spring"), 216–17, 406; "Da cheng zhong de xiao shiqing" ("A Small Matter in a Big City"), 105, 400; "Daigou," 116, 389; "Daxiao Ruan" ("Big Ruan and Little Ruan"), 109, 221, 419; "Deng" ("Lamp"), 98, 222, 401; "Disi" ("No. 4"), 216–17, 401; "Dushi yi furen" ("A Lady of the City"), 108, 406; "Fufu" ("The Lovers"), 181, 183, 400; "Fulan" ("Rot"), 173, 410; "Gengfu Ahan" ("Ahan the Night Watch"), 116, 161, 177, 184, 391; "Guisheng," 161–83 *passim*; "Guolingzhe" ("The One Who Crossed Over the Mountains"), 258, 411; "Guwenguan" ("Staff Adviser"), 44, 415; "Hei ye" ("Dark Night"), 168, 258, 407; "Huchu" ("Tiger Cub"), 222, 404; "Huiming," 163, 168f, 172–74, 180, 183, 400; "Jing" ("Quiet"), 222, 406; "Jueshi yihou" ("After Fasting"), 97, 103, 390; "Junzi," 106, 393; "Kan hong lu" ("Gazing at a Rainbow"), 193, 254–56, 257, 422; "Laba zhou" ("Holiday Fruit Congee"), 23, 115–16, 118, 391; "Laike" ("The Visitor"), 222, 408; "Lansheng tong Lansheng taitai" ("Lansheng and His Mrs."), 106, 394; "Láo mei, zuohen!" ("Maiden, How Beautiful You Are!"), 122, 393; "Laoshi ren" ("The Simpleton"), 135, 396; "Lianzhang" ("The Captain"), 43, 395; "Long Zhu," 141–42, 152–53, 155, 217, 224, 398; "Louluo" ("Outlaws"), 43, 395; "Lubian" ("Hearthside"), 23, 116, 393; "Lüdian" ("The Inn"), 163, 399; "Meigui yu Jiumei" ("Roses and Little Sister No. 9"), 115, 391; "Meijin, Baozi, yu na yang" ("Meijin, Baozi, and the White Kid"), 155–58, 399; "Mian xie" ("Cotton Shoes"), 73–74f, 88–

91, 94, 99, 133, 390; "Nitu" ("Mud"), 173, 405; "Niu" ("Ox"), 163, 168, 172, 174f, 180–81, 183, 400; "Pingfan gushi" [2] ("An Ordinary Story"), 221, 401; "Qi ge yeren yu zuihou yi ge yingchunjie" ("Seven Barbarians and the Last Rite of Spring"), 158, 399; "Qiaoxiu he Dongsheng" ("Qiaoxiu and Dongsheng"), 251, 258, 428; "Ruilong," 116, 391; "Ruomo yisheng" ("Dr. Ruomo"), 216–19, 406; "Rurui," 222, 408; "Ruwuhou" ("After Entering the Ranks"), 43, 51, 55, 98, 215, 394; "San Bei xiansheng jiaxun" ("The Family Precepts of Mr. San Bei"), 106, 389; "San ge nanren he yi ge nüren" ("Three Men and a Woman"), 44, 401; "San ge nüxing" ("Three Women"), 205, 214–15, 408; "Sansan," 115, 161–81 *passim*, 404; "Shangui" ("Mountain Spirit"), 163–64, 180, 395; "Shaobing" ("Sentry"), 44, 393; "Sheng" ("Living"), 222, 408; "Shenshi de taitai" ("The Gentry Wife"), 108, 402; "Shiji" ("At Market"), 116, 391; "Shizi chuan" ("The Marble Carrying Boat"), 105, 131, 403; "Shuiyun" ("Water and Clouds"), 256–57, 424; "Shuo gushi ren de gushi" ("A Tale of a Storyteller"), 37, 399; "Songzi jun" ("Master Songzi"), 98, 101, 393; "Tao de qian yi tian" ("The Day Before He Deserted"), 44, 49–50, 401; "Tuzhuobian" ("At the Butcher's Block"), 116, 389; "Wang Xie zidi" ("Sons of the Rich"), 221, 418; "Wangshi" ("Events Gone By"), 117, 394; "Wo de xiaoxue jiaoyu" ("My Primary School Education"), 25–27, 117, 393; "Xiang cheng" ("A Country Town"), 163, 248, 422; "Xianxian," 189, 405; "Xiaocao yu fuping" ("The Little Grass and the Duckweed"), 93, 394; "Xiaoxiao," 23, 115, 168, 173, 179, 181f, 400; "Xin yu jiu" ("The New and the Old"), 208–9, 414; "Xue ("Snow"), 131–33, 250, 396; "Xue qing" ("After Snow"), 258, 427; "Ye" [1] ("Night"), 43, 401; "Ye yu" [1] ("Night Fishing"), 116, 391; "Yong 'A' zi jixialai de shi" ("Events to Be Filed Under 'A' "), 73f, 88, 103, 390; "Yu" [1] ("Rain"), 100, 393; "Yu" ("Fishing"), 169–70, 403; "Yu hou" ("After Rain"), 144–45, 181, 213, 397; "Yuexia xiaojing" ("Under Moonlight"), 152–55, 408; "Zai bie yi ge guodu li" ("In a Separate Realm"), 43, 92, 392; "Zai sishu" ("In a Private School"), 25, 31–32, 92, 117, 396; "Zao" ("Restless"), 189, 405; "Zaoshang—yi dui tu yi ge bing" ("Morning: A Soldier on a Mound of Earth"), 258, 408; "Zhai xing lu" ("Plucking a Star"), 254, 266, 422; "Zhangfu" ("The Husband"), 181, 401; "Zhishi" ("Knowledge"), 168, 222, 412; "Zhong jun" ("Master Zhong"), 100f, 392; "Zhufu" [1] ("Housewife"), 189, 219–21, 420; "Zisha" ("Suicide"), 219, 415

—story collections: *Ahei xiaoshi* (*The Story of Ahei*), 139, 182; *Lüdian* (*The Inn*), 203; *Shizi chuan* (*The Marble Carrying Boat*), 203; *Yan* (*Nightmares*), 210, 257, 267; *Yazi* (*Duck*), 92; *Yuexia xiaojing* (*Under Moonlight*), 129, 191

—evaluations of, 1–2, 72, 146–48, 228, 245, 269–70, 273, 365f; by Kinkley, 2–3, 67, 109, 148–49, 160, 171, 183–84, 194, 245, 249, 279–80; by Shen himself, 67, 188–90, 211; by leftists, 161, 186ff, 191, 211

Shen Dieyu (younger brother), 20, 22, 40, 232, 238, 244–45, 249
Shen Hongfu (grandfather), 19–20, 21, 23, 29, 33, 40n, 62, 153
Shen Yunlu (older brother), 20, 22, 27, 71, 89, 115, 117, 232, 241, 248f, 253
Shen Zongsi (father), 14, 18–23 *passim*, 30–31, 34, 40, 117, 241
Shengming ("life"), 85, 222–24, 255
Shi Cuntong, 77
Shi Zhicun, 83, 112, 197, 200, 402

Shiwai Taoyuan (the Chinese Shangri-La), 15–16, 243
Shuixing (*Mercury*), 336
Shunshun, 135, 366
Sichuan province, 9, 28, 39, 56f, 63, 65, 76, 140, 198
Sima Qian, 59f, 80
Sisters of Shen, 117; younger (Shen Yuemeng, No. 9), 22, 77, 115, 214–15, 221, 292, 335; elder, 31
Situ Qiao, 76
Smedley, Agnes, 205, 315
Song Xilian, 263
Songs, *see* Folk songs
Southeastern China, *see* Jiangnan
Spirit soldiers (*shenbing*), 57, 65, 239, 243
Sterne, Laurence, 3, 93–94
Students, 6, 69–82, 92, 99–100, 243, 259, 266, 274
Su Wen (Dai Kechong), 197, 200–201
Su Xuelin, 146, 330
Subjective writing, 95–104, 109. *See also* Autobiographical writing
Suicide, 155f, 190, 213, 219, 264f, 267
Sun Fuyuan, 72
Sun Jianzhong, 366
Sun Ling, 314–15
Sun Xizhen, 358, 368
Sun Yatsen, 29, 39, 79
Symbolism (in Shen's works), 5–6, 75, 109, 115, 139, 147, 162f, 213–15, 257; religious and celestial, 81, 121–22, 145, 150f, 221f, 224, 226; sexual, 142–45, 216; political, 208–9, 214, 247; color, 210, 214, 222
Symbolist movement, 122, 200, 210, 214, 265

Tagore, Rabindranath, 80, 107, 119, 121, 150, 223f
Taiping Rebellion, 17, 19, 21, 39
Tang Tao, 200, 330
Tang Yongtong, 319
Tao Qian, 271–72
Taoism, 147, 159, 165, 192, 259
Taoyuan, 16, 61, 127, 234f

Tian family (Tian Xingshu and descendants), 19, 29, 31, 39–41, 56, 62
Tian Junjian, 248, 357
Tian Sannu, 241
Tian Tao, 419
Tongcheng School, 59
Tongren, 117, 135
Tongxin ("childlike mind"), 134–35, 160, 180, 234
Tongyangxi ("child bride"), 23, 182
Torture, 38, 42, 51ff, 58, 242, 298–99
Travelogue, 89, 167, 190, 232–35
Tribespeople, *see* Miao; Tujia
Tujia, 12, 20, 121, 133, 139, 142, 149, 154, 169f
Tuntian ("colony") system, 17–18, 33, 155, 230, 238f, 241
Turgenev, Ivan, 2, 80, 269
Tutelary deities, 25, 117, 161

Universities, 66–71, 100; Peking, 70–79 *passim*, 83, 192n, 231, 261, 266f; Yanjing, 70–71, 75f, 78, 112; Franco-Chinese, 70; Qinghua, 75, 82, 261; Peking Agricultural College, 75–76, 78; Woosung China Institute, 83, 185, 192; Qingdao, 83, 192n, 272; Wuhan, 83, 192, 203; Peking Women's Normal College, 106, 123; Southwestern Union, 192n; North China, 267; Furen, 267; Revolutionary, 268; Jishou, 281; Jinan, 318

Violence, 55, 65, 241, 262; condemned by Shen, 69, 204, 207–9, 246, 251–52, 258–61 *passim*; attractive to Shen, 103, 133–34

Wang Jizhen, 203
Wang Luyan, 252
Wang Xu, 267
Wang Yarong, 272
Wang Yuanhua, 262–64
Wang Zengqi, 265, 337
Wang Zhengya, 305
Wangcun, 231, 234, 239
War and civil conflict, 18, 280; Sino-Japanese War, 6, 188, 240–45, 248–

50, 252–53, 258; ethnic conflict, 9–14 passim, 133, 237–40, 242, 245, 247, 261–65; revolution, 29–30, 78, 233, 246, 263–65; civil war, 33, 39–41, 65, 233–36, 240, 246f, 263–65; general civil disorder, 37–38, 41, 65, 229, 234, 237–43, 247, 251–52, 262–65; massacres, 57, 65, 265; scorched earth, 63, 262; white terror, 107; feuds, 134, 170, 250–51; 1946–49 Civil War, 187, 248, 258–65; bombing, 239, 243
Wen Yiduo, 82–84, 120, 173, 214, 266, 349, 359, 363, 403
"Wenyi" ("Literature Supplement"), see Dagongbao
West Hunan (Xiangxi), 4–66, 133–58, 165f, 225–52 passim, 261–65, 280–81; writers of, 279
Western influences (literary), 60, 80, 87–95 passim, 107–8, 112–14, 119f, 187, 254, 275
Wife of Shen, see Zhang Zhaohe
Women (in Shen's works), 22f, 38; in romantic works, 74, 77, 98–102, 106–7, 118, 121, 135, 157–58, 211–20; country, 132–33, 162–64, 173, 178, 182, 229–30, 247, 251; dark beauties, 165, 214. See also Prostitutes
Women friends of Shen, 59, 68, 256, 349, 359–60
Writers: social position and role of, 85–86, 186, 195–200, 209–13, 215, 265f, 278, 281; persecution of, 104, 200, 202–7, 215
Wu Han, 84, 318–19
Wu Hengliang, 239f, 242, 263f
Wu Mi, 83, 191, 219, 317
Wu Xuenao, 366
Wu Zhihui, 269, 367

Xia Yan, 266
Xiandai (Les Contemporains), 200–201
Xiandai pinglun (Modern Critic), 73, 82
Xiang Kairan, 202
Xiangshan (Fragrant Hills), 72–74, 76, 89; Orphanage, 72–74, 81, 97, 103

Xiangtu wenxue ("native-soil, or rural, literature"), 274, 366
Xiao Qian, 84, 252, 412, 430
Xiaoshuo yuekan (The Story Monthly), 336
Xie Bingying, 321
Xiong family of Zhen'gan and Yuanzhou, 39–40, 40n, 56, 58f, 355; Xiong Xiling, 31, 39–40, 60, 63, 68–74 passim, 256, 367
Xiong Kewu, 307
Xu Dishan (Luo Huasheng), 85, 411
Xu Teli, 252
Xu Zhimo, 82–85 passim, 107, 113, 189, 201, 203, 224, 324, 336
Xue Yue, 244, 355

Yan Ruyi, 28
Yan Wenjing, 312, 339
Yan Xishan, 63, 174
Yang Zhensheng, 83, 269, 317–18, 337, 361
Yao Pengzi, 83
Yao Xueyin, 367
Yaoyao, 165, 240, 246
Ye Gongchao, 83
Ye Shaojun, 197
Yishibao (Social Welfare), 258
Yongsui, 16, 238–39, 243, 263
You River, 61, 167, 231, 239f, 264
Young China, 6–7, 42f, 56, 186, 277–78; West Hunan as, 6–7, 11–12, 140
Youth: as a bloc, 68f, 84–86, 95–106 passim, 137, 188, 207, 249–50, 278; literature to lead, 110, 227, 278; literature for, 153, 191, 197, 330. See also Students; Young China
Yu Dafu, 66, 68–70, 72, 81f, 94–96 passim, 100, 109, 403
Yuan Kejia, 265
Yuan River, 8; as a site of historical strife, 12f, 38, 62, 65, 72, 233f, 239; in Shen's works, 122, 131, 136, 164–67 passim
Yuan Shikai, 20, 33, 38f, 40, 277
Yuan Tongli, 73
Yuanling, see Chenzhou

Yuanzhou (Zhijiang), 41, 56, 58ff, 62, 65, 242f
Yue Daiyun, 337
Yushuwan, 41, 45, 51, 243
Yusi (*Threads of Talk*), 82, 99

Zang Kejia, 337, 359
Zawen or *zagan*, *see* Essays
Zeng Guofan, 28, 62
Zhang Caizhen, 76ff
Zhang Chonghe (sister-in-law), 336–37
Zhang Dongsun, 112, 350
Zhang Fangxu (Jinyi), 84, 336
Zhang Jingsheng, 95
Zhang Shizhao, 323
Zhang Tianyi, 84, 183
Zhang Tiesheng, 345
Zhang Xiruo, 270
Zhang Xueji, 39ff, 56f, 62, 65, 236
Zhang Yiping, 138
Zhang Zhang (brother-in-law), 271
Zhang Zhaohe (wife), 84, 165, 232, 267, 273f, 347, 350, 363; courtship and marriage of, 189, 204, 219, 257; in fiction, 214–15, 219–20, 222, 225f
Zhang Zhizhong, 237, 240, 355
Zhang Ziping, 138f, 195, 197, 403
Zhang Ziqing, 61, 64–65
Zhanguoce (*Intrigues of the Warring States*), 253, 359
Zhao Jingshen, 83
Zhao Shuli, 367
Zhao Taimou, 349
Zheng Zhenduo, 336
Zhen'gan, *see* Fenghuang
Zhijiang, *see* Yuanzhou
Zhou Enlai, 271, 273
Zhou Zuoren, 81f, 85, 94f, 112, 122–23, 125, 154, 199, 201
Zhu Guangqian, 85, 148, 216, 265, 269, 350, 361
Zhu Xiang, 82, 403
Zhu Ziqing, 337

Library of Congress Cataloging-in-Publication Data

Kinkley, Jeffrey C., 1948–
   The odyssey of Shen Congwen.

   Bibliography: p.
   "List of Shen Congwen's works": p.
   Includes index.
     1. Shen, Ts'ung-wen, 1902–   —Biography.
  2. Authors, Chinese—20th century—Biography.
I. Title.
PL2801.N18Z73   1987   895.1'35   87-2276
ISBN 0-8047-1372-3